Teverc

With best wishes

from

Fiona Cownie

& Tony Bradney

18. Feb. 2025

Elgar Concise Encyclopedia of Legal Education

ELGAR CONCISE ENCYCLOPEDIAS IN LAW

Elgar Concise Encyclopedias in Law are the definitive guides to a wide variety of subject areas in the field. The format is an invaluable reference source and essential research destination for academics, practitioners, and students alike.

Each encyclopedia is edited by one or more leading international scholars and contains a broad yet curated collection of entries written by key academics and practitioners. The result is concise, accessible coverage of each topic. Equally useful as reference tools or high-level introductions to specific topics, issues, cases, and debates, these encyclopedias are a unique, foundational contribution to the field.

For a full list of Edward Elgar published titles, including the titles in this series, visit our website at www.e-elgar.com.

Elgar Concise Encyclopedia of Legal Education

Edited by

Fiona Cownie

Professor of Law Emerita, School of Law, Keele University; Senior Associate Research Fellow, Institute of Advanced Legal Studies, School of Advanced Study, University of London, UK

Anthony Bradney

Emeritus Professor of Law, School of Law, Keele University; Senior Associate Research Fellow, Institute of Advanced Legal Studies, School of Advanced Study, University of London, UK

Emma Jones

Senior Lecturer in Law, School of Law, University of Sheffield, UK

ELGAR CONCISE ENCYCLOPEDIAS IN LAW

 Edward Elgar
PUBLISHING

Cheltenham, UK • Northampton, MA, USA

Published by
Edward Elgar Publishing Limited
The Lypiatts
15 Lansdown Road
Cheltenham
Glos GL50 2JA
UK

Edward Elgar Publishing, Inc.
William Pratt House
9 Dewey Court
Northampton
Massachusetts 01060
USA

A catalogue record for this book
is available from the British Library

Library of Congress Control Number: 2024948340

This book is available electronically in the **Elgar**online
Law subject collection
https://doi.org/10.4337/9781035302932

ISBN 978 1 0353 0292 5 (cased)
ISBN 978 1 0353 0293 2 (eBook)

Printed and bound by CPI Group (UK) Ltd, Croydon, CR0 4YY

Contents

Contributors

Shaimaa Abdelkarim, Assistant Professor in Postcolonial Legal Theory and Critical Race Studies, School of Law, University of Birmingham, UK

Sergio Iván Anzola-Rodríguez, Researcher at CEEAD (Centro de Estudios para la enseñanza y el aprendizaje del derecho), México and Adjunct Professor of Legal Ethics and Professional Responsibility at Universidad de los Andes, Colombia

Rachael Aplin, Senior Lecturer and Course Lead in Criminology, Leeds Law School, Leeds Beckett University, UK

Sarah Archer, Lecturer in Law, Solicitor (Non-practising), York Law School, University of York, UK

César Arjona, Independent Researcher

Seán Arthurs, Global education innovator and learner

Howard Atkin, Former Senior Lecturer in Policing, Department of Human and Health Sciences, University of Huddersfield, UK

Rosemary Auchmuty, Professor of Law, School of Law, University of Reading, UK

Stephen Bailey, Professor of Public Law, School of Law, University of Nottingham, UK

Felice Batlan, Professor of Law, Chicago-Kent College of Law, Illinois Tech, UK

Susan Bartie, Senior Lecturer in Law, College of Law, Australian National University, Australia

Lydia Bleasdale, Professor of Legal Education, School of Law, University of Leeds, UK

Martin Böhmer, Professor of Law, Faculty of Law, Universidad de Buenos Aires, Argentina

Sophie Boyron, Associate Professor of Law, Birmingham Law School, University of Birmingham, UK

Anthony Bradney, Emeritus Professor of Law, School of Law, Keele University, UK; Senior Associate Research Fellow, Institute of Advanced Legal Studies, School of Advanced Study, University of London, UK

Susan L. Brooks, Professor of Law, Drexel University Thomas R. Kline School of Law, USA

Peter Burdon, Professor of Law, Adelaide Law School, The University of Adelaide, Australia

Luke Campbell, Senior Lecturer in Law, Aston Law School, Aston University, UK

Kate Campbell-Pilling, Senior University Teacher, School of Law, University of Sheffield, UK

Susan Carle, Professor of Law, College of Law, American University Washington, USA

Helen Carr, Professor of Property Law and Social Justice, Southampton Law School, University of Southampton, UK

Jane Ching, Professor of Professional Legal Education, Nottingham Law School, Nottingham Trent University, UK

Richard Collier, Professor of Law and Social Theory, Newcastle Law School, Newcastle University, UK

Fiona Cownie, Professor of Law Emerita, School of Law, Keele University, UK; Senior Associate Research Fellow, Institute of Advanced Legal Studies, School of Advanced Study, University of London, UK

Dionne Cruickshank, Barrister-at-Law (Non-practicing), UK and Attorney-at-Law, Tutor/Legal Clinician, Norman Manley, Law School Legal Aid Clinic, Jamaica

Anthony Cullen, Associate Professor in Law, School of Law and Social Sciences, Middlesex University London, UK

Filip Cyuńczyk, Assistant Professor at SWPS University, Faculty of Law, SWPS University, Poland

Michael Doherty, Professor of Law and Associate Head, Law School, Lancaster University, UK

Nigel Duncan, Professor Emeritus of Legal Education, The City Law School, City St George's, University of London, UK

Carol Edwards, Senior Lecturer in Law and Student Experience Manager, School of Law, The Open University, UK

Rachael Field, Professor of Law, Faculty of Law, Bond University, Australia

Lila Zaire Flores-Fernandez, Director and Researcher at CEEAD (Centro de Estudios para la enseñanza y el aprendizaje del derecho), México

Kate Galloway, Adjunct Research Fellow, Griffith Law School, Griffith University, Australia

Caroline Gibby, Reader in Legal Education and Head of Law, School of Law, University of Hull, UK

Philip Girard, Emeritus Professor of Law and Senior Scholar, Osgoode Hall Law School, York University, Canada

Ben Golder, Professor of Law, School of Law, Society and Criminology, University of New South Wales, Australia

David Goosey, Registered social worker and experienced chair of several Safeguarding Children and Adults Boards

Lesley Greenbaum, Emeritus Associate Professor of Law, Faculty of Law, University of Cape Town, South Africa

Elaine Gregersen, Associate Professor of Law, Northumbria Law School, Northumbria University, UK

Elisabeth Griffiths, Associate Professor of Law, Northumbria Law School, Northumbria University, UK

Richard Grimes, Independent legal education and access to justice consultant and Visiting Professor of Law, Faculty of Law, Charles University, Czech Republic

Jessica Guth, Head of Law, School of Law, Leeds Trinity University, UK

María José Gutiérrez-Rodríguez, Coord i-nadora de proyecto de formación de líneas jurisprudenciales de la Corte Interamericana de Derechos Humanos, Centro de estudios

Constitucionales de la Suprema Corte de Justicia de la Nación, Mexico

Adrien Habermacher, Professeur agrégé, Faculté de droit, Université de Moncton, Canada

Jean-Louis Halpérin, Professeur de Droit, Département des Sciences Sociales, Ecole Normale Supérieure – PSL, France

Pamela Henderson, Senior Lecturer in Law, Nottingham Law School, Nottingham Trent University, UK

Nina Holvast, Associate Professor in Sociology of Law, Erasmus School of Law, Erasmus University Rotterdam, The Netherlands

Caroline Hunter, Professor of Law, York Law School, University of York, UK

Morten Hviid, Professor of Law, UEA Law School, University of East Anglia, UK

Claire Illingworth, Senior Lecturer in Law, Solicitor (Non-practising), York Law School, University of York, UK

Colin James, Solicitor and Honorary Senior Lecturer, ANU College of Law, The Australian National University, Australia

Emma Jones, Senior Lecturer in Law, School of Law, University of Sheffield, UK

Willem-Jan Kortleven, Assistant Professor in Sociology of Law, Erasmus School of Law, Erasmus University Rotterdam, The Netherlands

Helen Kruuse, Associate Professor of Law, Faculty of Law, Rhodes University, South Africa

Michele Leering, Visiting Scholar, Faculty of Law, Queen's University, Kingston, Ontario, Canada

Patricia Leighton, Professor of Law Emerita, South Wales Business School, University of South Wales, UK; Visiting Professor of Law, Nottingham Law School, Nottingham Trent University, UK

Carlos Lista, Emeritus Professor of Law, School of Law, Universidad Nacional de Córdoba, Argentina

Omar Madhloom, Associate Professor in Law and Legal Clinic Director, Southampton Law School, University of Southampton, UK

Mariana Anahí Manzo, Senior Researcher

at CEEAD (Centro de Estudios sobre la Enseñanza y el Aprendizaje del Derecho), Mexico and Professor at Universidad de Monterrey, Mexico

Andrew Maxfield, Lecturer and Student Experience Manager, School of Law, The Open University, UK

Gayle McKemey, Senior Lecturer in Law, Solicitor (Non-Practising), School of Law and Social Sciences, Oxford Brookes University, UK

Thomas McMorrow, Associate Professor of Legal Studies, Ontario Tech University, Canada

David Milward, Professor of Law, Faculty of Law, University of Victoria, Canada

Steven Montagu-Cairns, Associate Professor in Banking and Corporate Law, School of Law, University of Leeds, UK

Luis Alfonso Mora-Ruenes, Junior Researcher at CEEAD (Centro de Estudios para la enseñanza y el aprendizaje del derecho), México

Ann Nowak, Director of the Legal Writing Center and Adjunct Professor, Jacob D. Fuchsberg Law Center, Touro University, USA

Ernest Ojukwu, Professor of Law, Faculty of Law, Baze University, Nigeria

Abiodun Michael Olatokun, Associate Lecturer in Law, Goldsmiths, University of London; Barrister, 36 Group, London, UK

Michael Palmer, Emeritus Professor of Law, University of London; Senior Research Fellow (SOAS & IALS, London University); Editor, Amicus Curiae, Joint Editor, The Journal of Comparative Law; Senior Research Fellow Chinese University of Hong Kong; Cheng Yu Tung Visiting Professor of Law, University of Hong Kong

Aleksandra Partyk, Assistant Professor, Faculty of Law, Administration and International Relations, Andrzej Frycz Modrzewski Krakow University, Poland

Sebastian Peyer, Associate Professor of Law, UEA Law School, University of East Anglia, UK

Olga Piaskowska, Professor at SWPS University, Faculty of Law, SWPS University, Poland

Piotr Piesiewicz, Professor at SWPS University, Faculty of Law, SWPS University, Poland

Senthorun Raj, Reader in Human Rights Law, Manchester Law School, Manchester Metropolitan University, UK

Annie Rochette, Professor (Pedagogical Innovation) Faculté de droit civil, University of Ottawa, Canada

Andreas Rühmkorf, Professor of German and International Commercial Law, Westfälische Hochschule Gelsenkirchen, Bocholt, Recklinghausen, Germany and Honorary Professor of Law, School of Law, University of Sheffield, UK

Rebecca Samaras, Senior Lecturer in Law, Dundee Law School, University of Dundee, UK

David Sandomierski, Associate Professor, Faculty of Law, Western University, Canada

Shuvro Prosun Sarker, Assistant Professor, Rajiv Gandhi School of Intellectual Property, IIT Kharagpur, West Bengal, India

Ulrike Schultz, Lawyer and retired Senior Academic at the FernUniversität Hagen, Germany

Prakash Sharma, Assistant Professor, Rajiv Gandhi School of Intellectual Property, IIT Kharagpur, West Bengal, India

Avrom Sherr, Emeritus Professor of Law, Institute of Advanced Legal Studies, School of Advanced Study, University of London, UK

Carole Silver, Professor of Global Law and Practice Emerita, Northwestern University Pritzker School of Law, Northwestern University, USA

Natalie Skead, Professor of Law, Law School, The University of Western Australia, Australia and Dean of the Singapore Judicial College, Singapore

Gemma Smyth, Associate Professor and Externship Director, Faculty of Law, University of Windsor, Canada

Ekokoi Solomon, Senior Lecturer in Law, Faculty of Law, University of Uyo, Nigeria

Alex Steel, Professor of Law, Faculty of Law and Justice, University of New South Wales, Australia

Katie Steiner, Senior University Teacher, School of Law, University of Sheffield, UK

Carel Stolker, Former Rector & President of Leiden University (2013–2021), former Dean of Leiden Law School (2004–2011), and Professor-Emeritus of Private Law, Leiden University, The Netherlands

Caroline Strevens, Professor of Legal Education, School of Law, University of Portsmouth, UK

David Sugarman, Professor of Law Emeritus, Lancaster University Law School; Senior Associate Research Fellow, Institute of Advanced Legal Studies, School of Advanced Study, University of London; Senior Associate, Centre for Socio-Legal Studies, University of Oxford, UK

Gabriela Talancón-Villegas, Lecturer in Law, University of Monterrey, Mexico

Lynne Taylor, Professor of Law and Associate Dean (Academic), Faculty of Law, University of Canterbury, Christchurch, New Zealand

Ann Thanaraj, Associate Professor of Learning and Teaching & Assistant Director of Digital Transformation, Teesside University, UK

Linden Thomas, Reader in Clinical Legal Education and Pro Bono, Birmingham Law School, University of Birmingham, UK

Emanuel V. Towfigh, Professor, Chair in Public Law, Empirical Legal Research and Law & Economics, EBS Universität, Wiesbaden, Germany and Distinguished Scholar in Residence, Peking University School of Transnational Law, China

B. Robinson Turner, Lecturer in Law, School of Law and Politics, Cardiff University, UK

Steven Vaughan, Professor of Law, Faculty of Laws, UCL London, UK

Catherine Vincent, Assistant Professor of Law, Birmingham Law School, University of Birmingham, UK

Emily Walsh, Associate Professor in Landlord and Tenant Law and Legal Education, School of Law, University of Portsmouth, UK

Ben Waters, Principal Lecturer in Law, School of Law, Policing, and Social Sciences, Canterbury Christ Church University, UK

Dawn Watkins, Professor of Law, School of Law, University of Sheffield, UK

Gary Watt, Professor of Law, Warwick Law School, University of Warwick, UK

Julian Webb, Professor of Law, Melbourne Law School, University of Melbourne, Australia

Lisa Webley, Professor of Legal Education and Research, Birmingham Law School, University of Birmingham, UK

Helena Whalen-Bridge, Associate Professor of Law, Faculty of Law, National University of Singapore, Singapore

Sally Wheeler, Vice Chancellor, Birkbeck, University of London, UK

Ling Zhou, Assistant Professor, School of Foreign Languages, Shenzhen Technology University, China; Associate Research Fellow, Institute of Advanced Legal Studies, University of London, UK

Preface

This volume is an encyclopedia of legal education. Entries are intended to describe the range of issues debated in relation to legal education in the contemporary era. We have not restricted the coverage to those issues that are of personal concern to us as editors. The fact that something is discussed does not mean that we necessarily endorse what is said. It does not even mean that we always agree that the matter deserves serious consideration. Instead, we have relied upon contributors to use their knowledge to introduce readers to arguments and information that seem to them to be of pressing concern and that we know are regarded as being important by others.

Writing encyclopedia entries involves unique problems for contributors, particularly when they are experts in the field that they are writing about. Whilst all academics are familiar with the limitation and difficulties that come with constraints of space, writing for this volume takes this to challenge to a level that may be unique. On the one hand people have been asked to be comprehensive in what they say. At the same time the word limit that we have given them has been quite severe. They must write, as academics must always write, what they believe to be important and true. Yet they have only been able say a small fraction of what they are capable of saying. We are very grateful to our contributors for rising to this uncomfortable task and at the same time doing this within the unreasonable time pressures that academics always work under.

This having been said, an encyclopedia, still more a concise encyclopedia, will always involve a degree of selection. This is exemplified by the entries describing the different forms that legal education takes in various jurisdictions throughout the world. Nobody can truthfully gainsay the proposition that each jurisdiction's system of legal education reflects that unique confluence of culture, politics and history to be found in that jurisdiction. Examination of each jurisdiction's legal education thus brings some special features that are not to be found in examination of any other jurisdiction. Yet were an encyclopedia to seek to encompass all jurisdictions it would not merely fail to be concise it would end by being similar to the work of Borges' cartographers who, in seeking 'exactitude', 'struck a Map of the Empire whose size was that of the Empire' (Borges 'On Exactitude in Science'). Concision involves selection. In deciding which jurisdictions to discuss we have been guided by theoretical considerations such as issues relating to global history and the purely pragmatic such as the availability of contributors. But other jurisdictions could have been included and the jurisdictions to be found in this volume could have been omitted. So it is with all the other entries. The focus of this volume is on university legal education though some other forms of legal education also find a place. We think that there are compelling reasons for including what is to be found here. Others might find compelling reasons for writing about something else.

Encyclopedia entries are one way to start an enquiry. Each entry here includes references that will help take the enquiry further. Each entry, as with all discussion of law, is an argument. We hope that each entry, and the volume taken as a whole, will enable readers to take their own arguments further.

Professor of Law Emeritus Anthony Bradney
Professor of Law Emerita Fiona Cownie
Dr Emma Jones

1. Academic skills in legal education

Many legal academics agree that 'reasoning and analysis are central to the discipline of law' (Twining [1988] at 13) and form the basis of what it means to study law and to be a lawyer (broadly defined). Nonetheless the discussions about skills in legal education are contested and complex (Guth [2020], Solomon [2020]) and academic skills, with which this entry is concerned, must be considered alongside other skills such as soft skills [see Emotions and Soft Skills in Legal Education] and professional skills [see Professional Legal Education] and the overlap between them must be acknowledged.

What are academic skills in legal education?

The easiest way to think about skills is to conceptualise them as learning about how to do things rather than learning about things (Twining [1988]). Academic skills are those which allow us to make academic (as opposed to a legal practice) contributions and which will help students to become successful students and researchers of law over the course of their studies.

Research and Reasoning Skills

Academic (legal) skills are those which are 'focused on learning how to locate, access, read and use specific information and as well as learning how to think about particular issues in certain ways and construct cogent arguments about those issues' (Guth [2020]) and finally present those arguments in a variety of formats for different academic audiences. However, these definitions could be applied to many disciplines and the difference between academic skills in legal education and other fields is about context. The differences are the type of sources drawn on, the particular ways in which critical thought is identified and encouraged and the sort of conclusions that can and are drawn as well as the sort of outputs that might be written or otherwise produced. Legal academic skills are therefore focused on finding and using legal materials such as statutes and cases alongside commentary from (legal) academics. They are about reasoning in a particular way using rules of statutory interpretation and case law reasoning. The emphasis on how to reason and what materials to give more weight to will depend on the jurisdiction being studied with common law countries often being more focused on legal reasoning based on case law.

Legal Reasoning

It is worth flagging legal reasoning as a key academic skill as the hallmark of 'thinking like a lawyer' because it is both core to studying law (at any level) and has been recognised as problematic for a long time. Legal reasoning has been described thus: 'the ability to analyse facts and appreciate the shifting legal results produced by factual nuances, to separate a complicated problem into its component parts, to assemble facts into a meaningful whole; and, running through it all, a capacity of ferreting out of a problem those features relevant to its resolution' (Mudd [1983] at 705). However, this paints a particular picture of legal reasoning which ignores the fact that 'interpretation, we now know, is as much creation as discovery' (Posner [1992] at 435) and that when strictly applied this way of thinking will ignore the myriad of, for example, social and economic factors as well as differing experiences of legal situations by marginalised groups (Finley [1989] is just one relatively early example). Mudd therefore goes on to note that 'we legal educators might do well to state as our goal the training of our students to think well rather than to presume the assimilation of some new process that is unique to a lawyers' intellect' and that our emphasis should be on 'thinking clearly and precisely' (Mudd [1983] at 706).

Digital Skills

The nature and availability of information and therefore research has changed dramatically and continues to do so at pace (Ajevski et al [2024]). Academic skills must now include a range of digital skills that allow students to find electronic or digital sources and to navigate them [see Digital Skills in Legal Education]. Students (and researchers) must now be able to differentiate between different types of online content, quality assure that content and make decisions about the value of that content for their task at hand. In addition, students also need to understand how to use Artificial Intelligence (AI) tools in ways which help rather than hinder their academic endeavours and which are compliant with ever evolving institutional policies. Many of these skills are also directly relevant in practical and employability contexts and the lines between different groupings of skills become ever more blurred.

Assessment Literacy Skills

If academic skills are those which help students be successful students, then the ability to understand and decode assessment briefs, learning outcomes and marking criteria is also a key academic skill (Zhu and Evans [2024]). This skill is not explored in much detail in the legal education literature and the teaching of assessment literacy does not appear to be widespread.

When and how are skills taught?

It is now widely accepted that skills should be taught (see for example Turner, Bone and Ashton [2018]) rather than assuming that law students will somehow acquire the necessary skills by osmosis (Thornton [2012]). However, there is little consensus on the best way to teach skills. Some programmes provide legal skills courses which cover a variety of legal skills including academic ones. Others incorporate the teaching of academic skills into substantive law modules. Others still might distinguish between academic skills which are generic and can be outsourced to specialist academic skills teachers and those which are law specific which are covered by law teachers or other specialists such as librarians or [Legal Writing Instructors]. Examples here might include sessions on writing essays delivered by central university services and specific legal writing modules or classes incorporated into law programmes and essay writing skills being taught in any substantive law module. While there are several studies which suggest things that can be done in order to enhance students' legal skills, they are usually small scale and only a few focus explicitly on academic skills (for example Tyrell and Jowitt [2019], Sokhi-Bulley [2016], Del Mar [2016]). More research in this area is therefore necessary.

Often it is argued that skills should be taught in practical contexts and in 'real life' or clinical legal education [see Clinical Legal Education (Overview)] situations (Grimes

and Gibbons [2016]). This perhaps implies that academic skills are not legal skills in that sense. However, critical thinking, reading, interpreting and applying statutes and case law to build arguments and provide insights are real life skills of academic lawyers. Teaching these skills in an academic context is no less practical in the sense that it is about how to do something and learn it by doing it than any of the other possible approaches and as Wallace [2018] reminds us, all of them should be underpinned by relevant learning theories.

If academic skills are about how things are done, it is important to facilitate the development of them very early on. Overall, the dominant assumption in programme design appears to be that the necessary academic skills have been acquired by the end of the first year and need not be further developed explicitly. Substantive law modules that follow might encourage the development of more advanced and nuanced reasoning and writing skills but often do so implicitly. Research skills that are about the use of academic material rather than primary legal materials seem to feature less in early skills teaching and are often left to substantive law modules that follow the first year. This raises questions about the consistency with which more advanced research and reasoning skills are taught and whether students, while being taught the basics, are still expected to develop the required more advanced skills without ever being taught (or even told) that this is the case or what exactly is expected.

Overall, the development of academic skills in legal education is an area that would benefit from more research so we can fully understand what is and should be taught and how.

JESSICA GUTH

References

Ajevski, M., Barker, K., Gilbert, A., Hardie, L. and Ryan, F. (2023). 'ChatGPT and the future of legal education and practice', *The Law Teacher*, 57(3), p. 352.

Del Mar, M. (2016). 'Learning How to Read Cases: resources from the visual and dramatic arts', in Van Klink, B. and de Vries, U. (eds), *Academic Learning Law. Theoretical Positions, Teaching Experiments and Learning Experiences*, Edward Elgar Publishing.

Finley, L.M. (1989). 'Breaking Women's Silence in Law: The Dilemma of the Gendered Nature of Legal Reasoning', *Notre Dame L. Rev.*, 64, p. 886.

Grimes, R. and Gibbons, J. (2016) 'Assessing experiential learning – us, them and the others', *International Journal of Clinical Legal Education*, 23(1). Available at http://dx.doi.org/10.19164/ijcle.v23i1.492.

Guth, J. (2020). 'The past and futures of legal skills in English Law Schools', in Jones, E. and Cownie, F. (eds), *Key Directions in Legal Education: National and International Perspectives*, Routledge.

Mudd, J.O. (1983). 'Thinking Critically About "Thinking Like a Lawyer"', *Journal of Legal Education*, 33, p. 704.

Posner, R.A. (1992). 'Legal Reasoning from the Top down and from the Bottom up: The Question of Unenumerated Constitutional Rights', *The University of Chicago Law Review*, 59(1), p. 433.

Sokhi-Bulley, S. (2016). 'Learning Law Differently: the importance of theory and methodology', in Van Klink, B. and de Vries, U. (eds), *Academic Learning Law. Theoretical Positions, Teaching Experiments and Learning Experiences*, Edward Elgar Publishing.

Solomon, E. (2020). 'Legal Skills: Making a real change in Nigerian Legal Education', in Jones, E. and Cownie, F. (eds), *Key Directions in Legal Education: National and International Perspectives*, Routledge.

Thornton, M. (2012). *Privatising the Public University: The Case of Law*, Routledge.

Turner, J., Bone, A. and Ashton, J. (2018). 'Reasons why law students should have access to learning law through a skills-based approach', *The Law Teacher*, 52(1), p. 1.

Tyrrell, H. and Jowitt, J. (2019). 'Let them eat cases! Bridging the gap between school and degree level learning', *The Law Teacher*, 56(2), p. 271.

Twining, W. (1988). 'Legal Skills and Legal Education', *The Law Teacher*, 22(1), p. 4.

Wallace, C.J. (2018). 'The pedagogy of legal reasoning: democracy, discourse and community', *The Law Teacher*, 52(3), p. 260.

Xiaotong Z. and Evans, C. (2024). 'Enhancing the development and understanding of assessment literacy in higher education', *European Journal of Higher Education*, 14(1), p. 80.

2. Adjunct professors and legal pracademics

What are adjunct professors?

Adjunct professors are practising lawyers who spend part of their time teaching law students. They are very common in North American law schools. In the USA, for example, they form such a vital part of the workforce that were they to disappear, the resulting shortage of law teachers would pose an existential threat to most law schools in the United States (Funk, Boutros and Volokh ([2023] at 63). Adjunct professors are employed for a number of reasons, in addition to the obvious one of providing extra teaching resources. Adjuncts can, for example, provide cover while a legal academic is on sabbatical leave and they can also be used to provide specialist expertise and thus enable law schools to offer students a greater choice of specialist subjects than would otherwise be possible (Lemmer and Robak [2014] at 12).

The role of adjunct professors in the law school

North American law schools have made significant use of adjuncts for decades. Writing in 1997, Popper noted that in the greater Washington area it was not unusual for law schools to employ between 100 and 200 adjuncts, and in some law schools they could be carrying out just over one third of the upper-level teaching (Popper [1997] at 83). In 2023 Funk, Boutros and Volokh found a similar situation as regards the use of adjuncts: '…in the typical U.S. law school there are roughly two adjunct professors for each full-time professor listed on the law school's faculty page'. Many of these adjunct professors are likely to be teaching elective courses involving smaller numbers of students than the compulsory courses taught by full-time faculty). However, their overall contribution to the ability of law schools to offer a wide variety of courses is significant, with adjuncts often teaching over half of the courses offered to second and third-level students (Funk, Boutros and Volokh [2023] at 56). Despite (or perhaps because of) their major contribution to law school teaching,

organisations representing full-time faculty have opposed any reduction in the American Bar Association (ABA) Standard 403, '… which requires that full-time faculty perform at least 50% of *aggregate* law teaching – meaning classes provided during all three years of law school' (Funk, Boutros and Volokh [2023] at 61 [emphasis in original]). In a 2017 press release, the Association of American Law Schools (AALS), for example, said that part-time law teachers, while enriching the curriculum, '…cannot substitute for the focus of full-time faculty on teaching, availability to students, curriculum design and assessment, scholarship and sustained engagement for educating professionals for the multiple roles they will play as lawyers and leaders' (AALS, quoted in Funk, Boutros and Volokh [2023] at 61). While it appears likely that there is a certain amount of self-interest involved in such pronouncements, it is also the case that adjunct professors do not have the same skill-set (especially as regards pedagogical techniques) as full-time academics, and in general they do not carry out research, or become involved in the administrative tasks that full-time academics carry out, such as sitting on committees, involvement in recruitment of students or in alumni events.

What motivates adjunct professors?

Adjunct professors do not in general seem to take up these roles primarily for financial gain. Funk, Boutros and Volokh ([2023] at 57) emphasise the poor rates of pay in the USA for adjunct positions and argue that they provide their services with little or no support from the university which employs them. In their view: 'The typical adjunct prepares everything at home or work with little or no institutional support, arrives at the law school to teach the class, and then departs. In fact, it is not at all unusual for an adjunct to get through a full semester without receiving any but the most ministerial institutional assistance' (Funk, Boutros and Volokh [2023] at 59). However, there is evidence that adjunct professors who teach in Canadian universities enjoy significantly better conditions of employment than their counterparts in the USA (Chegg and Hannover Research [2023] at 11). Nevertheless, there are a number of advantages for legal practitioners in holding an adjunct position, which might go some way to explaining their significant presence, even in US law schools. These include the benefit of staying up-to-date in their field of expertise, the prestige associated with holding a position in a university law school and the satisfaction of sharing their knowledge and experience with the lawyers of the future. Lemmer and Robak, advising practitioners who are contemplating taking up an adjunct position, elaborate further on the business opportunities which may flow from the appointment. They point out that being an adjunct will enhance an individual's professional reputation, validating their expertise in a particular area of law. Consequently, adjuncts should update their website and all client marketing materials. The prestige of an adjunct position, they note '…may lead to referrals and even to opportunities for media commentary' (Lemmer and Robak [2014] at 12). Nevertheless, Lemmer and Robak also emphasise that taking up an adjunct position involves serious commitment of time and effort, so should not be entered into without serious consideration. They caution the intending adjunct that there are a lot of things to learn about the way in which a law school operates, including: the 'jargon' of higher education, how to design a course and get it approved (including appropriate assessment tasks), how to design materials to support learning, how to give feedback and how to interact with students. Essentially, the adjunct needs to understand the culture of higher education and develop their pedagogic expertise as well (Lemmer and Robak [2014] at 14). Popper, drawing on his experience as an associate dean responsible for the administration of adjunct faculty at the Washington College of Law, American University, takes a pragmatic view of the advice that he recommends adjuncts receive: 'Adjuncts need to be told that student performance will probably not be as high as they have fantasized, and that the task of teaching is more difficult and more time-consuming than they may have guessed' (Popper [1997] at 85).

Supporting adjunct professors

Despite the challenges, it is clear that adjunct teachers are an important part of the teaching resource in North American law schools. Nevertheless, there is evidence that in the USA in particular they lack support and training for their role, not only as teachers, but as student advisors which affects their ability to perform effectively (Chegg and Hanover Research [2023] at 22). Recognising this problem, the American Association of Law Schools runs an annual workshop for adjunct faculty, and has developed a website providing a range of resources intended to support the professional development of adjuncts in their teaching capacity (https://www.aals.org/faculty-staff-resources/adjunct/). The American Bar Association has an adjunct faculty committee, which '…provides a forum for law schools to discuss ways to better recruit, train, mentor and supervise adjunct faculty' and a section of its website provides a range of resources, including a sample adjunct faculty handbook (https://www.americanbar.org/groups/legal_education/committees/adjunct_faculty/). Such initiatives are clearly intended to support adjunct faculty in their academic role and help them to negotiate the culture of higher education, so that they can continue to provide a valuable resource for law schools and their students.

Legal pracademics

Although adjunct professors appear to be a largely North American phenomenon, it is also the case that some professors of law in European universities practise law, as well as teaching and researching. However, they tend to hold full faculty positions as academics (whether full-time or part-time), unlike adjunct professors in North America, who do not become part of the academic faculty. In England and Wales, some law schools employ full-time staff as legal academics who had previously pursued a career as legal practitioners. The term 'pracademic' has been coined to describe former practitioners of any profession or occupation who then take up a post in a university (see, for example, Posner [2009] at 16). In law schools, former legal practitioners who then take up an academic post are frequently involved in running law clinics or are otherwise engaged in activities designed to promote the employability of law students (see Employability and Legal Education entry).

As with adjunct professors, although legal practitioners and academic lawyers share some commonalities, pracademics who take up academic posts experience at first hand the tensions to their professional and personal values arising from differences between the two communities of practice to which they now belong. Collins and Collins comment that '…academic work is often perceived by practitioners as too focused, too esoteric or just simple common sense…In parallel, academics can perceive practice as dated, opinion driven and closed to innovation' (Collins and Collins [2019] at 7). To be effective, the pracademic must not only successfully straddle both the world of academia and that of practice, but they must establish sufficient legitimacy to be respected in both communities (see Wenger [1998] at 109 quoted in Kuhn ([2009] at 109). The experience of becoming a pracademic is complex, since individuals do not necessarily move seamlessly from one stable professional identity in practice to another in higher education (Dickinson, Fowler and Griffiths [2022] at 293). Dickinson, Fowler and Griffiths ([2022] at 292) argue that although some literature has enthusiastically emphasised the variety of pracademics' skillsets 'Other research has cautioned against over-championing the pracademic in this way, suggesting that both career academics and pracademics need to perceive each other as equals to fully benefit from their shared skills, experience and knowledge pools'. The path to achieving this parity of esteem is far from straightforward, however.

FIONA COWNIE

References

Chegg and Hanover Research (2023). 'Contingent Faculty: hidden assets, still underserved and underpaid' Center for Digital Learning', available at https://www.chegg.com/about/center-for-digital-learning/.

Collins, L. and Collins, D. (2019). 'The Role of "pracademics" in Education and Development of Adventure Sport Professionals', *Journal of Adventure Education and Outdoor Learning*, 19, p. 1.

Dickinson, J., Fowler, A. and Griffiths, T.L. (2022). 'Pracademics? Exploring Transitions and Professional Identities in Higher Education', *Studies in Higher Education*, 47, p. 290.

Funk, Markus, T., Boutros, A.S. and Volokh, E. (2023). 'The Hidden Life of Law School Adjuncts: Teaching Temps, Indispensable Instructors, Underappreciated Cash Cows, or Something Else?', *Texas Law Review Online*, 102, p. 44.

Kuhn, T. (2002). 'Negotiating Boundaries Between Scholars and Practitioners', *Management Communication Quarterly*, 16, p. 106.

Lemmer, C.A. and Robak, M.J. (2014). 'So, You Want to Be an Adjunct Professor? The Processes, Perils, and Potential', *New York State Bar Association Journal*, 86(6), p. 10.

Popper, A.F. (1997). 'The Uneasy Integration of Adjunct Teachers into American Legal Education', *Journal of Legal Education*, 47, p. 83.

Posner, P.L. (2009). 'The Pracademic: an agenda for re-engaging practitioners and academics', *Public Budgeting and Finance*, 29, p. 12.

Wenger, E. (1998). *Communities of Practice: Learning, meaning and identity*, Cambridge University Press.

3. AI literacies in legal education

Introduction

This entry argues that Artificial Intelligence (AI) literacies have now become a key aspect of legal education. The term AI refers to

> ...computer systems which are intended to replicate human cognitive functions. In particular it includes 'machine learning', where algorithms detect patterns in data, and apply these new patterns to automate certain tasks. (The Law Society of England and Wales, 2018)

Law students and legal academics have already become comfortable in use corrective AI every time they check their writing with spellcheck. They have become skilled in using extractive AI to find caselaw in legal research databases. Many also use collaborative AI to bring diverse thinking and practices together conveniently.

At the same time, AI is altering how lawyers work, influencing and changing the types of work lawyers do and the sorts of professional responsibilities, knowledge, skills and attributes necessary to thrive in an AI-mediated world of legal work. Today, we see many examples of where AI is already supporting legal professionals in key areas of work including service delivery, client care, legal research and advice, due diligence, and drafting and analysing legal documents. The power in an AI-mediated world of work is not the concern around machines replacing legal services delivered by lawyers, instead the focus is on how we will collaborate with AI technologies to be better lawyers, which is likely to require law students and legal students and academics to do some things differently.

AI and legal education

For law schools, AI provides an opportunity to reframing what we teach our students, what we value as part of the law curriculum, how much emphasis is placed on knowledge acquisition and application, the professional and tacit knowledge required, the sorts of competencies we ask of our learners and how we fully preparing students for a changing world (Simpson et al [2023]).

AI literacies refer to the knowledge, skills, and understanding necessary to effectively engage with and make informed decisions about the use and implications of AI technologies. An AI literate graduate typically possess an understanding and confidence around the capabilities, limitations, and ethical considerations associated with AI systems and the skills to adapt and thrive in this changing landscape (Ng et al [2021]). Within the AI landscape it is also necessary to continue to prepare students, albeit differently, to elevate their knowledge of the law, understanding of professional responsibilities, the various lawyering skills and the skills and attributes of what makes a professional, alongside learning how to be more human to thrive in an AI-mediated future.

Key principles for law schools around preparing students to be empowered in the age of AI are:

- Using AI as a companion for learning.
- Using AI responsibly, confidentially and critically in learning, teaching and research.
- Preparing learners to confidently thrive in a professional world of work that is permeated and mediated by AI across professions, industries and sectors.
- Creating relevance of our curriculum and the authenticity of our assessment means we need to bring these tools into the learning experiences and our assessments now.

Mapping AI literacies

It is essential that we ensure that law students are prepared to confidently thrive in a professional world of work that is permeated and mediated by AI across professions, industries and sectors. The headings below seek to outline what a future ready law graduate who is AI literate should be equipped with as part of their legal education journey (Thanaraj [2023]). A deep theoretical understanding is necessary in the age of generative AI and other forms of AI use in professional sectors, particularly where new kinds of technology and innovation-driven jobs are coming into the legal sector. It is also an opportunity for law schools and the legal profession to embrace an experimentation mindset. Much work in law schools and across the Higher Education sector needs to focus on supporting students to learn how professionals engage with AI outputs, how to use AI to creatively solve problems by questioning, verifying and scrutinising how AI is used and its intersection between efficiency and professional responsibilities of a lawyer.

Technical Understanding
- Familiarity with a glossary of algorithms, and techniques used in AI, such as machine learning, neural networks, and natural language processing.
- Recognising AI and distinguishing between technological artifacts that use and do not use AI.
- Being able to choose wisely: Knowing the various AI tools and their affordances, including whether generative AI is the right tool for this task, or whether earlier more reliable or predictable tools may better serve your needs.
- A basic understanding of how AI systems are trained including deep learning via supervised learning of feed forward networks.
- The architecture of large language models ('LLMs') and the methods involved in how they generate their outputs through different levels of training such as: (i) pre-training, (ii) supervised reinforcement where labelled datasets are used to train algorithms that classify data or predict outcomes accurately, and (iii) reinforcement learning from human feedback which takes into account the user's beliefs, preferences, and objectives.
- Understanding the significance of weights and how they produce an output through the influence input data has on the output product.
- Understanding word embeddings which are vectors or numbers which encode the meaning of words so that similar words or phrases have closer vector representations, enabling users to capture this similarity in meaning by placing these phrases close together in the embedding space, including efficiently capturing the semantics/meaning of inputs, which can be useful for tasks such as text searching.

Data Literacy
- An understanding that AI helps legal professionals to analyse and extract insights from large datasets, enabling data-driven decision-making.

- Knowledge of data collection, processing, and analysis methods. This includes understanding data formats, data quality, biases, and privacy issues.
- Prioritising explainability and transparency in decisions and outputs is essential. There is a need for law students to understand how an AI tool reaches its conclusions.
- Recognising that humans play an important role in programming, choosing models, and fine-tuning AI systems, therefore an awareness of how datasets were created, how data was collected, and what are the limitations of the dataset will help with the transparency of the decisions and outputs generated by AI.

Ethical Awareness
- Lawyers are highly trained professionals with unique skills and responsibilities that are exercised to provide professional judgement and well-informed advice to their clients. When using AI influenced technologies to undertake various forms of legal work, lawyers will need to take into consideration fairness, transparency, accountability, and the potential impacts of the AI generated information on society and individuals. Therefore, law students need to be aware of these potential ethical issues.
- Associated with the importance of ethical awareness is the need for competent representation from lawyers which includes the legal knowledge, skill, thoroughness and preparation reasonably necessary for the representation. To skilfully and competently represent clients, lawyers need to be keep abreast of changes to technology used in legal practice, develop reasonable skill and competency with technology, its affordances and limitations. This means introducing law students to key concepts and ethical debates.
- Understanding the international regulatory scene, how to apply ethical frameworks to machine learning.

Critical Thinking
- Developing the ability to evaluate and question AI applications critically. This involves understanding the strengths and limitations of AI systems, recognising their potential risks and biases, and being

able to assess the reliability and credibility of AI-generated information.

- Being able to determine when it is appropriate to use AI and when to leverage human skills.
- Acknowledging that technology should facilitate, not replace, legal knowledge. AI tools are great for efficiency but should not overshadow legal judgment or replace legal advice.

Human-centred Design

- Using technologies in alignment with human values, needs, and preferences. This includes understanding user experience design principles, considering accessibility and inclusivity, and involving diverse perspectives in the development and deployment of AI technologies.
- Introducing law students to problem solving challenges that allow them to take on real-world legal challenges or case studies and apply design thinking principles to come up with innovative solutions. This may require multidisciplinary problem-solving and innovation.
- Creating opportunities for law students to foster a mindset of creativity, empathy, and adaptability, with a strong emphasis on understanding and empathising with the needs of clients and other relevant groups.

Collaboration and Communication

- A deep understanding of the subject matter and the ability to communicate complex ideas clearly and concisely, including a strong foundation in AI technologies to determine the usefulness of its outputs.
- The ability to work effectively with interdisciplinary teams and communicate AI concepts and implications to a wide range of audiences.
- Building and crafting the ability to explain a problem to another person precisely and concisely, so that they can solve it themselves.

This is arguably the most critical skill needed for the appropriate use of generative AI. It involves compressing your understanding of the present problem into a detailed yet precise set of directions that ask for a solution, leaving out nothing important and including nothing irrelevant. The ability to effectively instruct – whether a human assistant or, more commonly from now on, an artificial one – is the key high-value skill required of lawyers in the AI age. It is also of value to law students in echoing some of the features (clarity, precision, relevance) most valued within typical law assessments. Whilst the focus of much AI-related discussion in legal academic has been on maintaining academic integrity (Hargreaves [2023]), this is an opportune time to harness the power of AI as a powerful catalyst for change. Specifically, it offers a generational incentive to review and reimagine course design, learning experiences and assessments.

To ensure the relevance of the law school curriculum and the authenticity of its assessment, it is imperative that AI literacies are incorporated into the learning experiences and also into such assessments. There is an opportunity to consider why we are assessing our students, what is being evaluated and how evidence of learning is being gathered and demonstrated, This enables law schools to raise awareness of the use of AI within the learning experience, be confident that the learning experiences help students build their knowledge, skills, academic and professional attributes for an AI mediated world of life and work and to be confidently innovative in course design and assessments.

Practical ways to develop students' AI literacies throughout the law degree can include:

- Exploring the capabilities and limitations of AI with students. Articulation of how it is aligned with disciplinary or professional values is key to integration success.
- Considering with students how learning to work with AI is rapidly becoming a critical capability of the professional world.
- Asking students for their critical reflections on the usefulness of appropriate AI tools and its outputs to highlight that information generated from AI may lack reliability and credibility.
- Considering formative assessments that facilitate the use of AI within the learning experience.
- Providing students with clear guidelines on what is considered acceptable use of AI tools within their studies and how its use should be acknowledged.
- Asking students to document/evidence/ reflect upon the process they followed to produce an AI 'output', acknowledging

and critiquing how AI was used as part of their work. Evidencing the process of learning can support a better understanding of the learning process such as making sense, how knowledge is being formed and then applied, how they have arrived at decisions and judgements – what they ultimately know and do.

Key considerations for legal academics in embedding AI into wider course design include asking:

- What value will AI add to what law students learn and how they learn?
- In what ways does AI in the curriculum support, develop and prepare students with the necessary skills and knowledge for assessments?
- How does it link to wider employability skills and graduate attributes?
- What AI literacies are you looking to develop in your students? Are these literacies generic or will they be tailored towards subject disciplines and professional identities?
- How will you communicate to students the benefit(s) of each of the above so they are able to appreciate the value of engaging with the tasks/learning to assist their learning and development?
- How are you planning to support your students to understand the technologies you are asking them to use so that they are able to use them optimally for their learning?
- When embedded into assessments, what is the expected output from the AI, and what sorts of solutions help achieve that?
- Can all students and staff have access to various AI platforms and solutions? How will using AI in learning activities link to other activities in the module and does it need to be done in a sequence?

Conclusion

Given the rapid advancements in AI technologies, continuously staying updated with the latest developments, exploring new AI applications, and understanding evolving ethical and legal frameworks is essential for law schools. This starts with thinking about the skills students will need to thrive and, perhaps more importantly, the skills they will need to lead in this age of AI. Law students will need a mindset and agility to deal with the inevitable changes AI and other technologies will bring. This mindset requires students to embrace curiosity, the desire to continuously learn, accept that we may not know everything and effectively deal with unknow challenges in an ethical and professional manner. It also requires them to apply creativity, problem finding and problem solving in new ways, acknowledging that innovation can fortify our position at a time of change Finally, it also requires collaboration, working across professional boundaries and disciplinary boundaries to equip oneself with new methodologies, research, and skillsets to view problems in new ways. In short, AI literacies are crucial within the contemporary law school.

ANN THANARAJ

References

Ng, D.T.K., Leung, J.K.L. Chu, S.K.W. and Qiao, M.S. (2021). 'Conceptualizing AI literacy: An exploratory review', *Computers and Education: Artificial Intelligence*, 2, available at https://www.sciencedirect.com/science/article/pii/S2666920X21000357.

Simpson, M., Thanaraj, A. and Durston, P. (2023). 'Learning how to be more human will prepare universities for an AI-mediated future', WONKHE, available at https://wonkhe.com/blogs/learning-how-to-be-more-human-will-prepare-universities-for-an-ai-mediated-future/.

Thanaraj, A. (2023). Model for AI literacies in legal education, presented at Westminster Legal Policy Forum.

The Law Society of England and Wales. (2018). *Artificial Intelligence (AI) and the Legal Profession – Horizon Scanning Report*, available at https://www.lawsociety.org.uk/en/topics/research/ai-artificial-intelligence-and-the-legal-profession.

4. Alternative Dispute Resolution and legal education

When referring to ADR and the teaching of it within university law schools, we are most commonly concerned with mediation, negotiation, and arbitration. Where ADR is taught within law schools there are good examples within UK universities where these aspects of ADR form part of the undergraduate law degree curriculum. For instance, at Canterbury Christ Church University, the year one 20 credit LLB module Dispute Resolution includes a focus on ADR processes, including negotiation, mediation, and arbitration, at year two the optional module Civil & Commercial Mediation is offered.

In England and Wales, the Civil Procedure Rules (CPR) have undoubtedly influenced the way in which lawyers advise their clients regarding dispute resolution. This is because since their introduction, the indications are that the adversarial vigour with which legal advisers pursued their clients' interests in the pre-Woolf era is now an unacceptable approach to take with regard to dispute resolution. Not only do the CPR signal a significant shift in the regulatory framework within which litigation occurs, they also attempt to change the way the process of litigation is viewed. This approach in practice has started to be reflected within law schools' curricula and the way in which 'dispute resolution' and ADR is being taught.

Judicial approaches including the emphasis now being placed on the promotion of settlement and the embedding of 'dispute resolution' opportunities within the CPR, indicate that lawyers' roles have changed. Within the UK, in the face of this kind of attitudinal change and the growing judicial support for the use and encouragement of ADR, dispute resolution as an academic subject has started to attract more attention in UK law schools. With this increased judicial intervention and commentary on the subject of mediation in particular, some law schools have started to take a more socio-critical curriculum approach and incorporate aspects of ADR, in the same way that their North American counterparts in USA and Canadian law schools have already embraced the teaching of ADR.

Within England and Wales, the recent introduction of the Solicitors' Qualification Examination (SQE) by the Solicitors Regulation Authority (SRA), replaces the Legal Practice Course as the academic stage of a solicitor's training. This introduction is perhaps an example of an attempt to provide future solicitors with 'day one competence' (a central aim of the new training approach) and include within the curriculum socio-legal themes that future solicitors are likely to experience in practice, hence, the introduction of Dispute Resolution for the first time as a discrete assessment area. The objectives of SQE 1 are to provide students with the skills required to apply relevant core legal principles and rules appropriately and effectively, at the level of a competent newly qualified solicitor in practice, to realistic client based and ethical problems and situations in a number of areas including arbitration, mediation, and litigation as an appropriate mechanism to resolve a dispute.

At SQE 2, the second stage of academic training and assessment, law students in England and Wales are required to take 5 Practical Legal Skills Assessments, including Client Interviewing, Advocacy/Persuasive Oral Communication, Case and Matter Analysis, Legal Research and Written Advice, and Legal Drafting. All five assessments must be taken and passed in the same two practice contexts, making a total of 10 assessments. The practice contexts are: Criminal Practice, Property, Wills and the Administration of Estates and Trusts, Business Practice, and Dispute Resolution. Again, the introduction of Dispute Resolution (including ADR) is a new area of assessment.

The SQE is taken postgraduate level, and where ADR is taught within UK law schools it tends to be either optional within legal education at undergraduate level or more commonly found at postgraduate level. Current examples of those UK law schools teaching aspects of ADR at postgraduate level (taught Master's) are Newcastle, King's College London, Queen Mary University of London, City University, Aberdeen University, Strathclyde, and the University of Law which offers a Master of Laws (LLM) in Mediation and Alternative Dispute Resolution. At undergraduate level, the situation is less developed. Canterbury Christ Church University probably leads the way with a defined dispute resolution pathway within the levels of the

LLB, teaching dispute resolution including ADR and specifically mediation, whilst other law schools such as York, Newcastle, Sussex, Kent, Swansea, the University of West of England, and Liverpool John Moores all teach ADR as optional modules at higher levels of study, although Northumbria has a compulsory level 5 Civil Dispute Resolution module.

In other common law jurisdictions, for example Australia, whilst ADR is not central to the law school curriculum, where it is taught the courses are 'stand-alone' and more commonly found as final year electives or optional courses. There are however examples of a more enlightened approach to the teaching of ADR in some other common law jurisdictions. For instance, of the top 10 ranked US law schools in 2022, as listed in the US News and World Report Rankings 2022/23 were: Yale, Stanford, Columbia, The University of Chicago, Harvard, The University of Pennsylvania, New York University, The University of Virginia, The University of California Berkeley, University of Michigan Ann Arbor, all of which teach 'stand-alone' courses on negotiation, mediation, and arbitration and some have 'live' clinics linked with these areas of the taught curriculum. Similarly, in Canada the top ranked law schools as listed by the QS World University Rankings 2022/23 were: The University of Toronto, McGill, The University of British Columbia, Osgoode Hall Law School, and the University of Montreal. All these law schools offer conflict or dispute resolution, mediation, and negotiation courses as part of their legal education curriculum provision.

Of those countries which adopt the civil law system (as opposed to the common law system of justice), the Postgraduate Centre at the University of Vienna offers an Arbitration and Mediation LLM. The LLM offered at The Sciences Po Law School in Paris offers an LLM in Transnational Arbitration & Dispute Settlement and is a truly 'international' flavoured course judging by the origins of faculty contributors drawn from Italy, Chile, China, Singapore, Greece, and Russia. Leiden University's Master of Laws in Advanced Studies in International Dispute Settlement and Arbitration (LLM) is a high-level postgraduate programme on the theory and practice of international dispute settlement and arbitration in international law. It focuses on public international law, but blends in private law dimensions, equip-

ping graduates with skills for a new legal landscape. There are currently 27 LLM programmes offered across European University law schools' LLM Programmes in Alternative Dispute Resolution/Arbitration/Mediation. The Programme on Negotiation (PON) based at Harvard Law School is a consortium of Harvard University, Massachusetts Institute of Technology, and Tufts University, and has led the way in dispute resolution pedagogy since its foundation in the early 1980s. The PON describes itself as an interdisciplinary research centre dedicated to developing the theory and practice of negotiation and dispute resolution including mediation and other related ADR processes, in a range of public and private settings. The PON has undoubtedly influenced many law schools in the development of dispute resolution courses. It has a vast range of educational materials available on its website to download for university classroom settings, including role-play simulations, videos, books, periodicals, and case studies.

Out of Harvard Law School and the PON has emerged a considerable body of dispute resolution literature including the seminal work *Getting to Yes* by Roger Fisher and William Ury, first published in 1981. It is a book that is widely used as a foundational text for negotiation and mediation classes and has become a valuable and influential legal education resource. There is a growing body of literature centred around dispute resolution and ADR, more-so perhaps in North America, but the interest is growing in the UK and other parts of the world. Some African nations such as Nigeria for instance have embraced ADR, so too Continental Europe where the literature emerging is evidence that ADR in its various process formats is being more widely used.

Graduate and other useful transferable skills can be effectively acquired through the study of dispute resolution and specific aspects of it as an academic subject at higher education level. This has been demonstrated through Clinical Legal Education (see entries on Clinical Legal Education). Situational learning within the context of dispute resolution-based modules can enable the participating students, through engagement with aspects of simulated role-play activity, that is, playing the roles of mediators and parties, to acquire and develop important key graduate skills, particularly organisational management, team-working and communication skills.

Research has shown that using simulation activities as part of Clinical Legal Education can provide a number of benefits therefore. These can be summarised as; deep and surface learning theory through immersion, confidence, motivation, or willingness to learn, the affective nature of the learning approach, preparation, graduate skills acquisition, learning enjoyment and an appreciation of the importance and benefit of reflection.

Mediation clinics

Mediation clinics, found more frequently in the US and Canadian law schools than in other jurisdictions, are places where theory meets practice. Depending on the model of clinic (simulated or 'live' experiential), these clinics provide great opportunities for observation of 'live' mediations and participation in simulated role play exercises. Law students benefit from these clinics through acquiring a number of graduate and employability transferrable skills including: personal and interpersonal skills, autonomy and confidence enhancement, independence of thought, problem-solving and decision making skills, and team working.

Some examples of law programmes which provide their law students with the opportunity to participate in legal education through engagement with well-established mediation clinics in Canada and the USA include: the Osgoode Hall Law School Mediation Clinical Program at York University Toronto, which bridges mediation theory and practice, while actively engaging students in the provision of conflict resolution services through an in-house mediation clinic, and The Gittis Centre at The University of Pennsylvania's Carey Law School, which provides law students with the opportunity to be mediators in a wide array of cases. With a faculty supervisor present, students co-mediate an average of four to five cases per semester at courthouses, government agencies, and within their law school in areas that include civil litigation, criminal, domestic, campus student discipline, international child custody disputes, and employment discrimination matters.

There are also examples of mediation and dispute resolution clinics having been established in UK law schools. Strathclyde University, The University of Central Lancashire, Canterbury Christ Church University, University of Sussex, and the Centre for Mediation and Conflict Management within Business and Law School at East London University, all have mediation clinics. Nottingham Law School has a Centre for Mediation and Dispute Resolution.

ADR competitions

Activities that are extra-curricular to the law school's main curriculum have for the past 20 years in the UK included the UK Student Mediation Competition, a competition for law students at both undergraduate and postgraduate level of study. The Worshipful Company of Arbitrators runs a mediation and arbitration competition in alternate years for law students and early years legal practitioners. The Willem C Vis International Commercial Arbitration Moot or Vis Moot is an international arbitration competition which has been running since the mid 1990s, the finals of which take place in Vienna, Austria. ADR-ODR International have in the past organised an online mediation competition, and CEDR, the London-based mediation training provider, runs a national negotiation competition for law students in the UK annually. The International Chamber of Commerce (ICC) International Commercial Mediation Competition is one of the biggest educational competitions worldwide for law students dedicated exclusively to international commercial mediation. In the US The International Academy of Dispute Resolution organises the annual International Law School Mediation Tournament which is generally held in March or April each year and features law school and graduate school participants from all over the world. The Consensual Dispute Resolution Competition in Mediation and Negotiation, is an international skills-based law school competition, which takes place annually over five days at the University of Vienna, combining the arts and skills of mediation and negotiation, and which includes mock mediations, educational programmes and social events.

BEN WATERS

References

Fisher, R., Ury, W. and Patton, B. (2011). *Getting to Yes, Negotiating Agreement Without Giving In*, Penguin.

Hodges, C., Creutzfeldt, N. and MacLeod, S. (2014). 'Reforming the EU Consumer ADR Landscape: Implementation and its Issues (policy brief from 2014 ADR conference in Oxford)'.

Ikubanni, O.O. and Saheed, A.A. (2022). 'Impact of Technology on Alternative Dispute Resolution in Nigeria and the Birth and Challenges of Online Dispute Resolution', *Global Journal of Politics and Law Research*, 10(4), p. 1.

Leiden University's Master of Laws in Advanced Studies in International Dispute Settlement and Arbitration (LL.M.), available at https://www.universiteitleiden.nl/en/education/study-programmes/master/international-dispute-settlement-and-arbitration.

LLM Programmes in Alternative Dispute Resolution at the University of Vienna' Law School, available at https://llm-guide.com/schools/austria/concentration/alternative-dispute-resolution-arbitration-mediation.

Ojo, S.O. (2023). 'Alternative Dispute Resolution (ADR): A Suitable Broad Based Dispute Resolution Model in Nigeria; Challenges and Prospects', *International Journal of Conflict Management*, 4(1), p. 50.

Po Sciences Law School's LLM In Transnational Arbitration & Dispute Settlement, available at https://www.sciencespo.fr/ecole-de-droit/en/content/llm-transnational-arbitration-dispute-settlement/students.

Terekhov, V. (2019). 'Online Mediation: A Game Changer or Much Abo about Nothing?', *Access to Just. E. Eur.*, p. 33.

Training for Tomorrow Policy Statement and SQE Assessment Specification 2020, both available at https://www.sra.org.uk/.

US News and World Report Rankings 2022/23, available at https://www.usnews.com/education/best-global-universities/rankings.

Waters, B.D. (2017). 'The Importance of Teaching Dispute Resolution in a 21st Century Law School', *The Law Teacher*, 51(2), p. 227.

5. Argentina (contemporary legal education)

To understand the macro-institutional aspects of contemporary legal education in Argentina it is crucial to acknowledge the tensions shaping the Argentine university system. Among them are the type of university management (public/private), student access (open admission/limited enrolment and selection of entrants) and financial contributions (tuition-free/fee-based).

These tensions originate from diverse perspectives on the university and its functions, giving rise to political disputes, along with both continuities and disruptions that characterise the country's higher education history.

Argentina's higher education system comprises universities and university institutes. The former offer a range of disciplines, while the latter focus on a single discipline.

Type of management: public vs private

Universities are the primary institutions for legal education, offering both undergraduate (law degree) and postgraduate (master's and doctoral programmes in law). They can be publicly or privately managed, with only two having an international/foreign character that lacks legal education units.

To practise as a lawyer, it is necessary to graduate from an undergraduate law programme and then enrol with the corresponding bar association in the corresponding jurisdiction. Bar associations regulate the legal profession and provide ongoing training for lawyers.

Argentina's higher education is characterised by the early and continuous development of the state or public sector and the late emergence of the private sector in the late 1950s. This distinguishes Argentina from other Latin American countries (Barsky and Corengia [2017] at 32). 'In Latin America, it is one of the countries that has one of the strongest traditions of public higher education' (Plotkin [2006] at 43).

State universities were established with the monopolistic power to issue nationally recognised professional degrees. This func-tion was also extended to private universities, justifying state control over them.

The current higher education system comprises 144 institutions, primarily universities (122) and 22 university institutes. Of these institutions, 56 per cent are state managed (national or provincial) and 44 per cent are privately managed (self-obtained data from the websites of universities and institutes of higher education [2023]).

Currently, legal education is almost exclusively conducted within universities. Private universities have a much higher presence of law programmes (78 per cent) compared to public universities (41 per cent) (self-obtained data from universities' websites [2023]). However, the number of law students and graduates from public institutions is much higher than that of private institutions. Thus, quantitatively, the responsibility for legal education in Argentina largely rests on the national state.

Undergraduate law programmes: number of students

In Argentina, government policies related to higher education have fluctuated, resulting in disparities and contrasts, particularly in the field of legal education. Public universities have historically registered a larger number of students compared to private institutions.

Historically, the law degree has been one of the most socially attractive fields of study within the university's academic offerings. Legal studies have played an active role in shaping the power elites (De Imaz [1965]) (Böhmer [1999]), 'which makes legal knowledge highly valued as a cultural capital due to its relationship with other forms of capital (political, economic and cultural)' (Lista [2005] at 602).

In Argentina, in 2021, the total number of law students exceeded 240,000 (Ministerio de Educación (ME) de Argentina (SEU-DIU) [2021]). It is the profession with the highest number of students after those of the field of economics as a whole.

The vast majority of law students (70 per cent) are enrolled in state universities, primarily national, with the remaining 30 per cent attending private universities (ME de Argentina (SEU-DIU) [2021]). This sets the country apart from observable trends in other countries in the region, such as Mexico and Brazil. It is worth noting that women make up the majority of undergraduate law programmes (Lista [2022] at 14).

Postgraduate law programmes: number of students

In Argentina's higher education system, postgraduate programmes come in three modalities: doctoral, master's and specialisation.

According to official data, in 2019, there were 2,977 postgraduate law programmes in the country, with 16 per cent being doctoral programmes, 36 per cent master's programmes and 48 per cent specialisations (Lista [2022] at 14).

In terms of postgraduate law studies, the trends are similar to those at the undergraduate level. State-managed institutions attract the highest number of students in all modalities: 61 per cent in doctoral programmes, 69 per cent in master's programmes and 81 per cent of those pursuing specialisations (ME de Argentina (SEU-DIU) [2021]).

Regarding the gender distribution of postgraduate law students, trends are similar to those at the undergraduate level, with slightly more than half being women, except in doctoral programs where men make up the majority (Lista [2022] at 15).

Organisation and governance of legal education: chairs, tuition-free education and open admission

The basic organisational model for both public and private universities consists of faculties subdivided into schools. In state universities, the department structure is less common and relatively recent.

The chair (*cátedra*) is the fundamental unit for organising teaching. It brings together professors with different hierarchical positions (full, associate and assistant). Chairs operate as differentiated and differentiating 'habitats', fostering strong loyalties within but fragmentation outside, making horizontal integration and articulation processes difficult (Lista and Brigido [2002] at 298).

In state universities and faculties, legislative functions are exercised (to varying degrees) by representatives of professors, students, graduates, and sometimes administrative staff. They collectively participate in decision-making and the election of authorities (rectors and deans). This fundamental

principle was established by the University Reform of 1918 and, since then, has been respected by democratic governments and suspended during dictatorial regimes.

State universities are financially and administratively autarkic and academically and pedagogically autonomous (Fucito [2000] at 74). While the national government retains significant decision-making power, universities, in exercising their autonomy, dictate their own statutes.

Two other principles of the 1918 Reform, firmly rooted, are the free public education and open admission of students to state universities. Policies that regulate and restrict these principles are viewed as undemocratic, as seen during military regimes that limited access and neoliberal governments that attempted to regulate tuition fees.

Curriculum: duration and structure

The formal or ideal duration of law degree programmes varies, with state programmes typically lasting five or six years and most private programmes lasting five. In practice, the actual duration tends to be longer, especially in public institutions.

A highly homogeneous aspect of law degree programmes is the organisation of subjects within a highly-structured curriculum structure, which compartmentalises legal knowledge into distinct and separate compartments. The core consists of subjects with legal content, which are obligatory by definition, while subjects considered extra-legal (sociology, history, philosophy, economics and so on) are confined to specialised courses, sometimes not mandatory. This curriculum matrix, organised according to different classification axes (public-private law, substantive-procedural law, legal-extra-legal knowledge), facilitates the establishment of hierarchies (Lista, Brigido [2002] at 111, 120).

Law degree programmes tend to be highly structured, with a large number of fixed and mandatory subjects. Recent curriculum reforms have introduced some flexibility by including optional subjects, giving students greater content choice. However, these reforms have not innovated in the fundamental features of the dominant pedagogical model.

Graduate profile

The debate about the ideal and actual graduate profile of law programmes has a long history. There is an ongoing discussion about whether the education should be strictly professional, whether students should graduate with strong theoretical foundation or a practical orientation, whether they should be mere recipients and reproducers of 'black letter' (doctrinal) law or professionals capable of solving problems and handling cases and whether they should also be reflexive and critical of the law and its practices and institutions (Cardinaux et al [2005]).

In practice, the prevailing profile is that of a generalist lawyer who, after obtaining a degree, enters the professional field and defines his or her profile according to the work he or she undertakes. Thus, law programmes open a relatively broad, undetermined and unplanned spectrum of occupational possibilities. In this context, tradition is highly influential.

Faculty

From the early 1980s, mass student enrolment increased the number of law professors disproportionately in state university law programmes. Professors are selected through open competitions, a principle established in the 1918 Reform that continued under subsequent democratic governments. To address implementation difficulties and costs, interim appointments became common, offering flexibility but less stability for teaching staff (Lista and Brigido [2002] at 96, 97).

Teaching hours for professors are categorised as full-time, part-time or time-limited, with full-time positions being rare in law programmes (Fucito [2000] at 326).

Traditionally, prior pedagogical training was not mandatory for law professors. While many law programmes now offer pedagogical training, it is not obligatory for obtaining a teaching position. Pedagogical and didactic skills are largely informally acquired through emulation of their own instructors (Cardinaux and Clérico [2005] at 34).

Dominant pedagogical discourse: main features

The legal tradition and its teaching in Argentina are mainly influenced by the Roman-Germanic legal system, often referred to as the continental legal system. This system is founded on the idea of a harmonious, abstract, rational, self-contained and coherent legal order, separate from the complex and conflicting social, political and cultural reality.

In recent decades, Argentina has undergone significant legal and judicial reforms, partly driven by global influences, which include the constitutional recognition of international human rights treaties in the 1994 constitutional reform, the adoption of a new Civil and Commercial Code in 2015 and reforms of procedural codes aimed at simplifying and improving judicial processes. Argentina has also integrated aspects of the Common Law system, such as jury trials, mediation and alternative dispute resolution, greater orality in criminal proceedings and increased transparency and access to judicial information. These changes reflect shifts in society and the economy and have become part of contemporary legal education, altering some traditional teaching methods.

The prevailing predominant legal education model follows the Roman-Germanic legal tradition, with variations among institutions but significant homogeneity. It is rooted in positivist legal formalism, prioritising the teaching of legal texts (laws, doctrine, and case law) and legal principles while promoting a dogmatic and exegetic view of law and positing the ethical and political neutrality of law (Lista, Brigido [2002] at 227) (Bianco and Carrera [2010] at 168). The emphasis is on developing cognitive-instrumental skills like understanding, analysing, and synthesising the law, while cognitive-critical and expressive skills are often neglected (Brigido et al [2009] at 154 et seq.).

The lecture, where professors orally present codes and laws, has been the traditional teaching method, remaining deeply established despite criticisms (Lista [2012] at 50, 55) (Bianco and Carrera [2010] at 164).

In recent decades, law degree curricula have placed greater emphasis on practical training, including legal clinics, professional internships, conflict resolution training and mock trials, among other teaching strategies.

Conclusion

Despite institutional ruptures and discontinuities, legal education in Argentina is characterised by remarkable consistency and stability. While it cannot be claimed that there is a single, unvaried approach to teaching and learning law, a dominant consensus combines several characteristics that shape it as a model. This model is highly effective in producing specialised ways of thinking, acting and perceiving the world, that leads to specialised professional identities.

From a traditional perspective, the dominant consensus represents the 'legally thinkable' in contradiction with alternative consensuses defined as the 'legally unthinkable'. Alternative views incorporate discourses based on critical values, philosophical, historical and social elements that highlight the tension between the materiality and formalism of the law and contribute to the understanding of law and facts in their wider social context.

In the twenty-first century, global and national social, political and economic changes have favoured legal education reforms that allowed the incorporation of alternative contents and practices, thus making legal education more flexible and diverse compared to the traditional model.

CARLOS LISTA

References

Barsky, O. and Corengia, Á. (2017). 'La educación universitaria privada en argentina', *Debate Universitario*, 10(31), p. 70.

Bianco, C. and Carrera, M.C. (2010). 'Proyecto institucional y prácticas de enseñanza en la carrera de Derecho. El proceso de formación universitaria y los debates pendientes', in González, M.G. and Cardinaux, N. (eds), *Los actores y las prácticas*, Editorial de la Universidad Nacional de La Plata.

Böhmer, F.M. (1999). *La enseñanza del derecho y el ejercicio de la abogacía*, Gedisa.

Brigido, A.M. and others. (2009). *La socialización de los estudiantes de abogacía. Crónica de una metaformosis*, Hispania Editorial.

Cardinaux, N. (2005). *De cursos y de formaciones docentes*, Universidad de Buenos Aires, Departamento de publicaciones.

Cardinaux, N. and Clérico, L. (2005). 'La formación docente universitaria y su relación con

los "modelos" de formación de abogados' in Cardinaux, N. and others, *De cursos y de formaciones docentes*, Universidad de Buenos Aires, Departamento de publicaciones, pp. 33–50.

De Imaz, J.L. (1965). *Los que mandan*, Eudeba.

Fucito, F. (2000). *El profesor de derecho de las universidades de Buenos Aires y Nacional de La Plata*, Editorial de la Universidad Nacional de La Plata.

Lista, C.A. (2022). 'La Educación Jurídica en Argentina: una revisión crítica', *Revista Pedagogía Universitaria y Didáctica del Derecho*, 9(1), p. 38.

Lista, C.A. (2012). '¿Derecho sin justicia? Los déficits de la educación jurídica en la socialización de los abogados en Argentina' in Ibarra Serrano, F.J., Rojas Castro, M.O. and Pineda Solorio, M.E. (eds), *La Educación Jurídica. Retos para el siglo XXI*, Centro de Investigaciones Jurídicas y Sociales, Facultad de Derecho y Ciencias Sociales de la Universidad Michoacana, pp. 35–73.

Lista, C.A. (2005). 'La educación jurídica en Argentina: genealogía de una crisis', *Anuario VIII*, Centro de Investigaciones Jurídicas y Sociales de la Universidad Nacional de Córdoba, pp. 601, 617.

Lista, C.A. and Brigido, A.M. (2002). *La enseñanza del derecho y la formación de la conciencia jurídica*, Sima Editora.

Ministerio de Educación de Argentina, Secretaría de Políticas Universitarias, Departamento de Información Universitaria. (2021). *Anuario Estadístico*, available at https://www.argentina.gob.ar/educacion/universidades/informacion/publicaciones/anuarios.

Plotkin, M.B. (2006). 'El desarrollo de la educación superior privada en la Argentina' in Plotkin, M.B. (ed), *La privatización de la educación superior y las ciencias sociales en Argentina. Un estudio de las carreras de Psicología y Economía*, CLACSO, pp. 43, 62.

6. Argentina (history of legal education)

The process of establishing the Argentine higher education system can be divided into two major periods: the colonial era under Spanish rule that extended until 1810 and the independent period that followed. In the current configuration of the system, it is essential to analyse the impact of the University Reform of 1918, which established the guiding principles that currently govern it. However, the validity of these principles was not stable, as they were highly resisted and suspended during extended periods of government throughout the twentieth century. Conflicts arising from different understandings of the university and its functions have led to various tensions that intersect the university policies implemented by successive governments, characterised by shifts, continuities, and ruptures that define the history of higher education in the country.

To comprehend the macro-institutional aspects of legal education in Argentina, it is necessary to analyse it in light of the various tensions present in the historical development of the Argentine university system. These tensions constitute institutional variables that have given specific structural features to legal education.

From the colonial period to independence

The origin of the Universidad de Córdoba, the first centre of higher education in what is now Argentine territory, predates the creation of the Viceroyalty of the Río de la Plata in 1776 by the Spanish crown. In 1613, based on what was the Colegio Máximo, a house of studies was founded under the direction of the Jesuits until their expulsion in 1767 by order of King Carlos III. Later, it was elevated to university status with authorisation from Pope Gregory XV and King Felipe III of Spain (Deckmann Fleck [2013] at 79).

During the colonial period, legal regulation was achieved through the application of Spanish laws, which were based on Roman and canonical law combined with medieval Castilian law and laws specifically created to administer and govern the American colonies, known as 'Leyes de Indias' and the 'Derecho Indiano', developed to address the unique circumstances of the colonies.

In 1791, the Chair of Instituta was established, marking the birth of the first Faculty of Jurisprudence in the viceroyalty, and in 1793, Chairs of Civil Jurisprudence and Canonical Jurisprudence were created. In 1795, the university was granted the authority to confer the degrees of Bachelor, Licentiate and Doctor in Civil Law (Ramírez [2013] at 61), (Aspell et al [1998] at 2).

Legal studies arose from 'the necessity of the colonial administrative system, which, with the creation of the Real Audiencia of Buenos Aires in August 1785, made it indispensable to train jurists to handle local legal matters in the distant region of the Río de la Plata' (Ramírez [2013] at 68).

In 1821, after the independence of Spain, the Universidad de Buenos Aires was established as the second institution of higher education in the country. Divided into six departments, including jurisprudence, it was created to address specific problems of the port of Buenos Aires, satisfying the interests of merchants, overseas trade, and local bureaucracy (Buchbinder [2005]).

The reception of the Roman-Germanic or Continental legal tradition, in its liberal version, occurred in the nineteenth century, leading to the establishment of the Constitution of 1853 and the Civil Code of 1869, among other legal developments. These reforms laid the foundations for the modern and contemporary Argentine legal system and legal education.

For the first time, in 1883, law graduates were legally authorised to enrol in a bar association.

During the civil wars that followed independence and until the mid-nineteenth century, the two universities continued to contribute to the education of the elites and provincial officials, among which the role played by the lawyers stood out. The universities fulfilled important institutional and political functions until their nationalisation in 1854, a year after the enactment of the National Constitution that established the Argentine state.

From then on, the national government initiated a process of university transformation. In 1870, during the presidency of Domingo Faustino Sarmiento, the Universidad Nacional de Córdoba underwent a significant change to give it a more scientific and secular character.

In the Faculty of Law, the curriculum was modified to expand and update its content (Aspell et al [1998] at 4, 5). The process of secularisation and the relative separation between the state and the Catholic Church, initiated during this period, strongly impacted university studies in general and legal studies in particular, ushering in a period of university modernisation.

As Argentina progressed towards building its modern legal system, legal education became more formalised and academic, adapted to the principles and values of European Continental law.

In 1885, the first university law, N° 1597, was enacted, establishing the organisational foundations of higher education institutions. This law represented a step toward university autonomy and self-governance, although more profound and sustained change was strongly resisted by conservative sectors until the twentieth century began.

At the end of the nineteenth century, the main function of the university was established as the education of professionals, certifying the abilities of graduates to practice liberal professions, including that of lawyer, on behalf of the state. The university became a crucial instrument for the social advancement of the emerging Argentine middle classes.

The university reform of 1918 and its opponents

The contemporary development of legal education in Argentina, as well as higher education in general, cannot be understood without analysing the democratising impact of the University Reform of 1918 and the subsequent counter-reform efforts, especially during the military and Peronist governments that followed. These governments aimed to reverse or at least suspend the central achievements of the reform, the effects of which continue to the present day.

The Reform began at the Universidad Nacional de Córdoba. It was led by a movement of university students who, at the beginning of the century, emerged as a confrontational alternative to a system of privileges benefiting elite professors and excluding student participation in academic decisions.

The student mobilisation was driven by the convergence of various factors. Internationally, World War I, the Russian Revolution, and echoes of the Mexican Revolution reflected profound changes on the global stage, encouraging political and social transformations. Nationally, the so-called Radical Party won the 1916 presidential elections, ending a period of conservative governments through universal male suffrage and the support of immigrants and their descendants, predominantly of European origin. Locally, the marked colonial, Catholic, and conservative tradition of Córdoba, with an aristocratic elite that embodied these traits and held significant influence in the university, played a role.

The 1918 Reform substantially altered higher education in the country, opening up institutions to new currents of thought and establishing the values and principles of the Argentine public university. Although the Reform extended beyond the faculties of law, law faculties were 'a paradigmatic example of the university system that the reformist students reacted against' (González et al [2011] at 301).

Legal education in particular was impacted by the demands of the reformists, which, not without tensions, were accepted by the national government: (a) university autonomy, academic freedom, and the end of clerical influence; (b) co-governance by professors, students, and graduates, with the election of university authorities through assemblies; (c) free attendance by students to avoid classes with authoritarian and conservative professors; (d) open competition for the selection of professors; (e) term limits on positions to end lifelong appointments; (f) tuition-free university education managed and financed by the state; and (g) university extension an engagement and society.

The university reform was not merely academic and pedagogical, but fundamentally political. Its influence spread throughout the country and extended to other Latin American countries and had a strong impact on legal education. Its principles were subsequently targeted and resisted by authoritarian governments.

Between 1918 and 1943, university administration followed reformist principles (Buchbinder [2005]), except for the period 1930–1932 during the military government of General Uriburu. In 1943–1946 a new conservative, nationalist and Catholic military government once again suppressed university autonomy and expelled opposing faculty and students. The government of General Perón (1946–1955) revoked university autonomy, abolished tuition fees and provided scholarships to students (Plotkin [2006] at 44). Opposing teachers were expelled and student involvement in university governance was restricted.

The military forces that overthrew Perón in 1955 reinstated university autonomy, but it was once again disrupted for an extended period: between 1966–1973, as a result of a new conservative military coup and between 1973–1976, during the democratically elected Peronist governments. This situation worsened during the period 1976–1983, due to a highly repressive new military coup. The goal was to dismantle the university reform. The law faculties were central to these policies as they were considered key institutions for the reproduction of legal culture.

This period was characterised by systematic state terrorism, disappearances and human rights violations. The universities were one of the main targets of state repression. Professors, students and university staff were persecuted, kidnapped, tortured, and killed, resulting in significant damage to academic life. This had a lasting effect on the quality of education and research in legal studies. Legal education and law faculties were profoundly affected, with many professors and students becoming victims of state violence.

The interruption of democracy by successive military coups and state violence sparked new debates and introduced new topics in legal education, such as the risks of the rule of law and its preservation, the role of jurists in legitimising dictatorships, law and democracy recovery and the prosecution of military juntas, among others.

The post-dictatorship period and beyond

In 1983, Argentina restored democracy with President Alfonsin's government. This marked a period of efforts to rebuild the university system, restore academic freedom, and address human rights violations from the dictatorship era. Universities faced the challenge of regaining autonomy, strengthening academic quality, and renewing their social commitment.

Legal education, like other disciplines, underwent renewal and reconstruction in the post-dictatorship era. Academic reform and new pedagogical approaches gained momentum. The 1994 constitutional reform enabled international human rights treaties to directly impact the Argentine legal system. Efforts were made to integrate human rights education into legal curricula for a more critical understanding of the law.

Carlos Menem's neoliberal government (1989–1999) initiated educational reforms which significantly impacted the university system. These aimed to promote academic assessment and allocate funds for enhancing university education quality but faced resistance from certain sectors. Arguments against the innovations included university autonomy, the national executive power's neoliberal inspiration, and the funding source (World Bank) (Echenique [2003]), (Coraggio and Torres [1997]).

Within law faculties, reform policies and the debates surrounding them had noteworthy effects, breaking their isolation and institutional inertia. 'Either they incorporated into the processes of reform, self-evaluation, and institutional assessment or they were reached by them' (González et al [2011] at 302). Some faculties adopted self-assessment and institutional evaluation processes deviating from the prevailing logic in Argentine legal education. Additionally, they faced the possibility of initiating curricular changes and shifts in teaching methods.

While some faculties initially reacted slowly to the prospect of introducing changes, and with reluctance and mistrust, 'because the evaluative culture and change itself have little foundation in legal education institutions, especially with criteria and standards that are traditionally foreign to them' (González et al [2011] at 302, 303) in others, authorities and more progressive sectors seized the opportunity to effect changes. Curricular adjustments, institutional self-assessment, and discussions on legal education took place.

The turn of the millennium saw a renewed emphasis on human rights education and transitional justice in legal studies, linked to efforts to address dictatorship-era atrocities and hold those responsible for human rights violations accountable. Legal education began to adopt a more critical perspective on the law, focusing on access to justice, human rights, and the role of law in shaping society.

Recent years have witnessed ongoing evolution in legal education in Argentina, reflecting broader societal changes and challenges.

Efforts continue to balance the traditional legal curriculum with contemporary issues, interdisciplinary approaches, and practical training. The digital transformation has also impacted legal education, with technology integration in teaching and learning methods. In 2020, this process accelerated significantly due to government-imposed forced isolation in response to the COVID-19 pandemic.

In conclusion, the development of legal education in Argentina has been shaped by a complex interplay of historical, political, social, and cultural factors. From its colonial origins to the struggles for university reform, from the challenges of military dictatorships to the pursuit of human rights education, legal education has adapted and transformed in response to the changing needs of society and the broader context. It remains an integral part of the Argentine higher education system, contributing to the training of legal professionals and the critical examination of law's role in society.

CARLOS LISTA

References

Aspell, M. and others. (1998). *Ciencia Derecho y Sociedad. Autoevaluación de la Carrera de Abogacía*, Universidad Nacional de Córdoba, Facultad de Derecho y Ciencias Sociales.

Buchbinder, P. (2005). *Historia de las Universidades Argentinas*, Editorial Sudamericana.

Coraggio, J.L. and Torres, M.R. (1997). *La Educación según el Banco Mundial*. Miño y Dávila.

Deckmann Fleck, E.C. (2013). 'Sobre el Colegio Jesuita de Río y "la Atenas de nuestros escolares": estudio comparativo entre los Colegios de Río de Janeiro y Córdoba (siglos XVII y XVIII)', in *UNC. Cuatrocientos Años de Historia*, Tomo I Universidad Nacional de Córdoba, pp. 79, 106.

Echenique, M. (2003). *La propuesta educativa neoliberal: Argentina (1980–2000)*, Homo Sapiens Ediciones.

González, M.G. and others. (2011). 'La formación de los abogados y la educación jurídica en Argentina', in González, M.G. and Lista, C.A. (eds), *Sociología Jurídica en Argentina. Tendencias y perspectivas*, Eudeba, pp. 297, 352

Plotkin, M.B. (2006). 'El desarrollo de la educación superior privada en la Argentina', in Plotkin, M.B. (ed), *La privatización de la educación superior y las ciencias sociales en Argentina. Un estudio de las carreras de Psicología y Economía*, CLACSO, pp. 43, 62.

Ramírez, H. (2013). 'Entre el cielo y la tierra. La Universidad de Córdoba como obra de hombres en los avatares del tiempo', in *UNC. Cuatrocientos Años de Historia*, Tomo I Universidad Nacional de Córdoba, pp. 59, 77.

7. Argentina (regulation of contemporary legal education)

Law in Argentina is pursued at undergraduate level, with students typically entering law schools directly after completing secondary education, usually around the age of 18. The educational system is divided between state and private universities, encompassing a total of 70 law schools. Of these, 34 are under the administration of the State mostly the Federal State, while 36 are private institutions managed by civil associations, foundations, and many of them by the Catholic Church. (See Argentina (Contemporary Legal Education))

Argentina is a federal state although a very centralised one. The federal government regulates universities under national law 24.521 Statute of Higher Education, enacted in 1995 (Ley 24521). According to its article 2 'The national State is responsible for providing financing, supervision and inspection of national universities, as well as supervision and inspection of private universities,' and only universities have the authority to award graduate and postgraduate degrees, such as Masters or Doctorates. Article 42 specifies that degrees recognised by the National Ministry of Education validate academic training and allow for professional practice. Thus, the national government delegate in universities the power to award professional degrees to practice professions such as law and the power to oversee professions and regulate their operations remains in the provincial governments.

Professions 'the exercise of which could compromise the public interest, directly putting at risk the health, safety, rights, property or training of the inhabitants' (Ley 24521, art. 43) are subject to regulation under special conditions. The National Ministry of Education, in conjunction with the National Council of Universities, sets out essential content and training standards for the curriculum to accredit degrees related to public interest. Accreditation processes for these degrees will be conducted periodically (Ley 24521, art. 43.a and 43.b).

In 2015, 20 years after the law was passed, the Council of Universities and the Ministry of Education decided to regulate the law degree as a public interest one, and in 2017 the Council accepted the minimum requirements on their law curricula, thus starting the accreditation process of law schools for the first time in Argentina (Resolución 340-E/2017).

State law schools do not require an entrance examination, and they are tuition-free, aligning with the explicit constitutional right to a free and equitable public education. Some private law schools do require an examination and charge tuition. The law programme has a duration of five years, culminating without a final global examination, granting the student the title of lawyer upon completion. Unlike some jurisdictions, Argentina does not have a Bar exam. However, to practice law, it is obligatory for individuals to be members of the Bar Association in the provincial jurisdiction where they intend to work.

The curriculum in Argentina's law schools has undergone limited changes over the past century and a half. Rooted in the civil law tradition, it is structured around a list of topics aligned with the legal Codes. These topics cover a broad spectrum, including civil law (legal entities, torts, contracts, property, family), commercial law, criminal law, administrative law, constitutional law, and legal procedure structured in 51 semester mandatory courses. The instructional approach in Argentina's legal education follows a Cartesian conception, emphasising the teaching of general principles before delving into specific issues within each area of law. This pedagogical model is structured to introduce foundational concepts before exploring more intricate aspects of legal domains. For instance, in the study of civil law, the curriculum typically begins with a course on the general principles, followed by a progression through specific topics such as obligations, contracts, and the various types of contracts. This sequential arrangement aims to provide students with a comprehensive understanding of the fundamental principles that underpin the legal system before immersing them in the nuances and complexities of individual legal domains (Parise [2021]).

While there are courses touching upon legal and political theory, economics, and, in select law schools, clinical legal education in the final year or semester, the overall structure has retained its historical framework.

The prevailing instructional method in these institutions is centered around lectures, where professors convey information through recitations or explanations, and students actively engage by taking notes. Consequently, assessments predominantly take the form of written, closed-book examinations, emphasising the retention of legal and doctrinal texts as well as memory recall. The architectural layout of classrooms aligns with this teaching approach, featuring benches arranged to face the professor's desk or platform, from which they deliver lectures. This traditional setup underscores the historical emphasis on didactic instruction (Böhmer [2005, 2012]).

The study and teaching loads in these law programmes are generally not overly demanding, contributing to a prevalence of part-time engagements for both students and professors. Many students opt for early entry into the workforce, eventually securing positions in legal-related roles such as paralegals or within the Judiciary.

Law professors, predominantly comprised of practicing lawyers and judges, typically dedicate their time to teaching as a part-time commitment. Such an arrangement provides law students with access to members of the legal professions and eventually to some acquaintance with legal practice. While this arrangement offers students an opportunity to connect with members of the legal community, the actual course load is frequently managed by teaching assistants. When classes are conducted by professors, the emphasis tends to be on theoretical and doctrinal aspects. Even in clinical settings, where practical experience is emphasised, professors often focus on teaching the theory of legal processes, while adjuncts take charge of actual cases and client interactions. Unfortunately, the structured transference of professional skills and ethics lacks a dedicated institutional framework. There remains a gap in the formalised inclusion of practical skills and ethical considerations within the curriculum (Ministerio de Justicia [2019]).

Within this context, legal research faces significant challenges in Argentina. Lawyers and legal issues, despite their societal importance, occupy a marginal position in the country's scientific endeavors. This is reflected in the public research system, such as CONICET, where a mere 0.5 per cent of researchers and scholarship holders specialise in law (Ministerio de Justicia [2019]).

While numerous law schools publish their own law reviews, the aspiration for these publications to be indexed remains a struggle. In fact, none of the top 25 ranked law reviews in Latin America hail from Argentina. This dearth of indexed publications suggests that the visibility and recognition of Argentine legal research on the regional stage are currently limited (Ministerio de Justicia [2019]).

The absence of independent legal scholarship poses a challenge to the strength of a constitutional democracy and its capacity to foster the rule of law. In essence, a vibrant democracy relies on a critical and autonomous perspective within the legal sphere. This independence is crucial for evaluating legal practices, ensuring accountability, and promoting the principles of justice. The inherent conflicts of interest within a system where lawyers and judges share classes can contribute to a lack of objectivity and impartiality. This intertwined relationship may impede the development of a truly independent legal scholarship that can scrutinise legal practices, challenge norms, and contribute to the evolution of the legal system.

Continuing legal education in Argentina is not mandatory, but over the past three decades, there has been a significant proliferation of postgraduate courses. These offerings range from individual courses focusing on current legal issues to comprehensive Master of Law programmes and even Doctorates. Law schools have expanded their academic offerings to cater to the growing demand for specialised knowledge and advanced qualifications.

This surge in postgraduate education aligns with the establishment of the Council of the Magistrates, both at federal and provincial levels in the 1990s, which holds responsibilities such as the selection of judges. Aspiring candidates for judicial positions are required to pass a written exam and personal interviews, but also have a strong academic background. Consequently, the demand for graduate courses has witnessed a notable increase, as individuals seek to enhance their academic qualifications to improve their prospects within the Judiciary.

Several significant factors have contributed to transformative changes in Argentina's legal landscape. One of the pivotal moments was the country's transition from dictatorship to democracy in 1983, marked by the resounding commitment to 'Never again'. This phrase became emblematic in rejecting military rule and embracing democratic values.

The famous 'Never again' also refers to the CONADEP (Argentina's truth commission) Report on the egregious human rights violations orchestrated by the military regime. This transition sparked a rejection of human rights abuses and a wholehearted embrace of constitutionalism. In 1994, Argentina underwent constitutional reform, ushering in substantial changes to its legal system. The constitutional text now incorporates eleven international human rights treaties, explicit recognition of new rights, regulations for legal procedures to enforce these rights, acknowledgment of the legal standing of social actors (both individual and collective), and the establishment of the Ombudsman's office, also with collective standing to sue and demand collective remedies and injunctions. These constitutional changes have led to a redefined role for the Judiciary within the political system, prompting shifts in the knowledge, attitudes, and skills expected from lawyers and judges. In response to this evolving landscape, a new generation of deans and professors in law schools is emerging, addressing the demand for a different kind of legal education.

Another catalyst for change stems from Argentina's decision, along with many Latin American countries, to transition its legal procedures from inquisitorial, written systems to adversarial, oral procedures. This transformation is particularly evident in criminal procedures and, in certain jurisdictions, extends to non-criminal procedures as well as the adoption of trials by jury. This shift reflects a broader movement towards more transparent, participatory, and adversarial legal processes, requiring legal professionals to adapt their knowledge and skills accordingly.

As mentioned above, in 2017 Argentina underwent a significant transformation with the initiation of the first nationwide accreditation process for law schools led by the National Commission of University Evaluation and Accreditation (CONEAU). This landmark event represented a crucial stride toward standardising legal education across the nation. As part of the accreditation process, law schools were mandated to conform to a minimum set of criteria concerning content and teaching methodologies.

One particularly noteworthy requirement mandated that law schools allocate a minimum of 30 per cent of courses to professional skills training. Although challenging, this directive was deemed immensely relevant in response to the evolving political climate and the dynamic nature of legal professions, necessitating a departure from traditional training methods (CONEAU). Recognising the need for legal professionals to possess a broader skill set beyond theoretical knowledge, law schools strategically incorporated aspects of clinical legal education into their curriculum. This included modules on legal writing, legal research, legal ethics, advocacy skills, moot courts, and clinics.

A notable development related to clinics stemmed from the 1994 constitutional reform, which prompted the creation of pro bono lawyer organisations tasked with litigating public interest cases alongside numerous NGOs advocating for human rights. Some of these entities evolved into public interest law clinics based in law schools, allowing institutions to leverage these experiences and introduce public interest law or human rights clinics within their curriculum, often in collaboration with human rights NGOs.

Given that a law degree serves as the sole gateway to practicing law, law schools bear the responsibility of adequately preparing future lawyers for the substantial responsibilities awaiting them in their professional journeys. The emphasis on professional skills training reflects a commitment to producing graduates equipped not only with theoretical legal knowledge but also with the practical skills and legal ethics essential to navigate the complexities of legal practice. This shift in accreditation criteria reflects a broader acknowledgment of the dynamic nature of the legal profession, highlighting the imperative for legal education to evolve in tandem with these changes.

The results of the evaluation process that preceded the accreditation focused on the same issues law schools should improve. The need to strengthen student retention mechanisms, the increase in academic research and full-time faculty and the creation of courses and clinical legal education in order to impart lawyering skills training were concerns the evaluators insisted on (CONEAU). Most law schools were accredited in 2020 and, depending on their performance, they were awarded three or six years before they must undergo the same process again. The pandemic delayed the schedule, but it is expected that a new cycle will be starting soon.

Argentina finds itself at a crossroads, as legal education endeavors to keep pace with societal changes and the demands of a dynamic environment. The challenge is considerable, given the inertia of massive institutions, prevailing social values, entrenched professional routines, and corporate interests that tend to resist change. The pace of transformation varies across law schools, influenced by factors such as size, budget, and leadership. Against a backdrop of economic turmoil, rising poverty levels, and institutional uncertainty, observing the efforts of the legal community to confront these challenges is a compelling and consequential endeavour.

MARTIN BÖHMER

References

Böhmer, M. (2005). 'Metas comunes: la enseñanza y la construcción del derecho en la Argentina', *Sistemas Judiciales*, 5(9), p. 26.

Böhmer, M. (2012). *Imagining the State: The Politics of Legal Education in Argentina, USA and Chile*, Doctoral dissertation, on file Yale Law School.

CONEAU, The comprehensive list of accredited law schools, along with their respective recommendations and deficits, is available for consultation here under Carrera, Abogacía, available at https://global.coneau.gob.ar/coneauglobal/publico/buscadores/acreditacion/.

Ministerio de Justicia de la República Argentina. (2019): 'La abogacía en la Argentina. Su enseñanza, investigación y difusión. Relevamientos y análisis del estado de situación', available at https://www.argentina.gob.ar/sites/default/files/la_abogacia_en_la_argentina_-_datos_consolidados_por_la_dnrecaso_minjus.pdf.

Parise, A. (2021). 'Legal Education in Argentina: A Plea for Comparative Law in a Multicultural Environment', *La. L. Rev.* 81, available at https://digitalcommons.law.lsu.edu/lalrev/vol81/iss4/9.

Ley 24.521 de Educación Superior, enacted in 1995, available at https://servicios.infoleg.gob.ar/infolegInternet/anexos/25000-29999/25394/texact.htm.

Resolución 340-E/2017, Ministerio de Justicia de la Nación, enacted 8 September 2017, available at https://www.coneau.gob.ar/archivos/resoluciones/rm-3401-e-2017-abogado-59ba9a63723e9.pdf.

8. Assessment in legal education

Assessment is the practice of documenting, evaluating, and measuring students' learning or achievement. Ideally, assessment methods should be aligned with learning objectives and teaching methods. Assessments can be formative (that is, occurring throughout a course) or summative (occurring at the culmination of a course). The purpose of formative assessment is to give feedback, which is essential to student learning. Summative assessments, on the other hand, are designed to evaluate student performance for the purpose of a grade.

Assessment often takes place at several points in students' professional journeys, as well as at an institutional level. Law schools are often assessed by governments or external professional regulators. Law students can be assessed at several points in their education, including upon entrance to law school, and again upon admission to the bar. This entry focuses on assessment of students within the law school curriculum itself.

Interest in assessment in legal education has ebbed and flowed over the years, but it remains relatively under-investigated around the world, leaving comparative or empirical examination of this subject difficult. Lack of scholarly attention to assessment is perhaps symbolic of the ongoing tensions regarding the social, economic, and political roles of legal education or symptomatic of an underdeveloped scholarship of teaching and learning in law (Rochette [2011], Stolker [2014]). Because of the relative lack of literature in this area, this entry does not draw global comparative conclusions. Instead, a high-level review, informed mostly by common law jurisdictions and mostly English language literature, is presented.

Legal education, and therefore assessment practices, are influenced by many factors including the regulation of higher education (e.g. the Bologna process in Europe (Reinalda and Kulesza [2006]), socioeconomic conditions, colonialism, corruption, privatisation, and other local conditions. Assessment is tightly connected to the culture and mission of an institution (Maranville et al [2015]), jurisdiction, legal system, government and professional regulatory requirements and the structure of legal education. For example, in most continental European jurisdictions, the UK, Australia, India, Russia, and many African and Latin American countries, law is an undergraduate university degree that takes anywhere from three to five years to complete (Stolker [2014]). For students wishing to get called as a lawyer, the university law degree is followed by practical skills training, a period of apprenticeship or pupillage, and further examinations. In this structure of legal education, legal knowledge is taught in the context of a university degree while practical skills are taught in a separate context. Further, in many continental European jurisdictions, where higher education is public and affordable or free, first year law classes take place in large lecture halls with hundreds of students. In these contexts, assessment in the law school, when mandatory, is mostly summative. It typically focuses on legal knowledge, often in the form of a formal written or oral examination. These summative assessments often require students to memorise and recall legal rules or explain concepts.

As noted above, assessment in legal education has been influenced by global shifts in colonial power. For example, in the mid-twentieth century, university-based, American approaches to legal education were also exported to other jurisdictions, including Canada, Japan and China (Stolker [2014]). Summative written examinations using fact scenarios or hypotheticals emerged as a common assessment method in this era, although more recent shifts in American legal education include more attention to experiential and applied methods. Summative assessment methods remain dominant in legal education in many jurisdictions around the world.

Assessment methods in legal education tend toward norm-referenced rather than criterion-referenced assessment. In norm-referenced assessment, the practice of 'curving' is common, whereby students are assessed in comparison with one another rather than being measured against an external standard. There are concerning impacts of this approach, including high-stakes assessment that lends itself to competitive rather than learning-focused relationships between students.

Thankfully, teaching methods in law have diversified significantly over the past several decades, notably with the rise of problem-based, applied, simulated, experiential, clinical, land-based, and community-engaged approaches. Alongside innovation in pedagogy, new forms of assessment have been introduced. These include learning and e-portfolios, reflective journals, simulations, peer and self-assessment, and many more. While many creative pedagogies have arisen, they remain less common than lecture-based pedagogies and summative, written assessments.

Greatest attention to assessment appears to come from the clinical and experiential learning community, perhaps because the context requires diversified teaching methods (Strevens et al [2014]). In the clinical and experiential context, debates are ongoing about the value of pass/fail methods, assessment of concepts such as professional identity formation and reflective practice, the competencies students should be learning in these contexts, effort-based grading, and the impact of grade adjustments or 'curves', the role of the 'standardized client' (Baron et al [2006]), among other issues. However, the degree to which clinical and experiential programs engage with constructive alignment, competencies, and other assessment theory remains a question (Stuckey et al [2007]).

More recent external events are also challenging legal education globally and, by extension, assessment. For example, during the pandemic, formal sit-down examinations were replaced by other forms of assessments such as take-home examinations or other assignments and online examinations. Many of these new forms of assessment are still in place today; however, the in-person sit-down final examination has been reinstated as the dominant form of assessment, largely due to security (i.e. cheating) issues. Globalisation and the concomitant push toward standardisation and portability of professional qualifications also remain an important consideration. 'Common' exams – whether this be at the point of entry to law school or entry to the profession – will undoubtedly continue to play an important standard-setting role in determining what law schools value and assess. Most recently, the prevalence of artificial intelligence has added a layer of complexity to law school assessment (Ajevski et al [2023]).

ANNIE ROCHETTE AND GEMMA SMYTH

References

Ajevski, M. et al. (2023). 'ChatGPT and the Future of Legal Education and Practice', *The Law Teacher*, 57(3), p. 352.

Baron, K. et al. (2006). 'Valuing What Clients Think: Standardized Clients and the Assessment of Communicative Competence', *Clinical L Rev*, 13(1), p. 1.

Bone, A. and Maharg, P. (2019). *Critical Perspectives on the Scholarship of Assessment and Learning in Law*, Australian National University Press.

Brustin, S. and Chavkin, D. (1997). 'Testing the Grades: Evaluating Grading Models in Clinical Legal Education', *Clinical L Rev*, 3, p. 299.

Cavazos, A.M. (2010–11). 'The Journey Toward Excellence in Clinical Legal Education: Developing, Utilizing and Evaluating Methodologies for Determining and Assessing the Effectiveness of Student Learning Outcomes', *Southwestern L Rev*, 40, p. 1.

Evans, A et al. (2016). 'Australian Clinical Legal Education: Designing and Operating a Best Practice Clinical Program in an Australian Law School', Acton: Australian National University Press, available at https://library.oapen.org/bitstream/handle/20.500.12657/31597/626828.pdf;jsessionid=72C760DBFB70F9F7CAA7FC39BFB1C7CF?sequence=1.

Grimes, R. and Gibbons, J. (2016). 'Assessing Experiential Learning – Us, Them and the Others', *Intl J of Clinical Legal Education*, 23(1), p. 107.

Light, G., Cox, R. and Calkins, S. (2009). *Learning and Teaching in Higher Education: The Reflective Professional*, 2nd edn, Sage.

Montoya, J. (2010). 'The Current State of Legal Education Reform in Latin America: A Critical Appraisal', *J of Legal Education*, 59, p. 545.

Pereira, D., Assunção Flores, M. and Niklasson, L. (2016). 'Assessment Revisited: A Review of Research', *Assessment and Evaluation in Higher Education*, 41(7), p. 1008.

Perez Hurtado, L.F. (2010). 'Content, Structure, and Growth of Mexican Legal Education', *J Legal Education*, 59(4), p. 567.

Reinaloda, B. et al. (2006). *The Bologna Process – Harmonizing Europe's Higher Education: Including the Essential Original Texts*, Verlag Barbara Budrich.

Rice, S. (2008). 'Assessing – But not Grading – Clinical Legal Education', *Legal Education Digest*, 16(2), p. 5.

Rochette, A. (2011). 'Teaching and Learning in Canadian Legal Education: An Empirical Exploration', DCL thesis, McGill University.

Standing Committee on Legal Education and Training. (April 2018). *Comprehensive Review of Legal Education and Training in Hong Kong: Final Report of the Consultants*, available at https://www.sclet.gov.hk/eng/pdf/final2018.pdf.

Stolker, C. (2014). *Rethinking the Law School: Education, Research, Outreach and Governance*, Cambridge University Press.

Strevens, C et al. (2014). *Legal Education: Simulation in Theory and Practice*, Ashgate.

Sullivan, W.M. et al. (2007). *Educating Lawyers: Preparation for the Profession of Law*, Jossey-Bass.

9. Australia (contemporary legal education)

Australia has nearly 40 law schools (https://cald.asn.au/contact-us/deans-law-schools/), and legal education is a vibrant field of activity and research. Legal education is seen as an elite form of university education with strong competition to gain places in the larger law schools. There is a strong emphasis on students engaging in critical analysis of doctrinal knowledge and its practical application, as well as understanding the broader social issues relevant to law and legal practice.

Degree structures

Admission to practice in Australia is for most students via a three year university degree. (see e.g. https://cald.asn.au/studying-law-in-australia-slia/) That degree can be either an undergraduate Bachelor of Laws (LLB), or a postgraduate Juris Doctor (JD). The LLB is the traditional degree with the JD becoming more popular in the last two decades. In some universities, the JD has replaced the LLB. In other universities the JD is primarily a full fee-paying option for those who do not gain entry to the LLB.

While standalone LLB degrees are offered at a number of universities, most Australian undergraduate law students enrol in an undergraduate joint-degree programme. That is, the students study law concurrently with another undergraduate degree – such as a Bachelor of Arts, Commerce, Science, etc. The way the two degrees are combined, the university's rules on progression and student choice mean a very wide variety of subject orderings occur.

A traditional pattern has been to structure joint degree programmes so that the non-law degree is completed in the first three/four years of enrolment. During that first three years students take the equivalent of the first year of a standalone law degree spread across the three years. The students thus finish their university career fully focussed on law subjects. Student choice and cost of living pressures however mean that student study pathways now are less predictable.

Thus, while the LLB is defined as an undergraduate degree, many students complete a substantial proportion of the degree after already completing three full years of study. What is expected of the students in years four and five is in many law schools at the same level as is expected of graduate students. As a result, there is substantial similarity between the LLB and JD degree – at least by the time a student graduates.

The JD is typically taken as a standalone degree. Thus, JD students complete a full year of law units in their first year, while LLB students complete those units more slowly over the course of three years. The elongated sequence across three years for LLB students means it is possible to stage the development of skills alongside content. For JD students this all occurs in the first year and this necessitates different approaches to teaching those courses. Despite this, formally the teaching methodology in both degrees is often the same.

Honours in some law schools were previously awarded based solely on an overall mark, but Commonwealth regulation now requires Honours to be research-based (cf https://cald.asn.au/wp-content/uploads/2023/11/CALD-Honours-Position-Statement-Final-28-August-2012.pdf). Most law schools offer a thesis subject as part of the suite of electives in the degree rather than as an additional year. As the JD is postgraduate it is not possible to award Honours.

Degree content

As discussed in Australia (Regulation of Legal Education), in Australia Admitting Authorities focus on a long list of legal content requirements in university degrees (Prescribed Areas of Academic Knowledge (AAK) https://legalservicescouncil.org.au/documents/prescribed-academic-areas-of-knowledge.pdf) are. They expressed as a list of 11 doctrinal areas (colloquially known as the 'Priestley 11' after the chair of the drafting committee), and an additional Statement on Required Understanding of Statutory Interpretation (https://www.legalservicescouncil.org.au/content/dam/dcj/legal-services-council/documents/LACC_-_Statement_on_Statutory_Interpretation_-_2009.pdf), and post-qualification practical legal training (PLT) (https://www.legalservicescouncil.org.au/content/dam/dcj/legal-services-council/documents/PLT-competency-standards-for-entry-level-lawyers-Oct-2017.pdf). The impact of these dual requirements in Australia is that typically law schools have a compulsory core set of units that account for two thirds of the degree to satisfy the content requirements, and students do not have significant opportunity to take up electives until their final year. This is in contrast to some other countries where the compulsory core of the degree is less and there is subsequently more room for agile, experimental elective units. Australian law schools are struggling with the need to teach new areas of content, and skills but yet continue to teach a wide set of compulsory areas.

The compulsory core covers 11 areas of law arranged into traditional doctrinal categories (such as contracts, torts, constitutional law, crime). Generally law school curriculum follows this categorisation and students learn each area as a separate unit. There has traditionally been little attempt to combine the knowledge across these units, though some law schools offer later year clinics or capstone units.

The existence of separate PLT programmes has also meant that Australian law schools have traditionally not emphasised the teaching of practice skills. This is changing, and many law schools now run community legal centres, or partner with one, and work-integrated-learning is becoming more commonplace – in fact it is becoming an expected part of a quality degree experience. Integration of skills across all subjects remains a work in progress, a project that is becoming more urgent with the emergence of generative AI and the need to work with that in practice.

Law school rankings, sizes and staff-student ratios

Law schools in Australia range from year cohorts of under 50 in smaller regional law schools, to some major city law schools that have over 800 students in a year cohort. Staff student ratios are also significantly higher in Australia than some other countries, with many Australian law schools having employed significant numbers of adjunct staff on casual contracts to teach law classes (https://www.timeshighereducation.com/world-university-rankings/2024/subject-ranking/law) The impact of recent work law changes may see this approach change in coming years (https://www.theguardian.com/australia-news/2023/jun/05/australian-universities-accused-of

-entrenched-non-compliance-with-workplace-law-over-staff-underpayment).

Class sizes vary. Some law schools maintain seminar-style classes of 40–60 students without lectures, others have large lectures with small tutorial classes of 20–30 students.

Tuition fees

A distinctive feature of Australian higher education is the fee structure for domestic students. If a law school offers both LLB and JD degrees, the JD degrees are predominantly full-fee paying. The cost of a full degree for a domestic student can be up to $140,000, and for an international student up to $155,000 depending on the university.

However the cost of undergraduate degrees in Australia for domestic students (and JD where that is the sole degree offered) is partly supported by the Commonwealth Government (CSP students) (CSP and HECS-HELP Booklet https://www.studyassist.gov.au/resources/2023-commonwealth-supported-places-and-hecs-help-information-booklet). Rather than pay up front tuition fees, students are required to pay a subsided 'contribution' – currently $45,426 for a three year law degree (with additional fees for any other degree combined). Students are eligible to enter into a loans scheme with the Commonwealth Government, the Higher Education Contribution Scheme (HELP). The loan is interest free (though the amount is indexed to inflation) and students repay the loan as a percentage of their income tax once their income reaches a threshold, currently $48,361 with annual tax surcharges ranging from 1–10 per cent based on income. Similar schemes exist for university amenities fees and overseas study. There is however a lifetime cap on the loans available, currently $113,028. Significantly this means that for local students studying the LLB, there is not a substantial financial debt to be repaid immediately on graduation. For JD students who exceed the HELP cap there can still be a substantial amount of up-front fees to pay.

While the cost of living in Australia is high, many Australian LLB students continue to live at home whilst studying – particularly those who live in the major cities – thus decreasing the financial implications of higher education. There is however a substantial proportion of students for whom such living arrangements are not possible. For these students, the costs of living and availability of accommodation are currently at a crisis point (https://www.smh.com.au/business/companies/student-accommodation-sector-faces-critical-shortage-crisis-20230906-p5e2f3.html). Significant building by private accommodation providers is underway in major cities, but overall cost of living pressures remain substantial.

Australian Law Schools have a strong commitment to student academic and wellbeing support. The Council of Australian Deans Voluntary Standards place great emphasis on student wellbeing and support (https://cald.asn.au/the-australian-law-schools-standards/). The Federal Government also has a strong focus on increasing access and support for students and has passed legislation requiring universities to publicise support for students policies (https://www.education.gov.au/new-requirements-support-students).

International students

Australian universities derive significant income from international student fees, and for many these fees are an essential aspect of their budget. This in turn has created significant pressure to increase the numbers of international students studying law. Most international students are attracted to the larger city law schools, and the majority have studied Masters degrees. However, significant numbers are now enrolling in JD degrees. Proposed legislative caps on international enrolments (https://ministers.education.gov.au/clare/improving-sustainability-international-education) are likely to mean increased enrolments in the JD which can attract higher fees than other degrees.

Teaching methods and approaches

Australian law schools until the 1960s were organised and taught students in the same way as English universities. This was primarily via lectures with 100 per cent final closed book examinations. The Langdellian form of Socratic questioning developed in the US (Weaver [1991]) (see Socratic Method) was not adopted. In the 1970s and 1980s a number of Australian law schools introduced smaller seminar style classes with a modified form of Socratic teaching that was based more around discussion rather than interrogation (Keyes and Johnstone [2004]). Today the practice varies across Australia with a mixture of lectures/tutorial and seminar approaches both across and within law schools. For those schools teaching a portion of the degree via lectures, teaching in other classes is strongly focussed on active learning with Socratic dialogue in some form predominant. Active learning is in fact a requirement of law school accreditation (Standard 4.5 https://legalservicescouncil.org.au/documents/accreditation-standards-for-law-courses.pdf).

Teaching face-to-face remains the most common teaching environment, though now strongly supplemented by online activities and materials. Asynchronous and synchronous teaching online as a primary method of instruction has post-COVID become more widely accepted, and most law schools now include some online components in their degree. Only a couple of law schools offer fully online degrees (van Caenegem and Mundy [2021]).

For many years, and in line with the case-method approach, students were set a printed textbook and a set of case extracts, either compiled by the lecturer, or more commonly from a commercially produced set. With the growth of learning management systems, and spurred on by COVID and practices in other disciplines, printed case materials are now being supplemented by more multi-modal materials, and links to electronic judgments and files held by university libraries. The high cost of legal textbooks is encouraging universities to find alternative approaches for student learning.

Some insight into the prevailing philosophy of teaching can be gained from the Threshold Learning Outcomes (https://cald.asn.au/wp-content/uploads/2024/04/LLB-TLOsKiftetalLTASStandardsStatement2010-TLOs-LLB2.pdf) and Australian Law School Standards (https://cald.asn.au/the-australian-law-schools-standards/). The Standards emphasise that a fundamental mission of legal education is a 'commitment to the rule of law, and the promotion of the highest standards of ethical conduct, professional responsibility, and community' (1.3.3). Students are to 'be active participants in the learning process and to engage with the law in an analytical and critical way' (2.2.2). Social justice and incorporation of indigenous perspectives on law are strong foci of curriculum development (2.3.3) as well as the impacts of technology on legal practice.

ALEX STEEL

The TLOs emphasis that legal education should not only teach legal principles and rules, but also the broader context in which those laws operate (TLO 1). In addition to thinking, research and communication skills, ethics and professional responsibility is seen as a core requirement of a legal education (TLO 2). Finally, self-management that allows students to work independently; reflecting on and assessing their capabilities and performance are seen as key graduate skills.

With a widespread epidemic of mental health issues, specific measures to protect student well-being have also been emphasised by both the Council of Australian Law Deans (https://cald.asn.au/wp-content/uploads/2023/11/Promoting-Law-Student-Well-Being-Good-Practice-Guidelines-for-Law-Schools.pdf) and the Law School Standards. There is also an ongoing project to increase the level of recognition by academics of diverse student needs (Israel et al [2017]).

All law schools endeavour to provide experiential learning opportunities for their students, and as mentioned above, many law schools have strong links with community legal centres where their students volunteer. Many students complete work-integrated learning courses in local or international law firms or social justice groups.

Assessment and grading

Approaches to grading vary across Australian law schools, but tight conformity to a distribution curve is rare, unlike the US. Law schools vary in the extent to which they moderate against an indicative distribution, and the extent to which they moderate individual assessment scores against overall performance. The predominant view across the higher education sector in Australia is that marking should be standards based. All assessment is now aligned with overall degree learning outcomes, and students are informed of this alignment in course outlines. This is both a government requirement (*Higher Education Standards Framework (Threshold Standards) 2021* 1.4) and core to the Australian Law School Standards (Standard 3).

Australia has a well-established expectation that there are multiple points of summative assessment in each subject, and it would be rare for any subjects to have final examinations that are greater than 50–60 per cent. Most subjects would have two to three assessments. Primarily assessments in both take-home and in exam settings are fact scenario-based problem questions or essays. Class discussion, mooting, and group projects are also traditional elements of the assessment landscape. Other forms of assessment are emerging, especially in digital formats. The recent emergence of generative AI has brought into question some traditional approaches to assessment and law schools are continuing to examine what assessment formats remain reliable.

ALEX STEEL

References

Australian Qualifications Framework Council. (2013). Australian Qualifications Framework 2nd edition, available at https://www.aqf.edu.au/framework/australian-qualifications-framework.

Barker, D. (2017). *History of Legal Education in Australia, Federation Press Sydney*.

Council of Australian Law Deans, available at https://cald.asn.au/.

Council of Australian Law Deans, Juris Doctor Threshold Learning Outcomes, available at https://cald.asn.au/wp-content/uploads/2024/04/JD-TLOs-March-2012-Andrew-Kenyon11.pdf.

Council of Australian Law Deans, Australian Law School Standards, available at https://cald.asn.au/the-australian-law-schools-standards/.

Israel, M. et al. (2017). 'Fostering "quiet inclusion": Interaction and diversity in the Australian law classroom', *Journal of Legal Education*, 66(2), pp. 332–356.

Keyes, M. and Johnstone, R. (2004). 'Changing Legal Education: Rhetoric, Realty, and Prospects for the Future', *Sydney L Rev*, 26, p. 537.

Kingsford Legal Centre Clinical Legal Education Guide, 13th edition, available at https://www.klc.unsw.edu.au/sites/default/files/documents/2924%20CLE%20guide-WEB.pdf.

Law Admission Consultative Committee. (2018). Accreditation Standards for Australian Law Courses, available at https://legalservicescouncil.org.au/documents/accreditation-standards-for-law-courses.pdf.

Learning and Teaching Academic Standards Project Bachelor of Laws Learning and Teaching Academic Standards Statement December 2010, available at https://cald.asn.au/wp-content/uploads/2024/04/LLB-TLOsKiftetalLTASStandardsStatement2010-TLOs-LLB2.pdf.

Legal Services Council, Prescribed Areas of Academic Knowledge (AAK), available at

https://legalservicescouncil.org.au/documents/prescribed-academic-areas-of-knowledge.pdf.

van Caenegem, W.A. and Mundy, T. (2021). Special Report on Online Legal Education in Australia, available at https://papers.ssrn.com/sol3/papers.cfm?abstract_id=3951659.

Weaver, R.L. (1991). 'Langdell's Legacy: Living with the Case Method', *Vill L Rev*, 36, p. 517.

10. Australia (history of university legal education)

Legal education has a long history in Australia, dating well before the invasion of the continent by the British in 1788. The Decolonising the Legal Curriculum entry of this encyclopedia provides an entry point into this history and its importance. The current entry concentrates on what has become the dominant form of formalised legal education in Australia, legal education for students within university law schools. It is important to note the limitations of this history. It does not record how First Nation's people have taught about lore for over 65,000 years, nor does it capture the numerous ways that people learn about law beyond university settings (Twining [2018]). These conceptions of legal education warrant greater attention. There are, nonetheless, reasons why university-based history remains important. Law Schools educate a powerful elite who occupy leadership roles in government and industry, and who are also engaged in social justice work. The growing number of law schools and law students has meant that they are responsible for the creation of a large professional class of 'virtue capitalists' (Forsyth [2023]). How law schools have contributed to the elevation of this class, maintained their status and shaped their ideas about the administration and creation of law provides important insights into the makeup of Australian society and the central ideas ruling that society.

The first four Australian universities were established in the middle and second half of the nineteenth century, created by 'self-confident settler elites who saw them as both symbols and disseminators of European civilisation in the colonies' (Pietsch [2015]). It was a time when convict transportation to the colony of New South Wales had been abolished and military tribunals had been replaced by a Supreme Court in New South Wales. In this period Australia's first two universities took different positions on how universities might contribute to the standing of lawyers. At the University of Sydney, the judges and barristers who first sat on the board of the university considered that the universities could aid the elevation of the profession by providing barristers, who would become future judges, with a classical and liberal education (Martin [1986], Bartie [2019]). In Victoria, concern over the 'poor quality of Melbourne's gold-era lawyers' and an awareness of 'recommendations for systematic legal education circulating in Britain' led Redmond Barry, justice of the Supreme Court of Victoria and Chancellor of the University of Melbourne, to smooth the way for university legal training (Waugh [2007]). This meant that although teaching about law first occurred at the University of Sydney, Melbourne was the first university to create a law school and degree programme in law. While law was taught from 1855 at Sydney it was not part of a formal law degree structure, nor housed within a law school. It was not until the 1880s, with a new Vice Chancellor who considered that the earlier conception of a university was 'better suited to a leisured class than to such a busy working world as ours,' that steps were taken to create a law school at Sydney (Martin [1986]). It began in 1890. The University of Adelaide was created in 1872 and the University of Tasmania in 1891.

English ideas played a prominent role in early university law teaching. For example, English law professors (Frederick Pollock and John Westlake) played a crucial role in setting the early law curriculum at Sydney, leaving the first law professor, William Pitt Cobbett, to defer to their directions (Martin [1986], Bartie [2019]). Prior to the 1950s, Australian law professors produced only a very small number of Australian law books, meaning that the vast bulk of law teaching at Australian law schools relied heavily on English textbooks with their emphasis on English law. The majority of full-time academics had been educated in the United Kingdom, most often in Oxbridge. Nonetheless there are signs of divergence from England. First, unlike the English elevation of private and common law, several of the early Australian law professors held a fascination with public and constitutional law and held interests in the potential of statutes. While for most of this period law schools had only one or two full time academic staff, Melbourne and Sydney each had Chairs in Public Law. Second, several were attracted, albeit cautiously, to the ideas and practices of US law schools, with two prominent professors, Jethro Brown (Adelaide Law School) and Harrison Moore (Melbourne Law School) touring US law schools and reporting on their findings. At Melbourne Law School we find several law professors in the 1920s and 1930s voicing sympathies for American Legal Realism (Bartie [2019]). Lunney detects among some members of this early generation of Australian legal academics, evidence of British race patriotism, suggesting that the professors held strong ties with English law professors, were well educated in English ideas and laws but also wanted to serve their local communities which sometimes meant departing from these English ideas and laws (Lunney [2018], Bartie [2019]).

The opportunity to experiment with ideas and create university legal education distinctive to Australian conditions did not arise until the 1950s. The injection of large amounts of funding into universities and law schools helped to employ a community of scholars to oversee a large student cohort. One of the central priorities of this generation was to create Australian law textbooks and to prioritise Australian law (Bartie [2010]). There are clear signs that this generation of scholars wanted to put Australian law on a global map, expressing frustration at the failure of English textbooks to refer to Australian law (Bartie [2010]). At Melbourne there even existed a belief that the law school could in time become as great as the elite US law schools, which due to their size and grandeur constituted a significant benchmark (Sawer [1950]). Several young legal scholars participated in exchanges to the US, often facilitated by Erwin Griswald of Harvard who seemed enthusiastic at the prospect of bringing the Harvard model to Australia (Bartie [2021]). However, none of the Australian academics seemed wholly taken by the US models, issuing criticisms and suggesting ways to improve on both the American and English systems (a tradition that began with the early writings of Jethro Brown). There were some significant innovators who drew from leading overseas theoretical schools and combined them with thinking drawn from the local context (Bartie [2019]) (Starr [1992]).

Until the 1970s law was taught in Australian law schools almost exclusively by men to classrooms full of men. The majority of these men were white, although it is important to recognise that several of the leading professors in the 1950s and 1960s were from minority (e.g. Jewish) and working class backgrounds. Several displayed a strong interest in social causes, however the idea

that women or men who were not white Anglo-Saxons should also be encouraged to prosper in law was not raised with any force until the critical ferment of the 1970s. Even then it was mostly raised by women. Margaret Thornton has provided several accounts of how women struggled to gain a foothold in the legal academy and legal profession (despite the first woman graduating from law in 1902, women did not join the profession in any significant number until the 1970s) and how strong masculine cultures prospered within Australian law schools throughout the twentieth century, influencing both the teaching and practice of law in numerous ways and making women students feel unwelcome (Thornton [1996], Thornton [2023]). While the number of women university law students equalled and then surpassed men in the 1990s, women remain underrepresented in leadership positions, such as barristers, judges and partners in law firms (Thornton [2023]).

The 1970s brought greater diversity among both student and staff cohorts in law schools, as well as new law schools which sought to differentiate themselves from the older order. Sometimes the differences were modest, while at other times, as in the case of Macquarie Law School, they were radical, with teaching and research based on critical legal studies tenets (Carrigan [2014], Thornton [2006]). In the history of Australian university legal education, Macquarie has been the only law school to openly proclaim a strong radical strain. A 1987 national discipline assessment which strongly criticised the school (despite strong student evaluations) (The Pearce Report [1987]) and the fact that several radical members were pushed out of the school discouraged the creation of future law schools of this kind (Carrigan [2014]).

The final two decades of the twentieth century marked a shift in university law schools, and universities more generally, which continues to be felt today (Bartie [2019]). During this period universities emerged as a mass system and large contributor to Australia's economy with research becoming one of its central commodities (Forsyth [2014]). Whereas in the 1950s and 1960s, Australian legal academics viewed law teaching as their primary responsibility, with the creation of a law textbook often qualifying an academic for promotion to professor, steadily over the 1980s and 1990s expectations grew that legal academics gain

PhDs, seek grant funding and concentrate on research and scholarship other than textbooks. Professional standards led to the homogenisation of the law curriculum, with all Australian law schools required to teach the same 11 compulsory subjects in order for their students to be admitted to practice law (Barker [2017]). This has meant that despite the number of law students and law schools continuing to grow in the final two decades of the twentieth century, the education students receive across the country is very similar. While since the 1970s various academics and law schools have sought to introduce offerings (most often electives) that challenge traditional legal paradigms and legal culture, and recognise the plurality of law (particularly acknowledging Indigenous law), broader managerial trends have discouraged legal academics from devoting significant energies to teaching and curriculum design.

SUSAN BARTIE

References

Barker, D. (2017). *A History of Australian Legal Education*, The Federation Press.

Bartie, S. (2021). 'Functionalism, Legal Process and the Transformation (and Subordination) of Australian Law Schools', in Bartie, S. and Sandomierski, D. (eds), *American Legal Education Abroad*, New York University Press.

Bartie, S. (2019). *Free Hands and Minds – Pioneering Australian Legal Scholars*, Hart Publishing.

Bartie, S. (2010). 'A Full Day's Work: A Study of Australia's First Legal Scholarly Community', *University of Queensland Law Journal*, 29(1), p. 67.

Carrigan, F. (2014). 'They Make a Desert and Call It Peace', *Legal Education Review*, 23, p. 313.

Forsyth, H. (2014). *A History of the Modern Australian University*, NewSouth.

Forsyth, H. (2023). *Virtue Capitalists: The Rise and Fall of the Professional Class in the Anglophone World, 1870–2008*, Cambridge University Press.

Lunney, M. (2018). *A History of Australian Tort Law 1901–1945: England's Obedient Servant?*, Cambridge University Press.

Martin, L. (1986). 'From Apprenticeship to Law School: A Social History of Legal Education in Nineteenth Century New South Wales', *University of New South Wales Law Journal*, 9, p. 111.

Pearce, D., Campbell, E. and Harding, D. (1987). *Australian Law Schools: A Discipline Assessment for the Commonwealth Tertiary Education Commission*, Canberra, Australian Government Publishing Service (The Pearce Report).

Pietsch, T. (2015). *Empire of Scholars – Universities, Networks and the British Academic World 1850–1939*, Manchester University Press.

Sawer, G. (1950). 'Legal Education in the United States', *University of Western Australia Annual Law Review*, 1, p. 398.

Starr, L. (1992). *Julius Stone – An Intellectual Life*, Oxford University Press.

Thornton, M. (2023). *Law and the Quest for Gender Equality*, ANU Press.

Thornton, M. (2006). 'The Dissolution of the Social in the Legal Academy', *Australian Feminist Law Journal*, 25, p. 3.

Thornton, M. (1996). *Dissonance and Distrust – Women and the Legal Profession*, Oxford University Press.

Twining, W. (2018). 'Rethinking Legal Education', *The Law Teacher*, 52, p. 241.

Waugh, J. (2007). *First Principles*, Miegunyah Press.

11. Australia (regulation of legal education)

Admission to practice as a solicitor or barrister in Australia is regulated by legislation in each State and Territory (e.g. Legal Profession Act NSW 2007) and administered by Admissions Boards set up by the various Supreme Courts (e.g. https://www.lawadmissions.vic.gov.au/). Admission is based on successful completion of a legal education qualification and certification of Practical Legal Training competencies. Where the legal education qualification is gained via a higher education provider, further Commonwealth Government regulations apply (Higher Education Standards (Threshold Standards) 2021). The Admissions Boards do not regulate non-qualifying degrees – such as Graduate Diplomas, Masters or PhD qualifications. A voluntary certification is also available for Law Schools through the Australian Law Schools Standards Committee (https://cald.asn.au/the-australian-law-schools-standards/).

Law degrees are offered in every State and mainland Territory of Australia, with Law Schools in 38 universities, both public and private (https://cald.asn.au/contact-us/deans-law-schools/). New South Wales also has one private Institute of Higher Education qualification, and one non-university qualification offered by the state's Legal Profession Admission Board (https://www.lpab.justice.nsw.gov.au/Pages/diploma-law-course/diploma-law-course.aspx). This Diploma in Law is the oldest Australian legal qualification. Unlike all other Australian legal qualifications, it is not registered with the Tertiary Education Qualifications Standards Agency but operates under specific statutory licence. The content is however governed by the same rules applying to other NSW university qualifications. It is strongly focussed on practice and doctrinal aspects and is designed to be an accessible route to a legal career for those for whom a university qualification is unattainable. For simplicity the discussion that follows will not refer to this qualification.

In Australia, there are no external admission examinations administered by the Admission Boards. Instead, all applicants must demonstrate successful graduation from both an accredited degree (Bachelor of Laws or Juris Doctor program) and an accredited practical legal training (PLT) program. Admission is initially limited to practising under the supervision of an experienced lawyer. Solo practice on admission is not permitted.

PLT programs are offered by two main independent colleges and a number of law schools also offer PLT programs either embedded in or subsequent to their law degrees. It is also possible to undertake the training via workplace supervision in Victoria and Queensland.

Admission board regulation

Victoria, New South Wales and Western Australia's regulatory schemes operate under a Uniform Law and Rules administered by the Legal Services Council (Law Admission Consultative Committee, Uniform Admission Rules 2008). Other States and Territories continue to maintain individual legislative schemes. All admitting authorities follow the same core set of requirements that have been developed by the Law Admissions Consultative Committee (LACC), a peak advisory group for all admitting authorities (https://www.legalservicescouncil.org.au/about-us/law-admissions-consultative-committee.html). LACC promulgates nationally agreed requirements for legal education and PLT content, and standards for accreditation.

The content requirements for legal education (Prescribed Areas of Academic Knowledge (AAK) https://legalservicescouncil.org.au/documents/prescribed-academic-areas-of-knowledge.pdf) are expressed as a list of 11 doctrinal areas (colloquially known as the 'Priestley 11' after the chair of the drafting committee), and an additional Statement on Required Understanding of Statutory Interpretation (https://www.legalservicescouncil.org.au/content/dam/dcj/legal-services-council/documents/LACC_-_Statement_on_Statutory_Interpretation_-_2009.pdf). The AAK are: Torts, Contracts, Property, Equity, Company Law, Administrative Law, Federal and State Constitutional Law, Civil Dispute Resolution, Evidence and Ethics and Professional Responsibility. The AAK is a combination of two previous lists of requirements, as a result each doctrinal area is described as both a list of specific elements to be taught and in the alternative a generalised list of topic areas. Law Schools can choose either, but most choose to teach the detailed list. Most law schools will devote at least one unit to each area, but some may teach more. Schools may also include additional areas in their compulsory core.

A second set of requirements relates to PLT (https://www.legalservicescouncil.org.au/content/dam/dcj/legal-services-council/documents/PLT-competency-standards-for-entry-level-lawyers-Oct-2017.pdf). Those seeking admission must satisfy competence in areas grouped into Skills, Practice Areas and Values. The competencies require new lawyers to be able to undertake a range of practical activities expected of practicing lawyers and to have the underlying skills and professional values to be able to discharge these tasks appropriately.

Supplementing both sets of requirements are detailed Standards for how the content is to be taught. For the qualifying degree a number of standards are worth emphasising: the degree must be the equivalent of three years, full time study in length; each of the AAK should receive at least 36 hours of direct interaction, and the degree should be primarily based on an active learning pedagogy. The PLT Standards include requirements for students to undertake both authentic competency-based assessments, and also set hours for workplace training of either six months or an integrated set of programmed training of 450 hours and three weeks of workplace experience.

Commonwealth regulation

Australian university degrees are regulated under the Australian Qualifications Framework Reference (https://www.aqf.edu.au/) – which regulates generic learning outcomes of degree levels, and the Higher Education Standards (Threshold Standards) 2021 (https://www.legislation.gov.au/Details/F2022C00105) which sets teaching quality and student support standards.

For many years Australian universities only offered law as an undergraduate degree – the Bachelor of Laws (LLB). In recent years, graduate entry JD degrees have begun to have been offered. All Australian JD degrees are three years in length and for accreditation purposes are required to contain the same content as the LLB degrees. Thus to admitting authorities there is no difference between the LLB and the JD. Given the importance of

training lawyers for practice and the need for accreditation it might be assumed that both LLB and JD students would be taught to the same levels of competence and skill.

However, under the Australian Qualifications Framework the LLB is required to meet the learning outcomes of Level 7 Bachelor degree and the JD must meet Level 9 Masters (Extended) degree learning outcomes. Those Level 9 learning outcomes require more understanding of recent developments and of research principles in the discipline, more mastery of theoretical and critical skills and a capstone or research project. Given the LLB is generally taught to similar levels (ie above Level 7) in practice the two degrees are substantially alike, though assessment may vary. Although the learning outcome of the degrees are differently described, the identical professional accreditation requirements mean that at most law schools, no practical difference in the required learning outcomes of the LLB and JD students exists.

Under the Higher Education Standards law degrees must have learning outcomes for each course of study and assessment that is consistent with those outcomes and are capable of confirming student attainment of those outcomes. Teaching staff must have up to date knowledge, skills in teaching, and a qualification one level higher than that taught (or equivalent experience). For JD teaching this means a PhD or equivalent academic or professional experience. Universities must have internal quality assurance processes, and the law degrees must be reviewed by a body including external members every seven years. Students must have opportunities to provide feedback on the courses.

Complementing these requirements, the Tertiary Education Quality and Standards Agency (https://www.teqsa.gov.au/) undertakes periodic review of universities and imposes sector wide reporting requirements.

Threshold learning outcomes

As part of a national project Kift, Israel and Field developed a set of six threshold learning outcomes (TLOs) for the Bachelor of Laws: Knowledge, Ethics and Professional Responsibility, Thinking Skills, Research Skills, Communication and collaboration and Self-Management (https://cald.asn.au/wp-content/uploads/2024/04/LLB-TLOsKiftetalLTASStandardsStatement2010

-TLOs-LLB2.pdf). These outcomes went significantly beyond the AAK. They were subsequently adopted by the Council of Australian Law Deans, and together with a variation for the Juris Doctor, have been incorporated into the learning outcomes of all Australian law degrees.

Australian law schools standards committee

The Council of Australian Law Deans has also developed a set of voluntary standards that provide a more holistic set of standards (https://cald .asn.au/the-australian-law-schools-standards/). There are 10 standards: Fundamental issues, mission and objectives; The law course (which incorporates the TLOs); Assessment of students; Course and subject evaluation; Academic staff; The nexus between teaching and research; The law library or law collection; Resources and infrastructure; Governance and administration; Continuous renewal and improvement. Many of the standards have sub-standards. Obtaining certification against these standards has required a written submission responding to each area covered and follow up discussions. The standards are notable in focusing on student and staff wellbeing; law school independence and academic freedom; and detailed requirements around curriculum and assessment mapping and quality control. Most law schools have obtained certification under these standards.

ALEX STEEL

References

Australian Qualifications Framework Council https://www.aqf.edu.au/.

Council of Australian Law Deans https://cald.asn.au/.

Council of Australian Law Deans, Juris Doctor Threshold Learning Outcomes https://cald.asn.au/wp-content/uploads/2024/04/JD-TLOs-March-2012-Andrew-Kenyon11.pdf.

Council of Australian Law Deans, Australian Law School Standards https://cald.asn.au/the-australian-law-schools-standards/.

Higher Education Standards (Threshold Standards) 2021 https://www.legislation.gov.au/Details/F2022C00105.

Law Admission Consultative Committee, Accreditation Standards for Australian Law Courses 2018 https://legalservicescouncil.org.au/documents/accreditation-standards-for-law-courses.pdf.

12. Building community in the law school classroom

Introduction

This entry presents an approach to legal education pedagogy focused on community building as an essential component of effective teaching and learning. It demonstrates how this approach radically departs from the norms of the traditional law school classroom, which emphasise hierarchy, competition, and conformity. Creating community requires law teachers to make an ongoing investment in prioritising relationships and wholeness through careful and deliberate attention to issues of equity, inclusion, belonging, and wellbeing. The entry begins with a description of traditional law school culture, and then traces important developments in the legal education field that have helped create a shift toward pedagogical methods that emphasise collaboration, experiential learning, and reflective practice. The entry goes on to identify six core ingredients for community building in the law school classroom, which also offer a framework for trauma-informed and healing-centred teaching and learning.

Reshaping classroom culture in law schools

The historical context for this discussion can be traced to Harvard Law professor Christopher Columbus Langdell, who is credited with establishing what is still considered the 'signature pedagogy' of legal education known as the Socratic method (Sullivan et al [2007]). This method is typically characterised by a stern professor standing at the podium of a large lecture hall who calls on unsuspecting students and proceeds to interrogate them in front of their peers. The professor's cross-examination presumably is intended to highlight a point of legal reasoning or analysis for the supposed benefit of the entire class, and yet it often creates immediate harm for individual students and contributes to an unhealthy classroom learning environment. The Socratic method is a major contributor to what has been described as the cultural 'Matrix' of legal education (Sturm and Guinier [2007]), which reproduces the dominant hierarchies of power and privilege, leading to widespread student alienation and disconnection, particularly among students from historically marginalised groups (Sturm and Guinier [2007]). For decades, these aspects of legal education have been widely critiqued as producing a culture of competition and conformity, and more recently as a 'white space' (Capers [2021]) and a 'straight space' (Balakrishnen [2022]).

While the dominant 'euroheteropatriarchal paradigms' continue to persist in legal education (Martinez [2015] at 596), a confluence of developments over the past few decades have led to more creative, democratic, and participatory teaching methods in law schools. These developments include the Critical Legal Studies (CLS) movement, which arose in legal academia in part as a critique of the individualistic rights-based approach underlying modern liberal legal systems, particularly that of the US (e.g. Gabel [2015]), and expanded over time to include other critical legal movements, including Critical Feminism, Critical Race Theory, and, more recently, Critical Disability Studies. Other related scholarly movements connected to CLS have focused on promoting wellbeing and greater satisfaction among people impacted by law and legal processes including Therapeutic Jurisprudence (TJ) (e.g. Wexler [1995]) and Procedural Justice (e.g. Tyler [2003]). Yet another scholarly field that has influenced law school pedagogy is the Law and Society movement (also known as socio-legal studies in the UK [see Socio-Legal Approaches to Legal Education], which has supported the emergence of new interdisciplinary fields such as Law and Emotions and Feminist Legal Studies. Alongside these developments in legal scholarship, legal education has undergone significant curricular expansion into areas such as clinical and experiential education (e.g. Bryant et al [2014], Wortham et al [2016]), alternative dispute resolution (Brooks [2020]), and formation of professional identity (e.g. Hamilton [2019]) [see Clinical Legal Education (Overview), Alternative Dispute Resolution and Legal Education, and Professional Identity Formation of Law Students].

Additionally, these developments have been supported by a wide variety of organisations, including mainstream entities like the American Bar Association (ABA), which regulates a vast number of law schools primarily in the US, and has launched initiatives such as the Taskforce on Lawyer Well Being, which issued a report in 2018 including specific guidance for law schools, and recent revisions to the ABA Standards that require students to be provided with substantial opportunities to engage with formation of their professional identities, anti-racism, and cross-cultural lawyering. Another large and influential organisation is the Association of American Law Schools (AALS), also based in the US, which has sections on Balance and Well-being and Teaching Methods. Alongside the contributions of larger institutions, efforts to 'humanise legal education' have been supported through a handful of smaller scale initiatives with a global reach, such as the Project for Integrating Spirituality, Law and Politics (PISLAP), Mindfulness in Law Society, the Global Alliance for Justice Education (GAJE), and the Centre for Study of Emotion and Law.

Taken together, these wide-ranging developments have paved the way for pedagogical changes in legal education that support greater attention to community building in law school classrooms. Nevertheless, even law teachers who care genuinely about the idea of creating community may either believe it will simply happen on its own or are convinced they cannot afford the time to devote to community building because it will unduly detract from their coverage of important subject matter. While some aspects of community may naturally emerge in a law school class, law teachers who make an ongoing commitment to being intentional and deliberate can create classroom learning communities where all students experience a sense of belonging, where creative dialogues can take place, and where conflicts that arise can lead to breakthroughs and transformative learning (Bliss, et al [2021]). The goal is to design courses in ways that prioritise concerns around equity and inclusion and support wellbeing and liberation. Community building requires law teachers to engage in ongoing reflective practices that model and foster an environment in which students are encouraged to connect intra- and interpersonal dimensions of their learning with systemic understandings, meaning, 'working within ourselves and between ourselves, and then work[ing] to change the larger systems and societies in which we live' (Bliss, et al [2021] at 2). Creating supportive learning conditions

allows students to gain transferable knowledge, skills, and values that will serve them well over the course of their professional lives and careers.

Six core ingredients for community building and healing-centred engagement

The next section outlines six ingredients for creating community in the law school classroom that draw from many sources both within and outside of the legal field, and represent a trauma-informed and healing centred teaching framework These six ingredients are as follows: (1) relational worldview; (2) safer/braver spaces; (3) contextualised, multi-dimensional lens; (4) strengths orientation; (5) agency; and (6) transparency and trustworthiness (Brooks [2023]).

Relational Worldview

A central theme in approaching community building in the classroom is the idea of relationship. A relational worldview embraces the ideas of human mutuality and interconnectedness and invites consideration of what it means to affirm those qualities through day-to-day interactions. Given this omni-presence of relationship, each moment in the classroom is an opportunity to cultivate relationships, including acknowledging past or present harm that has impacted relationships and investing in transforming relationships by harnessing core values and broad aspirations (Brooks and Carolin [2023]). To this end law teachers can draw on adrienne maree brown's idea that 'what we practice at the small scale sets the patterns for the whole system' (Brown [2017]). By spending time focusing on relationships and reflecting on interaction at all levels, interpersonal relationships and the classroom community as a whole can enrich the learning process.

Safer/Braver Spaces

It is critically important for law teachers to appreciate the challenges of supporting students to be able to show up as fully and authentically as possible. In safer/braver spaces, law teachers foster the conditions in which students can give voice to whatever is true for them, speaking from the heart and engaging in generous and whole body listening (Brooks [2020]). The more law teachers can create these conditions in the classroom, the more likely it is that students can transfer these lessons into their work and legal professionals through cultivating an ability to hold space for uncertainty while remaining open, caring, and compassionate toward others with whom they interact (Brooks [2023]).

This work of creating safer and braver spaces requires law teachers to meet students where they are, which means acknowledging that students arrive in their classrooms with a wide range of different levels of privilege and hardship, including individual and collective histories of trauma and oppression. (Brooks [2023]). It also requires devoting significant time to inviting and incorporating student input and feedback as a continuous practice before, during, and after the time frame of the course. Another important theme and set of practices that support this work is slowing down. Practicing slowness means responding to uncomfortable moments or conflicts by inviting curiosity and reflection rather than reactivity. By incorporating tools and activities that help build capacity among students to stay with discomfort in ways that draw upon their core values and 'best selves', difficult conversations can actually deepen relationships and lead to breakthroughs rather than contributing to separation and disconnection. The key takeaway is that law teachers cannot simply say or think the words 'safe space' and expect students magically to feel safe. It is necessary to invest significant time and energy to showing up and acting in ways that allow students to bring more of their full selves into the classroom to maximise their learning (Brooks [2023]).

Contextualised, Multi-Dimensional Lens

To gain a better understanding of themselves and their students, law teachers need to appreciate the various contexts each person brings into classroom encounters, which include individual and collective histories, a wide array of often intersectional identities, and immediate circumstances, among other considerations. It is also important to appreciate this richness of teachers' and students' various contexts from a complex, multi-dimensional, and multi-disciplinary lens that can incorporate a whole range of bio-psycho-social-spiritual perspectives (Brooks [2023]). To effectively create community in the law school classroom, law teachers need to take the time to appreciate their own and their students' contexts as fully as possible, and practice self-awareness around how their own contexts shape their decision making and the choices they make in interacting with their students.

Strengths Orientation

Shifting to a more relational way of being requires law teachers to view themselves and their students as whole people, which includes embracing their own as well as all their students' unique strengths and assets. (Brooks [2023], Brooks [2018]). This emphasis on strengths is especially important for law faculty, as so much of their disciplinary training and even the design of the law itself is built on scepticism and risk aversion, which tends to problematise everyone and everything. This shift in orientation toward strengths can contribute significantly to the creative reimagining of our work as law teachers, and our students' work as future legal professionals.

Agency

The notion of agency represents a fundamental belief in oneself, and the ability to act on the qualities of choice, voice, and empowerment, all of which have been identified as core elements of trauma-informed practice. To create classroom communities that promote healing, students need to experience themselves as being able to exercise the choice to speak or stay silent, and, if they choose to speak, to be able to express themselves authentically in a manner that feels aligned and truthful. It is therefore essential for law teachers to interact with students in ways that allow them to exercise as much choice as possible (Brooks [2023]).

One simple yet profound way to implement this idea is to use invitational language, meaning incorporating the words 'I invite you ...' when prompting an activity or giving instructions in the classroom. Of course, the use of this language only makes sense if the law teacher truly embraces the notion that students are fundamentally in choice at all times and accepts respectful presence and listening as meaningful forms of engagement and participation.

Transparency and Trustworthiness

Transparency and trustworthiness have also been identified as essential aspects of trauma-informed and healing-centred engagement. Law teachers can support the agency of their students through being transparent with them about their decision making as much as possible, which in turn will enhance the students' trust and ability to learn (Brooks [2023]).

For instance, at times a classroom discussion takes an unexpected turn, and it may be difficult for the teacher to respond in real time in a way that feels complete or fully in alignment with their values. Acting with transparency can mean initiating a follow-up conversation, acknowledging and accepting responsibility for their role in what took place, creating space to slow down, and inviting the class to share feedback and reflections around what happened. Offering this level of openness, transparency, and humility creates a learning environment in which students are often able to respond with appreciation and with similar relational qualities of kindness, empathy, and compassion. This example illustrates how transparency and trustworthiness can lead to more authentic communication and the possibility for deepening classroom connections, even in situations of tension or conflict.

Conclusion

Legal education has undergone significant changes since the time of Langdell, and yet, transforming the culture of competition and conformity remains an ongoing challenge. By devoting time and deliberate attention to community building informed by relational and wholehearted perspectives and practices, law teachers can create a trauma-informed and healing-centred experience for all students. Creating community in law school classrooms can maximise opportunities for meaningful and transferable student learning and professional development at the individual, interpersonal, and collective levels.

SUSAN L BROOKS

References

Balakrishnen, S.S. (2022). 'Law school as straight space', *Fordham Law Review*, 90, p. 1113.

Bliss, L., Brooks, S.L. and Huq, C. (2021). 'Creating Online Education Spaces to Support Equity, Inclusion, Belonging, and Wellbeing', *John Marshall Law Journal*, 14(2), p. 1.

Brooks, S.L. (2023). 'Reimagining lawyering: supporting well-being and liberation', *Hofstra Law Review*, 58, p. 1.

Brooks, S.L. (2021). *Fostering wholehearted lawyers through clinical legal education*, Best Practices for Legal Education (Blog), available at https://bestpracticeslegaled.com/2021/04/26/fostering-wholehearted-lawyers-through-clinical-legal-education/.

Brooks, S.L. (2020). 'Listening and relational lawyering', in Worthington, D.L. and Bodie, G.D. (eds), *The handbook of listening*, Wiley.

Brooks, S.L. (2019). 'Mindful engagement and relational lawyering', *Southwestern Law Journal*, 48, p. 267.

Brooks, S.L. (2018). 'Fostering wholehearted lawyers: Practical guidance for supporting law students' professional identity formation', *St Thomas Law Journal*, 14, p. 412.

Brooks, S.L. and Carolin, J. (2023). *Lawyering for social change*, Unpublished course materials, on file with author.

Brooks, S.L. and Madden, R.G. (eds) (2010). *Relationship-Centered Lawyering: Social Science Theory for Transforming Legal Practice*, Carolina Academic Press.

Brown, A.M. (2017). *Emergent Strategy: Shaping Change, Changing Worlds*, AK Press.

Brown, B. (2010). *The gifts of imperfection: let go of you think you're supposed to be and embrace who you are*, Hazeldon.

Bryant, S., Milstein, E. and Shalleck, A. (2014). *Transforming the Education of Lawyers: The Theory and Practice of Clinical Pedagogy*, Carolina Academic Press.

Burke, K. and Leben, S. (2007–08). 'Procedural fairness: A key ingredient in public satisfaction' [White paper of the American Judges Association], *Court review*, 44, p. 4.

Capers, B. (2021). 'The law school as a white space', *Minnesota Law Review*, 106, p. 7.

Gabel, P. (2015). *Another way of seeing: Essays on transforming law, politics and culture*, Quid Pro.

Ginwright, S.A. (2018). 'The future of healing: shifting from trauma-informed care to healing-centered engagement', available at https://ginwright.medium.com/the-future-of-healing-shifting-from-trauma-informed-care-to-healing-centered-engagement-634f557ce69c.

Hamilton, N. (2019). 'Leadership of self: Each student taking ownership of continuous professional development/self-directed learning', *Santa Clara Law Review*, 58(3), p. 567.

Hammond, S.A. (2013). *The thin book of appreciative inquiry*, Thin Book Publishing.

Magee, R.V. (2019). *The inner work of racial justice: healing ourselves and transform-*

ing our communities through mindfulness, TarcherPerigee.

Martínez, S.I.V. (2015). 'Towards an outcrit pedagogy of anti-subordination in the classroom', *Chicago Kent Law Review*, p. 585.

Spencer, R. and Brooks, S.L. (2019). 'Reflecting on reflection: A dialogue across the hemispheres on teaching and assessing reflective practice in clinical legal education', *The Law Teacher*, 53(4), pp. 458–474.

Sturm, S. and Guinier, L. (2007). 'The Law School Matrix: Reforming Legal Education in a Culture of Competition and Conformity', *Vanderbilt Law Review*, 60, p. 515.

Sullivan, W.M, Colby, A., Wegner, J.W., Bond, L. and Shulman, L.S. (2007). *Educating Lawyers: Preparation for the Profession of Law*, Jossey-Bass.

Tyler, T.R. (2003). 'Procedural justice, legitimacy, and the effective rule of law', *Crime and Justice*, 30, p. 283.

Wexler, D.B. (1995). 'Reflections on the scope of therapeutic jurisprudence', *Psychology, Public Policy, and Law*, 1(1), p. 220.

Wortham, L., Scherr, A., Brooks, S.L. and Maurer, N. (eds) (2016). *Learning from Practice: A Text for Experiential Legal Education*, 3rd edition West Academic.

13. Canada (contemporary legal education)

Canada is a federal state consisting of 10 provinces and three territories. Pursuant to the provincial constitutional power to legislate in matters of property and civil rights, private law – and the regulation of the legal profession – is a provincial concern (Constitution Act, 1867, ss 92(13), 94A). Law students in Quebec study the civil law; outside of Quebec, the common law.

University legal education as a pathway to practice

In all Canadian provinces, a licence to practice law requires a university law degree – in Quebec, a Bachelor of Laws; in the common law provinces, a Juris Doctor. Common law programmes are typically a second degree, with highly competitive admissions processes that often rely on a combination of postsecondary grades and Law School Admission Test (LSAT) results, with a varying number of spaces available at different faculties for alternative admissions pathways. Civil law programmes are typically first degree programmes. In addition to completing an approved degree, aspiring lawyers must also complete a provincial law society's training programme and some form of articling or approved substitute.

Universities are free, subject to their internal governing procedures and approval by provincial authorities, to offer these degrees; however, in order for their degrees to satisfy accreditation requirements, they must also be approved by provincial licensing bodies in concert with their umbrella organisation, the Federation of Law Societies of Canada [see Canada (Regulation of Legal Education)]. As of 2023, 24 universities offer approved degrees: seven universities offer a Bachelor in Civil Law, and 19 offer a JD. The University of Ottawa, which has a Faculty of Common Law, and a Faculty of Civil Law, offers approved degrees for the practice in both jurisdictions. McGill University offers an integrated programme whose graduates receive both a JD and a Bachelor of Civil Law.

Most approved law degree programmes in Canada have a long historical legacy [see Canada (History of Legal Education)], although four programmes are relatively new entrants. In British Columbia, Thomson Rivers University had its first JD class in 2011; in Ontario, the Bora Laskin Faculty of Law at Lakehead University opened in 2013 and the Lincoln Alexander School of Law at Toronto Metropolitan University opened in 2020; in Quebec, the Université du Québec en Outaouais began offering a Bachelor of Laws degree in Fall 2023. Trinity Western University, a private Christian university in British Columbia, sought approval for a JD programme in 2012, but was denied accreditation from the Law Society of British Columbia, a decision ultimately upheld by the Supreme Court of Canada (*Law Society of British Columbia v. Trinity Western University*, 2018 SCC 32).

As of 2023, therefore, all approved degrees for the practice in law in Canada are offered by programmes within publicly funded universities. Unlike in the USA, there are no law schools that rely exclusively on private funding or that operate independent of a university. The units offering approved degrees in Canada vary in nomenclature: a university may have a law *school*, a law *faculty*, or, less commonly, a *college* of law or a *department* of juridical science. Despite functional similarities, there may be important symbolic differences for this choice of label (Macdonald & McMorrow [2014]). The term 'law faculty' will be used generically for the remainder of this entry.

University legal education not on a pathway to practice

Canadian universities also offer legal education that does not lead to accreditation. Students may study law in dedicated undergraduate programmes, such as Law & Society or Legal Studies; many law-related courses are also offered by other departments (philosophy, political science, engineering, etc). Graduate legal education (LLM for law graduates, MSL for graduates of other disciplines, and doctorates, including DCL, PhD, and SJD degrees) is also typically outside of the accreditation pathway. The doctoral stream is research-intensive; graduates often serve in policy and academia, among other areas. Masters degrees are typically either research-focused, with a major paper or thesis, or course-based. Graduate programmes are for the most part relatively small in contrast to large course-based programmes in the USA, although in recent years some universities have created separate streams of graduate programmes to cater to professionals and foreign-trained lawyers looking to qualify to practice in Canada.

The political economy of Canadian legal education

As Harry Arthurs has written (1998), legal education in Canada 'is located in the borderlands between two powerful suzerains, the higher education sector and the legal profession'. This intersection is often characterised as a space of conflict and competition – historically, over the right to provide accredited legal education (Kyer & Bickenbach) and, more recently, over the content of the required curriculum (Arthurs [2019]). To the extent that Canadian law faculties are required to certify that their graduates have obtained competencies mandated by the Federation of Law Societies of Canada, one could say their scope for curricular innovation is somewhat constrained [see Canada (Regulation of Legal Education)].

At the same time, most law faculties experience fiscal and resource constraints, both through the central budgeting processes of the broader universities in which they are housed, and via governmental policies. Law tuition is regulated by provincial governments, resulting in variable tuition rates and governmental subsidies across the country and fluctuating abilities of law faculties to set their tuitions, depending on the policies of the day. For example, in Ontario, tuition fees for professional programmes were de-regulated in the late 1990s, leading to higher-than-national-average rates in that province (Frenette [2008]), only to be followed two decades later by a governmental policy that abruptly reduced and froze tuition rates (Jones [2023]).

Despite the structural limitations imposed by governments, universities, and law societies, Canadian law faculties offer an eclectic mix of educational offerings.

The JD curriculum

The standard JD programme is three years in length, although a one-year common law degree is available from some universities to graduates of a Canadian civil law programme (and vice-versa, in one case [Ottawa]), and the transsystemic programmes at McGill and the University of Victoria are slightly longer (3.5 and 4 years, respectively). The first-year curriculum is mostly compulsory and relatively uniform across the country, consisting of courses in Contracts, Property, Torts, Criminal Law, Constitutional Law, and Legal Research & Writing – although there are some variations in course title and focus at different schools (e.g. 'Fundamentals of Public Law'; 'Contracts and Judicial Decision-Making' at the Schulich School of Law at Dalhousie). The upper-year programme is much more variable, with a range in the number and type of required courses – although frequently, courses in civil procedure, ethics and professionalism, Indigenous legal studies, and administrative law are mandatory. Upper year courses are typically offered in the Fall or Winter Semester; most first-year programmes offer most courses throughout the full year, although a small number of programmes have semesterised their first-year offerings.

Electives

The trend over the past 40 years, ever since the publication of a flagship report on Canadian legal education that argued for increased interdisciplinary scholarship and teaching in pursuit of cultivating 'humane professionalism' (Consultative Group [1983]), is of an increasing number of interdisciplinary, critical, and perspectives-based courses. At some law schools studying one such course is compulsory, but usually they are elective. Among elective courses, no single discipline appears to predominate; offerings tend to reflect faculty research specialisation. Elective courses range from interdisciplinary courses, such as in law and economics, philosophy of law, law & public health, to courses in 'outsider pedagogy', such as those incorporating perspectives from, inter alia, critical race, feminist, queer, and disability theories (Bakht et al [2007]). [See also entries on Critical Legal Studies and Sexuality and Legal Education.] A large number of doctrinal courses are also typically offered on an elective basis or as electives within a required number of mandatory categories [see Doctrinal Legal Education].

Clinical and experiential legal education

Most law faculties in Canada have one or multiple legal clinics that provide legal advice or information to the general public. Usually through a selective process, students work at these clinics either for course credit or as summer employment, engaging in community education and supervised case work. Some law faculties host multiple clinics that cater to specific communities or areas of law, such as an Indigenous Community Legal Clinic (UBC, Toronto) or a Technology and Innovation Law Clinic (Dalhousie). Unlike in the US, there is typically no 'bifurcated' two-tier structure of clinical and doctrinal faculty (Richman [2020]), although there is a rich literature on Canadian clinical education (Hathaway [1987], Anderson [2013], Smyth et al [2017], Barkaskas & Buhler [2017]). Other experiential learning opportunities routinely offered include moot court competitions, as well as courses in trial advocacy and negotiation. Within the curriculum, experiential learning for course credit is typically elective, although a small number of faculties impose a requirement.

Indigenous legal education: legacy of the Truth and Reconciliation Commission of Canada

From approximately 1883 until 1969, although predating and extending beyond these dates, the Government of Canada partnered with various religious organisations to establish and operate a series of residential schools for Indigenous children. These schools forcibly separated First Nations, Métis, and Inuit children from their families, severed linguistic and cultural links between generations, and served as a venue for physical, sexual, and emotional abuse. A legal settlement recognising the harms perpetuated to children at 139 schools, as well as the policy of cultural genocide, established the Truth and Reconciliation Commission of Canada, which, in 1995, published numerous reports including a list of 94 'Calls to Action'. Recommendation 28 called on 'law schools in Canada to require all law students to take a course in Aboriginal

people and the law, which includes the history and legacy of residential schools, the *United Nations Declaration on the Rights of Indigenous Peoples*, Treaties and Aboriginal rights, Indigenous law, and Aboriginal-Crown relations.'

In response to the Call to Action 28, law faculties across Canada have increased the content of their course offerings in Indigenous and Aboriginal law to the point where the majority of schools (14 out of 24, as of 2023) have instituted a mandatory course, with the format, year of offering, and focus of the course varying between schools. In addition, there have been attempts to indigenise or, preferably to some, decolonise the standard law curriculum through incorporating Indigenous legal perspectives and experiences into doctrinal courses (Hewitt [2016]). Some instructors have published their initiatives (Lund [2016], Drake [2017], Hanna [2022]), and an informal website for sharing resources has been created (https://reconciliationsyllabus.wordpress.com/). [See entry on Decolonising the legal curriculum.]

On a more comprehensive level, the University of Victoria has offered a Joint Degree in Canadian Common Law and Indigenous Legal Orders since 2018. Students in this programme receive two degrees, JD/JID, and study Indigenous law and the common law in an integrated fashion. A new National Centre for Indigenous Law will be built on site in 2024 to expand the initiative. The transsystemic pedagogy was inspired by McGill University's 'McGill Program', founded in 1998, in which students study civil and common law in an integrated fashion (Borrows [2010], Macdonald & McLean [2005]) The University of Saskatchewan has run the Indigenous Law Centre (formerly the Native Law Centre) to facilitate access to legal education for Indigenous peoples since 1975, and offered on-site legal education in the Inuit territory of Nunavut via the Nunavut Law Program, from 2017 to 2021.

Bilingual legal education

The official languages of Canada are English and French. All but two of the common law programmes are offered primarily in English. The exceptions are the University of Ottawa (offering JD courses in both languages) and the Université de Moncton, which provides unilingual common law instruction in French as part of a deliberate policy to support bilingualism in the province and to ensure access to justice in both official languages. Other common law faculties (Manitoba, Calgary, Saskatchewan) offer some courses or certificate programmes in common law French. All of the civil law programmes are offered predominantly in French, except for McGill, where courses are offered in both French and English. Courses offered in a third language are rare.

DAVID SANDOMIERSKI

References

Anderson, J. (2013). 'Clinical Legal Education: Perspectives from Former Clinical Law Students', *Man LJ*, 37(1), p. 427.

Arnow-Richman, R. (2020). 'Integrated Learning, Integrated Facult', *Temp L Rev*, 92(4), p. 745.

Arthurs, H.W. (1998). 'The Political Economy of Canadian Legal Education', *Journal of Law and Society*, 25, p. 14.

Arthurs, H.W. (2019). 'The Tree of Knowledge, the Axe of Power: Le Dain and the Transformation of Canadian Legal Education' in Baker, B.G. and Janda, R. (eds), *Tracings of Gerald Le Dain's Life in the Law*, McGill-Queen's University Press.

Bakht, N. et al. (2007). 'Counting Outsiders: A Critical Exploration of Outsider Course Enrollment in Canadian Legal Education', *Osgoode Hall LJ*, 45(4), p. 667.

Barkaskas, P. and Buhler, S. (2017). 'Beyond Reconciliation: Decolonizing Clinical Legal Education', *Journal of Law and Social Policy*, 26, p. 1.

Borrows, J. (2010). *Canada's Indigenous Constitution*, University of Toronto Press.

Constitution Act 1867, 30 & 31 Vict, c 3.

Consultative Group on Research and Education in Law, *Law and Learning* (Report to the Social Sciences and Humanities Research Council of Canada, Chairman Harry Arthurs) (Social Sciences and Humanities Research Council of Canada, 1983).

'Courses and Requirements'. (2023). *Dalhousie University, Schulich School of Law*, available at https://www.dal.ca/faculty/law/current-students/jd-students/courses.html.

Drake, K. (2017). 'Finding a Path to Reconciliation: Mandatory Indigenous Law, Anishinaabe Pedagogy, and Academic Freedom', *Can B Rev*, 95(1), p. 9.

Frenette, M. (2008). 'University Access Amid Tuition Fee Deregulation: Evidence from Ontario Professional Programs', *Canadian Public Policy/Analyse de Politiques*, 34(1), p. 89.

Hanna, A. (2022). 'An Introduction to Indigenous and Aboriginal Laws', in Ben-Ishai, S. and Percy, D.R. (eds), *Contracts: Cases and Commentaries*, 11th edition, Thomson Reuters, p. 17.

Hathaway, J.C. (1987). 'Clinical Legal Education', *Osgoode Hall LJ*, 25(2), p. 239.

Hewitt, J.G. (2016). 'Decolonizing and Indigenizing: Some Considerations for Law Schools', *Windsor Y B Access Just*, 33(1), p. 65.

Jones, A. (2023). 'Ontario's tuition freeze on colleges, universities continues for 3rd straight year', CBC News, available at https://www.cbc.ca/news/canada/ottawa/ottawa-townhouse-arson-revenge-for-cop-call-victim-1.676595.

Kyer, C.I. and Bickenbach, J.E. (1987). *The Fiercest Debate: Cecil A Wright, the Benchers, and Legal Education in Ontario*, The Osgoode Society.

Law Society of British Columbia v. Trinity Western University, 2018 SCC 32.

Lund, A. et al. (2016). 'Reconciliation in the Corporate Commercial Classroom', *Lakehead LJ*, 2(1), p. 49.

Macdonald, R.A. and MacLean, J. (2005). 'No Toilets in Park', *McGill LJ*, 50(4), p. 721.

MacDonald, R.A. and McMorrow, T.B. (2014). 'Decolonizing Law School', *Alta Law Rev*, 51(4), p. 717.

Smyth, G., Hale, S. and Gold, N. (2017). 'Clinical and Experiential Learning in Canadian Law Schools: Current Perspectives', *Can B Rev*, 95(1), p. 151.

Sossin, L. (2014). 'Experience the Future of Legal Education', *Alta Law Rev*, 51(4), p. 849.

Truth and Reconciliation Commission of Canada. (2015). *Honouring the Truth, Reconciling for the Future: Summary of the Final Report of the Truth and Reconciliation Commission of Canada*, 1–6, available at _Summary_English_Web.pdf.

Truth and Reconciliation Commission of Canada. (2015). *Truth and Reconciliation Commission of Canada Calls to Action*, available at https://ehprnh2mwo3.exactdn.com/wp-content/uploads/2021/01/Calls_to_Action_English2.pdf.

14. Canada (history of legal education)

The legal professions in Canada have existed for some 400 years, beginning with the appearance of the first notaries in New France in the 1620s. Notaries in the civilian tradition, who draft certain private documents such as marriage and employment contracts, wills, and land transfers, and deal with the devolution of property on death, were the only legal profession in New France prior to the cession to the United Kingdom in 1763. Advocates were not formally banned under the French regime, but none are known to have practised, with the result that notaries informally took on the role of pleading in court. (Vachon [1961]) In 1764 the British introduced the profession of advocate (effectively, barrister) under that name, formalising the existence of two separate professions in Quebec which have continued down to the present day. An ordinance of 1785 forbade individuals from becoming members of both professions. Meanwhile, in the common law provinces, the American model of a unified profession took hold early on, with all 'attorneys' authorised to carry on both barrister and solicitor functions. (Girard [2014])

Under the French regime, no formal education for notaries existed. Some might informally apprentice with another notary, but this was not required, and most notaries were self-taught with the aid of existing French texts. Attorney General Louis-Guillaume Verrier, formerly an advocate in the Parlement of Paris, gave a course of lectures on law from the 1730s until his death in 1758, but it was aimed at members of the elite who desired some familiarity with the law, not at aspiring notaries. This unsystematic approach continued under the British until the ordinance of 1785, which required a five-year apprenticeship for both notaries and advocates capped with an examination by senior practitioners under judicial supervision. (Vachon [1961])

In the common law provinces too, an apprenticeship of between four and six years (the period initially being set by the judges) was long the norm, during which the student was expected to work through a reading list of classic texts before undergoing a final oral examination by the judges prior to admission to the profession. Some young men from elite backgrounds attended the Inns of Court and returned to British North America, but this was more to make connections useful in the securing of imperial patronage than to learn the law. (Bell [1992])

Legal education was taken most seriously in Upper Canada (later Ontario). An act of 1797 gave the newly created Law Society of Upper Canada control over the legal profession and a monopoly over legal education. It took this obligation seriously, requiring aspiring lawyers to serve an apprenticeship at York (later renamed Toronto) and attend a course of lectures given at the Law Society's headquarters, Osgoode Hall. The University of Toronto began offering some lectures in law by the mid-nineteenth century, but these were not recognised by the Law Society. Spurred on by the spread of university legal education in the United States, the Law Society created its own Osgoode Hall Law School in 1889 but discouraged the offering of law courses by provincial universities, a stance it would maintain until 1957. It offered a concurrent programme of lectures in the morning followed by office work with one's principal in the afternoon, as was also the case in Quebec after university legal education began there. (Baker [1981])

University legal education began in Quebec, at McGill in 1848, Laval in 1852, and a branch of Laval in Montreal in 1878 (which eventually became the Université de Montréal faculty of law in 1920). This education was aimed principally at those planning to become advocates. University programmes for notaries lagged, leaving apprenticeship long the mode of entry to that profession.

In the common law provinces, the Maritime provinces led the way as many aspiring lawyers had become familiar with university legal education by attending the east coast US law schools in the 1850s–70s. Dalhousie University's law school was founded in 1883, followed by the Saint John Law School in New Brunswick in 1892, affiliated for complex reasons with King's College in Windsor, Nova Scotia. In the Prairie provinces, the universities instituted law schools in quick succession: Alberta in 1912, Saskatchewan in 1913 and Manitoba in 1914. Manitoba's programme used the concurrent model, but the others required three years of full-time study. (Girard [2021] at 71–4) British Columbia was the laggard, with the bar running its own law school until the

University of British Columbia opened a law faculty in 1945. 'Night schools' and private law schools never appeared in Canada. (Pue [1995], Pue [2016])

The curricula at the common law schools offered a mix of private law, public law, and legal history, but in the early twentieth century they began to adopt what was understood as the Harvard model begun under Dean Christopher Columbus Langdell. Although historically Canadian common law was strongly influenced by English models, university legal education followed the US path. Hence, the case method, legal 'science,' and private law eventually took pride of place. Pre-law university study was insisted on from the 1920s, though entering the profession via apprenticeship continued to be possible until after World War II.

In one respect, however, Canadian law schools carved out a different path. Outside Quebec, with its three law schools, each province had only one for long stretches of time. This meant that the law of the home jurisdiction, along with federal law, was taught in preference to the disembodied 'national' approach developed by Langdell and widely imitated in US legal education. (Girard [2021]) McGill's attempt in the 1920s to create a 'national' programme in both civil and common law met with strong resistance from the bar. It was terminated after a few years and only resurrected in the 1960s. (Hobbins [2008])

Legal education at the francophone law schools in Quebec was long infused with religious values inspired by the Roman Catholic church, in contrast to the secular approach at McGill and elsewhere in Canada. An emphasis on natural law, Thomist philosophy, and the Civil Code of Lower Canada created an ideological bulwark against US influences and law reform initiatives, a trend especially evident during the interwar years when ultramontanism was at its peak in Quebec. Gradually, however, the study of case law, though not the case method itself, entered the curriculum in the twentieth century. (Normand [2005])

Although inspired by the US model, Canadian law schools were much more poorly resourced and enjoyed rather less autonomy from their respective provincial law societies than those south of the border. Until World War II most law schools in the common law provinces survived with two or three full-time professors, as did McGill, the rest of the courses being offered by local practitioners or judges. In Quebec all the law schools offered only concurrent programmes until McGill started a full-time programme in 1925, and the francophone law schools had no full-time professors until the first one was appointed in 1944. Prior to that, a judge usually acted as part-time dean. The Quebec bar kept the law schools on a very short leash, having been granted legislative authority to dictate the content of university law programmes and even the number of hours devoted to each course. Outside Quebec and Ontario, the law schools had more autonomy, but still had to maintain good relations with local law societies. In Canada, unlike the US, provincial law societies were guild-like bodies possessing statutory authority to supervise both lawyers and legal education. Canadian law societies still require a period of up to a year spent as an articling clerk prior to admission to the bar, such a requirement having long ago disappeared in the US.

In Ontario, the Law Society of Upper Canada remained the last holdout against university legal education in North America. It tolerated the law programme in the faculty of arts at the University of Toronto but did not grant any advanced standing to Toronto graduates. Matters came to a head in 1949 when almost the entire staff of Osgoode Hall Law School resigned in protest over the Law Society's continued resistance to a more academic approach to legal education. The disaffected staff, who included a future chief justice of Canada, Bora Laskin, all moved to the University of Toronto, where the law school had recently been organised as a separate faculty. This imbroglio led the Law Society finally to permit Ontario universities to create law faculties from 1957, and to reform its own law school in a more academic direction. (Kyer and Bickenbach [1987]) In 1968 it transferred Osgoode Hall Law School to the newly created York University in Toronto and ceased offering legal education of its own aside from a bar admission course to be completed after graduation with the LLB.

The postwar baby boom and strong economic growth generated a dramatic expansion in the numbers of law students and professors as well as the resources available to Canadian law schools. For the first time they faced excess demand for the available spaces, leading to the adoption of the US Law School Admission Test (LSAT) by all law schools outside Quebec as of the 1970–71 academic year. The postwar period also saw the requirement of at least two years of pre-law university study added as an admission requirement everywhere outside Quebec (though entry after obtaining a degree became common), while a law degree from a recognised university became required for bar admission across Canada, eclipsing the apprenticeship route. After Quebec reformed its secondary education system in the 1960s, it became possible for students to enter law school directly after three years of high school and two years of junior college, a lower bar than elsewhere in Canada but similar to European and British practice. (Brierley [1986]) Quebec students increasingly acquired a non-law university degree before entering law school, however.

To meet rising demand, four new law schools were created in Ontario after the barrier was removed by the Law Society in 1957, and two in Quebec, but only three elsewhere in Canada, including the Université de Moncton École de droit in 1978, the only law school in the world to offer the common law in French. By 1980 there were 19 recognised law faculties in Canada. The number would remain stable until the 2010s, sending overseas many Canadians who could not secure admission at home. The major change in the student body from about 1970 was a rapid increase in the number of women, who formed as much as half the student body in some law schools by the 1990s. There had long been a certain amount of ethnic diversity, but significant numbers of racialised and Indigenous students are a much more recent development. The Native Law Centre at the University of Saskatchewan, founded in 1975, provides a Head Start-type programme which has assisted hundreds of Indigenous students to become lawyers across Canada.

The 1960s and 1970s saw a considerable amount of law student activism, with demands for more social relevance and intellectual diversity in the curriculum and better student representation in faculty decision-making. These demands were particularly widespread in Quebec, where students also rebelled against standard magisterial teaching styles and rigid evaluation methods. Laval students went on strike twice in 1971 and 1973 to achieve their goals and by the later 1970s the reforms sought by Quebec students had been largely achieved.

The number of professorial positions in the legal academy increased fourfold between 1960 and 1970. Many non-Canadians, principally from the US, the United Kingdom and Commonwealth countries were hired given the dearth of qualified Canadians. This generation retired for the most part around 2000, and since that time non-Canadian faculty have tended to come from sub-Saharan Africa, especially Nigeria, continental Europe, Latin America, and Asia. An infusion of Indigenous faculty members has also added to the diversity of the legal academy. Female law professors met considerable resistance from the 1970s on, but most law faculties now feature a gender-balanced staff cohort.

The expanded professoriate prompted the offering of a wider spectrum of courses, and as of 1969 the law societies permitted the upper-year curriculum to become completely optional. 'Law-and' courses proliferated as part of a 'cafeteria-style' approach that contained little structuring of student choices. At the same time, clinical options became widely available, providing a practical adjunct to classroom theory. Graduate legal education was slow to develop as US, French and UK higher degrees were long seen as more prestigious, but by the turn of the twenty-first century high-quality graduate programmes existed at several Canadian law schools. Unlike the US, where higher degrees in law are not a route to academe, entering the Canadian professoriate has increasingly required a doctorate in law or another discipline.

The enlarged Canadian professoriate did not immediately lead to more valuable or original legal scholarship, much of it being conducted 'in' rather than 'on' law. A 1982 report on legal scholarship commissioned by the Social Sciences and Humanities Research Council of Canada reached disappointing conclusions about the quantity and quality of legal research conducted in law faculties, though its downplaying of the value of doctrinal scholarship was controversial. The report seems to have provoked some positive change as the variety, quality, and quantity of legal research now available in leading Canadian law journals and monograph form has increased markedly, as has the total funding secured from granting agencies, foundations, and other sources. After a slow start, it may be said that Canadian university legal education came of age in the 1970s and 1980s.

PHILIP GIRARD

References

Baker, G.B. (1983). 'Legal Education in Upper Canada: The Law Society as Educator, 1785–1889' in Flaherty, D.H. (ed), *Essays in the History of Canadian Law*, vol II, University of Toronto Press.

Bell, D.G. (1992). *Legal Education in New Brunswick: A History*, University of New Brunswick Faculty of Law.

Brierley, J.E.C. (1986–87). 'Quebec Legal Education Since 1945: Cultural Paradoxes and Traditional Ambiguities', *Dalhousie Law Journal*, 10, p. 5.

Girard, P. (2021). 'American Influences, Canadian Realities: How "American" is Canadian Legal Education?' in Bartie, S. and Sandomierski, D. (eds), *American Legal Education Abroad: Critical Histories*, NYU Press.

Girard, P. (2014). 'The Making of the Canadian Legal Profession: A Hybrid Heritage', *International Journal of the Legal Profession*, 21, p. 145.

Hobbins, A.H. (2008). '"A couple generations ahead of popular demand": The First National Law Programme at McGill University, 1918–1924', *Dalhousie Law Journal*, 31, p. 181.

Kyer, C.I. and Bickenbach, J.E. (1987). *The Fiercest Debate: Cecil A. Wright, the Benchers, and Legal Education in Ontario, 1923–1957*, The Osgoode Society.

Normand, S. (2005). *Le droit comme discipline universitaire: Une histoire de la Faculté de droit de l'Université Laval*, Presses de l'Université Laval.

Pue, W.W. (1995). *Law School: the story of legal education in British Columbia*, University of British Columbia Faculty of Law.

Pue, W.W. (2016). 'Common Law Legal Education in the Dominion of Canada's Moral Project' in Pue, W.W., *Lawyers' Empire: Legal Professions and Cultural Authority, 1780–1950*, UBC Press.

Vachon, A. (1962). *Histoire du notariat canadien, 1621–1960*, Presses de l'Université Laval.

15. Canada (regulation of legal education)

In Canada, the continuum of legal education comprises the following stages:

- Admission to law school
- Law school
- Bar admission courses and examinations
- Articling
- Call to the bar
- Professional development
- Retirement

Because of the mobility of lawyers between provinces and territories, provincial and territorial law societies created a national body to collaborate and coordinate national efforts around regulation: the Federation of Law Societies of Canada (Federation). As such, some parts of the continuum of legal education are regulated by provincial and territorial law societies and others are dealt with by the Federation.

Admission to law school and the accreditation of law schools in common law Canada (but not in Québec) are now regulated by the Federation, which applies the National Requirement to approve law school programmes. The National Requirement was adopted by the Federation in 2009 and the accreditation of law school programmes began in 2015. At the time, the Federation justified the regulation of law school programmes, which had largely been left alone by the regulators up until then, based on three main reasons. Before this initiative, there had been relatively little change in legal education (i.e. the number of law schools, the curriculum) since it had moved to universities, but the landscape was changing. The first reason given for regulating law school programmes was that there were proposals for new law schools for the first time in 25 years and 'recognition of their degrees as meeting the academic requirements for entry to bar admission programmes requires a more explicit statement of what is required' (FLSC [2009]). The second justification was the increasing number of internationally trained applicants for entry into bar admission programmes, along with new fairness legislation respecting access to regulated professions adopted by many provinces, which together required a standard for determining equivalency.

Finally, a national standard for law school programmes would enhance professional mobility between provinces and territories, which governments and law societies viewed as important.

The National Requirement lists some requirements as to length of programme, mode of delivery, learning resources, and the competencies required of law school graduates. The required competencies include mostly substantive knowledge competencies of the age-old law school first year curriculum (e.g. torts, contracts, property, criminal and Constitutional law) and some upper year courses (e.g. administrative law). It also includes skill competencies such as legal analysis, oral and written communication and legal research, as well as competencies related to ethics and professionalism. The National Requirement is in the process of being reviewed and will likely include new provisions regarding online and experiential learning, as well as competencies relating to Indigenous peoples and Indigenous legal orders.

The Federation accredits law schools using two possible models: the Programme Approval Model or the Individual Student Approval Model. As stated in its Conditions of Law School Approvals, Canadian law schools can choose either of these two models for accreditation purposes. If a law school chooses the Programme Approval Model, by definition every student granted a JD degree will have met the required competencies listed in the National Requirement. If a school chooses the Individual Student Approval Model, then the transcript of individual students must specify that the student has acquired the required competencies. Interestingly, all common law programmes, including those one-year common law programmes for students with a civil law degree, have opted for the Programme Approval Model.

The National Requirement also mandates that the admission requirements of law schools must include, at a minimum, successful completion of two years of post-secondary education at a recognised university or for Québec, recognised CEGEP. (A CEGEP is a Collège d'enseignement général et professionnel, which means general and professional teaching college). CEGEPS are post-secondary educational institutions that only exist in Québec. Any person in Québec wanting to go to university must first go through two years of CEGEP. This creates a difference in admission criteria between Québec civil and English common law programmes; one can attend law school in Québec having completed two years of CEGEP but no university.) Because of this requirement, the norm in common law programmes is that students enter law school having completed an undergraduate degree; law is considered a post-graduate degree similar to the United States. On the other hand, in Québec, the law degree is an undergraduate degree, more like in continental Europe. The National Requirement does not apply to civil law degrees in Québec law programmes.

National Committee on Accreditation

The Federation also regulates the educational requirements for those with foreign law degrees who want to enter a bar admission programme. Candidates with foreign law degrees must apply to the National Committee on Accreditation (NCA) for a certificate of equivalency and depending on the jurisdiction (and legal system) they are from and their work experience, the NCA will require them to complete their education or to write a certain number of examinations before they can be admitted to the next stage, a provincial bar admission programme.

Bar admission programmes, examinations and articling

Most provincial and territorial regulators require candidates to complete a bar admission programme and/or bar examinations before being called to the bar, as well as a period of apprenticeship which is called 'articling'. Because this stage of the legal education continuum is regulated by each provincial or territorial law societies and not the Federation, these two requirements vary in form and length. For example, in Ontario, candidates can choose from three different pathways to access the legal profession, but all pathways include both solicitor and barrister examinations. Some provinces require completion of an online bar admission course and a period of articling, but no examination, and some require all three. All jurisdictions require some form of experiential learning (articling, work placement or integrated curriculum) before one is called to the bar, which is different from most jurisdictions in the United States where writing bar examinations remains the only requirement for entry into the profession.

Continuing professional development

Provincial and territorial law societies also regulate the continuing professional development of lawyers. The requirement for continuing education is usually in the form of a required number of annual or bi-annual hours of professional development. Professional development can take many forms including taking courses, teaching courses, study groups and in some cases, mentoring. Some provinces have requirements mandating a certain number of hours in given areas such as ethics and professional responsibility, practice management, and more recently, equity, diversity and inclusion, and Reconciliation. (In Canada, the Truth and Reconciliation Commission issued its Final Report in 2015, which included 94 Calls to Action to 'redress the legacy of residential schools and advance the process of Canadian reconciliation'. Calls to Action #27 and #28 called upon the Federation and law schools in Canada to educate students and lawyers about residential schools, the United Nations Declaration on the Rights of Indigenous Peoples, Treaties and Aboriginal rights, Indigenous law, and to create cultural competency training.)

The province of Alberta is a notable exception to this method of regulating the continued competence of lawyers. Instead of reporting the number of hours, it requires lawyers to submit a Continuing Professional Development plan and to connect this plan to the provincial lawyer competency profile. This way of regulating continuing education emphasises self-assessment, reflective practice and lifelong learning and has the potential to radically change the way lawyers view continuing professional development.

ANNIE ROCHETTE

References

Federation of Law Societies of Canada (FLSC), Task Force on the Canadian Common Law Degree Final Report 2009, available at https://flsc-s3-storage-pub.s3.ca-central-1.amazonaws.com/Apprtaskforcereportoct2009.pdf?

_rt=MXwxfHRhc2sgZm9yY2UgY29tbW9u
IGxhd3wxNzAxNDU2ODU4&_rt_nonce=
9b5efa099d.

Federation of Law Societies of Canada (FLSC),
Common Law Degree Implementation Committee
Final Report 2011, available at https://flsc-s3
-storage-pub.s3.ca-central-1.amazonaws.com/AP
PROVALCommitteeFinalReport2011.pdf.

Federation of Law Societies of Canada (FLSC),
National Requirement 2018, available at https://
flsc-s3-storage-pub.s3.ca-central-1.amazonaws
.com/National-Requirement-Jan-2018-FIN.pdf.

Federation of Law Societies of Canada (FLSC),
Conditions of Law School Approvals, available at https://flsc-s3-storage-pub.s3.ca-central
-1.amazonaws.com/Conditions%20of%20Law
%20School%20Approvals.pdf.

Federation of Law Societies of Canada (FLSC),
Discussion Paper on the National Requirement
Review, June 26, 2023, available at https://
flsc.ca/wp-content/uploads/2023/06/NRRC
-Discussion-Paper-V3.pdf?_rt=MnwxfG
5hdGlvbmFsIHJlcXVpcmVtZW50IHJl
dmlld3wxNzAxNDYxNjY3&_rt_nonce=
e35a62ea3c.

Law Society of Alberta, Continuing Professional
Development, available at https://www.lawsociety
.ab.ca/lawyers-and-students/continuing-professional
-development/.

Truth and Reconciliation Commission of Canada:
Calls to Action, 2015, available at https://
ehprnh2mwo3.exactdn.com/wp-content/
uploads/2021/01/Calls_to_Action_English2
.pdf.

16. Children, schools and legal education

Introduction

The lives of all children are directly impacted by domestic laws in their nation states, and by the implementation (or lack of implementation) of international treaties. Yet the idea of 'legal education for children' remains a novel concept. Some obligations exist regarding states' responsibilities to educate children about their rights under domestic law and international treaties, but the extent to which these obligations are met varies. Pockets of activity exist nationally and internationally, but these are neither coherent nor coordinated.

In this entry we take an international perspective but focus on the United Kingdom as a discrete example. First of all, we consider states' obligations to deliver human rights education to children under international treaties, and how far these obligations are being met by the state. We then consider more discrete obligations arising under domestic law. We conclude by providing examples of work being done by non-governmental organisations (NGOs) to promote children's legal education.

States' obligations

The state's responsibility to educate children (and all people) about human rights was set out in the Universal Declaration of Human Rights 1948. Since then, a field of practice and scholarship known as 'Human Rights Education' (HRE) has developed internationally (Bajaj [2017]). Practices have varied widely (Council of Europe [2022]), but the same broad principles have been followed. These principles were reaffirmed more recently (United Nations [2011]), and are now defined as encompassing:

- education *about* human rights, which includes providing knowledge and understanding of human rights norms and principles, the values that underpin them and the mechanisms for their protection;
- education *through* human rights, which includes learning and teaching in a way that respects the rights of both educators and learners;
- education *for* human rights, which includes empowering persons to enjoy and exercise their rights and to respect and uphold the rights of others.

Education *for* human rights is also referred to as 'transformative' HRE in the literature (Bajaj et al. [2016]). Scholars working in this field have argued that for HRE to be truly transformative for children, knowledge of domestic law and legal processes is essential (Lundy and Martínez Sainz [2018], Watkins [2022]).

A significant further obligation for states to educate children about their human rights is set out in Article 42 of the United Nations Convention on the Rights of the Child (UNCRC). This convention has been described as 'the most complete statement of children's rights ever produced' (United Nations Children's Fund [2023]), and since its adoption by the United Nations General Assembly in 1989, it has been ratified by every UN member state, except the United States of America.

Article 42 requires all ratifying states 'to make the principles and provisions of the Convention widely known, by appropriate and active means, to adults and children alike.' The extent to which this, and other obligations are being met by states is monitored by the Committee on the Rights of the Child (CRC). In a recent report, this committee noted 'with concern' the relatively low level of knowledge about the UNCRC in the UK, and its recommendations include adopting a national strategy to raise public awareness concerning the UNCRC and including the teaching of children's rights within the national curriculum (CRC [2023] at 14, and at 47(i)). As highlighted by this recommendation, the teaching of children's rights is not a mandatory part of the national curriculum in the UK.

With regard to what *is* included in the curriculum around legal and rights education, the picture is complicated because schooling and education policy for the UK has been a devolved responsibility since 1999, and so approaches to curriculum vary across England, Northern Ireland, Scotland and Wales (Sibieta and Jerrim [2021]). For the sake of space, and in light of the authors' areas of expertise, we focus on England in the next section.

The situation in England

In England, there is currently no effective legal obligation for all schools to teach children about the law (Olatokun [2022]). However, there are two areas of practice which are relevant: (1) schools' responsibilities to teach fundamental British values, and (2) citizenship education in the school curriculum. We discuss these in turn.

Under section 78 of the Education Act 2002 (EA 2002), schools are required to provide a 'balanced and broadly based curriculum' which 'promotes the spiritual, moral, cultural, mental and physical development of pupils at the school and of society' (SMSC). Section 157(1)(b) EA 2002 provides that the relevant minister may use their powers to set standards for other schools, i.e. independent schools, in relation to SMSC. In 2014, DfE issued guidance which required SMSC to specifically include the promotion of the 'Fundamental British Values' which are described as democracy, the rule of law, individual liberty, and mutual respect and tolerance for those of different and no faiths (DfE [2014]).

It has been noted that the requirements for teaching fundamental British values focus on individual conformity to the law, and there is no requirement for children to be encouraged to consider how they might act collectively to influence change (Olatokun [2022]). For example, Regulation 5b of The Education (Independent School Standards) (England) Regulations 2010 states that SMSC requirements are met where independent schools 'enable pupils to distinguish right from wrong and to respect the law.'

Citizenship Education is a subject through which school-age children are taught about their legal rights as citizens in England. As the national public authority responsible for setting the curriculum, the DfE has devised programmes of study that set out the content to be taught according to children's age and key stage of education. The programme of study for younger children (key stages 1 and 2) in primary schools is non-compulsory (DfE [2015]). By contrast, the programmes of study (DfE [2013]) for those aged 11–14 years (Key Stage 3) and 15–16 years (Key Stage 4) are compulsory (at least in principle, as we explain further below).

At Key Stage 3, students are taught 'the precious liberties enjoyed by the citizens of the United Kingdom; the nature of rules and laws and the justice system; including the role of the police and the operation of courts and tribunals' (DfE [2013] at 2). The programmes of study also dictate that students should be taught about 'the roles played by public institutions and voluntary groups in society' (DfE [2013] at 2).

The programmes of study for Key Stage 4 require that students are taught 'key elements of the constitution of the United Kingdom, including the power of government, the role of citizens and Parliament in holding those in power to account, and the different roles of the executive, legislature and judiciary and a free press' (DfE [2013] at 2) as well as 'human rights and international law' (DfE [2013] at 2–3).

At first sight, our description of these programmes of study might be seen to contradict the earlier statement that in England, there is currently no legal obligation for schools to teach children about the law. Indeed, Citizenship education became a compulsory part of the national curriculum for key stages 3 and 4 in 2002. However, a few years later, under the Academies Act 2010, schools maintained by their local authority were permitted to become independent academies. Crucially, the large number of schools which have chosen to change to academy status are no longer obliged to follow the national curriculum (Roberts [2021]); meaning that Citizenship has become a non-compulsory subject in many settings. Because of this and other factors, it has been recognised that the implementation of the Citizenship curriculum has seriously limited its effectiveness (House of Lords Select Committee on Citizenship and Civic Engagement [2018], House of Lords Liaison Committee [2022]).

Work being done by non-governmental organisations

Organisations such as the United Nations Children's Fund (UNICEF) and Amnesty International are working internationally to promote children's understanding of their rights under international treaties. UNICEF provides resources and opportunities for schools (of various types and stages) to become accredited as Rights Respecting Schools, in categories of Bronze (rights committed), Silver (rights aware) and Gold (rights respecting), based on their commitment to embedding the principles of the UNCRC into the school's ethos and practices (UNICEF [2023]). Amnesty International provides resources to schools to assist them in becoming Human Rights Friendly Schools (Amnesty International [2023]). In the UK, civil society organisations such as the established citizenship education charity Young Citizens provide resources to schools to support Citizenship education both within and outside of the school curriculum. One of the key annual campaigns of that organisation and others is the 'big legal lesson' (Young Citizens [2023]), a call for teachers and lawyers to provide lessons on legal rights to children throughout England. Internationally, groups of university law students are involved in delivering legal education to children in schools, as part of a practice known as 'Street Law', which was founded in 1972 at Georgetown University in Washington DC (Street Law [2023]). This work overlaps to some extent with work being undertaken in the field of Public Legal Education (see entries on Public Legal Education (Prisons) and Public Legal Education (Community)

DAWN WATKINS AND ABIODUN MICHAEL OLATOKUN

References

Amnesty International, Human Rights Friendly Schools, available at https://www.amnesty.org/en/human-rights-education/human-rights-friendly-schools/.

Bajaj, M., Cislaghi, B. and Mackie, G. (2016). *Advancing Transformative human rights education. Appendix D to the Report of the Global Citizenship Commission*, Open Book.

Bajaj, M. (ed.) *Human Rights Education: Theory, Research, Praxis*, University of Pennsylvania Press.

Council of Europe, Introducing Human Rights Education, available at https://www.coe.int/en/web/compass/introducing-human-rights-education.

Department for Education, Promoting fundamental British values as part of SMSC in schools
Departmental advice for maintained schools (DFE-00679-2014).

Department for Education, Citizenship Programmes of Study for key stages 1 and 2 (DFE-00057-2015).

Department for Education, National curriculum in England: citizenship programmes of study for key stages 3 and 4 (DFE-00190-2013).

House of Lords Ad Hoc Select Committee on Citizenship and Civic Engagement, Report of Session 2017–2019, 'The Ties That Bind: Citizenship and Civic Engagement in the 21st Century', HL Paper 118 [2018].

House of Lords Liaison Committee, 5th Report of Session 2021–2022, 'The Ties that Bind: Citizenship and Civic Engagement in the 21st Century: Follow-up report', HL Paper 179' [2022].

Lundy, L. and Martínez Sainz, G. (2018). 'The role of law and legal knowledge for a transformative human rights education: addressing violations of children's rights in formal education', *Human Rights Education Review*, 1(2), p. 4.

Olatokun, A. (2022). 'The Journey To Legal Capability: Challenges for Public Law from Public Legal Education', *International Journal of Public Legal Education*, 6(1), p. 28.

Roberts, N. (2021). The school curriculum in England, House of Commons Briefing Paper (Number 06798, 26 March).

Sibieta, L. and Jerrim, J. (2021). *A Comparison of School Institutions and Policies across the UK*, Nuffield Foundation.

Street Law. (2023). What we do, available at https://streetlaw.org/who-we-are/about/.

UNICEF. (2023). The Rights Respecting Schools Award, available at https://www.unicef.org.uk/rights-respecting-schools/about-us-new.

United Nations Committee on the Rights of the Child, 'Concluding observations on the combined sixth and seventh periodic reports of the United Kingdom of Great Britain and Northern Ireland' (22 June 2023) CRC/C/GBR/CO/6–7.

United Nations Declaration on Human Rights Education and Training (Adopted by the General Assembly, Resolution 66/137, A/RES/66/137, 19 December 2011).

Universal Declaration of Human Rights 1948.

Watkins, D. (2022). 'Exploring the role of domestic law in human rights education', *Human Rights Education Review*, 5(2), p. 98.

Young Citizens. (2023). The Big Legal Lesson, available at https://www.youngcitizens.org/programmes/the-big-legal-lesson/.

17. China (contemporary legal education)

Introduction: context

Since the late 1970s, the People's Republic of China ('PRC'; 'China') has seen a re-emergence of the legal professions, the growth of legal education, and efforts to enhance legal consciousness across society. Although closely intertwined with the country's legal and economic reforms, mainstream legal education lacks a clear connection with the administration of justice and professional legal practice. It emphasises academic over practical law – the former is seen as being focused on *faxue* (法学) or 'academic law', and the latter on *falü* (法律) or 'positive law', and also reflects a broader 'political-legal' (政法: *zhengfa*) culture dominated by the Chinese Communist Party (CCP). Despite reforms, the CCP maintains strong control over the legal system and legal education, influencing law and justice administration through a political and administrative lens. The 1982 Constitution, and especially its 2018 revisions has been shaped by CCP values, reinforcing the Party's control of legal institutions.

Historically, imperial China's education system was designed to produce graduates for administrative roles, reinforcing an administrative approach to law that persists today. This focus is reinforced today by judicial and prosecutorial training programmes and encourages something of an 'administrative ethos' in legal education.

Over the past decade, China's emphasis on social stability has often overshadowed legal development, with measures like the 2018 constitutional amendments strengthening CCP leadership, raising concerns over 'delegalisation'. Despite pressures for legal freedoms, civil society expansion, and reduced party-state power from social and civic sectors, political policies continue to restrict legal education reforms. The legacy of the 1950s, when lawyers were stigmatised for their role as defence attorneys, persists, affecting legal practice by prioritising commercial matters. The shift to a socialist market economy in the 1990s further entrenched the perception of lawyers as facilitators of economic transactions rather than defenders of rights.

Overview of legal education

In the PRC, there is a notable lack of professional legal education, with a belief that skills are best learned through practice. Despite this, advanced law degrees such as International Economic Law are available, providing specialist knowledge useful in legal practice. Lawyers, judges, procurators, and notaries in the PRC all take the same national judicial examination, which faces significant criticism. Tuition fees for law degrees are lower than in many countries, and competition for university law school entry is becoming less intense. There are no nationwide evaluations of faculty performance, though internal appraisals exist. Legal ethics are underemphasised in undergraduate law degrees, while political education is heavily stressed, including courses on CCP policies and the importance of social service. The former Institutes of Politics and Law, especially important in the early years of the post-Mao reforms have been transformed into universities, and today, for example, the Chinese University of Politics and Law (Zhongguo Zhengfa Daxue: 中国政法大学), with 16,000 students and 1,000 law teachers, plays a key role in training legal administrators and professionals. Since the 1950s, it has educated over 100,000 students, preparing them for roles in the '*zhengfa*' system. It was the largest of the six political-legal institutes overseen by the Ministry of Justice crucial in reviving legal education after China decided to adopt policies of socialist-legality in the late 1970s. Biddulph ([2010]) provides an insightful account of the development of legal education in another such body: the East China University of Politics and Law.

In 2000, the leadership of China's political-legal colleges and over 600 law schools transitioned to the Ministry of Education, impacting the education of more than 300,000 law students. This shift led to the separation and later reintegration of law and public administration programmes. More specifically, there are three year 'academic' LLM degrees (*faxue shuoshi*: 法学硕士) or two or three year 'professional' JM degrees (*falü zhuanye shuoshi*: 法律专业硕士) (mainly for non-law graduates, similar to the 'JD' in the US). Those who take the academic LLM will perhaps attempt a PhD programme lasting three years or more, perhaps even to be followed by a post-doctoral scheme. As a result, many teachers in law schools are in their early 30s before they get their first teaching appointment.

University law schools continue to concentrate on academic legal studies, equipping students for careers in teaching and research but also for roles in government and the business sector. The former political-legal institutes, thanks to their traditionally stronger linkage with legal practice and the policy of economic reform and 'opening up' to the global economy, have managed to 'internationalise' more effectively. This is evident in initiatives like establishing joint programmes with international partners, despite their close ties to the PRC's 'political-legal' system.

In many law schools across the PRC, reform in the style of teaching is progressing slowly. The traditional view of teachers as all-knowing leaders persists, with insufficient emphasis on learning outcomes or student feedback. This culture extends into the professional network, where personal connections and being a student of a notable 'PhD' supervisor are highly valued. This network also benefits those in the justice administration, who pursue doctorates to advance their careers. Senior teachers often emphasise government recognition as 'PhD supervisors', elevating their status as leaders, and sometimes seek further appointment by the provincial government rather than their university, harking back to the traditional training of officials as 'scholar officials'.

Undergraduate law programmes offer both mandatory and optional subjects, the latter often shaped into 'subject groupings' or 'directions' (*fangxiang*: 方向) but carrying fewer credits and leading to a more superficial learning approach. To graduate in four years, students typically take eight or more courses per semester, particularly in their second and third years, due to a packed curriculum aimed at leaving the final year open for internships and job hunting. Despite the fact that the 1982 Constitution itself is not justiciable in Chinese courts, the importance of constitutional law as a first-year subject is stressed. The focus is more on legal theory and academic law than practical law, and only in recent years have some schools started to prepare students for the national Judicial Examination required for legal practice in China. During the final year of undergraduate law studies, students engage in professional placements or internships at law firms, courts, or arbitration commissions. This period serves as 'on-the-job' training, but is not closely monitored by the law school. The quality of these placements varies, with some providing valuable learning experiences, while others are less beneficial.

Legal clinics, often supported by foreign legal assistance, are linked to law schools, offering free legal help (Zheng Zhen [2002]; Baskir, Ma and Li [2015]). Students are encouraged to join the CCP to improve job prospects and satisfy parental expectations. Law schools gauge success by their graduates' employment rates and take measures to assist graduates in finding jobs post-graduation. Within the law school, the Party Secretary (*shuji*: 书记) bears a heavy responsibility for helping law graduates with the initial stages of their career. However, due to downsizing in the legal sector, law graduates face employment challenges, prompting them to broaden their academic profiles and improve employability.

The legal education system in China, overseen by the Ministry of Education in Beijing, is characterised by the dominance of northern law schools and a top-down approach in school assessment and funding. This system enforces strict success indicators and often yields research that lacks depth due to outdated research standards and simplistic measures of research output. Publications frequently require financial contributions, and the government controls university faculty salaries while providing research funding, encouraging political orthodoxy.

Popular and professional legal education

The Popular Legal Education (普法: *pufa*) or legal literacy campaign in China has been a key component of its legal education system, aiming to enhance legal awareness in a society historically ambivalent towards law. Launched in 1985, this national movement has focused on spreading knowledge about significant laws and new legislation through media like newspapers and TV, often using engaging examples to illustrate the importance of lawful conduct. In recent years a policy has been pursued of 'whoever enforces the law, teaches the law', imposing on many public organs a responsibility for popular legal education. This approach has not only broadened the public's understanding of law but also fostered the emergence of 'netizens' who use the internet to highlight and address injustices, reinforcing the message that laws must be obeyed, especially by officials.

Furthermore, in the early years of reform, many judges and prosecutors within the PRC were without the necessary legal qualifications, having been selected for legal work (法律工作: *falü gongzuo*) primarily because their military backgrounds meant they were accustomed to issuing and following orders. As a result, systems for education and on-the-job training through professional colleges affiliated with key legal institutions were established. For example , the National Judges College (国家法官学院: Guojia Faguan Xueyuan) and the '*zhengfa*' or 'Politics and Law' institutes have offered a variety of part-time and distance learning courses designed for individuals aspiring to pursue careers in the legal domain.

In 2012, China introduced a unified Judicial Examination (司法考试: *sifa kaoshi*) and made it a requirement for law students seeking to become lawyers, but mainly testing memorisation of law. This approach, mirroring reforms in other East Asian legal systems, produced a low pass rate of 15–20 per cent annually. While some argue that the exam effectively assesses legal potential, critics point out its failure to evaluate real-world legal analysis and application, highlighting the need for educational reform to better prepare students for legal practice (Guo Xiang [2010]). Subsequent reforms to the Examination have not resolved this problem. The reform of China's Judicial Examination did, however, spark a debate on the goals of legal education, questioning whether it should focus on nurturing well-rounded legal talent through academic law or preparing students to pass the Judicial Examination with a focus on positive law. There is also a view favouring a broad educational approach for all-around development in legal studies. Also, until recently international collaboration has been growing, with foreign law schools entering China and offering programmes aiming to produce multilingual, international legal practitioners to meet the demand for cross-border legal expertise.

The Ministry of Justice in China oversees the National Judicial Examination, controlling access to the legal professions and dominating the legal practice landscape, including the All-China Lawyers' Association. Law schools have adapted by offering preparatory programmes for students aiming to pass this examination, significantly increasing pass rates. Some schools suspend regular classes for exam preparation, while others view the exam as a student's private responsibility.

The Judicial Examination evolved from the 'Test for Lawyers' initiated in 1986, primarily aimed at qualifying lawyers. Later, the selection of judges and prosecutors followed separate criteria under the Judges Law and Procurators Law of 1995, leading to criticism for their leniency and informal nature (Xue and Luo [2017]). Throughout the 1980s and 1990s, many judges and prosecutors were appointed without legal examinations, often from retired military or administrative backgrounds, lacking legal education. This resulted in a disparity in professional quality between lawyers, and judges and prosecutors.

In 2001, China's Supreme People's Court, Supreme People's Procuratorate, and Ministry of Justice initiated the National Judicial Examination, consolidating examinations for judges, prosecutors, notaries, and lawyers into one unified test. This move, aimed at standardising qualifications for legal practitioners, saw its first examination in 2002 with 360,000 candidates, of whom 24,000 passed. This reform was preceded by amendments to the Judges' and Prosecutors' Laws, requiring these professionals to pass the national exam. The unified Judicial Examination has since been a crucial qualification for entering the legal professions in China.

After 2008, undergraduate law students were allowed to sit for the National Judicial Examination, leading to concerns from some scholars. They argued this shift caused students to focus more on exam preparation than on broader academic pursuits within law, such as jurisprudence and international law, potentially narrowing their education (Wang [2014]). In 2015, China introduced influential reforms, proposing a 'National Unified Legal Profession Qualification Examination' to replace the old National Judicial Examination. This initiative, detailed further in April 2018, expanded the selection criteria for legal practitioners to include a wider range of legal service providers beyond lawyers, judges, and notaries. However, it also tightened eligibility for examinees, now requiring a law degree (bachelors or masters) or three years of legal work experience.

The reform of 2018 de-emphasises multiple choice questions in favour of essay questions that encourage ideologically aligned answers. Previously, essay questions were a smaller portion of the exam, but now, candidates must pass an initial test of 'objective' questions before tackling the more 'subjective' essay questions – the 'subjective' exam is held on a separate date, and each candidate can attempt twice to pass. Since 2021, the subjective essay questions have been revised to emphasise socialist legal values and Xi Jinping's legal philosophy – the most important outcome of the Central Conference on Comprehensively Governing the Country by Law in November 2020.

There remains a significant gap between university legal education and practical legal training, despite many law students aiming for a career in law. Discussions on introducing specialised professional training programmes have been unsuccessful, leading to a lack of effective integration between academic and professional legal education.

International collaboration

Since the early 1980s, inspired by Deng Xiaoping, China has emphasised the importance of legal education abroad, unlike the former Soviet Union. This approach values the experience gained from living and working in legal communities outside mainland China, particularly through programmes in the UK and the US, such as the Lord Chancellor's Training Schemes and the EU-China Legal and Judicial Training Programme. These experiences are seen as crucial for Chinese legal professionals, offering a 'trans-systemic legal education' (Glenn [2005]) that enhances their prospects within China's major law firms.

Conclusions

In the PRC, efforts at legal reform face challenges due to the gap between academic and positive law, and the 'political-legal' nature of the legal system. Despite some progress towards reform, there remains a lack of development in professional legal education with a focus on skills, alongside difficulties in achieving legal profession autonomy. Globalisation is influencing legal education towards a more international approach but faces resistance due to generational divides and adherence to traditional political values. There is a pressing need for legal education in China to meet international standards, adopt practical teaching methods, and integrate academic and professional training while overcoming resistance to teaching foreign law. Drawing from reforms in East Asia could provide a model for improving China's legal education system.

LING ZHOU

References

Biddulph, S. (2010). 'Legal Education in the People's Republic of China', in Steele, S. and Taylor, K. (eds), *Legal Education in Asia: Globalization, Change and Contexts*, Routledge Law in Asia.

Baskir, C.E., Liqun, M. and Ao, L. (2015). 'Chinese Clinical Legal Education: Globalizing and Localizing', in Prosun Sarker, S. (ed), *Clinical Legal Education in Asia: Accessing Justice for the Underprivileged*, Palgrave Macmillan.

Glenn, P. (2005). 'Doin' the Transsystemic: Legal Systems and Legal Traditions', *McGill Law Journal*, 50, pp. 863–898.

Guo, X. (2010). 'Lun Sifa Kaoshi yu Faxue Jiaoyu de Guanxi – Jian yu Zhou Xiang, Qi Wenyuan Liangwei Xiansheng Shangque' [On the Relationship between the Judicial Examination and Legal Education: Discussion with Zhou Xiang and Qi Wenyuan], *Faxue* [*Law Science*], 2, pp. 62–68, 62–63.

Wang, A. (2014). 'Cong Riben Fake Daxue Yuan kan Woguo Sifa Kaoshi yu Faxue Jiaoyu zhi Guanxi,' [Interpreting the Relation between China's Judicial Exam and Legal Education from the Perspective of Japan Law School], *Dalian Daxue Xuebao* [Journal of Dalian University], 35(1), p. 119.

Xue, Z. and LUO, G. (2017). 'Falü Zhiye Zige Kaoshi Zhidu Bianqian yu Faxue Benke Jiaoyu Zhuanxing Tiaozheng' [Changes in the Legal Qualification Examination System and the Adjustment of Transformation of Undergraduate Education in Law], *Journal of Tianjin Academy of Educational Science*, 4, p. 23.

Zheng, H.R. (1988). 'The Evolving Role of Lawyers and Legal Practice in China', *The American Journal of Comparative Law*, 36(3), p. 473.

Zheng, Z. (2002). *Zhengsuo Falü Jiaoyu zai Zhongguo* (1988) [Clinical Legal Education in China]. Law Press China.

18. China (history of legal education)

Introduction

This entry considers the historical development of legal education in China, examining the system that prevailed during the Qing dynasty (1644–1911), then the reforms of the Republican era (1912–1949), and finally changes post-Liberation (1949 to present).

Late Imperial China

The dominant ideology and official belief system as defined by the state during the Qing dynasty (1644–1911) and earlier, was Confucianism. Confucianism emphasises education through virtue (礼：*li*) to create an ideal social order based on morality (德：*de*), contrasting with Legalists' focus on positive law (法：*fa*). Confucianists believe in governing with virtue, and this exemplary conduct encourages people to conduct themselves with goodness, and avoid disputes by compromise, that is by 'yielding' (让：*rang*). The ruler's exemplary conduct is pivotal for good governance and social stability. This 'harmony ideology' discouraged litigation in favour of mediation and honoured those skilled in mediation rather than those learned in law and legal practice. The Confucian view was that encouraging virtuous conduct was the preferred way for maintaining social order. Late imperial China did not have a private legal profession – those who performed such functions unofficially were looked down upon (Fuma [2007]), nor a structured training system for legal experts. Instead, it believed that teaching Confucian values through family and lineage education, and use of didactic mediation by third parties grounded in Confucian values, was the most effective way to instil these virtues, enforced by the penal codes.

Critically important institutions for the provision of Confucian education were called 'Academies' (书院: *shuyuan*). Initially rooted in rural areas with a focus on antiurban philosophy, as time progressed, these academies became more urban in place and outlook (Grimm [1977]). By studying classical texts such as the *Lunyu* (论语) or *Analects*, the Confucian educational ethos was to create within students the superior person or "Junzi"

(君子) virtues of benevolence (仁: *ren*), righteousness (义: yi), propriety (礼: *li*), wisdom (智: *zhi*), and integrity (信: *xin*).

Literacy was crucial for social mobility in traditional China, focusing on Confucian classics. Education centred on imperial exams for bureaucratic roles. The philosophy of Legalism influenced the legal system but transitioned to emphasise Confucian principles. Officials were appointed through success in the imperial exams, without any legal training. Formal legal education was not a common practice in imperial China. Nevertheless, various figures in the late imperial Chinese legal system played important roles in handling legal matters, including officials from the Board of Punishments, provincial judicial commissioners, and *yamen* (衙门) or magistrates' clerks (Li [2012]). Training was mainly conducted in-house, supplemented by self-study of legal texts and memoirs (Huang [1984]). The legal secretary to the local magistrate was crucial, providing essential legal support gained through apprenticeship. This secretary, known as the 'friend behind the curtain' (幕友: *muyou*) offered advice to the magistrate and specialised in legal knowledge, giving his legal advice from a discrete position in the courtroom. Many such legal secretaries came from Shaoxing, a wealthy area in central eastern China, and which developed a reputation for producing such legal experts.

Collapse of the Qing dynasty and developments in the Republican period (1911–1949)

Clashes between the Qing dynasty and Western powers in the eighteenth and nineteenth centuries resulted in the Opium Wars and unequal treaties. The Qing dynasty, under Western influence, enacted legal reforms before its collapse in 1911. Reformers sought to implement changes in laws and institutions inspired by emerging transplanted concepts of the rule of law, judicial independence, and due process. These reforms, carried through the Republican era (1912–1949), prompted the establishment of a formal legal education system, beginning with the founding of Peking University Law School in 1904. The Law Department's four-year curriculum encompassed law-specific and interdisciplinary courses. Topics including

Science of Jurisprudence, Chinese Criminal Law History, and Comparative Studies of Commercial Laws were taught, in addition to European law modules. Despite a tumultuous history during much of the twentieth century, the school stands today as the most esteemed law institution in mainland China.

Schools in China offering law courses after the 1905 abolition of the imperial examination system saw substantial expansion, especially after the 1910 Introduction of the Law on Organizing Courts lawyers in Chinese courts, and the introduction in 1912 by the Ministry of Justice of the first regulations on private lawyers, covering qualifications, ethics, supervision, and more. The Soochow Law School in Shanghai, sponsored by US missionaries, stood out for teaching foreign law using the case method. Graduates excelled in Shanghai's legal sphere with a focus on ethics. Despite interruptions by the Japanese Occupation and the Communist Party civil war against the Nationalist government, 1949, the school prioritised ethics and professional skills, preparing lawyers for political and commercial engagement. Furthermore, the institution underscored the significance of social accountability and public duty among its alumni. It acknowledged that a lawyer's role transcends mere legal advocacy, emphasising their obligation to utilise their expertise and abilities for societal development (Conner [1983]). Many other law schools adopted less innovative teaching methods.

The People's Republic of China

In 1949, the Communist Party took power in China, leading to the establishment of a one-Party led political system. Efforts to develop higher education were part of state initiatives, resulting in a top-down system under Party control. Legal education was reintroduced in the early 1950s, following a Soviet model, with a focus on training cadres for use by the state. Despite legal studies being influenced by Soviet and Chinese laws (some of which had been developed in the areas of China conquered by the Party prior to 1949), educational policy prioritised engineering and science over law due to the emphasis on heavy industry in the centrally planned economy.

Legal education in China faced challenges during the political turmoil that lasted from the late 1950s to mid-1970s. Leftist campaigns disrupted major legal institutions and halted university law programs during the Cultural Revolution. In the late 1970s, after Mao's death, leaders focused on stability and economic growth. Reforms brought new laws, leading to a revival of legal education through reopening law schools and foreign partnerships. This included reviving previously closed law programs and institutions.

Significant transformations in legal education have unfolded in China in recent years. The pace at which this rebuilding of legal education took place was remarkably swift. As China moved away from the Cultural Revolution, it introduced in 1976, a comprehensive legal development strategy. This initiative led to extensive codification of law, an increase in the number of courts, an expanded legal profession, and the reform and expansion of legal education. There are now more than 300,000 law students and 600 law schools in higher education. The growth of law schools in China, driven by increasing demand for legal professionals, has evolved alongside educational reforms. Initially overseen by the Ministry of Justice, legal education responsibilities shifted to the Ministry of Education and provincial governments in 1999. This transition led to the establishment of specialised law universities offering various degree programs. The focus has to some extent shifted towards practical training, bridging the gap between academic and practitioner-oriented approaches. Additionally, professional training centres within the public security system, courts, and procuratorates have emerged to meet the need for legal education among those with responsibility for the administration of justice.

Traditional teaching methods in Chinese law education persist despite some reforms. Lectures focus on formal law with limited student engagement. Graduates often seek non-legal jobs, and aspiring lawyers prioritise Bar Exam preparation. The system favours memorisation over practical legal skills. Some specific developments aim to bring change. One such advance has been the introduction of a specialised postgraduate law degree for non-law graduates, allowing them to earn a law degree in two to three years. This programme includes courses like Public International Law, International Economic Law, and Private International Law. Law schools compete to offer these prestigious LLM (or JM) degrees, for which a law school may receive more funding than undergraduate programmes. In China today, however, legal education mainly focuses on undergraduate LLB degrees, with about two-thirds of law students pursuing this path.

Clinical Legal Education (CLE) has grown significantly in China since 2000. This development, originating from voluntary legal aid associations, aims to provide practical legal experience to students while assisting underprivileged individuals. Although CLE has progressed considerably in the PRC, it continues to encounter obstacles such as the need for institutional backing, the advancement of a stronger public interest law sector, and the continuing disagreement between traditional and innovative legal education methods. Nevertheless, CLE plays a useful role in legal education in China, and is supported by the legal academics, judges and others involved in the administration of justice.

Thirdly, the Bar exam requirements in China have been expanded to cover various legal professions. The exam, known as the National Unified Legal Professional Qualification Examination, includes both objective and subjective tests on legal subjects. It is overseen by the Ministry of Justice and emphasises socialist legal theory. The exam has a political aspect with a focus on demonstrating loyalty to the ruling party. Since 2018, the pass rate has typically ranged between 10 per cent to 15 per cent.

Fourthly, PRC legal education has become more internationalised, with Chinese law students encouraged to study abroad (unlike law students in other socialist jurisdictions) since the early 1980s. This exposure to foreign and international law helps them bring new perspectives to legal education in China. Foreign legal scholars also contribute to Chinese academic institutions, despite facing political constraints on their teaching content.

However, the rise of China's global power is diversifying international engagement by Chinese law schools, transitioning legal education from one-way borrowing to multidirectional exchanges. BRICS nations offer insights for comparative legal training and potential innovations in investment practices through academic cooperation. The Belt and Road Initiative (BRI), led by the PRC, involves global agreements, investments, and infrastructure development. It is shaping new legal frameworks and processes for BRI disputes arising in courts and arbitration bodies and legal preparations for managing disputes. Research on the BRI, which is badly needed, may well come to inform international economic and transnational commercial law studies – issues in investment, trade, labour, intellectual property, environmental protection, as well as the settlement of disputes will need to be studied, especially as part of postgraduate legal education.

Over the past decade, China has shifted politically towards conservatism under President Xi Jinping's leadership. Efforts include discouraging Western governance concepts in education – some government directives have urged PRC students to report on professors promoting Western ideals of good governance, while other directives have emphasised adherence to the party's stance, rejecting Western notions like constitutional government and judicial independence crackdowns on human rights lawyers, and asserting control over foreign relations. These actions align with challenging the American-led global order but may impede legal education reform in China.

Conclusion

In China today, there are now many law schools, and an emphasis on legal rules – as opposed to the political mobilisation movements of the Maoist era. In addition, CLE, encouragement of overseas legal education, greater attention to foreign and international law, are important features of the current scene, but significant issues persist. Despite many years of reform, various challenges continue to face Chinese legal education, such as overexpansion leading to unemployment, degree devaluation, inadequate practical skills training and politicisation and institutional distortions. The historical transformation of Chinese legal education started in the late nineteenth century largely as a result of western impact and continues with global influences. As a result, there is always some ambivalence towards reforms that originate outside of China, even as the PRC continues to draw on foreign models for inspiration in its educational reform.

MICHAEL PALMER

References

Conner, A. (1993). 'Soochow Law School and the Shanghai Bar', *Hong Kong Law Journal*, 23(3), p. 395.

Fuma, S. (2007). 'Litigation Masters and the Litigation System of Ming and Qing China', *International Journal of Asian Studies*, 4(1), p. 79.

Grimm, T. (1977). 'Academies and Urban Systems in Kwangtung', in William Skinner, G. (ed), *The City in Late Imperial China*, Stanford University Press.

Huang L.-H. (1984). *A Complete Book Concerning Happiness and Benevolence: A Manual for Local Magistrates in Seventeenth-Century China*. Edited and translated by Djang Chu, University of Arizona Press.

Li C. (2012). 'Legal Specialists and Judicial Administration in Late Imperial China, 1651–1911', *Late Imperial China*, 33(1), p. 1.

MICHAEL PALMER

19. China (regulation of legal education)

Introduction

In the post-Mao reforms, commencing in the late 1970s, there have been significant developments in policies concerning legal education and its regulation, and today it is self-evident that the regulation of legal education in the People's Republic of China (PRC) is seen as crucial for enhancing quality in that education and meeting various domestic and international challenges. In the 1950s, China reformed its higher education system based on a Soviet model, leading to separation of teaching and research. Then, for nearly three decades after the Anti-Rightist movement of 1957, the Chinese leadership pursued insular policies that gave little attention to the value of law and legal education and their international standards, and many law schools were closed. In the 1980s and 1990s, China underwent 'de-Sovietization' reforms, focusing on general education, integrating teaching and research, and increasing university autonomy (Shen, Zhang, and Liu [2022]). This shift towards Western learning, particularly from the American experience, allowed Chinese universities to reconnect with the global academic community, shaping the development of modern universities in China. Recent efforts at legal education reform in the contemporary era include, for example, the 'Outstanding Legal Personnel Education Scheme' intended to improve legal education's structure and methods and thereby assist in the development of legal experts for better governing the country by law and ensuring social order (Shan [2014]). Despite progress, there is a continuing recognised need to address domestic and international demands more effectively.

Legal education and its regulation are vital for international and comparative legal studies in a globalising world, especially for China with its Cultural Revolution history of anti-law movements, closing down of law schools and related bodies, and insularity. China recognises the need to build legal attitudes that assist in engagement with a globalised world, and better understanding of general principles of law, transnational law dimensions of legal practice, different legal systems, critical thinking skills, and the need for many students to prepare for international legal practice. These aims are found in China but understood with nuances that reflect Chinese traditions and socialist values. In general, Chinese higher legal education focuses on a knowledge-centred education model rather than a skill-oriented education model.

Reforms and challenges

Over the past four decades or so, legal reforms in China have been significant, especially in legal education. China now emphasises the rule of law, with legal education playing a crucial role in its promotion. Legal education regulation and quality enhancement are emphasised. Efforts such as the 'Outstanding Legal Personnel Education Scheme', already noted, aim to enhance legal education quality, reflecting a strong commitment to improvement – this initiative aims to revamp the structure, content, and methods of legal education in China. Such changes can offer valuable insights into enhancing legal education quality. Additionally, analysing the distinctive features of legal education regulation and its reforms, the Chinese leadership argues, may even offer valuable lessons for other nations, providing insights into different legal systems, aiding global legal practice, and reflecting the country's commitment to the rule of law. Chinese legal education reforms have now begun to emphasise practical skills training. The reforms aim to diversify education models but face tension between academic freedom and government investment priorities. Pressures from international competition and low employment rates of law graduates are key drivers of the reforms (Li [2019]).

However, regulating legal education in China faces several challenges. First, the quality of legal education is a significant concern. There are issues with the curriculum setting and the lack of specialisation, that cases in law textbooks are too old, teachers' teaching methods lack interaction and opportunities for discussion, and courses are highly 'transplanted' with similar content even though they have different course names. For example, in the design of an experimental class in China University of Political Science and Law, the class' curriculum consists of four sections: 'basic lectures – case study – seminars – discussion on specific topics'.

However, in practice, because courses in each section are taught by teachers from different schools in the university (Commercial Law School, International Law School, Criminal Law School, etc), the contents of the courses greatly overlap, so students have complained that a similar body of knowledge in the curriculum has actually been taught to them four times (Xu [2016]).

In addition, there is a gap between the education provided and the demand for legal services in China's market-oriented economic development. There is a lack of emphasis on practical skills training in the current legal education system, and insufficient attention to modern methods of Alternative Dispute Resolution (Zhao [2018]). Indeed, in practice, not many schools in China have the capacity to offer courses on simulation of real legal practice such as mediation and negotiation, and strain to offer legal clinics for law students.

Thirdly, there is a lack of appreciation of the nature and value of the idea of professional education, and a lack of legal ethics education, which detract significantly from the professional development of law students. As for the 'Outstanding Legal Personnel Education Scheme', some scholars argue that the goal of the scheme is ambiguous, and many schools fail to put ethics courses in the curriculum. For example, among the 41 law schools in a survey, only 36.59 per cent of law schools have the capacity to offer the course on 'legal professionals' ethics', and only 9.76 per cent have made it a compulsory course in the curriculum (Liu [2014]). This is in great contrast to the legal education in many other jurisdictions around the world such as the USA, Australia, Canada, Japan and Korea, where the cultivation of professional ethics is seen as a must in their legal education.

So there continues to be a need for further reforms and improvements in the regulation of legal education in China. More generally, the party-state's policies on the 'rule of law' do not reflect understandings found elsewhere.

Regulatory agencies

Legal education in China is overseen by several pivotal agencies, of which the most significant in terms of functionality is the State Council. This body – or more specifically, the departments authorised by it for educational administration, especially the Ministry of Education and earlier, the Ministry of Justice – are required to formulate the principal regulations related to schools, educational institutions, educational formats, duration of studies, admission criteria, and educational goals. The Central Political and Legal Affairs Commission, together with the Ministry of Education, jointly publish measures such as the 'Outstanding Legal Personnel Education Scheme' to enhance the quality of legal education. The Commission and the State Council also emphasise that legal educational activities should benefit the public interests of state and society. In managing higher education, including any private legal training institutions, responsibilities are devolved to the People's government of provinces, autonomous regions, or municipalities directly under the central government.

When China's legal reforms were recommended in the early 1980s, there quickly developed a diversity of legal educational institutions. Professionalisation and standardisation became policy goals. Beginning in the late 1990s, authorities upgraded secondary technical schools of law and politics to institutes of higher education. The administration of the five specialised political institutes was transferred from the Ministry of Justice to the Ministry of Education and local governments. In 1998, educational authorities introduced a mandatory core curriculum of sixteen classes for undergraduate law majors. By 2002, Chinese authorities had combined the separate entrance exams for the bar, courts, and procuracy into a single national test. In 2002, Chinese authorities unified the previously separate entrance examinations for the bar, courts, and procuracy into a single national test.

Today the Ministry of Justice's main functions include oversight of the establishment of local judicial offices, people's mediation, community correction, local legal services, as well as assistance, education, and reintegration support for released prisoners, and for more than three decades ran the *poufa huodong* (普法活动) or 'popularisation of law' campaign, intended to raise levels of legal awareness among ordinary citizens. The Ministry of Justice is also responsible for administering the National Unified Legal Professional Qualification Examination, also known as the 'Bar Exam'. This is a rigorous test on subjects like legal theory, constitution, criminal law, and more. Preparation involves practice with exam-like questions, tutoring, and studying at private bodies which help students prepare for the exam. It has had a pass rate of 10 per cent to 15 per cent since its inception in 2018.

Secondly, the Supreme People's Court (SPC) and the Supreme People's Procuracy (SPP) provide in-house education and training. For judges, the SPC does this in particular through its National Judges College, as well as though issuing collections – both hard copy and online – of decided cases to assist the work of lower courts in meeting SPC standards and legal profession needs. The National Judges College is a government-sponsored institution directly under the SPC. It is one of the main institutes offering education and training programs for Chinese judges. In 1985, the SPC commenced its now well-established practice of publishing 'typical cases' in its official publication, and also now online. In addition, the Supreme People's Procuracy (SPP) plays a significant role in legal education. The SPP organises and guides the education and training of the staff of prosecution bodies and establishes training centres such as the National Procurators College. It also undertakes planning and provides guidance for its various training centres and their teaching staff. These roles are intended to ensure that the legal education provided aligns with the standards set by the SPP and meets the needs of the legal profession.

Thirdly, since 1986 the All-China Lawyers Association (ACLA) has borne responsibility for the profession. In its early years it was closely linked to the Ministry of Justice. As the official professional association for lawyers in China, the ACLA serves as a self-regulatory body responsible for monitoring the professional conduct and advancement of lawyers through China. All lawyers in China are required to register with the ACLA or its municipal and local counterparts. Law teachers from colleges and universities who possess the appropriate qualifications can be registered as part-time lawyers and admitted to membership in the ACLA. All lawyers in China are members of the ACLA and undergo further legal practice training through local branches of ACLA.

Fourthly, universities and other higher educational establishments also contribute to the governance of legal education, particularly in developing curricula and implementing educational strategies. These organisations are encouraged to collaborate in order to uphold the quality and credibility of legal education in China by establishing standards, regulating teacher conduct, and reforming educational programs so that they align better with what are seen as the profession's requirements.

Fifthly, the Chinese Communist Party (CCP) also plays a significant role in the regulation of legal education in China, in order to promote the development of a socialist rule of law and to ensure that the legal education provided aligns with the political objectives of the CCP. One aspect of this role is ideological control. In recent years, the CCP has ordered closer adherence to its policies and stronger support for leader Xi Jinping in legal education, advising that schools 'oppose and resist Western erroneous views' such as constitutional government, separation of powers, and judicial independence. In many cases textbooks used in teaching must be submitted to and approved by the teaching section of the university. The Party also plays a significant part in the appointment of judges and prosecutors and exerts influence on legal policymaking to ensure alignment with the party's political objectives. Recent structural changes allow a far greater degree of party influence in the day-to-day running of colleges and universities. Most law schools have a local CCP Party Secretary to assist in the governance of the school, to recruit new CCP members, and to assist in finding employment for graduates. The Party also plays a key role in the appointment of university presidents and party secretaries.

Conclusions

The field of legal education regulation in China is complex and continuously evolving. Key aspects encompass the significant growth of legal education, persistent quality concerns, implementation of the Outstanding Legal Personnel Education Scheme, the need for further reforms, the rise of new challenges in the legal field, and the influence of regulatory constraints as well as those of the CCP. These observations mirror the fluidity of legal education regulation in China and ongoing endeavours to elevate its quality and applicability.

LING ZHOU

References

Ruohan Li. (2019). 'Rethinking on China's Higher Legal Education Reform', *International Journal of Information and Education Technology*, 9(8), p. 553.

Kunlun Liu. (2014). *Zhongguo falü zhiye lunli jiaoyu kaocha* [Investigation of Legal Ethics Education in China], China University of Political Science & Law Press, p. 76.

Wenhua Shan. (2014). 'Legal Education in China: The New "Outstanding Legal Personnel Education Scheme" and Its Implications', *Legal Information Management*, 13(1), p. 10.

Shen, W., Zhang, H. and Liu, C. (2022). 'Toward a Chinese model: De-Sovietization reforms of China's higher education in the 1980s and 1990s', *International Journal of Chinese Education*, 11(3), p. 1.

Shenjian Xu. (2016). 'Zhuoyue falü rencai jiaoyu peiyang jihua zhi fansi yu chongsu' [Reflection and Reconstruction on the Outstanding Legal Personnel Education Scheme], *SJTU Law Review*, 3, p. 20.

Yun Zhao. (2016). 'Mediation in Contemporary China: Thinking About Reform', *Journal of Comparative Law* 2, p. 65.

20. Class in legal education

Class is a useful and longstanding social classification used across the social sciences. While some argue that class is less relevant now (Pakulski and Waters [1996]) and has been overtaken as a useful lens of analysis by other theoretical stances, there is still much we can learn from class-based analyses of law and legal education.

Higher Education and the legal sector globally have seen a lot of change in recent times, showing significant growth and claiming success in widening access and participation for groups of students whose background would have made it very difficult to enter those spaces just a few decades ago (Hussey and Smith [2010], Sommerlad et al [2015]). Recently working-class academics, students and graduates have begun speaking out to share their experiences of studying and working in spaces where they never quite feel like they fully belong (Waterfield et al [2019]). Most of the work on class in (legal) education and the (legal) academy utilises the work of Pierre Bourdieu (for example Bourdieu [1984], [1986]) on habitus and various forms of capital to make sense of the way working class students and academics experience law schools.

Class and law students

While some progress has been made in opening up legal education to students who have traditionally been underrepresented, coming from a working class or lower socio-economic background still represents a significant barrier to access, full participation and success in law school. In the English and Welsh context the Legal Education and Training Review (LETR) noted:

> ...progress on widening the socio-economic origins of the student population, particularly within elite universities has been slow, with consequences for social mobility and the diversity of the professions.

Research suggests that those from lower socio-economic backgrounds are less likely to apply to university and where they do apply are less likely to accepted. This is particularly the case where they are applying to top ranked or elite universities (Hussey and Smith [2010]). Reay et al [2009a], [2009b] have pointed out a widening gap between those universities attracting those from working class and minority ethnic backgrounds and those attracting traditional university students.

There are many reasons as to why working class student are less likely to apply including being more financially risk averse and reluctant to take on the significant debt required to study law (Kish-Gephardt [2017]), lack of role models and a perception that studying law is something that is not for them or possible in their contexts, prioritising work and/or family commitments as well as pressures from family and friends to enter the work place to earn money rather than 'waste time' going to university. The reasons why they are less likely to be accepted to their chosen university are also wide ranging and include the type of qualification obtained (Petrie and Gicheva [2018]) and the support and opportunities available to students right through education systems (Hussey and Smith [2010]). These patterns are familiar globally.

Even if accepted though, working class students are often at a disadvantage compared to more traditional students and while class divisions can be difficult to define they are often keenly felt by students (Reay [2021]). Working class students often lack the social and cultural capital others have gained simply by having parents, siblings and friends at university and in the legal professions; they are less familiar with what is expected from them and how to navigate a university environment and progression into the legal professions (Francis [2011], Sommerlad et al [2015]). Non-traditional students may lack the understanding and support needed to successfully transition into their legal education. In addition they may miss out on elements of the hidden curriculum and not fully understand the importance of extra-curricular activities such as mooting, law review, and work experience to their future employment prospects. Even where working class students understand the expectations, they are often not able to fully participate because they are more likely to have to work or work longer hours as well as have caring responsibilities which means their time for study is more limited than that of traditional students. They cannot take part in extra-curricular activities, unpaid internships or placements and they cannot take opportunities such as study trips or competitions because they cannot afford to take time off paid or care work. Many feel a sense of dislocation and remain the proverbial 'fish out of water' having knock on effects on well-being, university experience and success and ultimately also career prospects (Reay [2021]).

Class and legal academics

Given the experiences of working class students and the barriers faced by them it is perhaps unsurprising that those aspiring to careers in academia face further significant hurdles. These include the ability to access funded postgraduate research programmes, to survive on limited scholarships without relying on family support or savings; the need to move geographically in order to secure an academic job and often again for promotions as well as the precarity of many academic careers where short term, teaching term only contracts are not uncommon.

In addition the literature on working class academics identifies several issues including feelings of alienation or invisibility, imposter syndrome or exclusion, whether self-exclusion or exclusion by others (Crew [2021]). Working class academics also report being subjected to micro-aggressions such as colleagues and students making comments about their accents and many note that their choice of clothing or even sense of humour set them apart. Working class academics often feel in between worlds having working class roots but, by virtue of being an academic, having entered and learned to navigate at least superficially, a middle class world (Poole [2023]).

There is surprisingly little literature that focuses specifically on working class legal academics but recent work looking at the academy more generally suggests that little has changed since Deo [2015], Collier [2010] and Cownie [2004] noted some of the same issues in the specific context of law schools in the US and England.

Law school and the reproduction of hierarchies

Overall what we see across the world is not law schools helping to minimise socio-economic disadvantage but instead reproducing hierarchies – much like Kennedy outlined in his 1983 article. Put starkly (and simplistically)

elite law firms recruit from elite law schools where elite academics are teaching predominantly traditional law students who come from middle and upper class backgrounds, often having close family in the legal professions or academia. Students at less highly ranked institutions who are more likely to be from working class backgrounds are more likely to end up in less prestigious and lower paid (legal) roles. While this entry is concerned with class in law schools, what happens in law schools obviously has a direct knock on effect on the legal professions. The class divide between different types of law schools is therefore mirrored in the professions and many students at lower ranked institutions do not necessarily gain the cultural and social capital required by some of the elite firms they might aspire to. Socialisation into the elite has often already taken place before students reach law school and is simply reinforced once there, making it difficult for any outsider to break in.

While hierarchies are undoubtedly reproduced in law schools, class ceilings are also shattered. Success stories of working class students entering the highest ranked law schools or getting into elite law firms and working class academics climbing the career ladder to relative job security and seniority can now relatively easily be found. However, the individual success stories, while always worth celebrating, also distract from the structural barriers and the cultures found in academia and the professions that make it so hard for those with working class backgrounds to succeed. They also distract from the fact that these successes are often related to status and economic success and remove focus from the emotional cost paid and compromises entered into by those who 'make it'. They leave little room for discussions around belonging and well-being and how working class academics and students might thrive and not simply be economically successful.

Reclaiming working class identities

This entry so far has painted a bleak picture for those with working class backgrounds seeking entry into the legal academy as students or academics. It should however be noted that we are beginning to hear working class voices more strongly and that they are being amplified (see for example the Alliance of Working Class Academics). The focus is perhaps shifting away from ways in which law schools can help their working class students and academics better fit in and how they can be encouraged to make up for the lack of social and cultural capital. Instead more recent research, often auto-ethnographic, seeks to amplify the lived experience of those from working class backgrounds in order to foreground the importance of working class heritage, knowledge and experience (Michell et al [2015], Burnell Reilly [2022]). In the same way that contributions from women, racially marginalised and other minority groups are slowly being recognised, working class contributions are beginning to be seen as valuable and working class identities are beginning to be something to be celebrated rather than hidden.

Conclusion

Class is complex and always intertwined with other characteristics and inequalities. How class plays out for students and academics in law schools is equally complex and dependent on other characteristics and experiences. There is now a plethora of research about class in Higher Education and some about class in the legal professions but there is less that is specifically about the experience of legal academics and law students. More research which genuinely tries to engage with the lives of working class students and academics in context and which is not focused on them as somehow lacking in something that causes them to not quite fit but takes a more positive approach, considering how the different experiences can enrich our understanding of a myriad of issues, would go some way to fully understanding and being able to address how class plays out in law schools.

JESSICA GUTH

References

Bourdieu, P. (1984). *Distinction: A Social Critique of the Judgement of Taste*, Harvard University Press.

Bourdieu, P. (1986), 'The Forms of Capital', in Richardson, J.G. *Handbook of Theory and Research for the Sociology of Education*, edited by Greenwood Press, pp. 241–258.

Burnell, Reilly, I. (2022). *The Lives of Working Class Academics Getting Ideas Above your Station*, Emerald.

Collier, R. (2010). 'Legal Academics as Stakeholders: Reconceptualising Identity and Social Class', in Cownie, F. (ed), *Stakeholders in the Law School*, Hart Publishing.

Cownie, F. (2004). *Legal Academics: Culture and Identities*, Hart Publishing.

Crew, T. (2020). *Higher Education and Working-Class Academics: Precarity and Diversity in Academia*, Palgrave Macmillan Publishing.

Deo, M.E. (2015). 'The Ugly Truth about Legal Academia', *Brooklyn Law Review*, 80, p. 943 available at SSRN: https://ssrn.com/abstract= 2524097.

Francis, A. (2011). *At the Edge of Law: Emergent and Divergent Models of Legal Professionalism*, Routledge.

Hussey, T. and Smith, P. (2010). *The Trouble with Higher Education: A Critical Examination of our Universities*, Routledge.

Kennedy, D. (1982). 'Legal Education and the Reproduction of Hierarchy', *J. Legal Education*, 32, p. 591.

Kish-Gephart, J. (2017). 'Social class and risk preferences and behavior', *Current Opinion in Psychology*, 18, p. 89.

Legal Education and Training Review. (2013). 'Setting Standards: The Future of Legal Services Education and Training Regulation in England and Wales', available at http://letr.org.uk/wp-content/uploads/LETR-Report.pdf.

Michell, D., Wilson, J.Z. and Archer, V. (2015). *Bread and Roses: Voices of Australian Academics from the Working Class*, Brill.

Pakulski, J. and Waters, M. (1996). *The Death of Class*, SAGE.

Petrie, K. and Gicheva, N. (2018). *Vocation, Vocation, Vocation: The role of vocational routes into higher education*, Social Market Foundation Report (29 January) London.

Poole, A. (2023). 'From recalcitrance to rapprochement: tinkering with a working-class academic bricolage of "critical empathy"', *Discourse: Studies in the Cultural Politics of Education*, 44(4), p. 522.

Reay, D. (2021). 'The working classes and higher education: Meritocratic fallacies of upward mobility in the United Kingdom', *European Journal of Education*, 56(1), pp. 53–64.

Reay, D., Crozier, G. and Clayton, J. (2009a). '"Fitting in" or "standing out": working-class students in UK higher education', *British Educational Research Journal*, 32(1), p. 1.

Reay, D., Crozier, G. and Clayton, J. (2009b). '"Strangers in Paradise"? Working-class Students in Elite Universities', *Sociology*, 43(6), p. 1103.

Sommerlad, H., Young, R., Vaughan, S. and Harris-Short, S. (2015), 'The Futures of Legal Education and the Legal Profession' in Sommerlad, H., Young, R., Vaughan, S. and

Harris-Short, S. (eds), *The Futures of Legal Education and the Legal Profession*, Hart.

Waterfield, B., Beagan, B.L. and Mohamed, T. (2019). '"You Always Remain Slightly an Outsider": Workplace Experiences of Academics from Working-Class or Impoverished Backgrounds', *Canadian Review of Sociology/Revue canadienne de sociologie*, 56, p. 368.

https://www.workingclassacademics.com.

21. Client interviewing in legal education

Clinical legal education

Clinical Legal Education (CLE) is offered at the academic and/or vocational stage of reading for legal qualification at various universities around the world. CLE is seen by its adherents as a premier method of learning and teaching. Its intensive, one-on-one, or small group nature can allow students to apply legal theory and develop their lawyering skills to solve client legal problems, as mentioned in Curran & Foley [2014] [see Clinical Legal Education (Overview)].

In CLE, the lawyer-client interview module comprises strategies and skills that are integral in the foundation of the lawyer-client relationship. These strategies and skills are compatible with all legal systems around the world. The lawyer-client relationship sets the tone in determining whether the client has a possible law case, and if the lawyer has secured a legal retainer.

Through the exercise of lawyer-client interviews, it is important to appreciate that each client brings a unique and particular set of facts to the relationship; and despite the said area of law being tried and tested daily over hundreds of years, each lawyer-client interview produces information which turns on a unique set of facts.

Detailed research into the law, emotional awareness, cultural differences, patience, and attentive listening, combined with copious notetaking are features that should be appreciated in conducting a lawyer-client interview. Once these features are recognised and facilitated, an emotionally comfortable environment will be created for both parties; and it is through this experience, that information will be obtained from the client and legal advice will be tendered.

In this entry, discussions will focus on the lawyer-client relationship with each other; hence, the terms lawyer-client and client-lawyer will be used interchangeably.

What is client interviewing in legal education?

Client interviewing is one of the most important skills required of a lawyer – it is the practice of communicating with and advising a client on a legal matter. Client-interviewing modules allow law students to develop the skills needed to conduct legal interviews. 'Client-centered lawyers must consider and reflect in practice their client's values, feelings, and preferences' (Binder et al [2019] at 63).

Client interviewing modules allow you to develop the skills needed when conducting a legal interview, such as how to establish a relationship with the client, how to identify the nature of the legal problem, and then how to obtain the relevant information from the client to reach a potential solution.

In ensuring the productive exercise of the client interview, preparation is an essential component. This entry will discuss four stages that can be followed in conducting a successful client interview. Within a legal chambers/practice/firm environment the legal clerk would have communication with the client and receive preliminary information. This would be forwarded to the lawyer to facilitate the preparation of the lawyer-client interview. Practice varies within CLE, but students may receive a briefing from their instructor.

Stage 1: Preparation for Client-Lawyer Interview

'In practice terms, an initial interview can impact later follow-up interviews or contacts, rapport, trust, and confidence, as well as the conduct of any litigation or negotiations that may follow' (Curan & Foley [2014] at 77). 'No matter how many-lawyer client interviews you've conducted it is still important to prepare by reviewing the client's file. You will also need to plan the interview structure and prepare attorney-client interview questions' (Miki [2024]).

Soft and hard skills are important components in the teaching of client interviewing in CLE. Soft skills during an interview are demonstrated when a student is conscious of the emotions being felt by the client which has resulted in their quest for legal assistance. Similarly, hard skills include researching the law that pertains to the issue in question, and the possible questions that would be relevant in understanding the nature of the legal issue. The student has to be aware of employing both these skills before the client interview.

These skills have to be developed and practiced to maintain competence in this exercise as both are important in establishing the initial client-lawyer relationship. Additionally, both skills combined have to be tactically couched to achieve the best possible outcome for all parties.

A student when given a file or brief (in the case of a criminal matter) will need to enquire from the person who has instructed them to provide them with the following information:

- Name
- Age
- Marital Status
- Occupation
- Geographic location
- Any previous involvement with the legal system
- Means Test (for legal aid purposes)
- Disability (if any)
- Area of law that may surround the interview, ex Civil, Criminal, Family

This list is not exhaustive, but this basic information will prepare the student both emotionally and intellectually to conduct a successful interview.

The information required is categorised as client data. Many jurisdictions around the world have legislation that addresses how lawyers treat client biographical data such as the list above. Before commencing the lawyer-client interview, students typically need to inform clients that information received during the interview will be protected following the legislation of the land, for example, in the UK the Data Protection Act 2018.

Stage 2: The Format of and Skills in Lawyer Client-Interviewing

Once the student has received the information from their instructor, or a clinic administrator, and finalised the mode of communication, location, and time convenient to all parties it is now time for the student to conduct the interview. Depending on the way CLE is delivered within an individual law school, this may be conducted by one, two or a group of students. An instructor and/or qualified lawyer may also be present.

Salutations and introductions are the formalities that start the lawyer-client interview, by establishing the correct pronunciations of names and confirming the titles by which both parties prefer to be addressed. Once

that is completed the stage is now set for the commencement of the interview. Salinas suggests two things in her piece which are that in information gathering the professional (or, in this case, student) should sit quietly and listen to the client's story; and should try to limit close-ended questions at first so that the clients have the freedom to describe their problems as they see their problems (Salinas [2014]).

Allowing clients to freely express themselves is supported by the philosophy of existentialism, which highlights the life circumstances of persons. Nevertheless, within an existential framework, the client is encouraged to accept that it is she or he who has the responsibility to choose, the freedom to act, and will ultimately be accountable to him or herself for the outcomes (Boutle [2020]).

Once the interview is completed the student will usually ask the client if there are any questions or concerns which have arisen out of the interview. If there are no changes to be made to the information garnered from the interview, the information may be read over to the client at which time the client may be asked to sign an interview statement. The client will be informed what to expect after the interview, for example, the student may draft and send a letter of advice based on the interview.

Stage 3: Post Client Interview

After a client interview, the student will usually take time to review the information gleaned from the client and check it against the questions and the law researched before the interview. Some law clinics are then able to offer a retainer, creating an on-going lawyer-client relationship, while others will provide 'one-off' advice.

Stage 4: Client-Interviewing in a Technological Age

With the advent of the global COVID-19 pandemic, more so than ever before, CLE has begun to include virtual communication. Client interviewing has benefited greatly from virtual communication as it facilitates persons in a wider geographical net, and it serves as an excellent teaching and learning tool in the technological age for modules in the vocational arm of law schools.

In a virtual world, lawyer-client interviews are governed by netiquette practices while conducting client interviews virtually. According to the (Cambridge Dictionary[n.d.]), netiquette is described as a 'set of rules about behaviour that is acceptable when communicating with people over the internet'. These practices include the following, non-exhaustive list:

- Background setting
- Background noises
- Videos should always be on for clients and lawyers to identify each other
- The microphone should not be open outside of interviewing time
- Dress Code appropriate to that of face-to-face client-lawyer interviews

Both students and clients need to be aware of these guidelines in this new technological environment. For students, it provides a valuable grounding in skills which are increasingly required within legal practice.

Conclusion

In summary, the four stages addressed in this entry are critical for successful lawyer-client interviews and therefore are commonly emulated by students within CLE. The details of each should be followed carefully, the student should endeavour not to breach any aspect of this relationship and the client should be willing to adjust and embrace the etiquette demanded by the lawyer-client relationship. These steps provide a model for the conduct of a lawyer-client interview in legal education.

DIONNE CRUICKSHANK

References

Binder, D.A., Bergman, P., Price, S.C. and Tremblay, P. (2019). *Lawyers as Counselors: A Client-Centered Approach*, 5th edn, West Academic Publishing.

Boutle, G. (2020). 'Clients and Counselling – an Existential Approach', Counselling Directory, 17 November, available at https://www.counselling-directory.org.uk/memberarticles/clients-and-counselling-an-existential-approach.

Cambridge Dictionary, 'Netiquette | English Meaning – Cambridge Dictionary', *Cambridge Dictionary*, available at https://dictionary.cambridge.org/dictionary/english/netiquette.

Curran, L. and Foley, T. (2014). 'Integrating Two Measures of Quality Practice into Clinical and Practical Legal Education Assessment: Good Client Interviewing and Effective Community Legal Education', *International Journal of Clinical Legal Education*, 21, p. 69.

Data Protection Act 2018.

Hlass, L.L. and Harris, L.M. (2021). 'Critical Interviewing', Utah Law Digital Commons, p. 683, available at https://dc.law.utah.edu/ulr/vol2021/iss3/4/.

Miki, S. (2024). 'The Initial Consultation: Solicitor-Client Interview Questions', *Clio UK*, 27 March 2024, available at https://www.clio.com/uk/blog/solicitor-client-interview-questions/.

Salinas, O.J. (2014). 'Effective Client Interviewing and Counseling', UNC Legal Studies Research Paper No. 2401119, available at SSRN: https://ssrn.com/abstract=2401119 or http://dx.doi.org/10.2139/ssrn.2401119.

22. Clinical legal education (for commerce)

History of Commercial Law Clinics

Commercial Law Clinics have existed in the United States since the late 1970s. The earliest clinics focused on housing and community economic development – teaching business and property doctrine alongside lawyering skills (Jones and Lainez [2013]). In the 1990s, the number of Commercial Law Clinics in the United States grew rapidly, with greater emphasis on the needs of creative entrepreneurs and small businesses (Jones and Lainez [2013]).

The American Bar Association lists over 200 accredited law schools with formal pro bono or clinical programmes. There are at least 70 specific Commercial Law Clinics, and this figure does not include generalist clinic projects where commercial advice may form part of the service. The clinics cover an extensive array of legal issues, including incorporation and structuring, taxation, succession planning, governance, contract drafting and negotiation, real estate, intellectual property, and employment (American Bar Association [2023]). For example, at the University of Illinois College of Law IP Clinic each clinic participant meets and advises five assigned student companies on their trademark matters. This includes performing trademark searching services and preparing trademark applications. Another example is the Small Entrepreneur and Economic Development Legal Clinic at the University of Akron which provides low-cost legal and business assistance to small and emerging businesses in the local community. This assistance includes business planning, employment, contract/lease, tax, and entity formation information. However, as Jones ([2013] at 90) has noted, these examples cannot 'capture the richness and variation' of the Commercial Law Clinics in the United States.

Commercial Law Clinics beyond the United States

Outside of the United States, there is little scholarship on Commercial Law Clinics. This means that it can be challenging to map the scope of Commercial Law Clinics internationally. In the United Kingdom, the first Commercial Law Clinics were only established after the turn of the Millennium (Campbell [2016a; 2016b]). The Student Law Office at Northumbria University, for example, created its first Commercial Law Clinic in 2007. At the time, the clinic offered a small number of students the opportunity to advise on a range of business issues whilst supervised by members of academic staff who also held practising certificates (Campbell [2015]). In 2012, City, University of London launched Start-Ed, a pro bono law clinic for start-ups operating in London (Collins [2016]). Start-Ed was created in response to requests from law firms that trainees demonstrate commercial awareness, as well as a desire to increase entrepreneurial education at the University (Collins [2016]). The following year, Queen Mary University of London created qLegal – a scheme where postgraduate law students provide free support to start-ups and entrepreneurs under the supervision of qualified lawyers (Platts-Mills and Wapples [2023]). All of these clinical projects are still ongoing.

The development of clinics offering more commercially-oriented legal advice has been slow, but the 2020 Law School Pro Bono and Clinic Report suggests that 50 per cent of law clinics in the UK are advising on small business set up with a further 45 per cent dealing with 'other commercial' matters including intellectual property (Sandbach and Grimes [2020]).

Commercial Law Clinics can also be found in Israel, Ireland, and Australia. The Interdisciplinary Center Herzliya Legal Clinic for Start-Ups at Radzyner Law School is the first of its kind in Israel (Roper et al [2018]). The clinics assists technological entrepreneurs by providing free legal services, allowing entrepreneurs to download free legal documents, connecting entrepreneurs with experienced mentors and offering events geared towards entrepreneurs. Target communities include new immigrants to Israel, Arabs, ultra-orthodox Jews, peripheral residents and disabled people. Preference is also given to women (Roper et al [2018]). The IT Law Clinic at University College Cork also restricts its advice to issues of copyright law, web domain names, electronic commerce and data protection law. The client must have a low turnover – maximum €100,000 per year and the clinic can only deal with queries from January to April (University College Cork [2023]). In Australia, a major review of higher education in 2008 called for universities to do more to prepare graduates for the world of work. An example of a response to this call, is the Law Tech Clinic at Monash University. Designed in collaboration with a student-led start-up BotL, students work to build transformative legal technology for the enhancement of legal services (Weinberg [2023]). This innovative programme, which disrupts the law clinic model, works to educate law students on the intersectionality of technology and legal services, whilst still teaching client-centred techniques and strategies for effective legal research.

Commercial Law Clinics: charging clients

Unlike traditional pro bono legal advice provided to individuals (see Clinical Legal Education (for Individuals)), some Commercial Law Clinics asks clients to pay a fee for their services. For example, the University of Central Lancashire Business Law Clinic asks prospective clients to pay an administration fee of £50 plus VAT before an initial meeting can be arranged (University of Central Lancashire [2023]). There is no charge for any advice offered, however. The Business and Enterprise Law Service provided by NLS Legal at Nottingham Trent University does charge for legal advice. NLS Legal offers low-cost legal assistance on a range of issues across the life cycle of a business from inception to post-insolvency. There is a particular focus on dispute resolution and litigation (Nottingham Trent University [2023]). All legal work is undertaken by law student volunteers, legal assistance and paralegals, under the supervision of a Business and Enterprise Law Services solicitor (Nottingham Trent University [2023]).

Criticism of Commercial Law Clinics

Some academics believe that clinical legal education should focus on low-income individuals who are unable to afford legal advice. They argue that Commercial Law Clinics lack the social justice element inherent in the foundations of clinical legal education (see Clinical Legal Education (for Individuals)) because they offer legal assistance to for-profit businesses, many of whom could afford representation elsewhere. Nicholson [2006], in particular, criticises the willingness of some clinics to put education over community need as problematic when it leads to weak and vulnerable people being harmed. This happens, he argues, 'when clinics represent landlords or employers because of pedagogical benefits' ([2006] at 4). More generally, Wizner and Atkin [2004] ask whether supervised student representation of disadvantaged clients has been sacrificed in favour of skills training and guided reflection.

Other scholars believe that the traditional conceptualisation of social justice should be challenged (Campbell [2015; 2016a; 2016b]; Roper et al [2018]; Gregersen [2023]). They believe that Commercial Law Clinics fulfil a broader social justice agenda because the clinics offer opportunities to students who may face barriers pursuing a career in business law. In addition, some academics assert that the community as a whole benefits from thriving businesses. For example, Campbell [2015; 2016a; 2016b] contends that giving legal advice to established local companies for free means that the companies have more money to pay wages, to provide services to the community and to promote economic growth in the area.

ELAINE GREGERSEN

References

American Bar Association, 'Directory of Law School Public Interest & Pro Bono Programs', available at https://www.americanbar.org/groups/center-pro-bono/resources/directory_of_law_school_public_interest_pro_bono_programs/.

Campbell, E. (2015). 'A dangerous method? Defending the rise of business law clinics in the UK', *The Law Teacher*, 49, p. 165.

Campbell, E. and Murray, V. (2015). 'Mind the Gap: Clinic and the Access to Justice Dilemma', *International Journal of Legal and Social Studies*, 2, p. 94.

Campbell, E. (2016a). 'Taking Care of Business: Challenging the Traditional Conceptualisation of Social Justice in Clinical Legal Education' in Ashford, C. and McKeown, P. (eds), *Social Justice and Legal Education*, Cambridge Scholars Publishing.

Campbell, E. (2016b). 'Recognizing the Social and Economic Value of Transactional Law Clinics:

A View from the United Kingdom', *Journal of Legal Education*, 65, p. 580.

Collins, D., Klotz, E. and Robinson, B. (2016). 'Start-Ed: A Model for Commercial Clinical Legal Education', *International Journal of Clinical Legal Education*, 23, p. 80.

Jones, S.R. and Lainez, J. (2013). 'Enriching the Law School Curriculum: The Rise of Transactional Legal Clinics in U.S. Law Schools', *Washington University Journal of Law & Policy*, 43, p. 85.

Nicolson, D. (2006). 'Legal Education Or Community Service? The Extra-Curricular Student Law Clinic', *Web Journal of Current Legal Issues*, p. 3.

Nottingham Trent University, 'Our Services', available at https://www.ntu.ac.uk/study-and-courses/academic-schools/nottingham-law-school/nls-legal/our-services.

Platts-Mills, E. and Wapples, E. (2023). 'Thinking Like Entrepreneurs: Qlegal's Experience of Teaching Law Students to have an Entrepreneurial Mindset', *International Journal of Clinical Legal Education*, p. 73.

Roper, V. and others. (2018). 'Understanding the Scope of Business Law Clinics: Perspectives from the United Kingdom, Israel and the United States', *Journal of International and Comparative Law*, 5, p. 217.

Sandbach, J. and Grimes, R. (2020). 'Law School Pro Bono and Clinic Report 2020', *LawWorks and CLEO* (Clinical Legal Education Organisation), 12.

University College Cork, 'IT Law Clinic', available at https://www.ucc.ie/en/law/society/it-law-clinic/.

University of Central Lancashire, 'Business Law Clinic', available at https://www.uclan.ac.uk/professional-services/arc#law-clinic.

Weinberg, J. and Hyams, R. (2023). 'The Law Tech Clinic: Leading the way in Entrepreneurial Law Clinics', *International Journal of Clinical Legal Education*, p. 34.

Wizner, S. and Aiken, J. (2004). 'Teaching and doing: The role of law school clinics in enhancing access to justice', *Fordham Law Review*, 73, p. 997.

23. Clinical legal education (for individuals)

Introduction

Clinical Legal Education (CLE) is a methodology (Bellow [1973]) which incorporates a variety of experiential models such as live-client clinics, public legal education, and policy clinics. Although clinic clients can be community interest organisations, non-government organisations (NGOs), and for-profit corporations (see Clinical Legal Education (Overview) and Clinical Legal Education (for Commerce)) the focus here will be on the client as an individual, namely natural persons. This entry seeks to achieve three broad aims. First, to outline the general characteristics of a typical live-client clinic. Second, to argue that, generally, legal education excludes the concept of the individual client from the debate. Third, to identify an ethical model that can contribute to respecting the client's humanity irrespective of any defining characteristics such as age, religion, nationality, or sexual orientation.

Legal education

I argue that non-CLE pedagogies, such as the doctrinal approach, critical race theory, and feminist critique do not adequately prepare students for the complexities and uncertainties of legal practice. This is mainly due to the fact that legal education, especially in common law jurisdictions, is dominated by the study of appellate decisions where the focus of the inquiry is on legal arguments, concepts, and doctrines and not the individual. In her critique of legal education in the United States, Shalleck argues that clients occupy two worlds: the legal and the social ([1993] at 1731). She notes that absent from legal are 'clients with particular identities who are situated in distinctive ways within the social world, facing often critical choices about their participation in the legal world' (Shalleck [1993] at 1731). Consequently, students are not afforded the opportunity to engage with the social world or the client's position within it (Shalleck [1993] at 1734). Instead, legal education encourages students to construct client identities and experiences

only within the existing parameters of legal analysis, independent of the client's social world (Shalleck [1993] at 1737). Focusing on appellate decisions raises several issues. First, most aspiring lawyers will not deal with the appellate courts during their legal careers. Instead, they are likely to be advising clients in the lower courts. Excluded from class-room discussions are the realities of legal practice such as the lawyer-client relationship, the jury, and witness testimonies. It was these limitations that prompted the American legal realist, Frank, to advocate for the incorporation of law clinics into legal education (Frank [1933]). Second, educating students to construct a client purely within the appellate court's decision and version of the facts of the case strips the client from their identity and lived experience of both the social world and the legal world. This can give rise to the third issue, students view clients as 'walking bundles of legal rights and interests' rather than individuals whose legal problems are closely connected to other concerns such as relationships, emotions, and values (Kruse [2010] at 104). Fourth, by viewing the two worlds as separate, students may adopt a paternalistic approach to legal practice resulting from the fact that they may view themselves as the experts in the legal realm.

Characteristics of clinic clients

In 2000, Wizner lamented the fact that access to justice for the 'legally underprivileged' is a growing problem (Wizner [2000] at 328). However, Wizner does not define 'access to justice'. The United Nations Development Programme (UNDP) defines this as '[t]he ability of people to seek and obtain a remedy through formal or informal institutions of justice, and in conformity with human rights standards' (UNDP [2005] at 5). To determine whether access to justice is a growing problem, it is instructive to firstly examine the United Nations Sustainable Development Goals (SDGs), which lay various targets for national and global development policies to 2030, namely SDG 16, which promises to 'provide access to justice for all' (United Nations [2015] at 14). However, given the fact that approximately two-thirds of the world's population face a myriad of access to justice issues such as the inability to obtain justice for civil or criminal matters, being excluded from the protection of the law due to the lack of legal documents (for example, identification documents, land deeds, and work permits), and living in conditions of extreme injustice (World Justice Project [2019] at 5), it becomes clear that not only are the majority of individuals facing access to justice issues but that the world is far from achieving SDG 16 by the target year 2030. One could, therefore, conclude that individuals experiencing access to justice issues include some of the most vulnerable in society such as immigrants (such as asylum seekers, economic migrants, and refugees), victims of domestic sexual violence, and street-homeless individuals.

To develop a fuller picture of the archetypal clinic client, it is necessary to briefly examine the barriers they typically face when accessing the justice system. Drummond and McKeever ([2015] at 25) identify three barriers which clinic clients tend to experience. First, clients face intellectual challenges such as understanding legal formalities such as language and procedure. Second, practical issues such as knowing where to seek legal assistance and long waiting times. Third, emotional barriers, such as stress, anxiety, and frustration, can impact on clients' ability to gain access to justice.

The pedagogic benefits of live-client clinics

Unlike classroom-based legal education and other forms of CLE, such as policy clinics, the client has a key role in live-client clinics. The inclusion of the client benefits legal education in the following ways. First, students are provided with the opportunity to develop the client's case theory or theory of the case and to deal with evidential issues normally absent in appellate court decisions. Second, they experience first-hand the impact of the law on clients and are able to debate the content of the law with reference to their client. In other words, students can adopt a natural law approach to engage in critique of legal positivism echoing as Kelsen's claim that '[a]ny content whatever can be law' ([1997] at 56), irrespective of its moral quality. Third, students can view clients as individuals possessing unique characteristics (Shalleck [1993] at 1740). This allows students to reflect on the client's circumstances and their relationship to the legal world. In other words, CLE bridges the divide between the legal world

and the social world. Fourthly, students are less likely to be become paternalistic lawyers when they are trained to view their clients as autonomous decision makers who are actively involved in the legal process.

Fifth, a commitment to effectively utilising emotions in legal education (Jones [2019]) can be achieved through live-client clinics. Students can reflect on their own emotions, such as sympathy and compassion, and the feelings experienced by their clients, such as anger, fear, and anxiety. In relation to the student's emotions, sympathy to suffering can be a useful starting point regarding one's moral obligations to individuals in other parts of the world. Sixthly, students' reflective capacities are developed when they incorporate the impact of the law and political institutions on their client, for example when considering issues such as distributive justice (Madhloom and Preložnjak [2022]).

Ethical issues in live-client clinics

Notwithstanding the above pedagogic benefits of incorporating clients into legal education, several ethical issues present themselves in live-client clinics. Firstly, students working in university clinics are not qualified lawyers. In other words, clients, who are some of the most vulnerable in society, are being 'used' to develop students' legal and professional acumen. The second issue is concerned with moral obligations and the question of whether clinics owe obligations to individuals in other parts of the world. Thirdly, individuals, including students, are prone to bias (Donald and Anderson [2022]). This presents a challenge in terms of training students to ensure that they are cognizant of the fact that they may impose upon clients their own cultural norms.

To address the above ethical issues, I will draw on a normative model which I have developed elsewhere (Madhloom [2022]). This model is underpinned by Immanuel Kant's work and moral cosmopolitanism. The latter refers to the idea that a person is a member of a global moral community and owes responsibilities to their fellow members (Nussbaum [1996] at 4). In other words, a person's moral responsibilities are not confined to local obligations.

In addition to rejecting lawyer paternalism, it promotes lawyer rationality without sacrificing the value of emotions such as sympathy and compassion in developing students' moral perception.

With regards to the first ethical issue, it could be argued that allowing students to develop their lawyering skills is in direct violation of Kant's second formula, 'Act in such a way that you always treat humanity, whether in your own person or in the person of any other, never simply as a means, but always at the same time as an end' (Kant [1969]). However, provided clients are not treated purely for instrumental reasons and the student-client relationship is based on reciprocity, it becomes difficult to argue that a client is being treated as a mere mean. Moreover, according to Kant, a duty to assist those facing hardship, for example through the provision of legal assistance, is an imperfect duty (Kant [1969] at 84). Imperfect duties allow the agent to exercise discretion when fulling these duties. Thus, it is up to the individual supervisor to decide how best to discharge their duty to their client. Secondly, like utilitarianism, Kant's third formula (the kingdom of ends) is cosmopolitan in nature in that it views individuals as members of a moral community. This is a valuable concept for both clinicians and students. For the former it can help inform the CLE curriculum to include topics such as global justice, moral commitment to clients, and cultural competence. For students, moral cosmopolitanisms can help focus their reflection upon their own bias and their duties to clients in other parts of the world.

OMAR MADHLOOM

References

Bellow, G. (1973). 'On Teaching the Teachers: Some Preliminary Reflections on Clinical Education as Methodology', in Council on Legal Education for Professional Responsibility, *Clinical Education for The Law Student: Legal Education in a Service Setting* (Council on Legal Education for Professional Responsibility).

Drummond, O. and McKeever, G. (2015). *Access to Justice through University Law Clinics*, Ulster University Law School.

Frank, J. (1933). 'Why not a clinical lawyer-school?', *University of Pennsylvania Law Review*, 81(8), p. 907.

Jones, E. (2019). *Emotions in the Law School: Transforming Legal Education Through the Passions*, Routledge.

Kant, I. (1969). *The Moral Law*. (Paton, H.J. trans), The Open University.

Kelsen, H. (2009). *Introduction to the Problems of Legal Theory* (Paulson, B.L. and Paulson, S.L. trans), Oxford University Press.

Kruse, K.R. (2010). 'Beyond Cardboard Clients in Lega Ethics', *The Georgetown Journal of Legal Ethics*, 23(1), p. 103.

Madhloom, O. (2022). 'A Kantian Moral Cosmopolitan Approach to Teaching Professional Legal Ethics', *German Law Journal*, 23, p. 1139.

Madhloom, O. and Preložnjak, B. (2022). 'Applying Rawls' theory of justice to Clinical Legal Education in the Republic of Croatia', in Madhloom, O. and McFaul, H. (eds), *Thinking About Clinical Legal Education: Philosophical and Theoretical Perspectives*, Routledge.

Nussbaum, M.C. (1996). 'Patriotism and Cosmopolitanism', in Cohen, J. (ed), *For Love of Country: Debating the Limits of Patriotism*, Beacon Press.

Polden, D.J. and Anderson, J.M. (2022). 'Leadership to Address Implicit Bias in the Legal Profession', *Santa Clara Law Review*, 62(1), p. 63.

Ratnapala, S. (2009). *Jurisprudence*, Cambridge University Press.

Shalleck, A. (1993). 'Constructions of the Client within Legal Education', *Stanford Law Review*, 45(6), p. 1731.

United Nations Development Programme. (2005). Programming for Justice: Access for All, United Nations Development Programme.

United Nations. (2015). 'Transforming our world: the 2030 Agenda for Sustainable Development'.

Wizner. S. (2000). 'Beyond Skills Training', *Clinical Law Review*, 7, p. 327.

World Justice Project. (2019). 'Measuring the Justice Gap: A People-Centred Assessment of Unmet Justice Needs Around the World'.

24. Clinical legal education (overview)

Clinical legal education is a methodology for training law students to be lawyers by providing experiential opportunities for law students to practice and learn lawyering skills with real clients, cases, and facts. Though the broader concept of clinical education, where aspiring student practitioners work and interact with real people under the supervision of a trained professional, has been around for centuries in field such as medicine, the formal practice of clinical legal education is a relatively new and less developed phenomenon. In the last 60 years, however, the field of clinical legal education has gained significant traction within law schools across the globe and growing recognition as a best practice within the legal education community. This entry explains the concept of clinical legal education, considers the advantages and limitations of clinical legal education, and frames the relevance of clinical legal education to modern legal training.

Though legal education dates back to the time of the Romans, the concept of a modern law school did not take shape until the nineteenth century. The first wave of law schools focused on studying the law as written or codified within each domestic system. Apprenticeships, or studying and then practicing law under the supervision of a trained attorney were supplemental, or even alternative, components of many countries' early approaches to legal training. The emergence of the case method approach, popularised at Harvard by Dean Langdell in the 1870s, rapidly gained popularity both within the United States and across the globe as a best practice in legal education pedagogy (Stevens [1983]). The case method approach involved studying judicial decisions to identify the core principles of law as applied by judges. Studying these cases and how judges applied the written laws to different facts and actors was widely held to be the most effective way of training the next generation of lawyers. Despite calls from law students for more practical legal training, this commitment to learning how to be a lawyer through rigorous attention to the study of legal doctrine and appellate court holdings remained the predominant approach to the legal education until midway through the twentieth century (Stuckey [2004]).

In the 1960s, however, things would begin to shift. Amidst a backdrop of global social activism, widespread disillusionment with the status quo, and increased calls for more accessible and justice-oriented legal services, law schools and law students sought a new way to engage with both global and domestic justice movements. Legal clinics, where law students working under the supervision of trained attorneys or professors provide free legal services to those most in need, offered both an opportunity to bridge this gap and an opportunity to supplement the traditional legal education model (Barry et al [2000]).

Though examples of legal outreach and efforts, including informal legal aid advising and community education sessions, existed previously, these were informal, typically driven by volunteer law students, lacking academic credit, and loosely supervised. Beginning in the 1960s, law schools and law students began to more fully embrace both the potential and relevance of legal clinics and the clinical training model to preparation for the practice of law and furthering the goal of justice for all.

Clinical legal education is the methodology used within legal clinics for training law students how to be lawyers by providing experiential opportunities for law students to practice and learn lawyering skills with real clients, cases and facts. In contrast, the traditional law school approach, to teach law students how to 'think like a lawyer,' focuses on the study of the law as written and as interpreted through judicial decisions – skills that can be learned in the classroom and from law texts exclusively. Clinical legal education, however, focuses on the more practical side of lawyering, often referred to as how to 'act like a lawyer,' and involves working with real clients and unresolved situations. Working under the supervision of a law professor or trained lawyer, law students in legal clinics learn and practice a variety of hard and soft skills that can only be acquired through a cycle of preparation, practice, and reflection.

Though legal clinics vary in their content focus, approach, and range of representation, a constant through line is the unique, experiential opportunity to practice being a lawyer while still in law school. The skills students can learn through participation in a law school clinic include everything from how to greet a client and explain the lawyer-client relationship through to the submission of legal pleadings and appearances in court. Students can learn how to organise and formulate facts and arguments, how to negotiate and interact with other lawyers and judges, how to differentiate between the relevant and irrelevant, how to identify and choose between available legal claims, and how to negotiate, draft and file legal documents. These skills are all practiced and learned in real time with the law students simultaneously navigating the complex interplay between client expectations, legal realities and the demands and constraints of the legal system.

This clinical work does not occur in a vacuum or without adequate preparation and support. Law students must first enrol in a legal clinic at their law school – often highly competitive slots with prerequisites including foundational courses in legal procedure, jurisdiction, and the relevant legal content such as criminal or family law. Once in the clinic, law students work under the supervision of a law school professor or trained attorney in a classroom setting to learn about best practices in working with clients, advocacy, and legal procedure. Law students' subsequent interactions with clients are carefully structured and law students have to provide periodic updates and briefings as the representation proceeds. Clients are aware they are working with clinical students and also know that there is a formal supervision protocol and ongoing classroom learning. The supervisor reviews and approves any significant filings or actions with respect to each client and grades the law students on their performance.

The benefits of clinical legal education extend beyond the opportunity to 'act like a lawyer' and develop important oral and written communication skills, however. From a teaching and learning perspective, the cycle of study, practice, and reflect is a proven pedagogy and a more effective way to learn and practice any skill – including those required of the next generation of lawyers. Law students learn how to learn and how to transfer knowledge and apply problem-solving and analytical skills to new contexts – a core competency of any successful lawyer. Law students also develop a professional lawyering identity and ethos, gaining invaluable firsthand perspectives into how the law as written differs from the law as lived, and beginning to understand

the myriad interactions between the legal system and government entities (Goldfarb [2012]).

For many law students, while the advocacy, case planning, and practical skills learned through participating in a clinic are important, the real draw of clinical legal education is the opportunity to work on social justice issues and with clients most in need of help. The idea that the law can be a vehicle for social change and that lawyers are uniquely positioned to help create more just and equitable societies motivates many students to attend law school. This animating purpose can often seem distant as students wade through introductory courses in torts, jurisdiction, property, and business law. Participation in a clinic is a concrete opportunity to help make the law more accessible and understandable for those who often get forgotten or neglected by existing structures and systems. Almost all legal clinics offer their law student services at low or no cost and the clients and issues focused on are typically selected without regard to profitability or economic returns for the clinic. Indeed, the commitment to work on social, economic, racial, and other justice issues is often an explicitly stated aim of law school clinical programmes.

Today, law clinics exist for nearly every possible area of the law, from domestic violence to prisoners' rights, from landlord–tenant to public benefits, from family law to starting a business, and from legislative reform to environmental advocacy. The different legal framing and procedures involved in each situation mean law students in one clinic may be scheduling meetings based on a prison's visiting schedule while students in another clinic may be researching historical environmental data in preparation for a legal appeal on behalf of an advocacy organisation.

Just as each of these clinics focuses on different skills and requires different strategies, so do law schools differ in their decisions around what clinics to offer and how to build their clinical programs. Clinics can be housed in law schools or mobile clinics, can involve direct-client representation or complicated appellate filings, can be graduation requirements or entirely extracurricular, and anything in between. Law schools who offer clinics must also decide how to structure and schedule the classroom component, the grading and credit aspects, and the balance between doctrinal and clinical offerings.

SEÁN ARTHURS

In addition to these programmatic decisions, law schools must also consider the limitations or trade-offs involved in launching and sustaining a legal clinic. At the institutional level, adding clinical requirements – or even alternatives – can be seen as competition or displacement of more traditional classroom instruction. This is more than just a theoretical tension as law schools have limited budgets and staff – offering clinical programmes requires resources. Legal clinics are not as cost-efficient as standard classroom offerings, with clinical courses consisting of as few as 10–15 students per professor while large lecture courses often have more than 100 students. Legal cases, and the accompanying clinical work, also don't follow academic calendars and some cases can extend over years, requiring the active involvement of multiple classes of students. Supervising and training law students in clinical settings requires a blend of practical expertise and knowledge of clinical legal education pedagogy markedly different from what is expected of a traditional law professor. Additionally, despite the growth of the clinical legal education movement in the last half century, and in part due to the nature of the methodology itself, the field of clinical legal education still lacks standardised definition, methodology, assessment, and structure (Sandefur and Selbin [2009]).

Fortunately, proponents of clinical legal education are working to fill these gaps and to develop a more robust field of clinical legal education. Today, journals such as the Clinical Law Review and the International Journal of Clinical Legal Education publish peer-reviewed articles while organisations such as the Clinical Legal Education Organisation, the European Network for Clinical Legal Education, and the Global Alliance for Justice Education convene conferences and bring together practitioners and researchers to share best practices and learnings in the clinical legal education space. Legal accreditation organisations and professional societies have also begun to recognise and formalise the practice of clinical legal education as part of their standards and legal training structures. And while the first wave of clinical legal education was dominated by clinics in the United States, Canada, Britain, and Australia, legal clinics now exist across the globe (Wilson [2018]).

Clinical legal education is still a relatively young field but one that offers tremendous benefits to law students, law schools, and the clients they serve. The rapid rise of the clinical legal movement and the thousands of clinics that now exist around the world speak to both the appeal and relevance of this approach to training and preparing lawyers. As the demand for better prepared and more flexible, collaborative, and experienced law school graduates continues to grow, the value and import of legal clinics and clinical legal education will likewise continue to grow. Clinical legal education offers a unique value proposition within the broader legal education model and will help shape and influence the profession and practice of law for years to come.

SEÁN ARTHURS

References

Barry, M.M, Dubin, J.C. and Joy, P.A. (2007). 'Clinical Education for This Millenium: The Third Wave', Clinical L. Rev, 7, p. 2.

Goldfarb, P. (2012). 'Back to the Future of Clinical Legal Education', B.C. J.L. & Soc. Just., 32, p. 279.

Sandefur, R. and Selbin, J. (2009). 'The Clinic Effect', Clinical L. Rev., 16, p. 57.

Stevens, R. (1983). Law School: Legal Education in American from the 1850s to the 1980s, The University of North Carolina Press.

Stuckey, R. (2004). 'The Evolution of Legal Education in the United States and the United Kingdom: How one system became more faculty-oriented while the other became more consumer-oriented', Int. J. Clin. Leg. Educ., 6, p. 101.

Wilson, R.J. (2018). 'Legal Aid and Clinical Legal Education in Europe and the USA: Are They Compatible?', in Hammerslev, O. and Halvorsen Rønning, O. (eds), Outsourcing Legal Aid in the Nordic Welfare States, Palgrave.

25. Clinicians in legal education

'Clinician' is the term commonly used to denote an individual responsible for supervising, overseeing and/or coordinating clinical legal education activities provided on behalf of a law school.

The 'typical' clinician

There is no single or proscribed professional profile for the role of clinician. Just as there are many and varied models of clinical legal education, the professional backgrounds of those who oversee these activities are equally diverse. In many institutions the clinicians will be qualified and experienced legal practitioners. In others, they may be legal academics who entered academia via the traditional PhD route and have limited prior legal practice experience. In some law schools, legal practitioners and legal academics work side by side, both fulfilling the role of 'clinician' within the same clinic.

The employment status of clinicians is equally varied. Some will be employed by their university on an 'academic' contract of employment that includes an expectation to engage in research or scholarship and/or to take on other functions outside of the law clinic, that are connected with the running of the law school or wider institution. Others will be on 'professional services' or 'administrative' contracts, with no expectations or opportunities to engage in academic pursuits beyond their clinic teaching and supervision. As explored below, contract type can dictate opportunities for, and barriers to, career progression for clinicians.

Some clinicians who are qualified legal practitioners maintain an active legal practice outside of their clinical legal education activity, perhaps retaining part time employment with an external law firm or third sector organisation or working as a self-employed advocate. Others 'practise' only through the law school clinic, acting in a supervisory capacity to students engaged in the provision of legal services. And there are some legally qualified clinicians who do not practise law at all. The latter may establish and oversee law clinics in which supervision of the legal service being provided by students is done by others, such as external lawyers acting on a pro bono basis.

The clinician in academia

It has long been recognised in the scholarly literature on clinical legal education that the role of the clinician is multifaceted and can be complex. Many clinicians find themselves simultaneously fulfilling some or all of the following roles: lawyer; clinical legal educator; legal practice manager/administrator; researcher or scholar; 'mainstream' law teacher; personal academic tutor; and holder of other departmental and/or institutional management or leadership responsibilities. This complex arrangement can give rise to challenges, tensions and opportunities.

One such well-reported dimension is the position and standing of 'the clinician' within the legal academy. Indeed, no encyclopedia entry on this topic would be complete without a consideration of the role and status of the clinician, relative to their traditional academic counterpart. In 2003, Chavkin described an academic community in the USA that was 'generally hostile' towards clinical legal education, in large part down to the perception that teaching law through clinical methods is academically less rigorous and demanding than the doctrinal study of law (Chavkin [2003]). Similar experiences have been reported in many other (although notably, not all) jurisdictions (for example, (Giddings and Lyman [2011]). Twenty years on from Chavkin's description, that experience may not be universal, but it remains the case in many law schools that, even where there is consensus on the value of clinical legal education, it continues to be perceived as 'something apart from the regular law curriculum' (Hall and Kerrigan [2011]). One reported consequence of this can be a sense of isolation on the part of some clinicians who are uniquely responsible for teaching through legal practice in an otherwise traditional law school, and in doing so, utilising teaching methods which may not be widely adopted or understood elsewhere in the department (Kinghan and Knowles [2018]).

Historically, clinicians have been afforded lower status positions; faced more limited scope for career progression; encountered greater barriers to promotion; and enjoyed less secure employment than other members of the legal academy (Nicolson et al [2023]).

Factors contributing to this may include: the distinctiveness of the clinician role within the academy which means its contribution is less easily understood; the different qualifications and prior experience many clinicians hold compared with their academic counterparts, which may not be readily recognised by the wider institution and in some cases may be considered inferior to the doctoral route; and the multiple demands on clinicians' time which can make engaging in research and scholarship (a core element of most academic posts) challenging (Blackburn [2018]).

The three primary elements of the clinician role are explored in greater detail below, along with examples of the particular opportunities and challenges posed by each.

The clinician as educator

All clinicians are, to varying extents, involved in teaching students during their participation in clinic, whether as credit bearing or extra-curricular activity. A clinician's teaching may take the form of direct supervision of students' legal work; providing training in lawyering skills such as client interviewing, legal drafting and professional conduct; and/or prompting reflective exercises to deepen students' learning, helping them to link theory to practice and so on. In the light of this, a number of other terms have been coined and used interchangeably and, in some cases, in preference to, the term 'clinician'. For example, 'teaching practitioner' (Kinghan and Knowles [2018]), 'clinical legal educator' (Bryant et al. [2014]) and 'clinical teacher' (Giddings and Lyman [2013]).

Whilst teaching methods will vary from clinic to clinic and from clinician to clinician, the pedagogical approach at the heart of clinical legal education means it is highly likely that a clinician will ascribe to the constructivist theory of learning. They will consider that students learn best when they are active participants in their own learning and are given the opportunity to engage with and apply their knowledge in a real-world context. Clinicians will couple this opportunity to 'learn by doing' with dedicated time and space for reflection on their learning experience (for more on the role of reflection in learning by doing, see (Gibbs [1988])).

The clinician as practitioner

Not all jurisdictions require those who supervise law clinics to be qualified and licensed lawyers. Indeed, in jurisdictions where this is not mandatory, there are many examples of outstanding legal clinics established and overseen exclusively by academic lawyers. However, where a clinician *is* professionally qualified, they are likely to be subject to the rules of professional conduct and regulation applicable in their jurisdiction. This can be challenging in jurisdictions where regulators have developed rules without having lawyers who are practising in university law clinics in mind. For a detailed examination of where professional regulation failed to consider the position of lawyers supervising in university law clinics see Thomas [2017].

At some point in their career, many clinicians feel themselves caught up in what Kinghan and Knowles describe as 'uncomfortable positions'; balancing their concurrent and, arguably competing, professional duties as lawyers and as educators (Kinghan and Knowles [2018]). As legal practitioners, clinicians are likely to have a professional obligation to act in the best interest of their client. Additional obligations arise where that client is vulnerable or has a legal issue which is time sensitive. Running in parallel to this, clinicians have a duty as educators to promote opportunities for students to learn. This is often achieved best in clinic by enabling students to grapple with complex tasks over a period of time and having the opportunity to try out different approaches, reflect and revise their approach accordingly. There may well be occasions where efficient client service and maximised opportunities for student learning are at odds. The question then arises as to which obligation ought to take precedence and when. For some clinicians, the principal objective of university law clinics should be to pursue a social justice imperative and therefore the provision of legal advice to those in need ought to be the clinic's (and therefore, by proxy, the clinician's) primary goal (Nicolson [2006]). Others consider that as along as clients receive 'effective' or 'competent' representation the clinician's primary focus should shift to 'maximizing educational benefits for the students involved' (Chavkin [2003]). Whilst neither of these perspectives eradicates the potential for clinicians to find themselves facing competing priorities, some reassurance can be found in the wisdom of experienced clinicians who assert that it is possible to address both parties' needs and minimise potential for competing interests through careful consideration in the design and model of clinic adopted (Brayne et al [1998]).

The clinician as scholar

There is an ever-growing body of scholarship by and for clinicians, often referred to as 'clinical legal scholarship' (Gold and Plowden [2011]). As outlined above, many clinicians will have contractual obligations to engage in research and scholarship and those on academic contracts will likely be required to produce such work in order to achieve promotion. The field of clinical legal scholarship can and does encompass lawyering skills; law and social change; and the clinical methodology (Bloch [2004]). However, engaging in scholarship can be challenging for some clinicians. Many will have come from practice and will lack the training in research methods that their academic counterparts who came to their current positions via doctoral study will have benefited from. Furthermore, the shape of the clinician's academic calendar and the demands on their time may also differ. Many clinicians will have to balance the demands of ongoing casework against their teaching responsibilities during term time and may need to continue casework outside of term time (Bloch [2004]). These are pulls on clinicians' time and energy that their traditional academic counterparts may not have, and who may be better able to enjoy greater opportunities to focus on research and scholarship as a result.

Notwithstanding the above, the case in favour of clinicians engaging in clinical legal scholarship is compelling and includes individual career progression, security and status for those who engage in it (Bloch [2004]), as well as potential to influence broader understandings and practices in legal education and in the legal profession and to improve the discipline of clinical legal education itself.

Communities of clinicians

Thus far, this entry has considered the clinician as an individual. However, the clinical legal education community is a generous and welcoming one and therefore it is fitting to conclude with reference to the communities of clinicians that exist across the globe. There are numerous national and international networks, which provide opportunities for clinicians to come together, share experiences, disseminate good practice and offer mutual support. Such networks provide a valuable outlet and source of professional support for clinicians, many of whom, as outlined above, may have limited opportunities to engage with others from their shared profession within their own institution.

At international level, the Global Alliance for Justice Education (GAJE), which was established in 1997, holds a bi-annual conference which brings together clinicians from across the globe. There are also numerous regional and national networks which all those working in and/or with an interest in, the field of clinical legal education would be well served by engaging with (Barry et al [2011]).

LINDEN THOMAS

References

Barry, M.M., Czernicki, P., Krasnicka, I. and Ling, M. (2011). 'The Role of National and Regional Clinical Organizations in the Global Clinic Movement', in Bloch, F.S. (ed), *The Global Clinical Movement: Educating Lawyers for Social Justice*, Oxford University Press.

Blackburn, L. (2018). 'Reimagining the Clinician Profile', in Thomas, L. et al (eds), *Reimagining Clinical Legal Education*, Hart Publishing.

Bloch, F. (2004). 'The Case for Clinical Scholarship', *International Journal of Clinical Legal Education*, 4, p. 7.

Brayne, H., Duncan, N. and Grimes, R. (1998). *Clinical Legal Education: Active Learning in your Law School*, Blackstone Press Limited.

Bryant, S., Milstein, E.S. and Shalleck, A.C. (2014). *Transforming the Education of Lawyers: The Theory and Practice of Clinical Pedagogy*, Carolina Academic Press.

Chavkin, D.F. (2003). 'Spinning Straw into Gold: Exploring the legacy of Bellow and Moulton', *Clinical Law Review*, 10, p. 245.

Gibbs, G. (1988). *Learning by Doing: A Guide to Teaching and Learning Methods*, FEU.

Giddings, J. and Lyman, J. (2011). 'Bridging Different Interests: The Contributions of Clinics to Legal Education', in Bloch, F.S. (ed), *The Global Clinical Movement: Educating Lawyers for Social Justice*, Oxford University Press.

Gold, N. and Plowden, P. (2011). 'Clinical Legal Scholarship and the Development of the Global Clinical Movement', in Bloch, F.S. (ed), *The*

Global Clinical Movement: Educating Lawyers for Social Justice, Oxford University Press.

Hall, J. and Kerrigan, K. (2011). 'Clinic and the Wider Law Curriculum', *International Journal of Clinical Legal Education*, 15.

Kinghan, J. and Knowles, R. (2018). 'Striking a Balance in Legal Education: Reimagining the Role of the Teaching-Practitioner in Casework Partnerships', in Thomas, L. et al (eds), *Reimagining Clinical Legal Education*, Hart Publishing.

Nicolson, D. (2006). 'Legal Education or Community Service? The Extra-Curricular Student Law Clinic', *Web Journal of Current Legal Issues*.

Nicolson, D., Newman, J. and Grimes, R. (2023). *How to Set Up and Run a Law Clinic: Principles and Practice*, Edward Elgar Publishing.

Thomas, L. (2017). 'Law Clinics in England & Wales: A regulatory Blackhole', *The Law Teacher*, 51(4), p. 469.

26. Comparative legal education

Introduction

At its most basic, the study of comparative legal education involves, as the name suggests, comparing the legal education delivered in one legal system, or 'jurisdiction', with that delivered in another jurisdiction (or more than one other). The purpose of learning and teaching using a comparative approach, and of comparative research into legal education, is to draw out, by the process of comparison, knowledge that could not be obtained by considering the same phenomena in isolation, within the confines of one jurisdiction (Samuel [2018] at 124).

However, this is not a simple exercise. Both legal education and law are closely tied to the legal and educational cultures of the societies in which they occur. As far as legal education is concerned, this means that there are wide variations in the content of the curriculum, as well as its intended purpose (for instance, is an undergraduate degree in law primarily intended for aspiring legal practitioners or is it an academic degree similar to those in other social science or humanities disciplines?). Acknowledging the importance of the cultural context of law and legal education has led comparativists increasingly to adopt a cultural approach to their work, both in terms of the way they teach and the way they research. They pay close attention to the fact that the legal phenomena being studied are the products of their cultural context (Samuel [2018] at 125).

Definition

There are two main aspects to comparative legal education. The first is in the context of education and training. Law students may be taught about the laws in jurisdictions other than the one in which they are studying (for example, students in Brazil might learn about the ways in which the law of contract is different in England or China to that which operates in Brazil). Equally, practising lawyers whose work requires them to have an understanding of one or more jurisdictions outside the one in which they are situated will also need training to enable them to advise their clients accurately.

The other main aspect of comparative legal education is that researchers may compare curriculum content and approaches in different jurisdictions in order to gain further knowledge about the nature of legal education. This entry will illustrate both of these aspects.

Learning and teaching comparative law

Law Students

From the point of view of the law student, there can be a number of potential benefits to studying law using a comparative perspective. These include acquiring a better understanding of one's own legal system, and developing a critical approach to that system, as well as having a deeper understanding of problematic legal issues, and ways in which they could be addressed (Husa [2018] at 203–204). When comparative law teaching is taken seriously, the aim is to get the students to think in the same way as the lawyers in the foreign jurisdiction they are studying. To do this they must '…exit the domestic legal system and enter another…' (Valcke [2004] at 175). The students must not only try to understand how lawyers in the foreign culture think about law, but also work out why they think that way. In other words, they must try to understand the 'legal mentality' of the foreign lawyer (Samuel [2018] at 127).

From the point of view of the law school and the law teacher, there are a number of challenges which have to be overcome if comparative legal education is to be taken seriously. Taking the cultural approach to teaching comparatively means that a law teacher must have in-depth expertise in the foreign legal system that is being studied, in order to draw out the social, economic and political contexts in which the foreign law is located (Valcke [2004] at 176). Valcke argues that the best way for students to gain real expertise in a foreign legal system is to be immersed in it, by way of student exchanges or (better still) graduate studies. However, she concedes that while this might be ideal, it is not an opportunity open to all students, so law teachers need to use their pedagogic expertise to provide students with the best possible comparative legal education while they remain in a domestic setting (Valcke [2004] at 177–178).

In some jurisdictions, it is possible for students to undertake a 'dual degree', which generally involves a period of study in two different jurisdictions, taking slightly longer than the standard undergraduate law degree. The student then graduates with two degrees – one from their 'home' institution, and one from the other jurisdiction. In order to study a dual degree, students require sufficient competency in the relevant foreign language to enable them to study their discipline at the foreign university, so this is also not an opportunity which is available to all students. However, for those who possess the relevant skill, a dual degree brings with it a number of potential benefits, including increased competency in the foreign language, familiarity with two legal systems, enhanced problem-solving abilities and cultural awareness (Bosch [2009] at 285). There is also some evidence which suggests that students graduating with a dual degree increase their chance of graduating with an Upper Second or First Class degree, as compared with students undertaking a conventional domestic law degree (Caldwell [2020] at 159–160).

Legal practitioners

Globalisation has affected the legal profession as much as any other aspect of life. As Childress III et al say in their textbook, *Transnational Law and Practice* ([2020]) 'In an increasingly globalised world, individuals, businesses and governments are interacting more and more frequently across national borders' (Childress III, Ramsey & Whytock [2020] at xxiv). Lawyers, especially (though not exclusively) those working in large multinational law firms, are increasingly being called upon to advise their clients about transnational legal problems. This calls for knowledge which does not necessarily form part of the legal education undergraduate curriculum; while some individuals may go on to gain knowledge of other legal systems by taking a postgraduate degree, this is by no means universal. Consequently, commentators have expressed concern about the demands being placed on legal practitioners to advise clients on transnational legal problems which are not addressed by their academic or professional training.

Hafner singles out international commercial arbitration as a process which often involves participants from different sociocultural backgrounds. This means that various national, commercial and legal cultures come into contact as the arbitration process progresses (Hafner [2011] at 117). For example, the legal professionals involved in an arbitration may be drawn from a civil law tradition (see France (Contemporary Legal Education)) and a Common Law tradition (see Doctrinal Legal Education). Superficially, they are performing the same task (applying the relevant legal rules to the material facts of the case and reaching a legal conclusion). However, the two systems proceed on very different assumptions. Hafner concludes 'In order to overcome the potential for intercultural communication difficulties in this context there is a need for arbitrators to develop a facility with multiple linguistic, legal and cultural codes. Ideally, such intercultural communicative competence would allow arbitrators to operate flexibly and effectively in a range of cultural context of dispute resolution' (Hafner [2011] at 127). However, as Whalen-Bridge points out, despite considerable discussion of globalisation, and the consequent realisation that lawyers need to be trained to function across different jurisdictions effectively, the resources for those wishing to provide education or training in comparative legal skills are not substantial (Whalen-Bridge [2008] at 366).

Researching legal education using a comparative perspective

Any comparative legal research involves complex questions of method, as well as of the relevant theoretical perspectives and comparative techniques which are needed to produce high-quality analysis. Legrand argues that it involves:

> ...not the abolition of difference, but the deft management of cultural heteronomies, the assumption of pluralism, the acceptance and coexistence of non-harmonised rationalities and the steady practice of a politics of inclusion to enlarge the possibility of intelligible discourse between laws. In short, difference must be understood and the temptation to erase it withstood (Legrand [2006] 365 at 367–368).

The objective of comparative research in legal education is to understand aspects of one or more different systems of legal education in the same way as the law students and law teachers belonging to those systems think about them, and to understand why they think the way they do. Samuel, following Legrand, characterises this as understanding their 'legal mentalité' (Samuel [2018] at 127). Cotterrell explains the fundamental importance of culture as a kind of lens or filter, through which all aspects of the legal phenomena being studied must be examined (Cotterrell [2006, quoted in Samuel [2018] at 126).

While there is not a great amount of comparative research into legal education, some researchers have ventured into this challenging field. Stolker looks at law schools across the world; while acknowledging the limitations to this ambitious project, he is able to offer comparative insights into topics such as the place of law as a discipline in the university, educating law students, creativity in law schools and the economic and societal impact of law schools (Stolker [2014]). Pérez-Perdomo (2024) takes a cultural-historical approach when he examines legal education in the western world from classical times onwards, focusing in particular on comparison between civil law jurisdictions and common law jurisdictions. In a large comparative research project on the legal profession, Abel, Sommerlad, Hammerslev and Schultz have edited two substantial volumes, both of which contain comparative material on legal education (Abel, Hammerslev, Sommerlad and Schultz [2020] and Abel, Sommerlad, Hammerslev and Schultz [2022]). The first volume contains reports on the legal professions of 46 jurisdictions throughout the world, many of which include insights into legal education and training. In the second volume, authors draw on the national data to engage in discussion and analysis of some key comparative issues, including a chapter on legal education (Hammerslev [2022]). Cownie's comparative analysis of law teachers in England and Canada is an example of a study with a more specific focus on one set of actors within the law school – those involved in delivering legal education (Cownie [2009]).

Conclusion

Despite the considerable challenges of teaching and researching comparatively, there is some very interesting comparative work going on within the discipline of law around the world. As an increasing number of law teachers and researchers recognise the importance of adopting a cultural perspective, the prospects for comparative legal education look positive.

FIONA COWNIE

References

Abel, R.L., Hammerslev, O., Sommerlad, H. and Schultz, U. (eds). (2020). *Lawyers in 21st-Century Societies: Volume 1: National Reports*, Hart Publishing.

Abel, R.L., Hammerslev, O., Sommerlad, H. and Schultz, U. (eds). (2022). *Lawyers in 21st-Century Societies: Volume 2: Comparisons and Theories*, Hart Publishing.

Bosch, G.S. (2009). 'The "Internationalisation" of law degrees and enhancement of graduate employability: European dual qualification degrees in law', *The Law Teacher*, p. 285.

Caldwell, P.J. (2020). 'Does Studying Abroad Help Academic Achievement?', *European Journal of Higher Education*, p. 147.

Childress III, D.E., Ramsay M.D. and Whytock, C. (2020). *Transnational Law and Practice*, Aspen.

Cotterrell, R. (2006). 'Comparative Law and Legal Culture' in Reimann, M. and Zimmermann, R. (eds), *The Oxford Handbook of Comparative Law*, Oxford University Press.

Cownie, F. (2009). 'Teaching, professional identity and academic lawyers: Canada and England – a comparative perspective', *Canadian Legal Education Annual Review*, p. 37.

Hafner, C.A. (2011). 'Professional Cultures, Legal Reasoning and Arbitral Awards', *World Englishes*, p. 117.

Hammerslev, O. (2022). 'Globalisation and Education: Reconfigurations in Location, Scale, Form and Content' in Abel, R.L., Sommerlad, H., Hammerslev, O. and Schultz, U. (eds), *Lawyers in 21st-Century Societies: Volume 2: Comparisons and Theories*, Hart Publishing.

Husa, J. (2018). 'Comparative Law in legal education – building a legal mind for a transnational world', *The Law Teacher*, p. 201.

Legrand, P. (2006). 'Comparative Legal Studies and the Matter of Authenticity', *J Comp L*, 1, p. 365.

Pérez-Perdomo, R. (2024). *Legal Education in the Western World: a cultural and comparative history*, Stanford University Press.

Samuel, G. (2018). 'Comparative Law and its Methodology', in Watkins, D. and Burton,

M. (eds), *Research Methods in Law*, 2nd edn, Routledge.

Sommerlad, H. and Hammerslev, O. (2022). 'Studying lawyers comparatively in the 21st century: Issues in Method and Methodology', in Abel, R.L., Sommerlad, H., Hammerslev, O. and Schultz, U. (eds), *Lawyers in 21st-Century Societies. Volume. 2: Comparisons and Theories*, Hart Publishing.

Stolker, K. (2014). *Rethinking the Law School: Education, Research, Outreach and Governance*, Cambridge University Press.

Valcke, C. (2004). 'Global Law Teaching', *Journal of Legal Education*, p. 160.

Whalen-Bridge, H. (2008). 'The Reluctant Comparativist: Teaching Common Law Legal Reasoning to Civil Law Students and the Future of Comparative Legal Skills', *Journal of Legal Education*, 58, p. 364.

27. Contemplative practices in legal education

Introduction

The 'transformative potential' of contemplative practices for legal education has been emphasised in the work of Magee ([2013] at 32), Director of the Center for Contemplative Law and Ethics at the University of San Francisco. Magee referred to such practices as 'key to developing socially just classrooms capable of delivering transformative education that works for all' (Magee [2017] at 126). This entry will address how contemplative practices are defined, rationales for their incorporation into legal education, and challenges to the utilisation of such practices in the teaching of law.

What are contemplative practices?

Davidson and Dahl define contemplative practices as a form of mental training emphasising 'self-awareness, self-regulation, and/or self-inquiry to enact a process of psychological transformation.' (Davidson and Dahl [2017] at E1). Accordingly, 'contemplative practices are typically viewed as practical methods to bring about a state of enduring well-being or inner flourishing' (Davidson and Dahl [2017] at E1). The definition is necessarily a broad one. In the context of higher education, contemplative practices include the use of meditation (Cullen [2019]), journaling (Edwards [2019]), and approaches to reading and writing that encourage conscious reflection (Bach and Alexander [2015]). The 'Tree of Contemplative Practices' published by Centre for Contemplative Mind in Society (CMind [2021]) lists further examples – such as deep listening, visualisation and improvisation – that may be employed in the teaching of law. The pedagogic value of such practices in legal education is currently an underexplored area of enquiry.

Pedagogic rationale for the use of contemplative practices

The rationale for the incorporation of contemplative practices into legal education is reflected in the pedagogic value that is attributed to such practices more generally:

> Contemplative pedagogy not only provides a way of helping students to concentrate more effectively, it incorporates ways of teaching and learning that can provide a very different learning experience by opening up new ways of knowing. This is achieved by moving beyond a technical, scientific training to incorporate body, mind and spirit by allowing the space for students to incorporate who they are and to understand how they are changed by what they learn. (Barratt [2017])

In the context of legal education, the value added by contemplative practices is often characterised in terms of support for student well-being or as a way of ameliorating of the ill-effects of stress (Cullen and Kerin [2020]). Contemplative practices such as meditation are also known to enhance the capacity to focus. As noted by Vines and Morgan 'meditation can increase students' ability to focus, retain and retrieve information. These skills are important for law students who rely heavily on memory and recall, as well as on the ability to objectively analyse situations and arguments' (Vines and Morgan [2016] at 173). Meditation as a contemplative practice is also known to support the reflexivity enhancing an array of competencies 'related to lawyer effectiveness, including ... ethical and rational decision-making' (Buchanan et al [2017] at 53). The basis for the incorporation of such contemplative practices into legal education is thus one that is multi-faceted. While efficacy is supported by research in a variety of different contexts, the utilisation of completive practices in legal education is currently impeded by a number of issues.

Incorporating contemplative practices into legal education

Vines and Morgan state that '[t]he last forty years of neuroscience, psychology and meditation research has provided evidence for the benefits of contemplation generally and specifically in education ... These findings provided the initial impetus for teaching contemplative practices to law students and lawyers' (Vines and Morgan [2016] at 172). While the approach employed may be one that is evidence-based, the inclusion of contemplative practices in legal education has moved slowly for a number of reasons. First, academic staff are often not familiar with such practices. Without such familiarity, it is not possible to speak from personal experience of the benefits. Second, students sometimes place less value on that which is not subject to assessment or does not add to a CV. This is in part due to the creation of expectations concentrating more on the external measurement of performance and less on how the internal world of the student is shaped by the experience of law school. Third, the incorporation of contemplative practices does not align well with the neo-liberalist orientation of many institutions of higher education. Excessive workloads, extreme levels of competition, high levels of debt, and a lack of attention to individual well-being often result in academic environments that are less open to sustainable engagement with contemplation practices.

While each of the issues mentioned above is significant, none is insurmountable. Academic staff can be trained in completive practices and law students sensitised to the benefits. The most significant challenge is in the pervasive aspect of law school culture which focuses on 'extrinsic values of comparative worth, such as their class rank, grades, honors, and salary offers' (Huang [2018] at 458). As noted by Huang, 'Law school often alters law students in many truly fundamental ways, some that are very undesirable personally and societally. The displacement of intrinsic values by extrinsic values that happens to many law students reduces their subjective well-being, deep sense of meaning or purpose, and self-concordance' ([2018] at 458). A re-ordering of pedagogic priorities is required. Placing student well-being at the heart of legal education, the incorporation of contemplative practices would serve not only to strengthen personal efficacy in the study and practice of law, it could also serve to support the aim of education as stated in Article 26(2) of the Universal Declaration of Human Rights: 'the full development of the human personality'.

Conclusion

The use of contemplative practices to support student well-being is well-evidenced in scientific literature (Cullen and Kerin [2019]). In the context of legal education, the mental training involved is also known to enhance

focus and reflexivity. The transformative potential of contemplative practices is evident not only in the published research but also from first-person phenomenological accounts of such practices. In this context, contemplative practices engage a depth and breadth of experience which goes beyond that conventionally associated with the study of law, creating space for a more holistic approach to legal education. It is only by adopting such an approach that well-being can be accorded the place it deserves in curriculum design and legal pedagogy.

ANTHONY CULLEN

References

Bach, D.J. and Alexander, J. (2015). 'Contemplative Approaches to Reading and Writing: Cultivating Choice, Connectedness, and Wholeheartedness in the Critical Humanities', *The Journal of Contemplative Inquiry*, 2, p. 17.

Barbezat, D. and Bush, M. (2013). *Contemplative Practices in Higher Education: Powerful Methods to Transform Teaching and Learning*, Wiley.

Barratt, S.C. (2017). 'What is contemplative pedagogy?', Contemplative Pedagogy Network, available at https://contemplativepedagogynetwork.com/what-is-contemplative-pedagogy/.

Buchanan, B., Coyle, J., Brafford, A., Campbell, D, Camson, J., Gruber, C., Harrell, T., Jaffe, D., Kepler, T., and Krill, P. (2017). 'The Path to Lawyer Well-Being: Practical Recommendations for Positive Change (The Report of the National Task Force on Lawyer Well-Being), Part II, Recommendations for Law Schools'.

CMind. (2021). 'The Tree of Contemplative Practices [Illustration]', The Center for Contemplative Mind in Society, available at https://www.contemplativemind.org/practices/tree.

Cullen, A. (2019). 'Cultivating a Reflective Approach to the Practice of Law: The Use of Meditation in Legal Education', *Southwestern Law Review*, 48, p. 343.

Cullen, A. and Kerin, L. (2019). 'The incorporation of meditation into legal education', in Denley, E. and Kaur, T. (eds), *Consciousness in Management*, Heartfulness Education Trust, p. 182.

Cullen, A. and Kerin, L. (2020). 'Meditation in legal education: The value added toward the well-being of law students', in Strevens, C. and Field, R. (eds), *Educating for Well-Being in Law: Positive Professional Identities and Practice*,

Emerging Legal Education, Routledge, Taylor & Francis Group.

Davidson, R.J. and Dahl, C.J. (2017). 'Varieties of contemplative practice', *JAMA psychiatry*, 74, p. 121.

Edwards, S. (2019). 'Reflective journaling as contemplative practice', in Lin, J., Culham, T.E. and Edwards, S. (eds), *Contemplative Pedagogies for Transformative Teaching, Learning, and Being: Transforming Education for the Future*, IAP.

Huang, P.H. (2018). 'Adventures in Higher Education, Happiness, and Mindfulness', *British Journal of American Legal Studies*, 7, p. 427

Lewinbuk, K.P. (2015). 'Lawyer Heal Thy Self: Incorporating Mindfulness into Legal Education and Profession', *Journal of the Legal Profession*, 40, p. 1.

Magee, R. (2016). 'Legal Education as Contemplative Inquiry: An Integrative Approach to Legal Education, Law Practice, and the Substance of the Law We Make', *The Journal of Contemplative Inquiry*, 3, p. 7.

Magee, R. (2013). 'Contemplative practices and the renewal of legal education', *New Directions for Teaching and Learning*, 134, p. 31.

Magee, R. (2017). 'One Field, Different Doors In: Contemplative Higher Education, Transformative Education, and Education for Social Justice', *Social Justice, Inner Work & Contemplative Practice*, 1(1), p. 119.

Riskin, L.L. (2002). 'The contemplative lawyer: On the potential contributions of mindfulness meditation to law students, lawyers, and their clients', *Harvard Negotiation Law Review*, 7, p. 1.

Rogers, H.B. (2013). 'Mindfulness meditation for increasing resilience in college students', *Psychiatric Annals*, 43, p. 545.

Rogers, S.L. (2013). 'The Role of Mindfulness in the Ongoing Evolution of Legal Education', *University of Arkansas at Little Rock Law Review*, 36, p. 387.

Romaskiewicz, P. (2021). '"Teaching of" and "Teaching about" Meditation: The Legal Limits and Educational Prospects of a Contemplative Pedagogy', *The Wabash Center Journal on Teaching*, 2, p. 85.

Vines, P. and Morgan, P. (2016). 'Contemplative practice in the law school: Breaking barriers to learning and resilience', in Field, R., Duffy, J. and James, C. (eds), *Promoting law student and lawyer well-being in Australia and beyond*, Routledge.

28. Continuing professional development of legal professionals

Introduction

In common with many professions, regulators of legal practitioners usually require individuals to engage in continuing education after their initial training. The precise arrangements vary between jurisdictions and from regulator to regulator, and different models of continuing professional development (CPD) exist. While CPD aims to support individuals in maintaining the knowledge and skills they need to be competent to practice, there are barriers to achieving this. This entry considers CPD in the context of legal practitioners, including compliance and benefits CPD models, CPD activities and factors which impact upon whether these activities are accessible and effective.

CPD may be described as an ongoing process of formal and informal learning, undertaken after initial training, that supports an individual in maintaining and enhancing the knowledge, skills and professional standards they need to remain competent in their professional practice. It is often perceived to be a formal, structured process, even though informal learning also occurs, notably in the workplace.

The learning gained from CPD is not confined to maintaining competence. It may also be an essential part of developing competence in legal practitioners, particularly in jurisdictions where there is no requirement to undertake a period of supervised workplace training as a condition for admission to practice (Chakraborty & Gosh [2015]) or where individuals are moving into new areas of work.

Specific CPD requirements for legal practitioners are usually determined by the relevant regulatory bodies. Historically, the requirements in many jurisdictions have been largely compliance-focused. However, in more recent years there has been a shift towards benefits-focused arrangements.

CPD can be referred to using a range of different terminology, including continuing professional development, continuing professional education, continuing legal education, outcomes-focused, compliance model, benefits model, and maintaining competence.

Models of CPD

There are multiple models of CPD. Writing in the context of teachers, for example, Kennedy identifies nine models (Kennedy [2005]). However, for legal practitioners, there are two key CPD models: compliance and benefits.

A compliance model focuses on 'inputs' and mandates certain requirements, such as to spend a certain number of hours on CPD activities and/or to complete specified courses, for example in relation to ethics or advocacy. Sanctions for non-compliance act as both a deterrent and a punishment. A compliance model may help to maintain minimum standards and ensure that individuals undertake, and employers support, a certain level of CPD activity (Henderson et al [2012]). In jurisdictions where there is no requirement to complete a period of supervised training before being admitted to practice, or concerns about a lack of competence in the profession, a compliance model may be necessary to ensure that individuals engage in at least a minimum amount of CPD activity (Chakraborty & Gosh [2015]). However, the compliance model has been criticised for assuming that meaningful learning and development will result simply from undertaking a certain volume of activity (Webb et al [2013]). Stipulating that individuals must undertake a certain number of hours of CPD activities may create the impression that this is sufficient to ensure competence, or that undertaking fewer hours will diminish competence. A compliance model may lead individuals to focus upon activities that demonstrate compliance, rather than to develop knowledge and skills which they can then put into practice (Webb et al [2013]). In particular, a CPD model that focuses on quantifiable inputs can lead to a perception that learning and development is something which only happens in a formal (classroom) environment, so individuals may not recognise the informal learning which occurs elsewhere, notably in the workplace.

A benefits model focuses upon 'outcomes', though it may still include a requirement to complete a number of hours of CPD activity. This model aims to ensure that the burden of complying with regulations is not excessive, and that individuals are not obliged to undertake CPD activities that are not relevant to them. Therefore, a benefits model may result in more meaningful learning, by allowing individuals to determine their own development needs and identify activities that will meet those needs. With its focus upon outcomes, a benefits model encourages individuals to undertake a wider variety of activities, and to recognise their informal learning, which typically occurs in the workplace (Evers et al [2011]) and is a significant contributor to professional competence (Cheetham & Chivers [2001]). Even with a benefits model, however, there may be mandated activities, for example to ensure compliance with external regulations, such as those relating to anti-money laundering. Moreover, more precise planning and reviewing is required in relation to learning objectives and outcomes, to ensure that CPD is effective.

CPD regulations for legal practitioners vary between jurisdictions and between different types of legal practitioner, such that there is no single, consistent approach, nor a recognised model of international best practice. However, a benefits model is increasingly more likely to be used than a compliance model.

CPD activities

CPD activities are offered by a range of providers, including commercial organisations, academic institutions, regulatory bodies and legal practitioners. The activities that are offered largely reflect the regulations applicable to the provider's target market, as well as general market demand.

While CPD regulations vary in different jurisdictions and for different branches of the legal professions, many will encompass both formal and informal activities, including not just attendance at courses, but also delivering courses, participating in mentoring or coaching, writing books and papers, studying for academic and professional qualifications, and undertaking research. However, CPD regulations usually exclude work that is undertaken as part of the individual's routine legal practice, even though learning through experience can be significant for professionals in their acquisition of knowledge and development of skills (Cheetham & Chivers [2001]). This exclusion is presumably designed to avoid an individual claiming to have fulfilled regulatory requirements simply by performing their everyday role.

CPD activities are not confined to technical legal knowledge, but include a range of professional skills and standards, such as advocacy, equality and diversity, use of artificial intelligence, and management training. Increasingly, legal practitioners need to consider their readiness to operate in a globalised marketplace. Some countries, such as South Korea, recognise the importance for legal practitioners to have a working knowledge of different aspects of international law, and incorporate this into their core law school curriculum (Chakraborty & Gosh [2015]). Where this is not the case, however, there is potential for CPD activities to fill the gaps.

Moreover, regulators may mandate certain CPD activity, with the specific requirements varying between jurisdictions and professions. Mandatory requirements incline towards skills rather than doctrinal law. For example, for legal practitioners who undertake advocacy (e.g. barristers), it is common for regulators to impose requirements to undertake regular advocacy training. Ethics and professionalism are also areas where it is common for regulators to stipulate a certain amount of regular training.

Legal practitioners working in environments which are not exclusively 'legal' in nature may have additional training and development needs linked to the broader nature of their employing organisation. For example, a legal practitioner working within a public body will need not only the requisite legal expertise for the transactions they undertake on behalf of their employer, but also a detailed understanding of the legal structure and regulatory powers of the public body itself.

Furthermore, an individual's training and development needs are not static, but change over time, notably as they gain experience and seniority or move into a new role. Therefore, the nature and level of CPD activities they undertake needs to reflect this. For example, legal practitioners in the early stages of their careers may be primarily concerned with building their technical legal expertise (see, for example, Henderson et al [2012] in relation to solicitors in England & Wales). Indeed, a command of the law and the logical thought processes involved in using the law to address a client's problem are valuable to legal practitioners at all career stages, and many have traditionally valued CPD activities as contributing to this (Daley [2001]). However, legal practitioners may incorporate more CPD activity in relation to financial, business and people management as they progress into more senior roles, where a different skillset is required.

Factors impacting upon accessibility and effectiveness of CPD for legal practitioners

Despite the prevalence of CPD requirements for legal practitioners, this will not always assure ongoing competence or enhance their knowledge and skills. In particular, CPD may not result in learning that is meaningful, unless the individual actively applies that learning to their professional practice, combining it with existing knowledge and observing its effects in their interactions with clients (Eraut [1994] and Daley [2001]). For example, an individual may learn from attending a CPD course what the law says about a client's strict legal rights in relation to a breach of contract, but they also need to learn how to use that information to provide advice to a client that is not just legally correct, but can realistically be acted upon by that client (Ching [2015]). In this respect, formal learning via CPD, and informal learning in the workplace reinforce each other (Van der Heijden et al [2009]).

Despite its limitations, dispensing entirely with a requirement for legal practitioners to undertake CPD activity is unlikely to be palatable to the general public, who expect legal practitioners to be competent to provide client services. Moreover, it is not the case that CPD is never beneficial, but rather that there are factors which impact upon its accessibility and effectiveness that need to be recognised and addressed.

Regulators increasingly require individuals to undertake a process of planning, implementing, evaluating and reflecting, as part of an annual CPD process, especially where a benefits model is in place. This approach draws upon Kolb's work in experiential learning (Kolb [1984]) and while there are some criticisms of the learning cycle proposed by Kolb, its simplicity and adaptability (Kolb and Kolb [2018]) make it a useful tool in many learning contexts, including CPD.

Even with careful planning, however, where legal practitioners have limited funds available for CPD, this may drive them towards low-cost activities, which may be irrelevant or ineffective (see, for example, Henderson et al [2012]). This is particularly the case where regulators mandate certain activities or require some or all activities to be formally accredited. In such cases, the choice of CPD activity undertaken to comply with regulatory requirements may be dictated by what is available at a price that the individual can afford. CPD that is focused upon the development of skills such as advocacy, or niche and specialist areas, is typically more expensive to deliver, thus increasing the price that the provider needs to charge.

CPD activities may not be offered in all locations, thus limiting access for some individuals. For example, in England & Wales, more specialist or niche training may only be available in London or the larger cities. In Mongolia, where a high percentage of the population is concentrated in once city (Ulaanbaatar), there are obvious challenges in providing CPD opportunities to the lower numbers of legal practitioners in more remote areas. However, there is scope for innovative approaches by regulators and providers to improve access. While there are concerns around engagement with e-learning, this can facilitate access to CPD opportunities in areas where resources may be limited, as long as users perceive the offer to have useability, quality and value (Chiu et al [2005]). For example, the Mongolian Bar Association has developed an app which provides a wide range of online CPD activities to legal practitioners, available at any time and place, and which successfully blends regulatory objectives with an informed pedagogical stance (Ching and Henderson [2019]).

For legal practitioners generally, client work typically takes precedence, which may mean that CPD which an individual had planned to undertake is abandoned in favour of completing client work, especially urgent matters. The individual may later undertake whatever CPD activity is available that they can use to demonstrate at least nominal compliance with regulatory requirements, even if this is not relevant or useful to them. This problem may be mitigated by encouraging a work environment in which learning and growth is valued, aligning the needs of both the individual and the employer (Collin, Van der Heijden and Lewis [2012]).

PAMELA HENDERSON

Conclusion

CPD can contribute to ongoing competence for legal practitioners, but it is not without its challenges and limitations. A benefits model, coupled with a thoughtful planning process, is the approach most likely to support individuals in undertaking activities that will lead to meaningful learning and development.

PAMELA HENDERSON

References

Chakraborty, A. and Ghosh, Y. (2015). 'Promoting continuing legal education: a step towards implementing the second generation legal reforms for creating competent lawyers in the new century', *Asian Journal of Legal Education*, 2(1), p. 29.

Cheetham, G. and Chivers, G. (2001). 'How professionals learn in practice: an investigation of informal learning amongst people working in professions', *Journal of European Industrial Training*, 25(5), p. 247.

Ching, J. (2015). '"Favourable variations": towards a refreshed approach for the interviewing classroom', *Legal Education Review*, 25(1), p. 173.

Ching, J. and Henderson, P. (2019). Providing advisory support and training on best practices in education and training techniques for legal professionals, Ulaanbaatar, Mongolia: Asia Foundation, available at https://irep.ntu.ac.uk/id/eprint/37041/.

Chiu, C.M., Hsu, M.H., Sun, S.Y., Lin, T.C. and Sun, P.C. (2005). 'Usability, quality, value and e-learning continuance decisions', *Computers & Education*, 45(4), p. 399.

Collin, K., Van der Heijden, B. and Lewis, P. (2012). 'Continuing professional development', *International Journal of Training and Development*, 16, p. 155.

Daley, B.J. (2001). 'Learning and professional practice: A study of four professions', *Adult Education Quarterly*, 52(1), p. 39.

Eraut, M. (1994). *Developing professional knowledge and competence*, Psychology Press.

Evers, A.T., Van der Heijden, B.I., Kreijns, K. and Gerrichhauzen, J.T. (2011). 'Organisational factors and teachers' professional development in Dutch secondary schools', *Journal of European Industrial Training*, 35(1), p. 24.

Henderson, P., Wallace, S., Jarman, J. and Hodgson, J. (2012). Solicitors Regulation Authority: CPD Review, Nottingham: Nottingham Law School, available at https://irep.ntu.ac.uk/id/eprint/20486/.

Kennedy, A. (2005). 'Models of continuing professional development: A framework for analysis', *Journal of In-service Education*, 31(2), p. 235.

Kolb, D. (1984). *Experiential learning: experience as the source of learning and development*, Prentice Hill.

Kolb, A. and Kolb, D. (2018). 'Eight important things to know about the experiential learning cycle', *Australian Educational Leader*, 40(3), p. 8.

Van Der Heijden, B., Boon, J., Van der Klink, M. and Meijs, E. (2009). 'Employability enhancement through formal and informal learning: an empirical study among Dutch non-academic university staff members', *International Journal of Training and Development*, 13(1), p. 37.

Webb, J., Ching, J., Maharg, P. and Sherr, A. (2013). 'Setting standards: the future of legal services education and training regulation in England and Wales: the final report of the Legal Education and Training Review independent research team, June 2013', *Legal Education and Training Review*, available at https://irep.ntu.ac.uk/id/eprint/26418/.

29. Creativity in legal education

Introduction

Law can be characterised as a heavily text-based discipline. Students spend much time reading weighty textbooks, journal articles and appellate judgments. They are commonly assessed via written work, such as essays and problem-style questions. However, in recent years there have been a range of challenges to this conventional approach and an increasing emphasis on the need to integrate creative approaches to teaching and research and foster creativity amongst students.

The term 'creativity' has been defined in a range of ways but is generally accepted to refer to 'the production of novel and useful ideas and products' (Walia [2019] at 237). This does not necessarily infer a particular artistic focus, for example, in recent years the playing of educational video games has been found to improve student creativity, with suitable inspirational and instructional support in place (Rahimi & Shute [2021]).

This entry considers some of the ways in which different forms of creativity have been integrated into legal education, with a particular emphasis on the integration of non-text-based modalities into law teaching. In doing so, it echoes the argument of Bańkowski et al that:

> ...[T]he teaching and research of law can be experienced in ways that do not depend exclusively on text, but that have recourse to the full range and diversity of the sensory capacities of teachers, students, professionals and scholars' (Bańkowski et al [2013] at 1).

In other words, it argues that it is both possible and desirable for legal education to integrate creativity within its approaches to teaching and learning. Doing so can not only enhance student (and staff) motivation and engagement, but also have positive benefits in terms of students' graduate attributes and employability (Rampersad & Patel [2014]).

Creative methods within legal education

There is some evidence that traditional methods of teaching law do not foster creativity, or even actively discourage it. Research conducted at The Australian National University found that students' thinking styles altered during their first year of legal studies. Their rational thinking scores increased over the year, whereas their experiential thinking scores (which encompass intuitive thinking) decreased. In part at least this seemed to be due to the individualistic, competitive and isolating nature of their studies (Towness O'Brien et al [2011]). Given that intuitive thinking is an integral part of the creative process (Hardman [2021]), this suggests that law students' propensity for creativity is being reduced. The growing interest in creativity in legal education seeks to challenge many of these traditional norms within law schools and instead engage in innovative and creative pedagogical approaches.

One example of such approaches is the use of music in law teaching. For example, Collinson describes integrating into two undergraduate law modules at the University of Huddersfield in the UK ('Law in Society' and 'Immigration and Asylum Law'). He identifies five different ways in which music was used, namely '(a) as an icebreaker; (b) to set the tone; (c) to explore questions of representation; (d) to tell stories; and (e) to make theory tangible' (Collinson [2023] at 156). Theatre has also been used, for example, Sheikh ([2020]) describes designing an elective undergraduate law degree module on 'Legal Theatre: Exploring Gender and Sexuality through a Performative Lens' at the Jindal Global Law School in India. This involved both reading existing theatrical texts and judicial decisions and constructing and performing original play scripts (Sheikh [2020] at 116). Poetry, art, dance and many other forms of creativity can also be incorporated.

It should be noted that such creative methods are not restricted solely to degree-level legal studies. One of these is the adaption of the popular UK television show 'Taskmaster' in which five comedians are set a series of 'nonsensical and joyful' tasks. This has been used as the basis of widening participation work with primary aged children (approximately 4 to 11 years old) to provide them with an understanding of the law and encourage the development of relevant skills:

> We do not encourage rote learning of legal concepts or cases; we pose problems and encourage the children to think creatively, critically and collaboratively about their solutions. Is a Jaffa Cake a cake or a biscuit? If a car is placed on roller-skates on the road, is it actually on the road? If you bite off someone's nose, are you infringing a statute that prohibits assault with a weapon? (Struthers & McConnell [2023] at 2 and 4).

This can be characterised as one example of game based learning (see Game Based Learning in Legal Education), a creative pedagogy which is becoming increasingly engaged with throughout legal education. Another example of this is the development of the 'Mediation Game' piloted by law students at Chiang Mai University in Thailand. This is a board game designed to develop law students' skills in advocacy, negotiation and other skills relevant to mediation as a dispute resolution process (Luengvilai & Yodmongkol [2016]).

The development of digital technology has also led to new forms of creative engagement. This can be in terms of the medium used for teaching and learning, for example, developing an 'electronic roll-and-move board game, named the *Grade Inflation Game*' for students of tort law at Singapore Management University (designed by their Centre for Teaching Excellence) (Chan et al [2017] at 7). However, it can also be through harnessing some of the processes commonly used within technological development, such as the process of legal design. For example, research conducted in the Australian context suggests that incorporating design thinking methodologies into legal education can, through encouraging different perspectives on and approaches to problem-solving, foster 'empathic, creative, and innovative thinking skills as an alternative to the traditional institutionalised way of producing lawyers' (Hewes et al [2023] at 101352). Even the imaginative incorporation of AI literacies (see AI Literacies in Legal Education) can both demonstrate and foster creativity, in part, due to its interdisciplinary nature (using learning from computer science). Drawing upon other disciplines in addition to law can encourage students to think in new and different ways,

in other words, creatively (Moirano et al [2020]).

The examples discussed in this section suggest innovative fusions of disciplines and pedagogies. However, even within more traditional legal studies, there is still scope for creativity. For example, Nussbaum argues for the importance of developing students' 'narrative imagination' including 'the ability to think what it might be like to be in the shoes of a person different from oneself, to be an intelligent reader of that person's story, and to understand the emotions, wishes and desires that someone so placed might have' ([2003] at 270). This can be done through literature, as witnessed by the 'law and literature' movement. However, it is arguable that engagement with case law could also stimulate rich and imaginative responses in this way. Other common aspects of legal studies can also be used creatively, for example, James ([2012] at 80) describes how applying critical thinking to legal reasoning can shift its formalistic focus to encompass factors such as 'policy considerations, commercial realities, non-adversarial solutions and a concern for social justice and the wellbeing of others'.

A final aspect of creativity in legal education which should be acknowledged is the potential for law students to be assessed in a creative manner, moving away from the examinations and essay and problem-style questions often associated with legal studies. For example, asking students to create of audio-visual activities, write blog posts, design and construct artefacts and/or incorporating forms of authentic assessment (Bedford et al [2024]).

Conclusion

Creativity can exist, and be inspired by, numerous facets of legal education. Although traditional approaches have often ignored or stifled this potential, within contemporary law schools (and beyond) there are many examples of creativity being acknowledged and fostered. These examples range from incorporating artistic interests and methodologies into teaching, to applying games-based pedagogies to developing innovative uses of digital technology to introducing new forms of assessment. They cover both more traditional legal knowledge and skills and newer additions to the field in a way which indicates creativity is becoming increasingly embedded within legal pedagogy.

EMMA JONES

References

Bańkowski, Z., Del Mar, M. and Maharg, P. (2013). 'Introduction', in Bańkowski, Z., Del Mar, M. and Maharg, P. (eds), *The Arts & The Legal Academy: Beyond Text in Legal Education*, Ashgate Publishing Company.

Bedford, N., Bonython, W. and Taylor, A. (2024). 'Law as it is, and how it could be: law reform participation as authentic assessment and a pedagogical tool', *The Law Teacher*, 58(1).

Chan, K.Y.G., Tan, S.L., Hew, K.F.T., Koh, B.G., Lim, L.S. and Yong, J.C.* (2017). 'Knowledge for games, games for knowledge: designing a digital roll-and-move board game for a law of torts class', *Research and Practice in Technology Enhanced Learning*, 12, p. 7.

Collinson, C. (2023). 'Integrating music into the study of law to engage students', *The Law Teacher*, 57(2), 155.

Hardman, T.J. (2021). 'Understanding creative intuition', *Journal of Creativity*, 31, p. 100006.

Hews, R., Beligatamulla, G. and McNamara, J. (2023). 'Creative confidence and thinking skills for lawyers: Making sense of design thinking pedagogy in legal education', *Thinking Skills and Creativity*, 49, p. 101352.

James, N. (2012). 'Logical, critical and creative: Teaching "thinking skills" to law students', *Law and Justice Journal*, 12(1), p. 66.

Luengvilai, C. and Yodmongkol, P. (2016). 'Mediation Game When the Conflict Can Be Fun to Learn – A Legal Skill Learning Tool: The Integration of Knowledge Management, Learning Theory and Serious Game Concept', *International Education Studies*, 9(5), p. 219.

Moirano, R., Sánchez, M.A. and Štěpánek, L. (2020). 'Creative interdisciplinary collaboration: A systematic literature review', *Thinking Skills and Creativity*, 35, p. 100626.

Nussbaum, M.C. (2003). 'Cultivating Humanity in Legal Education', *University of Chicago Law Review*, 70(1), p. 265.

Townes O'Brien, M., Tang, S. and Hall, K. (2011). 'Changing our thinking: Empirical research on law student wellbeing, thinking styles and the law curriculum', *Legal Education Review*, 21(1/2), p. 149.

Rahimi, S. and Shute, V.J. (2021). 'First inspire, then instruct to improve students' creativity', *Computers & Education*, 174, p. 104312.

Rampersad G. and Patel, F. (2014). 'Creativity as a desirable graduate attribute: Implications for curriculum design and employability', *Asia-Pacific journal of cooperative education*, 15(1), p. 1.

Sheikh, D. (2020). 'Legal theatre: Staging critique in the law school', *Australian Feminist Law Journal*, 46(1), p. 115.

Struthers, A.E.C. and McConnell, S. (2024). 'Improve children's legal knowledge and skills through School Tasking: your time starts now', *The Law Teacher*, 58(1), p. 1.

Walia, C. (2019). 'A Dynamic Definition of Creativity', *Creativity Research Journal*, 31(1), p. 237.

30.   Critical legal studies

What is (or was, or could or should be) the relationship between legal education and critical legal studies? Surely all legal education, at least these days, aspires in some generic sense to be critical? (Another way of expressing this point would be to say that no self-respecting law teacher nowadays would describe their practice as the uncritical transmission of legal doctrine from teacher to student!) Contemporary legal education, indeed pretty much all university education in the humanities and social sciences, aspires in the broad sense to equip its students with a set of critical skills, orientations and dispositions – analytical and reading capacities, for example, but not only these – that will help them navigate and make sense of legal (and social, political, economic, etc.) texts and how they function in the world. Today's law student is encouraged to be a critic of legal text in this, broad, sense (which we often see embedded in course or programme learning outcomes, or graduate attributes, under the guise of 'Critical Thinking') (cf. Golder [2021]). Once the law student is trained in the arcane arts of 'thinking like a lawyer' (Mertz [2007], Seale [2020]) they are enjoined to deploy their newfound lawyerly skills on their own account and not to accept professorial dogma and doctrine – sapere aude (dare to think for yourself) could well be the motto of today's critical law student (cf. Kant (1784) [1996]). But as the course learning and programme outcomes, and the graduate attributes, teach us – this classic, Kantian conception of critical (legal) thinking is entirely consistent with (indeed, a prerequisite for) gainful future employment in the legal marketplace. No self-respecting partner of a law firm would admit to wanting to hire a young lawyer who did not think for herself.

But 'critical legal studies' refers to something more precise, and a little less conducive to future employment prospects, than the kind of critical thinking that helps one make analytical sense of ambiguous texts and navigate contested lines of precedent. Essentially, critical legal studies is a body of thought that critiques the presuppositions and founding tenets of the legal system itself. Critical legal studies in this more precise and radical sense criticises the law's pretensions to objectivity and neutrality and argues instead that law is inescapably political and that it is invested in maintaining social and economic hierarchies (of class, of race, of gender and sexuality, and so forth). It is critical of law and of the ways that its traditional reasoning processes and practices work to reproduce injustice and unfairness. Understood in this sense, we might well ask (indeed, many have), what business does such a body of thought have in the university law school? Might it not stand in some intellectual and institutional tension with the aspirations of the first kind of critical practice? Might it not get in the way of, disrupt even, the critical businesslike task of thinking like a lawyer? We could well go back several centuries to find the sources (both within and without law – including in philosophy and history, social theory and sociology, etc.) of this way of thinking critically about law. But one has to start somewhere and in a *Concise Encyclopedia* such as the one you are reading the brief is to be simultaneously concise and encyclopaedic. So the focus here is on an example of a particular group of critical legal scholars and teachers of the late twentieth century that is, despite its particularity, reflective of some of the common tensions of maintaining this project of critical thinking about law from within the law school. The example is the well-rehearsed one of the Critical Legal Studies (CLS) movement in the United States towards the end of the last century. It is important to stress that this is a particular example, because, given the hegemonic influence of the American legal academy, US-based examples are too readily used as synecdoches and I want to stress there are many more things in critical legal heaven and earth than are dreamt of in New Haven and Harvard Yard. CLS (uppercase) does not exhaust the meaning of critical legal studies (lowercase) – there were and are rival traditions of thinking critically about law (Goodrich [1999], Gearey [2006], van Marle and Modiri [2016]). However, this US-centric example is a useful example because the proponents of CLS, as it came to be called, drew a particularly close and interesting connection between legal education and critical legal thinking and because the efflorescence of CLS in American law schools in the late 1970s and 1980s tells us something interesting, important and ultimately salutary about this connection (and its future in our own time).

CLS had its heyday in American law classrooms of the late 1970s and 1980s and, according to received accounts, melded the methodological insights and political orientations of American legal realism (of the 1920s and 1930s), the New Left and the Marxist and theoretical traditions of post-War European social and political thought (phenomenology, structuralism, post-structuralism). There are a multitude of received accounts one could consult in order to pursue the intellectual genealogy of CLS and the vagaries of its short-lived institutionalisation and long-term influence over American (but not only American) legal thought and legal educational practice. For instance, the relevant chapter in *Asking the Law Question* (Davies [2017]) is both a rich and clear introduction to the movement. Secondly, less textual yet more intimate and anecdotal, is the podcast produced by Jon Hanson of Harvard Law School entitled 'Critical Legal Theory' and featuring long-form interviews with several of the lead protagonists of the original CLS (Duncan Kennedy and David Trubek). See here: https://criticallegaltheory.buzzsprout .com/.

CLS was led by a group of largely male, largely white, self-professedly radical law professors at a select group of elite US law schools (Yale and Harvard). One of the things that made it distinctive was the fact that it was legal theory written out of, about, and to, the law classroom. CLS as a body of critical legal thought was constitutively pedagogic. This is by no means a necessary connection, despite the fact that much legal theory (critical or otherwise) is authored by legal scholars (who when not theorising law are gainfully employed to teach it to university students). Yet whereas much legal theory either floated free of the classroom in (analytic or Germanic) abstraction, or productively moved beyond the classroom, CLS was a constitutively pedagogic enterprise. The law classroom was its métier. It explicitly addressed itself to the production, reproduction and transmission of legal knowledge. It was a critique of legal education. This was perhaps most clear, and polemically so, in Duncan Kennedy's justly famous pamphlet/manifesto, 'Legal Education and the Reproduction of Hierarchy' (1982), which analysed the internal workings of the American law school and showed how it reinforced existing class, racial and gendered dynamics in American capitalist society more broadly. But the CLS critique encompassed not only the material organisation of the law school and the ideological interpellation of law students into status hierarchies. Rather, it concerned itself with the founding methods of legal analysis taught in those spaces.

The form of analysis that CLS practised, and encouraged students themselves to practise, was a kind of immanent doctrinal critique that, in Mark Kelman's words, sought to 'take specific arguments very seriously in their own terms; discover they are actually *foolish* ([tragi]-*comic*); and then look for some (external observer's) order (not the germ of truth) in the internally contradictory, incoherent chaos we've exposed' ([1984] at 293, emphasis in original; discussing Kennedy [1979]). CLS worked on the level of exposure, as Kelman's classic article, 'Trashing,' articulates. It exposed the internal incoherences and inconsistencies of legal doctrine, disabusing students of any lingering faith they might have had in formalist myths of law's completeness, doctrinal coherence or truth. As its many doctrinal and liberal legalist detractors decried, this raised the spectre of nihilism (see Singer [1984]). If (according to what are by now the received CLS tenets of legal indeterminacy and the fundamentally political nature of law) law itself does not provide definite answers to legal questions, then what role is there for law, exactly? And does this sorry conclusion not enervate rather than energise the law classroom and its young denizens?

'One thing that people joined the movement enthusiastic to try to accomplish together,' Duncan Kennedy recently reflected, 'was reform of the educational practice of the classroom,' including the hierarchies and petty violences of 'the culture ... [of] the Socratic classroom' (Kennedy and Blalock [2022] at 378). There is, at the same time, something vaguely Socratic about the charges levelled at the CLS'ers of the 1980s with their allegedly nihilistic corruption of the youth. But, in truth, the CLS message to law students was profoundly affirmative. If the god of legal certitude was dead then this vacated the space for the savvy, disabused, post-realist, policy-wielding lawyer profoundly comfortable with the epistemic uncertainty of law and the interpretive margin that legal indeterminacy afforded them. Think, for example, of the Appendix to James Boyle's classic, 'Anatomy of a Torts Class,' entitled 'First Year Mystification and Legal Argument: How to Avoid the Former and Master the Latter' (Boyle [1985]). There, students are instructed in (better: inducted into) the subtle arts of wielding various internally inconsistent, to be sure, but legally cognizable, arguments based on doctrine and policy so as to achieve particular political ends. The purpose of trashing the orthodoxy of formalist legal reasoning and liberal legality was never to do away with legal reasoning but to reveal its irreducible political nature and its pliability. CLS never strayed too far from legal technique even as (especially when) it looked to deconstruct, or trash, it.

This pedagogic-institutional context is itself important and goes some way to explaining both the enormous appeal of CLS in its own time and (Ivied) places and its relatively short-lived time in the legal theoretical sun. CLS spoke directly to students and their experience of legal knowledge. But it also managed to cleverly twin both senses of 'critical legal studies' with which this entry began – the analytic-technical sense and the more radical, questioning sense. Indeed, it was in the relay between these two experiences of mastering legal technical competence and of nevertheless realising that law did not provide all the answers that CLS delivered its critique. Just as received wisdom traces CLS's genealogy back to legal realism, so too do reports of its demise some time in the late 1980s or 1990s gesture to its afterlives in waves of Critical Race Theory and feminist legal theory – or the institutional eclipse effected by its ideological bête noire, law and economics (which brings us closer to the neoliberal context of our own day) (Blalock [2022] at 226–227). Ultimately, the restriction of its critical attentions to the universe of the law classroom had both a catalysing and a restricting effect.

It is notable that the lead contender to accede to the critical mantle of CLS – at least in the US legal academy (in the UK, see Wall, Middleton, Shah and CLAW [2021]) – is the Law and Political Economy (LPE) movement, which frames itself as a pedagogic project (the 'Learn' section of the LPE website (https://lpeproject.org/learn/) has links to primers (texts on key topics written 'by students in consultation with faculty'), to LPE 101 recorded

lectures, and to a bank of syllabi of LPE and LPE-related texts. But the LPE project has greater ambitions than just to be a pedagogic project – it explicitly addresses 'the ways law enables capitalist forms of exploitation and domination' (Blalock [2022] at 223) and is thus training its sights on things CLS did not sufficiently emphasise and in ways that it did not. As Amy Kapczynski argues, 'one thing that sets the LPE formation somewhat apart from some of the critical legal scholarship on which it draws is a commitment to thinking institutionally and structurally, and also to generating projects of reform' (Brown and Kapczynski [2022] at 249). If the critical legal theory, or critical legal studies, of our own day does not (as did CLS in the past) start and end in the law classroom then this is perhaps because the grim apocalyptic realities of capitalist accumulation and climactic degradation impose themselves with unprecedented vigour in every aspect of our students' lives, putting the limits of the classroom (and much else besides) into question. Where does the law classroom begin and end in such a world? And perhaps the protocols of legal critique, too, need updating. Maybe the question is not, as it might have been in CLS's time, to unmask and reveal, to trash and to disabuse. To appropriate the words of philosopher, Jean-Luc Nancy, 'everyone can clearly see that it is time: the disaster of [capitalism] is sufficiently spread out, and sufficiently common, to steal anyone's innocence' (Nancy [2000] at 142) even law students'. Maybe law's complicity in today's crises is so patent and so outlandish that we do not so much need a critical hermeneutics of suspicion as we (or, better, our students) need a critical legal pedagogy of radical, creative and practical imagination, one that teaches them 'to think *about* law … *with* law but also *beyond* law' (Blalock [2022] at 223, emphasis in original) in the interests of radical democracy, economic equality and environmental sustainability. Where the critical legal project of CLS drew energy from the law classroom, today's critical legal projects need to speak to a context beyond, yet impinging on, that classroom.

BEN GOLDER

References

Blalock, C. (2022). 'Introduction: Law and the Critique of Capitalism', *SAQ*, 121(2), p. 223.

Boyle, J. (1985). 'The Anatomy of a Torts Class', *American Uni LR*, 34, p. 1003.

Brown, W., and Kapcyznski, A. (2022), 'A Conversation Between Wendy Brown and Amy Kapczynski', *SAQ*, 121(2), p. 239.

Davies, M. (2017). *Asking the Law Question*, 4th edn, Lawbook Co.

Gearey, A. (2006). 'Anxiety and Affirmation: Critical Legal Studies and the Critical "Tradition(s)"', *NYU Rev. L and Soc. Change*, 31, p. 585.

Golder, B. (2021). 'From the Crisis of Critique to the Critique of Crisis', *Uni Col LR*, 92(4), p. 1065.

Goodrich, P. (1999). 'The Critic's Love of the Law: Intimate Observations on an Insular Jurisdiction', *Law & Critique*, 10, p. 343.

Kant, I. (1996). 'An Answer to the Question: What is Enlightenment?', in Schmidt, J. (ed), *What is Enlightenment? Eighteenth-Century Answers and Twentieth-Century Questions*, University of California Press.

Kelman, M.G. (1984). 'Trashing', *Stanford LR*, 36(1/2), p. 293.

Kennedy, D. (1982). 'Legal Education and the Reproduction of Hierarchy', *J Legal Educ*, 32, p. 591.

Kennedy, D. (1979). 'The Structure of Blackstone's Commentaries', *Buff LR*, 28(2), p. 205.

Kennedy, D. and Blalock, C. (2022). 'Provocation as Strategy: An Interview with Duncan Kennedy', *SAQ*, 121(2), p. 377

Mertz, E. (2007). *The Language of Law School: Learning to 'Think Like a Lawyer'*, Oxford University Press.

Nancy, J.-L. (2000). *Being Singular Plural* (trans. Richardson, R.D. and O'Byrne, A.E.), Stanford.

rua Wall, I., Middleton, F., Shah, S., and CLAW. (2021). (eds), *Critical Legal Pocketbook*, Counterpress.

Seale, C. (2020). *Thinking Like a Lawyer: A Framework for Teaching Critical Thinking to all Students*, Routledge.

Singer, J.W. (1984). 'The Player and the Cards: Nihilism and Legal Theory', *Yale LJ*, 94(1), p. 1.

Van Marle, K., and Modiri, J. (2012). '"What does Changing the World Entail?" Law, Critique, and Legal Education in the Time of Post-Apartheid', *S African L.J.*, 129(2), p. 209.

31. Decolonising the legal curriculum

Introduction

This entry introduces the reader to the decolonising the legal curriculum movement. The movement initiated from student-led demands to acknowledge and respond to the contemporary effects of the apartheid regime in South African universities. The student-led movement traversed to various locations in order to question colonial sensibilities in knowledge production.

This entry treats the decolonising the legal curriculum as a student-led movement that advances decolonial legal analysis. Decolonial legal analysis is mapped through the plurality of approaches that examine the role of law and legal operations in the reproduction of coloniality and legacies of empire. The entry situates the impact of decolonising the legal curriculum beyond academic institutions and more broadly, acknowledging its societal impact in relation to how legal systems and operations are perceived as neutral and objective. It identifies direct impacts from the student-led demands of the decolonising the legal curriculum movement on law as a discipline and a profession. Such impact is seen in, first, the demand to question the function of law in the reproduction of race and racism; second, the need for critical languages that speak to intersecting experiences of marginalisation and exclusions through naturalised categories of identification like race, ethnicity, gender and sexuality; third, the demand for cultivating an intentionality to decolonisation beyond calls for diversification; and last, the call for equal dialogues between various geographies of knowledge, while interrogating the centricity of western, liberal ideals in legal education.

Background of the decolonising law movement

The decolonising the legal curriculum movement in the United Kingdom gained traction after the 2015 student protests in South African universities. It is important to contextualise the decolonising the legal curriculum movement in student mobilisations in South Africa that gave rise to the demand to decolonisation in the Global North. In doing so, the entry addresses one of the key demands of the South African student-led movement, which is to decolonise education everywhere. This demand speaks to the broader global impact of the movement on subverting knowledge production, in which universal legal values are predetermined in the Global North.

The South African student-led protests responded to the contemporary manifestations of the apartheid regime in curricula and knowledge production. South African students called for the removal of the statue of Cecil Rhodes in University of Cape Town, who facilitated the legal framework for the apartheid regime (Memon & Jivraj [2020]). Rhodes was responsible for the introduction of segregationist policy, the Glen Grey Act in 1894. The Act facilitated the entrenchment of colonial authority over land in the Cape region of South Africa (Ramutsindela [2012]). It functioned as a land tenure and labour supply framework. It identified majority black neighbourhoods in the Glen Grey district of the northern Cape as rural areas, enabling the exploitation of native labour forces in these neighbourhoods, while denying African possession of land that was regulated by colonial individuals. The Act followed a colonial pattern of controlling and displacement of black labour, enabling the accumulation of wealth in colonial metropoles through centring individual property rights and introducing racialised land tenure systems. Student protests calling for the removal of the Rhodes statue responded to the structural inequalities that persisted after the end of apartheid in 1991. Such inequalities are vivid in the current inequality of freehold land distribution in South Africa that is estimated at 72 per cent of white landowners (Rural Development and Land Reform [2017]).

The student-led collective movement also aims to reshape the vision of knowledge production in which the university plays an active role in maintaining unequal racial relations that mythologises the apartheid regime rather than engaging with its contemporary effects. Examples of these effects are unaffordable tuition fees and the dominance of English-language universities in South Africa. The movement sought to disrupt the function of the university and broaden the monolingual referential worldview in universities.

The impact of the South African student-led protests traversed elsewhere and in Europe, as a sense of urgencies towards reimagining the function of academic institutions. In Britian, the *Rhodes Must Fall* movement in Oxford University echoed the dissatisfactions with institutional racism and structural inequalities and the need for discussions on the legacies of empire, that other social mobilisations, like Black Lives Matter, have also highlighted.

Decolonial legal theory

In legal education, the decolonising the curriculum movement has shed light on the advancements in decolonial legal theory that give students the language and critical skills to navigate and articulate the function of law in propagating structural inequalities. Decolonial legal theory is marked by multiple approaches and modes of analysis that aim to contextualise the function of law and legal operations. Decolonial thought, as an intellectual project, has been developing in various geographies for a long period of time (Duara [2003]). Broadly, decolonial legal theory attends to a multiplicity of processes and developments that decentre western ideals, mainly that of liberalism, while unpacking structural inequalities in legal operations and processes. Such analysis treats coloniality as a logic of domination and exploitation that still has an effect on legal structures today (Quijano [2008]). Decolonial legal theory initiates from the position that colonised societies acquiring political sovereignty did not end colonial structures. Coloniality erupts as examining the historical imaginations that gave rise to epistemic inequalities.

There are two implications on the teaching of law while unpacking the concept of coloniality. The first one relates to the question of time and progress. Decolonial theory treats time as relational (Adebisi [2023]). It refuses time as a linear concept, negating the progressive narrative to history. It entangles progress and civilisation with coloniality, in which a progressive history has always reiterated the supremacy of western ideals and domination. Decoloniality treats the past, present, and future as intermingling relations that shape and construct contemporary agencies. Second, coloniality uncovers and articulates systematic oppression which is sustained through legal ideals, like that of rationality, objectivity and neutrality.

The aim of decolonial analysis is to recognise how legal concepts are essential for producing discursive practises of race, gender,

ethnicity, sexuality and class. It treats race as a social construct. To illustrate, the rule of law in its doctrinal sense defines the basis for equality and separation of power to safeguard individual liberties and freedom. Law also validates the construction of race and racism. For instance, in *Taiwo v Olaigbe and another*, the UK Supreme Court looked at whether the mistreatment of migrant domestic workers, who are on precarious migration status, amounts to direct or indirect race discrimination. While the Equality Act 2010 recognises race as a protected characteristic, it does not recognise immigrant as a protected characteristic (section 9). The court determined that the treatment of the appellants did not amount to racial discrimination under the Equality Act 2010 and, as such, they were not the subject of direct or indirect discrimination. In instances like this, legal operations validate racial relations as constitutive of societal relations, while displacing such legal discrepancies – or failures of the present legal frameworks to remedy harms that exceed the Equality Act 2010 – are framed as jurisdictional issues and not a matter for courts but ones for the parliament to debate (Zokaityte and Mbjoh [2023]). Decolonial analyses directs attention to such failures, not as failures, but as part of how law and legal operations naturalises and validates stratifying categories of identification, like race and gender, while maintaining neutrality and equality.

Decolonial legal theory questions and complicates the social foundations of equality in the rule of law. It complicates the single narrative story of courts and legal operations in drawing relevant facts of the case that are decoupled from their social, economic, and political context. To illustrate, decolonial legal theory highlights the inadequacies of doctrinal legal approaches in tackling structural inequalities. Doctrinal legal approaches are inadequate when the analyses delink law from other disciplines in favour of rationality and objectivity. Decolonial legal theory acknowledges interrelated agencies and relations. It negates the individualisation of agency in liberal thought and questions its universal rhetoric. It retrieves concepts that speak to the experiences of colonialism and contemporary racialisation (Matiluko [2020]). To do so, decolonial legal analysis situates lived experiences at the core of analysing and engaging with the function of legal rules and structures.

Impact on law as a discipline and a profession

This section outlines some of the various impacts of the demands to decolonising the legal curriculum on the legal discipline and legal practice. The demands implicate both the function of law and legal practices in reproducing race and racism in the production and the circulation of legal knowledge. The section addresses five threads of impact: first, the function of law in the reproduction of race and racism; second, the urgencies for understanding the intersecting nature of structural inequalities; third, the cultivation of intentionality in addressing epistemic injustice; fourth, the examination of the universal presumption of legal objectivity in doctrinal methods; fifth, the reimagining of function of legal education through decolonial pedagogies.

First, the decolonising the legal curriculum movement signposts that it is not enough to recognise and address structural inequalities within the legal realm. It redirects attention to experiences of exclusion and marginalisation. The movement moves beyond socio-legal approaches of putting legal relations in social context. It questions the function of law and legal operations in reproducing racialisation in the legal field. Decolonial legal analysis negates the assumption that legal practices are value-neutral and interrogates the detachment of law from the social, political and economic realm. It complicates the function of law and legal practices in which law is part of the flow of coloniality.

Second, the movement offers the critical language that enables students and legal practitioners to comprehend and articulate the contemporary manifestations of colonial relations. Decolonial legal theory offers a nuanced understanding of intersecting forms of exclusions and global disparities. It affirms multi-layered experiences and complex relations, avoiding reductionist arguments on equality and racism.

Third, decoloniality cultivates an intentionality to decolonisation. It exceeds demands for the diversification of curriculums. The movement questions processes of western-centred knowledge production. The intentionality affirms, for instance, the political role of citations in the assumptions that legal knowledge and expertise flow from the North to the South. Citations are seen as an intentional practice to highlight geographies of knowledge on relational perspectives, for instance through indigenous knowledge or Islamic jurisprudence through *fiqh*. *Fiqh* is usually reduced only to *Shariah* (Islamic Law) in mainstream western legal engagements due to the overemphasis on private legal relations, whereas *fiqh* reflects a nuanced engagement with the practices and knowledge of Islamic laws as an episteme of knowledge (El-Saadi [2020]). Engaging with non-western epistemes cultivates awareness of local histories, and different knowledge systems. It subverts erasures of colonial history, indigenous experiences, and marginalised lived experiences in law.

Fourth, the decolonising the legal curriculum movement implicates legal dialogues. It problematises the adversarial nature of the rule of law and the assumption of impartiality. It opens space for conversations that harness collaborative ethos and centres lived experiences. The movement harnesses dialogues between legal education and practice in the UK and various geographies. It unpacks the colonial foundations of the legal discipline through opening dialogue between various geographies of knowledge, while acknowledging the stratifying knowledge hierarchies within the North and South. The movement interrogates the universalised liberal assumptions on the nature of the rule of law and the function of legal institutions.

Last, the movement impacts the function of legal education and practice in affecting social change. For instance, the *Decolonise UoK* initiative aims to open space by problematising the lack of conversations on institutional racism in legal education (Memon and Jivraj [2020]). In its manifesto (Decolonise UoK [2019]), the initiative treats students as co-producers of knowledge, attending to the multiple positionalities that they bring into the classroom. The decolonial pedagogical initiative engages students with the aim of 'self-actualisation', as hooks puts it (Hooks [1994]). It builds on the complex lives and experiences of students and engages with their effects on their legal education. The decolonising the legal curriculum movement demands being responsive to experiences of structural inequalities that highlight the inadequacies of doctrinal legal approaches in addressing unequal power structures. The movement calls for a continuous and processual engagement with lived experiences in addressing the colonial matrix of power.

SHAIMAA ABDELKARIM

References

Adebisi, F. (2023). *Decolonisation and Legal Knowledge: Reflections on Power and Possibility*, Routledge.

Adebisi, F. (2021). 'Should We Rethink the Purposes of the Law School? A Case for Decolonial Thought in Legal Pedagogy', *Amicus Curiae*, p. 428.

Ahmed, S. (2017). *Living a Feminist Life*, Duke University Press Books.

AlAttar, M. and Abdelkarim, S. (2023). 'Decolonising the Curriculum in International Law: Entrapments in Praxis and Critical Thought', *Law Critique*, p. 34.

Barreto, J.-M. (2012). 'Decolonial Strategies and Dialogue in the Human Rights Field: A Manifesto', *Transnational Legal Theory*, 3(1), p. 1.

Boodia-Canoo, N.S. (2020). 'Researching colonialism and colonial legacies from a legal perspective', *The Law Teacher*, 54(4), p. 517.

Burman, A. (2017). 'The Political Ontology of Climate Change: Moral Meteorology, Climate Justice, and the Coloniality of Reality in the Bolivian Andes', *Journal of Political Ecology*, 24(1), p. 921.

Decolonise UoK, Decolonising the Curriculum Project: Through the Kaleidoscope, available at https://decoloniseukc.files.wordpress.com/ 2019/03/decolonising-the-curriculum-manifesto -final-2.pdf.

Duara, P. (2003). *Decolonization: Perspectives from Now and Then*, Routledge.

Dussel, E. (1995). 'Eurocentrism and Modernity (Introduction to the Frankfurt Lectures)', in Beverley, J., Oviedo, J. and Arona, M. (eds), *The Postmodernism Debate in Latin America*, Duke University Press, p. 65.

El-Saadi, H. (2020). 'Rulings and Gendering the Public Space: The Discrepancy between Written Formality and Daily Reality', in Reda, N. and Amin, Y. (eds), *Islamic Interpretive Tradition and Gender Justice: Processes of Canonization Subversion and Change*, McGill-Queen's University Press.

Hooks, B. (1994). *Teaching to Transgress: Education as the Practice of Freedom*, Routledge.

Jivraj, S. (2020). 'Decolonising the University: Success, Pitfalls and Next Steps', in Thomas, D.S. and Jivraj, S. (eds), *Towards Decolonising the University: A Kaleidoscope for Empowered Action*, Counterpress.

Lugones, M. (2008). 'The Coloniality of Gender', Worlds and Knowledges Otherwise.

Lugones, M. (2010). 'Toward a Decolonial Feminism', *Hypatia*, 25(4), p. 742.

Mamdani, M. (2016). 'Between the public intellectual and the scholar: Decolonization and some post-independence initiatives in African higher education', *Inter-Asia Cultural Studies*, 17(1), p. 68.

Matiluko, O. (2020). 'Decolonising the master's house: how Black Feminist epistemologies can be and are used in decolonial strategy', *The Law Teacher*, 54(4), p. 547.

Memon, A.R. and Jivraj, S. (2020). 'Trust, courage and silence: carving out decolonial spaces in higher education through student-staff partnerships', *The Law Teacher*, p. 475.

Mignolo, W. (2002). 'The Geopolitics of Knowledge and the Colonial Difference', *South Atlantic Quarterly*, 101(1), p. 57.

Moran, M. (2023). *Rethinking the Reasonable Person: An Egalitarian Reconstruction of the Objective*, Oxford University Press.

Pahuja, S. (2011). *Decolonising International Law: Development, Economic Growth and the Politics of Universality*, Cambridge University Press.

Quijano, A. (2007). 'Coloniality and Modernity/ Rationality', *Cultural Studies*, 21(2–3), p. 155.

Quijano, A. (2008). 'Coloniality of Power, Eurocentrism, and Social Classification', in Moraña, M., Dussel, E. and Jáuregui, C.A. (eds), *Coloniality at Large. Latin America and the Postcolonial Debate*, Duke University Press, p. 181.

Ramutsindela, M. (2012). 'Property rights, land tenure and the racial discourses', *GeoJournal*, 77, p. 753.

Rural Development and Land Reform. (2017). Land Audit Report, available at https://www .gov.za/sites/default/files/gcis_document/ 201802/landauditreport13feb2018.pdf.

Salaymeh, L. and Michaels, R. (2022). 'Decolonial Comparative Law: A Conceptual Beginning', *Rabel Journal of Comparative and International Private Law*, 86(1), p. 166.

Taiwo v Olaigbe and another [2016] UKSC 31.

Tapia Tapia, S. (2022). *Feminism, Violence Against Women, and Law Reform: Decolonial Lessons from Ecuador*, Routledge.

Tapia Tapia, S. (2023). 'Human Rights Penality and Violence Against Women: The Coloniality of Disembodied Justice', *Law Critique*.

Tendayi Achiume, E. and Last, T. (2021). 'Decolonial Regionalism: Reorienting Southern African Migration Policy', *Third World Approaches to International Law Review / TWAIL Review (TWAILR)*, 2, pp. 1-6.

Van Wagner, E. (2013). 'Putting Property in its Place: Relational Theory, Environmental Rights and Land Use Planning', *Revue générale de droit*, 43, p. 275.

Xavier, S., Jacobs, B., Waboose, V., Hewitt, J.G. and Bhatia, A. (2021). *Decolonizing Law Indigenous, Third World and Settler Perspectives*, Routledge.

Zokaityte, A. and Mbioh, W.R. (2023). 'Judicial production of racial injustice in Taiwo v Olaigbe: decolonising the incomplete story on race and contracting', *Social & Legal Studies*, p. 1.

32. Design in legal education

Legal design involves the application of design mindsets and methods to law. Its evolution goes back to the escape of design ideas from art and design schools (producing graphic and industrial designers) into a more generalised and widely applicable approach to problem solving through service design and design thinking. From the late twentieth century, design thinking has been used in addressing problems across many sectors such as technology, banking, healthcare, government services and, latterly, law and legal services.

Design thinking can be manifested in multiple ways through product, process and service design, user experience design, systems design etc. Where law is perceived as a service, a product, a process, as something that citizens experience, or as a system, then it is open to the impact of design.

The overarching ethos of design thinking is human-centredness – a desire to make the experience of using the product or service as accessible, useful and satisfactory as possible. This is why it places such an emphasis on user research; to try to understand user needs and the reality of how users interact with the product or service. It also promotes innovation and creativity in seeking solutions, experimentation and prototyping, and the rigorous testing of impacts.

As an illustrative example of legal design in practice, in 2019 the contracts innovation team at Airbus identified a problem: that the many small startup companies they interacted with struggled to understand and use non-disclosure agreements. The existing legal documents were in a traditional format of dense text and technical legalese. Working together with the legal design agencies, Let's Do Legal Design and Visual Contracts, they undertook detailed user research to understand the needs of Airbus and the start-ups, particularly in protecting their intellectual property. They prototyped and tested NDA contracts that had been shortened and simplified. These included explanations of key legal terms along with greater use of icons, diagrams and other visualisation tools. These changes increased the readability scores of the documents (on the Fleisch scale) from 22 to 51. Testing showed not just greater useability of the documents but also a deeper level of trust in the ongoing business relationship. (Kohlmeier [2019])

The methods that emerge from the design world are varied and fluid but the IDEO design agency and the Design School at Stanford University (the d.school) have played an important role in collating and simplifying these methods into scaleable problem-solving models. These are not the only ways in which people bring design into law but they have been a useful facilitator. The Stanford model of design thinking is a flexible and iterative way of undertaking design projects. It involves:

- empathising – this might involve diverse methods of user experience research, focus groups, participant and ethnographic approaches;
- problem definition – design spends a lot more time in the 'problem space', trying to understand where the problem genuinely lies, than traditional legal approaches which emphasise immediate expert-led solutions;
- ideation – generating a broad range of innovative possibilities, co-creating with diverse groups, and then clustering and ranking options;
- prototyping – making ideas visible and tangible (often through rough models, diagrams, wireframe websites) so that they can be understood, explored and evaluated; and
- testing – monitoring the real-world impact of the interventions and iterating to seek further improvements.

The development of legal design education

Looking at the development of legal design as a field of practice and an academic sub-discipline, the first known use of the term 'legal design' was in the early 1990s by Colette Brunschwig, a researcher at the Legal Vizualization Unit, University of Zurich. The key stages in the development of legal design and legal design education, though, have happened since the early 2010s.

Law schools played a central role in the development of legal design in the United States, particularly through the creation of innovation 'labs' that have been focussed on social justice and access to justice issues. An early example is NuLawLab at Northeastern University which runs a regular seminar in Applied and Critical Legal Design along with placement and student-led projects working with (mainly) local communities on issues such as housing displacement and voting rights. The Stanford Legal Design Lab was founded in 2013. It is a research and development lab but it offers workshops and design sprints (short intensive programmes aimed at addressing real-world problems) for both students and external legal organisations, courts and legal aid groups. These have focussed on issues such as helping self-represented litigants navigate court proceedings and leveraging AI for legal advice. Other notable legal design and innovation labs have been created at Vanderbilt University (with its Program on Law and Innovation), Brigham Young University (LawX legal design clinic) and the New Jersey Housing Justice and Legal Design Clinic at Seton Hall University.

The development of legal design education in Europe has the same timeframe but a different context. The pioneers of legal design in Europe are people such as Helena Haapio and Stefania Passera (based in Helsinki), Astrid Kohlmeier (Munich), Marie Potel-Saville (Paris) and Lieke Beelen (Amsterdam). They have all been involved in the provision of legal design education within universities. Haapio, for example, holds positions at the Universities of Vaasa and Lapland. In general, though, they have come from (and often primarily stayed) in practice and consultancy. Their work has had a more commercial focus than the US tradition, often working with major clients on contract design, consumer terms and conditions, and privacy policies.

Despite these different starting points there is relatively high degree of coherence and common purpose in the legal design movement. This has been aided by inclusive and integrative organisations (such as the Legal Design Alliance), events (such as the series of Legal Design Summits held in Helsinki since 2017) and platforms (such as the Legal Design Journal launched in 2023).

The pace of development in legal design education has also picked up in recent years. As of 2023 there are least 40 modules or programmes at higher education institutions that have a main legal design focus. Legal design also forms part of most legal innovation courses and some legal tech programmes.

The legal design courses are split, more or less equally, between undergraduate, postgraduate and project-based / microcredential courses. The most courses by country are in the US, but there are also multiple providers in Australia, Brazil, Finland, France, Germany and the UK.

Most regions of the world have some sort of legal education provision now, with programmes in South Africa, Turkey, Hong Kong and Singapore, Colombia and Chile and various European countries.

In the UK, there have been three key centres of development. The work of Emily Allbon at City University, London on visualisation of legal resources through projects such as Lawbore predates involvement in the legal design movement, and now incorporates legal design publications, events and a legal design-focussed gallery – tl;dr (the Less Textual Legal Gallery). Amanda Perry-Kessaris, at the University of Kent, is the leading voice on connecting designerly ways of thinking and doing with socio-legal work, including via events such as the Pop-Up Museum of Legal Objects and a legal design option in the undergraduate curriculum. Michael Doherty led education-focussed legal design projects at the University of Central Lancashire and has continued work on legal design culture and the development of legal design disciplinarity (e.g. by leading the development of the Legal Design Journal) at Lancaster University. Other important developments have taken place at Queen Mary University, London on integrating legal design with clinic work and at South Bank University on interdisciplinary approaches to legal innovation education.

One particularly prominent feature of the legal design movement is that it consciously has very porous boundaries between the academic and professional practice sectors. This is reflected in legal design education. Some of the most impactful educational offerings have come from private providers or as an element of the work of legal design consultancies. Legal Creatives, for example, is based in Canada but operates digitally and globally, and offers legal design training, bootcamps and immersions. Helsinki, again, has been an important centre of this private provision with both the Legal Design School and the Lawyers Design School providing training in practical-focussed legal design methods.

MICHAEL DOHERTY

Why teach legal design?

Legal design offers a distinctive set of opportunities for legal change, and challenges against established ways of doing law. This is reflected in how and why higher education institutions have developed programmes (or indeed why they have not yet done so).

The challenges include the fact that legal design is so new and has been so little known and understood. This is compounded by a range of misconceptions about and trivialisations of legal design, e.g. that it is just concerned with making legal documents look pretty. What is true is that design has values that are in tension with many existing cultural norms in legal education. It values co-creation and collective approaches, is creative, and embraces experimentation and failure. Many approaches to legal design education are interdisciplinary, project-based, community-engaged and relatively resource intensive. All these things can make it harder to get approval and resources for curriculum development proposals.

The opportunities mirror the challenges. Legal design is an energising and exciting field of practice. There is a shortage of law graduates with appropriate skills and the opportunities for people practicing in this area are considerable. For many students, exposure to the different ways of thinking about and doing law is a liberating and empowering experience. Students may have existing skills, values and worldviews that are in tension with traditionally received notions of legal education and lawyering that make them feel like outsiders in their own chosen field. Finding legal design approaches can show that there is a place for them in the law. Finally, there is a conscious thread of radicalism in legal design (including within the more corporate part of the movement). It springs from a dissatisfaction with current modes of learning about law and providing legal services and believes that there are user-centred, more human and more socially responsible ways of doing law. This can be a terribly attractive proposition for educators and students.

What is taught in legal design?

There is no standard syllabus for legal design education. Most courses seem to involve consideration of practical case studies, an introduction to the key concepts, mindsets and methods of legal design and an opportunity to apply some of those methods to a problem. The problem could be a simulation or working with a live client. The methods can include undertaking user experience research through desk research, surveys or focus groups. They can extend to more ethnographic techniques of data collection such as participant observation ('a day in the life of …') and online ethnography ('be a mystery shopper of this online legal process'). Students can be shown different ways of synthesising this research e.g. via user personas (that personify characteristics and motives of archetypal users of legal services), or journey maps (that visualise the timeline of interactions between a user and a legal process). The balance between which methods are simply taught and which are also applied by students will vary widely, with more opportunities in project-based programmes.

Courses will typically give students experience of the sorts of ideation methods used in practical legal design projects such as 'how might we …?' questions (e.g. 'how might we make it easier for people to apply for Personal Independence Payments without help completing the form?'), co-creating maps and timelines, brain writing (noting down as many ideas as possible in silence in a limited time). In physical terms, these ways of working look very different from those traditionally associated with a law classroom. They are likely to feature what have become familiar tropes of legal design: Post-It notes, flip chart paper and Sharpie pens, using the walls of the classroom to display ideas, huddles of people standing and discussing some concrete artefact rather than sat at desks looking at their own notes. Legal design education is generally weakest at communicating and giving experience of the end stages of the design process. Often students are just tasked with creating new ideas without having to test them with users, push them through implementation or evaluate impact.

How is legal design taught?

It may be possible to teach legal design through a broadly traditional pedagogical structure of lectures, plus seminars with activities based around a reading list and discursive questions, but existing courses largely eschew this approach. They mostly seem to be grounded in an understanding of how legal design projects are done in practice, though they may also draw from sophisticated traditions of thought in socio-legal studies, Critical Legal Studies, radical lawyering, and the wider access to justice literature. Students are often tasked with working in teams, applying the methods outlined above and proposing and justifying potential solutions. This may call on them to produce work using creative and visual methods, though the written report still seems the most common form of output.

Some project-based programmes, such as the Legal Design Masterclass at NuLawLab and the legal technology module at South Bank University pair law students with those from other disciplines such as computer science, architecture, or games design.

Service design approaches to wider legal education

One final entanglement of design and legal education to outline here does not relate to the process of teaching legal design skills and knowledge. It involves applying service and design thinking to the design of wider law curricula, student support and experience. It is founded on the notion that legal education is a service, albeit not a simple service provider-service user relationship. It acknowledges the wider social purpose of education and the diversity of stakeholders but argues that the service design methods outlined above can be used to better understand the real lives and educational needs of law students, to co-create curricula and pedagogies alongside students rather than as a purely top-down expert-perspective approach and produce imaginative and challenging ideas on directions in legal education. There currently only seems to have been one attempt to apply service design to a wider law curriculum review in any systematic way (at the University of Central Lancashire). There is though, beyond law, a wider movement led by the Service Design in Higher Education network seeking to apply design thinking to a range of university systems (such as developing data systems to respect preferred names and genders), library and student support services, transition to HE, and methods for obtaining and responding to student feedback.

Michael Doherty

References

Allbon, E. and Perry-Kessaris, A. (2022). *Design in Legal Education*, Routledge.

Allbon, E. *tl;dr The Less Textual Legal Gallery*, available at https://tldr.legal/home.html.

Corrales, M., Haapio, H., Hagan, M. and Doherty, M. (2021). *Legal Design: Integrating Business, Design and Legal Thinking*, Edward Elgar Publishing.

Kohlmeier, A. (2019). 'How to create usercentric NDAs for startup companies', available at https://astridkohlmeier.de/portfolio/nda-startups/.

Kohlmeier, A. and Klemola, M. (2021). *The Legal Design Book*, Klemola & Kohlmeier.

33. Digital learning and legal education

Introduction

Digital learning refers to use of digital technology in the education experience. In legal education, as in the rest of our daily lives, digital technologies have become omnipresent in many societies across the world. Digital learning covers a wide spectrum of possibilities, ranging from the innocuous presence of digital tools in everyday activities to more profound transformations of legal education. The sort of digital tools that might be used in everyday activities would encompass visual, audio and/or materials, taking notes on electronic devices and email communications. In terms of the more fundamental developments in legal education one would find legal research in databases and the availability of vast amounts of information on the internet, learning management systems (LMSs), video-conferencing and web-based asynchronous modules, as well as emerging artificial intelligence tools for drafting and analysing documents. The diverse aspects of digital learning combine in endless options. Some are sustaining, i.e. they support and enhance traditional ways of teaching and learning law, and others are disruptive, i.e. profoundly transformative in the sector (Susskind [2023] at 63). The various forms of digital technology that are now part of legal education modify the experience of education, creating new opportunities and novel challenges. Some consequences of this new reality are specific to legal education due to its historical development, current paradigms and unique objectives.

The ways and extent to which digital technologies permeate legal education first and foremost varies depending on their prevalence in a given society at large. This became evident in the wake of the COVID-19 pandemic when nearly all countries instituted public health measures temporarily banning in-person gatherings, including in-class teaching. In some jurisdictions, the pre-existing infrastructure and skills made for a smooth transition to an all-digital education whereas in others, law students simply halted their learning until they could physically come together in classroom again (Nottage and Ibusuki [2023]). Another illustration lies in the great varia-tion in responses across continents when law students and teachers are asked about the main technical difficulty they encountered in a context of online or hybrid learning (one form of digital learning among others) (IALS [2020]): some cite the low bandwidth or even the lack of adequate electronic devices, when others have the comparative luxury of mentioning the lack of training to make the best of the available infrastructure.

The issues and considerations stemming from digital learning also vary at different stages of legal education (undergraduate and graduate university programs in law, initial professional training and continuing legal education) and even with each element within each of these stages (e.g. a theoretical versus a practical course, a first-year vs upper-year course, etc). A legal education is the sum of a wide array of educational attainments, and the learning objectives and context differ throughout this continuum. As many jurisdictions are developing frameworks to identify learning outcomes that student lawyers should demonstrate at different stages of their education (sometimes called competency profiles or graduates attributes), our capacity to engage with digital learning at a more granular level rather than with blanket reflections increases.

Current knowledge about digital learning in law

A major obstacle in deciding whether and how digital learning enhances or hinders the development of the learning outcomes that legal education aims at fostering is the paucity of robust empirical research on legal education in general. While there is a large collection of publications sharing anecdotal experiences, it is only sometimes supported by data corroborating the conclusions regarding students' learning. Even among data-grounded publications, the lack of common parameters or even sound methodology in many cases results in the impossibility of compiling meta-analyses, generalising results or drawing conclusions, whether at the scale of regional or country-wide level. In the current state of the literature, it is not possible to answer with any confidence whether, how, why, nor under which conditions different modalities of digital learning enhance or inhibit the teaching and learning of legal competencies (Maharg [2016] at 18).

However, legal education can look outside of its own perimeter to learn from the existing and robust literature on digital learning more broadly. For instance, Means et al. [2010] for the US Department of Education offered robust conclusions on the effectiveness of online learning, based on 1,000+ studies between 1996–2008 (none of them related to legal education). The Association for Medication Education in Europe has published over 100 evidence-based guides on diverse aspects and modalities of medical education (AMEE), including some directly connected to digital technologies in education. Although there is no equivalent in legal education, studies such as these shed light on many aspects of learning that are shared across diverse disciplines and settings.

The task becomes more difficult once we focus on specifically legal competencies, such as identifying legally relevant facts, formulating convincing arguments to apply rules to new situations and critiquing the state of the law on a given topic. However, some robust data does exist, including the Law School Student Survey of Engagement (LSSSE), a yearly US-based survey eliciting thousands of student responses and exploring diverse aspects of the legal education experience including in relation to digital learning (see e.g. Petzold et al. [2022]). The COVID-19 pandemic and forced experiment with web-based remote delivery of legal education programs in most countries triggered ad hoc surveys to test students' perceptions of diverse digital learning strategies, on a global scale (IALS [2020], reproduced yearly thereafter) and in a national context (Murchison et al. [2022]). This growing body of literature is starting to shed light on how legal education stakeholders perceive the efficiency and desirability of various digital learning possibilities.

One area that requires special attention is the socialisation aspect of legal education. In many jurisdictions, legal education is not only seen as learning legal knowledge and legal analysis skills; it is also considered to be a process of socialisation into the professional group constituted by lawyers (Mertz [2007]). More than competencies like analysing a judgment or formulating a legal opinion on a new situation, it is probably in this intangible aspect of legal education that digital learning makes the most profound changes.

Issues, challenges and opportunities specific to legal education

Digital learning, in its many forms, raises new issues, creates new challenges and creates new possibilities that may put to the test or enhance aspects that are specific to legal education as opposed to other fields.

Digital remote learning ('e-learning'), by way of web-based synchronous ('online learning') or asynchronous ('distance learning') pedagogy, has attracted most commentaries. Around 2010, a form of distance education called Massive Online Open Courses (MOOCs) emerged on the education market. The excitement was short-lived. Stakeholders soon realised that law MOOCs could advance public legal education by making information about and understanding of the legal system available to a very large public but they were not gaining recognition as a credentialing option for law professionals. Some jurisdictions nonetheless established online education options for university law degrees alongside other in-person options (e.g. UK, Australia). Recorded lectures, online classes and at-home assignments opened the doors of university legal education to students with family or work responsibilities that would not allow them to pursue a more traditional format of education.

Nonetheless, by the end of the 2010s, some countries with the infrastructure that would make it possible and the geography that might also make it desirable had nonetheless showed great reluctance to integrate online legal education in their range of options available to law students. In the USA and Canada in particular, this reluctance could perhaps be explained by the attachment to the Socratic Method of teaching and the historical construction of on-campus, full-time university education on elitist grounds.

In addition to making in-person or remote legal education more accessible to students with diverse disabilities or family and work situations, E-learning options enable participation in legal education by students whose medical conditions, family responsibilities or work commitments do not permit them to commit to being physically present in the classroom for the duration of each class. Fully asynchronous modules and recordings of live classes diminish the impact that the contingencies of life can have on a student's ability to achieve the requisite knowledge and skills to succeed. Digital technologies in education more broadly can help neurodivergent students, students with a variety of learning styles and preferences as well as those whose cultural background or generational habits make it easier to learn when digital formats are used to enhance or supplant traditional teaching.

Even for in-person education, digital technologies open new possibilities to enhance or disrupt the traditional law school pedagogies, whether the Socratic Method, lectures or other approaches. Digital visual or audio-video materials complementing the teachers' oral presentations are now widespread in classrooms. Less frequently perhaps, teachers also leverage the fact that many students take notes on a mobile electronic device to engage all of them at once in active-learning activities through live polling and collaborations on shared documents. Some teachers use a 'flipped classroom' model, recording lectures for students to study ahead of time so that the time spent in class can be used for activities designed to further develop the students' legal knowledge and skills.

In many jurisdictions, there is increasing demand for experiential learning opportunities in the form of law clinics, moot court competition, placements in court or law firm settings, etc. Such learning environments are resource-intensive compared to traditional lecture formats. Emerging tools for simulating lawyer-client interaction or even court room proceedings have the potential to make experiential learning opportunities cheaper and more prevalent in legal education. It is the kind of e-learning that Susskind predicts will prove disruptive in the near future (Susskind [2023] at 68).

The increasing prevalence of digital technologies in everyday legal practice adds pressure on law schools to train their students in the mastery of tools such as online research in databases, e-discovery, artificial intelligence-powered document review and even drafting and remote hearings. Law schools may also wonder how best to equip their students to think critically about the use and the ethical implications of such tools.

Law, as a social phenomenon, profession and field of knowledge is essentially grounded in embodied, human to human experience. More than many other disciplines, it involves human interactions, emotions, relationships of trust. The omnipresence of digital mediation in exchanges about law and justice in legal education may challenges learners' relationship to this essential aspect of what law and becoming a lawyer entail.

Regulation of digital technology in legal education

In many jurisdictions, university legal education must meet some accreditation requirements for their graduates to have access to the legal professions. The regulatory frameworks often require a minimum level of digital technology in the law school's environment to match the local perceptions of what constitutes a quality education given the available technologies. On the other hand, the same regulatory frameworks may place restrictions on online and web-based distance education possibilities (see ABA Standards 306 [2022]). Such regulatory framework may inhibit the adoption of digital learning options as much as other factors in the political economy of legal education.

Conclusion

To conclude, some key questions can guide us to develop further our own reflections and the much-needed research on digital learning and legal education. First, we can ask what is lost and gained for students and teachers when we remove one specific modality of digital learning from the experience? Conversely, what is lost and gained when we digitalise all aspects of the teaching and learning of law? Answering this double question can help us distinguish the digital tools and strategy that actually enhance legal education from those amounting to gadgetry used for the sake of novelty. Second, we can ask which, if any, digital technologies have proven or will prove pivotal for legal education? Some digital technologies have had a lasting and profound impact in the way law is learned and practiced, such as the switch to online legal research instead of solely using a physical library; other digital tools quickly faded away after some early excitement. Time will tell whether cutting edge developments in virtual reality and artificial intelligence will fall in the former or the latter category as far as legal education is concerned.

Adrien Habermacher

References

American Bar Association, *Standards and Rules of Procedure for Approval of Law Schools 2022–2023*, available at https://www.americanbar.org/groups/legal_education/resources/standards/.

International Association of Law Schools. (2020). *Transitioning to Online Legal Education – The Student Voice*, available at https://www.ialsnet.org/surveyreports/.

Maharg, P. (2016). 'Editorial: Learning/Technology', 50(1), *The Law Teacher*.

Mertz, E. (2007). *The Language of Law School: Learning to 'Think Like a Lawyer'*, Oxford University Press.

Murchison, M. et al (2022). 'Remote Learning in Law School During the Pandemic: A Canadian Survey', 8, CJCCL, available at https://www.cjccl.ca/wp-content/uploads/2022/7-Murchison-et-al.pdf.

Nottage, L. and Ibusuki, M. (2023). *Comparing Online Legal Education: Past, Present and Future*, Intersentia.

Petzold, J., Deo, M.E. and Christensen, C. (2022). *LSSSE 2022 Annual Report: Success With Online Education*, available at https://lssse.indiana.edu/annual-results/.

Susskind, R. (2023). *Tomorrow's Lawyers: An Introduction to Your Future*, Oxford University Press.

34. Digital skills in legal education

Introduction

Over the past 20 years, technology has developed at an unprecedented rate, with the legal sector increasingly adopting greater digitalisation. This integration of technology is not simply limited to the use of emails rather than physical post and the prevalence of digitised legal research repositories, but to ever more diverse applications (Jones [2021]). Documents can, for example, now be generated and completed by Artificial Intelligence (Thanaraj [2021]), and dispute resolution services are ever more frequently being delivered online (Rabinovich-Einy [2021]). Indeed, the greater integration of technology is not confined to law, with professions such as medicine, consultancy and even clerical positions taking advantage of technological integration (Susskind and Susskind [2015]).

It is, therefore, apparent that law graduates, not of the future but of *now*, require both legal knowledge and technological nous to thrive. Therefore, the law degree requires the development of both competencies. This entry will use the UK as a case study, examining the Solicitors Regulation Authority (SRA) and Bar Standards Board (BSB) skill requirements for the LLB law degree, as well as those of the Quality Assurance Agency (QAA). These institutions represent the regulatory bodies of the legal profession in England and Wales (the SRA regulating solicitors, and the BSB regulating barristers), as well as setting the subjects to be studied on, and – alongside the QAA standards body – ensuring the required standards of the LLB. It will consider these vis-à-vis digital skills development, as well as provide an international perspective on digital skills in legal education.

Technological developments: the current legal landscape

The development and implementation of Legal Tech is a global endeavour. Perhaps most obviously, Legal tech has been well received in order to drive business efficiencies for legal practices and the courts. For example, Canada was a relatively early adopter of online dispute resolution (ODR), with the UK, US and China also adopt-

ing similar systems later on (Salter [2017]; Menezes, Mocheva and Shankar [2020]). In Australia, firms are utilising technological systems such as automated document generation and 'cloud-based practice management software' to achieve efficiencies (Jones and Pearson [2020]). In Singapore, firms are utilising advanced technological systems to improve client experience, improve administrative efficiency (such as time billing) and document retrieval software (Ang and Ng [2021]). Meanwhile in Nigeria, software is being introduced that provides enhanced legal analytics, and in South Africa, LexisNexis has integrated AI into their offerings to help make legal research more efficient (Egeruoh-Adindu [2021]). Clearly, the use of technology here is motivated by the drive to seek cost efficiencies.

Indeed, it is not just in the areas of business efficiencies, automation, and provision enhancement where digital technologies are making an impact. Law firms and chambers are still businesses that require publicity and advertisement to obtain clients. In this respect, law firms are utilising their online presence to generate business and attract clients (Jones [2021]). Blogs from firms offering publicly accessible legal expertise and authored by a firm's lawyers have become commonplace; as have advertisements and marketing strategies on social media platforms such as LinkedIn (Ryan [2021]).

Furthermore, the rapid development and integration of technology has led to the development of a new branch of the legal profession, legal technologists. Legal technologists lie somewhere between lawyer and computer specialist, often utilising their legal knowledge to create, implement and operate innovative technological legal solutions (Allen and Overy n.d.). Some firms offer this route as a specific qualification route for solicitors (Westland [2021]).

Digital skills in the LLB: requirements of regulatory bodies and standards agencies

Despite the prevalence of technology within the legal profession and within the legal academy, there is little mention of digital skills within the QAA's guidance or the SRA-BSB's Academic Stage Handbook. The SRA-BSB joint statement mentions technology regarding the provisions of the provider institution, namely that there must be sufficient IT infrastructure and digital resources for the students (SRA [2021]).

The QAA Subject Benchmarks are a little more detailed. Paragraphs 1.17 and 1.18 suggest the need for providers to engage students in the understanding of technology's role in areas such as access to justice and the increasing use of technology within the legal profession (QAA [2023] at 5). It also notes at 2.6 and 4.4 the need to inculcate within students the appropriate use of technology in different situations and its use in the collection, analysis and presentation of data (QAA [2023]). Importantly, the QAA statement makes specific reference to Artificial Intelligence (AI) and its potential impact on the legal profession at 1.18 (QAA [2023]). However, the paragraph still remains quite broad in its addressing of AI.

Basic digital literacy

The requirements and suggestions of the QAA and SRA-BSB statements can be broadly divided into two categories: basic digital literacy and further technological skills. The subject of this section is that of basic digital literacy. This is the idea that law students need to have a basic grasp of the fundamental digital applications that lawyers use within practice and, without which, a firm would unlikely be able to function. These include text editing software such as Microsoft Word, digital legal research databases like Westlaw and Practical Law, and email.

As a result of the wholesale changes made to communication due to the COVID-19 pandemic in 2020/21, video-call and video-conferencing could also be included in this section. Applications such as Microsoft Teams, Zoom and Skype for Business have become a standard feature of many lawyers' practices and other workplaces.

While these applications can be categorised as 'basic' in that they are a fundamental part of the legal profession, to consider the knowledge of their use as second nature is a mistake. Indeed, the concept of the 'digital native' is occasionally utilised to suggest the idea that younger generations are automatically *au fait* with the use of, at least, these basic technologies, often due to the fact that they have grown up in a society which has integrated them. While it is true that younger

generations are utilising technology more than previous generations, there still exists significant digital inequalities, even in more developed nations (Eynon [2020]).

In this respect, many universities offer digital skills courses as part of their provision. For example Lancaster University offers the Digital Skills Certificate (2023), Edinburgh University offers a Digital Skills Programme (2023), and Oxford has a bank of digital skills courses (2023). These courses are commonplace globally, including in Australia (Griffiths [2023]; Wollogong [2023]), Canada (Waterloo [2023]) and the Netherlands (Amsterdam [2023]).

Additionally, some of the more legal focused basic skills such as legal database use are taught by the companies who developed them. For example, LexisNexis offers a suite of training, including legal research certification (LexisNexis). Similarly, Westlaw offers basic, advanced, international and practical training and certification for law school students (Westlaw).

Further technological skills

On the other hand, the legal profession – including the legal academy – has begun to further integrate more advanced technologies in their practice. As a result, the skills provision within law schools has needed development to effectively and ethically utilise these technologies. Indeed, from the standpoint of England and Wales, the QAA requires development of such skills (QAA [2023]).

Of note, the QAA specifically mentions the need to develop skills relevant to AI and its integration within the legal profession (QAA [2023]). Clearly, the rapid integration of AI within the legal profession does give law schools a mandate to help their students develop the skills to utilise it effectively and ethically. For example, the University of Manchester has developed the 'Law and Technology Initiative' in conjunction with legal and corporate partners in order to enhance students' digital skills through the creation of a relevant law and technology curriculum (Manchester [2023]).

However, skills development in this area is still likely to be less of a priority for law schools than the 'basic skills' noted above. While the development of basic digital skills for law students is vital to ensure that the day-to-day running of a legal practice continues, more specialist applications such as AI are likely to be overseen by outside technology support or more specialist 'in-house' support, such as legal technologists (Hallowell [2021]).

Conclusion

Clearly, there is both a national and international effort to further enhance students' digital skills within law school. This is a natural response to the ever-increasing digitisation of the legal profession, which in itself requires lawyers to have a working knowledge of basic digital applications, as well as other non-legal professions. Furthermore, regulatory bodies are also heeding these developments, mandating that law schools prepare their students for a digitalised profession.

However, while there is an effort to integrate high level technological applications such as AI into the legal profession, the requirements for law students to fully understand these technologies is perhaps less critical. These technologies will likely be overseen by those with specialist skills in this area, either 'in-house' by IT teams and legal technologists, or outside specialist companies. Law students, it must be remembered, are taking a law degree not a computer science degree, and while some may well opt to further their specialist digital knowledge, for others a basic working knowledge of essential technologies may well be sufficient.

B. ROBINSON TURNER

References

Ang, P. and Ng, M. (2021). 'Singapore: A Fertile Ground for Legaltech Innovation', *Asian Legal Business*, available at https://www.legalbusinessonline.com/other-news/singapore-fertile-ground-legaltech-innovation.

Egeruoh-Adindu, I.E. (2018/2019). 'Technology and the Law: The Impact of Artificial Intelligence (AI) on Litigation and Dispute Resolution in Africa', *Nigerian Yearbook of International Law*, p. 413.

Eynon, R. (2020). 'The Myth of the Digital Native: Why it Persists and the Harm it Inflicts', in Burns, T. and Gottschalk, F. (eds), *Education in the Digital Age*, OECD.

Hallowell, S. (2021). 'How law schools can incorporate LegalTech into their curriculum', LexisNexis, available at https://www.lexisnexis.co.uk/blog/future-of-law/how-law-schools-can-incorporate-legaltech-into-their-curriculum.

Jones, E.J. (2021). 'The 21st Century Legal Professional' in Jones, E., Ryan, F., Thanaraj, A. and Wong, T. (eds), *Digital Lawyering: Technology and Legal Practice in the 21st Century*, Routledge.

Jones, L.J. and Pearson, A. (2020). 'The Use of Technology by Gold Coast Legal Practitioners', *Law, Technology and Humans*, 2(1).

'Law Tech Graduate Programme' (n.d.), available at https://www.aograduate.com/lawtech-programme.

LexisNexis, 'Lexis Advanced Training for Law School Students', available at https://www.lexisnexis.com/community/lawschool/student/training.

Menezes, A., Mocheva, N. and Shankar, S.S. (2020). '"Under Pressure": Integrating Online Dispute Resolution Platforms into Preinsolvency Processes and Early Warning Tools to Save Distressed Small Businesses', *Vikalpa*, 45(2).

Quality Assurance Agency. (2023). 'Subject Benchmark Statement: Law', available at https://www.qaa.ac.uk/docs/qaa/sbs/sbs-law-23.pdf?sfvrsn=c271a881_6.

Rabinovich-Einstein, O. (2021). 'The Past, Present and Future of Online Dispute Resolution', *Current Legal Problems*, 74(1), p. 125.

Ryan, F. (2021). 'The Use and Practice of Social Media', in Jones, E., Ryan, F., Thanaraj, A. and Wong, T. (eds), *Digital Lawyering: Technology and Legal Practice in the 21st Century*, Routledge.

Salter, S. (2017). 'Online Dispute Resolution and Justice System Integration: British Columbia's Civil Resolution Tribunal', *Windsor Yearbook of Access to Justice*, p. 112.

Solicitors Regulation Authority (SRA). (2014). 'Academic Stage Handbook', available at https://www.sra.org.uk/become-solicitor/legal-practice-course-route/qualifying-law-degree-common-professional-examination/.

Susskind, R. and Susskind, D. (2015). *The Future of the Professions*, OUP.

Thanaraj, A. (2021). 'Using Artificial Intelligence to Enhance and Augment the Delivery of Legal Services', in Jones, E., Ryan, F., Thanaraj, A. and Wong, T. (eds), *Digital Lawyering: Technology and Legal Practice in the 21st Century*, Routledge.

University of Manchester, 'About Us', available at https://www.law-tech.manchester.ac.uk/about-us/.

Westland, K. (2021). 'Legal Technology – A Career Path Less Trodden? (For Now)', available at https://www.addleshawgoddard.com/en/insights/insights-briefings/tech-talks/

legal-technology--a-career-path-less-trodden -for-now/.

Westlaw, 'Get certified in Westlaw and Practical Law', available at https://legalsolutions.thomsonreuters .co.uk/en/products-services/uk-law-student/get -certified-westlaw-uk.html.

35. Disability and legal education

Disability in law schools and legal education is relatively underexplored and there is a paucity of literature on disability and legal education in the UK. Issues to do with disability in law school have probably always existed but disclosure of disability has not always been easy for a number of reasons (Griffiths [2021]). Disclosure of a disability has increased generally in higher education in the last few years. A sizeable minority of the student population are disabled and in 2018–2019, 14.3 per cent of students studying in England and Wales declared at least one disability (Office for Students [2020]). In Law 12.9 per cent of students disclosed a disability (12,295 in total) (Advance HE [2020]) revealing a change in attitudes amongst the student population.

There is a small body of work on disability and legal education in the United States (Rothstein [2014]; Payne-Tsoupros [2020]) and this sits alongside studies, often labelled as 'wellbeing studies', on growing levels of anxiety and depression reported during law school in Australia and the United States (Krieger [2002]; Sheldon and Krieger [2004]; Lester, England, and Antolak-Saper [2011]; Larcombe, Tumbaga, Malkin, and Nicholson [2013]). More generalist reviews of disability in Higher Education are prevalent in the United States where ableist practices in Higher Education are reported (Dolmage [2017]). Disability in Higher Education generally is now being considered more widely in the UK where there is a reported widespread 'unevenness of understanding of disabled students' needs' across Higher Education (Vickerman and Blundell [2010] at 26). Real engagement with the issues faced by disabled students has started to gather traction with the work of the Office for Students (OFS) and the Disabled Students Commission (DSC) which was established for a three-year period by the Universities Minister in 2020 to address disability inclusion in higher education. Disability as a concept is often linked to the wellbeing and mental health of law students (see Wellbeing/Mental Health of Law Students) (Jones et al [2019]; Cage et al [2021]) rather than being a standalone issue requiring further scrutiny. Disability is much broader than wellbeing or mental health and some understanding of the legal definition of disability alongside the various models of disability is needed to understand the nature of disability in law school, legal education and the legal profession.

The legal definition of disability in England, Wales and Scotland

The Equality Act 2010, and before it the Disability Discrimination Act 1995, legislates for the complex phenomenon of disability. This legislation frames disability using an anti-discrimination framework linked to Equality, Diversity and Inclusion (EDI) (see Equality, Diversity and Inclusion (EDI) and the Law School). The aim of the Equality Act 2010 is principally equal treatment and non-discrimination and it forms part of the law in England, Wales and for the purposes of education and work, Scotland. Section 4 of the Equality Act brings all 'protected characteristics' together into one piece of legislation (whereas previously these were separate), all separate 'silos' (Solanke [2011]) but in theory equal before the law. A single body, the Equality and Human Rights Commission, oversees promoting and protecting the codified rights. Disability, defined in Section 6 of the Equality Act 2010, is a physical or mental impairment, which has a substantial and long-term adverse effect on the disabled person's ability to carry out normal day to day activities. The definition in the Equality Act 2010 concentrates on the medical impairment model of disability and places emphasis on the individual and a diagnosis to prove disability. The nature and severity of the impairment and its long-term effects are often the subject of medical evidence in any dispute about disability and when disabled people seek reasonable adjustments.

The notion of impairment rests solely with the individual which invariably means that the disabled person cannot participate in society fully without some accommodation (Duff and Ferguson [2007]). That accommodation in the Equality Act 2010 is defined as a 'reasonable adjustment' in Section 20. This duty enables disabled individuals to participate fully with some adjustments, albeit only those adjustments deemed reasonable. Lawson [2008] provides a full account of the duty of reasonable adjustments linking it to the duty of 'reasonable accommodation' in the United States. The duty provides for the removal of disadvantage experienced by the disabled student by the education provider taking any reasonable step, or combination of steps, necessary. The duty allows for the inclusion of disabled people and values them as equals (Lawson [2008] at 235). The 'reasonable adjustment' duty is reactive, and knowledge of disability is crucial, which puts disabled students under pressure to disclose both during their time at university in terms of learning and assessment and when looking for work experience, placement, or graduate employment. The reasonable adjustment duty can also cause tension in the classroom for law teachers, particularly in relation to assessment and understanding the nature and extent of the entitlements under the Equality Act 2010 for disabled law students where a 'one size fits all approach' to assessment can be problematic (Cameron et al [2019]).

Models of disability

Disability is often framed using various 'models' of disability. The medical model is used in the Equality Act 2010 where disability is understood as an individual impairment issue that needs to be rectified in some way by a reasonable adjustment to allow equal participation. The social model of disability challenges the medical model of disability and is led largely by the disabled people's movement (Oliver [1990]; Oliver and Barnes [2012]). The social model positions disability as a collective issue suggesting that disabled people are disabled not by their own impairments but by the disabling barriers in society. The social model at times seems to ignore the reality of the symptoms of some impairments (Shakespeare [2014]; Thomas [1999]; Thomas [2004]) but nevertheless it challenges the socially constructed barriers faced by disabled people in society. The human rights model of disability is derived from the protection offered by the United Nations Convention on the Rights of Persons with Disabilities (CRPD) and its Optional Protocol and complements the social model of disability suggesting that it is the interaction between the impairment and the societal barriers which is important (Lawson and Beckett [2021]; Kanter [2015]). The CRPD includes rights to 'reasonable accommodations' and 'inclusive education.' The social model is widely accepted as the most effective way that

Higher Education Institutions can respond to the needs of disabled students (Barnes [2007]; Office for Students [2019]). The UK's Office for Students [2019] advocates for more inclusion of disabled students through curriculum development, assessment, accommodation, and academic services (Office for Students [2019]) all of which are relevant to law school and legal education. Critical Disability Studies (Shildrik [2009]; Goodley [2014]) requires an intersectional approach to disability where the effect of prejudice is multiplied by other marginalised social identities such as class, race, sexuality and so on.

Disability in higher education and law schools

Recent literature identifies both the barriers (negative attitudes displayed by faculty members, doubting the students have a disability, not adapting teaching practices, and questioning the student's capacity to study in university) and the support available during disabled students' university experiences (Morina [2017]). Similar barriers were identified by Griffiths [2021] who specifically explored the lived experience of disability in an English law school. This research revealed a complex transition through law school where identities are constructed and re-constructed on multiple occasions in different contexts (Griffiths [2021]). Disability as a word or identity was often rejected or re-packaged by the law student participants and equality laws played only a small part in identity construction (Griffiths [2021]). Disability significantly impacted the time spent in law school in terms of relationships with others, particularly law tutors who doubted their non-visible disability or questioned their need for reasonable adjustments, their grades, their ability to socialise and network like other law students and their future becoming as a lawyer (Griffiths [2021]). Stigma associated with disability runs deep in disabled law students who suggested that they would not declare a disability during recruitment exercises with law firms or barristers' chambers for fear of being overlooked for training contracts and pupillage (Griffiths [2021]). The future of legal education in England and Wales is uncertain with the development of new routes to the profession through the apprenticeship programme and a new Solicitors Qualifying Examination (SQE), which has already garnered controversy in its attitude towards disabled people (Reyes [2021]). On a more positive note, the new UK Quality Assurance Agency Subject Benchmark Statement for law [2023] includes Accessibility and specific reference to disability for the first time. The Law Society of England and Wales's Disabled Solicitors Network Committee has recently published guidance for disabled law students (The Law Society [2023]) seeking employment. These advances support disability issues becoming more mainstream when considering EDI and disability in law school and legal education. They also support the idea of a disabled professional identity so that disabled law students can see themselves in the legal profession (see Professional Identity Formation of Law Students) and they can start to experience a sense of belonging in that profession which has not always been so welcoming (Foster and Hirst [2020]; Jones et al [2020]) and where mental health and wellbeing has been under scrutiny (Collier [2016]; Jones et al [2020]) in the last few years.

ELISABETH GRIFFITHS

References

Advance HE (2020). *Students Statistical Report*, Advance HE, available at https://www.advance -he.ac.uk/knowledge-hub/equality-higher -education-statistical-report-2020.

Barnes, C. (2007). 'Disability, higher education and the inclusive society', *British Journal of Sociology of Education*, 28(1), p. 135.

Cage, E., Jones, E., Ryan, G., Hughes, G. and Spanner, L. (2021). 'Student mental health and transitions into, through and out of university: student and staff perspectives', *Journal of Further and Higher Education*, 45(8), p. 1076.

Cameron, H., Coleman, B., Hervey, T., Rahman, S. and Rostant, P. (2019). 'Equality law obligations in higher education: reasonable adjustments under the Equality Act 2010 in assessment of students' unseen disabilities', *Legal Studies*, 39(2), p. 204.

Collier, R. (2016). 'Wellbeing in the legal profession: Reflections on recent developments (or, what do we talk about, when we talk about wellbeing?)', *International Journal of the Legal Profession*, 23(1), p. 41.

Disabled Students' Commission. (2020). *Annual report 2020–2021: Enhancing the Disabled Student Experience*, Advance HE.

Dolmage, J.T. (2017). *Academic ableism: Disability and Higher Education*, 1st edn, University of Michigan Press.

Duff, A. and Ferguson, J. (2007). 'Disability and accounting firms: Evidence from the UK', *Critical Perspectives on Accounting*, 18(2), p. 139.

Foster, D. and Hirst, N. (2020). *Legally Disabled? The Career Experiences of Disabled People Working in the Legal Profession*, Cardiff University Business School.

Goodley, D. (2014). *Dis/ability Studies. Theorising Disablism and Ableism*, Routledge.

Griffiths, E. (2021). 'The lived experience of disabled students in law school: present realities and possible futures', DLaw Thesis, The University of Northumbria at Newcastle, available at https://nrl.northumbria.ac.uk/id/eprint/48811/.

Jones, E., Samra, R. and Mathijs, L. (2019). 'The World at Their Fingertips? The Mental Wellbeing of Online Distance-Based Law Students', *The Law Teacher*, 53(1), pp. 49–69.

Jones, E., Graffin, N., Samra, R. and Lucassen, M. (2020). *Mental Health and Wellbeing in the Legal Professions*, 1st edn, Bristol University Press.

Kanter, A.S. (2015). *The Development of Disability Rights under International Law: From Charity to Human Rights*, 1st edn, Routledge.

Krieger, L.S. (2002). 'Institutional Denial about the Dark Side of Law School, and Fresh Empirical Guidance for Constructively Breaking the Silence', *Journal of Legal Education*, 52(2), p. 112.

Larcombe, W., Tumbaga, L., Malkin, I. and Nicholson, P. (2013). 'Does an Improved Experience of Law School Protect Students Against Depression, Anxiety and Stress? An Empirical Study of Wellbeing and the Law School Experience of LLB and JD Students', *Sydney Law Review*, 35(2), p. 407.

Lawson, A. (2008). *Disability and Equality Law in Britain: The Role of Reasonable Adjustment*, Bloomsbury Publishing.

Lawson, A. (2020). 'Disability Law as an Academic Discipline: Towards Cohesion and Mainstreaming', *Journal of Law and Society*, 47(4), p. 558.

Lawson, A. and Beckett, A.E. (2021). 'The Social and Human Rights Models of Disability: Towards a Complementary Thesis', *The International Journal of Human Rights*, 25(2), p. 348.

Lester, A., England, L. and Antolak-Saper, N. (2011). 'Health and Wellbeing in the First Year: The Law School Experience', *Alternative Law Journal*, 36(1), p. 47.

Morina, A. (2017). 'Inclusive Education in Higher Education: Challenges and Opportunities', *European Journal of Special Needs Education*, 32(1), p. 3.

Office for Students. (2019). *Insight: Beyond the bare minimum: Are colleges and universities doing enough for disabled students?*, Office for Students.

Office for Students. (2020). *Coronavirus Briefing Note*, Office for Students, available at https://

www.officeforstudents.org.uk/publications/
coronavirus-briefing-note-disabled-students/#.

Oliver, M. (1990). *The Politics of Disablement*, Macmillan.

Oliver, M. and Barnes, C. (2012). *The New Politics of Disablement*, Palgrave Macmillan.

Payne-Tsoupros, C. (2020). 'A Starting Point for Disability Justice in Legal Education', *Journal Committed to Social Change on Race and Ethnicity*, 6(1), p. 164.

Quality Assurance Agency Subject Benchmark Statement – Law. (2023), available at https://www.qaa.ac.uk/the-quality-code/subject -benchmark-statements/subject-benchmark -statement-law#.

Reyes, E. (2021). 'Disabled People "Wilfully Excluded" in New Super-exam', *The Law Society Gazette*.

Rothstein, L. (2014). 'Forty Years of Disability Policy in Legal Education and the Legal Profession: What has Changed and What are the New Issues', *American University Journal of Gender Social Policy and Law*, 22(3), p. 519.

Shakespeare, T. (2014). *Disability Rights and Wrongs Revisited*, Routledge.

Sheldon, K.M. and Krieger, L.S. (2004). 'Does Legal Education have Negative Effects on Law Students? Evaluating Changes in Motivation,

Values, and Well-being', *Behavioral Sciences and the Law*, 22, p. 261.

Sheldon, K. and Krieger, L.S. (2007). 'Understanding the negative effects of legal education on law students: a longitudinal test of self-determination theory', *Personality and Social Psychology Bulletin*, 33, p. 883.

Shildrik, M. (2009). *Dangerous Discourse of Disability, Subjectivity and Sexuality*, Palgrave Macmillan.

Solanke, I. (2011). 'Infusing the Silos in the Equality Act 2010 with Synergy', *Industrial Law Journal*, 40, p. 336.

The Law Society. (2023). Becoming a solicitor as a disabled student, available at https://www.lawsociety.org.uk/career-advice/becoming-a-solicitor/disabled-students.

Thomas, C. (1999). *Female Forms: Experiencing and Understanding Disability*, Open University Press.

Thomas C. (2004). 'Developing the Social Relational in the Social Model of Disability: A Theoretical Agenda', in Barnes, C. and Mercer, G. (eds), *Implementing the Social Model of Disability: Theory and Research*, Disability Press, p. 32.

Vickerman, P. and Blundell, M. (2010). 'Hearing the voices of disabled students in higher education', *Disability & Society*, 25(1), p. 21.

36. Doctrinal legal education

Overview

Education about legal doctrine is well established in society and as part of higher education. At all levels the main focus of doctrinal legal education is on the rules applicable within a particular jurisdiction. The effective study of those rules, certainly at the level of higher education, requires the development of specialist skills in the identification and application of the rules relevant to determining legal questions and in the evaluation of those rules.

Introduction

The word 'doctrinal' in the context of law, and in particular in the phrases 'doctrinal legal education' and 'doctrinal legal research' generally has a broader meaning than one associated with 'a doctrine' or 'doctrines' of the law. It applies where attention is focussed on the whole body of principles or rules of law (grand and otherwise; common law and statutory; clear and unclear) that apply to a specified area of interest. That area may, for example, be a particular legal dispute between two parties, a stage of life (e.g. child law; the law and the dead), a kind of event (e.g. the law relating to road accidents) or a kind of law (e.g. criminal law, the law of tort).

Forms of law

In a common law system, such as that in England, a rule of law that applies to resolve a legal issue can be derived from primary or secondary legislation or from a decision or series of decisions of one of the superior courts (the 'common law'). In both cases the relevant rule may be very precise and the answer needed to resolve the legal issue obvious. Some people may believe that all law is like that, and that legal education is simply a matter of learning and remembering a large number of rules that they can recite when asked to do so in the manner of a quiz contestant and that can be assessed solely by multiple choice questions. This is nonsense, for a number of reasons. The whole body of law is immense and ever-increasing in size and complexity. Identifying which rule or

rules are relevant for solving a legal issue can be a major task. Identifying the applicable version of a heavily amended legislative text can be technically difficult; modern legal databases are of an enormous help here but still sometimes make mistakes. Many legal rules, both legislative and common law, are couched in general rather than specific terms. The wording of a rule may be ambiguous. It will often be the case that a rule was designed to deal with a specific situation in mind and the question will arise whether a different situation should be regarded as analogous. Special skills are needed to read and interpret case law. The proper approach to be adopted to interpreting statutes (and indeed a constitution) is itself subject to a great deal of case law and legal literature. Accordingly, a great deal of intellectual work will often be needed to get to a plausible answer. Law students need to be equipped with the skills to work out what the answers are and indeed should be.

Doctrinal legal education in higher education

It is axiomatic that any law degree will include the study of a range of legal subjects, commonly (but not necessarily) tied to a particular legal jurisdiction. Usually, students will be required to study subjects regarded as foundational. In the UK, for instance, these generally include public law, criminal law, the law of obligations and property law. Many law degrees also require some study of legal theory. The development of legal skills may be both the subject of separate teaching and integrated within substantive law courses. These compulsory subjects are complemented by a wide range of options. The study of most of these subjects will necessarily include an account of the substantive rules of law applicable to them in some part of the real world, usually today but sometimes in the past – for example the study of Roman law can be regarded as a valuable introduction for new law students to how law works.

A convenient starting point for considering the role of doctrinal legal education in higher education is to use the UK as an example. In the UK the benchmark statement for Law is produced with the key involvement of, and wide support from, academic lawyers by the Quality Assurance Agency for Higher Education. This provides guidance for curriculum design but is not a regulatory requirement. A key statement is that:

> Law degrees provide opportunities for developing proficiency in legal understanding. This means knowledge and comprehension of, and the capacity to question and apply, theories, concepts, values, principles and rules of public and private laws within a range of contexts.... Legal understanding also includes the ability to recognise ambiguity and deal with legal uncertainty. It involves offering evidenced conclusions via the application of knowledge to address actual or hypothetical problems in different contexts, and developing the capacity to produce syntheses of relevant doctrinal, policy and contextual issues, present reasoned choices between alternative solutions, and make critical judgements on the merits of particular arguments....[I]t is expected that legal study will include detailed engagement with substantive areas of law. (QAA Benchmark for Law [2023] at para.3.2)

Similar statements are made about US legal education: 'The analysis, critique and development of legal doctrine..., in combination, constitute the first, essential element of legal education (Sullivan [2007] at 13) and see USA (Contemporary Legal Education). The same is true of other jurisdictions: see for example legal education in Mexico (Contemporary Legal Education) and South Africa (Contemporary Legal Education). Accordingly, it seems that the study of doctrine is both an essential part of legal study in higher education and in itself not enough. However, is it necessary, desirable or even possible to put a hard line around the 'study of doctrine' on the one hand and everything else contemplated by the benchmark on the other? It is suggested that the answer to all three questions is no. The effective study of doctrine will clearly include engagement with the key rules of law applicable in the subject in question. And many of them may be reasonably clear-cut. But there will inevitably be a need to pay attention to how areas of uncertainty within those rules should be resolved, whether through a process of statutory interpretation (the modern process in the UK being contextual and purposive (Burrows [2022] at 4) or case law reasoning. There is then the dimension of evaluation. What is the purpose of the rule? Is that a proper purpose? Is the rule appropriately designed to achieve that purpose? Does the rule achieve that purpose

in real life? These matters can be relevant both to determining what the rule should be where there is uncertainty and whether a rule, once it is established what it is, needs to be reformed. And there are many further perspectives from which law can be evaluated.

When it comes to teaching it is hard, if not impossible, to understand a rule without an appreciation of its purpose. It is difficult to see how there can be effective doctrinal teaching without any context (see Twining [1994], [1997] and [2019]). The balance of emphasis as between rule and context will depend very much on the subject and the personal interests of the teacher, subject to any constraints set by professional bodies. Another variable is the depth at which substantive law subjects are taught.

The relationship between the study of law in Higher Education and the professional education and training of lawyers

In many jurisdictions in the world, possession of a law degree from a university or other institution of higher education is a necessary although not always sufficient requirement for qualification as a lawyer. The content of law degrees becomes a matter in which both legal academics and the relevant legal profession(s) have legitimate interests; this can give rise to tension if not dispute. This can play directly into the content of the law degree, with professional bodies stipulating what subjects have to be covered and in what depth. For example, an important difference between the US and the UK is that, in the US, a three-year postgraduate JD (Juris Doctor) law degree from a law school accredited by the American Bar Association is normally a requirement for qualification as a lawyer (in addition to passing subsequently a State Bar Examination) and is taken after a non-law degree. There is a high level of prescription (ABA Standards of Approval [2023]). In the UK, law degrees, of many kinds, are established undergraduate degrees and it is the case that probably only a minority of law graduates will go on to qualify as a lawyer; the extent of professional prescription in England and Wales is relatively limited and less than that in Scotland and Northern Ireland. In the case of the solicitors' profession in England and Wales, professional regulation of law degrees no longer exists (see England (Regulation of Legal Education) and Professional Legal Education.

The delivery of doctrinal legal education in Higher Education

In the UK, standard teaching methods in HE involve in-person lectures to large classes (law schools tend to be large as law is a very popular subject with applicants and is one of the least expensive subjects to provide for vice-chancellors). They may be reinforced by seminars with, say, 20 or so students or tutorials with smaller numbers. These are designed to be for discussion, but the larger the group the more difficult it is for discussion to be generated. In addition, smaller options are often taught solely by seminars, designed to incorporate both exposition and discussion. York Law School has chosen to adopt problem-based learning for key subjects, a distinctive approach adapted from its established use in some UK medical schools (see Problem-based Learning). Here, students in groups, supported by tutor-facilitators, address practical problems that are 'simulated real-life examples brought…by virtual clients'. The students have to 'identify the legal principles involved in the problem and unravel the legal and contextual issues that lie at the heart of it, which will typically involve more than one area of law' (York Law School [2023]). In the past, there has in the UK been some use of case-method teaching ('Socratic case-dialogue instruction' (Sullivan [2007] at 3) (and see Socratic Method), modelled on practice in US law schools, where this is, albeit in a wide variety of forms, the 'signature' teaching method for at least first year classes (Turow [1977]; Duxbury [1995]; Sullivan [2007] Ch 2). For example, the late Professor Sir John Smith and other colleagues taught contract, criminal law and tort by the case method at the University of Nottingham, using materials that developed into commercially published casebooks (e.g. Smith and Thomas [1957]). However, this ceased to be viable with increases in student numbers and pressure on teaching resources. A recent development has been the pervasive development of online teaching, forced upon all law schools by the global pandemic. The response by students to its continuation after the pandemic has been mixed. Lectures tend also to be recorded, leading to a reduction in attendances in person. There remains a school of thought that holds that for many, although admittedly not all, a subject is best understood if it is explained to them by another human being.

Assessment of doctrinal legal education in Higher Education

Assessment methods for substantive law subjects tend to include the 'signature' model of 'problem questions', which set out a set of facts and ask the student to apply the relevant law to those facts and commonly to evaluate that law as well. These tend to co-exist with evaluative essays, purely descriptive questions being out of fashion. In some instances, multiple choice (or single best answer) questions are used. These are easy to mark and work well in testing the application of clear law; whether they can do much if anything more is contested and they are in practice only used in conjunction with other methods of assessment. (See Assessment in Legal Education).

Conclusion

There have been some scholars, particularly in the US, who have claimed that legal doctrines are a fiction behind which judges can hide when in reality they are deciding legal issues in cases according to their own social or political inclinations or prejudices (see Critical Legal Studies). This has been contested as providing an inaccurate depiction of judging in the US and it is very difficult to see it as holding good for judges in the three UK legal systems. Legal doctrine is a reality. It is also the case that 'doctrinal' seems to be used by some in the context of legal research in a pejorative fashion, asserting or insinuating that doctrinal legal research can never rise above the second rate, a position consistently challenged by both the academic panels that periodically pass judgment on the quality of legal research in the UK, now in Research Excellence Framework (REF 2021 [2022] at 109), and by others (Fentiman [2022]). In the context of legal education the study of doctrine is both a necessary feature of a significant part of the curriculum and necessarily integrated with an understanding of policy and context (see Cownie [2004] at 55).

STEPHEN BAILEY

References

ABA Standards of Approval [2023] https://www.americanbar.org/content/dam/aba/administrative/legal_education_and_admissions_to_the_bar/standards/2023-2024/2023-2024-aba-standards-rules-for-approval.pdf.

Burrows. (2022). Lord Burrows, 'Statutory Interpretation in the Courts Today' (Sir Christopher Staughton Memorial Lecture 2022).

Cownie, F. (2004). *Legal Academics: culture and identities*, Hart Publishing.

Duxbury, N. (1995). *Patterns of American Jurisprudence*, Clarendon Press.

Fentiman, R. (2022). 'Citadels of the Law: Law Schools and the Defence of Doctrine', The Queens' Distinguished Lecture in Law.

QAA Benchmark for Law. (2023), available at https://www.qaa.ac.uk/the-quality-code/subject-benchmark-statements/subject-benchmark-statement-law.

REF 2021. (2022). Overview report by Main Panel C and Sub-panels 13 to 24.

Smith, J.C. and Thomas, J.A.C. (1957). *A Casebook on Contract*, Sweet & Maxwell, 1st edn.

Sullivan, W.M. et al (2007). *Educating Lawyers*, Jossey-Bass.

Turow, S. (1977). *One L: An Inside Account of Life in the First Year at Harvard Law School*, G Putnam.

Twining, W. (1994). *Blackstone's Tower: The English Law School*, Sweet & Maxwell.

Twining, W. (1997). *Law in Context*, Clarendon Press.

Twining, W. (2019). *Jurist in Context: A Memoir*, Cambridge University Press.

York Law School. (2023). https://www.york.ac.uk/law/undergraduate/pbl/.

37. Emeriti positions

The story of UC Hastings' Sixty-Five Club

UC Hastings College of the Law in San Francisco (today UC Law San Francisco), where I taught and researched in 1991, got it right. Hastings has had its Sixty-Five Club for a long time. Its history is linked to young men who had to fight in World War II. As a result, the law school had a shortage of teachers, with young men even scarcer than before so the Dean, David Ellington Snodgrass, appointed experienced faculty, many of whom had involuntarily retired at age 65. (Tobriner [1962–1964] at 8). When, after World War II, the number of law students began to rise rapidly, the faculty remembered the success of the Sixty-Five Club. Thus, the earlier solution developed into a long-term programme, which became a tradition and the faculty's hallmark. This practice meant that Hastings was also able to attract big names and even became one of the nation's strongest law schools.

The Sixty-Five Club has always stayed with me. Not only because of its many advantages, but also because of the possible disadvantages of a more structural deployment of emeriti. I still remember my question to the dean about when these emeriti, often well into their seventies, would have to leave. His sobering answer: 'As soon as the students can no longer understand them.'

Professor, more than a job: an identity

The question of what exactly 'emeritus professor' means is not so easy to answer (Crow 2021), and the definition is not the same everywhere. In some countries, the emerita/emeritus status is an honorary title awarded by the President of the university for distinguished service to the academic community; elsewhere every retired professor is an emeritus professor. For this entry, 'emeritus professor' and 'academic retirement' are understood to mean the same thing: the termination of the formal employment contract between an academic and the university, whereby the payment of a salary by the university stops and changes to an income from a pension because one has reached a certain age. The exact age may vary from country to country.

A professor for whom retirement is in sight can often look back on a long commitment to the university: a union that by no means took place only between eight o'clock in the morning and six o'clock in the evening. After all, new scientific and scholarly insights and ideas continue to flow, even after a professor has reached retirement age, or, what the late American Law Dean William L. Prosser once called, the 'age of statutory senility'. In addition, academics not only have a bond with their university, their faculty, and their department, but also with colleagues nationally and internationally. Their discipline is not retiring. Their personal identity – some call it a vocation (Crow [2021]) – is strongly linked to their discipline and to the colleagues, former PhD candidates, and students who are part of that discipline and that network. For some, therefore, the concept of academic retirement should be reframed from a static question of 'when' to a more dynamic process of 'how' (Xie and Ali [2023]).

Many will therefore choose to remain active – but without any formal payment in return. Others see retirement as requiring a clean break, leaving academia and academic identity behind (Crow [2021]).

Why emeriti professors are important

A good Law Dean can see well in advance that a professor will retire. This means that they must think about succession in good time. But also, about the question of how the departing academic can still contribute to the law school after retirement. On the one hand, a professor's departure at the end of their career contributes to the necessary rejuvenation and renewal of the academic staff. On the other hand, the leaving of a very experienced teacher is also a loss, especially in the case of a tight labour market and in countries with a rapidly changing demographic, such as East Africa (Inter-university Council for East Africa [2023]).

In many universities, the number of students is growing rapidly, and the workload is high. This is certainly true for law schools, with their strong focus on education and student well-being. In general, the teaching will be taken over by the successor; it does not seem wise to depend on emeriti for the regular curriculum. Yet emeriti can contribute to alleviating the workload in education. They may be available for specialist electives and for supervising theses. This gives early-career academics more opportunity to divide their time more evenly between research and education.

Moreover, with the emeritus, it is not only an experienced lecturer who leaves, but often also a productive researcher who is still professionally active. It is precisely in the field of research that the end of an academic career will take place quite gradually: articles still have to be completed and published, the last PhD candidates still have to be guided to the finishing line, editorial memberships continue, requests to peer review articles and books continue to pour in, and members of scientific societies and editors of journals often do not have a retirement age.

Emeriti are also assailed by invitations to sit on external review committees of other universities or scientific juries, or they are invited to join supervisory boards of universities and academic institutions. In this way, too, in management, administration, and quality assurance, they can be an important source of information for their university by sharing their experiences.

The freedom that comes with retirement also allows the emeritus to explore entirely new research avenues, which may be important for a future research agenda of the law school. Sometimes these are publications of a more reflective nature, for example about the prospects of one's own field (Stolker [2014]). With all this, they continue to add directly to the national and international reputation of both their discipline and their school. They also contribute to this by accepting invitations to give lectures, and by writing articles in special issues of magazines and in *Festschriften* for other retirees. Recognitions such as honorary doctorates and prizes do not stop when you reach retirement age; quite the contrary.

Moreover, they are also an important source in the provision of information *within* the law school or their department. Research shows that faculty often rely more on their peers than on department chairs, websites, or faculty handbooks for information. Also, there is an almost endless need for advice and coaching among the early-career faculty. Emeriti can be a valuable source to meet that need as well. Some universities use their retired faculty as

a reliable source of information, asking them to conduct sessions for faculty thinking about retirement (Van Ummersen [2023]).

Furthermore, happy emeriti can be crucial ambassadors in their contacts with alumni and other friends of the institution, and from that position contribute to fundraising for the school. The University of California is a fine example of this, where retiree associations establish endowments to fund scholarships and make additional donations to campus groups (CUCRA [2020]).

Finally, consider other volunteer work within the law school or the broader university. At Leiden University, for example, emeriti act as chairs in the defence of university dissertations, they are still part of many university committees, for example in the field of academic integrity, and they work as confidential advisers for PhD candidates and students. Retired lawyers from the law school are also popular as chairpersons of whistleblower committees and other complaints committees within the university.

Yet there is still little policy

Research increasingly shows that it is important to rethink the position of emeriti and that higher education leaders need to adapt more quickly (Van Ummersen et al [2023], Baldwin [2018]).

Most universities limit their information for future retirees mainly to advice such as the financial planning of retirement, insurance issues, and possibly also to the loss or retention of a university email address. Too often university policies do not go much further than this. This lack of policy seems to stem from discomfort. When you retire as a professor, you have to learn to play second fiddle, which includes giving space to the new generation of professors and administrators. Everyone at the university knows examples of retired professors who find it difficult to distance themselves from the day-to-day management of the department. An emeritus professor who arranges weekly lunches with his (former) staff, with the best of intentions, is nevertheless likely to be very subversive for his successor.

That's wrong. The retirement of an academic not only creates space for the retiree. It should do the same for the law school – for example, to break new ground, to reorganise education, to recalibrate the organisation or culture within a department or institute, or to change ingrained patterns of behaviour. Emeriti should never get in the way of incumbent colleagues. This is all the truer if the emeritus professor in question has also been an administrator or a director. To facilitate this, emeriti who want to remain active will have to be prepared to lower their voices in all these areas, or even to remain silent altogether, at least for some time.

And that's where it gets tricky: who will have that at times complicated conversation? And who will be willing to lay down the law when things don't go well? These conversations rarely appear easy for a dean or a department chair. A few schools acknowledge that their department chairs and deans need training to become more comfortable in discussing retirement plans with faculty. These leaders must understand the dynamics of these changes and the necessity of developing win-win solutions for both the faculty's and the institution's long-term success (Van Ummersen et al [2023]).

In several universities, there is a development from reluctance towards emeriti to keeping emeriti actively involved. Emeriti associations play a key role in this, as the experiences of the University of California show, for example. It has such a retirement association on nine of its ten campuses, and even physical retirement centres on eight. With its regular Retiree Surveys, the university demonstrates a great deal of experience in what a good retirement policy can yield for a university (CUCRA [2020]). The *Faculty Retirement* book and the research by Graham Crow and others also provide inspiring examples.

What is needed

As we have seen, retired academics can still contribute to the intellectual, organisational, and social life of the university and its law school. But never forget that the interests of the faculty, the department and in particular the successor should be central. It is key to have an open, comprehensive, and timely policy concerning academic retirement. This starts with the law school knowing what the wishes of its leaving academics are. These wishes can vary widely, as research among scholars has shown (Crow [2021]). Not everyone wants the same thing: discuss mutual needs, possibilities, and aspirations.

It is also important to consider the possible different aspirations of men and women (Cahill and Galvin [2022], Sharpe [2020]). Given that in some countries the number of women professors is still quite low, a good policy for women emeriti may help to some extent there as well (Doralt [2021]), although it can never be a solution in case of a possible gender inequality within a law school.

What retired faculty are generally entitled to, by default, is the retention of an email address and account, and a web page on which their publications can be found. IT support, access to the faculty building, access to the physical and digital library, and the opportunity to complete the supervision of ongoing PhD research and research assignments are also facilities that emeriti can expect to continue to enjoy. All these basic and essential facilities are part of the 'post-contractual rights' of an emeritus. Clear agreements should be made about the use of telephones, secretarial assistance, financial support for conferences, and the possibility of using physical spaces in the university. Some universities have so-called 'emeriti rooms', where emeriti can meet, socialise, and study. Also, it is important to be clear that university integrity and behavioural rules apply to emeriti insofar as they still participate in the institution's research and teaching, supervise PhD candidates, or publicise their research using the institution's name.

Navigating between the needs of an institution and those of loyal emeriti is a balancing act – but a potentially happy one. All those involved should be aware of the often-unspoken concern that retired faculty may find it difficult to resist somehow co-governing or influencing the direction of education and research. Be open on this and on other potential pitfalls when discussing the topic of retirement with a faculty member. It is important for the school and the university to have a clear and transparent written policy, effective communication, and a few active emeriti who, together with the deans, the department chairs, and the chief academic officers, want to take the lead (Van Ummersen et al [2023]). Perhaps, when developing a good emeriti policy, it would also be beneficial to pay attention to the differences between disciplines, each of which, such as Law, has its own individual identity and culture (Cownie [2006], Stolker [2014]). Where emeriti associations exist, they can play a significant role (Bugge et al [2021]). In addition, it may be wise for the dean to meet with the emeriti with some regularity.

To conclude, a carefully drafted policy, a mutually open attitude, and clear agreements between the school and the emeritus are essential for a win-win.

CAREL STOLKER

References

Baldwin, R.G. (ed), co-editors: Barefoot, B.O. and Kinzie, J.L. (2018). *Reinventing Academic Retirement, New Directions for Higher Education*, Wiley.

Bugge, J., Goldberg, C.E. and Say, B.H. (2018). 'Winning Support for New Visions of Academic Retirement', in Baldwin, R.G. (ed), *Reinventing Academic Retirement, New Directions for Higher Education*, Wiley.

Cahill, M. and Galvin, R. (2022). 'Being an academic retiree: a qualitative, follow-up study of women academics in the Republic of Ireland', *Irish Journal of Occupational Therapy*, 50(1).

Cownie, F. (2004). *Legal Academics – Culture and Identities*, Hart Publishing.

Crow, G. (2021). 'Academics Retiring, Scunnered or Otherwise, Project Managing Career Endings and the Transition to Retirement: The Case of Academics', the University of Edinburgh.

CUCRA. (2020). Council of University of California Retiree Associations, 'UC Retirees – Generous Talents, Enduring Community'.

Doralt, W. (2021). 'Akademische Karrierewege für Juristen in Deutschland und Österreich', Graz Law Working Paper No 09–2021.

Inter-university Council for East Africa. (2023). 'Demographics of African Faculty – Lessons from East African Community'.

Sharpe, D.L. (2021). 'Reinventing Retirement', *Journal of Family and Economic Issues*, 42 (Suppl 1).

Shenchu Xie, J. and Javed Ali, M. (2023). 'Academic Retirement: Changing Paradigms from "When" to "How"', *Seminars in Ophthalmology*, 38(6).

Stolker, C. (2014). *Rethinking the Law School: Education, Research, Outreach and Governance*, Cambridge University Press.

Tobriner, M.D. (1963–1964). 'In Memoriam David E Snodgrass (1894–1963)', *Hastings Law Journal*, 15, p. 8.

Van Ummersen, C. et al. (2023). *Faculty Retirement, Best Practices for Navigating the Transition*, Routledge.

38. Emotions and soft skills in legal education

Introduction

Traditionally, emotions have not been viewed as valuable, or even relevant, within legal education. The emphasis of the law upon reason and rationality led to the development of norms which encouraged the disregard and suppression of emotions within both legal education and legal practice. Emotions have been commonly characterised as illogical, irrational, antithetical to legal reasoning. As such, they have not been viewed as a fitting topic for the law degree, but rather something of an unpleasant type of quirk which must be ironed out to socialise students appropriately into being fledgling lawyers (Jones [2019]; Jones [2023]).

However, despite the persistence of this traditional approach, recent years have seen a gradual shift in attitudes. This has stemmed, at least in part, from the development of a body of 'law and emotions' scholarship (Bandes [1999]) and the existence of strong neuroscientific evidence on the value of emotions within learning (Immordino-Yang [2016]). It has also been encouraged by the increasing importance of so-called soft skills within the legal profession (Kiser [2017]). This entry will focus upon the key aspects of legal education where emotions are now becoming incorporated, including through an acknowledgment of such soft skills, arguing that there has been vital progress, but that there are still aspects where emotions and soft skills require further acknowledgment and utilisation.

Emotions as soft skills

The aspect of legal education in which emotions are now arguably most fully incorporated is skills development. This is often encapsulated in the term 'soft skills'. Although definitions of this term vary, in the context of legal education, Tsaoussi ([2020] at 2) describes them as 'learning about the social environment of the law and how to maximise performance in it, through better communication and forging strong interpersonal rela-

tionships with colleagues, clients'. They are also sometimes referred to as 'human skills' or even 'power skills' (Runyon [2022]). This reflects the fact usage of the term 'soft' has been critiqued as implying an 'otherness' about this set of skills which implies they are not of equal value to traditional 'hard' legal skills, such as legal reasoning and analysis.

There are several reasons for the growing interest in soft skills, one being the gradual acknowledgment of the role of emotions within legal practice. In the UK, this was encapsulated in the Legal Education and Training Review's acknowledgment of the affective domain as key to legal practice (LETR [2012]). In the US, the American Bar Association [2017] has promoted the importance of emotional intelligence and globally, the International Bar Association has promoted its importance (Botsford [Undated]). Another connected reason is the continued growth of clinical legal education as a component of legal education [see entry on Clinical Legal Education (Overview)]. There is a need for students in clinical settings to be emotionally prepared and supported as they are exposed to real-world scenarios and clients.

Effective engagement with clients requires students and legal professionals to be able to interpret and regulate their own emotions and those of their clients and colleagues. There is a need to show empathy and build rapport, whilst maintaining appropriate personal boundaries. This requires a set of complex but teachable skills requiring emotions. Examples of such skills development in legal education range from Brooke's [2015] focus on 'relational' lawyering (drawing on principles from social work in the US) to the global growth of interest in trauma-informed legal education and practice [see entry on Trauma-informed Legal Education].

The growing interest in reflection in legal education [see entry on Reflection and Legal Education] could also be seen as encouraging acknowledgment and incorporation of emotions as part of students' skills development. Clinical legal education programmes have been pioneers in such reflective practice and Spencer [2014] (in the Australian context) has argued that such reflection should explicitly include an acknowledgment of, and reflection upon, emotions. However, the extent to which this is currently done is unclear.

Emotions as content

The ever-increasing body of law and emotions scholarship referred to in the Introduction to this entry demonstrates the potential for emotions to be considered within the taught content of legal education. For example, Grossi [2019] has written on the inter-relationship between emotions and contract law in Australia. Raj has written about the experience of convening an optional undergraduate module titled 'Law and Emotion' in a UK University ([2021] at 128).

Although there are isolated examples of courses with an explicit focus on emotions, such as Raj's, these remain relatively sparse. However, the strength of socio-legal studies (also known as 'law and society' approaches) suggests that this could change in future. Law and emotions scholarship is an example of the type of inter-disciplinary work which is prized by this approach. Nevertheless, whilst well established in terms of research, its prevalence in terms of teaching is unclear. There have been arguments that law schools still have a tendency to adopt a vocational focus which prizes the 'know how' required for legal practice, focusing upon those subjects and approaches which will facilitate students' eventual entry into the legal profession (Thornton [2022]). Conversely, there is some evidence of interdisciplinarity and diversity within law teaching, for example, Prihandono and Yuniarti [2020] suggest that the average percentage of interdisciplinary law courses in the Association of Southeast Asian Nations Universities is 43.4 per cent (with Indonesia somewhat lower at around 27 per cent). Therefore it will be interesting to see if, and how, the content of the law curricula may continue to develop to incorporate emotions.

Emotions within pedagogy

In addition to (some) examples of emotions being incorporated into the content of a law degree, there is also some suggestions that it is increasingly being acknowledged in terms of the pedagogies applied within law teaching. This can also be put into the context of wider concerns over student wellbeing generally. For example, in the UK the University Mental Health Charter calls for a 'whole university' approach to promoting wellbeing which includes all aspects of teaching, learning and assessment (Hughes and Spanner [2019]). Given the strong links between emotional wellbeing and teaching and learning this suggests that there should be some form of pedagogical engagement with emotions. This is echoed in the literature on higher education which increasingly argues for emotions and affect to be acknowledged and incorporated within all aspects of university life, including pedagogy. For example, in the context of Indian higher education, Aithal and Aithal ([2023] at 372) argue: 'Emotional infrastructure enriches the overall learning experience by creating an environment where students feel safe to express their thoughts, ask questions, and engage in discussions. This sense of emotional security fosters active participation and a deeper understanding of course materials'.

Incorporating emotions into law pedagogy can involve factoring students' emotional responses into specific aspects of teaching. One example of this is providing assessment feedback in a way which elicits positive and motivating emotional responses from students, avoiding generating negative and de-motivating emotions (Turnbull [2022]). Another example is role-modelling appropriate use and regulation of emotions to students (Juergens [2005]).

A particular aspect of legal education which arguably allows for the inclusion of emotions, is the growing use of so-called 'trigger warnings' designed to alert students to the presence of sensitive content within the curricula. This is of particular relevance to law students, where topics may cover a range of violent and sexual offences and other potentially distressing subject-matter. It is important that such warnings or notices are accompanied by support and resources to assist students in navigating their emotional responses and developing healthy forms of emotional resilience. Without these, students may simply avoid the material in question, or may have a response which impedes their ability to absorb the relevant information. Avoiding this by incorporating emotions into pedagogy is important in terms of both students' studies and their psychological health. Indeed, Chanbonpin ([2015] at 616–617) argues that 'trigger warnings' present a critique of traditional legal education (in the US context) in a way which can stimulate new pedagogic approaches and staff-student partnerships.

Conclusion

The incorporation of emotions into legal education remains incomplete and uneven. While there is strong evidence to support their explicit acknowledgment and utilisation, there is not yet a full acknowledgment and acceptance of this within law schools. There are potentially promising developments which may result in the greater integration of emotions, including the increasing prominence of 'soft skills' within the legal profession, growing understanding of the importance of emotions in clinical legal education, the introduction broader, inter-disciplinary content within legal curricula and pedagogic imperatives for incorporating emotions. Whilst at an early stage, these provide indications that there remains scope for further developments in this area.

EMMA JONES

References

Aithal, P.S. and Aithal, S. (2023). 'How to Increase Emotional Infrastructure of Higher Education Institutions', *International Journal of Management, Technology, and Social Sciences*, 8(3), p. 356.

American Bar Association. (2017). *How emotional intelligence makes you a better lawyer*, available at https://www.americanbar.org/news/abanews/publications/youraba/2017/october-2017/how-successful-lawyers-use-emotional-intelligence-to-their-advan/.

Bandes, S. (ed) (1999). *The passions of law* (Vol. 67), NYU Press.

Botsford, P. (Undated). 'Why lawyers need to be taught more about emotional intelligence', *International Bar Association*, available at https://www.ibanet.org/article/bc769d24-a76e-447a-aff1-fd92903bbd60.

Brooks, S.L. (2015). 'Teaching Relational Lawyering', *Rich. J.L. & Pub. Int.*, 19, p. 401.

Chanbonpin, K.D. (2015). 'Crisis and Trigger Warnings: Reflections on Legal Education and the Social Value of the Law', *Chi.-Kent L. Rev.*, 90, p. 615.

Grossi, R. (2019). 'The discomfort of Thorne v Kennedy: Law, love and money', *Alternative Law Journal*, 44(4), p. 281.

Hughes, G. and Spanner, L. (2019). The University Mental Health Charter, available at https://hub.studentminds.org.uk/university-mental-health-charter/.

Immordino-Yang, H. (2016). *Emotions, learning, and the brain: Exploring the educational impli-cations of affective neuroscience*, W.W. Norton & Company.

Jones, E. (2019). *Emotions in the Law School: Transforming Legal Education through the Passions*, Routledge 2019.

Jones, E. (2023). 'Incorporating an affective framework into liberal legal education to achieve the development of a "better person" and "good citizen"', *European Journal of Legal Education*, 4(1).

Juergens, A. (2005). 'Practicing what we teach: The importance of emotion and community connection in law work and law teaching', *Clinical L. Rev.*, 11, p. 413.

Kiser, R. (2017). *Soft Skills for the Effective Lawyer*, Cambridge University Press.

Legal Education and Training Review. (2013). *Setting Standards: The future of legal services education and training regulation in England and Wales*, available at https://letr.org.uk/the-report/index.html.

Prihandono, I. and Yuniarti, D.S. (2020). 'Interdisciplinary teaching in law: study on Indonesian law schools', *Utopía y praxis latinoamericana: revista internacional de filosofía iberoamericana y teoría social*, 6, p. 268.

Raj, S. (2021). 'Teaching feeling: bringing emotion into the law school', *The Law Teacher*, 55(2), p. 128.

Runyon, N. (2022). 'Why "power skills" is the new term for soft skills in the hybrid work world', Thomson Reuters, available at https://www.thomsonreuters.com/en-us/posts/legal/power-skills-rebranding/.

Spencer, R. (2014). ' "*First they tell us to ignore our emotions, then they tell us to reflect*": the development of a reflective writing pedagogy in clinical legal education through an analysis of student perceptions of reflective writing', *International Journal of Clinical Legal Education*, 21(2), p. 33.

Thornton, M. (2022). 'What is the Law School for in a Post-Pandemic World?', in Dunn, R.A., Maharg, P. and Roper, V. (eds), *What is Legal Education For? Re-assessing the Purposes of Early Twenty-First Century Learning and Law Schools*, Routledge.

Turnbull, A. (2022). 'Feeling feedback: screencasting assessment feedback for tutor and student well-being', *The Law Teacher*, 56(1), p. 105.

Tsaoussi, A.I. (2020). 'Using soft skills courses to inspire law teachers: a new methodology for a more humanistic legal education', *The Law Teacher*, 54(1), p. 1.

39. Employability and legal education

The meaning of employability

There is no single agreed meaning of employability. To add to the challenge, both policy and scholarly literature also refer to 'work readiness', 'career readiness', 'graduate skills', and 'graduate employment'. Higher education literature also engages with related concepts of work integrated learning, clinics, placements, and internships.

For these purposes, the latter concepts support development of the former. They may occur within (for credit) curriculum or via extra-curricular activities either with the support of the law school or on the student's own initiative. The focus here is on the first group of concepts, described as 'employability', taken to embrace work- or career-readiness and graduate skills.

At its narrowest, employability can be understood as the acquisition of and competence in skills identified by stakeholders as necessary for work in their industry. While graduates' threshold discipline knowledge might be taken for granted, this narrower view of employability can be understood as extending beyond knowledge per se to 'higher-order transferrable skills that are applicable and common to a range of contexts across all specific fields, and include[ing] communication, analytical and problem-solving skills, interpersonal relations and the ability to use information technology' (Pitan [2017]).

By contrast Bridgstock, for example, suggests a broader definition of employability that includes: 'self-belief and an ability to secure and retain employment' and 'competencies necessary for a successful life and well-functioning society' (Bridgstock [2009] at 34). She observes that an essential and often overlooked component employability skillset is that of career management. A broader conception of employability thus implies a multitude of further component knowledge, skills, and dispositions (Bridgstock [2009]). Given the desirability of 'transferrable' skills, an individual's own choices, and the state of the employment market, the work for which a graduate is prepared need not be within their discipline. Further complicating the meaning of employability, Francis (2015) observes the inherent contradiction

that one might be employable without being employed. Educators may be able to assess the knowledge, skills, and dispositions constituting employability, while remaining unable to measure success solely through data on graduate employment.

Against this context this entry adopts a broad conceptualisation of employability in legal education. The term here is taken to mean the knowledge, skills and dispositions in the law graduate that equip them to:

- gain and retain meaningful employment in the legal profession or law-related contexts; and
- contribute purposefully to the community in alignment with the norms of the profession.

Although not necessary from a purely pedagogical perspective, a further facet of the policy environment is the involvement of industry in student learning. In Australia, for example, government definitions of work integrated learning require some industry nexus to qualify (TEQSA [2022]).

Acknowledging the contestation around what employability might mean, what knowledge skills and dispositions might constitute employability, and how it may be measured, this entry provides an overview of strategies for the design, analysis, evaluation, and overall response to the imperative of graduate employability in legal education. The goal is explicit preparation of graduates for a career in law, and participation in an engaged citizenry as an expanded conception of the professional in society.

Employability in legal education

One challenge for law academics in designing a curriculum for employability lies in implicit assumptions about the nature of legal education and its nexus with legal practice. Jurisdictional accreditation requirements for identified graduate knowledge, skills, and dispositions provide an expectation of what is necessary to become a lawyer. However, they do not speak to graduates' capabilities to find and succeed in legal work and a legal career i.e. their employability. Translating accreditation standards into employability requires attention to curriculum and pedagogy beyond threshold knowledge areas and skills. There is scope beyond accreditation requirements for a law school to determine the parameters of employability through knowledge, skills, and dispositions, in a curriculum suited to their own context (Galloway, Castan and Steel [2023]). Despite this potential, many law academics are specialists in discipline knowledge and accustomed to the traditional emphasis on acquisition of doctrinal knowledge. It can be expected that not all law schools or law teachers will embrace employability with enthusiasm.

Despite debates around what legal knowledge should properly be mandated in a law degree, there is likely consensus over the need for a 'coherent body of discipline knowledge' (Kift, Israel and Field [2010] at 10) as the foundation for employability in law graduates. Further, dispositions including ethics and service might be broadly agreed upon as part of a graduate's comprehension of the nature of the profession and the role of a lawyer. Beyond this foundation lies potential for programme differentiation in terms of additional knowledge such as other discipline or Indigenous knowledges, and dispositions that might reflect institutional imperatives, such as sustainability or global mindedness. In New Zealand, for example, 2025 will see a new accreditation requirement for the teaching and assessment of Tikanga Māori |Māori Māori Laws and philosophy. See *Professional Examinations in Law Regulations 2008* (NZ).

Apart from legal problem solving, many skills have traditionally been implicit within the law curriculum. The Australian Discipline Standards (Kift, Israel and Field [2010]) provide a helpful framework of threshold graduate skills that might inform an explicit and scaffolded skills curriculum:

• thinking skills;
• research skills;
• communication and collaboration;
• self-management.

In their fuller descriptions, some of these skills represent *legal* skills e.g. 'identify and articulate legal issues and apply legal reasoning and research to generate appropriate responses to legal issues' (Kift, Israel and Field [2010] at 10). Others are *transferrable* skills, such as 'collaborate effectively'.

In addition, most universities provide for graduate attributes and so-called transferrable skills which are also features of the broad conceptualisation of employability. Such

transferrable skills might be mapped onto the Discipline Standards (Galloway [2017]) providing a means of translating generic skills into *law* graduate capabilities necessary for career readiness.

In considering what skills to include in a law programme's focus on employability it is helpful also to comprehend how students will develop those skills. For example, mooting is often seen as a quintessential legal skill emblematic of graduates' threshold competency. Mooting is, rather, a collection of legal skills that themselves are grounded in transferrable skills, many of which overlap (Galloway et al [2016]). Component skills in mooting might comprise research, thinking skills, writing and speaking. An introductory level might require simply locating cited cases and legislation, progressing to locating law relevant to solving a bounded legal problem, and at an advanced level, locating cases and legislation to answer an unbounded question. Similarly, speaking might start by emphasising oral communication, while an advanced level engages with court-room advocacy practice. Employability in legal education therefore requires attention to the breakdown of skills that comprise complex law-specific or transferrable tasks, ensuring that students can develop them during the programme.

A whole-curriculum approach to employability

Knowing *what* skills (or knowledge and dispositions) comprise employability leaves open the question of how to organise curriculum to support coherent learning to achieve the goal of graduate employability. Nor does it address how to engage students in broader contextual questions of what a career in or with the law looks like, and the skills of navigating one's career.

To develop a coherent approach to employability it is worth considering the components of the broader approach and how they manifest as a student progresses. This suggests a matrix of criteria: occupation specific skills and knowledge, understanding the nature of the profession, self-understanding, and career management skills (Jones, Millar and Chuck [2019]). Each can be described at progressive levels of competency. Such a whole of programme rubric (James and Burton [2017]) can provide a framework for intentional scaffolding of employability within a law curriculum.

Where the nexus between employability and industry is important, the levels of attainment of criteria can also suggest degrees of workplace proximity (Bosco and Fern [2014]). The introductory level might occur in the classroom (low proximity). Students can be introduced to workplace specific examples, perhaps with guest lecturers, to demonstrate an explicit link between the classroom and the workplace. They might explore the 'why' of the learning outcome and the role it plays in professional life (Jones, Miller and Chuck [2019] at Appendix A). The aim at this level is to build a sense of professional identity so that students can link their classroom learning with their career orientation.

The intermediate level might take place in classroom activities, including simulations such as a moot or client interview, or may have closer workplace proximity via field trips or other 'real-world' encounters, such as a court visit. Although the advanced level may take place within the classroom, high workplace proximity might involve a clinic or internship, or project-based learning in conjunction with industry or community. How this occurs in a curriculum will depend on resources and scalability of programmes.

Conclusion

Even where all law schools are required to engage with graduate employability, adopting a principles-based approach to employability in curriculum design allows for differentiation between programmes. Existing frameworks such as the Australian Discipline Standards can be given form through the application of an institution's own values and priorities to signal how that curriculum will deliver on employability.

Further, the resultant priorities can be structured to afford a coherent learning experience for students. Such a framework can assist law academics in making explicit how students are preparing for their lives beyond graduation.

KATE GALLOWAY

References

Bosco, A.M. and Ferns, F. (2014). 'Embedding of Authentic Assessment in Work-Integrated Learning Curriculum', *Asia-Pacific Journal of Cooperative Education*, 15(4), p. 281.

Bridgstock, R. (2009). 'The Graduate Attributes We've Overlooked: Enhancing Graduate Employability through Career Management Skills', *Higher Education Research and Development*, 28(1), p. 31.

Francis, A. (2015). 'Legal Education, Social Mobility and Employability: Possible Selves, Curriculum Intervention and the Role of Legal Work Experience', *J of Law and Society*, 41(2), p. 173.

Galloway, K. (2017). 'Disrupted Law Degree: Future Competencies for Legal Service Delivery', available at http://dx.doi.org/10.2139/ssrn.3082486.

Galloway, K. et al (2016). 'Working the Nexus: Teaching Students to Think, Read and Problem-solve Like a Lawyer', *Legal Education Review*, 26 (1 & 2), p. 95.

Galloway, K., Castan, M. and Steel, A. (2023). 'Hacking the Priestleys', in Gibbon, H. et al (eds), *Critical Legal Education as a Subversive Activity*, Routledge.

James, N. and Burton, K. (2017). 'Measuring the Critical Thinking Skills of Law Students Using a Whole-of-Curriculum Approach', *Legal Education Review*, 27(1), p. 1.

Jones, C.E., Millar, T.J. and Chuck, J.-A. (2019). 'Development of a Rubric for Identifying and Characterizing Work-Integrated Learning Activities in Science Undergraduate Courses', *International Journal of Work-Integrated Learning*, 20(4), p. 351.

Kift, S., Israel, M. and Field, R. (2010). 'Bachelor of laws: Learning and Teaching Academic Standards Statement', Australian Learning and Teaching Council.

Pitan, O.S. (2017). 'Graduate Employees' Generic Skills and Training Needs', *Higher Education, Skills and Work Based Learning*, 7(3), p. 290.

Tertiary Education Quality and Standards Agency ('TEQSA'). (2022). 'Guidance Note: Work-Integrated Learning' Version 2.0.

40. England (contemporary legal education)

Introduction

Formal legal education in England is both an academic study and a precursor to qualification as a lawyer. English Law can be studied at school as an A and AS level subject. But most formal legal education takes place at the university, or tertiary level. In 2020–21, 31,585 UK students applied to study law at undergraduate level in England and Wales, out of whom 21,650 UK students were accepted. 92 universities in England and Wales offer law degrees (UCAS 2024). In 2021 18,927 students graduated in law including twice as many women as men. Only about 25 per cent of those who take law degrees subsequently qualify and practice as solicitors (The Law Society Annual Statistical Report [2022] at 32).

The new apprenticeship route

Until recently, all those wishing to practice as lawyers had to possess a law degree or, if they were a non-law graduate, obtain a qualification in law known as the Common Professional Examination or Graduate Diploma in Law. It is now also possible for school leavers to take an apprenticeship route into legal practice as a solicitor through a six-year apprenticeship. The apprenticeship involves working in a law firm and studying for a law undergraduate degree and an LLM whilst working. However, a university degree remains the most common route to qualification. Chartered Legal Executives follow a slightly different route to qualify as a solicitor.

Law courses in university

In England, legal education at undergraduate university level is generally very similar in all universities, usually including courses in Public Law, Criminal Law, Law of Obligations (contract, restitution and tort), Property Law, Trusts and Equity and European Union Law (despite Brexit, European Law still is important for the UK). However, law departments and faculties differ in the way these and other subjects are taught. Some law teachers consider that a 'black-letter law' approach, studying the law as it is written (the law in books), is appropriate (see Doctrinal Legal Education) and others adopt more of a 'law in society' approach (see entry on Socio-legal Studies) looking at the effect of law in the real world, the role and importance of law, lawyers and judges and how law affects ordinary people. Cownie's empirical study of law teachers in England suggests that they are becoming much more 'contextualist' in approach (2004).

Liberal and vocational

Because the basic law degree can be used to satisfy requirements for entry to the legal professions and is also a degree involving the academic study of law within the humanities or the social sciences, it has become something of a battle ground between the profession and the academy as to whose needs are paramount. Only a minority of law graduates will take or find jobs in the profession, and there is a strong argument for a more open or varied legal education. The debate centres on whether a 'liberal' and a vocational education can co-exist.

Kahn-Freund (1966) criticised the 'superstition that only that which is of practical importance is worthy to be taught' and 'the perhaps even more pernicious superstition that the less a thing has to do with practice the better it is for the so-called training of the mind'. English scholars like Cownie (2005) and Bradney (2003) have argued for a more liberal education approach at university level as do Roger Brownsword, Bob Hepple and the ACLEC Report (Brownsword [1999], Hepple [1996], ACLEC [1996]). Twining (1994) would seem to want both a liberal education *and* one that will suit the profession, as would Sherr (1998), Ching (2018) and Boon and Webb (2008), although Twining's 'vocatio praecox' (premature vocationalism) is a warning against bringing too much early vocationalism into the academic programme. The Legal Education and Training Review (2013) in England and Wales, funded by and written for the professions, promoted a liberal education. And Tony King (2015), a partner at Clifford Chance, said on behalf of the profession that it was 'perfectly legitimate' that law should be 'a liberal arts degree'.

For Kahn-Freund the goal of legal education was to teach the ability to accept authority while simultaneously questioning it (1966). He also thought that the use of hypothetical legal problems in examinations was a poor approach to teaching law. And the focus on case law in common law jurisdictions emphasised the marginal rather than the typical phenomena, which are the subject of other social sciences (and feature in the civil law approach in which Kahn-Freund was trained). Kahn-Freund's solution was to add 'descriptive economics' and sociology to English law courses. Twining (2018) describes 'a constant tension between positivist and normative perspectives and between doctrinal and empirical approaches' but finds that the mainstream of academic law is 'committed to the values of liberal education' (see also Arthurs' idea of 'humane professionalism' [1972]).

Coupled with this is the question whether law really belongs in the academy or should be taught in a 'trade school'. Twining (1994) described how law moved from the Inns of Court to the academy. The 'science of law' approach and the case method of Christopher Columbus Langdell, Dean of Harvard Law School from 1870 to 1895, systematised and simplified legal education by focusing on cases that exemplified principles or doctrines. As a legal realist, Karl Llewellyn had proclaimed the need to teach law students more about what lawyers do. Medicine similarly expects students to learn a large number of facts and be able to regurgitate these in context. Yet law has lagged behind some of the more practical and conceptual developments in medical education where objective, structured, clinical examination (OSCEs) and similar practical tests are a major part of assessment for qualification (Stern [2005] and Philips [2008]). Where law tries similar approaches at the professional stage it sometimes finds itself dogged by cultural and diversity difficulties (see the Barrow Report [1994]).

Course content

A different literature asks whether legal educators are teaching the law and the practice of law as it is today (or when they themselves practised, if they did) or are preparing students for the future? Richard and Daniel Susskind (2015) and other futurologists have suggested that the work of lawyers will change radically with the further development of information technology and artificial intelligence. In some ways this issue is overcome by the growth of continuing legal education for lawyers. Unlike doctors, lawyers do not have to be reappraised periodically. Since 1988 English solicitors have been mandated to carry out between 12 and 16 hours of continuing legal education per year, and many large law firms instituted their own internal training systems in order to provide such training and promote their own approach and methods to staff. Directors of Training were appointed to lead Continuing Professional Development (CPD) in each firm and assist the partners and senior staff in carrying out training. The LETR (2013) suggested that this might be carried out much more informally than previously, and sometimes continuing legal education regulation has been considered as mere window dressing.

Different conceptual subject categorisations in the training of lawyers have also appeared, including relative need, risk, right, relationship, responsibility, remedy and quality of life. Some of these are products of the critique of legal positivism and the flowering of socio-legal, critical and feminist studies. In addition, some legal subject classifications are appearing, including the state, the individual, the family, the corporate body, the trust, the environment, capacity and conflict. However, the dominant theme is the movement from law for the people toward law for commerce and capital (Sherr and Webb [1989]).

Three phases – solicitors

Apart from the apprenticeship and chartered legal executive routes, the three phases of legal education qualification to become a solicitor in England remain:

1. the Academic element – satisfied either by a law degree or a non-law degree and conversion course;
3. professional knowledge element – satisfied by the Solicitors' Qualifying Examination (SQE) Parts 1 and 2 (or the LPC for those who began their degree before 2021); and
3. the Practical Professional training element – satisfied by a training contract usually of two years or Qualifying Work Experience.

SQE 1 begins with an assessment of Functioning Legal Knowledge (FLK) through multiple choice questions (MCQs) over a two-day period. It covers business law and practice; dispute resolution; contract; tort; legal system of England and Wales; constitutional and administrative law and EU law and legal services; property practice; wills and the administration of estates; solicitors' accounts; land law; trusts; criminal law and practice.

The SQE2 is taken over five days and assesses core legal skills through a combination of written and oral tasks. The skills assessed are Client interview and attendance note/legal analysis, Advocacy, Case and matter analysis, Legal research, Legal writing and Legal drafting. For those with a law degree it is possible to qualify as a solicitor within 6 years, without a law degree it will take seven years.

Three phases – barristers

Barristers do not have an apprenticeship route. They therefore need:

1. the Academic element – satisfied either by a law degree or a non-law degree and 'conversion course';
2. the Professional knowledge element – satisfied by the Bar Professional Training Course; and
3. the Practical Professional training element – satisfied by pupillage at a barrister set or two sets of chambers lasting a year in total.

For those with a law degree it is possible to qualify as a barrister within five years, without a law degree it will take six years.

Specialisation

Beyond the basic education courses leading to initial qualification there are a number of other specialist qualification opportunities for solicitors in different areas of law. Criminal defence solicitors may take a course to become a duty solicitor in the police station (a qualification also available to non-solicitors) and a separate qualification as a duty solicitor in court. The police station qualification is necessary to attend on clients who are being held by the police for investigation, advising them on the evidence against them and how to react to questioning in the police station. There is now no complete 'right of silence'. Therefore, sometimes it may be better to refuse to answer questions, sometimes it is

better to answer and sometimes it is best to provide a prepared statement. This complexity certainly needs the presence of a trained person to assist. Duty solicitors in courts will pick up any criminal defendants who do not have representation on their rota day, and therefore court duty solicitors need to know a wide range of criminal law and how to deal with bail applications and negotiating with the Crown Prosecution Service. There are also courses for panel membership relating to juvenile law, public law family cases, and supervisor status in housing, immigration and mental health. Additional qualifications also exist for insolvency law practitioners, patent and other intellectual property law specialists as well as separate qualifications for those who only practice in those areas.

Ethical perspectives

Another debate is whether law should be taught as an instrument to be used in whichever way the lawyer wished or as value neutral. As Burridge and Webb point out (2007), for law to be 'morally neutral' is not the same as law being 'value free'. Judith Shklar ([1964] at 1) described legalism as an 'ethical attitude that holds moral conduct to be a matter of rule following, and moral relationships to consist of duties and rights determined by rules'. Pue ([2006] at 210) observed that 'morality went out of fashion at some point, leaving utility as the only credible measure of educational aspiration'. A recent judicial scandal arose in England from a defective computational system adopted by the Post Office to keep account of sub-postmasters. The 'Horizon' system wrongly showed false accounting and theft against 736 sub-postmasters many of whom were sent to prison following convictions, losing their livelihoods and some their lives. Though some of the senior internal lawyers of the Post Office were aware of the flawed system they continued prosecutions and kept quiet about other defendants. Lawyers for the accused advised them to plead guilty to avoid longer sentences. It has taken 20 years for this issue to come to a public Inquiry (Moorhead [2021]). The role of lawyers in perpetuating the intransigence of the Post Office over the IT system's problems has been central. In terms of a judicial crisis this is of similar proportions to Watergate in the USA, where so many lawyers were involved. It is clear that more attention needs to be paid to teaching ethical behaviour to law students from the outset.

Conclusion

For the Common Law world the English system of legal education has been the predominant model and the system of qualification has also been copied elsewhere. However, 'decolonisation' movements have begun to shift law curricula away from the English approach and the US and Canadian models have been different for a long time. In England, despite the recent changes on the SQE, the subjects studied seem not to have changed much, although there is a shift towards commercial law away from law for the individual, partly a reaction to the decrease in legal aid funding. In England and Wales the bifurcation of solicitors and barristers still remains a predominant feature both in the profession and in the legal education leading to qualification.

AVROM SHERR

References

Arthurs. H. (1972). 'Towards a humane professionalism – Lawyering and the Convivial Society', available at https://digitalcommons.osgoode.yorku.ca/scholarly_works/31.

Barrow Report. (1994). The Bar Council.

Boon, A. and Webb, J. (2008). 'Back to the Future', *Journal of Legal Education*, 58, p. 79.

Bradney, A. (2003). *The Liberal Law School in the Twenty-First Century*, Bloomsbury.

Brownsword, R. (1999). 'Law Schools for Lawyers, Citizens and People', in Cownie, F. (ed), *The Law School: Global Issues, Local Questions*, Ashgate.

Burridge, R. and Webb, J. (2007). 'The Values of Common Law Legal Education: Rethinking Rules, Responsibilities, Relationships and Roles in the Law School', *Legal Ethics*, 10(1), p. 72.

Ching, J. (2018). 'A Five Year Retrospective', *The Law Teacher*, 52, p. 384.

Cownie, F. (2004). *Legal Academics: Culture and Identities*, Bloomsbury.

Kahn-Freund, O. (1966). 'Reflections on Legal Education', *The Modern Law Review*, 29, p. 121.

Hepple, B. (1996). 'The Renewal of the Liberal Law Degree', *The Cambridge Law Journal*, p. 470.

King, T. (2015). 'Clinical Legal Education: A view from Practice', Univ. of Birmingham Workshop on LETR.

Legal Education and Training Review (LETR), available at https://letr.org.uk.

Lord Chancellor's Committee on Legal Education and conduct, First Report – ACLEC Report (1996).

Moorhead, R. (2021). 'The Conduct of Horizon Prosecutions'. SSRN 3894944.

Pue, W. (2006). 'Educating the Total Jurist', *Journal of Legal Ethics*, 8, p. 208.

Sherr, A. (1998). 'Legal Education, Legal Competence and Little Bo Peep', *The Law Teacher*, 32, p. 37.

Sherr, A. and Webb, J. (1989). 'Law Students, the External Market, and Socialisation', *Journal of Law and Society*, 16, p. 225.

Shklar, J. (1964). *Legalism*, Harvard University Press.

Solicitors Regulation Authority – SRA. (2023).

Susskind, R. and Susskind, D. (2015). *The Future of the Professions*, Oxford University Press.

The Law Society Statistics. (2021).

The Law Society. (2022). *Trends in the Solicitors Profession; annual statistics report 2022*.

Twining, W. (1994). Blackstone's Tower: *The English Law School*, Sweet and Maxwell.

Twining, W. (2018). 'Rethinking Legal Education', *The Law Teacher*, 52, p. 241.

UCAS. (2024), available at https://digital.ucas.com/coursedisplay/results/courses?searchTerm=Law&studyYear=2024&destination=Undergraduate&postcodeDistanceSystem=imperial&pageNumber=1&sort=MostRelevant&clearingPreference=None.

41. England (history of legal education)

Legal education in medieval England

In the twelfth century an oral education in Roman and canon law (the laws of the church) was already available for canon lawyer advocates and judges in the English ecclesiastical courts, and it was also at this time that Roman and canon law were first taught at the newly emerging University of Oxford (Brand [2003] at 555).

Early direct evidence for the existence of oral legal instruction in the common law is a set of lectures delivered, probably close to the Court of Common Pleas at Westminster, in the mid-1270s by an anonymous law lecturer to a group of students (Brand [2003] at 51–52). However, in 1234 Henry III ordered the mayor and sheriffs of London to proclaim and prohibit the teaching in the City of London of 'laws' whose intention and meaning are the subject of debate.

University law schools then 'chose to confine their teaching to universal jurisprudence, dismissing English law as unwritten local custom beneath their notice' (Baker [2013] at 273). That this void was filled by the Inns of Court 'for better or worse, altered the course of world legal history for the common lawyers retaliated by excluding the Roman laws from their canon of authority, and English law was pointed irrevocably along its unique path' (Baker [2013] at 273).

Hence, the long-standing tension in English legal education between the practical and the academic approach, between legal education as principally for (and controlled by) legal practitioners versus legal education as a fully-fledged university subject producing more than would-be lawyers.

A division in the work of professional lawyers was established by 1272. Serjeants (subsequently, barristers) pleaded in court; counsellors or attorneys (subsequently, solicitors) dealt with the preliminaries of litigation.

By 1292, apprentices of the Bench were established, probably being apprenticed to the court, rather than a particular master, with the Court of Common Bench (c.1291–1307) allocating space in court, 'the crib', where apprentices could watch and learn. Evidence shows that some justices of the court took time to explain points of law during proceedings for their benefit.

Legal education in early modern England

The inns of court and chancery in London (created in the late thirteenth and fourteenth centuries) became the principal institutional home of the legal profession as well as places of learning and training. Legal education was a combination of lectures, learning exercises, private reading and practical experience (Baker [2000]).

Although far less is known about the inns of chancery, during the fourteenth and fifteenth centuries some Masters in Chancery provided some education in writs and common practice.

Not until the 1590s did the call to the Bar at a legal inn become an essential qualification to plead in court. The call was achieved, however, not by following a programme of studies, but rather by eating the requisite number of dinners in hall. Despite this, by 1600, the Inns possessed sufficient intellectual vivacity to be regarded by some as the 'third university of England', alongside Oxford and Cambridge. During the fifteenth and sixteenth centuries, lectures were given, vocational exercises in pleading and debates on cases were held. There remained no teaching of the common law.

Contemporary and modern commentaries have frequently been highly critical of the legal inns as educational institutions. There was no monitoring of progress and hardly any compulsory provision. Some students employed private tutors to teach them the law. 'Contemporary sources do not merely catalogue or condemn student delinquency, ignorance and laziness. They also identified two prime causes: inadequate supervision and the difficulty of the common law as a subject of study' (Prest [2023] at 179). For contemporaries, the common law was '... a foreign language, a barbarous dialect, an uncouth method, a mystique comprehended only by those who had diligently applied themselves to its subtleties over many years' (Prest [2023] at 183–184).

The educational role of the Inns was terminated in the 1640s by the civil wars; and after the 1670s, law students were left entirely to their own devices. Whilst the growth and persistence of apprenticeship (or pupillage) within the profession may have mitigated this to some extent, it was a poor substitute, usually requiring 'less mental expiation even than clerkship' (Baker [2013] at 284). It gave pupils access to their master's chambers, books and papers for copying, and whilst 'the more caring pupil-masters would exceptionally condescend to discuss law with their pupils and have them produce drafts…[pupillage] seems…to have been little more than self-help pursued on the edge of real practice' (Baker [2013] at 284 and 286).

Printed texts had become the default method for disseminating legal texts by the early seventeenth century. These and the circulation of manuscript sources helped fill the gap in legal education, with instruction beyond the court room becoming increasingly available as individual law reports with summaries of agreed facts, annotations and conclusions were being produced for educational purposes (Ross [1998] at 323; Williams [2022] at 243). Nonetheless, formal legal education had ceased. It was to be reinvented in the nineteenth century.

Legal education in modern England

The Dublin Law Institute was created in 1839 to offer legal education to both branches of the profession. With the financial support of the benchers of Kings Inn, five professors were appointed. Running into financial problems after the benchers withdrew their financial backing, it nonetheless attracted much attention in England. By the mid-1840s both branches of the profession were demanding better legal education.

A watershed moment came in 1846 when a House of Commons select committee on legal education concluded that, 'no legal education worthy of the name, is at this moment to be had in either England or Ireland' (Report of Select Committee [1846]). The woeful condition of law as an intellectual discipline and the poverty of English legal literature relative to that produced in the United States or on the Continent were allied concerns. The committee proposed that legal education should be offered at university level and available to non-vocational students as well as those intending to practice. A law degree should be the qualification for jobs currently reserved for barristers of seven years' standing. Those

seeking a legal career would then proceed to a second stage at a new school centred on the inns of court. Attracting insufficient support from the profession, these recommendations were not acted on by Parliament.

With their degree of self-government unique to English professions, the inns (notably, the benchers) opposed legislative and other outside interference. They frowned on challenges to the professional hierarchy (including the elevated position of the judiciary, and the separation of the upper (barristers) and lower branches (attorneys and solicitors) of the profession), their control of the Bar, and their nurturing of 'gentlemanly independence'.

The Council of Legal Education, established in 1852 and offering instruction to students as an alternative to the newly constituted bar examination, failed to attract large numbers of students. In 1967, the Inns of Court School of Law (ICSL) was established and a permanent teaching staff was first appointed. It remained the sole provider of training for the English Bar until 1997 when several universities were finally validated to deliver the successor to the finals course.

When the Bar examinations were made compulsory in 1872, students quickly turned to private crammers (tutors), a practice that remained virtually unchanged until the 1960s.

By the 1820s, legal education was seen by members of the lower branch as a vital means of improving the reputation of the profession. It was a high priority of the Law Society established in 1825 to better regulate and educate attorneys and solicitors. In 1833 the Society initiated regular lectures for articled clerks. From 1836 onwards, the Law Society gradually wrested control of professional examinations from the court, creating a three-tier system of examinations under the Solicitors Act 1860. Periodicals aimed at attorneys which republished the lectures given at the Law Society, led to clerks corresponding between themselves and the establishment in several provincial towns of debating clubs and law student societies (Polden [2010] at 1179). Some local law societies also set up courses of lectures.

Exams were introduced as an addition to existing apprenticeship requirements, and so study had to be undertaken around the training period (called 'articles'). In 1922, the society introduced a compulsory year of lectures prior to the intermediate examination and increased its subsidy of provincial law faculties to allow clerks articled outside London to attend. 'Attendance at the latter grew rapidly, both because provincial universities welcomed the income and because most provincial clerks did not have the alternative of a private crammer. But the Law Society's trump card was to merge with its principal competitor (Gibson and Weldon) in 1962, creating the College of Law' (Abel [1988] at 146). But the system proved impractical, and in the early 1960s, the Law Society had to reinstate its externally provided courses.

Developing legal education

Blackstone's *Commentaries* (Blackstone [1765–69]) were the first comprehensive, readable account of English law. But neither its international success nor Blackstone's election as Oxford's first professor of the common law (1758) established the study of English law on a secure footing. A law degree was not a prerequisite for admission to the Inns, and along with poor teaching, bedevilled the development of university legal education until well into the twentieth century.

The Downing Chair at Cambridge, founded in 1800, fared no better, being a sinecure for much of the nineteenth century. University College, London (1826) started well but rapidly declined.

During the period c. 1875–1914, a few full-time jurists in a small number of elite institutions (Harvard, Oxford and Cambridge) constituted, transmitted and legitimated modern university-based legal education and scholarship for the legal establishment. These new professional law professors detailed, simplified and synthesised leading cases of the common law, identifying the core principles of which the leading cases were illustrative. They sought to demonstrate that the apparent chaos of the law was grounded in a few general principles (Sugarman [2021] at 39–40).

This body of work established the dominant tradition of English legal education and scholarship until the late twentieth century and remains a powerful influence. Whilst producing some influential works, it largely failed to attract large numbers of able students or gain full acceptance by fellow academics or the practising profession.

By 1909 there were eight law faculties in England and Wales, mostly characterised by low student and staff numbers taught largely by part-time practitioners. The provincial law schools were especially dependent on preparing students for the solicitors' examinations.

Since World War II, and especially since the mid-1960s, university legal education and scholarship have changed dramatically. The numbers and characteristics of teachers, students and law schools, the media through which scholarship is communicated and the methods and subject-matter of legal scholarship have significantly increased and become more heterogeneous. Law teachers have gained greater acceptance by fellow academics and by the practising profession. Law schools and academic law have become more diverse, more outward looking regarding both foreign and international law, and other academic disciplines, and more prepared to employ the methods of the humanities and social sciences. The dominant expository formalist tradition has been supplemented by other approaches including socio-legal studies (see Socio-Legal Approaches to Legal Education), law and humanities, feminism (see Feminist Legal Education) and critical legal studies.

The student body and teaching staff in law grew slowly from 1945 to the mid-1960s, most notably in the older provincial universities and the new provincial universities (most founded since the war), rather than Oxbridge and London. The founding of polytechnics offering law degrees at the end of the 1960s, and the consequent explosion of enrolments in polytechnic degrees in the 1970s was of particular significance. This reflected the huge expansion of the legal profession, and the fact that a first degree in law had become a prerequisite for admission to the profession. By the 1980s there were more than 50 law schools. Polytechnics (subsequently designated universities) were the largest employers of law teachers, with significant numbers being located at the newer and old provincial universities. The age profile of the teaching profession drifted downwards, included more women and, to a lesser extent, ethnic minorities. The student body, similarly, became more diverse. The number of part-time teachers significantly declined and postgraduate legal education grew (Cownie [2004]).

Despite important changes since the mid-1960s, significant elements of university legal education remain the same. Importantly, the conditions that sustain current models of university legal education have remained constant: notably, student demand and finance; the cost of education; and the need for legal education to be sufficiently harmonious with the interests of the legal profession, of their principal clients, universities and government. Innovation in legal education operates within these confines (Sugarman [2021]).

DAVID SUGARMAN

References

Abel, R.L. (1988). *The Legal Profession in England and Wales*, Blackwell.

Baker, J.H. (ed). (2000). *Readers and Readings in the Inns of Court and Inns of Chancery*, Selden Society, Supplementary Series, vol. 13.

Sir John Baker. (2013). *Collected Papers in English Legal History*, Cambridge University Press, vol. I.

Blackstone, W. (2016). *Commentaries on the Laws of England* (1765–69), The Oxford Edition, Oxford University Press.

Brand, P. (1999). 'Legal Education in England before the Inns of Court', in Bush, J.A. and Wijffels, A. (eds), *Learning the Law: Teaching and the Transmission of Law in England, 1150–1900*, Hambledon Press.

Brooks, C. and Lobban, M. (1999). 'Apprenticeship or academy? The idea of a law university, 1830–1860' in Bush, J.A. and Wijffels, A. (eds), *Learning the Law: Teaching and the Transmission of Law in England, 1150–1900*, Hambledon Press.

Cownie, F. (2004). *Legal Academics: Culture and Identities*, Bloomsbury.

Polden, P. (2010). 'The Education of Lawyers', in Cornish, W. et al., *The Oxford History of the Laws of England vol. XI*, Oxford University Press.

Prest, W.R. (2011). 'Readers dinners and the culture of the early modern Inns of Court', in

Archer, J.E., Goldring, E. and Knight, S. (eds), *The Intellectual and Cultural World of the Early Modern Inns of Court*, Manchester University Press.

Prest, W.R. (2023). *The Inns of Court under Elizabeth I and the Early Stuarts:1590–1640*, Cambridge University Press.

Report of Select Committee on Legal Education no.686. (1846). B.P.P. vol.10.

Ross, R. (1998).'The commoning of the common law: the Renaissance debate over printing English law, 1520–1640', *University of Pennsylvania Law Review*, 146, p. 323.

Sugarman, D. (2021). 'How America Did (and Didn't) Influence English Legal Education, circa 1870–1965' in Bartie, S. and Sandomierski, D. (eds), *American Legal Education Abroad: Critical Histories*, New York University Press.

Sugarman, D. (2021). 'Twining's Tower and the Challenges of Making Law a Humanistic Discipline', *Amicus Curiae* (the official journal of the Society for Advanced Legal Studies and the Institute of Advanced Legal Studies, University of London) Series 2, 2(3), p. 337.

Twining, W. (1994). *Blackstone's Tower: the English Law School*, Stevens.

Williams, I. (2022). 'Learning the "New Law of the Star Chamber": Legal Education and Legal Literature in Early-Stuart England', *JLH*, 43, p. 243, available at https://onesearch .lancaster-university.uk/primo-explore/ fulldisplay?docid=TN_cdi_informaworld _taylorfrancis_310_1080_01440365_2022 _2140493&context=PC&vid=LUL_VU1& lang=en_US&search_scope=LSCOP_44LAN _ELEC&adaptor=primo_central_multiple _fe&tab=electronic&query=any%2Ccontains %2Clegal%20education%20and%20the %20Star%20Chamber&offset=0.

42. England (regulation of legal education)

This entry sets out how law degrees are regulated in England. There is a longer and a short form of this entry. The shorter form goes: there is not much specific regulation of the law degree in England. The longer form follows. The reason there is a shorter form is because of the recent introduction by the Solicitors Regulation Authority ('the SRA') of a new, centrally assessed mode of entry: the Solicitors Qualifying Examination, whose first assessments began in November 2021. As a result of the SQE, the regulatory gaze of the largest part of the legal profession in England (where solicitors outnumber barristers 10:1) has turned away from the 'qualifying law degree' and instead towards point of entry. The SRA is no longer interested, in regulatory terms, in what happens in law schools.

Below, I set out how law degrees in England were specifically regulated before the winter of 2021, and a few words on the SQE. I then turn to ongoing direct regulation of the law degree by the Bar Standards Board ('the BSB') – the regulator of barristers – and via the Quality Assurance Agency's Subject Benchmark Statement for Law.

The position before the SQE

Ever since English law began as a discipline in higher education (at University College London in 1826), there has been a sometimes challenging, sometimes strained relationship between those in the legal profession and those in legal academia (Bradney [1992]; Boon and Webb [2008]). How much control should the legal profession and its regulators have over what happens inside English law schools? Are law schools producing, in the evocative words of William Twining (1998), Pericles (wise care givers) or plumbers (legal mechanics)? These questions arise despite the fact that a degree in law has never, and is not currently, a requirement to practise as a solicitor and that around half of those entering the solicitor branch of the profession do not have law degrees (but instead some other degree and then 'convert' (on which, see below) or come via an apprenticeship route (Thomas and Mungham [1972] and Law Society Statistical Report [2014]).

In 1922, the Law Society (the professional body then responsible for the training of solicitors) made attendance at a law school compulsory for at least one year for those wishing to qualify as solicitors, and recognised university law schools alongside 'professional law schools' for the purposes of the scheme (Gower [1950]). Between the 1920s and the early 1970s, English law schools were said to bristle at a perceived 'constrictive effect' of the Law Society's approach to regulation of legal education, despite that regulation being, as Bradney notes, 'fairly slight, involving little more than a check on the subjects covered' ([1992] at 12).

The Ormerod Committee, which reported in 1971, brought into sharp focus a demarcation between what it labelled the academic, vocational, and continuing education aspects of legal education; with 'the universities being primarily responsible for the academic stage (but not fully in control)' (Hepple [1996] at 477). For the academic stage, the Committee report set out that anyone who had studied five 'core' subjects – those already compulsory in 'almost all' existing law degrees at the time – Tort, Contract, Crime, Constitutional Law, and Land Law – should be deemed to have satisfied the academic stage of professional development. While many in legal academia felt that *any* law degree should be sufficient for professional recognition, the 'professional bodies refused to accept any degree that did not include the…core subjects required by the professions in their Part I examination' (Boon and Webb [2008] at 91). What would and would not be required and accepted was negotiated and then published in a series of Joint Announcements or Joint Statements on Qualifying Law Degrees. Equity and Trusts, for example, was added as the sixth 'core' subject in 1979.

Until 1990, the Joint Announcements set out prescribed and detailed syllabi for each of six core subjects, prescribed assessment methods, and minimum teaching hours of core subjects for universities if they wanted their law degrees to be 'qualifying law degrees' (i.e. qualifying a student to pass the academic stage and to be passported into the vocational stage). As from 1990, the requirements in the Joint Announcement were relaxed (detailed syllabi becoming broader subject statements etc) and then, in 1995, a revised Joint Announcement liberalised the regulation of qualifying law degrees even further (even if some academics, like Peter Birks ([1995]) felt the new approach was still heavy-handed): more flexibly defining the newly-titled 'Foundations of Legal Knowledge' (or 'FOLK subjects'; still known to many as 'the core'); but also broadening their scope (e.g. including human rights in Public Law), adding in European Community law as a seventh compulsory FOLK subject, and reducing the amount of time required across the law degree for the FOLK subjects. A re-revised 1999 Joint Statement listed the seven FOLK subjects and required that at least 240 of 360 credits of a law degree must be in 'legal subjects', including at least 180 credits of FOLK subjects. This statement said nothing about the content of the FOLK subjects, although there was 'considerable mythology' and misunderstanding among academics around this (Guth and Ashford [2014] at 9); nor did the 1999 statement say anything about preferred modes of, or approaches to, assessment of the FOLK subjects.

The Legal Services Act 2007 significantly changed the regulatory landscape for legal services in England & Wales. The representative (or trade union) and regulatory functions of the professions were split and a new regulator of regulators (the Legal Services Board) created. The Law Society and Bar Council kept their representative roles, but new frontline regulators – including the Solicitors Regulation Authority and the Bar Standards Board – were brought into being. In January 2011, the Solicitors Regulation Authority, the Bar Standards Board and ILEX Professional Standards (the regulator of legal executives) announced the establishment of a joint fundamental review of the legal education and training requirements of those delivering legal services, known as LETR (the Legal Education and Training Review). On the law degree, the 2013 LETR report (Webb [2013]) acknowledged that, 'the QLD serves multiple purposes and should not be over-regulated', but also suggested a little more prescription as regards content description (following the approach in Australia with the 'Priestly 11'). The researchers also found that there was 'a high degree of support for the existing Foundation subjects' from those in both practice and academia.

Partly as a result of LETR, as from December 2015 the SRA ran a series of dedicated consultations on how solicitors might qualify in the future. These proposed a new approach – the Solicitors Qualifying Examination (SQE) – which would respond to the regulator's concerns about a lack of consistency or comparable standards in relation to assessment at the point of qualification. On the academic stage, the SRA spoke about the lack of common performance standards across the more than 100 providers of the qualifying law degree, the lack of content specified in the Joint Statement (which meant it was not possible to easily know who had been taught what), and that substantive law was being taught in law schools in a 'procedural vacuum'.

In introducing the SQE, the SRA decided not to regulate for any particular form of preparation for the new central examinations, not believing, they said, that 'that specifying particular courses or qualifications...can be the best way to encourage high quality teaching'. The only higher education requirement the SRA included for the SQE was the rule that would-be solicitors have a degree (of any kind) or equivalent. This means it is theoretically possible for someone to sit and pass the SQE with, say, a degree in mathematics and no formal legal education training of any kind (if, for example, they taught themselves law through textbooks or other materials). The SRA no longer regulating the qualifying law degree should have meant a sigh of relief for English law schools. This was, in theory, an opportunity for those schools to do whatever they liked. That does not, however, seem to have been the case. Many law schools still teach what they did to comply with the 1999 Joint Statement (possibly because of path dependency) and some others have made lesser or greater changes to align their syllabi and modes of assessment with the SQE (to be, they hope, more attractive to potential students). So while the SRA has formally moved away from any regulation at all of the English law degree, the spectre of the SQE has a continuing impact on at least some law schools.

Would-be barristers and the Bar Standards Board

The 1999 Joint Statement no longer applies to either profession; and ended, for would-be solicitors, with courses that started before 31 December 2021. For would-be barristers, Part 2 of the Bar Qualification Manual sets out the requirements on the 'Academic Component of Bar Training'. These rules apply to courses starting from September 2019. The seven FOLK subjects are required (with an explanatory note from the BSB saying that while the UK has left the EU, 'EU Law still has significant relevance to the laws of England and Wales and therefore practise as a barrister'; on which see Guth and Hervey (2018)); and there are some short rules on pass marks in FOLK subjects (40 per cent or above), marginal fails, deemed passes, and maximum number of attempts at passing. Law degrees must also include the 'skills associated with graduate legal work such as legal research'. The BSB does not set any rules on the syllabi or otherwise on the content or approach of the FOLK subjects being taught, on the credits to be allocated, on preferred modes of assessment for FOLK subjects, etc.

A lower second-class honours overall award is required in the law degree for entry to Bar, meaning that a student has (usually) an overall average of 50 per cent or more. The Bar Qualification Manual also sets out, in Section 2.B, that a student's law degree must be awarded at Level 6 (or above) of the 'Framework for Higher Education Qualifications' by a recognised degree-awarding body, and that the degree must comply with the QAA Benchmark Statement for Law (discussed in the following section).

What is hopefully clear from the preceding two paragraphs is that this new approach by the BSB is different and less prescriptive than that under the 1999 Joint Statement. This was quite intentional, with the regulator explicitly commenting in its Qualification Manual that it, 'reduced its regulatory involvement in legal academic learning to a minimum' (Section 2G(4)).

Instead of a law degree (a three- or four-year undergraduate course), students with a degree in another subject (English, mathematics, history etc) can undertake a one year 'conversion course' to satisfy the legal education academic component of Bar training. This was also true for would-be solicitors before the introduction of the SQE. The conversion course has many titles, depending on the provider: Graduate Diploma in Law (GDL), Common Professional Examination (CPE), and Postgraduate Diploma in Law (PGDL). This is a 12-month full-time programme (or part-time equivalent), in which students cram the FOLK subjects and not much else. In 2012, the LETR research team noted that,

'there is a risk that the GDL, whatever its merits or demerits, rests like a dead hand over the debate [on review and reform of legal education]' (Webb [2012] at 18). This was partly because, in a yearlong course, there is only so much that can be done by way of innovation if all of the FOLK subjects need to be taught.

There is a curious thing about the BSB continuing to regulate qualifying law degrees in England. And it is that very few people qualify each year as barristers. In 2021, only 514 people began pupillage, the trainee stage of barrister qualification. In the same year, there were 18,927 law graduates (and, as noted above, many lawyers do not have law degrees but instead 'convert'). This curiosity is part explained by law students not often knowing what they want to do when they start university (many say they might want to be barristers but then change their minds), and part explained by the allure of being a barrister (and where university law schools capitalise on this allure by offering law degrees that assist with potential qualification). Still, it is an odd thing to have a regulator shaping degree content for almost 20,000 students a year where no more than a few hundred of those students go on to become professionals eventually regulated by that regulator.

The Quality Assurance Agency Benchmark Statement for Law

The 1999 Joint Statement and the Bar's current rules both required compliance by law schools with the QAA Subject Benchmark Statement for Law. The Quality Assurance Agency says that Subject Benchmark Statements 'describe the nature of study and the academic standards expected of graduates in specific subject areas'. Written by subject area experts (and so unlike the Joint Statements/Announcements), and facilitated by the QAA, Benchmark Statements for Law were published in 2000, 2007, 2015, and 2023. As with the Joint Statements/Announcements, we see a general liberalising tendency with each version published. And so the 2015 Benchmark Statement for Law broke away from the mould of knowledge categories in law and spoke, instead, of 'a law student's skills and qualities of mind'. The 2023 Statement for Law goes even further, introducing, for example, cross-cutting themes including equality and diversity and education for sustainable development. The most recent Statement is so permissive that its impact on law schools and the design of law degrees is likely to be limited.

Conclusion

While the SRA has moved away from regulating the qualifying law degree, its new central assessment for qualification as a solicitor, the SQE, has an ongoing impact on what some law schools feel they must teach in order to attract students to their courses. This belief about in-effect regulation from the SRA sits alongside ongoing – admittedly light touch – rules by the BSB which prescribe what is required for the academic stage of training to be a barrister (even though only a tiny percentage of all law students end up as barristers). What should have been an opportunity for curriculum innovation and ownership of the liberal law degree post the introduction of the SQE seems to have been, for now at least, a damp squib.

STEVEN VAUGHAN

References

Birks, P. (1995). 'Shallow Foundations', *LQR*, p. 371.

Boon, A. and Webb, J. (2008). 'Legal education and training in England and Wales: Back to the future', *J. Legal Educ.*, 58, p. 79.

Bradney, A. (1992). 'Ivory towers and satanic mills: Choices for university law schools', *Studies in Higher Education*, 17, p. 5.

Gower, L.C.B. (1950). 'English Legal Training', *The Modern Law Review*, 13, p. 137.

Guth, J. and Hervey, T. (2018). 'Threats to internationalised legal education in the twenty-first century UK', *The Law Teacher*, 52, p. 350.

Hepple, B. (1996). 'The renewal of the liberal law degree', *CLJ*, 55, p. 470.

Law Society. (2014). *Annual Statistical Report 2014*.

SRA, 'A new route to qualification: The Solicitors Qualifying Examination (October 2016 Consultation Paper).

Thomas, P. and Mungham, G. (1972). 'English legal education: a commentary on the Ormrod report', *Val. UL Rev.*, p. 87.

Twining, W. (1998). 'Pericles regained?', *Legal Ethics*, 1, p. 131.

Webb, J. (2013). *Legal Education and Training Review Report*.

43. Equality, diversity and inclusion (EDI) and the law school

Equality, diversity, and inclusion (EDI) in the context of legal education refer to the principles and practices that are used to promote fairness, representation, and a welcoming environment within a university setting.

This statement can be broken down into component parts. Equality in legal education means ensuring that all individuals, regardless of their background, identity or status have equal opportunities to access and succeed at law school. This includes eliminating discrimination and providing fair treatment to all students and staff. Diversity involves recognising and valuing differences among students and staff in terms of race, gender, ethnicity, sexual orientation, socioeconomic status, disability, and more. The prominence of these values reflects a growing commitment amongst law schools to create a diverse community that reflects the broader society. Finally, inclusion focuses on creating an environment where everyone is respected, supported, and encouraged to participate fully in legal education. It entails actively addressing barriers to participation and fostering a sense of belonging for all individuals, especially those from underrepresented groups. Incorporating these principles into legal education helps to produce more inclusive and equitable legal professionals who are better prepared to serve diverse client populations and contribute to a just legal system.

EDI has increased in prominence as a counterbalance to the view that legal education perpetuates social and economic hierarchies within society. Duncan Kennedy ([1983] at 2) popularised this analysis in his argument that legal education, particularly in elite law schools, reinforces existing power structures and inequalities. This argument goes beyond the demographic make-up of law schools to suggest that the curriculum and pedagogy are designed to serve the interests of the owning class. Kennedy argued further that the legal profession prioritises technical expertise and conservative values, which can marginalise and exclude individuals from disadvantaged backgrounds. This can be noted when a topic fails to identify the ways that social and economic injustice make subjects vulnerable to the authority of law i.e. laws that criminalise the homeless for loitering or begging for money. A curriculum that taught law in a way that is divorced from the social, economic, and ethic plight of the homeless would, according to Kennedy, tacitly endorse existing power structures that maintain the status quo. In response, Kennedy called for a more critical and socially aware approach to legal education that encourages students to question how law operated in society and suggest reforms that encourage a more equitable and just legal system. Implicit in this view is the argument that law schools ought to be more than a training ground for technical skills and should equip students with the knowledge and skills required for democratic citizenship.

This provocation is consistent with legal obligations that are placed on law schools to refrain from engaging in any form of prohibited discrimination against their students. While legislation is jurisdictionally specific, these obligations tend to cover discrimination based on sex, chosen gender, race, colour, nationality, cultural or ethnic background, sexual orientation, gender identity, age, marital status, and pregnancy. Additionally, law schools are generally required to make accommodations for students with disabilities and other diverse needs. Beyond these formal legal obligations, it has been argued that law schools have a moral obligation to value a more expansive understanding of diversity that is connected with the social purpose of a university to serve the public good (Israel et al [2017] at 335). For example, the Law Council of Australia (2015) has articulated an obligation on law schools to foster a culture of professionals that is not only 'strong and fair' but also accommodates and encourages a 'diverse range of individuals and views'. In similar terms, the American Bar Association (2021) issued a statement requiring all law schools to take 'effective action to diversity students, faculty, and staff and foster an inclusive and fair environment for everyone'. These actions may encompass initiatives such as establishing and making public objectives pertaining to diversity and inclusion, implementing pipeline programs, and enhancing outreach to marginalised communities.

One of the most successful mechanisms for diversifying a student cohort are access scholarships. An example is the Diversity Access Scheme (DAS) offered by the Law Society UK (https://www.lawsociety.org.uk/

campaigns/diversity-access-scheme/).   The programme is designed to promote diversity and inclusion within the legal profession by providing opportunities for individuals from underrepresented backgrounds to pursue a career in law. The scheme aims to address barriers to entry faced by candidates from diverse ethnic, socio-economic, and other marginalised groups by offering financial support, mentorship, and networking opportunities. Through the DAS, participants receive assistance with law school tuition fees, training contracts, and other costs associated with qualifying as a solicitor. Additionally, the programme provides mentorship from experienced legal professionals and access to networking events to help participants build connections within the legal community. Similar funding opportunities are available in the United States. For instance, the American Bar Association (ABA) provides scholarships through its Legal Scholarship Opportunity Fund (https://www.americanbar.org/groups/departments_offices/FJE/aba-legal-opportunity-scholarship/) while   individual law schools often have their own diversity initiatives offering financial aid and support.

Today it is also common for law schools to have their own diversity and inclusion statements which are supported by university policy and measured with reference to external accreditation frameworks. A prominent example is Athena SWAN which is an accreditation programme run by AdvanceHE, based in the UK that recognises and celebrates commitment to advancing gender equality in higher education (https://www.advance-he.ac.uk/equality-charters/athena-swan-charter). The programme encourages universities to assess their policies, practices, and culture to identify and address gender disparities across all academic disciplines and career stages. Institutions applying for Athena SWAN accreditation typically undergo a rigorous self-assessment process, followed by the development and implementation of action plans to promote gender equality. However, programmes like this have been critiqued for placing a significant administrative burden on marginalised staff (Grove [2018]). Sara Ahmed (2021) has also critiqued accreditation programs as a shallow approach to diversity. Ahmed ([2021] at 63) argues that 'going for an equality award can be used to justify delaying the effort to deal with the problem of harassment and bulling' and can also incentivise an institution to conceal issues. For Ahmed, a complaint is not simply an expression of personal dissatisfaction. It is a moment when systemic issues of inequality, discrimination, and injustice are bought to the surface. For Universities to have a substantive response to EDI, it is necessary that marginalised voices are respected and protected. Ahmed argues for a revaluation of how we understand and respond to grievances. She encourages a shift towards creating more inclusive and equitable systems that address the root causes of complaint, rather than dismissing or silencing those who voice them.

Further to active listening, in parts of the United States EDI has developed through the use of affirmative action and the maintenance of quotas for minority groups. However, in 2023 the US Supreme Court prohibited public and private colleges and universities from considering race when admitting students (see *Students for Fair Admissions, Inc v President and Fellows of Harvard College* 600 US_(2023)). To fulfill commitments to EDI, law schools now rely primarily on pathway programmes and scholarships for disadvantaged groups. For example, the American Bar Association has introduced a Disability Programs Directory (https://www.americanbar.org/groups/diversity/disabilityrights/resources/law_school_programs/) that compiles information about programmes related to disabilities. Additionally, the Law School Admission Council gathers data from law schools in the United States and Canada to aid LGBTQ+ candidates in their journeys towards enrolling in law schools. These and other initiatives aim to make legal education accessible to a broad spectrum of students. As the number of available positions in law schools increases scholars have argued that institutions that do not embrace diversity and inclusivity may experience reduced competitiveness and a decline in the quality of their programs (Israel et al [2017] and Pearsall [2015]).

In some law schools, EDI has been further developed through initiatives that tackle social justice in the community. This work not only seeks to challenge key sites of discrimination but also sends a signal to prospective students that the school is committed to a substantive notion of inclusivity. For example, in the United States the Association of American Law Schools launched the Law Deans Antiracist Clearinghouse project in response to the impact racism has on the Rule of Law (https://www.aals.org/antiracist-clearinghouse/). And in the United Kingdom the Law Society offers a robust scholarship programme that provides funding and mentorship opportunities for students from underrepresented social groups.

Finally, EDI is increasingly part of a law school curriculum. While law degrees tend to be dominated by compulsory subjects required for accreditation, in some jurisdictions there is now a basic expectation that issues related to EDI are woven into core courses and offered as stand-alone elective subjects. An early demand for this inclusion can be noted in 1994 when the Australian Law Reform Commission recommended that schools amend their curriculum to include 'content on how each area of the law in substance and operation affects women and reflects their experiences'. Today this has been extended to include issues related to gender, sexuality culture and forms of disability. The emphasis placed on EDI in the curriculum reflects the fact that law gradates need to understand and be capable of engaging with the diverse members of their community.

PETER BURDON

References

AdvanceHE Athena Swan Charter, available at https://www.advance-he.ac.uk/equality-charters/athena-swan-charter.
Ahmed, S. (2021). *Complaint!*, Duke University Press.
American Bar Association. (2021). 'Council moves to strengthen law school diversity mandates', available at https://www.americanbar.org/news/abanews/aba-news-archives/2021/11/law-school-diversity/.
Association of American Law Schools, 'Law Deans Antiracist Clearinghouse', available at https://www.aals.org/antiracist-clearinghouse/.
Australian Law Reform Commission. (1994). 'Equality Before the Law: Women's Equality', available at https://www.alrc.gov.au/publication/equality-before-the-law-justice-for-women-alrc-report-69-part-1/.
Diversity Access Scheme (The Law Society), available at https://www.lawsociety.org.uk/campaigns/diversity-access-scheme/.
Grove, J. (2018). 'Complaints of "excessive" Athena SWAN workload as review launched', *Times Higher Education*, available at https://www.timeshighereducation.com/news/complaints-excessive-athena-swan-workload-review-launched.
Israel, M., Skead, N., Health, M., Hewitt, A., Galloway, K. and Steel, A. (2017). 'Fostering "Quiet Inclusion": Interaction and Diversity in the Australian Law Classroom', *Journal of Legal Education*, 66(2), p. 332.
Kennedy, D. (1983). *Legal Education and the Reproduction of Hierarchy*, Harvard University Press.
Law Council of Australia. (2015). 'Diversity and Equality Charter', available at https://lawcouncil.au/files/pdf/policy-guideline/Diversity%20Charter-Updated.pdf.
Pearsal, G. (2015). 'The Human Side of Law School: The Case for Socializing Minority Recruitment and Retention Programs', *Journal of Legal Education*, 64, p. 688.
Students for Fair Admissions, Inc, v President and Fellows of Harvard College 600 US (2023).

44. Ethnicity and legal education

In the context of legal education, ethnicity refers to an individual's cultural, social, and historical background, often based on shared characteristics such as nationality, language, and cultural heritage. As described in the entry on Equality, Diversity and Inclusion (EDI) and the Law School, understanding and acknowledging ethnicity is important to promote diversity, inclusivity, and a better understanding of how legal systems and institutions can impact different ethnic groups. It involves recognising the unique perspectives and challenges that individuals from various ethnic backgrounds bring to the legal field and working to ensure that legal education programs are responsive to and representative of this diversity.

More generally, ethnicity and legal education refers to the diverse racial and cultural backgrounds of the students, faculty, and staff within the legal education institution. It encompasses the racial and ethnic identities of individuals who are studying, teaching, and working in law schools. Recognising ethnicity in law school is significant for several reasons. First, law schools aim to have a diverse student body and faculty that reflects the broader society. A diverse law school community enriches discussions, perspectives, and the overall learning experience. Second, acknowledging ethnicity in law school is a fundamental aspect of creating an inclusive environment where individuals from various racial and ethnic backgrounds feel welcomed, valued, and supported in their educational journey. Third, it is essential to address issues of equity in legal education, including representation and access for underrepresented ethnic groups. Ethnicity plays a role in addressing disparities and promoting fairness. Finally, understanding the ethnic and cultural backgrounds of students and legal professionals is crucial for promoting cultural competency within the legal profession, as lawyers will need to serve clients from diverse backgrounds. Incorporating discussions about ethnicity in law school helps to foster a more inclusive and equitable learning environment, prepares future legal professionals to work effectively in a diverse society, and contributes to the broader goal of achieving justice and fairness within the legal system.

As noted in the entry on Equality, Diversity and Inclusion (EDI) and the Law School, law schools have taken proactive steps to address discrimination and diversify the demographic of students and staff. As a result, schools have shifted from being overwhelmingly white, middle-class, and English-speaking to reflect a greater measure of diversity. Key factors that have contributed to diversity include a rise in the number of law schools and the percentage of the population who can now access a legal education. For example, statistics collected from the Higher Education Statistics Authority (2023) in the UK show that 35 per cent of new law students come from culturally diverse backgrounds. Similarly, in 2023 the Law School Admission Council in the United States noted that 40.2 per cent of the incoming class consisted of students from diverse racial backgrounds, an increase from last year's 39 per cent, which was previously the highest on record (Leipold [2023]). Access to legal education has been aided, in part, by scholarships that are designed to promote diversity and inclusion within the legal profession by providing opportunities for individuals from underrepresented backgrounds to pursue a career in law.

Against this trend, first nations people continue to be underrepresented in legal education and have higher attrition rates than other social groups ([Melville [2014], Mahuteau [2015]). The reasons for this are complex and place specific. However, Rodgers-Falk (2011) argued that 'cultural disrespect, lateral violence and/or racial discrimination' are '[p]robably the biggest contributor to the high levels of attrition of [First Nations] law students within a university environment.' While dated now, the largest survey on this topic was conducted in British Columbia (Dolman [1997]). It found that '66% of BC Indigenous law graduates indicated that they had experienced some form of discriminatory barrier as a result of their aboriginal ancestry at law school.' In addition, 'three quarters of these indicated that insensitivity to aboriginal issues in course materials and the behaviour of the instructor was the most significant problem (Dolman [1997]).'

One evidence-based response to these conditions is cultural awareness and sensitivity training which aims to heighten awareness and understanding of the prejudices experienced by first nations students and staff. This approach was endorsed by Larissa Behrend et al ([2012] at xxiv) in the Review of Higher Education Access and Outcomes for Aboriginal and Torres Strait Islander People. The report makes a formal recommendation that 'universities continue to develop and implement a range of strategies to: improve the cultural understanding and awareness of staff, students and researchers within their institution, including the provision of cultural competency training.' In support of this statement, Mark Israel et al ([2017] at 339) argue that law schools should focus on fostering inclusive teaching methods and enhancing their ability to deliver justice for Indigenous communities. This involves encouraging Indigenous involvement in legal service provision and promoting broader awareness within the legal profession of the needs and goals of Indigenous users of legal services. Through these methods law schools can help students understand the broader Indigenous perspective on law, along with the experiences Indigenous individuals have within the existing legal framework.

Concomitant to this analysis, the issue of ethnicity also features within the law curriculum. Most expansively, this can be noted in the instruction of critical race theory (CRT) which examines the ways in which race and racism intersect with the law and legal institutions. Scholarship in this area varies widely but most approaches can be linked by three intersecting themes. The first is intersectionality – emphasises that race does not exist in isolation but intersects with other social identities such as gender, class, and sexuality, leading to unique experiences of oppression and privilege. The second is structural inequality and the ways racism is embedded in social structures, laws, and institutions, resulting in systemic and structural inequalities that persist over time. This theme was most prominent in response to the #blacklives matter movement which highlighted the relationship between structural violence and the way people of colour are policed. Finally, CRT investigates interest convergence and the contention that racial progress in the law is more likely to occur when it aligns with the interests of the political class (Crenshaw et al [1996]). For example, historically white institutions, such as law schools, might only adopt diversity measures for their own benefit i.e. economic advantage or the prestige of

their brand. Such motivations do not reflect a genuine commitment to racial equality but rather a strategic move to maintain power or gain benefits (Bell [1980]). While not denying the value of personal motivation, advocates of CRT highlight the substantive ethical motivations for action.

With respect to the second point on structural inequality, CRT provides a critique of the so-called neutrality or colour blindness of law and the suggestion that neutrality will lead to racial inequality. Demonstrating its interdisciplinarity, CRT draws on branches of political theory to suggest that indifference to the powers that organise society is to side with the status quo. Neutrality sounds prejudice free. But if ethnicity, for example, is a site of social power and something that limits a person's access to certain opportunities, experiences, and institutions, then for the law to insist on blindness is to side with privilege. This is most evident in laws which purport to represent everyone as free and equal. While undoubtedly an advancement from overtly discriminatory practices, equality before the law might also be limited and unable to provide emancipation to marginalised groups. This is because formal equality does not address the material conditions that led to disadvantage. Equality before the law holds out an abstract view of reality where we are all free and equal. This is a vision that is divorced from the lived experience of marginalised people. Issues of ethnicity and inequality are pushed into civil society where they are not named as political but are seen as the product of bad luck, the absence of hard work, or as natural. Some advocates of CRT seek responses that combine law reform with substantive changes to material society and economic disadvantages. These are mechanisms that can provide for a fuller vision of human emancipation (Bridges [2021]).

The inclusion of issues surrounding ethnicity into the curriculum has been widely supported by the legal profession and governing bodies. These groups have taken proactive steps to increase the representation of marginalised groups within the profession. More broadly, they have expressed an interest in graduates who understand issues of ethnicity and can engage with the lived experience of culturally diverse people. It is for this reason that Paul Tremblay (2002–2003) has argued that a 'culturally competent lawyer can anticipate the areas where difference is most likely to arise, and, equally importantly, the direction in which the differences are most likely to proceed.' The essential skill here is the development of a capacity to see the world from another's perspective. This is critical for contemporary practice because it aids listening and understanding which are fundamental skills if a lawyer is to discharge their responsibilities to the public.

PETER BURDON

References

Bell Jr, D.A. (1980). 'Brown v. Board of Education and the Interest-Convergence Dilemma', *Harvard Law Review*, 93(3), p. 518.

Bridges, K. (2021). 'Critical Race Theory and the Rule of Law', in Meierhenrich, J. and Loughlin, M. (eds), *The Rule of Law*, Cambridge University Press.

Crenshaw, K., Gotanda, N., Peller, G. and Thomas, K. (1996). *Critical Race Theory: The Key Writings That Formed the Movement*, The New Press.

Dolman, K. (1997). 'Indigenous lawyers: Success or Sacrifice?', *Indigenous Law Bulletin*, 4(1).

Higher Education Statistics Authority. (2023). 'Higher Education Student Statistics', available at https://www.hesa.ac.uk/news/19-01-2023/higher-education-student-statistics-uk-202122 -released.

Israel, M., Skead, N., Health, M., Hewitt, A., Galloway, K. and Steel, A. (2017). 'Fostering "Quiet Inclusion": Interaction and Diversity in the Australian Law Classroom', *Journal of Legal Education*, 66(2), p. 332.

Leipold, J. (2023). 'Incoming Class of 2023 Is the Most Diverse Ever, But More Work Remains', Law School Admission Council, available at https://www.lsac.org/blog/incoming-class-2023 -most-diverse-ever-more-work-remains.

Mahuteau, S., Karmel, T., Mavromaras K. and Zhu, R. (2015). 'Educational Outcomes of Young Indigenous Australians', National Centre for Student Equity in Higher Education, p. 7, available at https://www.ncsehe.edu.au/ research-database/educational-outcomes-of -young-indigenous-australians/.

Melville, A. (2014). 'Barriers to Entry into Law School: An Examination of Socio-Economic and Indigenous Disadvantage', *Legal Education Review*, 24, p. 44.

Rodgers-Falk, P. (2011). 'Growing the Number of Aboriginal and Torres Strait Islander Law Graduates: Barriers to the Profession', p. 2, available at https://www.education.gov.au/ access-and-participation/resources/growing -number-aboriginal-and-torres-strait-islander -law-graduates-barriers-profession.

45. Feminist legal education

Feminist legal education focuses on law's relationship to women and the relationship of men to women as enacted through law. Specifically, it explores the role that law plays in creating, defending and perpetuating men's dominance and women's subordination in society but also men's power *over* women. It exposes the purported neutrality and objectivity not only of laws and their enforcement but of a traditional doctrinal legal education by showing how the omission of a feminist perspective operates to serve men's interests. Despite receiving considerable attention from feminist legal scholars over the past 40 years, feminist legal education is still a Utopian project. Legal education delivered by universities and professional bodies worldwide remains resistant to feminist ideas; whether law students are exposed to elements of feminist knowledge and practice in their studies is largely a matter of choice or chance.

Comparison with traditional legal education

A traditional legal education consists of the acquisition of a knowledge of the rules of law in selected areas and the learning of techniques of application of that law to fact situations. As such, it is stripped of social and political context, any critical perspectives being confined to an analysis of a court's inconsistency of application or incorrect interpretation of or failure to draw on relevant precedent or statute. Questions of justice are dismissed as irrelevant or simply regrettable in a particular case. Gender is never mentioned except where it cannot be avoided, as in discussions of rape, for instance; even in such discussions, attention is invariably focused on the female victim rather than the male perpetrator. 'Woman' is constructed in stereotyped ways that reflect men's perceptions and serve their interests.

The greater part of the law curriculum in institutions across the world is still delivered in this way, with socio-legal perspectives confined to a few niche modules, and feminism even more marginalised in, at most, one or two options. In such a setting, a feminist approach tends to be characterised, at best, as one viewpoint among many or, at worst, as narrow and partisan, while traditional legal education is never so labelled even though it represents the viewpoint of the men who originally developed it and ignores the experience of half the population. As Catharine MacKinnon has noted, 'It is thought possible to know a subject while maintaining illiteracy on questions of gender' (MacKinnon [2003] at 200).

One does not have to be a feminist to recognise that, historically, law treated women less favourably than men, for example by excluding them from participation in the legal process or by restricting their access to property or reproductive autonomy. Traditional accounts tend to ignore or skate over these topics, however, or to admit past injustice but present the law as if those days were long gone, one's sex being now irrelevant and women 'equal' in almost all contexts. A feminist legal education, by contrast, looks closely at how and why these inequalities and injustices arose, how and why reforms occurred (highlighting feminist activism as well as changing social circumstances and sympathetic male lawmakers), and what inequalities and injustices remain. It asks students to consider what more needs to be done to achieve genuine justice and equality beyond formal consistency in law. It does not simply provide a novel perspective on legal studies but a corrected and more complete one.

Structure and content

Feminist legal education may appear in individual modules on law degrees, generally in specific options devoted to 'Gender and Law' (formerly 'Women and Law'), or on Women's Studies and Gender Studies modules and courses in countries where these are taught. Though it may sometimes be found (if taught by feminist academics) in the core curriculum – the subjects that students must study to become qualified lawyers – it is rare for it to be other than optional, so the great majority of law students will not have to engage with or, indeed, encounter any feminism unless they specifically choose to study it.

There are two main approaches to content in feminist legal education. The first, influenced by Women's Studies scholarship, takes the idea of 'woman' in her various roles (for example, woman as wife, woman as worker, woman as criminal or victim) and relationships to law (for example, woman and property, woman and pornography) and examines the law that applies to that role or relationship and how it constructs and affects women, especially, in relation to men. The other approach takes the traditional categories of legal studies and subjects the legal principles and authorities to a feminist analysis. Such an approach starts from the standard syllabus, the better to convince students of the 'relevance' of feminism to the 'real' law they must know as lawyers, but treats the principles contained therein in a critical and contextual way. Other ways to introduce feminist legal education include inserting the occasional special research-based topic into a conventional module (for example, focusing on Land Law's treatment of gender in a particular case or issue such as implied co-ownership or undue influence in mortgage situations) or creating an entire module composed of 'issues' concerning women (for example, 'Black Lives Matter', looking at the intersection of race and gender).

One of the most effective ways that men have maintained control over women has been by treating the masculine perspective as universal and overlooking women's different situation. (This helps to account for law's longstanding indifference to women's suffering in the private sphere.) Feminist legal education, by contrast, poses the 'woman question', asking, for example, how a particular legal provision affects women differently from men, or how the way it is interpreted or enforced reinforces male power, or why certain subjects are privileged in legal education and others ignored or less valued.

By emphasising the importance of context, feminist legal education shares common features with socio-legal and critical legal approaches (see Socio-Legal Approaches to Legal Education and Critical Legal Studies) and, like them, is implicitly and often explicitly political. It is often linked to feminist activism in campaigns around, for example, the low prosecution and conviction rates for rape or the inequality of punishment for male killers of women and female killers of men.

History of feminist legal education

Feminist activists have always understood the role law plays in perpetuating the injustices they campaign against. Even before women were allowed to study law at university or enter the legal profession, they wrote and published accounts of the law as it applied to particular issues with which they were engaging (e.g. Bodichon [1854]; Norton [1854]). After their admission to the legal profession, several early women lawyers, recognising the importance of wider public education on legal matters, wrote articles and books explaining how the law applied to women (e.g. Crofts [1924]; Normanton [1932]). Even after women's admission to the profession, scholars working in a relatively small, male-dominated discipline, in close relationship with practitioners in a relatively small, male-dominated profession, contrived to keep both the operation of the law and the teaching of it firmly patriarchal until the last years of the twentieth century. Learning to 'think like a lawyer', as students were enjoined: 'Law students must learn the rules so that as lawyers they may apply them; students who wish to learn *about* the rules and pass (subjective) judgment on them are in the wrong faculty' (O'Brien and McIntyre [1986] at 379).

A conjunction of factors, different in different contexts, broke down the near-total male monopoly on both the practice and teaching of law. In the UK, the move towards making law a graduate profession, together with the expansion of higher education in the 1960s, led to an influx of women students. By the late 1980s they outnumbered the men and have continued to do so. A similar demographic shift occurred a generation later in relation to law teachers, with numbers of male and female lecturers gradually equalising, initially at the lower ranks but now spreading to professorial level too. Similar changes have occurred in other jurisdictions.

The second significant influence was that of the second wave of feminism which, starting in the late 1960s in north America, focused attention on both law and education as sites of women's oppression. The movement prompted a great deal of research, largely outside the legal academy, into legal areas affecting women and their gendered treatment within educational institutions. A further decisive factor was the introduction in many jurisdictions of research exercises leading to government funding. From being an optional extra, research and publishing became mandatory for recruitment and promotion to most academic posts. Law schools began to seek out good researchers whatever their sex or area of work, and doors were opened to feminist researchers. Feminist research became acceptable – respectable, even. Today there is a huge body of feminist legal research, including journals devoted wholly to feminist scholarship (e.g. *Canadian Journal of Women and the Law*; *Feminist Legal Studies*) and special issues of standard academic journals. Teachers can draw on these materials in developing a feminist module or perspective on their courses.

The creation of specifically teaching-focused materials, however, has never matched the research. A promising start was made in the UK with the ground-breaking *Women and the Law* (Atkins and Hoggett [Hale, later President of the UK Supreme Court] [1984]) which tackled the subject of women's legal inequality and oppression in chapters that could be used on both the newly-developing 'Women and Law' modules and as supplements to traditional core subjects like Property Law. Further resources appeared in the 1990s (e.g. Graycar and Morgan [1990]; Bridgeman and Millns [1998]). An innovative series from British publisher Cavendish was inaugurated with *Feminist Perspectives on the Foundational Subjects of Law* (Bottomley [1996]), comprising essays showing how feminist content could be used in each of the legal core curriculum subjects. In the following decade, starting in Canada and spreading to many other jurisdictions, came the 'feminist judgments' projects that law teachers found useful to use in their teaching (Hunter [2012]). Palgrave Macmillan's *Great Debates* series included feminist perspectives in some (but not all) of its books, as well as one volume entirely devoted to *Great Debates in Gender and Law* (Auchmuty [2018]).

Reasons for limited impact

Many factors have limited the impact of feminist legal education. In many jurisdictions the legal profession exercises control over what is taught on law degrees and how it is taught. Even where that influence has waned, as in the UK, the fixed curriculum may be maintained by heavy reliance on textbooks, whose successive editions (often by successive authors) generally confine themselves simply to updating the existing canon. While from time to time a (very rare) feminist-inspired textbook has appeared, it is noteworthy that when their authors retire, the titles tend to be retired too, rather than going into new editions under new authorship.

The more recent absorption of able feminist scholars into managerial roles has removed many outstanding educators from face-to-face teaching, while simultaneously imposing a new set of constraints on their ability to support feminist endeavours. Priority is given to financial exigencies, market competition, league tables, and diversity and inclusion agendas in which every other group seems to need more urgent attention than women. In countries like the UK, instruction has become more and more basic as law schools are forced for commercial reasons to take greater numbers of ill-prepared and emotionally fragile students. Attempts to introduce innovative pedagogies collapse in the face of the pressures of pastoral care. Departures from the traditional curriculum cause student anxiety and negative feedback, leading in turn to censure of the teacher by management.

The future of feminist legal education

There is some ground for optimism about opportunities for greater incorporation of feminist ideas into legal education. In jurisdictions like the UK where the undergraduate and professional trainings are separate, and where increasing numbers of law students are not proceeding to a career in law, space may open up for increasingly liberal-arts-style degrees with greater social and political content that students will find accessible and 'relevant'. A broader core curriculum – one that includes family law and employment law, for example, where so much of women's inequality and oppression are located – could extend (or replace part of) the heavily male-influenced syllabus students currently study. An increase in the number of feminists in the legal profession and judiciary, especially its senior branches, may yet (as Lady Hale's example showed in the UK) force teachers and students to discuss feminist ideas where they arise in case law taught on mainstream courses. As students become less inclined to read around the subjects they study, the textbook may also decline in importance; students who rely solely on an individual's teacher's class materials may receive more feminist influence than they realise.

The case for feminist legal education is as compelling as it has ever been. Across the world, women remain segregated into roles that are underpaid and under-valued, particularly in the home where they may be subjected to men's economic control and physical violence. Even in the most advanced countries women are still subject to injustices in the courts; globally, they suffer disproportionate oppression. Rights that we thought had been won are being withdrawn (abortion, for example); laws passed to benefit us are watered down or simply not enforced (rape, for example). Women are routinely objectified and subjected to unwanted sexual attentions and abuse from men; they are trafficked and sold for men's sexual pleasure. To arm them for the world they are growing up in, students need to know about these inequalities and injustices and to understand the mechanisms that are used to create and perpetuate them, including the effect of a traditional legal education that not only encourages complacency with the status quo but renders critique irrelevant.

ROSEMARY AUCHMUTY

References

Atkins, S. and Hoggett, B. (1984). *Women and the Law*, Basil Blackwell.

Auchmuty, R. (2003). 'Agenda for a Feminist Legal Education', *Legal Studies*, 23, p. 375.

Auchmuty, R. (2018) ed. *Great Debates in Gender and Law*, Palgrave Macmillan.

Bodichon, B. (1854). *A Brief Summary in Plain Language of the Most Important Laws Concerning Women*, Chapman.

Bottomley, A. (1996) ed. *Feminist Perspectives on the Foundational Subjects of Law*, Cavendish.

Bridgman, J. and Millns, S. (1998). *Feminist Perspectives on Law: Law's Engagement with the Female Body*, Sweet & Maxwell.

Conaghan, J. (2000). 'Re-assessing the Feminist Theoretical Project in Law', *Journal of Law and Society*, 27, p. 354.

Crofts, M. (1924). *Women under English Law*, National Council of Women.

Graycar, R. and Morgan, J. (1990). *The Hidden Gender of Law*, Federation Press.

Hunter, R. (2012). 'Feminist judgments as teaching resources', *Onati Socio-Legal Series*, 2, p. 47.

MacKinnon, C.A. (2003). 'Mainstreaming Feminism in Legal Education', *Journal of Legal Education*, 53, p. 99.

Menkel-Meadow, C. (1988). 'Feminist Legal Theory, Critical Legal Studies, and Legal Education or "The Fem-Crits Go to Law School"', *Journal of Legal Education*, 38, p. 61.

Normanton, H. (1932). *Everyday Law for Women*, Ivor Nicholson and Watson.

Norton, C. (1854) English Laws for English Women, privately printed.

Norton, C. (1854). *English Laws for Women in the Nineteenth Century*, privately published.

O'Brien, M. and McIntyre, S. (1986). 'Patriarchal Hegemony and Legal Education', *Canadian Journal of Women and the Law*, 2, p. 81.

Rhode, D. (1993). 'Missing Questions: Feminist Perspectives on Legal Education', *Stanford Law Review*, 45, p. 1547.

46. France (contemporary legal education)

Introduction

In 2022, a law degree was the most sought-after programme on Parcoursup, the French higher education admissions platform (https://www.parcoursup.gouv.fr/). In 2023, there were 218,400 students in French law faculties, with approximately 60 per cent pursuing a Licence en droit (a three-year degree equivalent to an LLB) and 36 per cent registered on a Master en droit. It is notable that as of 2023, over 70 per cent of French law students are women (https://www.insee.fr/fr/statistiques/6047727?sommaire=6047805).

The organisation of legal education

Across the key legal professions, the typical path in France involves four or five years studying for a law degree at university, followed by an entrance exam or competition in order to undertake further and more practical training. For example, students training to become barristers undergo 18 months of professional training at an École de formation du barreau (bar school), culminating in the bar exam (Certificat d'aptitude à la profession d'avocat – CAPA).

Therefore, in the realm of legal training, a distinction exists between theoretical legal education primarily provided by law faculties, which focus on teaching the fundamental principles of French law and the subsequent professional training geared towards preparing for a legal career whether it be as avocat, notaire or magistrat (translated loosely as barrister, solicitor and judge). The professional training offers more specialised and practical knowledge.

The initial university education

Following the three-cycle higher education Bologna reform that France started to implement in 2002, university education is organised according to the 'LMD (Licence-Master-Doctorat translated as Bachelor-Master-PhD)' structure (https://eua.eu/issues/10:bologna-process.html). The LMD reform aimed to harmonise higher education courses across Europe and facilitate student mobility at European level.

The first two cycles of the initial university legal education entail a three-year Bachelor of laws programme followed by a two-year Master's degree split into two parts – Master 1 and Master 2 (respectively fourth and fifth year of study).

Due to France's civil law culture and historical legal traditions, law faculties play a distinct role in training lawyers in comparison to common law countries such as the United Kingdom.

While universities in France no longer hold a monopoly on teaching law, as higher education institutions teaching law have diversified in recent years (Sciences-Po has its own law school and some leading business schools offer legal programmes), universities continue to be the primary institutions for training lawyers. Still, there is a potential threat to their role in terms of quality.

A traditional legal education

Over the course of the three-year Licence programme, which spans six semesters and totals 180 European credits (European Credit Transfer and Accumulation System – ECTS credits, equivalent to 360 credits in the UK), the curriculum focuses on French positive law, encompassing the general principles constituting the French legislative framework and their interpretation by judges. This highly theoretical and abstract approach to teaching law is partially influenced by the sources of law in France, tracing back to the French Revolution of 1789 and Napoleonic codification (see France (History of Legal Education)). Since then, legislation has been the main source of law in France, much of which is found in code. The first successful and most influential example is the Code civil, which introduced a unified structure to French law. This statutory framework forms the basis of the law taught in French universities, subject by subject, mainly through cours magistraux (lectures), during which students are confined to the relatively passive listener role. Seminars, however, offer students opportunities to engage in legal exercises, closely tied to the sources of law such as legal dissertations and case commentaries. In French law schools, there is still a strong emphasis on a particular form of legal writing and the construction of logical argument. French law essays typically follow a two-part format, consisting of two main balanced sections, further divided into two subsections each. This rigid stylistic approach requires clear identification of each part of the essay, using numbers or letters followed by sub-headings. Furthermore, it is essential that this prescribed structure aligns with and supports the student's specific interpretation or perspective on the essay title.

The role of judges and of case law in legal sources also contributes to the relatively lesser solicitation of critical and independent thinking and creative faculties of law students in France (by nature, the content of French law is less debated than in common law jurisdictions such as the UK or the USA), particularly during the first four years of students' education. Legal education in France focuses more on what the law is rather than on the reasons for the law or what it should be ('L'enseignement du droit en France et en Angleterre: leçons d'une comparaison?' John Cartwright dans les cahiers de Portalis 2023/1 (n. 10), pages 99 à 108, Editions Presses Univ ersitaires d'Aix-Marseille). Independent and critical thinking typically comes to the forefront during the second year of the Master's degree.

The marked theoretical nature of law teaching, especially in the initial three years, can also be attributed to the substantial number of students enrolled in the Licence en droit and the resultant low teacher/student ratio, acting as a hindrance to the development of more innovative teaching techniques.

In terms of a typical timetable for a law student in France, there are more contact hours than in the UK, for example, averaging 30 hours per week. This includes three to four-and-a-half hours dedicated to seminars (each seminar lasts one hour and 30 minutes, with students having two to three seminars per week). The initial three years include a broad range of compulsory modules, such as employment law and family law.

Access to legal studies has undergone changes due to reforms introduced by the 2007 law on university freedoms and responsibilities (Loi n. 2007–1199 du 10 août 2007 relative aux libertés et responsabilités des universités) and the ORE law of 8 March 2018 (Loi n. 2018–166 du 8 mars 2018 relative à l'orientation et à la réussite des étudiants), undermining the principle of free access for all baccalaureate holders to the undergraduate course of their choice.

While the traditional three-year law degree course theoretically remains non-selective, with the only prerequisite being the bacca-lauréat, the recent reforms have facilitated the offering of selective courses, including the College de droit programmes that some universities offer to undergraduate law students and double degrees. For example, the University of Paris 1 Panthéon-Sorbonne offers dual qualification law degrees in partnership with British institutions (https://univ-droit.fr/formations/28676-licence-bi-disciplinaire-droit-specialite-droit-francais-anglais-ecole-de-droit-de-la-sorbonne-paris-1) or dual bachelor's programmes in law and economics (https://formations.pantheonsorbonne.fr/fr/catalogue-des-formations/licence-L/licence-droit-KBT8CDAC/double-licence-droit-economie-KBT8CEW8.html).These selective programmes recruit high-level students and contribute to the diversification of legal offerings in French universities.

Additionally, a selection process during the first year of law studies results in only approximately 40 per cent of students enrolled in the first year progressing to the second year (https://www.letudiant.fr/etudes/fac/fac-par-fac-ou-reussit-on-le-mieux-sa-premiere-annee-de-licence.html).

The next steps to professional legal training

Upon successful completion and validation of all 180 ECTS credits for the award of a Licence en droit, students aspiring to pursue careers as solicitors, barristers, in-house lawyers, judges, notaries or senior civil servants typically apply for a Master 1, followed by a Master 2 in many cases. (This allows students to specialise in a particular area of law, such as business law, public law or international law.)

It is worth noting that a Licence en droit does not grant access to the entrance examinations for Bar schools or the École Nationale de la Magistrature, which trains professional judges and prosecutors. Many professional entrance examinations or competitions require completion of a Master 1 as a prerequisite. Entry to these programmes has become highly selective since a law passed on 23 December 2016 (Loi n. 2016–1828 du 23 décembre 2016 portant adaptation du deuxième cycle de l'enseignement supérieur français au système Licence-Master-Doctorat (1).

SOPHIE BOYRON AND CATHERINE VINCENT

In conclusion, despite facing challenges such as the large number of students and low tuition fees, the quality of legal education in French universities remains high. This educational environment also fosters a diverse social mix, particularly during the initial three years, due to the non-selective admission process and low tuition fees.

SOPHIE BOYRON AND CATHERINE VINCENT

References

Loi n. 2007–1199 du 10 août 2007 relative aux libertés et responsabilités des universités.

Loi n. 2016–1828 du 23 décembre 2016 portant adaptation du deuxième cycle de l'enseignement supérieur français au système Licence-Master-Doctorat (1).

Loi n. 2018–166 du 8 mars 2018 relative à l'orientation et à la réussite des étudiants.

https://univ-droit.fr/institutions/les-institutions -representatives/conseil-national-du-droit: Conférence Nationale du droit.

https://www.enseignementsup-recherche.gouv.fr/ fr/effectifs-universitaires-en-2022-2023-91085.

https://univ-droit.fr/formations/28676-licence-bi -disciplinaire-droit-specialite-droit-francais -anglais-ecole-de-droit-de-la-sorbonne-paris-1.

https://formations.pantheonsorbonne.fr/fr/ catalogue-des-formations/licence-L/licence -droit-KBT8CDAC/double-licence-droit -economie-KBT8CEW8.html.

https://www.letudiant.fr/etudes/fac/fac-par-fac -ou-reussit-on-le-mieux-sa-premiere-annee-de -licence.html.

47. France (history of legal education)

Introduction

Legal education has a long history in France. It began in the Middle Ages, was linked with the construction of the royal State and was reframed, after a decade's break during the French Revolution, following a Napoleonic model.

Legal education in France until the French Revolution: from medieval universities to State law schools

Seven centuries after the fourth century manuscript of Autun (which contains extracts from Gaius' *Institutes*) legal education began in France with the rediscovery of Justinian's *Digest,* with the teaching model coming from Bologna at the end of the eleventh century. After lessons given in Mantua, Placentinus taught Roman law at Montpellier for twenty years in the second half of the twelfth century. In Paris, a small group of jurists, including some English masters, taught Canon and Roman laws at the end of the twelfth century and at the beginning of the thirteenth century. Then a University was created through a process that led to the recognition of four faculties (theology, arts, law, medicine) by papal bulls in the middle of the thirteenth century. In 1219 the papal bull *Super speculam* banished courses in Roman law in Paris, in order to preserve the theology faculty's prestige. Canon law continued to be studied in Paris (inside the 'Faculty of *Decretum*' where decrees were studied, probably with some lessons of Roman law alongside Gratian's *Decretum* and papal decrees). Masters and students wanting to study Roman law inside the royal domain went to Orléans, where the university was created during the 1230s and was made famous by Jacques de Révigny and Pierre de Belleperche at the end of the thirteenth century and at the beginning of the fourteenth century (Bassano [2022]). Roman law was also studied in Angers, whereas both Canon and Roman law were studied in the Universities of Montpellier and Toulouse (created in 1223 after the crusade against the Cathars), and in the last centuries of the Middle Ages in Avignon, Cahors, Grenoble, Orange, Aix, Poitiers, Nantes, Caen, Bourges and Bordeaux. In these universities legal education consisted of a long training based on the study of the two corpora of Roman and Canon law and evidenced by the awards of baccalaureate, the *licencia docendi* and the doctorate. Roman law was a source of law in the South of France (which explains the great number of southern Universities) and considered as the best way to educate jurists even in Northern provinces (which were governed by customs in the field of private law). Teaching was delivered in Latin, although there are some testimonies about the use of French words and probably some hints of customary law in the universities (Kuskowski [2022]).

New developments occurred in the sixteenth century, with more interventions from the secular powers in universities and the development of legal humanism. Influences from Italy, especially with Alciato coming to the University of Bourges in the 1520s and the 1530s, triggered debates about the best way to learn Roman law, with more attention to history and a better use of the Latin language. Later legal historians have created the wording *mos gallicus jura docendi* as opposed to the *mos italicus*. Recent studies, especially concerning Cujas and his teaching, have nuanced the range of change in legal studies, but it remained long (between six and eight years) and traditional with the same limitations relating to Roman and Canon laws (Prévost [2011]).

In the sixteenth century, the increasingly nationalist atmosphere restrained the number of foreign students in French universities (although Grotius obtained very quickly a doctorate in Orléans in 1598) and favoured the beginnings of a legal literature in the French language outside the University. The first half of the seventeenth century witnessed a clear decline in student enrolment and of the activity of professors (who were called *docteurs-régents)*. Facing a strong decline in the number of *docteurs-régents* at the Paris law school (*école de droit*) and a relaxation of the discipline, Louis XIV decided to reform all university teaching of law throughout France by his edict of April 1679. This edict enshrined the principle of the State monopoly for legal education through the prohibition of private lessons given by professors, required the attainment of the three years degree of *licence* for all royal judges (it was also the case for advocates from 1519), re-established the teaching of Roman law in

Paris and created professors of French law in order to teach royal laws and customary laws (written down in the sixteenth century in the North and Centre of France) in the French language. Canon law continued to be taught with Gallican doctrines, while the teaching of Roman law was concentrated on Justinian's *Institutes* with the probable use of French translations of the *Digest* (Halpérin [2019]), whereas professors of French law (among this group the best known was Pothier in the middle of the eighteenth century) developed innovative courses proposing some synthesis of Roman, customary and statutory laws.

In 1789 there were 21 law schools in France (*écoles* or *facultés de droit* or *des droits* because of the association between Canon and Roman law) and probably 3000 students, with a great discrepancy between Paris (700 students), Toulouse (400 students) and the other universities where the student body numbered between 50 and 200 law students (Kagan [1975]). Legal training, which was the sole higher education organized except medicine, attracted not only future advocates, judges and administrators but also social and intellectual elites, with the example of many French writers (like Marivaux, Voltaire or D'Alembert) enrolled in the law school.

The Napoleonic model and its evolution

The French Revolution broke this *Ancien Régime* of legal education. The closure of all universities in 1793 created a ten-year vacuum of legal education in France, apart from an attempt in 1795 to create courses of legislation inside the *écoles centrales*, which were a kind of high school giving a general education in each French department (Halpérin [1986]). Through the law of 13 March 1804, Bonaparte (a few days before the promulgation of the Civil Code and a few months before the establishment of the Empire) re-established 11 law schools (*écoles de droit*, later called *Facultés de droit* in 1808). Three of these were outside the 1792 frontiers in France (in Brussels, Torino and Coblentz, but they were suppressed after the collapse of the Napoleonic Empire). Many features of the 1679 edict were resumed: the State monopoly of legal education (justified by the training of judges, advocates and high officials), the recruitment of professors (at the beginning five in each faculty) as members of the public service

through local competitions, the three year degree of *licence* (for young undergraduates after the social selection of the baccalaureate at the end of secondary schools), with the possibility of a fourth year of doctorate that was necessary only in order to become a law professor. Taking account of the codification process, the mandatory syllabus focused on the Civil Code (taught in every year of the *licence*, according to the order of its articles), with a small amount of Roman law (but no Canon law) and a smaller amount of criminal and procedural law. Despite a decree being passed in 1804 which aimed to introduce the teaching of natural and public law, it was not implemented, so natural law and public law were not taught in the law schools.

This very rigid framing remained largely unchanged until the 1880s. The first attempts to create courses in administrative law, legal history or political economy failed, and the teaching of the Civil Code by the exegetic method was one of the main components of a large, but not very original, legal literature of courses and treatises. The Paris law school was the first example (with that of Vienna) of mass teaching: the number of enrolled students grew from 500 in 1805 to more than 2,400 after 1815 (there were 4,150 law students in the whole of France), reached a summit in 1835–1836 with 3,454 students, before diminishing (because of an overflow of graduates and the creation of a tax on advocates in 1850) to less than 2,000 at the beginning of the Third Republic (Halpérin [2011]). But enrollments increased again in the 1900s, exceeding 6000 (15,000 for the whole of France) and more than 10,000 in the inter-wars period: at this time the *Faculté de droit de Paris* was the largest law school in the world. The first women were enrolled at the end of the nineteenth century (there were 150 in 1910) and many foreign students came from Greece, Egypt, Romania or Russia (more than 2,000 in the 1930s). The fees to be enrolled and to pass the examinations (responsibility for oral examinations throughout the year contributed to the high salary of Parisian professors until 1876) were costly and thus legal studies were reserved to the upper and middle classes, except for some rare examples of social promotion, since there were no State fellowships. In the provincial towns (the older nine law schools, apart from Strasbourg, which was annexed to the German Empire between 1871 and 1918, completed by the new law schools of Douai/Lille, Bordeaux, Lyon, Montpellier and Algiers) the law school was a smaller *milieu* with just a dozen professors and a few hundred students. Despite the creation of universities in 1896 to gather all the faculties in the same location, law faculties remained largely separated and governed centrally by the Minister of Public Instruction. From 1880, however, law professors could nominate two candidates for the role of dean.

From the middle of the nineteenth century, law professors were recruited by a national competition called the *agrégation*. In 1896 the *agrégation* was divided into four sections (private law including criminal law, public law, legal history and political economy), giving French higher education a structure that has been retained until today. Law programmes and syllabi were nationally reformed through governmental decrees during the Third Republic (in 1880, 1889, 1905, 1922) with the suppression of the Latin thesis of *licence* in 1880, the introduction of new subjects (constitutional law, legal history, industrial law, international law, colonial law), and the beginning of written examinations (1922) as well as the development of the importance of the written thesis as part of the doctoral studies (in 1895 and 1925). By 1914 there were about 100 law professors. All these transformations favoured a clear improvement of the research involvement of professors, evidenced by the blossoming of legal reviews and of handbooks and a limited expansion of the social background of teachers and students (the very large Catholic and rather conservative majority being expanded by the presence of some Protestants and Jews, as well as two women becoming professors before 1945). In addition, it had been possible to create private (in fact Catholic) law faculties since 1875. Legal education in French universities also benefited from some contact with other social sciences (through the teaching of political economy).

After the hardships of the two World Wars (700 Paris students died during World War I, 12 Jewish professors were excluded during World War II), the number of law students increased again after 1945 (40,000 in the 1950s, 60,000 in the 1960s) and the 1954 reform modified the *licence* programme to four years' duration as well as establishing tutorial classes. This was the origin of the two-part plan (three years' study leading to the award of a *licence en droit* followed by a further year of study to gain a Master's degree (*maitrise en droit*) which has become the recommended path for all law students in France today.

The 1968 students revolt triggered a general reform of the Universities which purported to break the system of law faculties and to make Universities more autonomous (Audren et Halpérin [2022]). But many historical features of the nineteenth century and of the first half of the twentieth century remained in place, for example the mass education, the recruitment of academics as civil servants and the two-part plan that was in fact a creation of the 1940s.

JEAN-LOUIS HALPÉRIN

References

Audren, F. and Halpérin, J.-L. (2022). *La Culture juridique française XIXᵉ-XXᵉ siècles*, 2nd edition, CNRS éditions.
Bassano, M. (2022). *De maître à élève. Enseigner le droit à Orléans (c.1230–c.1320)*, Brill.
Halpérin, J.-L. (1986). 'Une enquête du ministère de l'Intérieur sous le Directoire sur les cours de législation dans les écoles centrales', *Annales d'histoire des facultés de droit*, 3, p. 57.
Halpérin, J.-L. (ed). (2011). *Paris, capitale juridique (1804–1950)*, éditions rue d'Ulm.
Halpérin, J.-L. (2019). 'L'insegnamento del diritto romano nella Francia del XVIII sec.: un declino?', in Bonin, P., Hakim, N., Nasti, F. and Schiavone, A. (dir.), Pensiero giuridico occidentale e Giuristi Romani, G. Giappichelli.
Kagan, R.L. (1975). 'Law Students and Legal Careers in Eighteenth Century France', *Past and Present*, p. 38.
Kuskowski, A.M. (2022). *Vernacular Law. Writing and the Reinvention of Customary in Medieval France*, Oxford University Press.
Prévost, X. (2011). 'Mos Gallicus jura docendi. Le réforme humaniste de la formation des juristes', *Revue historique de droit français et étranger*, p. 491.

48. France (regulation of legal education)

In France, the regulation of legal education aims largely at determining entry to the legal professions and to make provisions for the professions' continuing education. Each legal profession has different and multiple entry routes in a bid to provide a degree of diversity and to allow professionals to move between professions. Having said that, entry to the key legal professions follows a similar educational pattern: as explained in the entry on France (Contemporary Legal Education) key legal professions require both a university degree in law, often at Masters year one or year two level. A Masters in Law is a two-year postgraduate university degree that allows students to specialise in a particular area of law and a further period of professional training. University (law) degrees are created under the control of the minister for higher education and research. The national character of the degree ensures that the qualification is recognised equally across the country. The professional training stage is specific to each legal profession and framed by separate legislations and regulations. Together Parliament and Government set down the requirements and routes for the legal professions in France. Yet, the professional training stage is often conceived by or with the participation of the professional body that represents the profession.

As it is not possible to present here the educational regulations of all legal professions that make up the French legal landscape, we focus on three key professions, those that members of the public are most likely to encounter during their lifetime, namely the avocats, notaires and magistrats.

Avocats (loosely translated as barristers)

The profession of avocats is regulated by the law of 31 December 1971. Among other things, this legislation – amended at regular intervals – spells out the conditions for becoming an avocat. Beyond the requirement of nationality, morality, ethics etc., one finds the main educational requirements in article 11: aspiring avocats must have passed the first year of a Master. In addition, a regulation lists other equivalent degrees or titles that will meet the entry requirement. Importantly, a university law degree does not give direct access to the profession, as article 11 specifies that any aspiring avocat needs to obtain the Certificat d'Aptitude à la Profession d'Avocat, the diploma that is required to qualify as an avocat. The 1971 legislation has delegated the organisation of this diploma to the Conseil national des barreaux (National Council of Bars) (https://www.cnb.avocat.fr). Consequently, the National Council organises this professional training, the latest regulation dating from 17 November 2023. The Council has set up 12 regional schools: Ecole du Centre-Ouest des Avocats (Poitiers), Ecole des Avocats Aliénor (Bordeaux), Ecole des Avocats Centre-Sud (Montpellier), Ecole des Avocats du Grand-Ouest (Bruz), Ecole des Avocats Rhône-Alpes (Lyon), Ecole des Avocats Sud-Est (Marseille), Ecole des Avocats Sud-Ouest Pyrénées (Toulouse), Ecole de formation professionnnelle des barreaux de la Cour d'Appel de Paris (Issy-les-Moulineaux), Ecole Régionale des Avocats du Grand-Est (Strasbourg), Haute Ecole des Avocats Conseils de la Cour d'Appel de Versailles (Viroflay) and Ecole des Avocats du Nord-ouest (Lille). They provide the teaching and supervise the training of the aspiring avocats. To be admitted to one of these schools, aspiring avocats must pass an entrance examination; universities have dedicated programmes that prepare students for this examination. Once admitted, trainee avocats study for 18 months. The programme is divided into three periods of six months: the first period focuses on theoretical teaching of professional modules (in person and online); the second period requires the trainee avocat to devise a professional project (it can range from an internship in a charity, working abroad or to studying for a further law degree); the third period must be an internship in a law firm. All three periods are assessed and together these marks will determine whether the trainee avocat has obtained the certificate. The newly qualified avocat will be able to register with a Court of Appeal to practice. From January 2025, it will be necessary to have completed a Masters in Law to obtain the certificate. This is the main route to become an avocat, but there are other routes available to people who have relevant professional experience.

Notaires (loosely translated as notaries)

Most French people will have dealings with a notaire at least once in their lives. The profession of notaire is entirely regulated by legislation, in the main by the ordinance of 2 November 1945. The notaire is a public officer that has several missions; in particular, when drafting legal documents (such as wills, real estate contracts etc), the notaire ensures both their validity and their enforceability. Recently, access to the profession was reformed and the two academic and professional routes were merged by the decree of 7 October 2022. Since then, only one route remains to become a notaire. First, an aspiring notaire needs to obtain a Master in Law at university, and preferably a specialist Master preparing for the profession of notaire as this will give the candidate automatic admission to the study of the postgraduate diploma which is required to enter the profession. If the candidate holds a Master with another legal specialisation, admission to study for the diploma requires an application and an interview. The diploma requires 24 months of study at the Institut des formations notariales (Training institute for notaries; https://www.infn.fr). This period is split into three separate study periods that investigate the different angles of the profession. Alongside this theoretical training, the trainee notaire undertakes an internship part-time with a firm of notaire. It is possible to take an educational break during this period to acquire further professional experiences, but the qualification needs to be completed in ten years.

Magistrats (loosely translated as judges)

By and large, the French have chosen to organise their judges into separate careers that mirror the dual court structure. For this reason, aspiring judges are trained separately to become private and criminal law judges (magistrats judiciaires) or administrative law judges (magistrats administratifs).

Magistrats Judiciaires (Judges with Jurisdiction over Private and Criminal Law Cases)

There are well over 8,000 magistrats judiciaires in France (Answer to a senatorial question by the Ministry of Justice on 02/03/23

https://www.senat.fr/questions/base/2022/qSEQ220701722.html). The great majority of these magistrats will have trained in the Ecole Nationale de la Magistrature – the national school for the private law courts (https://www.enm.justice.fr/). Articles 15 to 21-1 of the ordinance of 22 December 1958 list the routes available to join this career judiciary via the Ecole Nationale de la Magistrature. Furthermore, the decree of 4 May 1972 which was last amended on 10 June 2022, regulates this Grande Ecole. This 'School' is a public body under the supervision of the Ministry of Justice. Admission is organised through three annual (and highly selective) entrance competitions. Each year the ministry of justice determines the number of places; these match the number of positions offered at the end of the training. The main competition is reserved for law graduates who have passed the first year of their Masters. The other two competitions are reserved to: one, civil servants with four years' experience and the other, to legal professionals with eight years' experience. In 2023, the school recruited 353 trainee judges with 292 for the graduate competition, 47 and 14 the other two competitions respectively (see https://www.enm.justice.fr/actu-20122023-concours-dacces-2023-felicitations-aux-353-candidats-admis). The selection is high: in 2021, the success rate for the graduate competition was 11.2 per cent (with 1,722 candidates and 196 admitted; see https://www.enm.justice.fr/api/getFile/sites/default/files/2023-03/Profil_promo_ADJ_2021.pdf). From 2025, there will only be two competitions: one for law graduates and the second for professionals with relevant experience. To increase their chances, aspiring magistrats judiciaires will normally follow a preparatory programme offered by the majority of universities. Special preparatory programmes were introduced in 2008 to help candidates from disadvantaged backgrounds prepare for the competition. Every year several deserving and aspiring candidates are admitted to these programmes and given a scholarship.

Once admitted to the school, she or he is a trainee judge, sworn in and fully part of the judiciary. Trainee judges are paid a salary while training for 31 months; this period is split 30 per cent in class learning and 70 per cent in internships (with the police, the prison service, law firms etc) with a minimum of 13 months spent in court. At the end of the training period, the trainee will be evaluated (through a combination of examinations and internship assessment) and ranked. Each trainee chooses in order of ranking his or her first judicial position from the list established by the minister of justice. Trainee judges that have come through the graduate competition will have a limited choice of judicial positions; more choices are offered to trainee judges that have come through the professional competitions. Still, some entry level positions are notoriously challenging such as the one of juge des enfants or juge d'instruction.

Magistrats Administratifs

There are over 1,200 magistrats administratifs in France; this excludes the 234 members of the Conseil d'Etat (see https://www.justice.gouv.fr/justice-france/acteurs-justice/magistrats/magistrats-administratifs). Magistrats administratifs are trained differently from their private law colleagues (although several mechanisms allow judges from the private law courts 'to move' to the administrative courts). At present, there are two main routes to becoming an administrative judge; in both cases, the aspiring magistrat administratif only needs a Licence en droit. The aspiring magistrat administratif can be admitted to the Institut National du Service Public (https://insp.gouv.fr/) after a highly selective entrance competition; the National Institute for the Public Service trains together top civil servants and magistrats administratifs. It was created by article 5 of the ordinance of 2 June 2021. It replaces the Ecole Nationale d'Administration that had been criticised for its elitism.

There are preparatory classes to help candidates from disadvantaged backgrounds prepare for the competition; they receive both a scholarship and free university accommodation. Successful candidates admitted to the School are paid a salary and train for 24 months. On completing their training, they are ranked and offered a choice of positions in the civil service or the administrative courts.

Alternatively, the aspiring magistrat administratif can be recruited directly into the administrative courts through two highly selective competitions organised annually by the Conseil d'Etat (the top administrative court). The number of recruits matches the needs of the administrative courts year on year. The external competition aims at recruiting graduates while the internal competition is reserved for civil servants that have several years of relevant professional experience.

Once the trainee magistrat administratif has chosen to join the administrative courts, the centre de formation des juridictions administratives (Training Institute of the Administrative Courts) will give newly appointed judges six months of initial training. Due to the collegiate nature of the judicial decision-making process in the administrative courts, the new appointees learn the job largely from practice. Importantly, during their careers, magistrats administratifs are required to go on secondment for a minimum of two periods of two years to a managerial position in the civil service or to a similar position in the private sector. This seeks to widen the experience of these judges.

One may question the requirement for a (long) university education in addition to passing a highly selective entrance examination or competition for admission to any legal professions' training/qualifying programme. This certainly lengthens the period of legal education and creates numerous obstacles to entry to the legal professions.

SOPHIE BOYRON AND CATHERINE VINCENT

References

Law n. 71–1130 of 31 December 1971 on the reform of some judicial and legal professions.
Ordinance n. 45–2590 of 2 November 1945 concerning the status of the notariate.
Ordinance n. 58–1270 of 22 December 1958 enacting the organic law relative to the status of the Judiciary.
Decree n. 72–355 of 4 May 1972 concerning the National School for the Judiciary.
Ordinance n. 2021–702 of 2 June 2021 reforming the management of the State's Civil Service.
Decree n. 2022–1298 of 7 October 2022 concerning the notariate's higher education diploma.
Decree n. 2022–881 of 10 June 2022 amending the decree 72–355 of 4 May 1972 concerning the

National School for the Judiciary to allow the organisation of diplomas and certificates.

https://www.senat.fr/questions/base/2022/qSEQ220701722.html.

https://www.enm.justice.fr/.

https://www.enm.justice.fr/actu-20122023-concours-dacces-2023-felicitations-aux-353-candidats-admis.

https://www.enm.justice.fr/api/getFile/sites/default/files/2023-03/Profil_promo_ADJ_2021.pdf.

https://www.justice.gouv.fr/justice-france/acteurs-justice/magistrats/magistrats-administratifs-:~:text=1 230 juges siègent dans,et cours administratives d'appel.

https://insp.gouv.fr/.

SOPHIE BOYRON AND CATHERINE VINCENT

49. Further education

This entry explores further education (FE) provision in law focusing on both the academic and the vocational courses available prior to possible undergraduate study or employment. Examples of options are provided from a range of countries allowing for comparisons to be made. The UK Government defines further education as 'any study after secondary education that's not part of higher (that is, not taken as part of an undergraduate or graduate degree)', while the Cambridge Dictionary defines it as 'education below the level of university degree for people who have left school' . Usually, FE involves study below undergraduate but above compulsory education. For the purpose of this entry the authors define FE as the study after compulsory education, at any stage in a person's life before they undertake undergraduate studies. This entry is not intended as a comprehensive overview but provides information on a range of opportunities available to study law at this level in different countries.

Not all countries provide opportunities for the study of Law within FE, but where they are provided, the options available fall into two categories, the academic and the practical. In most of the UK, for example, both these pathways are offered, students make a choice depending on their career aspiration. Most young people will attend secondary school until they are 16 with the possible option of studying the Advanced Level of the General Certificate of Education (A Level) at a school sixth form, a sixth form college or FE college. The A Level is considered by some to be the 'Gold Standard' for post compulsory education, although there have been suggestions that it is in need of reform. Politicians have referred to the possibility of reform of A levels and further introduction of T (technical) levels but this is currently not part of the UK Government's legislative programme. Law is offered at A level by the exam boards, including AQA and OCR, and is generally assessed by examinations of a mixture of compulsory and optional modules, including the Legal System, Criminal Law, Contract, Tort and Human Rights. Students will study a two year qualification aimed at providing the skills needed for undergraduate study. The grading for A level is A* to E.

Another path of UK FE study is a vocational course provided by the Business and Technical Education Council (BTEC) which oversees the BTEC National Certificate or Diploma in Applied Law. BTEC courses are designed to be more practical in nature, and employers engage in the design of the curriculum to ensure the qualification meets industry needs and thus has a broader range than at A Level. BTEC students can elect to study a certificate or extended diploma depending on the number of units studied. The units are internally assessed within the school or college and externally by the exam board, and the grading is a pass, merit or distinction. Another option for more mature students returning to education in the UK is the Access in Law course offered by many FE colleges and some universities, such as The Open University. Access courses involve subject knowledge and the development of key study skills, such as time management, referencing and writing skills, which are necessary for undergraduate studies. A range of assessment methods may mirror those used by the local Higher Education providers to prepare potential students for these institutions. An alternative option for a student wishing to follow a more work-based programme is the T Level, which was introduced in 2020 in the UK to sit alongside apprenticeships. The courses are equivalent to three A levels but focus on practical learning for a job and include a minimum of 45 days, industry placement. The T Level for Legal Services was delivered for the first time in 2023. There is continuing discussion around the impact these courses may have on BTEC qualifications.

The other category is the professional practical option. This is overseen by the National Association of Licenced Paralegals (NALP) and the Chartered Institute of Legal Executives (CILEX). NALP offers courses at both level 3 and level 4, assessment is done through assignments and not examinations. This is often the option for paralegals, those qualified by education, training or work experience to perform legal work which requires a basic knowledge of the law.

Paralegal courses are popular in the United States of America (USA). The traditional route into legal education is from High School with a Secondary School diploma. However, there are a number of Community Colleges which provide alternative ways of studying and look a little more like the UK FE institutions. At a Community College students can study a range of courses that can prepare them for Higher Education or help prepare them for work. The vocational type of course within the legal field includes Paralegal Courses. These qualify the student to work as a paralegal and, dependent upon the Community College selected, an internship may also be available to gain greater work experience. Many of the Paralegal courses at the Community Colleges are approved by the American Bar Association who support the development of a Paralegal career. Some also offer a range of short courses within legal areas for example employment law. These courses may form part of a bigger qualification.

A different approach is undertaken in Scotland, which although part of the UK is a separate legal jurisdiction. There is no Law A Level option, as in England and Wales, but students can elect to study, via distance learning, a course entitled Law Making in Scotland to enhance their application to study law at university. Alternatively, students can opt to study the Scottish Vocational Qualifications in a range of legal related areas, such as Court Operations and Court and Prosecution Administration. These are employment-based qualifications and focus on developing work-based skills and meeting industry standards. A student must have suitable employment or work experience to study these courses.

Other countries offer the option of Law as a FE academic subject but provide no direct vocational route. In India, the Higher Secondary Examination is the entry qualification for university, and within the curriculum there is the optional subject of Legal Studies. Conversely, other countries provide the vocational route and there appear to be no academic options at this level. In South Africa, students complete the Upper Secondary phase (comparable to FE) which appears to have no options to study Law. However, a Paralegal course is available, either full or part time, and the course will cover a range of legal related options.

In some countries the option of studying law as a FE subject is not available. In France, from the age of 15, students attend the Lycée General or Lycée Technical (both of which cater for students wishing to pursue a more academic programme) or the Lycée Professional (which is more vocational in nature) but none of the courses offer law before a degree. In Russia, students can elect to attend one of the two types of vocational schools which prepare them for a career. In order to attend university students must graduate from school with a Unified State Examination (EGE). There are two mandatory subjects, Russian and mathematics, then students have a choice of subjects that can be studied. Law is not offered as an option at this level and can only be studied at university. There is a similar situation in Poland, where students who wish to study Law at university first need to pass examinations in Polish, Modern Languages and Mathematics.

Many countries have a role of legal secretary, an individual who provides administrative support to a lawyer. Often, they are qualified in this role and have studied at the countries, equivalent of an FE college. For example, in the UK students can study a Level 3 Diploma for Legal Secretaries which covers such things as typing, transcription, information processing and an overview of the legal system. In Australia students can elect to study the Certificate IV in Legal Services which covers a range of key areas including legal communication, research evidence law and drafting legal documents. With the ever-growing use of online tuition students from any country can elect to join and train as a legal secretary with a professional organisation, for example the Institute of Legal Secretaries and PAs. The Institute not only acts as a professional body but members can study the Legal Secretaries Diploma online to enhance and develop their career. There are no formal entry requirements but students are expected to have good typing skills.

In summary, the opportunities to study law in FE are diverse reflecting the history and needs of different countries. Some offer options to experience through either academic or vocational pathways an introduction to law before committing to a degree. Vocational courses are offered by many countries allowing students to gain practical work-based skills. It also appeared that there were more opportunities to change career in some countries, for example in the UK or USA. For those countries where change is not so easy the opening up of the digital world will provide many more opportunities to study.

Legal education is not static, and many countries are reforming their education

CAROL EDWARDS AND ANDREW MAXFIELD

systems to meet the needs of the ever-changing workforce.

CAROL EDWARDS AND ANDREW MAXFIELD

References

America Bar Association, 2023, Guidelines for the Approval of Paralegal Education, available at guidelines-for-the-approval-of-paralegal-education-programs-2023 (americanbar.org).

Elwood, J. (1999). 'Gender, achievement and the "Gold Standard": differential performance in the GCE A level examination', *The Curriculum Journal*, 10(2), p. 189.

Nikolaev, D. and Chugunove, D. (2012). *Education System in the Russian Federation: Education Brief*, World Bank Publications.

Rogers, L. and Spours, K. (2020). 'The great stagnation of upper secondary education in England: A historical and system perspective', *British Educational Research Journal*, 46(6).

50. Game based learning in legal education

What is game based learning?

Game based learning (GBL) is a pedagogical approach that leverages games to deliver subject-specific content and achieve key learning outcomes. It has emerged as an innovative, active learning approach across various fields, including legal education. GBL harnesses the innate human proclivity for play to foster a rich, engaging, and effective educational experience. GBL helps to support the development of key graduate skills alongside the delivery of subject specific content (Subhash & Cudney [2018]). At this point it is important to distinguish game based learning from gamification. In game based learning the intrinsic motivation of the game itself is the vehicle for learning, and educational content is integrated directly into the gameplay. Gamification, on the other hand, applies game-like elements to non-game contexts to engage and extrinsically motivate people to achieve their goals (Capp [2012]). It does not necessarily involve creating an actual game but instead uses elements like points, badges, leaderboards, and achievements to encourage desired behaviours. The core intent of GBL is to provide learners with an immersive learning experience that can improve their knowledge or skills in a particular area through the mechanics and narrative of the game.

Why use game based learning in law?

Game based learning offers an alternative to the pedagogical conservatism that has permeated legal education for the past 200 years. The traditional approach to legal education predominantly revolves around didactic lectures followed by Socratic seminars, a model that has its origins in the nineteenth century and Langdell's casebook method. Whilst the Socratic method does have some pedagogical value it alone cannot deliver all the key skills that are required of the modern legal graduate. At its core, game based learning harnesses the interactive nature of games to promote active learning (Bergman [1986]), where students become agents of their educational journey, navigating through complex problems and scenarios that could potentially mirror real-world challenges. Unlike passive absorption of knowledge typical in the didactic lecture, game-based learning kindles critical thinking, adaptability, and decision-making skills, as students must constantly assess situations and recalibrate their strategies in response to dynamic game environments (Lameras [2017]). This active engagement catalyses deeper cognitive processing and aids in the retention and application of knowledge, effectively anchoring academic concepts within practical, memorable contexts.

Graduates lacking the skills for the world of work is an overused trope that has permeated the higher education sector for decades. However there is some evidence to support the argument that graduates are not equipped with the sufficient skill sets for the world of work. Millennial lawyers have been described as having the '…inability to receive feedback, lack of organisational loyalty, being incapable of anything other than instant gratification, and generally less robust in taking criticism' (Bleasdale & Francis [2020]). Variation in pedagogic delivery of content is imperative if we are to equip graduates with all of the key skills required for the world of work. GBL offers one opportunity for this variation as it has the potential to engage and motivate learners, foster creativity in thinking, facilitate knowledge retention and transfer, and cultivate critical thinking and decision-making skills. Analog and digital methods have both been employed to teach critical legal skills, aligning with the skills and cognitive attributes outlined in the quality standards such as the UK's QAA subject benchmark standards for Law.

How can game based learning be deployed within a legal context?

Utilising GBL within legal education can serve as a potent method, offering immersive and dynamic experiences that bolster comprehension and memory retention of intricate legal principles. Below are some suggestions for implementing game based learning in this setting:

Mooting

Whilst not traditionally thought of as GBL, Mooting constitutes a pedagogical exercise wherein students engage in mock judicial proceedings. This entails the preparation of legal documents, such as memorials or briefs, followed by participation in oral advocacy. The term 'moot' denotes a fictitious legal scenario or issue which the participants are required to deliberate upon before a bench comprising a judge or multiple judges, often within the setting of an appellate court or an arbitration context. The objective of this exercise is to facilitate the acquisition and enhancement of the students' skills in advocacy, research, and legal writing. Additionally, it aids in honing their competencies in formulating and counteracting legal arguments. The inclusion of mooting in legal education is deemed critical, as it equips students with practical experience and familiarises them with the procedural and substantive aspects of law, thereby preparing them for actual legal practice.

Simulations

Legal simulation games are interactive games that mimic real-life legal scenarios and processes (Mozier et al [2006]). These games are designed to provide players with a hypothetical environment where they can practice and develop legal skills, such as argumentation, legal reasoning, and decision-making. In these simulations, players might take on roles such as lawyers, judges, or other legal professionals, and navigate through various legal challenges, from negotiating contracts to arguing cases in court. The games often incorporate elements of real legal cases, require players to research and apply relevant laws, and make decisions that affect the outcome of the cases they are handling.

Escape Rooms

An escape room refers to an immersive, collaborative game wherein participants work together to discover clues, solve puzzles, and overcome various challenges within enclosed spaces, all with the objective of achieving a specific goal, typically escaping from the room, within a predetermined time limit. Escape rooms offer a valuable opportunity for skills development, particularly in legal education (Montagu-Cairns [2023b]). They foster critical thinking by prompting analysis, pattern recognition and logical deductions. Problem-solving skills are honed as players navigate challenges and think creatively. Teamwork is emphasised, promoting effective communication and cooperation. Time management is essential to meet the escape room's time limit. Stress management skills are developed as players handle pressure. Attention to detail improves through careful observation. Adaptability is tested as circumstances change and perseverance is cultivated through multiple attempts.

Board Games

Board games are tabletop games that typically use pieces moved or placed on a pre-marked surface or 'board', according to a set of rules. The objective can vary from achieving a certain layout, accumulating points, completing a mission, or besting opponents. Board games can be designed as either a co-operative or competitive experience and can be deployed in legal education as an innovative pedagogical tool to enhance learning, engagement, and understanding of legal concepts (Montagu-Cairns [2023a]). Custom-designed board games can help reinforce legal principles and terminology, promote soft skills, encouraging students to develop strategies, anticipate opponents' moves, and make decisions under pressure (Yuratich [2021]). Many board games require teamwork and communication encouraging students to work together, share knowledge, and develop a collective strategy, mirroring the collaborative nature of legal practice.

Digital Ethics Dilemmas and Decision-making Games

Digital games can be either designed or adapted to simulate a real world or hypothetical ethical scenario. Ethics constitutes a fundamental element of legal pedagogy. The concept of serious play can be employed to confront students with ethical quandaries and complex decision-making situations (Traczykowski [2021]). Within this framework, students are compelled to traverse the intricacies associated with legal ethics, professional duty, and moral contemplation. Such pedagogical approaches facilitate the cultivation of ethical reasoning (Razook [2018]) and assist students in constructing a robust ethical foundation for their impending legal careers.

Table Top Role Playing Games (TTRPG)

TTRPGs are a type of game where players act out the roles of specific characters, making decisions and performing actions through verbal description. The fate of these actions and decisions is guided by the individual traits of the characters, which can be defined by the players themselves or by pre-established character sheets. The outcome of these actions is governed by a structured set of rules known as the game system. Co-operative in nature they encourage teamwork and collective problem solving. Due to their immersive nature, pen-and-paper RPGs are more than a game, they are an experience (Yee [1999]). TTRPGs often necessitate the resolution of disputes, the interpretation of regulation, and the representation of one's character, which can facilitate the cultivation of adept persuasive communication, negotiation, and argumentation capabilities (Phillips [2012]). Moreover, the imperative to address ethical quandaries, manage equivocal circumstances and comply with the established norms of the game can prompt participants to develop a robust ethical compass, imbued with fairness and respect for procedural justice. Consequently, this fosters an enriched comprehension of fundamental principles such as justice, equity, and adherence to the rule of law.

Game based learning can significantly enhance the learning experience and outcomes for students. The examples above are a small snapshot that correspond to active, cooperative, and constructivist educational methods, involving students in hands-on and reflective exercises that are essential for legal studies. Moreover, they can be combined with generative AI technologies to increase interaction and customisation [see AI Literacies in Legal Education], providing a contemporary and inventive educational experience.

STEVEN MONTAGU-CAIRNS

References

Bergman, P., Sherr, A. and Burridge, R. (1986). 'Games law teachers play', *The Law Teacher*, 20(1), p. 21.

Bleasdale, L. and Andrew, F. (2020). 'Great expectations: millennial lawyers and the structures of contemporary legal practice', *Legal Studies*, p. 1.

De Freitas, S. (2006). 'Learning in immersive worlds: a review of game-based learning', Bristol: Joint Information Systems Committee, available at https://pureportal.coventry.ac.uk/ files/4017131/learning%20in%20immersive %20worlds.pdf.

Kapp, K.M. (2012). *The Gamification of Learning and Instruction: Game-Based Methods and Strategies for Training and Education*, Wiley.

Lameras, P. et al. (2017). 'Essential features of serious games design in higher education: Linking learning attributes to game mechanics', *British Journal of Educational Technology*, 48, p. 972.

Moizer, J., Lean, M., Towler, M. and Abbey, C. (2006). 'Simulations and Games: Overcoming the Barriers to their use in Higher Education', *Active Learning in Higher Education*, 10(3), p. 207.

Montagu-Cairns, S. (2003a). 'Merchants of Briberia: A Case Study In Adapting Commercial Boardgames To Increase Creativity In Legal Education', in *Creativity in the Law School*, ALT Publication Series.

Montagu-Cairns, S. (2003b). 'You wake up in a locked room...Using digital escape rooms to promote student engagement' THES, available at https://www.timeshighereducation.com/ campus/you-wake-locked-room-using-digital -escape-rooms-promote-student-engagement.

Newbery-Jones, C.J. (2015). 'Answering the Call of Duty: the Phenomenology of Justice in Twenty-First-Century Video Games', *Law and Humanities*, 9(1), p. 78.

Newbery-Jones, C.J. (2016). 'Ethical experiments with the D-pad: exploring the potential of video games as a phenomenological tool for experiential legal education', *The Law Teacher*, 50(1), p. 61.

Phillips, E. (2012). 'Law Games – Role Play and Simulation in Teaching Legal Case Studies. Application and Practical Skills: A Case study', *Compass: The Journal of Learning and Teaching at the University of Greenwich*, 5, available at: https://journals.gre.ac.uk/index .php/compass/article/viewFile/66/110.

Razook, N. (1998). 'Looking for leviathan: Students embrace and resist co-operative norms in a prisoners' dilemma game', *The Law Teacher*, 32(2), p. 157.

Subhash, S. and Cudney, E.A. (2018). 'Gamified learning in higher education: A systematic review of the literature', *Computers in Human Behaviour*, 87, p. 192.

Traczykowski, L. (2021). 'Disaster ethics!', available at https://www.radixonline.org/blog/disaster -ethics.

Yuratich, D. (2021). 'Ratio! A Game of Judgment: Using Game-Based Learning to Teach Legal Reasoning', *The Law Teacher*, 55(2), p. 213.

51. Gender and the law school

Introduction

Law is taught and studied at a whole range of levels in many jurisdictions, from schools and colleges to universities and institutions offering professional training for lawyers. In this entry the term 'law school' is used to mean university departments, schools or faculties which provide credit-bearing legal education and in which scholarly legal education research may also be undertaken. What will become clear is that there has been a dramatic shift in the demography of the university law student and legal academic population over the past century and that this is beginning to reshape the legal education curriculum and scholarship.

History of gender and law schools

Until relatively recently law schools were male-dominated environments in many jurisdictions. Consequently, there has been limited engagement either with topics of particular relevance to women, or gender critiques of the law or the legal system. The history of women's admission to law schools is an interesting one. For example, in the UK, women's colleges, set up in the mid to late 1800s at the Universities of Cambridge (1869, Girton and Newnham) and Oxford (1879, Sommerville and Lady Margaret Hall) led to young women being permitted to read law soon thereafter (Auchmuty [2008]) although they could not yet be awarded with degrees. University College London permitted women to take the same exams and to be awarded law degrees in the same way as men from 1878 (UoL Constituent Colleges at 345–59). In 1888 Eliza Orme in England and Laetitia Walkington in Ireland were the first women to gain law degrees (First Hundred Years) whereas women in Oxford and Cambridge were not awarded degrees until the twentieth century (Webley and Duff [2021]). In Australia, the first female student, Flos Greig, enrolled in arts and law in 1897 at the University of Melbourne, graduating in 1903, and Ada Evans graduated in law from the University of Sydney in 1902.

Even though women were permitted in a number of jurisdictions to read law at university from the late 1800s, they could not yet enter the legal profession as the profession did not permit them to sit for professional qualifying exams. In Australia, the first woman, Greig, practiced law from 1905 following her and others' successful campaign which led to the Women's Disabilities Removal Act 1903 in Victoria, Australia. The sex-qualification bar had been removed a few decades earlier in Canada in 1892, with Clara Brett Martin in 1897 becoming the first female lawyer to practice law in Canada (Backhouse [2021]). In 1912 Gwyneth Bebb, a de facto first-class honours law graduand from Oxford (the University permitted women to sit for the examinations, but not to be awarded a degree on passing them), was chosen as a test case to take the Law Society of England and Wales to court for its refusal to admit women to the profession (Auchmuty [2011]). She lost the case, although the cause gained much-needed support and just after the end of World War I the Sex Disqualification (Removal) Act 1919 was enacted, making it possible for women in the UK to enter the professions including as solicitors (Cruickshank [2019]), barristers (Bourne [2019], Goldthorpe [2019]), magistrates (Logan [2019]) and to sit as a juror. This change also encouraged the University of Oxford to award degrees to women; Cambridge held out until 1949.

The legal academy was not that much in advance of the legal profession, even though it had admitted women to study back in the 1870s. Ivy Williams was the first woman recorded as teaching law in a British law school context, having been the first woman to qualify as a barrister in 1920 but choosing an academic career in place of practice (Auchmuty [2008]). Frances Moran was appointed Professor of Law at Trinity College, Dublin (Ireland), in 1925 (Hutchinson [2019]). The number of women teaching in university law schools remained stubbornly low until the second half of the twentieth century. In the UK the first woman law professor, Claire Palley, was not appointed until 1970, at Queen's University, Belfast (Cownie [2019]; Wells [2001]). A whole number of first women law professors were appointed or promoted around the world within a similar 50-year period, including Inkeri Anttila, the first woman law professor in Finland (Silius [2021]); Aisha Rateb, Egypt's first female law professor (Mehanna and Sonneveld [2021]) and Badria Al-Awadhi, the first female law student and law professor in Kuwait (Maktabi [2021]).

Law student and legal academic demographics

Law student demographics have changed markedly since the early days of female admission into law schools. By the end of the 1980s in England and Wales the gender balance was broadly equal. Now, that balance has tipped heavily in favour of female entry, with 69 per cent of student entrants to law degrees being women (Trends in the Solicitors' Profession Annual Statistics Report [2021]). This trend has been noted in a number of other jurisdictions. This has changed the nature of the practising profession at initial entry stage too with similar proportions of women to men entering the profession as trainee solicitors, legal executives and pupil barristers. The speed with which women are reaching the most senior positions in the profession remains slower, particularly in the context of law firm partnership and senior judicial roles (Webley [2017]). A range of initiatives are in place to try to address the unequal dispersion of women through different levels of seniority although their likelihood of success remains moot.

Law schools have also come a long way since the first female academics were admitted in the twentieth century and contemporary law schools benefit from having a diverse teaching and research faculty. McGlynn's early study of the situation in England and Wales in the late 1990s revealed that only four per cent of law professors were women, compared to nine per cent across all disciplines, but that the proportion of women was increasing in law schools and they accounted for more than a third of law academics (McGlynn [1999]). Cownie's study in the early 2000s found there was limited awareness about gender inequality in law schools, making it challenging to instantiate gender critiques into the curriculum or teaching practice (Cownie [2004] at 91). Contemporaneously in Australia, Thornton's studies identified that a male-dominated senior management culture in universities was implicated in a lack of understanding of patterned gender inequality between academics (Thornton [2004]). Some feminist legal academics were seeking to disrupt this through their research into the academy as well as in other pro-fessional contexts, including through legal historical perspectives of women as legal practitioners and law academics (Rackley and Auchmuty [2019] at 7–11). In England and Wales the demographic position gradually improved. By 2016 the legal academy was 50 per cent female, women being slightly over-represented in the more junior roles and under-represented in senior roles (Webley and Duff [2021]). These findings were in keeping with Collier's previous study, which had identified the importance of being perceived to be excellent and productive in research in order to secure advancement within the legal academy (Collier [2002] at 8–9) and Cownie's informants, who noted that for promotion to a Chair research was the key factor whereas good citizenship was neither necessary nor seemingly valued (Cownie [2004] at 81–88).

Gender in the legal curriculum and in scholarship

The law degree curriculum in many jurisdictions remains relatively conservatively drawn, partly due to the way in which law has historically been considered to be gender neutral in its application, and partly because the award of a law degree has been associated with professional exemption from other forms of legal education, training and examination for entry into the legal profession (see, for example, entries on Australia (Contemporary Legal Education), South Africa (Contemporary Legal Education) and China (Contemporary Legal Education)). The building blocks of law, seven in England and Wales, eleven in Australia and ten in Canada, for example, have dominated the curriculum. They have largely been taught using a doctrinal approach, with some sporadic disruption to this model through interventions by small groups of feminist and/or critical legal pioneers in law schools (see entries on Doctrinal Legal Education, Feminist Legal Education and Critical Legal Studies). Optional modules have provided more scope for gender critiques of the law, and for reimagining the law and decentring dominant narratives.

Academic legal research and the publications that flow from it have shifted focus more substantially during the period, in part as a function of changing understandings of high quality scholarly work as drawn by the various national research assessment exercises that have considered the contribution of academic publications and which have become drivers for quality assessment and university metrics (Genn, Wheeler and Partington [2006]; Cownie and Bradney [2013]). Research projects diversified and some began to consider the lived experience of law, including the experience of women and girls. However, although some of these findings are included in reading lists for undergraduate and postgraduate modules in law schools, they have yet to make substantive changes to the nature of curriculum other than in specialist postgraduate taught and research programmes.

Conclusion

The gender make-up of law schools has changed dramatically over the past century. Far more women are reading law, they constitute the majority of law students in a number of jurisdictions. Women are also numerically above half of the entrants to the legal profession and at least half of entrants to the legal academy. As yet they do not account for half of those in senior positions including decision-making positions. Their presence has made a difference to the elective, optional, curriculum available to students and in some instances has provided a gender lens through which to consider the core cannon of law that law students must study. Their influence is clear within legal scholarship and research which has positioned the experience of women at the centre of many studies of the law, the legal system and of access to justice. The gender dimensions of law are now recognised.

LISA WEBLEY

References

Auchmuty, R. (2008). 'Early Women Law Students at Cambridge and Oxford', *The Journal of Legal History*, 29(1), p. 63.

Auchmuty, R. (2011). 'Whatever Happened to Miss Bebb? Bebb v The Law Society and women's legal history', *Legal Studies*, 31, p. 199.

Backhouse, C. (2021). *Deux grandes dames: Bertha Wilson et Claire L'Heureux-Dubé à la Cour suprême du Canada*, University of Ottawa Press.

Bourne, J. (2019). 'First Woman to be admitted to an Inn of Court, Helena Normanton, 1919', in Rackley, E. and Auchmuty, R. (eds), *Women's Legal Landmarks: Celebrating the History of Women and Law in the UK and Ireland*, Hart Publishing.

Collier, R. (1998). '"Nutty Professors", "Men in Suits" and "New Entrepreneurs": Corporeality, Subjectivity and Change in the Law School and Legal Practice', *Social and Legal Studies*, 7, p. 27.

Collier, R. (2002). 'The Changing University and the (Legal) Academic Career – Rethinking the Relationship between Women, Men and the "Private Life" of the Law School', *Legal Studies*, 22, p. 1.

Cownie, F. (1998). 'Women Legal Academics – A New Research Agenda', *Journal of Law and Society*, 25(1), p. 10.

Cownie, F. (2000). 'Women in the Law School – Shoals of Fish, Starfish or Fish Out of Water', in Thomas, P. (ed), *Discriminating Lawyers*, Routledge-Cavendish.

Cownie, F. (2004). *Legal Academics: Culture and Identities*, Hart Publishing.

Cownie, F. (2004). 'Two jobs, two lives and a funeral: Legal academics and work-life balance', *Web Journal of Current Legal Issues*, p. 5.

Cownie, F. and Bradney, A. (2013). 'Socio-legal Studies: a challenge to the doctrinal approach', in Watkins, D. and Burton, M., *Research Methods in Law*, Routledge.

Cownie, F. (2019). 'First Woman Law Professor in the UK, Claire Palley, 1970', in Rackley, E. and Auchmuty, R. (eds), *Women's Legal Landmarks: Celebrating the History of Women and Law in the UK and Ireland*, Hart Publishing.

Cruickshank, E. (2019). 'First Woman Solicitor in the UK, Carrie Morrison, 1922', in Rackley, E. and Auchmuty, R. (eds), *Women's Legal Landmarks: Celebrating the History of Women and Law in the UK and Ireland*, Hart Publishing.

First Hundred Years Project, available at https://first100years.org.uk/digital-museum/timeline/.

Genn, H., Wheeler, S. and Partington, M. (2006). *Law in the Real World: Improving Our Understanding of How Law Works: Final Report and Recommendations*, The Nuffield Foundation.

Goldthorpe, L. (2019). 'First Woman to Practise as a Barrister in Ireland and the (then) United Kingdom, Averil Deverell, 1921', in Rackley, E. and Auchmuty, R. (eds), *Women's Legal Landmarks: Celebrating the History of Women and Law in the UK and Ireland*, Hart Publishing.

Hutchinson, E. (2019). 'First Woman Professor of Law in Ireland, Frances Moran, 1925', in Rackley, E. and Auchmuty, R. (eds), *Women's Legal Landmarks: Celebrating the History of Women and Law in the UK and Ireland*, Hart Publishing.

Logan, A. (2019). 'First Women Justices of the Police, 1919', in Rackley, E. and Auchmuty, R. (eds), *Women's Legal Landmarks: Celebrating the History of Women and Law in the UK and Ireland*, Hart Publishing.

McGlynn, C. (1999). 'Women, Representation and the Legal Academy', *Legal Studies*, 19, p. 68.

McGlynn, C. (2003). 'The Status of Women Lawyers in the United Kingdom' and 'Strategies for Reforming the English Solicitors' Profession: An Analysis of the Business Case for Sex Equality', in Schultz, U. and Shaw, G. (eds), *Women in the World's Legal Professions*, Hart Publishing.

Maktabi, R. (2021). 'Chapter 21 First Female Law Student and Law Professor in Kuwait: Badria Al-Awadhi Opens Doors for Women in Law 1967–2020', in Schultz, U., Shaw, G., Auchmuty, R. and Thornton, M. (eds), *Gender and Careers in the Legal Academy*, Onati Book Series, Hart Publishing.

Mehanna, O. and Sonneveld, N. (2021). 'Chapter 20 Why Aisha Rateb could not become Egypt's First Female Judge, and became Egypt's First Female Law Professor Instead', in Schultz, U., Shaw, G., Auchmuty, R. and Thornton, M. (eds), *Gender and Careers in the Legal Academy*, Onati Book Series, Hart Publishing.

Melbourne Law School, 'First Woman Lawyer in Victoria', available at https://law.unimelb.edu.au/about/history/first-woman-lawyer-in-victoria.

Rackley, E. and Auchmuty, R. (2019). 'Introduction', in Rackley, E. and Auchmuty, R. (eds), *Women's Legal Landmarks: Celebrating the History of Women and Law in the UK and Ireland*, Hart Publishing.

Silius, H. (2021). 'Chapter 15 Inkeri Anttila, the First Woman Law Professor in Finland (1916–2013)', in Schultz, U., Shaw, G., Auchmuty, R. and Thornton, M. (eds), *Gender and Careers in the Legal Academy*, Onati Book Series, Hart Publishing.

Thornton, M. (2004). 'Neo-liberal Melancholia: The Case of Feminist Legal Scholarship', *Australian Feminist Law Journal*, 20(1), p. 77.

Thornton, M. (2004). 'Corrosive Leadership (or Bullying by Another Name): A Corollary of the Corporatised Academy', *Australian Journal of Labour Law*, 17, p. 161.

Trends in the Solicitors' Profession Annual Statistics Report 2021. (2022). The Law Society of England and Wales.

Webley, L. (2017). 'Great Debates in Gender and the Legal Profession', in Auchmuty, R. (ed), *Great Debates in Gender and Law*, Palgrave MacMillan.

Webley, L. and Duff, L. (2021). 'Chapter 2 Gender and the legal academy in the UK: a product of proxies and hiring and promotion practices', in Schultz, U., Shaw, G., Auchmuty, R. and Thornton, M. (eds), *Gender and Careers in the Legal Academy*, Onati Book Series, Hart Publishing.

Wells, C. (2001). 'Ladies in Waiting: The Women Law Professors' Story', *Sydney Law Review*, 23, p. 167.

University of London, 'The University of London: the Constituent Colleges' Bedford College, available at www.british-history.ac.uk/vch/middx/vol1/, pp. 345–59.

52. Germany (contemporary legal education)

Legal education in Germany

The 'classical' legal education in Germany is split into two phases, a theoretical part and a practical part (Germany (Regulation of Legal Education)) (Wernsmann [2016]). To become a fully-fledged jurist (*Volljurist*) which gives the qualification for judicial office, prosecution, notariat, advocacy and leading positions in the civil service ('higher civil service') both parts must be completed. The training is focussed on the skills a judge needs and the examinations at the end of both parts are organised by the judiciary. This is the concept of *Einheitsjurist* which is unique in the world, a remainder of the Prussian authoritarian state (*Obrigkeitsstaat*) (Schultz [2012a]; see Germany (History of Legal Education)).

Two phases of legal training

The first phase is a more theoretical training at university in which legal contents and the structure of the legal system are taught with a focus on the methodology of applying law to the case (*Subsumtion*) and the technique of legal reasoning (*Gutachtentechnik*). Teaching is divided into three areas: civil law, criminal law and public (constitutional and administrative) law. Teaching mainly deals with fictional cases. The students have to take a fixed number of certificates for which they write papers in a defined period of time and sit exams; most of these focus on solving cases with the exception of papers in the foundation courses (legal history, sociology of law, philosophy of law, law and economics) and 'key qualifications' (soft skills) courses. The state legal education acts describe contents which the students have to master for the examination, but there is no set curriculum. No competencies are defined, there is little room for subjective elements and experiences. Legal education is expected to train for practice in which university teachers however only have limited expertise. The faculties try to fill this theory-practice gap – at least partly – by employing lecturers with practical experience.

The second phase comprises a practical training as an apprentice in the various fields of legal occupations under the supervision of practitioners, and real files are used. The young lawyers learn to write indictments, judgments and any other kind of legal decisions; in civil law they have to apply a special technique of distilling the legal case out of the known facts and dealing with evidence and burden of proof (*Relationstechnik*). The practical training is accompanied by weekly classes taught by practitioners.

About 10 per cent of the students do not go on to the practical training (which takes two years). This part is called *Referendariat* or *Referendarzeit* and the young lawyers are called *Referendare*. They are state employees who get a state subsidy. On average young lawyers need 8–10 years to get the full qualification. After the second examination they can call themselves Assessor (*iuris*).

Although legal education is regulated by acts of the federal states (which also leave some discretion to the law faculties), structure and contents are quite homogeneous throughout Germany.

Learning law

Law is a mass subject at university, there are about 120,000 law students at 43 law faculties with 10 to 35 law professors each. The ratio of law professor per student is around one law professor per 130 students. Traditional teaching still takes place in the lecture theatre in large groups of often several hundred students and additionally in working groups led by research assistants. Many students decide not to attend the lectures, and the great majority of students, up to 90 per cent, take courses with private tutors (*Repetitor*) instead (or additionally) – a pattern which has existed for centuries, although meanwhile universities also offer repetition courses. There are also private tutors for the second examination. The tutors edit teaching materials which may have a greater impact than textbooks from law teachers although they also distribute 'grey papers' accompanying their lectures. Since the Corona pandemic teaching materials are increasingly made available online, including podcasts and recorded lectures to support the teaching and learning process. The most effective way to prepare for the exam is by writing up to 50 or more mock exams on test cases. In Germany there are no tuition fees at universities except for the two private law schools, but students spend on an average 2,000 to 3,000 Euro on private tutors.

Examinations

Students study on an average five years plus the examination period which may take half a year. The main part of the examination is organised by the appeal courts of the ordinary jurisdiction in the federal states. The examination traditionally consisted of three parts, a legal paper on a constructed case for which the students had four or six weeks of time (*Hausarbeit*), three to five examination papers and an oral examination. When computers, internet and e-mails helped to connect students across the federal states and case solutions were circulated more easily, the legal paper was abolished. To compensate for it and also to give students a chance to specialise, an elective unit at university was introduced (*Schwerpunkt*) which counts for 30 per cent of the overall grade in the first examination. The grade in the 'state part' is however given greater weight, as the assessment in the elective subjects is inconsistent and only few students fail it. For the state part the students have to write six to seven examination papers. The second examination is organised by the appeal courts and the Ministries of Justice.

Gate keeping and rite of passage

Legal education has many elements of a perseverance training: a high time pressure for all assignments and the most rigid marking system of all subjects. This is part of the so-called 'hidden curriculum'. In the first examination only two per cent of students get very good and good, 15 per cent the special mark 'fully satisfactory'. This is seen as the threshold state grade (*Staatsnote*), the prerequisite for a position in the judiciary. Between 25 and 35 per cent fail, women proportionally more than men. This effect which has been relatively stable over the decades has been closely examined in recent years (Schultz [2021]). The difference is difficult to explain for the anonymously written test papers. For the oral part it has been found out that a greater number of women in examination panels helps to reduce the effect. In the second examination the failure quota is lower,

the marks a little higher, and the gender effect almost levelled out.

The overall drop-out number amounts to 50 per cent. After the de facto study period had become longer and longer, it was feared that young lawyers could suffer disadvantages in international competition due to their long training period; the practical training was cut to two years and a so-called free shot (*Freischuss*) was introduced. Students who take the exam after eight semesters are not penalised if they fail, i.e. the failure does not count. Otherwise, they may only repeat the examination once.

Regular study surveys have dealt with the psychological effects of legal education. They show that many students complain of a poor study structure which leads to orientation problems and feelings of insecurity. Students have doubts about their ability to study. They have a high study motivation geared towards high marks and good positions, but they complain a competitive working and learning culture, little contact with their teachers and the non-discursive style of teaching. The two legal examinations can be considered as initiation rituals, and they have the function of conformity tests.

The examination grades are of great importance for the professional career. The 17 per cent with the fully satisfactory plus the statistically hardly countable good and very good in the first examination are on the safe side and will hardly have problems finding their first position. In recent years career prospects were overall good, as there are not enough qualified young lawyers in the market, although the number of law students has doubled in the past 50 years.

Women in legal education

The first women were admitted to legal education only at the beginning of the twentieth century (Schultz [2022] and [2023]). They had been considered too emotional, not objective enough for legal decisions, also too soft for the serious legal work, and also unwanted competitors in a narrow legal market. In the Nazi era, legal education was characterised by the Nazi masculinity cult and the few women in law were expelled from legal education and practice. After World War II their numbers developed slowly, and only increased rapidly since the 1980s. Meanwhile women make up to 60 and more per cent of law students, and also the majority of judges and prosecutors are women, the legal profession lagging behind with 37 per cent. Only few faculties offer gender contents (Schultz [2012a]), and sexism in legal education is complained about. (Schultz [2020 and 2022])

Law teachers

Law in Germany is an authoritarian discipline with dominance attitudes and a charismatic teaching culture. Positions in the academy and particularly in law are (still) prestigious. The road to a law professorship is long and rocky. It is characterised by patronage and social reproduction. In addition to the two state examinations the German doctorate is needed followed by the 'second big book', the habilitation. This phase is characterised by job insecurity and a low to moderate income. There is no graduated procedure. The introduction of junior professors with the perspective of tenure has led to a slight erosion at the fringes but not real change. The young *Privatdozenten* then have to apply to another university than that where they have qualified. House appointments (*Hausberufungen*) are taboo. The average age at the call is 36. (Schultz [2021])

Women in legal academia are still a rare species. The first female law professor was admitted in 1965; in the past two decades their numbers rose noticeably and is now at 20 per cent. The long and tough qualification procedure and the male culture at law faculties has deterred women and they lack role models. Less women than men do the doctorate and few the habilitation. Many women prefer the judiciary as a good alternative. Due to strict equal opportunities regulations and practices in the past years slightly more women have been appointed to a professorship than their share of habilitations, but progress is slow. Important Chairs have several research assistants, and law professors may generate a good additional income from publications, expert opinions and legal commentaries.

Bachelors and masters in (business) law

In the 1990s the growing number of universities of applied sciences (*Fachhochschulen*), which were offering diplomas in business studies, wanted to expand their area of activity and offer law. This met with great resistance from the Ministries of Justice and the legal profession who saw the quality and the state-centred monopoly of legal education endangered. By and by diplomas in 'business studies, specialisation law' were pushed through. With the introduction of bachelors and masters in the Bologna process the diploma courses were transformed into bachelors and masters-in-business law and related subjects. In recent years also the range of distance learning courses in law at the growing number of private universities of applied sciences has increased and law courses in private distance teaching institutions are mushrooming. 20.000 (i.e. about 1/7 of all law students) study at universities of applied sciences. Although their degrees do not allow them to practice in the traditional fields of lawyers as advocates, judges, prosecutors and notaries they find positions in the economy, the civil service, the non-profit sector and also in special functions in big law firms.

Some law faculties at universities have introduced Bachelors degrees as a kind of intermediate examination, which could become a model for legal education, as to date students who drop out after years of studying law have nothing in their pockets. Since the 1990s law faculties have introduced a wide range of specialised masters for which they can (and have to) charge study fees as these are not regular study programmes.

Legal education a socially exclusive subject and identity building process

The German state-centred legal education was and is a backbone of the German legal system and the legalistic culture of the German *Rechtsstaat*. Young lawyers come on an average from higher social strata than students of other disciplines, which is a homogenising factor, making law a socially exclusive discipline. The long time they spend together in their university and practical education is a welding process creating a strong esprit du corps. The result is an effective socialisation in tune with the qualities expected from civil servants. Young lawyers do not only learn law but also inhale the profession specific identity with its special cultural codes and habitus and an overall conservative perception of society. A lack of emancipatory potential has been shown, leading to a civil service mentality and subservient attitudes. On the other hand legal education conveys valuable informal qualifications: a high commitment to professional work, an outstanding dedication to tasks, high resilience, the ability to cope with consuming tasks and with time pressure.

Until about three decades ago leading positions in public functions as well as in the economy tended to be held by lawyers which was described by the notion of lawyers' monopoly. For many leading public functions like heads of cities or chancellors at universities a legal qualification was even a prerequisite. With the diversification of study subjects and university degrees the dominance of lawyers has been weakened but is still noticeable and they are still seen as generalists who are well trained or suitable for leading positions.

Since its inception legal education has been under discussion and been criticised: to be too broad, too judge centred, to have too much contents, too many assessment, that too few foundations are being taught. Changes have been made regularly, but rather minor ones, the basic structure has remained untouched.

ULRIKE SCHULTZ

References

Schultz, U. (2012a). 'Legal Education in Germany – an ever (never?) ending story of resistance to change', 4, 1–24 *RED,* Revista de Educación y Derecho, available at http://revistes.ub.edu/index.php/RED/article/view/2212.

Schultz, U. (2012b). 'Gender Curricula Law', Netzwerk Frauen und Geschlechterforschung NRW, available at https://www.gender-curricula.com/en/curriculum/rechtswissenschaften.

Schultz, U. (2020). 'Gender in Socio-Legal Teaching and Research in Germany', *German Law Journal,* 21(7), p. 1345.

Schultz, U. (2021). 'Gender and Careers in the Legal Academy in Germany – Women's difficult path from pioneers to a (still contested) minority', in Schultz, U., Shaw, G., Thornton, M. and Auchmuty, R. (eds), *Gender and Careers in the Legal Academy,* Hart Publishing.

Schultz, U. (2022). '"Breaking the Bowl": Integrating women's, gender and socio-legal issues into teaching and research in law', in Ramstedt, M. (ed), *IISL Memory Lectures,* OSLS Series.

Schultz, U. (2023). 'Women Jurists Under the Swastika', in Barnes, V., Honkala, N. and Wheeler, S. (eds), *Women, their lives and the law: Essays in honour of Rosemary Auchmuty,* Hart Publishing.

Wernsmann, R. (2016). 'The Structure, Purposes and Methods of German Legal Education', in Gane, C. and Huang, H.R. (eds), *Legal Education in the Global Context,* Routledge.

53. History of legal education in Germany

The guiding principle of the 'Einheitsjurist'

The German system of legal education is dedicated to creating the so-called 'uniform jurist' (Einheitsjurist). All law students undergo the same legal education, regardless of their intended career path; judges, prosecutors, attorneys, civil servants, and future academics study together. The curriculum generally does not differentiate into specialisations, neither regarding certain occupations nor content-wise. Whoever completes the state examination law programme and the two-year preparatory training (Referendariat) is eligible to work in any of these legal professions. Overall responsibility for this programme does not lie with the universities, but the state.

The origin of this model dates back as far as the late eighteenth century, when the Corpus Juris Fridericianum (1781) was the first codification to set uniform regulations for legal education. After two amendments in 1793 and 1815 it became the General Court Code for the Prussian States (Allgemeine Gerichtsordnung der Preussischen Staaten). Thus, together with the General State Laws for the Prussian States (Allgemeines Landrecht fuer die Preussischen Staaten) it contributed to the unification of the State of Prussia, which at that time consisted of many different territories. The General Court Code as well as setting standards for legal procedures also set out the framework for the training of judicial officials and civil servants within the administration.

The Prussian model thus turned away from the Bolognese school of law, which had shaped and influenced legal education within Europe until then. In the twelfth century the University of Bologna established the first separate faculty of law and soon became the centre of European legal education, attracting students from all over Europe, including Germany, teaching canon law and also the Corpus iuris civilis and its digests, as it was valid throughout Europe and therefore formed the basis of legal education across and beyond Italy's national borders. With the founding of the universities of Heidelberg (1386) and Cologne (1388), this model of legal education also came to Germany.

With the Prussian model of legal education, the focus of the legal education shifted from university studies to practical training which was added and given greater weight. The students had to pass three exams, the first after their studies at university, the second after their one year as an 'Auskultator', where they acquired basic knowledge for practice by listening in hearings at court and by performing auxiliary activities for the court. Before the third exam they underwent preparatory training and worked as an assistant judge for four years. The third exam, known as the 'Grand State Examination' took place centrally in Berlin, where the candidates were examined in all their knowledge and character with exhaustive thoroughness. This system guaranteed the training as a generalist through precise theoretical and solid practical knowledge which could be used in any position in the civil service. The best lawyers went into the states administration, thus corresponding to the overriding importance of public administration for the stability and unity of Prussia. The judiciary was left with the second-best graduates and the less capable were employed by the state as judicial commissioners (Justizkommissar). (Hattenhauer [1989])

Later, the number of exams was reduced to one state-administered exam as an entry requirement for the preparatory training and one final examination to become a fully qualified lawyer.

When the German Empire was formed, from 1890 onwards, the success story of the Prussian legal education continued, its general structure remaining intact, despite the resistance of those states that were formerly influenced by the French system. The principle of the dualistic education became obligatory. To exercise any legal profession, it was obligatory to acquire an essential qualification: the 'qualification to be a judge' (Befähigung zum Richteramt), which could only be obtained after academic training at university, completed by the first state law examination, a legal preparatory training, and the second grand state examination.

Since the end of the nineteenth century, this system has remained in place, largely unchanged until the end of World War II, when Germany was divided into the Federal Republic of Germany and the German

Democratic Republic (GDR). While the Federal Republic of Germany maintained the two-tiered system, the German Democratic Republic established a one-stage training that qualified graduates to practice law. Legal education in the GDR was different for future lawyers or for judges and prosecutors; only the latter had to complete a one-year clerkship after graduation, and the degree awarded was that of a Diplom-Jurist. After the reunification of Germany in 1990, the legal education system of the GDR was gradually integrated into that of the Federal Republic of Germany, introducing the two-tiered system and the state exams.

The need for reform of legal education in the Federal Republic of Germany has constantly been articulated since the nineteenth century. In the 1970s proposals were put forward to establish a one-tiered legal education and shift the focus of legal education (back) to the universities, but none of the efforts prevailed, and the attempt was discontinued. (Geck [1977]) Only minor changes came about over recent decades, leaving the concept of the 'Einheitsjurist' and the role and influence of the State firmly in place. A minor change is that in 2002 the First State Exam was re-named the First Law Exam, as it consists of two parts – namely one part of the exam administered by the State and accounting for 70 per cent of the degree, and a second part of the exam administered by the universities, covering elective subjects, and making up 30 per cent of the overall grade.

The Bologna process of the European Union, established in 1999, aiming at a Europe-wide harmonisation of study programmes and degrees, which has shaped the European higher education landscape, has had hardly any impact on legal education in Germany. Within the legal community in Germany the two-tier system with bachelor's and master's degrees and modularisation of study content was widely deemed inappropriate for studying law; the fear mainly being that the qualification of the well-rounded Einheitsjurist were endangered by a modulised and shorter university education. Therefore, the state examination law programme as the training for all legal professions is still firmly in place.

Curriculum

Following the tradition of the Bolognese Law School, in the Middle Ages the main topic of the legal curriculum at universities in Germany was Roman Law, which developed as a basis for the emerging legal systems of Europe. By studying the Corpus iuris civilis and its digests, the students learned to interpret, further develop, and apply a multitude of legal principles and case solutions to various current contexts. They were less trained for specific legal professions but rather indispensable specialists for decision-making and legitimation.

The nineteenth century marked a significant turning point in legal education in Germany. This period saw the rise of the German Pandectists, legal scholars who sought to reform legal education and the legal system itself. Their name is derived from the term 'Pandectae,' which denotes the Pandects, a compilation of Roman Law construed by the Byzantine emperor Justinian I in the sixth century. The Pandectists advocated for a move away from exclusive reliance on Roman Law and emphasised a more systematic, scientific approach to law. They sought to engage in scientific and comprehensive examinations of legal principles with the goal of creating a unified and coherent legal system based on Roman law, leading to the incorporation of various legal subjects into the curriculum, including civil law, criminal law, and administrative law, subjects that till today are at the core of legal education in Germany.

During the Nazi Era, the fact that legal education was in large part a state matter made it easy for the totalitarian regime to exert their influence and shape legal education according to its ideology. The training of lawyers was no longer the responsibility of the federal states but was centralised at the Reich Ministry of Justice. Parts of the training and even the examination were outsourced to 'Gemeinschaftslager Hanns Kerrl', a camp for indoctrination. This led to systematic devaluation of intellectual engagement and subjects such as philosophy of law and history of law were particularly susceptible to its ideology, and all too often served to spread National-Socialist legal views. Legal education in the German Democratic Republic faced a similar fate; Marxism–Leninism became a compulsory subject. Jurisprudence

EMANUEL V. TOWFIGH

was supposed to be deprived of its actual object, the (relative) independence of law, by reducing it to the application of Marxism–Leninism and the question of the political power. (Frassek [2004])

While the main subjects (civil law, public law and criminal law) remain the foundation of the curriculum, emphases in the curriculum shift and adaptations can be observed, that react either to societal developments or to needs of the professions. Thus, with the rising significance of the European Union in general and European legislation for the Member States in particular, the role of European Law changed over time, from only being taught in its basic features to becoming an essential component also of constitutional law classes. And with the introduction of focus areas (Schwerpunktbereiche) that determine the university-administered part of the exam, the range of electives has broadened the curricula to more specialised topics and interdisciplinary subjects such as Digitalisation and Law, International Law, Legal History, Arbitration, Tax Law, Intellectual Property, Data Protection, etc.

Academic degrees

In the Middle Ages, the academic degree obtained qualified the graduate not for a certain legal profession, but was aimed at granting a teaching license, as only qualified individuals were supposed to teach law. The examination in Bologna required a lecture on a passage of Roman or canon law, to determine the candidate's suitability to teach law. Those who passed were granted the 'licentia docendi', i.e. the teaching licence. It was not until the seventeenth century that the examinations took on more of the character of a final exam and not a lecture, because entry into the legal professions depended on the applicant possessing a university examination. (Kaiser [2009])

With the introduction of the State Examination by the Prussians, law students no longer earned a university degree. Instead, with the Grand State Examination, they earned the title of an 'Rechtsassessor' (assessor of law). In the late Roman Empire, this was the name given to the emperor's legal advisors; since the Middle Ages and early modern times, it was used to designate assistant judges.

Outlook

Since Prussian times legal education in Germany has basically been under constant pressure to justify and reform itself, though significant reforms were not in fact implemented. With declining numbers of graduates and rising numbers of dropouts, the pressure to act has increased. A major weakness of legal education in Germany is the fact that failure to pass the State Examinations leaves students empty-handed. In this case, the many years of study end without any academic or professional qualification. This has been criticised and problematised for decades, and only now are efforts slowly being made to change this situation. It needed private law schools to introduce an integrated bachelor's degree into the State Examination Programme to open a new path within legal education. This integrated bachelor's degree has twofold advantages: on the one hand, it opens new career paths beyond the traditional legal professions, for which the qualification to be a judge is still a prerequisite; and on the other hand, those students who fail the law exam definitely, do not end up empty-handed and without any formal qualification. The bachelor's degree only requires writing a bachelor's thesis as an additional element to the regular law curriculum, which will be credited towards this degree.

Also alternative or supplementary programmes of legal education are slowly emerging, such as the Bachelor of Laws (LLB) and the Master of Laws (LLM) degrees, directed at students who wish to pursue a career in law-related fields, such as business, administration, or academia, or who wish to specialise in a specific area of law, such as European law, international law, or business law, without being qualified for legal professions in Germany.

Another aspect in dire need of reform is the pedagogy used in law schools. Unimpressed by developments in university pedagogy, formal lectures as one-way 'chalk and talk' presentations are the prevailing teaching 'method'. Again, changes are slowly emerging, with modern concepts such as sequentialisation, blended learning and/or 'flipped classrooms' making their way into law schools. For instance, the private EBS University Law School has dedicated itself to reforming pedagogy. In following insights from modern university pedagogy, it has introduced sequentialised, integrated modules spanning short five weeks and concluding with an exam, as well as blended learning courses (i.e. a combination of e-learning and face-to-face teaching). At EBS, online units are a second, independent part of the lecture in addition to classroom units, i.e. it is not merely a matter of 'enriching' a classroom lecture with digital elements. The online unit as a self-learning phase is on an equal footing with the classroom unit as a group learning phase. The aim of linking the two units is to stimulate, structure and control the learning process to trigger a self-directed acquisition of skills by the learners – and thus not merely to impart knowledge. In combination with the inverted classroom method, the self-learning phase precedes the face-to-face-lecture, allowing the students to control their acquisition of knowledge. The goal of the self-learning phase, which, if done in combination with blended learning can be using e-learning tools, is for the students to acquire (in advance) the essential factual knowledge, so that the face-to-face lecture will be rather a context- and development-oriented, in-depth examination of the knowledge already acquired. (Towfigh/Keesen/Ulrich [2022])

EMANUEL V. TOWFIGH

References

Frassek, R. (2004). 'Juristenausbildung im Nationalsozialismus', *Kritische Justiz*, 37, p. 85.

Geck, W.K. (1977). 'The Reform of Legal Education in the Federal Republic of Germany', *The American Journal of Comparative Law*, 25, p. 86.

Hattenhauer, H. (1989). 'Juristenausbildung – Geschichte und Probleme', *Juristische Schulung*, p. 513.

Kaiser, T. (2009). 'Der andere Bologna-Prozess: Ursprünge europäischer Juristenausbildung im Mittelalter', *Juristishe Ausbildung*, p. 353.

Keilmann, A. (2006). '*The Einheitsjurist:* A German Phenomenon', *German Law Journal*, 7, p. 293.

Towfigh, E.V., Keesen, J. and Ulrich, J. (2022). 'Blended Learning und Flipped Classroom in der grundständigen Lehre', *Zeitschrift für Didaktik der Rechtswissenschaft*, p. 87.

54. Germany (regulation of legal education)

In a broad sense, legal education in Germany takes place at three levels. At the top level, there is the State Examination law programme at German universities (public and private), qualifying graduates for the traditional legal jobs (judge, public prosecutor, lawyer, notary public). One level below are study programmes at universities of applied sciences (Fachhochschulen) and bachelor's degree programmes at universities, whose degrees qualify graduates for legal jobs outside the aforementioned 'traditional' legal jobs (for example as compliance or data protection officers). Last but not least, there is vocational training which paralegals and judicial clerks undergo.

Since the nineteenth century, when legal education in Germany became a state matter and the main goal was to educate future public servants, legal education has been regulated by law. The first codification of its kind was the Corpus Iuris Fridericianum of 1781, Prussia's first code of civil procedure, that after two amendments in 1793 and 1815 and its renaming to Allgemeine Gerichtsordnung became not only the foundation of civil procedure, but also implemented essential elements of German legal education, which continue to be in place to this day. (See Chapter 53 (Germany (History of Legal Education)).

State Examination Law Programme

The Allgemeine Gerichtsordnung established the two-phase legal education that still characterises legal education in Germany and provides a uniform training programme for all traditional legal professions, imparting a broad base of knowledge in core fields of law. To be able to exercise any legal profession, it is necessary to acquire a qualification, known legally as the 'qualification to be a judge' (Befähigung zum Richteramt). This qualification goes beyond its actual purpose and has the reputation of producing generalists who can be used as 'all-purpose employees' on the labour market for management tasks in business and the public sector alike, comparable to the reputation that engineers have in France.

This qualification can only be obtained after academic training at university, concluded by the First Law Examination, consisting of a State-administered exam that determines 70 per cent of the grade and an exam administered by the universities, covering elective subjects, and making up the remaining 30 per cent of the overall grade (the exact ratio varies a little among the German Länder). This exam is followed by a two-year preparatory training in the different legal professions (similar to a clerkship or a set of internships, called Referendariat or Vorbereitungsdienst) and the second law examination. To ensure uniform, equivalent legal education throughout the country, the regulatory foundation is differentiated accordingly, setting a framework by both federal and state law that comprehensively regulates legal education in Germany. Federal and state regulations are in a tiered relationship in which the federal law forms the foundation and framework and the state legislation, divided into two stages, fills this framework with content and then, in a further stage by way of implementing ordinance, sets procedural rules.

Federal regulation

The relevant source of law at the federal level is the German Judiciary Act (Deutsches Richtergesetz) first promulgated in 1972. Although the main purpose of this Act is to regulate the legal status of judges in the federal and state service, it also sets the framework and the foundations of legal education. It ensures that the states' legislation, where the responsibility for the organisation of the legal training both on the university level but also the preparatory training lies, creates comparable conditions regarding examination requirements and performance assessment (section 5d para. 1) but especially in setting the standard requirements that have to be met in order to qualify for judicial office (section 5 para. 1):

1. Qualification to hold judicial office is acquired by anyone who concludes their legal studies at a university by taking the first state examination and completes a subsequent period of preparatory training; the first state examination comprises a university examination covering areas of specialisation and a state examination covering compulsory subjects.

2. The content of the university studies and preparatory training is to be coordinated.

The German Judiciary Act is therefore setting the scene for the more detailed regulations by the federal states. Though section 5 of the Act explicitly refers to the necessary qualifications for judicial office, the qualification to be a judge is also a prerequisite for appointment as a public prosecutor (section 122 para. 1 German Judiciary Act), for admission to the Bar (section 4 of the Federal Code for Lawyers/Bundesrechtsanwaltsordnung) and appointment as a notary public (section 5 of the Federal Code for Notaries/ Bundesnotarordnung), as well as for employment as a lawyer in the higher administrative service (e.g. section 21 para. 2 Federal Career Regulation/Bundeslaufbahnverordnung). The respective laws refer to this section of the German Judiciary Act, therefore the provisions of sections 5–7 of the German Judiciary Act relate to the training of lawyers in general. For commercial lawyers in the generally usual sense and lawyers of other kinds, the qualification for the office of judge is regularly required in practice, though not legally.

While section 5 of the German Judiciary Act establishes the necessary conditions to qualify to hold judicial office, sections 5a, 5b and 5d specify the course of legal education, section 5a covering university studies, section 5b the preparatory training and section 5d setting the framework for the state law exam, including the authorisation of the states to issue necessary statutory instruments.

Section 5a para. 2 outlines the minimum standard of study content necessary for preparation for the legal professions, the exact lists of subjects traditionally being included in the examination regulations of the federal states. It specifies the necessary length of university studies, compulsory subjects ('core areas of civil law, criminal law, public law and the law of procedure, including their links to European law, the methodology of legal science and the philosophical, historical and social foundations') and necessary key qualifications that are non-legal in nature, but of particular importance for most legal professions ('such as negotiation management, negotiation skills, rhetoric, conciliation, mediation, questioning techniques and communication skills'). The requirement to demonstrate foreign language competence was added in 2003 and since 2021 a critical analysis of the injustices of the National Socialist regime and of the Communist dictatorship in Germany is to be included in the teaching of the compulsory subjects.

The purpose of the preparatory training is to provide a step-by-step introduction to the professional world of legal careers that is as practical as possible. Every legal trainee must complete mandatory and elective periods of practical training. Section 5b of the German Judiciary Act implements this by specifying the different trainings that need to be completed, as with a court of ordinary jurisdiction in civil matters, a public prosecutor's office or a court with jurisdiction in criminal matters, an administrative authority, an attorney (Rechtsanwalt) and an elective period of training at an institution where appropriate training is guaranteed. Section 5b para. 1 sets the duration of the preparatory training at two years, including the examination period. Due to the organisational structure of the preparatory training, it is not possible to reduce this period and an extension is only possible in individual cases for compelling reasons (but not on account of inadequate performance).

According to para. 3, the training can take place to a reasonable extent at non-German, namely supranational, intergovernmental or foreign institutions, or at a foreign lawyer's office, both for mandatory and elective training. The criteria for when it is 'appropriate' is determined by the state law or the responsible examination office.

In 2021 a para. 6 was added to sec. 5b of the German Judiciary Act, obliging the states to allow part-time preparatory training – at least for trainees who are caring for one or more children or close family members. This extends the duration of the legal clerkship to 30 months and the second state law exam will also be taken at a later date.

Section 5 para. d specifies the examinations at universities and in the state examination, that must comply with the content requirements of section 5a para. 3. Furthermore, the uniformity of the examination requirements and the performance evaluation must be ensured by the federal states. One means of doing this is through the authority of the Federal Ministry of Justice and Consumer Protection to establish a scale of grades and points for the individual and overall grades of all examinations.

State regulation

The responsibility for the detailed regulation of legal training and examination as well as their conduct lies solely with the federal states. In doing so, they are bound by the aforementioned specifications of the German Judiciary Act, but still enjoy a certain freedom regarding the details of the curriculum or the specifics of the exams. This leads to minor differences between the states, but overall, they follow the same path.

Usually, an Act on Legal Education forms the core of the state legislation and defines the requirements for the university studies, the state administered examinations and the preparatory training. It establishes necessary authorities and bodies, such as a Judicial Examination Office that is either part of the State Ministry of Justice (e.g. in Berlin or Hesse) or the Higher Regional Court (Oberlandesgericht) (e.g. in North Rhine-Westphalia or Schleswig-Holstein) and passes authority to establish the necessary regulations for the university administered part of the first law exam to the universities.

The state legislation regulates in detail the study requirements, the entrance requirements for the first or second law examination and its distinct terms such as type of examinations and specific assessment load. With this it substantiates the requirements laid out in the German Judiciary Act regarding the compulsory subject matters by detailing which areas of civil, criminal and public law constitute the core areas, which have to be subject of the university studies and the examinations according to the German Judiciary Act.

The same applies to the preparatory training. It is within the sole responsibility of the federal states, therefore the Act of Legal Education also covers the details of the training and examination, as well as the financial support of the trainees who receive a subsistence allowance as they are trainees in public service.

University regulation

Within the State Examination Law Programme, universities have the authority to regulate the university-administered part of the first law examination. Here, they have broad discretion over subjects and specialisations that they may use to establish certain focus areas and to introduce interdisciplinary subjects such as Digitalisation and Law, International Law, Arbitration, Tax Law, Criminology etc. The universities issue study and examination regulations, which are in accordance with the guidelines of the federal state's Act of Legal Education, that might require certain forms of examination, such as the preparation of a scientific homework assignment.

Bachelors and Masters degrees and university of applied sciences

Beyond the strict regulation of the state examination law programme, universities have, within the legal parameters of the Higher Education Act of the respective federal state, the authority to establish degree programmes and award academic degrees. Recently universities have begun to make use of the EU's Bologna process and to establish law-related Bachelors (LLB) or Masters (LLM) programs, usually specialising in certain fields of law. The legal framework for these courses of study is no different from any other bachelor's or master's degree programme, consisting of a combination of federal state laws, supplementary legal ordinances and university-set exam regulations.

Universities of applied science are also offering courses of study that conclude with the academic degree of Diplomjurist (Dipl.-Jur.). They often specialise in business law, preparing their graduates to take on professions that are outside the scope of the German Judiciary Act, such as data protection officer or in the area of compliance.

Paralegals and judicial clerks

Paralegals and judicial clerks undergo vocational training, they do not acquire an academic qualification. While paralegals are trained in law firms, judicial clerks are trained in a public body such as a court. They are both regulated by their own training regulations, in which the contents of the training as well as the examination requirements are specified. The legislative responsibility for this lies initially with the federal government, though the exam regulations are within the authority of the federal states (for judicial clerks) and the Bar Associations (paralegals).

Emanuel V. Towfigh

References

Federal Code for Lawyers [Bundesrechtsanwalts ordnung] in the amended version published in the Federal Law Gazette Part III, Section 303–8, last amended by Article 1 of the Act of January 17, 2024 (Federal Law Gazette Part I, 2024, No. 12).

Federal Code for Notaries [Bundesnotarordnung] in the consolidated version published in the Federal Law Gazette III, Index No. 303–1, as last amended by Article 3 of the Act of 20 December 2023 (Federal Law Gazette I, 2023, No. 389).

Federal Career Regulation [Bundeslaufbahnvero rdnung] of February 12, 2009 (Federal Law Gazette I, 2009 p. 284), which was last amended by Article 1 of the Ordinance of January 27, 2023 (Federal Law Gazette I, 2023, No. 30).

German Judiciary Act [Deutsches Richtergesetz], in the version promulgated on April 19, 1972 (Federal Law Gazette Part l, 1972, p. 713), last amended by Article 2 of the Act of December 20, 2023 (Federal Law Gazette Part I, 2023 No. 389).

55. Health justice partnerships

This entry explains the term health justice partnerships and elaborates on its current and potential uses in undergraduate (and post-graduate) legal education. It is aligned to the entries on Clinical Legal Education (General) and Public Legal Education (Community/General).

Health justice partnerships have operated in Australia, USA (where they are known as medical-legal partnerships) and Canada and have also been operating in the UK since the 1980s. A working definition has been provided by Professor Hazel Genn, a leading UK academic researching in this area:

> Health-Justice Partnerships are practitioner-led collaborations between free social welfare legal services and healthcare services to better address the health-harming unmet legal needs of patients. (Genn & Beardon 2021)

The usual format involves a legal professional working in a health care setting in order to provide access to legal advice to patients who present symptoms accompanied by a context that flags a potential legal need. The process involves the health care expert acquiring the knowledge and skills to recognise the potential legal issues amidst the story delivered by the patient. Not only does this result in the patient receiving advice on a problem that they did not realise was legal in nature, it also increases the legal knowledge of the healthcare professional due to proactive training being provided to healthcare providers to help them screen for potential legal issues, from secondary consultations and/or from joint problem-solving. A further benefit can include an increased trust in the legal professional, but most importantly addressing the legal problem has a direct impact upon the health of the patient.

Genn (2021) tells us that unmet legal needs can impact health and thus fall within the list of factors, such as low income, social conflict, and poor housing that comprise the social determinants of health.

According to the World Health Organisation, the social determinants of health are:

the non-medical factors that influence health outcomes. They are the conditions in which people are born, grow, work, live, and age, and the wider set of forces and systems shaping the conditions of daily life.

The professional practice of combining health with legal advice has developed piecemeal and differs in the various jurisdictions as a result largely of funding and economic differences in access to medical and to legal advice that particularly impact the disadvantaged. Its development has also been influenced by growing concerns over racial injustice and structural determinants of health. In the USA, medical care is variably accessed by a population dependent upon the finance to pay for medical insurance or treatment, or access to charitable institutions. The populations of Canada and the UK have access to national healthcare systems whereas Australia has a mixture of public and private health coverage. Access to free legal advice and to legal advice centres is severely limited in the UK as a result of state funding cuts, with organisations such as Citizen's Advice and university law clinics moving in to fill some of the gaps. Legal Aid is provided in Australia through a system of State Commissioners and there are in additional about 200 community legal centres, together with other independent charities, running free legal advice clinics as well as University law clinics. In the USA, Congress established the Legal Services Corporation in 1974 and this provides funding to most states in America to support non-profit legal aid organisations, although a range of other sources of funding also exist for medical-legal partnerships. There are 61 American law schools involved in such partnerships, with a recent edition of *The Journal of Law, Medicine and Ethics* including a wide range of articles on this topic. The level of discourse on this topic in USA law and medical schools, together with resources put into curriculum development, have supported this growth (see e.g. Tobin-Tyler & Teitelbaum [2023]). One example is the work of Yale Law School and Yale School of Public Health which jointly created a 'Global Health Justice Partnership' in 2012 (Yale Law School [Undated]). In Canada, there are a mixture of government funded, independent legal clinics and University law school clinics but health justice partnerships are yet to be fully established within legal education.

Genn [2019] reviews research findings from the USA and UK indicating the positive impact of health justice partnerships and describes how the field of health justice research is emerging in order to investigate questions around the bidirectional connection between legal advice and health:

> A central question is how joining together legal and health services can transform provision for disadvantaged and vulnerable groups to improve wellbeing and alleviate health inequalities.

For a comprehensive review of the history of the development of these partnerships together with a comparison of international practice, challenges and outcomes see Tobin-Tyler et al [2023]. As far as undergraduate legal education is concerned, an interdisciplinary clinic that brings medical and law students together, although considered (Curran, Ryder and Strevens [2018]) has not yet been established or, if it has, there is no publication documenting an evaluation of such. The Law Works 2020 survey on UK Law clinics fails to reveal this type of development. A planned Portsmouth Law School proposal was derailed by the Covid pandemic. Nonetheless there remain strong arguments in favour of developing undergraduate interdisciplinary clinics (Bliss, Caley & Pettignano [2012]; Benfer [2014]; Canon [2023]). First there is the potential to break down silo thinking in professional students and to build trust in the health and legal systems. There is the possibility of exposing health professional and law students to holistic and therapeutic approaches to problem solving, fostering multi-disciplinary teamwork and addressing negative stereotypes that could be taken on into professional careers. Such clinics also provide systemic advocacy opportunities, give students the opportunity to advance structural change and offer rich potential for interdisciplinary scholarship and research. Healton et al [2021] note:

> Institutions of higher learning are well positioned to integrate MLPs [medical-legal partnerships] into education and training and to assess the effects of such partnerships on students knowledge, attitudes, skills, and career choices. They are also ideally resourced to help build the evidence base regarding MLPs

outcomes at the student, patient, and system's levels...

In addition, there are considerable differences in skills development approaches between disciplines which can also provide learning for legal educators. Healthcare education seeks to develop, for example, motivational client interviewing and peer to peer learning skills and also use more advanced reflection skills than the common reflection on action approach in assessed legal clinic programmes.

Academics from the USA have developed ideas for interdisciplinary clinics with an enhanced team model proposed by Weinberg and Harding [2004] and with what Lerner and Talati [2006] describe an 'experientially integrated team'. Both require the commitment and active involvement of disciplinary academics and students in the design and delivery of an interdisciplinary curriculum.

The challenges are great. The time involved in planning and recruiting academics from across the different curriculum is easily underestimated particularly since Universities remain divided into disciplines by teaching and research imperatives.

Tobin-Tyler et al [2023] suggest a strategy of seeking common skills and abilities in the Subject benchmark statements and other regulatory requirements, such as around teamworking and communication, as a foundation for interprofessional curricula. Elective and optional modules and simulation exercises may also offer conduits, provided academic connections can be made and resource provided.

Interest in and adoption of health justice partnerships is growing (Tobin-Tyler et al [2023]) and with the development of international networks and scholarship there is the opportunity to learn and implement best practice. It is hoped that as a result health and legal injustices will be understood and addressed to a far greater extent than at present, addressing client/patient needs holistically. Legal advice and intervention might directly alleviate a case of, say, damp from a leaking roof causing breathing problems. Understanding that there is a legal issue to be addressed and proactively providing access to help may reduce anxiety and improve physical and mental health. Access to justice is fundamental to the rule of law and more people who understand their rights will enable more to assert those rights to be treated fairly and without discrimination.

CAROLINE STREVENS

References

Beardon, S., Woodhead, C., Cooper, S., Ingram, E., Genn H. and Raine, R. (2021). 'International Evidence on the Impact of Health-Justice Partnerships: A Systematic Scoping Review', *Public Health Reviews*, 42, p. 1603976.

Benfer, E. (2014). 'Educating the Next Generation of Health Leaders: Medical-Legal Partnership and Interprofessional Graduate Education', *Journal of Legal Medicine*, 35(1), p. 113.

Bliss, L., Caley, S. and Pettignano, R. (2012). 'A Model for Interdisciplinary Clinical Education: Medical and Legal Professionals Learning and Working Together to Promote Public Health', *International Journal of Clinical Legal Education*, 18, p. 149.

Cannon, Y. (2023). 'Medical-Legal Partnership As a Model for Access to Justice', *Stanford Law Review*, 75, p. 73.

Curran, E., Ryder, I. and Strevens, C. (2018). 'Reframing Legal Problems: Educating Future Practitioners through an Interdisciplinary Student Clinic', *Int'l J Clinical Legal Educ*, 25, p. 4.

Genn, H. and Beardon, S. (2021). 'Health Justice Partnerships', available at www.ucl.ac.uk/health-of-public/sites/health_of_public/files/health_justice_partnerships_integrating_welfare_rights_advice_with_patient_care.pdf.

Genn, H. (2019). 'When Law is Good for Your Health: Mitigating the Social Determinants of Health through Access to Justice', *Current Legal Problems*, 72(1), p. 159.

Healton, E., Treanor, W., DeGioia, J. and Girard, V. (2023). 'Training Future Health Justice Leaders – A Role for Medical-Legal Partnerships', *New England Journal of Medicine*, 384(20), p. 1879.

Lerner, A.M. and Talati, E. (2006). 'Teaching Law and Educating Lawyers: Closing the Gap Through Multidisciplinary Experimental Learning', *Int'l J Clinical Legal Educ*, 10, p. 96.

Rosen Valverde, J. (2018). 'Preparing Tomorrow's Lawyers to Tackle Twenty-First Century Health and Social Justice Issues', *Denv L Rev*, 95, p. 539.

Sandbach, J. and Grimes, R. (2020). 'Law School Pro Bono and Clinic Report 2020', *LawWorks and CLEO (Clinical Legal Education Organisation)*, 12.

Teitelbaum, J. and Lawton, E. (2017). 'The roots and branches of the medical-legal partnership approach to health: from collegiality to civil rights to health equity', *Yale J Health Pol'y L & Ethics*, 17, p. 343.

Tobin-Tyler, E., Boyd-Caine, T., Genn, H. and Ries, N.M. (2023). 'Health Justice Partnerships: An International Comparison of Approaches to Employing Law to Promote Prevention and Health Equity', *Journal of Law, Medicine & Ethics*, 51(2), p. 332.

Tobin-Tyler, E. and Teitelbaum, J.B. (2023). *Essentials of Health Justice: A Primer. Essentials of Health Justice: Law, Policy and Structural Change*, 2nd Edition, Jones and Bartlett.

University of Toronto Faculty of Law. 'Health Justice Program (HJP) Client Intake Project'.

Weinberg, A. and Harding, C. (2004). 'Interdisciplinary teaching and collaboration in higher education: A concept whose time has come', *Wash UJL & Pol'y*, 14, p. 15.

Wettach, J.R. (2007). 'The Law School Clinic as a Partner in a Medical-Legal Partnership', *Tenn L Rev*, 75, p. 305.

WHO Commission on Social Determinants of Health, World Health Organization. (2008). *Closing the gap in a generation: health equity through action on the social determinants of health: Commission on Social Determinants of Health final report*. World Health Organization.

Yale Law School. 'About Us'. (Undated). Available at https://law.yale.edu/ghjp/about-us.

56. Higher education

Legal education commonly comprises three developmental components: a foundation stage of academic knowledge and intellectual skills; a second professional legal education phase focussed on preparation for practice, and, lastly, career-long continuing professional development (CPD). The work of the higher (university or equivalent) education sector tends to concentrate most on the first of these elements, though in some systems university law schools may also deliver professional training. For present purposes, higher legal education can thus be said to include, chiefly:

- Undergraduate and graduate taught degrees in law or legal studies that provide a general (liberal) education in law.
- Undergraduate or graduate taught degrees that are accredited as providing a part or (rather less commonly) the entirety of formal legal education for intending legal practitioners.
- A sufficient concentration of legal subjects to constitute a 'major' or 'minor' component of a joint or combined studies degree.
- The teaching of discrete legal subjects within 'non-law' programmes: see Service Teaching in Legal Education.
- Preparation of candidates for research higher degrees in legal and socio-legal subjects.

These categories are not all mutually exclusive. For example, there is often considerable functional overlap between 'liberal' and 'professional' academic programmes, with most undergraduate law degrees fulfilling both objectives. A joint honours degree in law and another discipline might also provide sufficient legal study to meet some or all of the requirements of a qualifying degree for the profession.

Undergraduate legal education has tended to constitute the core work of law schools, certainly within the Anglo-European tradition and its derivatives, though academic graduate degrees have become an increasingly important part of the globalised law school. This entry sets out to explain the emergence of this modern higher legal education system, and to explore some important current developments.

A short history of university legal education

(See also national entries on the history of legal education)

The modern law school is largely a product of Western industrial society. In continental Europe, the growing nationalism and imperialism of the eighteenth and nineteenth centuries saw the widespread systematisation and codification of the (Roman-influenced) *ius commune* along national lines. This gave the universities, active in teaching Roman and canon (church) law since the thirteenth century, a new mission in propagating and interpreting state law, and educating new generations in its use.

University legal education was less significant in the development of the English common law system, which remained primarily apprenticeship based until the mid-twentieth century. William Blackstone's appointment to the first Vinerian Chair of English Law at Oxford in 1758 represented a landmark, insofar as his historical and taxonomic approach to common law had lasting impacts on Anglophone systems of law teaching and curriculum (see, e.g., Prest [2006]). However, it took more than another century before law teaching became established in English universities, and until the 1920s for the national Law Society to exempt law graduates from the initial stage of professional qualification (Gower [1950]).

These contrasting civil and common law models also came to be reflected across the developing world, largely displacing indigenous or earlier customary or religious legal traditions. Local law schools were often established as part of the colonial project; for example, a network of universities, modelled on the University of Salamanca and teaching Roman Law, had been established across the Spanish Americas by the eighteenth century, catering exclusively for the 'pure blood old Christian' social elite (Pérez-Perdomo [2023]). Local schools were established in Delhi and Mumbai in the 1850s, but these lacked the prestige and resources of their English counterparts, and so had limited impact in pre-independence India. While this status difference was less pronounced for local universities in the white settler societies of Canada, Australia and New Zealand, the elite British and, later, US law schools nonetheless had a profound and continuing influence on domestic scholars and scholarship (Pue [2016], Bartie and Sandomierski [2021]). One way or another, legal education thus became a mechanism for legitimising colonial rule, maintaining links to the 'mother country', and reinforcing the colonisers' superior occupation of local juridical space (Pue [2016], Likhovski [2002]). The gravitational pull of European power also meant that by the late nineteenth century, countries like China and Japan, that were never fully colonised, also 'modernised' their systems along European lines (Chesterman [2017]).

The relative decline of the imperial powers following World War II had two major consequences for academic legal education. First, many colonies acquired greater autonomy, or independence in this period. Some repressive regimes sought to keep the legal profession under-developed or even reduce its influence, with often negative consequences for legal education. Others retained significant features of the colonial system, but found that the ongoing need to localise and re-imagine legal education and scholarship for a post-colonial society led to some significant innovations in thinking and teaching about law, including in the creation of legal pluralist and indigenous legal education perspectives. These developments also had some reflexive influence on teaching and scholarship in the colonising and settler societies, notably in developing 'law and society' and critical approaches to Western law.

Second, much of the gap left by the old empires has been filled by American law schools. This reflects both general US economic and political influence, and the active work of law schools, NGOs, international financial institutions and aid organisations in advancing US-centric Rule of Law interventions in developing economies (Hammerslev [2022]). This has advanced the diffusion of US teaching approaches, including the Socratic method, and widespread adoption of clinical legal education since the 1980s. The US graduate law degree model has also been exported into Canada, across the Pacific to Australia and into Asia, influencing developments in Hong Kong, Japan, and South Korea. US legal education through these processes has become a powerful imaginary, shaping the idea of a law school perhaps even more than the reality (Bartie and Sandomierski [2021]).

Current trends

In reviewing international developments, Hammerslev [2022] has suggested that recent reconfigurations in academic legal education can be best understood in terms of changes to its 'location, scale, form and content'. These reflect academic legal education's attempts to negotiate a space for itself between the state, the profession, and the global market.

Location

Higher legal education is becoming more internationalised. This involves three key structural trends. First has been the growth in popularity of Anglo-American qualifications as a form of cultural capital. In addition to the LLB/JD degree, graduate degrees have become a significant international market for the larger common law jurisdictions, and especially the USA, in what Garth [2015] describes as a continuation of the 'competition of empires' to credentialise the global corporate lawyer. Continental European schools are now starting to close the gap, notably by delivering postgraduate offerings in English. Secondly, there has been a related rise in student and faculty exchanges, facilitated by regional agreements (e.g. the European Bologna process) which have streamlined diploma recognition and credit transfer. Third, the campus itself has also become de-localised. This reflects two processes: first is the opening of physical campuses by (mostly) elite US, Australian and UK schools in European capitals or established Asian markets, such as China, Malaysia, and Indonesia. The second involves the rise of the virtual campus. Wholly online legal education is thus now widespread in Australia, and even in the US, where the American Bar Association had long held-out against distance education, law school accreditation standards were changed in 2023 to allow students to earn up to 50 per cent of their necessary credits through online or distance learning.

Internationalisation, combined with policies of massification (discussed below) has been significant in making law schools more cosmopolitan and diverse in composition. Access policies have substantially benefitted women, who now commonly comprise over 50 per cent of the student body, and a growing proportion of faculty. In some jurisdictions the recruitment of domestic ethnic and cultural minorities has lagged behind internationalisation and gender diversification. Moves to online education are seen as an important, if somewhat contestable, mechanism for widening access to underrepresented groups.

Scale

Higher education since the late twentieth century has been characterised by a shift from elite to mass participation. The push to create a global 'knowledge economy' saw national and regional education policies in the 1980s and 90s geared to increasing access to university as a mechanism for both collective and individual economic success. This framing has helped the legal education sector grow significantly. It also reflects the fact that law degrees in most jurisdictions are relatively low cost to provide, and popular with prospective students. Such 'massification' has, however, raised public and regulatory concerns about the quality and over-supply of graduates. These underpin many of the continuing calls for legal education reform (Pérez-Perdomo [2023]; Webb [2018]).

Massification has also underpinned higher education's marketisation and privatisation. Privatisation has involved both the re-making of public universities into quasi-corporate operations (Thornton [2012]), and the construction of a mixed economy in which public and private institutions compete. The latter has, in some jurisdictions, radically changed the scale and location of legal education offerings. In Brazil and Russia, for example, the number of private institutions now greatly exceeds the number of state universities (see, e.g., Hammerslev [2022]), and this has intensified stratification and competition across the legal education sector.

Massification and marketisation have also brought with them increasing managerialism and performance measurement. Law schools are now commonly subject to quality targets for research, quality assurance controls over teaching, and financial targets for recruitment, particularly from lucrative international markets. These changes have led to increases in bureaucracy, greater inter- and intra-faculty and inter-institutional competition for resources, and some significant changes to academic career expectations. The latter has undoubtedly led to greater professionalisation across legal academia, including more emphasis on the quality of research and teaching. However, some of these gains have been offset by increased casualisation of the academic workforce. How much these changes have had a direct impact on the form and content of academic legal education remains moot.

Form and Content

Massification, privatisation and the demands of an increasingly diverse employment market have increased pressure on law schools to make their offerings more 'relevant'; on the other side, as Hammerslev [2022] observes, 'the persistence of traditional social traits and elite lawyers' strategies of social closure' may act as counterweights to reform.

The 'core' legal curriculum internationally has remained stable and relatively consistent, built around the expectation that all law students need a foundation in the essentials of public and private law. Civil law and mixed jurisdictions, commonly, impose a larger core curriculum than their common law counterparts, with much of the variation accounted for by the different treatment of international law, and of vocational subjects, like procedure and evidence. There has also been some decline in 'metajuridical' topics like Roman law, comparative law, legal history and jurisprudence, and a largely demand-led drift towards commercial law. Notwithstanding the impacts of globalisation, and experiments with trans-systemic (notably at McGill University, Montreal) and transnational legal education, curriculum tends to remain heavily jurisdiction specific. University legal education also still prioritises theoretical knowledge over practical know-how, though there has been greater integration of transferable and professional skills into curricula since the 1990s, a trend that can be linked to the growth in clinical legal education.

Structurally, there are at least three longer term trends and debates of note. First, a declining proportion of students are entering the traditional legal professions, and the legal services market itself is becoming more segmented and subject to ongoing technological disruption (Susskind & Susskind [2017]). Law schools may thus find themselves caught between a public interest (in preparing competent professionals) rock and the hard place of preparing students for a highly diversified employment market. This complexity raises, again, the question, 'what are law schools for?', and arguably strengthens proponents' claims that the primary function of academic law can only be to provide a liberal rather than vocational education. However, other current debates seem to be pushing in a contrary direction. Thus, and secondly, the move to 'competence-based' models of legal education, particularly in the common law world (see Webb [2018]), reifies the neoliberal focus on 'useful knowledge' and professional skills. It arguably has benefits in offering students and employers greater transparency regarding student capabilities for the 'real world', but it can also be criticised for relying on a narrow, instrumental, conception of professional competence. Thirdly, and relatedly, there is ongoing debate about the externalisation of professional assessment, and its impact on academic legal education. Externalised assessment is exemplified by the national Bar Examination model. This approach is widespread in civil law and mixed systems. Outside the USA, it is less common in Anglophone systems, but has been introduced for those qualifying as solicitors in England and Wales. Such models are intended to provide a reliable baseline of professional competence and can indirectly regulate academic curricula. However, they may also act as a 'dead hand' over curriculum, have possibly negative effects on access and diversity (e.g., Devito et al [2022]) and undermine the legal education system's capacity for structural change (e.g., Sato [2016]). How these debates play out may tell us much about the autonomy and adaptability of academic legal education, and the ongoing power of the profession to control the production of graduates.

JULIAN WEBB

References

Bartie, S. and Sandomierski, D. (eds). (2021). *American Legal Education Abroad: Critical Histories*, NYU Press.
Chesterman, S. (2017). 'The Fall and Rise of Legal Education in Asia: Inhibition, Imitation, Innovation', in Harding, A.J. et al (eds), *Legal Education in Asia: From Imitation to Innovation*, Brill, p. 1.
Devito, S., Hample, K. and Lain, E. (2022). 'Examining the Bar Exam: An Empirical Analysis of Racial Bias in the Uniform Bar Examination', *University of Michigan Journal of Law Reform*, 55, p. 597.
Garth, B.G. (2015). 'Notes Toward an Understanding of the U.S. Market in Foreign LL.M. Students: From the British Empire and the Inns of Court to the U.S. LL.M.', *Indiana Journal of Global Legal Studies*, 22, p. 67.
Gower, L.C.B. (1950). 'English Legal Training: A Critical Survey', *MLR*, 13, p. 137.
Hammerslev, O. (2022). 'Globalisation and Education: Reconfigurations in Location, Scale, Form and Content', in Abel, R.L. et al (eds), *Lawyers in 21st Century Societies: Comparisons and Theories*, Hart Publishing, p. 253.
Likhovski, A. (2002). 'Colonialism, Nationalism and Legal Education: The Case of Mandatory Palestine', in Harris, R. et al (eds), *The History of Law in a Multicultural Society: Israel 1917–1967*, Ashgate, p. 75.
Pérez-Perdomo, R. (2023). 'Legal Education and the Legal Profession', in Mirow, M.C. and Uribe-Uran, V. (eds), *A Companion to Latin American Legal History*, Brill.
Prest, W. (2006). 'Legal History in Australian Law Schools: 1982 and 2005', *Adelaide Law Review*, 27, p. 267.
Pue, W.W. (2016). *Lawyers' Empire: Legal Professions and Cultural Authority*, UBC Press.
Sato, N. (2016). 'The State of Legal Education in Japan: Problems and "Re"-Renovations in JD Law Schools', *Asian Journal of Law and Society*, 3, p. 213.
Susskind, R. and Susskind, D. (2022). *The Future of the Professions*, revised 1st edn, Oxford University Press.
Thornton, M. (2012). *Privatizing the Public University: The Case of Law*, Routledge.
Webb, J. (2018). 'Preparing for Practice in the 21st Century: The Role of Legal Education and Its Regulation', in Bergmans, B. (ed), *Jahrbuch der Rechtsdidaktik 2017 / Yearbook of Legal Education 2017*, Berliner Wissenschafts-Verlag, p. 11.

57. India (contemporary legal education)

Introduction

Today, the concept of law and its learning occupies a prominent place in India, so much so that law learning has in fact opened the possibilities of expanding the frontiers of other arenas of knowledge scholarships. Since the establishment of the national law school (NLS) (India (History of Legal Education)), the primary goals of Indian legal education have been twofold: to cultivate the necessary abilities for dealing with the intricacies and variations of legal practice, and to instil ethical and social ideals in practitioners. At the same time, India has been making remarkable progress in both its economic and social growth. Due to the implementation of a liberalisation strategy and the opening of the economy to global competition in the early 1990s, the country is making efforts to transition into a knowledge-based economy. There are abundant resources, such as availability of skilled human capital, a democratic system, widespread use of English, macroeconomic stability, a dynamic private sector, institutions of a free market economy, a well-developed financial sector, and a broad and diversified science and technology infrastructure (Dahlman and Utz [2005] at ix). However, the key is to carefully allocate them to achieve optimal results. This necessitates the enhancement of legislation, such as intellectual property rights, labour regulations, land acquisition, foreign investment, tax laws, information and technology laws, etc. Simultaneously, it is essential for law schools to adapt to the increasing global aspects of legal education and the legal profession in order to effectively disseminate and ensure appropriate comprehension of legal concepts (National Knowledge Commission [2007]). From this standpoint, it is important to analyse the evolution of Indian legal education and assess India's efforts in achieving the ultimate goal of legal education, which is to shape law students into socially conscious and justice-driven legal professionals.

Legal education in India

India is positioned as the fifth largest economy among the top 20 economies worldwide and boasts the second largest higher education system and is the second largest source of international students (International Monetary Fund [2024]; Altbach [2022]). Recognising the significance of education and educational institutions, India is actively striving to improve its global standing with her institutions achieving significant recognition. In fact, in the QS World University Rankings: Asia 2024, India manages to represent 148 universities in the Rankings (TNN [2023]). India is making considerable progress in the field of legal education too. It is accurate to state that legal education in India has made significant progress and is seen as a method of social control and a mechanism for societal change (Chakraborty and Krishna [2022]). Of course, with the rise of corporate culture, this notion of legal education is getting challenged as well (Wilkins et al [2018], hereinafter *Indian Legal Profession in the Age of Globalization*). Nevertheless, the corporate legal structure still forms a minuscule fraction of the Indian legal profession, particularly in terms of the number of legal professionals (Chandrachud [2018]).

However, this does not imply that the processes of globalisation have not changed the standards. In fact, the phenomenon of globalisation is impacting the framework of legal education, its governance, and most significantly, raising concerns about the role of education in promoting ethical norms. This highlights the possible drawback of using one's strengths to take advantage of opportunities. B.S. Chmini ([2006] at 20–21) examines this predicament and cautions against the inclination to establish a division of 'two Indias' – one that welcomes and benefits from globalisation, while the other is denied of essential necessities (see also Sarker and Sharma [2022]).

There is minimal uncertainty that the management of globalisation offers few benefits to the impoverished. Baxi argues that 'people are not naturally poor, but are made poor' through a 'a dynamic process of public decision-making in which it is considered just, right and fair that some people may become or stay impoverished' (Baxi [1985] at viii). The facade of global competitiveness has generated a profound divide of injustice. This phenomenon is most evident in the way India has managed its legal education. Presently, there exists a disproportionate number of both law schools and law students, with one being significantly greater than the other (Cottrell [1986]). The difference among these legal schools is readily obvious. Whereas a few have managed to gain well-established reputations, the majority of law schools are still struggling in terms of maintaining infrastructure and other operational expenses. Owing to greater demand, prestigious legal schools do not hesitate in demanding exorbitant fees (Increasing Diversity by Increasing Access to Legal Education [2022]). As a result, individuals aspiring to pursue law at prestigious institutions are forced to obtain loans, and the repayment plan is designed in such a manner that it compels students, even though they wish to test the waters of litigation, to seek employment in the corporate sector. This is a significant issue, especially when there is a demand and necessity for social engineers who can create a substantial and influential change in society.

Likewise, there are concerns over the quality of the teaching, the teachers, and the facilities (Sarker and Sharma [2020]). Furthermore, there is a belief that what is taught is of marginal relevance to the needs of most of the students, and of even less value to the country and its aspirations (Sarker and Sharma [2020] at 69–72). This perhaps, reflects upon the sad reality of not living in the present. In fact, way back in the late 1970s, Baxi reflected on this aspect and cautioned that 'any grandiose plan to recast legal education demands a proper grasp of present realities' (Baxi [1975–1977]).

Conclusion

Our analysis indicates that every effort towards transformation of legal education in India is wholeheartedly accepted; and as the depth and pace of social change expand, the understanding of law as a form of social architecture is also liberally welcomed. However, India has not yet been successful in implementing a desirable approach to guiding its educational, economic, and political institutions with a social philosophy. Perhaps it is high time for the policy makers to realise that legal education in India could still serve as a unifying factor in a society beset by internal divisions.

In order to achieve the goal of becoming a knowledge-based economy, it is imperative that India enhances its economic and institutional framework. Here, the role of law schools is vital as they not only cultivate a group of knowledgeable lawyers but also contribute to the establishment of an effective system of innovation. To have a highly adaptable infrastructure, law schools require substantial investment and government backing. Nevertheless, it is crucial to exercise caution while restructuring legal education, as ambitious initiatives often falter if they disregard a thorough understanding of existing realities.

SHUVRO PROSUN SARKER AND PRAKASH SHARMA

References

Altbach, P.G. (2022). 'India's higher education is opening up. But is it ready?', University World News, available at: https://universityworldnews .com/post.php?story=20221102093858736.
Baxi, U. (1988). *Law and Poverty: Critical Essays*, N.M. Tripathi, Bombay.
Baxi, U. (1979). 'Notes Towards a Socially Relevant Legal Education: A Working Paper for the UGC Regional Workshops in Law 1975–1977', in *Towards a Socially Relevant Legal Education: A Consolidated Report of the University Grant Commission's Workshop on Modernisation of Legal Education*, available at: https://www.ugc.gov.in/oldpdf/pub/report/1 .pdf.
Chakraborty, S.K. and Krishna, T. (2022). 'Promises and Prospects of Legal Education in India in the Context of the New Education Policy: A Reality Check', *Asian Journal of Legal Education*, 9(1), p. 64.
Chandrachud, D.Y. (2019). *The Future of the Indian Legal Profession*, available at https:// clp.law.harvard.edu/knowledge-hub/magazine/ issues/indian-legal-profession/the-future-of-the -indian-legal-profession/.
Chmini, B.S. (2006). 'A Just World Under Law: A View from the South', *Proceedings of the Annual Meeting (American Society of International Law)*, 100, p. 20.
Cottrell, J. (1986). '10+2+5: A Change in the Structure of Indian Legal Education', *Journal of Legal Education*, 36(3), p. 331.
Dahlman, C. and Utz, A. (2005). *India and the Knowledge Economy: Leveraging Strengths and Opportunities*, World Bank, Washington D.C.
Increasing Diversity by Increasing Access to legal education. (2022). *IDIA Diversity Survey Report: 2020–2021*, IDIA, Bengaluru, available at https://www.idialaw.org.
International Monetary Fund, *GDP, Current Prices*. (2024), available at https://www.imf .org/external/datamapper/NGDPD@WEO/ OEMDC/ADVEC/WEOWORLD.
National Knowledge Commission, *Report to the Nation* (2007), available at https://epsiindia

.org/wp-content/uploads/2019/02/Knowledge-Commission-Report-20071.pdf.

Sarker, S.P. and Sharma, P. (2020). 'Bridging the Gap: Understanding the Trends in Indian Legal Education from Recent Developments', *Asian Journal of Legal Education*, 7, p. 65.

Sarker, S.P. and Sharma, P. (2022). 'Teaching and Research of International Law in an Expanded World: Understanding from the Indian Perspective', *Revista de Direito Internacional*, 19(2), p. 295.

TNN. (2023). 'India's Higher Education Soars and surpasses Mainland China for Numbers of Ranked Universities', *The Times of India*, available at: http://timesofindia.indiatimes.com/articleshow/105066269.cms?utm_source=contentofinterest&utm_medium=text&utm_campaign=cppst.

Wilkins, D.B., Vikramaditya S.K. and Trubek, D.M. (eds), *The Indian Legal Profession in the Age of Globalization: The Rise of the Corporate Legal Sector and its Impact on Lawyers and Society*, Cambridge University Press, New Delhi.

58. India (history of legal education)

An overview of historical developments

Indian legal education is probably the oldest in the world, and yet very little has been written on this (Bar Council of India [Undated]. Amongst academic legal writings, the historical aspect is either found limited or mentioned briefly. Nevertheless, a remarkable effort was made in Justice Dr. M. Rama Jois in a series of works ([1990], [2011], [2022]). Another major effort is made by Banaras Hindu University with its Centre for Vedic Sciences (Tripathi & Kumar [2022]).

That being said, legal education in India has witnessed massive transitions (from informal or formal legal education setup). Today, the concept of law and its learning occupies a prominent place in India, so much so that law learning has in fact opened the possibilities of expanding the frontiers of other arenas of knowledge scholarships. In this perspective, it is quite fascinating to unravel this journey of Indian legal education, which of course has its own ebb and flow. For instance, much like Western civilisation, the early understanding of law in India was on religious lines, which over the course of time traversed into secular, common, and now onto constitutional norms. In other words, the concept of law has been developed over ages via careful articulation and a deep grasp of suitable legal and political systems. Furthermore, after gaining independence, India recognised the importance of education, including legal education, in promoting national development and reducing poverty. However, the efforts made fell well short of achieving the expected results. One reason for this deficiency was increased government control and lack of institutional autonomy. Nevertheless, the pursuit of reform persisted, and it was soon recognised that the importance and impact of law school, especially in creating socially relevant lawyers, is vital. As result, the idea of National Law Schools was conceived.

Key phrases of historical development

As per Indian heritage, education is considered as the process of introducing individuals to the spiritual aspects of life, and teaching their souls to seek truth and engage in virtuous behaviour. It is not solely seen as a means of livelihood or a place for developing thoughts and citizenship, but considered as second birth (divitiyam janma) (Government of India [1963] [hereinafter the *Report of the University Education Commission*]). Having said this, Indian legal education has had its own reputation since its beginning. The concept of legal education in India goes back to the *Vedic* age when it was essentially based on the concept of Dharma. The training was self-acquired, wherein importance is given to the fact that those involved in matters connected to impart justice must possess or are known for their righteousness and justness and have the reputation of being fair and impartial. Of course, there are no records to suggest how such informal education was imparted, nevertheless, there was a lot of evidence that suggests that the society remained peaceful – with its own indigenous thinking on dispute resolution.

That being stated, the records of formal legal education in India began with the establishment of the Government Law College at Bombay in 1855 (Aggarwal [1962] at 232). And soon thereafter, there were series of other universities established in many other major cities across India. The greater idea was to firmly establish a 'traditional pattern of English education' (Aggarwal [1962] at 231). Critically commenting on this aspect, Arthur Taylor said that 'the imported system was brought to societies having fundamentally different cultural and social assumptions' (Taylor von Mehren [1965] at 1180). Policies were adopted wherein public employment in every case was preferred for those who had been educated in Western science and were familiar with the English language.

Of course, there were course corrections, however, they were piece-meal. By the end of colonial rule, although India was successful in realising the fact that legal order can make a significant contribution in releasing human energy and talent towards the betterment of the society, its reflection in higher education in general and legal education in particular was largely misplaced. This happened even when many of the freedom fighters belonged to the legal fraternity and were successful in creating a legal and political consciousness that led people to participate in the political process against colonial rule This aspect fairly reflects upon what Krishnan [2006] argues as a case for cause lawyering. Getman ([1969] at 153) opined that the 'legal education in India has a proud heritage', and as a matter fact, lawyers played a prominent role in the creation of the widely praised Indian Constitution. In fact, at the time when the Constitution was framed, there was a common understanding amongst the drafters that the document must be in tune with deep social-justice and public-policy values. Perhaps, the intention was to promote legal education in a way that aligns with the goals and principles of the Indian Constitution.

Post-Independence, the journey of Indian legal education is divided into various phases. For simplicity, we consider them into three phases. These transitions can be appreciated into three phases firstly, owing to multiple reasons, learning of law was not considered prestigious, secondly, where it was perceived as an alternate to another degree, and thirdly, wherein it is witnessing immense potential to act as a global leader in imparting quality as well as socially relevant legal education.

The First Phase

The initial phases saw legal education as a preparation for something other than practice. Part of the reason was the fact that, for a significant period of time, Indian law schools were unable to attract motivated students. As previously stated, education, and institutions connected with the same, was not a priority for colonial rulers. This resulted in a lack of interest in studying law. In almost all law schools, the vast majority of students did not intend to practice law or even if they did intend to practice the options available were limited. This aspect was aptly covered in the *Report of the University Education Commission* ([1963] at 244):

> Our colleges of law do not hold a place of high esteems either at home or abroad, nor has law become an area of profound scholarship or enlightened research. This is probably no reflection upon us as it arose from conditions inherent in our position as a dependent nation. There were eminent legal scholars in our ancient universities, and faculties of law were among the first established in the early modern universities at Calcutta, Bombay and Madras. The opportunity, however, for original, stimulating study of law hardly existed; certainly, no demand was created for it while the

burden of Government, public service and legal transactions were carried by others.

The primary focus of the *Report of the University Education Commission* was on teachers; the improvement of law schools and the lives of students. For example, one significant recommendation given by the Commission was that 'a three-year degree course be offered in special legal subjects, the last year to be given over largely to practical work, such as apprenticeship in advocates' chambers ([1963] at 228)). The overall objective was to prioritise the significance of distinguished professors who actively participated in significant research, regularly produced scholarly work, and excelled in teaching. Arguably, the concerns so raised were the main factors that led to the alteration in the course of legal education in the country. In this case, the Constitution offered an identical incentive. The main purpose of establishing a forward-looking Constitution was to effectively advance its specified objectives and ideals by promoting education that strengthened the democratic system. This event served as the catalyst for the establishment of rule-based institutions such as the Indian Institute of Technology (IIT), and Indian Institute of Management (IIM), and other like organisations.

With respect to legal education, this phase saw establishment of the important institutions, namely, the University Grants Commission (1956), the Indian Law Institute (ILI) (1956); and the Bar Council of India (BCI) (1961). In this period rather than focussing on how legal education must concern itself with the training of lawyers, the focus was towards establishing the institutions. A 1958 report by the Law Commission of India noted that almost every aspect of law schools appears to be 'extremely defective'. The report appeared in agreement with the *Report of the University Education Commission* and emphasised how the legal educational environment must enhance its scholarly reputation. It also called for the standardisation of legal education through regulatory intervention ([1958] at 548).

Another important aspect noticed was the involvement of the Ford foundation which played a huge role in establishing the ILI and ensuring acceptance of the proposal to make law a three-year degree course (Krishnan [2005]). The idea was to establish a pool of lawyers and judges, who could interpret the law and provide legal assistance to citizens. Owing to these and many other pathbreaking academic exercises, India managed to gather confidence in identifying scattered legal research work and thereafter disseminate it to the rest of the world. For instance, in the early part of its inception, ILI undertook research activity in constitutional and administrative law, which was considered 'solid and encouraging progress' (Merillat [1959] at 524).

The Second Phase

The second phase was characterised by two notable developments: (i) the global observation of the phenomena of regaining rights, and (ii) the introduction of liberalisation measures. These advancements necessitated the implementation of reforms at many levels, particularly to meet international standards. In this setting, the goal was to consider societal aspirations while adhering to international standards. These advancements necessitated adjustments in the structure of legal programmes. For example, the establishment of the National Law School of India University (NLSIU) introduced the five-year integrated law degree. The primary emphasis of this structure was on implementing changes in curriculum, teaching techniques, selection processes, accreditation standards, and autonomy. Additionally, significant attention was placed on promoting specialisation. The successful implementation of the NLSIU experiment paved the way for subsequent experiments, heralding the onset of educational breakthroughs and leading to most states in India creating National Law Schools (Sivakumar et al [2021]). Despite a focus on specialisation, the three-year degree continues to be offered and is equally recognised as an eligible qualification for practicing law in India. Currently, both the holders of the three-year degree and of the five-year integrated degree are eligible for enrolment with the BCI upon the fulfilment of eligibility conditions and upon enrolment, to appear before any court in India.

During this time frame, a noteworthy accomplishment was the merging of clinical procedures with legal instruction. It was seen as advantageous to promote the development of legal clinics. Furthermore, the focus on legal assistance and fairness in the law curriculum requires the development of advanced skills in law school. In recognition of the significance of law clinics in offering education that is both professional and ethical, the BCI issued a circular mandating all universities and law schools to assess and enhance their curricula by incorporating four practical papers beginning in the academic year 1998–1999 (Bar Council of India, Circular No. 4/1997). The idea was twofold i.e., (a) to promote professional skills training, and (b) to equip law schools with social justice involvement.

The Third Phase

Presently, expansion in the third phase has created a substantial excess of legal professionals. This is partly due to the accomplishments of the National Law School system, resulting in the idea that legal education alone can actively contribute to the legal aid movement. Law school legal aid clinics were tasked with the dual purpose of offering legal assistance and advancing legal education. However, because faculty members and students were unable to serve as advocates for clients, the primary emphasis of the law school again shifted towards enhancing legal knowledge. As a result, the operations of the legal aid clinics became ad-hoc and sporadic. Moreover, due to the absence of incentives for faculty members and the student community, as well as insufficient recognition, the legal aid clinics are currently seen solely as a necessary exercise for incorporating essential skills. The current situation emphasises this perception to a great extent (Prasanna [2020]), wherein the concept of social justice is replaced by the theory of skill development. Although law schools have raised their standards and set lofty aims, there are still hurdles that must be overcome to attain the intended outcomes. Linked to these concerns are matters of professional discontent, health-related problems, and so on. This phase is discussed further in India (Contemporary Legal Education).

Shuvro Prosun Sarker and Prakash Sharma

References

Aggarwal, A. P. (1962). 'Legal Education in India', *Journal of the Indian Law Institute*, 12, p. 232.
Bar Council of India (Undated), 'Brief History of Law in India', available at http://www.barcouncilofindia.org/about/about-the-legal

-profession/legal-education-in-the-united
-kingdom/.

Bar Council of India, Circular No. 4/1997.

Getman, J.G. (1969). 'The Development of Indian Legal Education: The Impact of the Language Problem', *Journal of Legal Education*, 21, p. 513.

Government of India. (1963). *The Report of University Education Commission-I, December 1948–August 1949*, The Manager Government of India Press, Simla, p. 38, available at https://www.educationforallinindia.com/1949%20Report%20of%20the%20University%20Education%20Commission.pdf.

Jois, M.R. (1990). *Seeds of Modern Public Law in Ancient Indian Jurisprudence*, Eastern Book Company.

Jois, M.R. (2011). *Raja Dharma with Lessons on Raja Neeti*, Universal Law Publishing.

Jois, M.R. (2022). *Legal and Constitutional History of India: Ancient Legal, Judicial and Constitutional System*, Lexis Nexis.

Krishnan, K.J. (2006). 'Lawyering for a Cause and Experiences from Abroad', *California Law Review*, 94(2), p. 575.

Krishnan, K.J. (2005). 'From the ALI to the ILI: The Efforts to Export an American Legal Institution', *Vanderbilt Journal of Transnational Law*, 38, p. 1265.

Merillat, H.C.L. (1959). 'The Indian Law Institute', *The American Journal of Comparative Law*, 8(4), p. 524.

Prasanna, P. (2020). 'Time for States to Go Vocal for Local in Legal Education', Vidhi: Centre for Legal Policy Blog, available at https://vidhilegalpolicy.in/blog/time-for-states-to-go-vocal-for-local-in-legal-education/.

Sivakumar, S., Sharma, P. and Pandey, A.K. (2021). (eds), *Clinical and Continuing Legal Education: A Roadmap for India*, Thomson Reuters & CLEA.

Taylor von Mehren, A. (1965). 'Law and Legal Education in India: Some Observations', *Harvard Law Review*, 78(6), p. 1180.

The Law Commission of India. (1958). '14th Report on Reform of Judicial Administration'.

Tripathi, U.K. and Kumar, A. (2022). (eds), *Vedic Tradition of Law & Legal System*, Centre for Vedic Sciences.

59. India (regulation of legal education)

The regulation of legal education in India

Legal education in India is imparted by a law university, or by a deemed-to-be university, or by a university law department, or by a law college that is an integral part of a university, or by an affiliated law college. The term deemed-to-be university refers to a designation awarded by the Indian Ministry of Education where a higher education institution is working to a very high standard in a particular subject and grants the institution the status and privileges of a university. In total, there are currently 1,662 law schools (Government of India [2023]). Now, the primary body dealing with legal education is the Bar Council of India (BCI) which has the function to promote legal education, safeguard the rights, privileges, and interest of advocates, organise legal aid, etc (The Advocates Act 1961, s. 7). Further, since 1965, the BCI in consultation with the Universities and State Bar Councils prepares Rules on the standards of legal education and recognition of degrees in law for the purpose of enrolment as an advocate. It also undertakes inspection of universities for the purpose of recognising its law degree (The Advocates Act 1961, ss. 7(1)(h) and (i); 24(1)(c)(iii), and (iiia); 49 (1) (af), (ag), and (d)). Schedule III of the Rules of Legal Education, framed by the BCI elaborately provides the minimum infrastructure required for any Law College to apply for permission to run law courses. Under the said rules (Rule 11), it is mandatory for every law school to establish and run a legal aid clinic. Besides the BCI mandate, the government has directed district legal services authorities to promote legal services clinics across the country (National Legal Services Authority (Legal Services Clinics) Regulations 2011, Regulation 3).

Another body, the University Grants Commission (UGC), is authorised to take steps for the 'promotion and co-ordination of University education and for the determination and maintenance of standards of teaching, examination and research in universities' under section 12 of the University Grants Commission Act 1956. In section 22 of this Act, it also states that the 'right of conferring or granting degrees shall be exercised only by a University established or incorporated by or under a Central Act, a Provincial Act or a State Act or an institution deemed to be a University'. As a result, there exist two regulatory agencies, ie, BCI and UGC, wherein the former sets the standards of legal education, and the latter validates the degree programmes (Avasthi [2004]). The Law Commission [2002] thoroughly examined this aspect in its 184th Report, emphasising that while the regulatory authorities may have distinct mandates, they ultimately have shared objectives.

That said, with the 2020 introduction of the National Education Policy ('NEP 2020') (Ministry of Human Resource and Development [2020]), there are a few further significant developments emerging. For instance, the UGC sets the framework for private universities setting up and running centres away from their on-campus provision (Establishment of and Maintenance of Standards in Private Universities) Regulation, 2003). The move was long overdue as earlier some privately owned deemed-to-be universities had been allowed to start off-campus centres with UGC approval (UGC (Institutions Deemed to be Universities) Regulations, 2022). This move was also in alignment with the evolving educational landscape outlined in the NEP 2020, which aims towards enhancing regulatory facilitation and supporting the expansion of higher education (Mitra & Sinha [2023]; Roy & Sharma [2024]). However, there are concerns over strict compliance. For instance, the UGC in 2023 had requested that higher education institutions (HEIs) allow a full refund of the college fees within a specified period, allowing students to opt out of the course they initially choose (UGC Redressal of Grievances of Students Regulation, 2023). This was not adhered to by a number of HEIs, and thereupon in 2024, the UGC was compelled to bring notice wherein it reiterated that any HEIs violating the UGC fee refund policy would face punitive action (Education Desk [2024]). Similarly, there is uncertainty over the function of the BCI in relation to the objectives of the NEP 2020. One reason for this is that the NEP 2020 does not explicitly establish or identify a specific regulatory body for law. Instead, it indirectly emphasises that legal education should be globally competitive, including the best methods and using new technology to ensure that more people have timely access to justice.

SHUVRO PROSUN SARKER AND PRAKASH SHARMA

References

Avasthi, A.K. (2004). 'Powerlessness of the BCI to Improve Standards of Legal Education', *Journal of the Indian Law Institute*, 46, p. 72.

Bar Council of India, Rules of Legal Education.

Education Desk. (2024). 'UGC directs universities to refund fees, implement provisions of UGC Act', *The Indian Express*, available at https://indianexpress.com/article/education/ugc-directs-universities-to-refund-fees-implement-provisions-ugc-act-9196435/.

Establishment of and Maintenance of Standards in Private Universities) Regulation 2003.

Government of India, Ministry of Law & Justice Department of Legal Affairs. (2023). Unstarred Question No. 3955, Rajya Sabha, available at https://legalaffairs.gov.in/sites/default/files/AU3955.pdf.

Law Commission. (2002). *184th Report on Legal Education & Professional Training and Proposals for amendments to the Advocates Act, 1961 and the University Grants Commission Act, 1956.*

Ministry of Human Resource and Development, National Education Policy. (2020), available at https://www.education.gov.in/sites/upload_files/mhrd/files/NEP_Final_English_0.pdf.

Mitra, N.L. and Sinha, M.K. (2023). 'National Education Policy 2020 and Challenges to the Bar Council of India', *Asian Journal of Legal Education*, 10(1), p. 7.

National Legal Services Authority (Legal Services Clinics) Regulations 2011.

Roy, R. and Sharma, P. (2024). 'The National Education Policy (NEP) of 2020 and the Hybrid Learning Paradigm: Revising Strategies for An Evolving Legal Education Environment', *Asian Journal of Legal Education*, 11(1), p. 44.

The Advocates Act 1961.

UGC (Institutions Deemed to be Universities) Regulations 2022.

UGC Redressal of Grievances of Students Regulation 2023.

University Grants Commission Act 1956.

60. Indigenous legal education

Indigenous legal education broadly speaking means the study and teaching of laws that have relevancy to Indigenous peoples. It traditionally included the teaching of laws created by nation states that have colonised Indigenous peoples and that were directed specifically towards Indigenous people. For example, Canadian Indigenous legal education often focused on the constitutional rights of Indigenous peoples under section 35 of the Constitution Act 1982. These rights include rights to ancestral practices, land title to lands held exclusively by an Indigenous society through time, and treaty rights through an agreement between an Indigenous society and the Crown. The Indian Act is also a frequent object of study (Isaac). American Indigenous legal studies often focus on the inherent sovereignty of American Indian tribes, the plenary jurisdiction doctrine that allows only Congress but not state legislatures to pass laws that limit tribal sovereignty, and legislation such as the Major Crimes Act and the Indian Civil Rights Act that place restrictions on tribal sovereignty (Gretches et al). Likewise New Zealand Indigenous legal studies places a lot of focus on the Treaty of Waitangi between the Crown and the Maori people (Orange).

A consistent theme in these lines of study is to explore how those state laws contribute to the ongoing colonisation of Indigenous peoples. For example, one test for inherent Indigenous rights to ancestral practices under section 35 of the Constitution Act 1982, in Canada limits rights to practices that were used prior to contact with Europeans. The test has been criticised for placing an artificial constraint that denies Indigenous cultures any capacity or right to evolve over time. Another criticism is a denial of general Indigenous rights, like an Indigenous right to self-determination for example, and instead on insistence on Indigenous peoples only being able to claim rights to very specific past practices. That would force Indigenous peoples into lengthy series of cost-prohibitive litigations to claim rights to a collection of specific governing practices instead of one litigation to claim a right to self-determination (Barsh and Henderson). Likewise the American plenary jurisdiction doctrine has been criticised as containing so many exceptions (tribal laws not applying to non-Indians on reserve land, or not applying to members of another tribe on reservation land) that in substance very little remains of tribal sovereignty (Steele).

Another traditional theme of Indigenous legal studies has been to study standard laws that on the surface appear to apply equally to everyone, but in truth have inordinately severe effects on Indigenous peoples as compared to non-Indigenous peoples. The theme also includes an exploration of legal alternatives administered by Indigenous peoples themselves that are perceived to be more constructive compared to standard state laws. There is almost no sphere of life in which demands for Indigenous self-determination have not been made. For example, it has been argued that self-determination over education is necessary so that Indigenous students receive adequate education with culturally appropriate pedagogies and curriculum, and to improve educational outcomes and economic prospects for Indigenous students (Stonechild). Demands for Indigenous self-determination over child welfare are made with reference to the problem of Indigenous over-representation in child welfare apprehensions, with the hope that extended family networks can be utilised as a resource that will minimise the need for apprehension and familial disruption (Blackstock; Blackstock and Trocmé). Indigenous self-determination over criminal justice, based on Indigenous justice traditions that parallel restorative justice, is often touted as a solution to Indigenous over-incarceration.

Indigenous legal studies, although not altogether abandoning analysis of state laws as applied to Indigenous peoples, has in recent years embraced the study of Indigenous legal orders as they existed prior to contact with Europeans and how they have remained in active evolution after colonisation. A source of law for many Indigenous peoples has been traditional stories. Stories in many Indigenous cultures center around a trickster figure, Wasakaychuk among the Cree, Napi among the Blackfeet, or Nanabush among the Anishnabe, among other examples. The stories frequently depict the trickster as engaging in harmful or questionable behaviour, and then suffering a misfortune at the end of the narrative. The behaviour described by the narrative also describes behaviour that is deemed unacceptable by the Indigenous society that produced the story. The misfortune often describes punishments or sanctions used by the Indigenous society. A particular trend in Indigenous legal studies has been to apply the common law method of casebook analysis to Indigenous stories by describing the facts of the narrative, and identifying the parties, the legal issues, the legal principles, and the outcome. It is a method of legitimating Indigenous orders as sophisticated bodies of law that existed prior to contact that are not less worthy of respect and study than state legal systems (Borrows [1995]; Napoleon and Friedland [2016]).

A parallel trend in Indigenous legal education is an advocacy for state laws to recognise and make room for Indigenous legal orders not only because they have intrinsic value in their own right, but because they can offer possibly better alternatives than state law for Indigenous social problems. John Borrows argues that the depiction of Canada as founded by two legal traditions, common law and civil law, is inaccurate because it fails to recognise Indigenous legal traditions as a third and equally important legal foundation for the formation of Canada. And giving effect to that recognition also demands that Indigenous peoples have the freedom to apply their own laws and traditions in addressing their own needs (Borrows [2010]).

The study of Indigenous legal orders is an endeavour that is being actively pursued. The revitalisation of Indigenous legal orders is an emerging academic field that is being pursued by law professors such as Val Napoleon, Hadley Friedland (Friedland and Napoleon [2017]), and Tracey Lindberg. But it is not just a field of academic study. The University of Victoria has started the world's first ever joint degree in both Common Law and Indigenous legal orders (JID/JD Programme). One of the key themes of the curriculum is that core subjects that would be taught in the first year of a mainstream law degree programme are taught over the course of the first two years of the joint degree programme. And those courses instruct students in Common Law but also the principles of multiple Indigenous legal orders, with the intention that at least some of the programme's graduates will use their knowledge to aid in the revitalisation of Indigenous legal orders. For example, John Borrows has in past years taught a course that

includes both Canadian constitutional law and Anishnabe law. Val Napoleon teaches a course that includes both Canadian property law and Gixtsan property law. David Milward teaches a course that includes both Canadian criminal law and Cree law as applied to social conflicts.

Another key component of the JID/JD Programme are mandatory field schools in the third and fourth years of the programme. A field school requires students to reside in a host Indigenous community for a period of time during a semester. Community elders and leaders instruct students in the laws of the community's Indigenous legal order. The instruction often includes land-based learning where students visit sacred sites, participate in caretaking activities with respect to the community's land, receive instruction on the role of plants and animals in the community's laws, or participate in ceremonies with legal significance. The students themselves will assist the community with projects that contribute to the revitalisation of the community's laws. The field school is meant to impress upon the students that Indigenous legal orders are daily lived experiences, and not so much the stereotyped expectations of statutes and judicial decisions that are associated with state legal systems.

The University of Victoria also has the Indigenous Law Research Unit, which has a team of dedicated researchers who assist Indigenous communities in the reclamation of their past laws for contemporary use and adaptation (University of Victoria). The University of Alberta likewise has an equivalent programme that is operated as a partnership between its Faculty of Law and its Native Studies Department, the Wahkohtowin Law and Governance Lodge (University of Alberta).

DAVID MILWARD

References

Barsh, R.L. and Henderson, S. (1997). 'The Supreme Court's *Van der Peet* Trilogy: Naïve Imperialism and Ropes of Sand', *McGill L.J.*, 42, p. 993.

Blackstock, C. (2007). 'Residential Schools: Did They Really Close or Just Morph into Child Welfare?', *Aboriginal L.J.*, 6, p. 71.

Blackstock, C. and Trocmé, N. (2005). 'Community-Based Child Welfare for Aboriginal Children: Supporting Resilience

Through Structural Change', *Social Policy Journal of New Zealand*, 24, p. 12.

Borrows, J. (1995). 'With or without you: First Nations law (in Canada)', *Mcgill L.J.*, 41, p. 629.

Borrows, J. (2010). *Canada's Aboriginal Constitution*, Toronto: University of Toronto Press.

Friedland, H. and Napoleon, V. (2015). 'Gathering the Threads: Developing a Methodology for Researching and Rebuilding Indigenous Legal Traditions' *Lakehead L.J.*, 1(1), p. 17.

Gretches, D. et al. (2016). *Federal Indian Law: Cases and Commentary*, 7th edition, West Academic Publishing.

Isaac, T. (2016). *Aboriginal Law: Supreme Court Decisions*, Toronto: Thomson Reuters.

Lindberg, T. (2015). *Birdie*, New York: Harper Collins.

Indian Act, R.S.C.c. I-5.

Milward, D. (2012). *Aboriginal Justice and the Charter*, UBC Press.

Napoleon, V. and Friedland, H. (2016). 'An inside job: Engaging with Indigenous legal traditions through stories', *McGill L.J.*, 61(4), p. 725.

Orange, C. (2011). *The Treaty of Waitangi*, Wellington, New Zealand: Bridget Williams Books.

Steele, M. (2016). 'Plenary Power, Political Questions, and Sovereignty in Indian Affairs', *U.C.L.A. L. Rev.*, 63, p. 666.

Stonechild, B. (2006). *The New Buffalo: The Struggle for Aboriginal Post-Secondary Education in Canada*, University of Manitoba Press.

The Constitution Act 1982, Schedule B to the Canada Act 1982 (UK) 1982, c 11

University of Alberta, 'Wahkohtowin Law and Governance Lodge', available at https://www.ualberta.ca/wahkohtowin/index.html.

University of Victoria, Faculty of Law, 'Indigenous Law Research Unit (ILRU)', available at https://www.uvic.ca/law/about/indigenous/indigenouslawresearchunit/index.php.

61. Law and economics

Introduction

The teaching and use of economic arguments in legal education is mainstream in the United States, but it is more niche elsewhere, including the United Kingdom (UK). The exception to this is competition law, where some economics is generally seen as an essential ingredient in the understanding of what competition does and why it needs protection. The situation is similar in research. While there is an American, Asian, and European Law and Economics Association and a number of national law and economics societies in continental Europe, there is no UK-based learned society, nor is there currently a specialist subject section in the UK academic legal associations.

What exactly is it?

Law and Economics (L&E) is the application of economic analysis to legal problems or any area of law except those areas where its application would be obvious (Garoupa and Ulen [2008]), i.e. it would not include competition law, regulated industries, and taxation. The economics typically used is micro-economics, the part of economics which focuses on individual choice (Cooter and Ulen [2012]). In this regard, individuals can be consumers, firms, or other organisations. Economics is generally concerned with the allocation of scarce resources. Because resources are scarce, it is desirable that these are used efficiently (Posner [2014]). A lot of early L&E scholarship has focused on whether or not law is efficient or supports the achievement of efficient outcomes for society (Dnes [2018]). Since the role of law in this context is to provide the 'right' incentives for people, the focus is often shifted to incentives and how statutory provisions or court decisions affect incentives. Because of this focus on incentives, procedural law is as much of interest to L&E as substantive law. The difference to classic, problem-based legal analysis is a focus on the consequences of legal rules or decision, thus, offering an external framework that assists with the critical assessment of legal decisions (Veljanovski [2007]).

The advance of technology has led to an increased availability of data and more powerful methods of data analysis with the result that an increasing number of L&E theories are being tested empirically (Gelbach and Klick [2017]). The other shift in the teaching of L&E is the growth of behavioural economics (Jolls [2017]). This strand of economic and psychological research considers predictable aberrations from rational behaviour as it is assumed in classic microeconomic theory.

Typical module coverage

Almost all L&E modules cover the basic private law areas: property rights, contract, and tort. Material on litigation is also commonly covered. On the other hand, the L&E for crime is covered in textbooks but may not feature in all L&E modules. Topics such as intellectual property law, family law, and environmental law may also be covered depending on the interests of the teaching team (Posner [2014], Dnes [2018]).

Generally, L&E modules start with lectures on the economics of individual choice, including rational choice theory, behavioural economics, choice under uncertainty and game theory before covering the legal subjects. L&E modules typically cover the intuition and insights provided by economic theory but do not always cover the formal proof or require in-depth knowledge of statistics to critically analyse empirical research.

Benefits of teaching L&E and how to reap them

A question often asked by students is what the benefits of learning L&E are, as there is no particular legal dispute to solve. One of the advantages of L&E is the use of an incentives-based approach to assess rules. Without making it explicit, policy makers and courts usually rest their decisions on assumptions about the potential effects that those decisions may have on the incentives of individuals. For example, imposing liability is frequently assumed to increase the level of caretaking and reduce the number and/or cost of accidents. L&E provides the springboard to analyse those assumptions systematically by using both theoretical and empirical approaches (Landes and Posner [1987], Veljanovski [2021], Panthöfer [2022]). Another advantage of L&E is that it affords a look across legal silos. Theories to explain the allocation of property rights (Coase [1960]) also foster the understanding of the effects of liability rules. This enables students to make better connections across legal sub-disciplines. In addition to a better understanding of incentive effects, theoretical and empirical evidence, L&E teaches numeracy and improves law students' strained relationship with mathematics. Generally, modules provide an opportunity to discuss quantitative research – something that is not normally part of the law syllabus – and introduce students to literature that is outside their comfort zone. The relevant microeconomics offer illustrative examples of what might work or more typically, what might not. Game theoretical models improve students' understanding of decision-making, for example, in litigation (Cooter and Rubinfeld [1989]). Thus, there are a number of potential benefits to the study of L&E.

Challenges and some suggestions on how to tackle them

In our experience, law students are unsure about the use of mathematics and formal notations. Law tends to be discursive whereas economics is rather formalistic. To ease our students into using models we tend to introduce models with the help of analogies such as maps, e.g. the London underground, or fables, following Rose's concept of simple stories with a purpose (Rose [1990]). We have found that Gary Becker's model of crime is a particularly good starting point for students to see the value and pitfalls of using models and we teach the law and economics of crime together with the introductory lectures on choice theory (Becker [1968]).

One clear advantage of economic thinking is that assumptions about human behaviour (and causation) are clearly spelled out. Lawyers tend to assume that humans behave in a particular way, without these assumptions being made explicit or subject to theoretical or empirical testing. The challenge is to focus students' attention on this weakness of legal analysis and turn it into a strength of their assessment of a given problem. At the same time, simplified assumptions and artificial frameworks often spark debate as to the realism and usefulness of economic models.

The diverse objectives of the law vis-à-vis clearly set objectives in the economic analysis of law tend to confuse students and hamper the analysis of (common) law. Criminal law is a good example where L&E presumes a deter-rence objective against which the effectiveness and efficiency of legal rules is measured (Shavell [2004]). The legal reality is more nuanced with criminal law aiming to prevent crime, protect the public, punish wrongdoers, pursue justice, and rehabilitate offenders. L&E has less to say about the other goals, which is perceived as a gap in the analysis. We tend to highlight those shortcomings and argue that L&E contributes to the understanding of legal systems rather than being the sole rational for a given legal construct.

For L&E teaching outside the United States (US), one of the difficulties is to identify national case law that explicitly references or implicitly uses economic concepts. While the general principles of L&E can be applied to any jurisdiction, the question occasionally arises how this is relevant in the context of national, non-US law. US judges tend to incorporate L&E thinking more openly, for example, by using the Hand formula when establishing negligence. In many other jurisdictions explicit considerations of precaution cost and the expected reduction of accident when precautions are improved are disguised in legal principles of negligence liability. National differences are also important when we deal with economic analysis where institutional details matter – a typical example would be (the cost of) private healthcare in the US compared with public healthcare systems in European countries.

As students' economic background in European law schools is limited, reading and evaluating economic contributions poses some difficulties. This applies to both evaluating theoretical and empirical insights published in economics journals. The L&E literature has evolved drastically over the last 65 years, and it is important not to focus on the simplicity of the early, seminal, contributions. Both theory and empirical analysis have evolved over time with more recent contributions being both more nuanced and also more advanced (in technical terms). This is particularly so with the extensive use of game theory and behavioural insights in theoretical models (Sunstein [2000], Teilbaum and Zeiler [2019], Zamir and Teichman [2018]), and the access to better data to test assumptions and predictions (Ho and Kramer [2013], Gelbach and Klick [2017]). We use references to classical L&E papers to scan for the most recent papers citing them.

SEBASTIAN PEYER AND MORTEN HVIID

Key concepts and key thinkers

Virtually all L&E modules will cover Becker's model of rational crime (Becker [1968]). The idea is intuitive to students and allows the introduction of an easy model that has been expanded theoretically and tested empirically (e.g. Ehrlich [1973], [1975], [1981] and with a summary of the empirical literature Ehrlich [2017]). Becker states that the rational person considering a career in crime will consider the probability of getting caught and the severity of the potential sanction, weighing those costs of crime against any benefit derived from committing an illegal action.

Similarly intuitive for the students is Learned Hand's negligence formula in tort law where a behaviour is considered negligent if the expected accident costs outweigh the costs of precaution to lower the risk of accidents. Calabresi's seminal work on risk distribution in tort law poses slightly more challenges to students but is also part of core L&E teaching (Calabresi [1961], Calabresi and Melamed [1972]). Another seminal idea that is part of the core catalogue is Coase's idea of allocation of property rights and transaction cost (Coase [1960]). It is a powerful theory to explain the consequences of awarding ownership and associated rights and how parties would deal with what they perceive as nuisance. The challenge for students is often to assume that property rights have not been allocated when, in reality, few such situations exist, and to correctly understand the purpose of transaction costs. The Coase theorem framework has been repeatedly tested, expanded and analysed (Posner and Parisi [2013], Elickson et al [2023]).

Richard Posner's work as judge and academic has contributed to the rise of L&E. As a judge, his decisions have been clearly influenced by L&E thinking and some of those cases lend themselves to classroom discussions due to the clear references to economic concepts. His seminal textbook is easily accessible to the novice and offers a good starting point for students of L&E (Posner [2014]).

L&E analysis has made immense progress since those founding concepts were established. Economic thinking is now applied to many areas of law including Intellectual Property Law, Family Law, International Law, Employment Law, Corporate Law, the legal process (procedure) and constitutional problems (Paris [2017]). There is not only an increasing number of legal areas that are subject to L&E research, but the methods of analysis have been refined too, including experimental economics and psychology (Hold and Sullivan [2017]). As better data has become available, empirical findings are added to the theoretical foundations of L&E. Insights into human behaviour challenge the rationality assumption that underpins classic L&E leading to a relatively new branch of behavioural L&E (Zamir and Teichman [2018], Jolls [2017]). This strand of research is based on the insight that humans predictably deviated from pure rationality and applies this insight to law and legal decision making, exploring, for example, heuristics and biases. Advances in artificial intelligence will open the field for research further (Kantorowicz [2022]).

SEBASTIAN PEYER AND MORTEN HVIID

References

Becker, G. (1968). 'Crime and punishment: an economic approach', *Journal of Political Economy*, 76(2), p. 169.

Calabresi, G. (1961). 'Some Thoughts on Risk Distribution and the Law of Torts', *Yale Law Journal*, 70(4), p. 499.

Calabresi, G. and Douglas Melamed, A. (1972). 'Property Rules, Liability Rules and Inalienability: One View of the Cathedral', *Harvard Law Review*, 58, p. 1089.

Coase, R. (1960). 'The Problem of Social Cost', *The Journal of Law and Economics*, 3(1), p. 1.

Cooter, R.D. and Ulen, T. (2012). *Law and Economics*, 6th edition, Prentice Hall.

Cooter, R.D. and Rubinfeld, D.L. (1989). 'Economic Analysis of Legal Disputes and their Resolution', *Journal of Economic Literature*, 27, p. 1067.

Dnes, A.W. (2018). *Principles of Law and Economics*, 3rd edition, Edward Elgar.

Ehrlich, I. (1973). 'Participation in Illegitimate Activities: Theoretical and Empirical Investigation', *Journal of Political Economy*, 81, p. 521.

Ehrlich, I. (1975). 'The Deterrent Effect of Capital Punishment: A Question of Life and Death', *American Economic Review*, 65, p. 397.

Ehrlich, I. (1981). 'On the Usefulness of Controlling Individuals: An Economic Analysis of Rehabilitation, Incapacitation and Deterrence', *American Economic Review*, 71, p. 307.

Ehrlich, I. (2017). 'Economics of Criminal Law: Crime and Punishment', in Parisi, F. (ed), *The Oxford Handbook of Law and Economics:*

Volume 3: Public Law and Legal Institutions, Oxford University Press.

Ellickson, R.C., Rose, C.M. and Smith, H.E. (eds), *Perspectives on Property Law*, 5th edition, Aspen Publishing.

Garoupa, N. and Ulen, T.S. (2008). 'The Market for Legal Innovation: Law and Economics in Europe and the United States', *Ala L Rev*, 59, p. 1555.

Gelbach, J.B. and Klick, J. (2017). 'Empirical Law and Economics', in Parisi, F. (ed), *The Oxford Handbook of Law and Economics: Volume 1: Methodology and Concepts*, Oxford University Press.

Ho, D.E. and Kramer, L. (2013). 'Introduction: The Empirical Revolution in Law', *Stanford Law Review*, 65(6), p. 1195.

Hold, C. and Sullivan, S.P. (2017). 'Experimental Economics and the Law', in Parisi, F. (ed), *The Oxford Handbook of Law and Economics: Volume 1: Methodology and Concepts*, Oxford University Press.

Jolls, C. (2017). 'Bounded Rationality, Behavioral Economics, and the Law', in Parisi, F. (ed), *The Oxford Handbook of Law and Economics: Volume 1: Methodology and Concepts*, Oxford University Press.

Kantorowicz, J. and Kantorowicz-Reznichenko, E. (2022). 'Law & Economics at Sixty: Mapping the Field with Bibliometric and Machine Learning Tools', available at https://ssrn.com/abstract=4041885.

Panthöfer, S. (2022). 'Do doctors prescribe antibiotics out of fear of malpractice?', *Journal of Empirical Legal Studies*, p. 340.

Posner, R.A. (2014). *Economic Analysis of Law*, 9th edition, Wolters Kluwer.

Posner, R.A. and Parisi, F. (2013). (eds), *The Coase Theorem – Volume I: Origins, Restatements and Extensions; Volume II: Criticisms and Applications*, Edward Elgar.

Rose, C.M. (1990). 'Property as Storytelling: Perspectives from Game Theory, Narrative Theory, Feminist Theory', *Yale JL & Human*, 2, p. 37.

Shavell, S. (2004). *Foundations of Economic Analysis of Law*, Harvard University Press.

Sunstein, C.R. (2000). *Behavioural Law and Economics*, Cambridge University Press.

Teilbaum, J.C. and Zeiler, K. (2019). *Research Handbook on Behavioral Law and Economics*, Edward Elgar.

Veljanovski, C. (2007). *Economic Principles of Law*, Cambridge University Press.

Veljanovski, C. (2021). 'The Impact of Employers' Liability on 19th-Century U.K. Coalmining Fatalities', *Journal of Empirical Legal Studies*, 18(3), p. 660.

Zamir, E. and Teichman, D. (2018). *Behavioral Law and Economics*, Oxford University Press.

62. Law and humanities

Law and humanities – topics and traditions

Interdisciplinary education in law and humanities assumes that legal practices and habits of juristic thought are as much at home with the arts and humanities as with the social sciences. One reason for the assumption is law's long association with the arts of rhetoric, going back to the original 'rhetors' who disputed legal and political issues in ancient Greece. Another reason is the perceived benefit to law students of engaging with the sorts of imaginative and critical practices in which the humanities excel, including deep reading, careful drafting, and public performance. Students who arrive at law school with educational backgrounds in the humanities and with a personal passion for the arts can pursue those interests through law and humanities. Opportunities can come in the shape of dedicated offerings, for example on 'law and literature' or 'law and cinema', and innovative approaches to more traditional legal topics. There might be opportunities to study with humanities students on cross-departmental modules, although law schools are often physically and institutionally isolated in universities or else grouped with the social sciences (Goodrich [1996]). There is evident willingness to engage with law from scholars in the humanities schools. Of the 46 academics who contributed to the book *Teaching Law and Literature* (Sarat et al [2011]) only eleven were principally affiliated with a law school. The situation is similar in mainland Europe where the number of law school scholars active in the humanities is small compared to the number of humanities scholars who engage with law.

The label 'humanities' is a contestable one. For present purposes, it describes scholastic disciplines that engage with artistic practices including rhetoric, prose, poetry, storytelling, painting, drawing, emblems, skin art, street art, comic strip, photography, television, film, video, music, sculpture, dance, architecture, weaving, pottery, cuisine, couture, masking, mime, theatre, and many more. The ancient Greek label technē is useful here because it drew no strict distinction between arts and crafts. It applied to any such skill that could be taught. The fact that technē could be taught

by humans in theory distinguished them from mousikē (poem, music, dance) which were attributed to the divine inspiration of the muses. On this view, rhetoric was technē, but the original practitioners of rhetoric looked to mousikē for exemplars of attractive composition and performance (Murray and Wilson [2010]). The rhetoricians' habit of looking to the arts continued with the orators of ancient Rome and into the early modern period. Thomas Elyot writes in *The Boke named the Gouernour* (1537) that mooting at London's Inns of Court, the original site of common law education, was 'a shadow or figure of the ancient rhetoric' (fol. 53r–v). He adds that mooting entailed good practice in 'the sharp wits of logicians, the grave sentences of philosophers, the elegancy of poets, the memory of civilians [civil lawyers], the voice and gesture of them that pronounce comedies' (fol. 54r–v). Another valuable attribute of mooting, as also of theatrical performance, is that it involves cooperative work within a group or ensemble.

In law's long tradition of engaging with the arts, it has never been clear where art stops and law starts. For all the benefits this closeness can bring, it has been a source of anxiety for those rhetoricians and lawyers who fear that association with drama injures the dignity of their profession. The Attic orator Aeschines, a former actor, relied upon theatricality in his rhetoric, whereas his rival Demosthenes denounced it as unworthy of the political sphere (Peters [2022] at 28). Under the decadence of Nero, the question was asked, 'would justice be furthered and would…knights better fulfil their noble function as jurors for having listened with a virtuoso's ear to falsetto notes and melodious voices?' (Yardley and Barrett [2008] at 313–4). These ancient anxieties continued even as the practice of rhetoric, law, and drama enjoyed a shared renaissance in the early modern period. It is therefore unsurprising that with the coming of the Enlightenment in the long eighteenth century, the paradigm of the arts and humanities was usurped in the legal imagination by the paradigm of empirical science. The prestige of the medical profession grew in this period as its methods became more scientifically accountable, and this seems to have prompted a rivalry and respect in legal professionals which led them to suppose that they might also diagnose and cure social ills by scientific means. There is a place for a scientific ambition in law, but the experienced reality of law in practice, especially in the common law, is that it does not yield solutions with algorithmic predictability. If it did, we might find fewer cases overturned on appeal and overturned another way on further appeal. In practice, the judicial process seems more akin to the responsive crafting of an artefact within a creative community. We might compare it to the epics that were developed by the Homer clan over generations. Ronald Dworkin likened it to writing a chain novel (Dworkin [1986] at 245). Judge Learned Hand said that the work of a judge, is 'what a poet does, it is what a sculptor does' (Shanks [1968] at xiii). It is typically when legal questions are most difficult that the judicial response is most creative. Existing law is not so much applied to hard cases as refigured by them. This, at least, is how the common law might be taught from a humanities perspective. The attraction for the law student is that the often hopeless and pointless task of reconciling divergent judicial decisions is replaced with an appreciation for the motivations and methods by which the judges crafted them. It is these motivations and methods, at least as much as any doctrine or rule, that will be active in the next case.

Law and literature

The dominant topic or territory of law school education in the humanities has been the literary arts, and this has for the most part entailed practice in textual critique. Done well, this will ask not only what a passage 'means' (originally, potentially), but also what it means for the reader and for the communities in which they live and work. This is a key insight of James Boyd White's pioneering book *The Legal Imagination* (White [1973]), which brought the study of law and literature into the modern law school as a set of teaching materials (comprising both legal and other literary texts) which students were called upon to engage with imaginatively, appreciatively, and critically. Where a typical law school seminar will ask, 'what is the law here?', a literary critical approach might ask, 'does the imagery used in this statement reflect an unspoken assumption or prejudice on the part of the speaker?'. A tutor might invite law students to redraft an existing judicial statement in a more humane manner, perhaps by employing different metaphors.

Owen Barfield, a member of the celebrated Oxford 'Inklings' literary fellowship, warned that 'really dreadful pitfalls open at the feet of the unpoetic critic' (Barfield [1928] at 166). The point is that to be an effective reader of law and literature one must read texts in the spirit of an active co-creator. There is a sense of this in Julen Etxabe's belief that 'law is not a thing that can be studied apart from the *jurisgenerative* capacities of actors and interpreters' (Etxabe [2019] at 19). Owen Barfield was a poetic writer, essayist, and solicitor. In his book, *This Ever Diverse Pair* (Barfield [1950]) he imagined Burgeon, avatar of his poetic self, to be engaged in an ongoing improving dialogue with Burden, representative of his legal self. Of course, we shouldn't go so far as to romanticise the humanities and demonise the law. We should instead appreciate more deeply the artistic and rhetorical richness of everyday legal language and literature as well as the commonplace materials of legal performance. In the latter category we can include official and professional dress, legal props (the 'law book' is one), and law's performance spaces (courtrooms, prisons, and so forth). Close reading of the most basic elements of legal language will reveal law's fictive processes at work in quite wonderful ways. Take the word 'mortgage'. Are we surprised to find that behind a label meaning 'death gage', the real mortgage died centuries ago. It was replaced in the jurisdiction of England and Wales by a creature called a 'charge *by way of* legal mortgage'. The legal thing we take for granted is therefore a fiction masquerading before our eyes in clothes inherited from a dead ancestor.

Educational ethos

As there is a danger that the humanities will be romanticised in the law school, so there is a danger that they will be colonised by law. American judge Guido Calabresi, former Dean of Yale Law School, wrote in his introductory letter to the first issue of the Yale Journal of Law & the Humanities of the need for 'mutual nurturing between law and liberal arts' (Calabresi [1988]). If, on the other hand, law simply captures the arts and humanities to sustain its own project, it will merely produce a greedier, grosser form of law. The legal philosopher Hans Kelsen once compared law's colonising effects to the magical touch of King Midas: 'Just as everything King Midas touched turned into gold, everything to which law refers becomes law' (Kelsen [1967] at 161). We must be wary of the label 'law and humanities' being applied decoratively and instrumentality to initiatives that seek to use the arts and humanities instead of engaging with them to challenge received legal habits and ideas. As a law school venture, law and humanities is not so much a set of topics as an educational ethos (Bradney [2003]). It leads the law student to appreciate and critique law from the outside. Recall that the etymology of 'education' is 'leading out' (ex-ducare), whereas a student's time at law school often begins with the opposite process of induction into legal ways of thinking. 'What are those ways of thinking?' and 'are they healthy ways of thinking?' are questions asked by a law and humanities approach.

Materials and the matter of culture

Law and humanities can be as imaginative in its educational methods and materials as in the topics with which it engages. Classes might entail performing, re-enacting, mooting, vlogging, cartooning, 'battle rapping', outdoor walking, crafting, music making, and much more. Building on the school exercise of 'show and tell', law students might be invited to bring to class a personal item that speaks to them of law, or to bring in a thing they regard as 'a thing of beauty' (Weisberg [2014]). Courtrooms, prisons, and other performance spaces of law can be visited in person and appreciated as sites directed at the legal education of society at large. Imaginative modes of assessment should follow from imaginative teaching practices. Even when assessed work is submitted as text, small innovative steps can lead to significant enhancements. Students might be invited to rewrite an extract from an historic judgment, or to write a journalistic report on a legally relevant event. An essay or dissertation could be submitted in the form of a poem, playscript, or dramatic dialogue instead of in the standard format (Raffield [2009]; Watt [2009]). The students' educational journey might be represented in a journal, scrapbook, zine, or commonplace book to include images and artwork in addition to text. Even further beyond text, work

may be submitted in the form of moots, debates, speeches and even songs and dance. Admittedly, it helps if students offer textual annotations to explain why they painted, drew, or danced as they did. Purists might object that non-textual art needs no text, but the practical need for accountability in university work assessed for credit will normally require explanation in words. Many a musical concert supplies a written programme and many an art exhibition a catalogue, so the purist's objection might start there. Another significant benefit of law and humanities education is that it can open up legal education and 'Western' ideas of law to a richer appreciation of the artistic and cultural practices of First Nations peoples (Johnson [2020]). When the Māori Whanganui iwi sing and dance a waiata in the New Zealand parliament, and when the Haida Nation of the North-East Pacific carve totems and totemic canoes to express their constitutional values, they are demonstrating the sort of deep cultural connection between law and arts which law and humanities is seeking to recover.

GARY WATT

References

Bankowski, Z., Del Mar, M. and Maharg, P. (2013). (eds), *The Arts and the Legal Academy: Beyond Text in Legal Education*, Routledge.
Barfield, O. (2010). *Poetic Diction: A Study in Meaning* (1928), Barfield Press.
Barfield, O. (2010). *This Ever Diverse Pair* (1950), Barfield Press.
Berger, L.A. (201). 'Studying and Teaching "Law as Rhetoric": A Place to Stand', *J. Legal Writing Inst.*, 16, p. 3.
Bradney, A. (2003). *Conversations, Choices and Chances: The Liberal Law School in the Twenty-First Century*, Hart Publishing.
Dworkin, R. (1986). *Law's Empire*, Harvard University Press.
Etxabe, J. (2019). *A Cultural History of Law in Antiquity*, Bloomsbury.
Goodrich, P. (1996). 'Of Blackstone's Tower: Metaphors of Distance and Histories of the English Law School', in Birks, P. (ed), *Pressing Problems in the Law Vol II: What are Law Schools For?*, Oxford University Press.
Hermida, J. (2022). *Teaching law and criminal justice through popular culture: a deep learning*

approach in the streaming era, Apple Academic Press.

Johnson, R. (2020). 'Questions About Questions: Law and Film Reflections on the Duty to Learn', *The Northern Review*, 50, p. 83.

Kelsen, H. (1967). *Pure Theory of Law*, University of California Press.

Law and Humanities (UK).

Law, Culture and the Humanities (US).

Law & Literature (US).

Law, Text, Culture (Australia).

Murray, P. and Wilson, P. (2010). (eds), *Music and the Muses: The Culture of Mousike in the Classical Athenian City*, Oxford University Press.

Peters, J.S. (2022). *Law as Performance: Theatricality, Spectatorship, and the Making of Law in Ancient, Medieval, and Early Modern Europe*, Oxford University Press.

Pòlemos: Journal of Law, Literature and Culture (Italy).

Raffield, P. (2009). 'Sunday's Child: Drama, Ensemble and the Community of Law', *Law and Humanities*, 3(2), p. 231.

Sarat, A., Frank, C.O. and Anderson, M. (2011). (eds), *Teaching Law and Literature*, The Modern Language Association of America.

Shanks, H. (1968). (ed), *The Art and Craft of Judging: The Decisions of Judge Learned Hand*, Macmillan.

Watt, G. (2009). 'Reflections on Creative Writing within a Law and Literature Module', *Law and Humanities*, 3(2), p. 257.

Weisberg, M. (2014). 'A Gift in Yellow Clothing: Learning and Teaching with *The Legal Imagination*', in Etxabe, J. and Watt, G. (eds), *Living In a Law Transformed: Encounters with the Works of James Boyd White*, Maize-Fulcrum, University of Michigan Press.

White, J.B. (1973). *The Legal Imagination*, Little, Brown.

Yale Journal of Law & the Humanities (US).

Yardley, J.C. and Barrett, A. (2008). (eds), *Tacitus: The Annals*, Oxford University Press.

63. Learned societies and associations of legal academics

Introduction

Academics have gathered together to study law for many centuries. In the Western tradition, for example, salaries for professors of law were first paid in Bologna in the 1220s (Grendler [1999] at 475). The Chinese and Indian traditions are as old or even older (Lui [2020] at 477) (China (History of Legal Education), India (History of Legal Education)). The history of learned societies and associations for legal academics is much shorter than this. Part of the reason for this may lie in the fact that in at least some jurisdictions the history of those who are pure academic lawyers is relatively short. Thus, for example, Schlegel suggests that prior to the end of the nineteenth century 'there was no profession [of academic lawyers] (Schlegel [1985] at 315). Instead, he argues, university law schools in the USA were dominated by practitioners or former practitioners. Practitioners commonly have had their own associations obviating the need for separate academic fora. In a similar fashion in the United Kingdom Holdsworth argued that a separate academic association for legal academics, the Society of Public Teachers of Law, was needed because of 'the recognition of the fact that there had arisen, alongside the two established branches of the legal profession, a third branch – the Public Teachers of Law – which needed its own organisation for the discussion of its problems and the furtherance of its aims. We are all members of the legal profession...' (Holdsworth [1925] at 1).

The key point here is the argument about the distinctiveness of those who were pure legal academics not their number. When the Society was founded it has been estimated that there were little more than 100 potential members in the United Kingdom (Cownie and Cocks [2009] at 4).

Whatever the reason for their comparatively short history the picture of learned societies and associations of legal academics is nevertheless now an important feature of legal education. This entry will look at the variety of such bodies and discuss both the pragmatic and theoretical consequences of their work.

The role of learned associations

Learned societies for legal academics are an example of a much bigger phenomenon, academic learned associations. Bennett notes that

> primary reasons for joining a learned association are the opportunity to attend annual meetings, online interaction with fellow researchers, receipt of a peer-reviewed journal and other publications and access to communications about jobs. (Bennett [2013] at 33)

Whilst Bennett's comments relate to learned associations in the humanities her remarks seem applicable to associations for legal academics. Thus, for example, the Association of American Law Schools not only has information on how to become a legal academic on its website but a Faculty Appointments Register, 'an online database of applications submitted by individuals interested in becoming a legal academic' (Association of American Law Schools, nd). Similarly, the Law and Society Association, founded in 1964, has an annual meeting which averages 2,255 attendees and its members receive the Law and Society Review (Law and Society, nd). Learned associations in law thus offer a variety of pragmatic advantages to their members. However, the societies can also say something about what it means to be a legal academic.

The Australasian Law Academics Association, founded in 2019 having previously been the Australasian Law Teachers Association, which was established in 1946, offers the practical advantages of an annual conference and various publications and special interest groups for members. Membership is open not only to legal academics but also to law librarians in a tertiary institution and 'all persons who have duties and interests which are relevant to legal education' (Australasian Law Academics Association, nd). However, the Society of Legal Scholars, which describes itself as being 'the oldest as well as the largest learned society in the field of law' having been founded in 1908, is open to those who teach law 'at or beyond degree level' and those in 'academic-related posts ancillary to the teaching of law, such as law librarians' (Society of Legal Scholars, nd). The slightly different membership criteria involve a greater stress on the centrality of the academic nature of the association in the case of the Society of Legal Scholars. Although this being said, the Society is also open to 'practitioners who are engaged in legal scholarship' whilst the website of the Australasian Law Academics Association stresses that the Association is 'a platform for Australasian law teachers and legal scholars to network, collaborate and share expertise'. Differences in the membership criteria are about degrees of nuance relating to what it means to be a legal academic. If the reason for creating learned associations for legal academics, as is argued above, was recognising the distinctive interests of legal academics specifying who it is who have these distinctive interests has troubled the associations. Thus, for example, membership of the All India Law Teachers Congress is baldly said to be open to 'teachers of law, in various universities and colleges in India' (All India Law Teachers Congress, nd) (see India (Contemporary Legal Education)). By contrast The Association of Law Teachers describes itself as a 'community of academics, professionals and practitioners engaged in legal education across countries' (The Association of Law Teachers, nd). To what degree the puzzle is caused by problems in intellectually articulating the reasons justifying a description of difference or in socially justifying a claim for special status is not clear.

The range of learned associations

Societies for legal academics may be general in their nature, being open to anyone who comes within the definition of academic for the purposes of the particular society. However, they can also be focussed on specific areas of academic interest as in the case of the American Society for Legal History (American Society for Legal History, nd). Alternatively, they can be focussed on particular methodologies as in the instance of the European Society for Empirical Legal Studies (Empirical Legal Studies, nd). Multiple associations can sometimes be found in the same country with overlapping memberships. Thus,

for example in the United Kingdom there are, amongst others, the Association of Law Teachers, the Society of Legal Scholars and the Socio-Legal Studies Association. Each of these is a relatively large organisation with British legal academics not infrequently being a member of more than one of them. In this instance accidents of history and arguments about the appropriate methodology for legal research and teaching explain the range of organisations open to legal academics.

Borders between academic professional associations and other types of organisation are porous. The distinction between a trade union and an academic association is for example not straightforward. In the United Kingdom for many decades the leading trade union for academics in universities was the Association of University Teachers (Perkin [1969]). Yet it has also been said that the union 'was an elite professional association for academics from "old" British research universities' (Ackers [2015] at 115).

Conclusion

Membership of academic professional associations is a voluntary matter. Individuals decide to join because of perceptions of individual advantage or duty to the academic community. Some learned societies have paid employees. However, they are under the control of their members who will be elected to positions of office. It is these members who will undertake the majority of the work in most societies and associations. Given this the fact that such associations continue to prosper is testimony to the value that legal academics see in them.

Anthony Bradney

References

Ackers, P. (2015). 'Trade unions as professional associations', in Johnson, S. and Ackers, P. (eds), *Finding a Voice at Work: New Perspectives on Employment Relations*, Oxford University Press.

All India Law Teachers Congress, available at http://ailtc.org/ailtc_profile.htm.

American Society for Legal History, available at https://aslh.net/.

Association of American Law Schools, available at https://www.aals.org/recruitment/current-faculty-staff/far/.

Australasian Law Academics Association, available at https://www.alaa.asn.au/membership.

Bennett, E. (2013). 'The future of learned associations in the humanities', *Learned Associations*, 26, p. 32.

Cownie, F. and Cocks, R. (2009). *'A Great and Noble Occupation!' The History of the Society of Legal Scholars*, Hart Publishing.

European Society for Empirical Legal Studies, available at https://esels.eu/.

Grendler, P. (1999). 'The university of Bologna, the city and the papacy', *Renaissance Studies*, 13(4), p. 475.

Holdsworth, W. (1925). 'The Vocation of a Public Teacher of Law', *Journal of the Society of Public Teachers of Law*, p. 1.

Law and Society, available at https://www.lawandsociety.org/about-lsa/.

Lui, S. (2020). 'Confucius and the Chinese Legal Tradition', *Michigan State International Law Review*, 28(3), p. 477.

Perkin, H. (1969). *Key Profession: The History of the Association of University Teachers*, Routledge and Kegan Paul.

Schlegel, J.H. (1985). 'Between the Harvard Founders and the American Legal Realists: The Professionalization of the American Law Professor', *Journal of Legal Education*, 35, p. 311.

Society of Legal Scholars, available at https://www.legalscholars.ac.uk/membership-guidance/.

The Association of Law Teachers, available at https://www.lawteacher.ac.uk/.

64. Legal education journals

Introduction

While many people might think of legal education solely in terms of the delivery of law teaching, it is also a topic which attracts academic researchers (Research into Legal Education (Empirical) and Research into Legal Education (Non-Empirical). The topics on which they work vary from investigations of teaching methods to the purpose of the university law school. The characteristics of the students and staff who inhabit the law school are also of interest to researchers, as is the potential of innovations such as artificial intelligence (AI) to enhance the delivery of law teaching (AI Literacies in Legal Education). These are just a few of the many topics which legal education researchers are interested in. When academic researchers wish to share the results of their research, they may publish it as a book (or 'monograph'), or as a chapter in a collection of essays, but the primary location of published research into legal education can be found in academic journals, which are the focus of this entry.

Legal education research in generalist and specialist journals

Research into legal education may be published in a specialist journal, which only publishes articles concerned with aspects of legal education, or it may be published in a generalist journal, which publishes articles on all the topics found within the discipline of law. In the generalist journals, an article on legal education might be found alongside articles on company law, intellectual property law, comparative law and, indeed, any one of the vast array of topics which go to make up the discipline of law. For example, the generalist journal, *Legal Studies*, based in the United Kingdom, occasionally publishes articles on legal education, although the majority of its content is concerned with areas of substantive law. In 2024, for example, *Legal Studies* published an article about embedding workplace experiences in law degrees (Perry and Spencer [2024]) while in 2022 an article considered judicial education in Ireland (Howlin, Coen, Barry and Lynch [2022]). However, the majority of research about legal education is published in specialist journals. These are mainly based in jurisdictions such as Australia, the United States and the United Kingdom, which have a strong common law tradition, although the *European Journal of Legal Education* includes contributions from scholars outside that tradition (https://ejle .eu/index.php/ejle). Many of the specialist legal education journals belong to legal academic associations which have a particular interest in legal education. This is true of *The Journal of Legal Education* (https://jle .aahttps://jle.aals.org/home/about.htmlls.org/ home/) which is published quarterly on behalf of the American Association of Law Schools. The Canadian Association of Law Teachers (CALT) publishes the *Canadian Legal Education Annual Review* (CLEAR) (https:// www.acpd-calt.org/clear_redac#Canadian %20Legal%20Education%20Annual %20Review), while in the United Kingdom, the specialist journal, *The Law Teacher*, is published on behalf of the Association of Law Teachers (https://www.lawteacher.ac.uk/). The European Journal of Legal Education is published by the *European Law Faculties Association* (ELFA) (https://elfa-edu.org/) and the *Legal Education Review* (https://ler .scholasticahq.com/about) is associated with the Australasian Law Academics Association. The *Journal of Commonwealth Law and Legal Education* (https://law-school.open.ac .uk/overview/journal-commonwealth-law -and-legal-education) is the journal of the Commonwealth Legal Education Association, but as its title indicates its scope is something of a hybrid, encompassing both the generalist and specialist. Although *The Journal of Legal Education* was first published in 1948 (https://jle.aals.org/home/about.html) several of the other specialist journals have a more recent history: *The Law Teacher* was first published in 1967 (Duncan [2006] at 313), while the *Legal Education Review* was established in 1989 (https://ler.scholasticahq .com/about). While all these journals are independent of each other, they share the common aim of disseminating research into legal education, using a broad interpretation of that concept. Often, examples of the areas which might be covered are indicated in the description of the journal. The *Journal of Legal Education* mentions that it is interested in 'emerging areas of scholarship and teaching' (https://jle.aals.org/home/about.html). The *Law Teacher* is unique in emphasising that it is '...concerned with the teaching of law and issues affecting legal education at all academic levels' and is therefore not exclusively concerned with legal education delivered in institutions of higher education (https://www.tandfonline.com/action/journalInformation?show=aimsScope&journalCode=ralt20).

The *European Journal of Legal Education* specifically refers to its interest in publishing articles about 'the issues surrounding the regulation and political influences on law faculties' (https://ejle.eu/index.php/EJLE/about). Both from these examples, and from the scope of this encyclopaedia, it is clear that the concept of legal education is one which offers researchers the potential to investigate an extremely broad range of topics.

The developing content of specialist legal education journals

The remainder of this entry will focus upon specialist legal education journals as important outlets for the publication of the broad range of topics around the concept of legal education. The content of such journals can be influenced by a wide range of factors, including the focus of specific associations and societies, the presence of specific publication metrics and the general positioning of law as a discipline within higher education.

The previous section identified that specialist legal education journals are commonly owned by associations and societies which exist to promote legal education, and which will have their own particular aims and objectives relating to this purpose. For example, the UK's Association of Law Teachers was founded in 1965 and as noted above its journal, then titled 'The Journal of the Association of Law Teachers' was launched in 1967 (Duncan [2006]). Some such journals are published 'in-house', for example, the *European Journal of Legal Education* is published open access on the ELFA website. Others are published by mainstream academic publishers, for example, the *Legal Education Review* is published by Scholastica, and therefore must navigate the bibliometrics (publication metrics) which are influential within academic publishing. These metrics may also influence the choices of topics and outlets made by prospective authors (Fire and Guestrin [2019]).

It is arguable that both of these influences can impact upon the content of such journals.

For example, *The Law Teacher* initially included a section on Current Legal Developments, giving information on substantive law topics which may impact their teaching. Its first issue included an article titled 'United Kingdom sovereignty & law vis-a-vis Britain's entry into the common market'. Indeed, the inclusion of such topics continued for a considerable period of time, with an article on 'Consumer Protection Laws for the 1990s' published in 1987 (Borrie [1987]). It was not until a change of editorship in 1988 that it was explicitly decided to focus upon articles which discussed the development of legal education itself (Duncan [2006] at 320). This reflected the growing maturity of the Association of Law Teachers as an organisation and its desire to continue to further its overall aims.

Law can be seen as a highly vocational discipline, focused upon producing the next generation of legal professionals. Alternatively, it can be viewed as a form of liberal arts study, akin to others within the academy (Bradney [2003]). Such positioning can vary both within and between jurisdictions. However, in a number of jurisdictions, there appear to have been moves to integrate law more fully into universities, moving it from a possible 'outsider' to an important part of a university's offering. Such a shift has arguably exposed law schools to a wider range of intellectual influences, fostering inter and multi-disciplinary work and enriching their academic vibrancy. Therefore, as the content in specialist legal education journals has generally shifted away from reviews and descriptions of the substantive law, there has instead been a positive shift towards fully embracing the breadth of topics which fall under the concept of legal education. For example, scholarship on the wellbeing of law students and staff (see Wellbeing/Mental Health of Law Students and Wellbeing/Mental Health of Legal Academics) draws upon both neuroscience and psychology to explore their implications for the legal academy (Jones and Strevens [2022]).

A final point worthy of note in relation to the content is the emergence of a small number of journals focused upon specific sub-categories of legal education. Examples of these include *The International Journal of Clinical Legal Education* (https://www.northumbriajournals.co.uk/index.php/ijcle) and *The International Journal of Public Legal*

Education (https://www.northumbriajournals
.co.uk/index.php/ijple/issue/archive),
founded in 2000 and 2017 respectively by
the University of Northumbria, UK. These
amplify the interest in, and research upon,
particular facets of legal education in a way
which can facilitate greater engagement and
foster a sense of community amongst those
working within this field.

Current challenges for specialist legal education journals

In common with all academic journals,
specialist legal education journals experience a range of challenges. A key one in
recent years has been navigating the growth
of open access publishing. This challenges
the traditional format of journal publishing
where readers subscribe to access the content.
Instead, the author (or their institution) pay
for the articles to be published open access,
so it is freely available online. Writing in
the Canadian context, Price and Puddephatt
([2017] at 102) note that 'new forms of publishing, peer-review, copyright, journal business models, and even styles of knowledge
production seem to be emerging continuously'. While some specialist legal education
journals are already open access, including
the *Journal of Commonwealth Law and Legal
Education* and the *European Journal of Legal
Education*, those which are produced by
mainstream publishers will increasingly need
to consider the comparative merits of sub-
scription and open access models. This can
be further complicated if the journal is owned
by an association or society which relies upon
income from the journal to help support its
wider activities.

Another challenge is around the quality
of work being published. In particular, some
legal education research has suffered from
the criticisms levied at some higher education
research more generally, namely, that '…
it is descriptive, rather than analytical, does
not pay sufficient attention to method (and in
particular, fails to justify use of a case-study
approach) and tends to repeat existing knowledge (albeit sometimes in a new context)
rather than contributing new knowledge'
(Cownie and Jones [2021] at 327; see also
Murray [2008]). To avoid the risk of all legal
education being viewed as subject to these
flaws, it is necessary to ensure that the standard of articles published by specialist legal

education journals is high. This requires sufficient numbers of researchers with appropriate
expertise, rigorous standards of peer review
and strong editorial teams.

Conclusion

While legal education research can be published in generalist law journals alongside
articles on substantive areas of law, specialist journals enable the dissemination of the
majority of articles which focus on legal education. These journals, often linked to specific
associations or societies, showcase the broad
range of topics that the concept of legal education encompasses. The content of these journals has developed and broadened over time,
as a result of a range of influences. Challenges
still exist, including navigating open access
publishing models and ensuring high quality
content. However, the breadth of content in
contemporary publications indicates that,
overall, the picture is one of a vibrant and
growing field of academic interest.

FIONA COWNIE AND EMMA JONES

References

Borrie, G. (1987). 'Consumer protection laws for
the 1990s', *The Law Teacher*, 21(3), p. 239.
Bradney, A. (2003). *Conversations, choices
and chances: The liberal law school in the
twenty-first century*, Hart Publishing.
Cownie, F. and Jones, E. (2021). 'Blackstone's
Tower in Context', *Amicus Curiae*, 2(3),
pp. 314–333.
Duncan, N.J. (2006). 'Pro Bono Legis Doctorum:
40 Years of the Law Teacher', *The Law Teacher*,
40(3), p. 313.
Fire, M. and Guestrin, C. (2019). 'Over-optimization
of academic publishing metrics: observing
Goodhart's Law in action', *GigaScience*, 8(6),
giz053.
Howlin, N., Coen, M., Barry, C. and Lynch, J.
(2022). '"Robinson Crusoe on a Desert Island?"
Judicial Education in Ireland, 1995–2019',
Legal Studies, 42, p. 525.
Jones, E. and Strevens, C. (2022). 'Legal education
for wellbeing: design, delivery and evaluation',
The Law Teacher, 56(1), p. 1.
Murray, R. (2008). 'Writing for Publication about
Teaching and Learning in Higher Education', in
Murray, R. (ed), *The Scholarship of Teaching
and Learning in Higher Education*, Open
University Press.
Perry, C. and Spencer, N. (2024). 'The Importance
of "Acting Yourself into New Ways of
Thinking": Preliminary Findings on the Impact
of Embedding Workplace Experiences in Law

Degrees to Positively Impact Student Skills Growth, Degree Results and Employment Outcomes before and during a Global Pandemic', *Legal Studies*, 44, p. 99.

Price, T. and Puddephatt, A. (2017). 'Power, emergence, and the meanings of resistance: Open access scholarly publishing in Canada', in Mulsolf, G.R. (ed), *Oppression and Resistance: Structure, Agency, Transformation*, Emerald Publishing Limited.

Wilson, E.-F. (1967). 'United Kingdom sovereignty & law vis-a-vis Britain's entry into the common market', *The Law Teacher*, 1(1), p. 41.

65. Legal writing instructors

Introduction

During the last 50 years, legal writing courses have become a core component of the first-year curriculum at law schools in the United States. These courses play a vital role in developing practice-ready lawyers, yet the professionals hired to teach legal writing often make much less money and have far less job security than other members of the faculty. In law schools outside the United States, legal writing courses are nowhere near as prevalent, although in some common law countries, they are included as part of the required curriculum. Law schools in civil law countries generally do not require students to take legal writing courses, although that is beginning to change.

Background

Legal writing serves as the backbone of the legal system in the United States, providing the framework for understanding, applying, and interpreting the law. It is important not only for conveying information but for shaping legal arguments and decisions. For example, lawyers use legal writing to create memoranda to help other lawyers in their law firms decide whether to take cases, how to manage those cases and how to advise clients on those cases. Additionally, lawyers write legal briefs to help judges decide how to rule on those cases. (Osbeck [2012])

In the United States, legal writing courses usually span the first two semesters of law school. These courses are sometimes called 'Legal Research and Writing', 'Legal Process' or 'Legal Methods' and include instruction in legal research as well as legal writing. The majority of these courses are taught by full-time instructors who were hired specifically to teach this – as opposed to faculty members who were hired to teach lecture-style courses in other subjects but who also teach this. (ALWD/LWI [2022])

In some law schools, however, the course instructors are not full-time; they are adjuncts, hired part-time at a small fraction of the salary of their full-time counterparts – often with the same teaching load but no job security or benefits such as health insurance. Increasingly, law schools in the United States are moving to use full-time legal writing instructors in response to pressure from national organisations of legal writing professionals seeking pay equity, status parity and tenure.

Legal writing courses typically include instruction in organisational paradigms such as IRAC (Issue-Rule-Analysis-Conclusion) and CREAC (Conclusion-Rule-Explanation of Rule-Analysis-Conclusion). Lawyers use these constructs to apply judicial conclusions and reasoning from past cases to the facts of a current case, discuss how the facts of the past case are or are not similar to the facts of the current case, and, based on this, conclude how the judge should decide the current case. Legal writing courses also train law students in oral advocacy skills, negotiating skills, and a wide range of writing to inform and persuade – memoranda, briefs, motions, client letters, etc. These courses are taught by lawyers who generally have experience practicing law.

History

Law schools in the United States did not always include legal writing courses as part of the core curriculum. Prior to the 1980s, lecture-based courses dominated the curriculum. In 1985, legal writing professors founded the Legal Writing Institute (known as LWI), a nonprofit organisation dedicated to 'building the discipline of legal writing, and improving the status of legal writing faculty across the country'. The organisation now has more than 1,700 members. In 1996, legal writing professors formed an additional nonprofit organisation, the Association of Legal Writing Directors (known as ALWD), to support the development of legal writing programmes in law schools and promote the effective teaching of legal writing. That organisation has more than 400 members at more than 130 law schools in North America.

Pressure to improve the legal writing skills of law students in the United States increased in 1989 when the ABA Section of Legal Education and Admission to the Bar formed a task force to examine the deficiencies of legal education in skills needed by practicing lawyers. (Osbeck [2012]) This resulted in what is commonly referred to as the MacCrate report, issued by the American Bar Association in 1992; the report called for an enhancement of skills instruction, including legal writing, in law schools. (ABA [1992])

Change, however, was slow. In 2007, the Carnegie Foundation for the Advancement of Teaching issued a report concluding that there was still an 'urgent' need for skills instruction in law schools to better prepare students for law practice. (Osbeck [2012])

Meanwhile, economics pushed law firms to cut back on their training of new associates. Starting salaries were rising, and firms could not assign the new lawyers to work on case files until the firms taught the new lawyers practice skills – including legal writing. This meant that the firms could not bill clients to offset the salaries of the new lawyers. Thus, the firms began to pressure law schools to take over the training and produce practice-ready graduates. (Dauphinais [2011])

Law schools were then faced with the challenge of finding people to teach legal writing. Law professors generally did not want to teach legal writing because legal writing courses were labour-intensive, requiring a great deal of individual attention to students' writing throughout the semester. (Stanchi and Levine [2001]) Law professors in other types of courses were used to assigning casebooks and lecturing, not meeting individually with students and reviewing their writing throughout the semester. As a result, law schools were forced to hire additional faculty to teach legal writing. Faced with this new expense, the law schools sought to economise on the salaries to be paid to the new hires.

Luckily, the law schools found a ready source of employees to fill these new positions: young female lawyers who were working for firms but who were married and wanted more time to be with their babies and young children. (Stanchi and Levine [2001]) Typically, these women had husbands who were employed, so the women were willing to work part-time at a salary that was far lower than the prorated salaries of the casebook professors.

Law schools also discriminated against the new hires in another way. Law professors in the United States traditionally had been awarded titles that included the word 'professor' (e.g, 'associate professor' or 'assistant professor'), but law schools gave the legal writing faculty members titles that clearly conveyed a lower status (e.g., 'instructor' or 'lecturer'). This situation has changed substantially over the years, but not entirely. Many law schools now give legal writing faculty titles that include the word 'professor', but the schools modify it to signal that these faculty members are not part of the casebook faculty. As an example, full professors who teach casebook courses are generally called either 'Professor' or 'Professor of Law', but legal writing professors often have titles like 'Professor of Legal Process'. This discrepancy in titles reinforces the divide between the casebook faculty and the skills faculty, perpetuating the second-class status of those who teach legal writing.

Pink ghetto

This early hiring of legal writing faculty gave rise to the term 'pink ghetto' because a large percentage were female. (Allen [2019]) Although practicing lawyers and judges have widely stated that legal writing is one of the most important foundational skills needed for the practice of law, law schools have traditionally relegated the teaching of legal writing to those with the lowest status, salary, and job security. And those largely have continued to be women. This pervasive discrimination is the 'dirty secret' of law schools (Stanchi and Levine [2001]) – institutions that train their students to fight discrimination. This caste system (Dauphinais [2011]) lingers today, even though legal writing professors have pushed, and are still pushing, for change.

Change has occurred, but it has been slow. In 1984, the American Bar Association added a provision to its Standards and Rules of Procedure for Approval of Law Schools to give some job security to the clinical faculty. (Joy [2017]) The provision, Standard 405(c), stated that law schools 'should' offer either long-term contracts or a separate tenure track from the one afforded to casebook faculty members. Although this addition was progress, its language reinforced the second-class status of the legal writing faculty – i.e., that they still weren't good enough or deserving enough to be eligible for the same tenure protection as the casebook faculty.

Another step toward equality occurred in 1994, when the American Bar Association changed Standard 405(c) from 'should' (aspirational) to 'shall' (mandatory). But, still, the Standard did not require law schools to award regular tenure to the legal writing faculty.

In 1996, the American Bar Association adopted Standard 405(d), ostensibly to address security of position for legal writing faculty. It stated that law schools employing full-time legal writing instructors or directors 'shall provide conditions sufficient to attract well-qualified' people. The standard was revised in 2001, but the revision still did not provide the security of position given to casebook faculty. (Weresh [2020])

To obtain even this second-class type of job security, legal writing faculty had to fight to prove that their scholarship was as worthy – that scholarship about legal writing contained the same type of analysis that was present in scholarship written by faculty who taught casebook courses such as contract law, constitutional law, criminal law, etc.

Despite these small steps, the 2021–2022 report of a survey of United States law schools by the Association of Legal Writing Directors and the Legal Writing Institute showed that only 30 percent of the full-time legal writing faculty had tenure or tenure-track status with traditional tenure. (ALWD/LWI [2022])

In 2023, ALWD and LWI jointly submitted a proposal to the American Bar Association calling for a uniform standard for all full-time faculty members. As of early 2024, the American Bar Association was moving forward with consideration of the proposal.

Outside the United States

The inclusion of legal writing courses in law school curricula is not widespread outside the United States. A large part of the reason is that in civil law countries, law is not based on judicial decisions from past cases. Thus, there is much less need for lawyers to know how to write a detailed analyses of precedential cases and write explanations of why judicial decisions in those cases should or should not apply to the current case. In some common law countries, such as Canada, Australia and New Zealand, legal writing courses are the norm in law schools. In the UK, legal writing is sometimes, but not always, part of the curriculum, often within a module such as 'Introduction to Law', 'Legal Skills', 'Legal System' or 'Legal Method'.

Countries where law schools have incorporated US-style legal writing courses into the required curriculum include: Canada, Australia, New Zealand, UK, Bhutan, Qatar, Kenya, and India. A smattering of law schools in civil law countries – e.g., Turkey – have also begun to add legal writing instruction to

prepare students for careers in international law firms where strong legal writing skills are necessary. Nonetheless, the addition of legal writing courses to law school curricula in civil law countries is not yet widespread.

ANN NOWAK

References

Allen, R.N. (2019). 'The "Pink Ghetto" Pipeline: Challenges and Opportunities for Women in Legal Education', *U. Det. Mercy L. Rev.*, 96, p. 525.

ALWD/LWI Legal Writing Survey. (2022), available at https://www.alwd.org/.

American Bar Association. (1992). 'Legal Education and Professional Development – an Educational Continuum, Report of the Task Force on Law Schools and the Profession: Narrowing the Gap (known as the MacCrate Report).

American Bar Association. (2023). Standards and Rules of Procedure for Approval of Law Schools, available at https://www.americanbar.org/groups/legal_education/resources/standards/.

Beazley, M.B. (2021). 'Shouting into the Wind: How the ABA Standards Promote Inequality in Legal Education, and What Law Students and Faculty Should Do About It', *Vill. L. Rev.*, 65, p. 1037

Beazley, M.B. (2000). 'Riddikulus!: Tenure-Track Legal Writing Faculty and the Boggart in the Wardrobe', *Scribes J. Leg. Writing*, 7, p. 797.

Chused, R.H. (1988). 'The Hiring and Retention of Minorities and Women on American Law School Faculties', *U. Pa. L. Rev.*, 137, p. 537.

Dauphinais, K.A. (2011). 'Sea Change: The Seismic Shift in the Legal Profession and How Legal Writing Professors Will Keep Legal Education Afloat in its Wake', *Seattle Journal for Social Justice*, 10(1), p. 49.

Durako, J.A. (2000). 'Second-Class Citizens in the Pink Ghetto: Gender Bias in Legal Writing', *J. Legal Educ.*, 50(1), p. 562.

Joy, P.A. (2017). 'ABA Standard 405(c): Two Steps Forward and One Step Back for Legal Education', *J. Legal Educ.*, 66(3), p. 606.

Kraft, D.B. (2015). 'CREAC in the Real World', *Clev. St. L. Rev.*, 63, p. 567.

Levine, J.M. (2020). 'Legal Writing as a Discipline: Past, Present, and Future', in *ABA Legal Writing Sourcebook*, 3rd edition, Duquesne University School of Law Research Paper No. 2020–05, available at https://papers.ssrn.com/sol3/papers.cfm?abstract_id=3605640.

McElroy, L.T., Coughlin, C.N. and Gordon, D.S. (2011). 'The Carnegie Report and Legal

Writing: Does the Report Go Far Enough?', *Legal Writing*, 17, p. 279.

Osbeck, M. (2012). 'What is "Good Legal Writing" and Why Does It Matter?', *Drexel L. Rev.*, 4(2), p. 417.

Ritchie, D.T. (2007). 'Who Is On the Outside Looking In, and What Do They See?: Metaphors of Exclusion in Legal Education', *Mercer L. Rev.*, 58, p. 991.

Stanchi, K.M. (2017). 'The Problem with ABA Standard 405(c)', *J. Legal Educ.*, 66(3), p. 558.

Stanchi, K.M. and Levine, J.M. (2001). 'Gender and Legal Writing: Law Schools' Dirty Little Secrets', *Berkeley Women's Law Journal*, 16, p. 3.

Sullivan, W.M. et al. (2007). 'Educating Lawyers Preparation for the Profession of Law' (The Carnegie Foundation for the Advancement of Teaching, Preparation for the Professions Program).

Todd, A. (2013). 'Writing Lessons from Abroad: A Comparative Perspective on the Teaching of Legal Writing', *Washburn L.J.*, 53, p. 295.

Weresh, M.H. (2020). 'The History of American Bar Association Standard 405(D): One Step Forward, Two Steps Back', *Legal Writing*, 24, p. 125.

66. Mexico (contemporary legal education)

Introduction

Mexico's legal education system is made up of law schools and their programmes, professors, students, and the government institutions that rule and oversee their performance. This entry will only refer to the characteristics of law schools and their law degree programmes. (See also entries on the history of legal education in Mexico and the regulation of legal education in Mexico.)

The law degree in Mexico is an undergraduate programme. Obtaining a professional license to practice law requires the completion of a Bachelor of Law programme (from now on, referred to as 'LLB') at a higher education institution that is part of the national education system (Pérez-Hurtado [2009]).

There are many institutions where one can pursue a law degree. In the 2022–2023 academic year, 2119 law schools offered at least one active LLB programme (CEEAD [2023]) with an enrolment of 361,419 students (ANUIES [2023]). However, some institutions of higher education offer more than one LLB programme, differing from each other in their schedule, pedagogical methodologies, or curriculum.

Of these law schools, only 9.4 per cent are public institutions of higher education with 187,094 students enrolled in them, while 90.6 per cent are private institutions with 174,325 students enrolled in them. The law school with the highest number of students is the National Autonomous University of Mexico with 15,636 students enrolled (ANUIES [2023]).

Increase in law schools and law students

Over the last 30 years, law schools and law students have been growing. While in 1992 118 higher education institutions were offering LLB degrees (CEEAD [2014]), in 2022 there were 2119 (CEEAD [2023]). It means that during this period the number of law schools in Mexico grew at a rate of one new law school every week. However, while the number of law schools continues to increase,

it has begun to slow down. By the 2022–2023 academic year, the average growth was one new law school per month (CEEAD [2023]). The number of LLB students rose from 116,160 in 1992 (ANUIES [1992]) to 361,419 in 2022, a 211 per cent increase. It is important to point out the increase, within this percentage, of female students. In 1992, 43.84 per cent of the total law students were women; in 2022, this number rose to 55.56 per cent.

This accelerated growth has several causes. One is the generalised increase in higher education enrolment throughout the country with the opening of more private universities.

Not only has the number of law students expanded, but also the number of programmes. In the last ten years, there has been a 34.83 per cent growth in enrolment in higher education (ANUIES [2013]).

A significant reason for the growth of private institutions is the incapacity of public institutions to meet the substantial demand for higher education. It opens a door for private institutions to adapt their programmes to the market needs. Some offer the LLB in a shorter period, ranging between two to five years, have fewer requirements to obtain the diploma, and some offer specialised programmes. Furthermore, most of these institutions use an 'open door' admission policy. They require only a high school diploma and a modest Grade Point Average (GPA) in order to attract the highest number of applicants possible (Pérez-Hurtado [2009]). In addition, law schools do not require extensive or expensive facilities or full-time professors. These conditions favour the expansion of private higher education.

Another cause of the growth of legal education is the demand from potential students. Law programmes are among the bachelor's degree programmes with the most students (ANUIES [2023]). This may be related to the reasons why students choose to study law. Research led by Perez-Hurtado involving almost 22,000 Mexican law students in 2004 provides some explanations. According to the students, the legal profession means '… professionally, a broad range of opportunities for different types of professional practice and locations in which to work; personally, it represents an appropriate income, access to certain social networks, as well as prestige; and socially, it offers the opportunity to expand democracy, social justice, and the common good' (Pérez-Hurtado [2009]). Furthermore, the study reveals that one of the main experiences that fuels students' interest in studying law is '… that they were victims of violations of their rights, or they perceived their environment as marked by injustice, corruption and impunity' (Pérez-Hurtado [2009]).

In summary, during the past 30 years, legal education in Mexico has transitioned from being centralised in public universities to being widely distributed, due to its growth within private institutions.

The LLB programmes

To offer an LLB programme, an institution must have government authorisation and be part of the national education system. There are two ways to join the system: one is for public universities to have private institutions incorporated with them; the second is for the remaining private institutions to obtain authorisation through the Ministry of Public Education or the education office of local governments. To understand this process in more detail, you can refer to the entry on the Regulation of Legal Education in Mexico.

Many institutions offer more than one LLB programme. By the academic year 2022–2023, there were 2,506 'active' LLB programmes (with students enrolled on them) in the 2119 law schools. Of these, 47 per cent were authorised through the Recognition of Official Validity of Studies (RVOE) granted by administrative authorities such as the President of Mexico or the federal government through the Ministry of Public Education; another 39 per cent were authorised through the RVOE granted by a state government through their public education offices (those programmes can only be offered within that particular state); 11 per cent were authorised by presidential decree and 3 per cent were incorporated into a public university. Of the total programmes incorporated, 44 per cent are offered by the National Autonomous University of Mexico (CEEAD [2023]). A presidential decree gives institutions special autonomy to define their academic programmes, while institutions of higher education with a Federal or State RVOE submit their study plans and pro-

grammes to the corresponding authority for approval.

LLB programmes are offered with 66 different titles around the country, such as 'Bachelor of Legal Sciences', 'Bachelor of Corporate Law' or 'Bachelor of Laws with specialisation in Criminal Law'. However, 90 per cent are offered using the title 'Licenciatura en Derecho'.

There are other differences in LLB programmes such as the duration, modality of their curriculum, and schedule. The General Law of Higher Education recognises three different modes of higher education:

- Full-time, where studies are taught in higher education institutions with a coinciding time and space between professors and students.
- Open or distance education, where there is a time overlap between professors and students and it can be carried out through digital platforms or didactic resources for distance learning.
- Part-time, as a combination of the on-campus and non-campus-based modes. It requires student attendance on certain days for short periods to participate in some programme components while the rest of the programme involves self-study and tutoring.

In the academic year 2022–2023 59 per cent of LLB programmes were taught full-time; 34 per cent were part-time; and 7 per cent were taught by open or distance mode (CEEAD [2023]). The delivery of LLB programmes varies: 64 per cent are taught in four-month periods; 30 per cent in semesters, and 2 per cent use other types of periods such as years, bimesters, trimesters, or modules. There is some flexibility in setting the length of an LLB programme, and it can last between two and five years (CEEAD [2023]). According to the Ministry of Public Education, the programme must only have a minimum of 300 credits, in which each hour of learning under teaching guidance or independent study is equivalent to 0.0625 credits. In addition to this, the number of weekly learning hours must be less than 50 and at least 2400 of study should be under teaching guidance (Agreement number 17/11/17 of the Ministry of Public Education [2017]).

Content of the LLB programmes

There is no regulation relating specifically to the content of the LLB programme. Each public university can freely design its law programmes, and private universities need only to establish programmes which correspond to their objectives and graduate profiles to obtain an RVOE.

Although there is no detailed data available on the precise content of the law curricula in different institutions, research led in 2009 by Pérez-Hurtado provides evidence that most law programmes contain between 40 and 70 mandatory courses, including courses related to legal context, Mexican legal history, the traditional areas of legal practice, and the professional context.

As mentioned earlier, law programmes are taught under 66 different names, including some programmes specialised in specific areas of professional practice. Consequently, there needs to be a particular regulation regarding the type of practice graduates of these programmes can engage in and the minimum content necessary to ensure the quality of professional practice. The decision about who can practice law in a particular court is often left to the discretion of jurisdictional authorities. Nevertheless, there are efforts to promote quality in higher education through accreditation mechanisms granted by institutions recognised by the Ministry of Education. The first of these efforts is the Interinstitutional Committees for the Evaluation of Higher Education (CIEES), created in 1991 to ensure the quality of Mexican higher education through a self-regulation mechanism for quality (Pérez-Hurtado [2008]).

Some recognised accreditation organisations include the Council for the Accreditation of Higher Education (COPAES), the National Council for Accreditation of Higher Education in Law (CONFEDE), and the National Council for the Accreditation of Teaching in Law (CONAED). This is a voluntary process that aims to recognise institutions that have made significant progress in fulfilling their mission and stated objectives. It involves self-assessment and evaluation, and accreditation is granted to institutions that meet specific requirements, such as qualified professors, a curriculum consistent with the mission and objectives, and coherent teaching methodologies. By the 2022–2023 academic year, only 8.7 per cent of LLB programmes had at least one accreditation from a national or international recognised institution (CEEAD [2023]).

In summary, the legal education system in Mexico is very complex, due to the quantity and diversity of institutions offering law degrees. In addition to this, other components such as faculty members, student characteristics, the content of specific programmes, and continuing education and postgraduate processes require broader and updated qualitative research processes to enable greater understanding of the ways in which they function. This entry provides an overview of the characteristics of law schools regarding their creation, operation, and development over the last 30 years, as well as the general features of LLB programmes in Mexico.

LILA ZAIRE FLORES-FERNANDEZ AND LUIS
ALFONSO MORA-RUENES

References

Agreement No. 17/11/17 which Establishes the Formalities and Procedures related to the Recognition of Official Validity of Studies (D.O.F., 13 November 2017).
ANUIES, 'Statistical Yearbook of Higher Education, Academic year 1991–1992'.
ANUIES, 'Statistical Yearbook of Higher Education, Academic year 2012–2013', available at http://www.anuies.mx/informacion-y-servicios/informacion-estadistica-de-educacion-superior/anuario-estadistico-de-educacion-superior.
ANUIES, 'Statistical Yearbook of Higher Education, Academic year 2022–2023', available at http://www.anuies.mx/informacion-y-servicios/informacion-estadistica-de-educacion-superior/anuario-estadistico-de-educacion-superior.
CEEAD, 'Law schools in Mexico infographic, Academic year 2013–2014', available at https://www.ceead.org.mx/.
CEEAD, 'Law schools in Mexico infographic, Academic year 2022–2023', available at https://www.ceead.org.mx/.
Fix-Fierro, H. and López-Ayllón, S. (2006). '¿Muchos abogados, pero poca profesión? Derecho y Profesión Jurídica en México', in Fix-Fierro, H. (ed), Del Gobierno de los abogados al imperio de las leyes: Estudios sociojurídicos sobre educación y profesiones jurídicas en el México contemporáneo, Oxford University Press.
General Education Law (Ley General de Educación Superior) (D.O.F., 20 April 2021).
Pérez-Hurtado, L. (2009). 'An Overview of Mexico's System of Legal Education', Mexican Law Review, 1(2), available at https://revistas

.juridicas.unam.mx/index.php/mexican-law
-review/article/view/7722.

Pérez-Hurtado, L. (2008). 'Evaluación, recono-
cimiento y acreditación educativa en México:
Espacios para la innovación en la enseñanza del
Derecho', *Cuadernos Unimetanos*, p. 237.

Pérez-Hurtado, L. (2009). *La futura generación
de abogados mexicanos. Estudio de las escuelas y los estudiantes de derecho en México*,
IIJUNAM-CEEAD, Oxford University Press.

67. Mexico (history of legal education)

Introduction

Mexico has a complex legal history. It has been a sovereign country since 1821; however, its political and legal history dates back to different pre-Hispanic civilisations. For this entry, we considered the Aztec civilisation the first in the territory to institutionalise legal education. When the Crown of Castile conquered the territory and founded the Viceroyalty of New Spain, a new legal system began. Consequently, the duties and knowledge required for the legal profession changed drastically. The War of Independence and the Mexican Revolution also impacted legal education because of the regime change and the economic and political viability of creating and operating universities within these contexts.

In modern times, there has been a push for higher education institutions to be accessible to a broader range of populations, both geographically and economically, which has led to the rapid growth of private law schools throughout Mexican territory. Although this effort has allowed for the student population of law schools to be more diverse, it has brought new challenges to the quality control and evaluation of legal education.

Pre Hispanic era

We can trace back legal education in México to an Aztec institution called *Calmecac*. It was a higher education institution dedicated to training young noblemen in general culture and some specialised disciplines, such as public administration, militia, and law. The clergy supervised the training processes held in the *Calmecac*. (González A. Carrancá [2016] at 707–708)

Although there is testimonial evidence that texts were used to teach law at the *Calmecac*, law courses were mainly oral. Legal education was theoretical and practical. In addition to the teaching lessons received at *Calmecac*, students visited the courts and learned firsthand about the administration of justice. (González A. Carrancá [2016] at 707–708)

Colonial era

The colonisation of the indigenous population in Mexico occurred during 1519–1521, after the fall of the Aztec Empire. The Crown of Castille founded the Viceroyalty of New Spain in 1535. The legal system was Indian law, composed of Hispanic and pre-Hispanic law. (Lizardi Tort [2022])

The complexity of Indian Law, the lack of systematisation, the constant actualisation, and the lack of libraries in the territory posed an obstacle to the study of law. (González A. Carranca [2016]) Lawyers were self-taught and learned through practice. To officially become a lawyer, one had to obtain the authorisation of the Real Audiencia de México [Court of Mexico]. (Guerrero [1998] at 133)

The Real y Pontífica Universidad de México [Royal and Pontifical University of Mexico] was founded in 1553, and legal education began to be institutionalised. The sons of the Spanish, a small native minority, could now access formal legal education and, hence, the possibility of occupying public positions. (Lizardi [2022]) Legal education focused on Roman Law and Canon Law. Classes consisted of lectures that relied heavily on the student's memorisation capacity, for it was uncommon to use textbooks. (Guerrero [1998])

Interested students had to complete three years of primary literature and Latin before studying law; then, they could enrol in law lectures. The law programme lasted five additional years. To obtain their law bachelor's degree, students needed to take an exam before three doctorates; if they sought a doctoral degree they needed to defend a thesis. However, to become a practicing lawyer, they had to do a two to four-year additional apprenticeship and be examined by the Real Audiencia de México [Court of Mexico]. (Guerrero [1998])

In 1741, during the reign of Carl III of the Borbon House, Royal Law was incorporated into legal education. By the eighteenth century, law was taught in five universities: Real y Pontífica Universidad de México [Royal and Potifical University of Mexico], Colegio Carolino de Puebla [Carolinian College of Puebla], Seminario de Valladolid [Seminar of Valladolid], Seminario de Monterrey [Seminar of Monterrey], and the Universidad de Guadalajara [University of Guadalajara]. (Guerrero [1998])

Post independence and modern times

Mexico began developing its legal system after gaining independence from Spain in 1821. The political instability of the time had an impact on formal legal education. The Real Audiencia de México [Court of Mexico] was constantly criticised by the liberals at the time, who saw it as an institution of the old colonial regime, and it was closed in 1865. Formal legal education was put on hold after this event. (Pérez Hurtado and Rivera Villegas [2022] at 4)

The Escuela de Nacional de Jurisprudencia [National School of Jurisprudence]

On 2 December 1867, the Organic Law of Public Instruction was published. It created several professional schools, including the Escuela Nacional de Jurisprudencia [National School of Jurisprudence], an institution authorised to provide legal education. (Pérez Hurtado and Rivera Villegas [2022] at 4) The professional degrees offered were Lawyer, Notary, and Business Agent. (Guerrero [1998] at 137)

The law programme lasted six years, and the 1867 curriculum consisted of the following classes: Natural Law, Roman Law, Canon Law, Patriotic Law, Constitutional and Administrative Law, International and Maritime Law, Civil Procedures, Criminal Procedures, and Comparative Law. (Colín Martínez [2022]) The requirements to obtain the law degree were the following: (1) cover all studies and complete the professional exam; (2) carry out a six-month internship in a law firm or civil court; (3) carry out a six-month internship at a criminal court; and (4) attend the Jurisprudence Academy of the National Bar Association and join the said institution. (Guerrero [1998] at 137)

The law programme at the Escuela Nacional de Jurisprudencia [National School of Jurisprudence] was the basis for developing the curriculum at the emerging public law schools in state entities. By 1874, legal education had spread throughout most of the country. (Guerrero [1998] at 140) Between 1867 and 1897, the curriculum of the law degree of the *Escuela Nacional de Jurisprudencia* [National School of Jurisprudence] experienced numerous changes in response to the legal developments that were taking place in the country to incorporate the teaching of new areas of law, such as Civil Law, Commercial Law, and Mining Law. (Colín Martínez [2022])

It is worth noting that the first woman who studied law did so at the Escuela Nacional de Jurisprudencia [National School of Jurisprudence] through a government scholarship in 1892 (Lira Alonso).

The opening of new public and private law schools

On 22 September 1910, after several political initiatives to unify the various professional schools into a comprehensive university model, the Universidad Nacional Autónoma de México (UNAM) [National Autonomous University of Mexico] was founded. However, the Mexican Revolution began in November 1910, and the university could not exercise its academic functions. Once the armed conflict was over in 1920, it consolidated its educational and institutional model. However, due to the complicated political and social context, the university saw its academic functions disrupted numerous times. During this period, various student movements organised strikes demanding greater regularity and certainty regarding the functioning of the institution and the teaching of classes. (Pérez Hurtado and Rivera Villegas [2022] at 5)

Another important moment in the history of legal education in Mexico was the creation of the *Escuela Libre de Derecho* [Free Law School] in 1912, the first private law school in the country. It was founded by distinguished law professors and as a separate entity to the Escuela Nacional de Jurisprudencia [National School of Jurisprudence] after a student strike paralysed it for months. The education authorities at the time authorised its creation, and the Colegio Nacional de Abogados [National Bar Association] endorsed it. (Guerrero [1998] at 142–143) This event represented an enormous step for the academic autonomy of legal education in Mexico.

Post-revolutionary stability encouraged several state entities to adopt state-level university models and establish their public higher education institutions. However, UNAM continued to be the primary law school in the country despite its budgetary limitations. In 1945, a new University Organic Law was adopted, and it recognised the UNAM as a decentralised institution of the Mexican State, guaranteeing the university a budget and autonomy in exercising its functions. In the years following, UNAM would continue to be the model for legal education at the national level and the institution with the most students enrolled. (Pérez Hurtado and Rivera Villegas [2022] at 5)

It is important to note that in the post-revolutionary period, to be part of the legal educational system, a law school could be created through either of these processes: (1) be established as a public education institution; (2) obtain an extraordinary authorisation from the Federal Government to establish a private law school, such as the Escuela Libre de Derecho [Free Law School]; or (3) be established as a private institution that incorporates itself to UNAM's study programme. (Pérez Hurtado and Rivera Villegas [2022] at 5–6)

Contemporary history

In the following years, public higher education institutions from other state entities gained the facility to incorporate private institutions in order to expand academic coverage in their federal entity. The option of incorporation into the Mexican legal education system peaked between 1970 and 1980. In 1973, the Federal Education Law was adopted, granting education authorities, at the federal and state levels, the power to authorise private institutions to offer higher-level education through the Recognition of Official Validity of Studies (RVOE in Spanish). (Pérez Hurtado and Rivera Villegas [2022] at 6)

In the 1980s, the World Bank and the Organisation for Economic Co-operation and Development (OECD) pushed for a policy to diversify funding in higher education institutions. During the administration of 1988–1994, the government adopted a system for decentralised education authorisation, which gained strength. (Pérez Hurtado and Rivera Villegas [2022] at 7) It facilitated administrative processes for the creation of higher education institutions. However, it lacked a quality control and evaluation system for the educational services. (Pérez Hurtado and Rivera Villegas [2022] at 9)

In turn, a rapid growth of private higher education institutions began. In 1985, 93 higher education institutions offered a law degree. (Pérez Hurtado and Rivera Villegas [2022] at 8) In the academic year 2022–2023, 2119 higher education institutions offer a law degree, of which 1920 are private and 199 are public. (CEEAD [2023])

Some of these private law schools represent a viable opportunity for law students in Mexico. They are affordable and flexible, do not require further prerequisites other than a high school certificate and the tuition payment, and are usually near work centres or in communities with few other higher education offerings. (Pérez Hurtado and Rivera Villegas [2022] at 9)

In general, most law schools in Mexico offer programmes that include extracurricular modules or requirements for students to have a space of professional practice, such as internships in governmental agencies or private practices and moot courts. (Pérez Hurtado and Rivera Villegas [2022] at 21) And in a few, mostly elite universities, law clinics are part of the law programme.

A significant effort to address the diversity of the student population in Mexican legal education are the Intercultural Universities. Federal and state governments created them as a response to the political demand of indigenous groups for higher education in their native languages and cultures. In 2001, the first Intercultural University was founded: the Universidad Autónoma Indígena de México [Autonomous Indigenous University of Mexico] in Mochicahui, Sinaloa. (Lloyd, Hernández Fierro [2021]) As of 2023, there are 11 campuses, most located in rural areas marginalised by universities that offer higher education programmes with an occidental view. (Dietz and Mateos Cortés [2019] at 166–167) In these schools, legal education has an intercultural approach. The curriculum design tries to balance the historical lack of access to education of indigenous communities as well as including matters of local and cultural relevance. (Dietz and Mateos Cortés [2019] at 173) Regulatory pluralism in Mexico makes the Law course especially relevant for these institutions. (CEEAD [2015])

Although the contemporary diversity of law schools in Mexico represents an opportunity in terms of accessibility for a diverse student population, the quality control of legal education, particularly of the institutions and their programmes, has not been thoroughly addressed. (Mexico (Regulation of Legal Education)) Consequently, students leave law schools with an uneven set of professional skills and knowledge.

The institutions and practices used to educate Mexican legal professionals have evolved alongside political and social changes in Mexico. Mexico's legal education history shows the place lawyers have had in society and the diversification of the population with access to this professional path.

GABRIELA TALANCÓN-VILLEGAS AND MARÍA JOSÉ GUTIÉRREZ-RODRÍGUEZ

References

Centro de Estudios sobre la Enseñanza y el Aprendizaje del Derecho, A.C. (2015). 'Fortaleciendo a las escuelas de derecho indígenas para que impulsen el desarrollo de sus comunidades. Propuesta de licenciatura en Derecho con enfoque intercultural', Centro de Estudios sobre la Enseñanza y el Aprendizaje del Derecho, A.C.

Centro de Estudios sobre la Enseñanza y el Aprendizaje del Derecho, A.C. (2023). 'Las escuelas de derecho en México, Instituciones de Educación Superior (IES) que ofrecen la Licenciatura en Derecho (LAD), Ciclo académico 2022–2023', Centro de Estudios sobre la Enseñanza y el Aprendizaje del Derecho, A.C.

Colín Martínez, J. (2022). 'La educación jurídica en México. Prácticas y saberes desde la Escuela Nacional de Jurisprudencia, 1867–1897', LXXII(284) Revista de la Facultad de Derecho de México, available at https://revistas.unam.mx/index.php/rfdm/article/download/81234/74137/253958.

Dietz, G. and Mateos Cortés, L.S. (2019). 'Las universidades interculturales en México, logros y retos de un nuevo subsistema de educación superior', XXV(49) Estudios sobre las Culturas Contemporáneas, available at https://www.redalyc.org/journal/316/31658531008/31658531008.pdf.

González, A.J. (2016). 'Carrancá', in *Comentarios sobre la evolución de la enseñanza del derecho en México. En Estudios en homenaje a Jorge Barrera Graf*, Volume I, UNAM-Instituto de Investigaciones Jurídicas.

Guerrero, O. (1998). *El funcionario, el diplomático y el juez*, Universidad de Guanajuato, Instituto de Administración Pública de Guanajuato, Instituto Nacional de Administración Pública, Plaza y Valdés Editores.

Lira Alonso, M.P. (2008). 'Un acercamiento a la biografía de María Asunción Sandoval, la primera abogada mexicana', available at https://coordinacioneditorialfacultadderecho.com/assets/la_primera_abogada-mexicana_un_acercamiento-a-su-biograf%C3%ADa.pdf.

Lizardi Tort, S. (2022). *Algunas consideraciones sobre la enseñanza y el aprendizaje del derecho*, Centro de Estudios Sobre la Enseñanza y el Aprendizaje, A.C.

Lloyd, M. and Hernández Fierro, V. (2021). 'Los egresados de la primera universidad indígena en México. Entre utopías, retos y realidades del mercado laboral', Perfiles educativos, 43(173).

Pérez Hurtado, L.F. and Rivera Villegas, H. (2022). 'Panorama de la educación jurídica mexicana', *Revista Pedagogía Universitaria y Didáctica Del Derecho*, 9(2), available at https://pedagogiaderecho.uchile.cl/index.php/RPUD/article/view/69235/72057.

68. Regulation of legal education in Mexico

Introduction

Mexico, a federal country with a population of 126,014,024 people (INEGI [2020]), is probably one of the countries with the most law schools in the world. According to data collected by the Centro de Estudios sobre la Enseñanza y el Aprendizaje del Derecho (CEEAD) in the 2022–2023 academic cycle there were 2,553 Higher Education Institutions authorised to offer a Bachelor of law degree (LLB) programme. Of those, 2,119 offered a law degree programme in practice. It is important to note that some Higher Education Institutions offer two or more law degree programmes. For example, in the same academic year an institution can offer an online degree programme while at the same time offering an in-person programme. During the academic cycle 2022–2023, 3,440 law degree programmes were offered. On average, during this academic cycle, one law school was opened each month. According to CEEAD 90 per cent of Mexican Law Schools are private (CEEAD [2023]). Probably, this high number of law schools and law degree programmes is due to a very loose and relaxed regulation of legal education and legal profession partnered with a fragmented and confusing control of access to the legal profession.

The Mexican constitution allows each of the 32 states to decide which professions require a professional licence to practice. All 32 states require a licence in order to practice law. In order to become an authorised law practitioner in México, a person must complete an undergraduate degree in law offered by an Institution of Higher Education which has to be part of the National Education System. According to Pérez Hurtado, there are three common requirements in law schools which must be met in order to obtain an academic title. The most common one is the 'option zero' which basically consists of passing all the courses and doing the social service mandated by law. The second one is the passing of the 'General Undergraduate Exit Exam' which started operating in 2000. This is a standardised exam, not officially required, that evaluates the knowledge, skills and attitudes that a law graduate needs to begin a professional career. The third require-ment consists of proving, before the educational institution, that the person has worked, for at least five years, on law related issues (Pérez Hurtado [2009]).

Once a person receives the academic title, they must register it with the General Directorate of Professions (Dirección General de Profesiones) in order to receive their professional card, which will state the exact academic title that the person was granted. As recently as 2022 there was no Bar exam or any other entry requirements for entry to the legal professions, although there are other mechanisms that indirectly influence the regulation of the profession, such as the Bar Associations through their regulatory and disciplinary responsibilities for the profession.

Holding a professional card is not an assurance that a person will be allowed to litigate before a court or judge. Judges decide, based on the professional card, whether its holder has the competencies and the right to litigate before their court. This is important since, in México, law degrees are not mandated to have a single and unique name (such as 'Licenciatura en Derecho' – Attorney at law) neither are law schools mandated by law to teach a specific set of minimum contents (such as constitutional law, contracts, criminal law, etc). In the 2022–2023 academic cycle, for example, 90 per cent of LLB's were offered under the name 'Licenciatura en Derecho'. The remaining 10 per cent were offered under different names such as 'Licenciado en derecho indígena', 'Licenciado en Derecho Fiscal' (Attorney at law on indigenous law and Attorney at law on tax law) (CEEAD [2023]). This means that it could be the case that a judge from a Criminal Court would have to decide whether a lawyer in front of him with a professional card stating that he is a 'Licenciado en derecho laboral' (Attorney at law on labour law) would have the right to litigate before his court. In short, this means that access to the legal profession is controlled in part by the executive branch, which administers the National Education System and decides which law schools are part of it; in part by law schools which determine the contents of legal education and the mechanisms to decide when and how to grant an academic title, and in part by each judge individually.

There is, however, an exception to the process described above. A person can also obtain a professional card by demonstrating their competencies in law before an authorised evaluating institution without completing an LLB. These competencies could be acquired either by professional experience or by being self-taught. The executive branch oversees this process. However, it is quite infrequent to hear of lawyers who have obtained their professional card via this process.

As stated above, there are no regulations regarding legal education in Mexico. Public and private law schools can freely design their law programmes without any legal norm establishing the minimum contents to be taught or the methodologies to be used. However, curricula across law schools are in fact quite homogenous and most programmes include 50 to 70 mandatory courses (Pérez Hurtado [2009]). Mexican legal education has been criticised with regards to its content for being too encyclopaedic, doctrinal and removed from real world practice. With regards to its pedagogy it has been criticised for being too lecture-centred, authoritarian and relying on rote-learning (Madrazo [2006]).

As with degrees in other disciplines, the opening and operation of law schools and law degrees is regulated by the General Law on Education (Ley General de Educación) and the Law for the Coordination of Higher Education (Ley para la Coordinación de la Educación Superior). According to the General Law on Education, only educational institutions that are part of the National Educational System are authorised by the State to grant academic degrees valid among the Mexican Republic. Public Institutions of Higher Education are automatically, and from their inception, part of the National Education System. On the other hand private institutions of higher education require a Recognition of Official Validity of Studies (Reconocimiento de Validez Oficial de Estudios) or incorporation into a Public Institution of Higher Education in order to become part of the National Education System. The academic and administrative autonomy that an institution of higher education has, depends in large part on whether it is public or private. If the institution is private, its autonomy will also depend on whether it was incorporated into a public institution or (if it obtained a Recognition) which type of Recognition.

Public institutions

From their inception, public institutions of higher education are part of the National Education System regulated by the General Law on Education and the Law for the Coordination of Higher Education. They are regulated by the Higher Education Secretary (SEP) and the Education Secretaries of each federal entity. Development and promotion actions are carried out within the framework of respect for university autonomy that is guaranteed by the Constitution (Article 3 of the Political Constitution of the United Mexican States summarises the educational purposes of education). There are different public institutions depending on the type of relationship they have with the federal or state administration. Article 29 of the General Law in Higher Education speaks of: (a) Federal Public University, (b) State Public University, (c) State Public University with Solidarity Support, (d) Intercultural University.

Thus, there are law schools that are created by the federal government and others created by state governments. Also there are Intercultural Universities, which are public higher institutions characterised by their ethnic, cultural and linguistic relevance. These universities seek to provide opportunities to populations of diverse cultural origin. According to CEEAD´s data, in the academic year 2022–2023 there were 2,119 Law school offering a degree in law. 199 of these were public law schools and 1920 were private schools. Although only 9.4 per cent of the total were public law schools, they contained the largest number of students (CEEAD [2023]).

Private institutions

The Recognition of Official Validity of Studies (Reconocimiento de Validez Oficial de Estudios also known as RVOE) is an administrative act which recognises that the programme offered by a private institution (either at the undergraduate or postgraduate level) satisfies the minimum requirements of the National Law of Education and therefore is part of the National Education System which implies that the titled granted by the institution will be valid for obtaining a professional card.

State authorities authorised to grant a Recognition are: (a) the federal government (by this meaning the President of the Mexican Republic); (b) the federal government via the Secretary of Education; (c) the state authorities via their Secretaries of Education but only with regards to the institutions of higher education operating in their territories.

A Recognition granted by the Federal Government allows a Private Higher Education Institution to freely create and design as many educational programmes (at undergraduate or postgraduate level) as it wants. In order to offer them the Institution only requires an authorisation from the Secretary of Education. According to Pérez Hurtado, very few institutions have obtained recognition from the Federal Government. In these cases, the reputation and economic solvency of the institution have been relevant factors influencing the decision of the executive to grant this recognition (Pérez Hurtado [2009]). On the other hand, recognitions granted by the federal or State Secretaries of Education, only authorise the operation of a specific educational programme. This means that a private Higher Education Institution will need a Recognition for each undergraduate and postgraduate degree it intends to offer. Federal and State Secretaries of Education grant or deny Recognitions based on three factors: (a) the structure and contents of the educational programme; (b) the security and functionality of the physical infrastructure of the institution; (c) the quality of the professors and academic personnel. However, each institution establishes its own requirements to obtain its academic title (i.e., whether it will require a thesis, final exams, clinical programmes, etc).

Incorporation

Incorporations can be granted by public universities of the federal or state levels which are authorised by the law that created them to do so. An incorporation occurs when a public institution recognises that the educational plan of a private institution follows the same plans, programmes and methodologies as it does itself.

There are different types of incorporations. If it is carried out by a federal public university, the regulations apply throughout the federal territory. A clear example is the private law schools incorporated into UNAM (National Autonomous University of México) which indicates that the degrees awarded by those private schools are endorsed by a prestigious university. However, if the incorporation is done by a state public university, it can only incorporate a private school within its own state.

In both types of incorporation, this indicates that the private institutions will be supervised, academically and administratively, by the public institution. In other words, this means that the private institution becomes an extension of the public institution offering exactly the same educational model and requirements for obtaining the academic title. It is important to remember that all RVOE (federal or state) and incorporations correspond only to private law schools. However, executive power decrees can be granted by both types of institution, public or private.

According to CEEAD's data, for the academic cycle 2022–2023, there were 3,440 programmes authorised to offer legal education. There were 2,506 'active' programmes, meaning that they had students enrolled on the course. In the academic cycle 2022–2023 active legal education programmes obtained authorisation to offer university studies as follows:

- 1,181 programmes were authorised through a federal RVOE;
- 962 programmes were authorised through a state RVOE;
- 82 programmes were incorporated into a public university, of which 38 are incorporated into UNAM;
- 281 programmes were authorised through a decree (73 are private programmes and 208 public).

Conclusion

This entry has looked at the intricate landscape of legal education in Mexico, a country with an extensive array of law schools, where on average one new programme per month is established. The 2022–2023 academic cycle witnessed 2,553 Higher Education Institutions offering a Bachelor of Law degree, with a staggering 90 per cent being private institutions. This proliferation of law schools is accompanied by a lack of regulatory oversight on legal education contents and methodologies.

Mariana Anahí Manzo and Sergio Iván Anzola-Rodríguez

References

CEEAD. (2022–2023). Las escuelas de Derecho en México Instituciones de Educación Superior (IES) que ofrecen la Licenciatura en Derecho (LED), Ciclo académico, available at https://

ceead.org.mx/como-transformamos/biblioteca -digital.

Fernando Pérez Hurtado, L. (2009). 'La Futura Generación de Abogados Mexicanos', Instituto de Investigaciones Jurídicas de la UNAM & CEEAD.

INEGI. (2020). 'Censo de Población y Vivienda', available at https://www.inegi.org.mx/programas/ ccpv/2020/.

Madrazo, A. (2006), '¿Qué?, ¿Cómo? y ¿Para qué? análisis y crítica al modelo tradicional de enseñanza del Derecho en México', Academia: revista sobre enseñanza del derecho de Buenos Aires, available at http://www.derecho.uba.ar/ publicaciones/rev_academia/revistas/07/que -como-y-para-que-analisis-y-critica-al-modelo -tradicional-de-ensenanza-del-derecho-en -mexico.pdf.

69. Mooting and legal education

The verb to moot means 'to suggest something for discussion' (Cambridge Dictionary).

In a legal educational context a moot is a fictitious and hypothetical court case where two competing parties appear before a judge to argue opposing points. The case is often an appeal against an original decision previously made in a lower court. Each party will put forward their argument, either that the final decision was correct and should be upheld or that it was incorrect and should be reversed. The judge then decides the winning party based upon their arguments. The winning party does not necessarily need to win the case legally but will be the party who presents their arguments most persuasively (Lynch [1996]).

The parties to the moot are given their roles in advance. In, for example a criminal appeal case, the parties are allocated a role to argue for the 'appellant' who is bringing the appeal or the 'respondent' who is defending the appeal in the hypothetical case.

The parties to a moot are referred to as 'counsel'. Often there are two counsel for each role, they are known as the 'lead counsel' and the 'junior counsel'.

A moot aims to simulate a court hearing as closely as possible so the parties usually dress formally, often in black court robes. Counsel will stand as the judge enters the room to replicate a court room and will wait until the judge directs them to sit down. There is a strict etiquette in a moot and parties should be polite and respectful throughout the case. All parties will use formal language to address each other, for example in a Court of Appeal case the judge should be addressed as 'my Lord/my Lordship' or 'my Lady/my Ladyship' and each party will stand up when addressing the judge. Counsel will refer to each other as 'my learned friend'. It is important to correctly and consistently use these formalities throughout the moot.

In advance of the moot the parties are provided with instructions, which will include a set of facts setting out a legal issue, usually known as the scenario. It can relate to any area of law, often in an unsettled area or where there have been new developments and whilst the case itself is fictitious and hypothetical it may be similar to reported cases and may include references to and citations for actual reported cases.

In preparation for the moot the parties need to be clear on the points of law in question that they will be arguing. As it is usually an appeal there will be no questions on evidence or fact as they have already been determined by the lower courts. The parties will need to first read and consider the cases referred to in the scenario which will aid them with existing principles, statutes and judgments to develop their legal arguments. They may also research other relevant authorities to aid them in preparing the legal arguments that they will submit. These submissions form the basis of the oral arguments they will present in the moot itself. There are usually two points of appeal and where there is a lead counsel and a junior counsel they will decide between themselves as to which point they will each argue. It is good preparation to consider what arguments the other party will raise so that such arguments can be pre-empted or argued against.

Depending on the type of moot, the parties may be required to draft a skeleton argument. This is a written document setting out the arguments each party will raise and the materials and cases, fully referenced, which will be referred to in the oral submissions. Skeleton arguments are similarly used in actual court cases. The skeleton argument will be given to, or as it is known, served on the judge and the other parties in advance of the moot. This enables the parties to consider the opposing arguments and be prepared to argue against them, known as rebutting, during the moot itself. The skeleton argument will be referred to during the moot. Template skeleton arguments are widely available.

The parties will also prepare a bundle in advance of the moot. This is the cases and materials they are going to rely on in their arguments and which were referred to in the skeleton argument. There are also template bundles widely available as a well-ordered bundle with a contents page, pagination, clearly marked sections and tabs will be well received by a judge. During the moot anything that is quoted by a party should be contained in the bundle so that the judge can follow it themselves. It is common to highlight specific parts of a judgment for example to aid the judge in finding the relevant text, although the party should also be able to direct the judge to the correct page and section of text. There can be strict rules on how a bundle should be presented so it is essential to check this information.

There is an established order for a moot, the lead counsel will speak first to present their argument in relation to the first point of appeal. They will usually speak for longer than the junior counsel who will speak second and argue the second point of appeal. The terms lead and junior do not indicate the experience of the parties, nor necessarily the importance of the points being argued. The traditional order of speaking in a moot is that the lead counsel for the appellant begins and will introduce the case and the parties before presenting their argument. They are then followed by the junior counsel for the appellant. Next to speak will be the lead counsel for the respondent followed by the junior counsel for the respondent. The lead counsel for the appellant then has a short amount of time for a rebuttal.

The formal language continues as each counsel begins their oral argument which is their submission. Once the counsel has introduced themselves and reminded the judge of their role, a common opening phrase in the UK is 'If it pleases my Lord/my Lordship, I will now begin with my submission'.

During their submission the counsel will refer to the relevant cases they have researched and are using to support their points. When first referring to a case the full name and citation should be used. There is a convention that when doing this the counsel will ask whether or not the judge needs the case information, again this is done formally and a common phrase to ask in the UK is 'Does my Lady/my Ladyship need a brief summary of the facts of the case?'. Thereafter the case name alone can be used.

There is usually a strict timescale for the moot and where there is a lead and junior counsel they will divide their overall time between themselves. It is usual for the judge to ask questions of counsel during their submissions which counsel are expected to be able to answer, using the correct formalities and still keep to their allocated time.

Some moots may have a clerk who is responsible for assisting the judge with note taking, ensuring that the parties keep to time and the general running of the moot.

Mooting is an excellent activity for law students and any other students considering a career in the law to get involved in as it develops and demonstrates a wide skill set (Thomas and Cradduck [2013]) [Professional Legal Education]. Some of the skills a student can gain through mooting are:

- Legal research, in preparing for the moot students will undertake legal research which will require finding and then close reading of cases.
- Critical analysis, as students must carefully analyse points of law from the relevant cases and then apply those to the scenario in question to develop a legal argument in support of the role.
- Assimilating information with context, students will assimilate the facts of the scenario and relevant cases to establish succinct points and develop legal arguments which puts the legal issues into a wider real-world context.
- Drafting, students will be required to correctly draft their skeleton argument using cases and statutes to support their arguments which will be advanced in the oral submissions.
- Presenting a legal argument, in delivering their submissions students will have to present the legal arguments they have developed in an appropriate and accessible audible manner.
- Advocacy and public speaking, the students must deliver their oral submissions by speaking at an appropriate pace, tone and volume whilst maintaining eye contact with the judge. In addition, the students must interact with the judge and other parties appropriately and with the correct etiquette.
- Organisation and time management, many students carry out moots as an extra curricula activity requiring them to manage their academic studies and other time commitments around the time required for the moot. They must also demonstrate time management during the moot itself.
- Teamwork, most moots will have a lead and junior counsel which requires the students to work together.

There are widely accepted common errors to avoid whilst mooting such as never speaking whilst the judge is speaking or interrupting the judge and avoiding reading from script.

Most UK Law Schools will offer the opportunity to be involved with mooting, many will have a mooting society and may hold internal mooting competitions. In England, the four Inns of Court hold mooting competitions or have mooting societies and there are numerous national and international competitions students can take part in, for example, the Commonwealth Legal Education Association's annual Commonwealth Moot.

Participating in a variety of competitions gives students a broad experience and the opportunity to practice and hone their skills which in addition to helping their academic studies are also transferable skills which can be employed beyond the traditional legal professions.

KATE CAMPBELL-PILLING AND KATIE STEINER

References

Cambridge Dictionary, available at: https://dictionary.cambridge.org/dictionary/english/moot.

Lynch, A. (1996). 'Why Do We Moot – Exploring the Role of Mooting in Legal Education', *Legal Educ. Rev.*, 7, p. 67.

Thomas, M. and Cradduck, L. (2013). 'The art of mooting: mooting and the cognitive domain', *International Journal of the Legal Profession*, 20(2), p. 223.

70. Negotiation and legal education

Negotiation: 'an interpersonal decision-making process necessary whenever we cannot achieve our objectives single-handedly'. (Thompson [2015])

Negotiation in legal education is the process of teaching law students the skills and strategies needed to effectively negotiate in various legal contexts. This includes understanding negotiation theory, practicing effective communication, problem-solving, and conflict resolution skills, as well as learning how to advocate for a client's interests while also seeking mutually beneficial solutions. Many law schools offer courses or workshops specifically focused on negotiations to help students develop these important skills.

Traditionally, law school curriculums have focused heavily on legal theory and case analysis. The legal profession today demands more than just a mastery of the law. By equipping graduates with strong negotiation skills, law schools are preparing them for the realities of the modern legal profession and empowering them to be successful advocates for their clients.

Legal education integrates negotiation skills into the law school curriculum in various ways. Negotiation skills can be offered through specific courses where students learn about negotiation theory, strategies, and gain practical techniques through role-playing and simulated negotiations. (Strevens, Grimes and Phillips [2014])

An increasing number of law schools have clinical legal education courses where students work with real clients under the supervision of experienced lawyers. These courses often involve negotiating on behalf of clients in various legal matters. Negotiation skills training will have been provided as part of the clinical course to prepare students fully for the client facing role.

Another way in which students can gain negotiation skills is for them to undertake internships or externships at law firms, law centres, charities, or other government and non-governmental agencies where they can observe and participate in negotiations first-hand under the guidance of legal professionals.

In some instances, instead of or in addition to standalone courses, law schools often invite practitioners and negotiation experts to conduct workshops or seminars on negotiation skills, providing students with practical insights and real-world examples.

Student negotiation competitions also play a vital role in supplementing legal education in the UK and internationally. These have become very popular throughout law schools and consist of simulated scenarios which require teams from each law school to negotiate on behalf of their 'client'. Competitions offer law students a valuable platform to practice their skills in a dynamic and competitive environment. They are offered at university, national and international levels. For example, winners of national university law school competitions will represent their country at the International Negotiation Competition (INC) which provides a truly global platform for students to test their skills and network with peers from diverse legal backgrounds (https://law-competitions.com/).

Law schools typically equip students with a variety of negotiation styles, allowing them to adapt their approach based on the situation and the other party. The common negotiation styles encountered in legal education include:

1. Competitive (positional) negotiation

This is the classic 'win-lose' approach. Negotiators take a firm stance on their initial position and fight for the best possible outcome for their side, often using concessions as leverage.

2. Collaborative (interest-based) negotiation

This approach focuses on identifying and understanding the underlying interests of both parties. Negotiators work together to find creative solutions that satisfy both parties' needs.

3. Integrative negotiation

Negotiators brainstorm solutions that benefit both sides and might involve concessions or trade-offs.

4. Principled negotiation

Where fairness, ethics, and long-term relationships are emphasised. Here, negotiators focus on using objective criteria and building trust while still advocating for their client's interests. (Fisher, Ury and Patton [1991])

5.   Concession negotiation

This style involves a strategic use of concessions to build rapport and move the negotiation forward. Negotiators offer something of value in exchange for concessions from the other side.

In addition to these core styles, some law schools might delve into more specific approaches, such as 'Hardball Negotiation' which is an aggressive form of competitive negotiation, often used when there's little trust or time, and 'Soft Negotiation' where a more cooperative style that prioritises building rapport and finding common ground is suggested.

The styles and terms may differ, but what is key is that law schools don't advocate for a single 'best' style. Instead, they equip students with a diverse and versatile range of styles and teach them how to choose the most appropriate approach for a given situation.

Regulatory authorities can also play a vital role in how negotiation skills are taught and tested in legal education. For example, England, Wales and Scotland are all part of the United Kingdom (UK), but Scotland has a separate legal system and regulatory body to that of England and Wales.

There is a distinction to be made between England and Wales which follows the Solicitors Qualifying Examination (SQE) for legal education and Scotland whose legal education is regulated by the Law Society of Scotland (LSS).

The SQE, introduced in 2021 for aspiring solicitors in England and Wales does not explicitly test negotiation skills. However, there is a strong connection between the SQE's requirements and the importance of negotiation skills in legal education.

While negotiation isn't directly tested, the skills assessed in SQE2, like legal research, client interviewing, and advocacy, all have a strong foundation in negotiation. (Solicitors Regulation Authority [2023]) The SQE encourages a client-centred approach, which is crucial for effective negotiation. The theory is that lawyers who understand their clients' needs and goals can negotiate more effectively on their behalf.

While the SQE doesn't directly test negotiation skills, the emphasis on practical skills

and a client-centred approach aligns with the importance of negotiation in legal practice. Law schools are bridging the gap by offering dedicated courses, simulations, and integrating negotiation principles into other subjects, ensuring graduates are well-equipped to negotiate effectively in their future careers.

The LSS does have a single, official statement outlining a specific stance on negotiation skills in legal education for aspiring solicitors in Scotland. The value of negotiation skills is set out in the outcomes for PEAT (Professional Education and Training), which is the mandatory qualification for aspiring solicitors in Scotland and set by the LSS. The PEAT guidelines [2023] explicitly mention negotiation skills, with outcomes for PEAT 1 alignment with core negotiation competencies. These outcomes include understanding different approaches to the theory of legal negotiation including facilitated negotiation and communicating with a client throughout a negotiation. Similar to the SQE in England and Wales, aspiring solicitors following the PEAT 1 standards will abide by ethical standards and negotiate according to practice conventions of at least one area of law.

The importance of negotiation skills in UK legal education is clear, and internationally there are similarities and differences.

Similar to the UK, legal education systems around the world are increasingly recognising the importance of negotiation skills. Law schools such as Harvard University in the US and the University of Melbourne, Australia have incorporated dedicated negotiation courses and simulations into their curriculums. The client-centred approach to negotiation is a global trend with law schools worldwide emphasising how negotiation skills allow lawyers to better understand and advocate for their clients' needs.

That said, certain countries might have an emphasis on specific negotiation styles. For example, the US legal education system might place a greater focus on positional negotiation, while some European countries might emphasise a more collaborative approach. The ability to negotiate across borders is becoming increasingly important and more law schools are offering specific courses or modules that focus on international negotiation.

The UK's emphasis on negotiation skills is a positive step towards preparing lawyers for the demands of the modern profession, and by fostering a broader understanding of negotiation in a global context, legal education in the UK as well as elsewhere can further empower graduates to navigate the complexities of the international legal world.

REBECCA SAMARAS

References

Fisher, R., Ury, W. and Patton, B. (1991). *Getting to Yes: Negotiating Agreement Without Giving In*, Penguin Books.

Law Society of Scotland. (2023). *Professional Diploma in Legal Education*, available at Diploma in Professional Legal Practice | Law Society of Scotland (lawscot.org.uk).

Solicitors Regulation Authority. (2023). *SQE 2 Assessment Specification*, available at https://sqe.sra.org.uk/exam-arrangements/assessment-information/sqe2-assessment-specification#Practice%20Areas.

Strevens, C., Grimes, R. and Phillips, E. (2014). *Legal Education: Simulation in Theory and Practice*, Ashgate.

Thompson, L.L. (2015). *The Mind and Heart of the Negotiator*, Pearson.

71. Neurodiversity and legal education

Language

Language that defines, describes, and explains the experience of neurodivergent individuals rests with the individuals. Whilst it may not be possible to get the use of language right, it is important to seek to do so.

In this entry, reference is made to neurodiversity, neurodivergence, neurodivergent, and neurotypical. The medical diagnostic term is used when referring to specific examples of neurodivergence. However, the use of such terms is often debated and sometimes rejected due to a focus on deficits and impairments. The description of particular deficits and impairments explored below should in no way detract from the numerous strengths of neurodivergent individuals.

Introduction

The entry seeks to advance the development of knowledge on neurodivergence in legal education by noting frequently used terms; setting out examples of neurodivergence; considering common challenges experienced by those that are neurodivergent, identified as executive functioning impairments; and offering some limited comments on the barriers that executive functioning impairments may present within law schools.

In the UK context, the Quality Assurance Agency for Higher Education (QAA) was established in response to independent recommendations that higher education providers improve widening participation for underrepresented groups, including disabled students (Abbott-Jones [2022] at 34–36).

A revised Benchmark Statement for Law (Benchmark Statement) published in 2023, provides some guidance on how accessibility may be achieved for the neurodivergent law student as members of the disabled community in higher education. To realise inclusivity, the Benchmark Statement calls on providers to understand and respond to the multiple disabled identities and disabilities found in the law school (QAA [2023] at para 1.11). Inclusivity lies in a design, delivery and assessment of the law curriculum and law school environments which embraces neurological diversity (QAA [2023] at paras 1.9–1.11 and 3.6).

Frequently encountered terms

Neurodiversity as a term captures the sheer diversity of human neuro-types. Neuro-types can be understood as the collection of cognitive abilities and cognitive functions possessed by a person to varying degrees. In this sense everyone is neurodiverse. However, not all humans are neurotypical, some are neurodivergent.

Neurotypical, also referred to as the predominant neuro-type (Marshall [2023] at 16), encompasses those with 'typical' cognitive abilities and cognitive functions. It is perceived that the majority of the population are neurotypical (Marshall [2023] at 16).

Neurodivergent represents the perceived minority whose neuro-type diverges significantly from the 'typical'. The neurodivergence is usually present from birth and is largely genetic and innate (e.g., dyslexia) but it can also be acquired as a result of subsequent events (e.g., a stroke) (Marshall [2023] at 14). Those falling within the minority may elect to use the term neurodivergent to refer to their neuro-type but may also be referred to as the minority neuro-type.

Another commonly encountered term is Specific Learning Differences (SpLD). The term is used to collectively refer to the associated learning differences (also referred to as difficulties) associated with neurodivergence (British Dyslexia Association et al [2018] at 2–3). The term focuses on the experience, challenges and corresponding needs, of neurodivergent students when it comes to learning.

Examples of neurodivergence

There is a wide range of neuro-types recognised under neurodivergence, what follows is a brief overview of commonly occurring neurodivergence: Autism Spectrum Disorder (ASD), Attention Deficit Hyperactivity Disorder (ADHD), dyslexia, and dyspraxia.

There are some common points.

First, as evident from the examples below, definitions of neurodivergence are linked to medical diagnostics which focus on deficits and symptoms, which cause significant impairments in several domains (e.g., social, occupation, education), whilst making no inherent statements as to strengths and abilities, including cognitive abilities (Attwood [2007] at p 241; Brown [2013] at 71–72).

Strengths may include: Autistic Spectrum Disorder – reliability, persistence, attention to detail, accuracy, integrity and honesty, logical thinking, deep knowledge on specific areas, original problem solving (Attwood [2007] at 307); Attention Deficit Hyperactivity Disorder – creative, resourceful, willing to explore alternative options, outcomes and solutions, strong sense of justice, enthusiasm (British Dyslexia Association et al [2018] 22); Dyslexia – spatial reasoning including spatial perspectives, lateral and holistic thinkers in terms of strategies and problem solving, highly motivated and determined, creative, good verbal communication skills, deeper empathy (British Dyslexia Association et al [2018] at 6; Abbott-Jones [2022] at 171–176); Dyspraxia – creative, deeper empathy, determined, loyal, attention to detail, lateral and strategic thinking (British Dyslexia Association et al [2018] at 9).

Second, there are significant overlaps and co-occurrence rates between different types of neurodivergence (British Dyslexia Association et al [2018] at 1 (diagram: common issues); Brown [2013] at 130–131; Bignell [2018] at 97).

Third, no two individuals' neurodivergence will present in the same way: neurodivergence is not linear, moving from mild to severe, but is a continuum. However, it is possible to focus on shared strengths and difficulties across neurodivergent students.

Finally, therefore, definitions and examples are inherently limited resulting in a confusing number of terms (e.g., Autism, Autistic Disorder, Asperger's Syndrome, High and Low Functioning Autism) (Bignell [2018] at 3).

Autism Spectrum Disorder

ASD captures a 'quadrad of impairments', namely: (i) social interaction deficits; (ii) verbal and non-verbal communication deficits; (iii) social imagination deficits – the existence of restrictive, repetitive, and stereotyped patterns of behaviours; and (iv) hyper or hypo reactivity to sensory input (Bignell [2018] at 31–32; Attwood [2007] at 15–16).

Attention Deficit Hyperactivity Disorder

ADHD (also referred to as Attention Deficit Disorder) is increasingly understood as a chronic developmental neurological and executive functioning impairments, rather than a behavioural impairment (Bignell [2018] at 11; Brown [2013] at 180; also Brown [2022] at 135–136).

Diagnostically, ADHD is defined via symptoms clustered around difficulties or differences in attention, hyperactivity, and impulse control (Bignell [2018] at 10 and 77). The prevalence of symptoms will determine whether an individual is characterised as hyperactive-impulsive type, inattentive type, or combined type (Bignell [2018] at 10).

Dyslexia

Dyslexia is characterised by impaired accurate and fluent word reading and spelling. Difficulties may also be experienced in organisation, phonological awareness, verbal memory and verbal processing speed (Abbott-Jones [2022] at 7; British Dyslexia Association et al [2018] at 4–6).

Dyspraxia

Dyspraxia is recognised primarily as a developmental coordination disorder impacting fine and/or gross motor coordination. Other significant impairments include poor planning, organising and the sequencing of ideas and writing activities (British Dyslexia Association et al [2018] at pp 8–9; Moody [2007] at 136).

Executive functioning: a common challenge

Executive functions (also cognitive functions or cognitive actions in the literature) collectively describes the aspects of the self-management system of the human brain. Executive functions typically work together, in different combinations, at speed and without conscious thought, with proficiency gradually developing from early school years through to late adolescence and early adulthood (Brown [2022] at 135 and 137; Abbott-Jones [2022] at 50).

These executive functions are responsible for the level of cognition inherent in a law student's ability to independently manage themselves: to get going on academic tasks (activation i.e., organising, prioritising, planning, and time-management); to manage their focus and attention to keep going on academic tasks (focus i.e., focusing, sustaining, shifting, controlling attention to tasks); and to ultimately complete academic tasks by getting the tasks done (action i.e., monitoring and regulating inhibition and impulse control, self-reflection, using new strategies) (Abbott-Jones [2022] at 50; Attwood [2007] at 246; Brown [2022] at 136).

To engage the executive functions relating to activation, focus and action, to complete academic tasks, a law student needs to engage further executive functions relating to: processing (i.e., regulating alertness, managing energy, and processing speeds, including understanding complex and abstract concepts); memory (i.e., utilising working memory and accessing information recall); and emotion regulation. These functions play essential roles in getting going, keeping going, and completing academic tasks (Abbott-Jones [2022] at 50; Attwood [2007] at 246; Brown [2022] at 136).

Chronic and significant impairments in executive functioning are a common occurrence across ASD, ADHD, dyslexia, and dyspraxia (British Dyslexia Association et al [2018] at 1 (diagram: common issues)). These impairments cause extreme difficulties in the executive functioning (as illustrated below), which adversely impacts outcomes across social, occupational, and educational domains. The impairments experienced by neurodivergent individuals, however, are not necessarily reflective of skills, will power, motivation or intellectual ability limitations (Brown [2022] at 149). Research shows that executive functioning impairments in neurodivergent individuals becomes more apparent and has greater adverse impact as they transition through educational stages (Attwood [2007] at 247; Brown [2022] at 136; Brown [2013] at 6, and 29–30). Furthermore, misalignments between executive functioning impairments and expectations may cause external and internal criticism for the neurodivergent individual (Attwood [2007] at 247). This can in turn result in the adoption of maladaptive coping strategies in an attempt to overcome the impairments (e.g., perfectionism and overworking) (Abbott-Jones [2022] at 168).

Executive functioning impairments and the Benchmark Statement threshold levels

Executive functioning impairments for every neurodivergent student will be unique to them. The impairments experienced by neurodivergent law students, when compared to the neurotypical law student, will present challenges to engaging in the academic tasks required by a law degree and the acquisition of skills and qualities of mind expected by threshold standards, such as the Subject Benchmark in the UK, the Council of Australian Law Dean's Bachelor of Laws Academic Standards [2010] in Australia and the requirements developed by US law schools in adherence to the American Bar Association's *Standards and Rules of Procedure for Approval of Law Schools* (2023/24). Such standards are often transposed into assessment criteria, consequently impacting grades and degree classifications.

Below are a limited number of hypothetical examples that illustrate a snapshot of some of the challenges.

1. 'Synthesise information from a number of primary and secondary legal sources to appreciate their relative value and to achieve knowledge and understanding of complex legal issues.' (QAA [2023] at para 4.3)

Student A (SA) has attended all of the lectures and made extra independently researched notes in a determination to have a perfect understanding of the topic. SA, now daunted by the amount of information acquired, looks through the notes, rereading over again. SA is attempting to synthesise their notes ready for use in an assignment. SA's mind goes blank, this frustrates SA. In response, despite working for many hours, SA neglects to take a break.

Despite the student's significant motivation, the difficulties in synthesising knowledge could be attributed to impairments in the following executive functions: focus – the shifting of attention and focus between the different sources of information and transitioning between work and rest; processing – processing speeds and understanding complex and abstract tasks and information; and memory – utilising working memory to access, recall, and synthesise information. Difficulties in emotion regulation may be engaged and in response common maladaptive coping strategies are deployed – overworking and perfectionism (Abbott-Jones [2022] at 168).

2. 'Apply legal knowledge to problem scenarios and draw reasoned conclusions supported by legal authority.' (QAA [2023] at para 4.3)

Student B (SB), struggling to organise and plan their study time, has yet to start answering a problem question for an imminent seminar. SB's reading of the facts is laboured. SB is interrupted. SB sits for a significant period of time unable to regain focus. Once focus is regained, SB looks back at the problem question and struggles to apply their knowledge of the topic to the facts. SB leaves the workspace and the problem question remains unanswered.

The student's difficulties may be linked to the executive function impairments: activation – organising, planning, time management, and generally getting going on the academic tasks; focus – sustaining and controlling attention; memory – retaining recently obtained information in working memory for recall purposes; and action – self monitoring and regulating impulse control to navigate distraction and ultimately get the task done. Slow and laboured processing speeds results in a need to spend additional time on a task. Barriers are, therefore, created to applying knowledge, which are compounded by further activation and processing difficulties relating to the organising and prioritising of complex concepts.

3. 'Communicate effectively and appropriately verbally and/or non-verbally.' (QAA [2023] at para 4.4)

Student C (SC), as part of an assessed presentation, is asked a question by the tutor. SC struggles to articulate the vast knowledge in their head. SC starts to answer the question but is conscious of their disjointed speech and the uncomfortable pauses and stumbles that occur. Feedback raised areas for improvement in communication – addressing inadequate clarity in speech, poor eye contact and
fidgeting. SC is discouraged and does not seek further support.

Perceived limitations in the student's communication may be a result of executive functioning impairments: processing – particularly difficulties with processing speeds means the student takes longer to formulate an answer and the sequencing of the answer may be disjointed; memory – using working memory to recall and respond to the question is inhibited; and emotion regulation – to recognise and modulate the range of emotions felt in the circumstances. Further, a neurodivergent trait, a lack of eye contact, is being interpreted as a communication deficit: the trait is not within the control of the student. Moreover, actions such as fidgeting may be an attempt to modulate executive functioning impairments relating to focus, emotion, and action. Finally, neurodivergent students can be emotionally triggered by criticism in earlier education and, therefore, find it additionally challenging to modulate executive function impairments relating to emotions and action to engage with feedback (Abbott-Jones [2022] at 157).

Conclusion

Law school communities are places of abundant neurodiversity. Within that diversity, there will be a minority that are neurodivergent. To realise accessibility and inclusivity for the minority, a foundation of knowledge on neurodivergence should be built within law schools. In building this knowledge, it may appear that the experience of the neurodivergent community is so diverse that to respond is difficult. However, by focusing on common areas of challenge – such as executive functioning impairments and considering their interaction with relevant threshold standards – barriers may be addressed to permit neurodivergent students' strengths to flourish.

LUKE CAMPBELL AND GAYLE MCKEMEY

References

Abbott-Jones, A.T. (2022). *Dyslexia In Higher Education, Anxiety and Coping Skills*, Cambridge University Press.

American Bar Association. (2023/24). *Standards and Rules of Procedure for Approval of Law Schools*, available at https://www.americanbar

.org/groups/legal_education/resources/
standards/.

Attwood, T.A. (2015). *Complete Guide to Asperger's Syndrome*, 2nd edition, Jessica Kingsley Publishers.

Bignell, S. (2018). *Autism, Asperger's and ADHD: A Guide for Parents, Students, and Other Professionals*, MyChild Services Publishing.

British Dyslexia Association et al. (2018). 'Understanding Neurodiversity. A guide to Specific learning differences', 2nd edition, available at https://cdn.bdadyslexia.org.uk/uploads/documents/Dyslexia/A_Guide_to_SpLD_2nd_ed.pdf?v=1554931179.

Brown, T.E. (2013). *A New Understanding of ADHD in Children and Adults: Executive Function Impairments*, Routledge.

Brown, T.E. (2021). *ADHD and Asperger Syndrome in Smart Kids and Adults: Twelve Stories of Struggle, Support and Treatment*, Routledge.

Council of Australian Law Deans. (2010). *Learning and Teaching Academic Standards Project Bachelor of Laws Learning and Teaching Academic Standards Statement*, available at https://cald.asn.au/wp-content/uploads/2024/04/LLB-TLOsKiftetalLTASStandardsStatement2010-TLOs-LLB2.pdf.

Marshall, B. et al. (2023). 'You, Me and Neurodiversity', available at https://www.scci.org.uk/Data/About_Downloads/You,MeandNeurodiversityEbook.pdf?date=31/05/2023%2006:53:37.

Moody, S. (2007). *Dyslexia: Surviving and succeeding at college*, Routledge.

QAA Membership. (2023). 'Subject Benchmark Statement: Law', available at https://www.qaa.ac.uk/docs/qaa/sbs/sbs-law-23.pdf?sfvrsn=c271a881_6.

72. Nigeria (contemporary legal education)

Introduction

The idea underpinning legal education goes beyond law and an organised legal system (Woodward and Dalton [1990] at 130). Therefore, the role of legal education in the ordering of society cannot be overemphasised (Ndulo [2002] at 488), as the failure to institute an effective legal education system can result in the failure of the legal profession, with society as the ultimate victim (Solomon [2020] at 174). Indeed, legal education plays a critical role in society. Legal education ranks high in the Nigerian education system as it is among the most competitive fields of study due to the versatile career opportunities that the LLB degree provide.

It is usually the practice to link the aptitude of legal professionals to the quality of legal education. This is so even when it is uncertain that the competence of legal professionals necessarily flows from their legal training. Thus, the calls for reform of the legal education system as a necessary condition for an efficient legal profession in Nigeria is not misplaced, as the totality of legal education entails the orientation of aspirants to the legal profession to what lawyers do through teaching/learning for the development of knowledge, functional skills and values.

The legal education system

In Nigeria, the transition from the law office and English Inns systems of educating lawyers to the contemporary system of legal education can be traced to the Report of the Committee on the Future of the Nigerian Legal Profession 1959 (Unsworth Committee Report) (Nigeria (History of Legal Education)). The Unsworth Committee was set up by the federal government of Nigeria in April 1959 to examine the state of the legal profession in Nigeria and make recommendations to remedy the deficiencies, with particular regard to legal education and admission to practice law in Nigeria. The Nigerian government accepted many of the committee's recommendations, which constitute the foundation for the two-tier legal education system in Nigeria. The efficacy of the two-tier system has been interrogated in view of the changes in the legal profession, which have 'created a new context for legal education' (Oko [2021] at 134).

Law students who graduate from an accredited faculty of law are awarded an LLB degree after a successful completion of their academic legal studies, which take between four and five academic sessions. They are awarded professional qualifying certificates on passing the bar examination after completing at least one academic session of vocational legal training at the Nigerian Law School (NLS) with a formal residency arrangement for the bar examination. Nigeria's legal education system allows persons admitted to the Nigerian Bar to practice as barristers and solicitors. The fusion of the two aspects of the legal profession was borne out of the necessity to fill the gap created by the lack of qualified legal professionals during the early developments of legal education in Nigeria (Manteaw [2008] at 912–913). This feature of the Nigerian legal system was maintained by the Unsworth Committee Report ([1959] at para 12). The nucleus of Nigeria's legal education system is predicated on the principles of common law However, Islamic law is accommodated in the curriculum of some university faculties of law, particularly in northern Nigeria.

Beginning in the late-2000s, efforts have been made to move away from the application of traditional methods to clinical or experiential methods of teaching/learning in Nigerian faculties of law and the NLS. The advocacy for the application of clinical teaching/learning methods is championed by the Network of University Legal Aid Institutions (NULAI) Nigeria led by Professor Ernest Ojukwu (SAN), a leading advocate of clinical legal education. The challenge, however, lies in the sustainability of clinical approach in Nigerian universities.

Mandatory continuing legal education is another article of legal education in Nigeria, which responsibility is vested in the Council of Legal Education (CLE) (Legal Education Consolidation Act, section 3). This aspect of legal education has not been activated by the CLE since its inception. However, while the Nigerian Bar Association (NBA) through its Institute of CLE has taken up the mandatory legal education of legal practitioners (Rules of Professional Conduct for Legal Practitioners [2023] Rule 11), accredited faculties of law of Nigerian universities offer postgraduate programmes leading to the award of the LLM and PhD degrees, which are largely research-based.

Despite the poor funding of legal education in Nigeria, the number of persons seeking legal education keeps rising at an exponential rate. This puts enormous pressure on existing infrastructure of law faculties (particularly in public universities), resulting in overcrowded classrooms, insufficient library facilities, overworked law teachers and pitiable teacher-students ratio. Yet successive NUC accreditation reports do not reflect the true state of affairs in many public universities in Nigeria (Ibijola [2014] at 649), and law faculties in particular. While the CLE tries to improve the standard of legal education through a more objective and coordinated accreditation system, the problem remains unresolved primarily due to lack of institutional cooperation between the NUC and CLE (Nigeria (Regulation of Legal Education)).

The typical response from policymakers to the upsurge in the demand for legal education has been to establish new universities and law faculties. This has led to the quandary whereby the national and sub-national governments are unable to fund university/legal education. The National Open University of Nigeria (NOUN) (including its law programme) – conceived as an alternative to the traditional university system by offering university education with the aid of technology – has also not been spared the funding problem. Indeed, poor funding has serious negative impact on Nigeria's legal education, including concerns about the capacity (or the lack thereof) of law graduates to find their place in the legal profession.

The gap between expectation and reality

Nigeria's legal education seeks to equip law students to become functional legal professionals. However, as in many aspects of Nigerian society, there appears to be a failure to align the prospects and realities of legal education. Thus, and perhaps related to the funding issue, legal education in Nigeria is plagued by three major setbacks.

First, there are gaps in policy. While Nigeria's legal education policy emphasises the application of clinical or experiential teaching/learning methods in the training of law students (NUC [2009], NUC [2018] at 45, CLE [2009]), it fails to address a key issue of training and re-training of law teachers on how to teach. At a time when experiential teaching/learning methods trump the traditional methods, the issue as to why law teachers in Nigeria are not taught how to teach was recently voiced (Ojukwu [2023]). And since the transfer of skills is neither simple nor automatic (Kift [1997]), many law teachers in Nigeria still dictate notes in class due to lack of clinical or experiential teaching skills. In terms of learning, this method promotes the stenographic tendency in, and provides an inappropriate nurturing environment for, law students.

Also, despite a large student population, law teachers in Nigeria are paid the same salary as other university teachers. This is counter-productive and tends to push some law teachers into private law practice because of its higher earning potential. By and large, Nigerian public universities are unable to entice, with lucrative compensation packages, many highly suitable and qualified persons into legal academia or encourage those in legal academia to be fully committed to teaching and research.

Second, there is the failure to respond to changes regarding the application of technology in legal education to enable law students understand to 'how technology works to effectively engage with the legal issues' (Ryan and McFaul [2020] at 70). While the purpose of legal education is to inculcate legal knowledge, skills and values in law students, in this age of technology law students also need digital skills to help them navigate the changes taking place in society and prepare for the marketplace. Regrettably, many law faculties in Nigeria do not offer law students the opportunity to learn and develop digital competence due to the failure to provide innovative technologies in legal education.

Third, there is lack of involvement of the Nigerian bar in legal education. Rather, in recent years, there has been a needless and unlawful attempt by the NBA to segment the legal profession by creating a distinction between the teaching and practice of law. This appears to have further reduced the level of participation of law teachers in the activities of the NBA, which cost of participation is borne by the individual law teacher. The bickering and lack of synergy between the bar and legal academia in Nigeria create a gap – the failure of the two segments of the legal profession to work together to find solutions to problems plaguing legal education in Nigeria (Kana [2016] at 48–53).

The state of legal education

There are concerns about the declining quality of legal education in Nigeria, in terms of the transferability of knowledge, functional skills and values, which ultimately impact the legal profession. While the focus has been on the physical infrastructure or the lack thereof and law students' performance, little or no consideration is given to the socio-economic and psychological factors that impact on legal education in Nigeria. The socio-economic factor (social background) appears to affect the learning capacity of many law students in Nigeria, whose focus is often divided between learning and fending for their needs in the course of the law programme.

Also, many law students in Nigeria do not have a good grasp of the English language, which is the lingua franca of legal education in Nigeria. The need to understand the use of English in legal education cannot be overemphasised as 'law is fundamentally a matter of language and there are some things one cannot understand about law if one does not understand language – and the limits of speech [as well as thought]' (Constable [2014] at 64). Thus, the inability of many law students in Nigeria to effectively use the language of law impacts negatively on their ability to engage in effective learning (Solomon [2017]), with dire consequences for legal education (Solomon [2020] at 180–181).

The psychological factor involves the capacity of law students to learn and assimilate what is being taught. In their work on 'threshold concept in law', Feld and Meyer recognised the nexus between student well-being and learning success, noting that, 'the psychological health of students, at all levels of learning, is a critical component of their capacity to learn effectively' (Feld and Meyer [2021] at 142). This is because the cognitive activity of law students appears to have some co-relation to age (Navarro, García-Rubio and Olivares [2015]). As earlier alluded, legal education in Nigeria commences from a university faculty of law, which offers the LLB programme.

A substantial number of applicants for admission into the LLB programme are secondary school leavers, with the middling age of between 16 and 17 years old. Perhaps the apparent deterioration in the quality of legal education (and by extension the legal profession) in Nigeria may be connected with the psychological state of law students, many of whom are emotionally or mentally unprepared for the study of law at the time of being admitted into the LLB programme. Worse still, there is no official and regulated pupillage system to support new entrants into the legal profession during the early period of transition from legal education to law practice (particularly courtroom advocacy).

Conclusion

While Nigeria's legal education has made progress since the inception of formal legal training in 1962, it is not in doubt that the legal education system is in dire need of, among others things, result-focused reforms aimed at improving teaching/learning experience, investments in infrastructure (including innovative technologies), a new model for the accreditation of legal education and training, overhaul of admission requirements for the LLB programme and effective collaboration by stakeholders in the legal profession.

EKOKOI SOLOMON

References

Constable, M. (2014). 'Law as language', *Critical Analysis of Law*, 1(1), p. 63.

Council of Legal Education. (2009). 'Nigerian law school curriculum', Nigerian Law School.

Feld, R. and Meyer, J. (2020). 'Threshold concepts in law: Intentional curriculum reform to support law student learning success and well-being', in Jones, E. and Cownie, F. (eds), *Key Directions in Legal Education: National and International Perspectives*, Routledge.

Ibijola, E. (2014). 'Accreditation role of the National Universities Commission and the quality of the educational inputs into Nigerian university system', *Universal Journal of Educational Research*, 2(9), p. 648.

Kana, A. (2016). 'Can law teachers practice and act as consultants for free or for a fee?', *Nigerian Law Journal*, 19(1), p. 35.

Kift, S. (1997). 'Lawyering skills: Finding their place in legal education', *Legal Education Review*, 8(1), art 2, available at https://www.researchgate.net/publication/352687020

_Lawyering_Skills_Finding_their_Place_in _Legal_Education.

Legal Education (Consolidation, etc.) Act, Cap L10 Laws of the Federation of Nigeria (LFN) 2004.

Manteaw, S. (2008). 'Legal education in Africa: What type of lawyers does Africa need', *McGeorge Law Review*, 39, p. 903.

National Universities Commission. (2009). 'Guidelines and conditions for the establishment of faculties of law in Nigeria'.

National Universities Commission. (2018). 'Benchmark minimum academic standards for undergraduate programmes in Nigerian universities – Law'.

Navarro, J., García-Rubio, J. and Olivares, P. (2015). 'The relative age effect and its influence on academic performance', *PLoS One*, 10(1), available at https://www.ncbi.nlm.nih.gov/pmc/articles/PMC4627818/.

Ndulo, M. (2002). 'Legal education in Africa in the era of globalization and structural adjustment', *Penn St. Int'l L. Rev*, 20(3), p. 487.

Ojukwu, E. (2023). '54th Nigerian association of law teachers conference: The challenge of NALT's reimage', Lead paper at the 54th Conference of the Nigerian Association of Law Teachers, Abia State University, Umuahia 12 July.

Oko, O. (2021). 'Legal education reform in Africa: Time to revisit the two-tier legal education system', *U. Miami Int'l & Comp. L. Rev*, 29(1), p. 130.

Report of the Committee on the Future of the Nigerian Legal Profession. (1959). Lagos, Federal Government Press.

Rules of Professional Conduct for Legal Practitioners 2023, Rule 11 – a subsidiary legislation made pursuant to the Legal Practitioners Act, Cap L11 LFN 2004.

Ryan, F. and McFaul, H. (2020). 'Innovative technologies in UK legal education', in Jones, E. and Cownie, F. (eds), *Key Directions in Legal Education: National and International Perspectives*, Routledge.

Solomon, E. (2017). 'Towards effective legal writing in Nigeria', *Journal of Commonwealth Law and Legal Education*, 12(1), p. 65.

Solomon, E. (2020). 'Legal skills: Making a real change in Nigerian legal education', in Jones, E. and Cownie, F. (eds), *Key Directions in Legal Education: National and International Perspectives*, Routledge.

Woodward, P. and Dalton, P. (1990). 'Green papers, black letters, grey matter', *Journal of the Association of Law Teachers*, p. 124.

73. Nigeria (history of legal education)

Introduction

Nigeria became an independent nation in 1960 having been colonised by Great Britain for nearly 100 years.

The colonial rule brought in legal pluralism as the English Common law and doctrines of equity and many English statutes of general application extant in England as of 1 January 1900 became applicable laws to Nigeria. By the first Ordinance No. 3 of 1863, it became enacted that all laws and statutes which were enforced within the realm of England on the 1st day of January, 1863, not being inconsistent with any ordinance in force in the Colony, or with any rule made in pursuance of any such Ordinance, should be deemed and taken to be in force in the Colony, and should be applied in the administration of justice, so far as local circumstances would permit.

These laws were applicable as well as Customary laws (including Muslim personal laws) if they were not contrary to public policy or repugnant to Natural justice, equity, and good conscience. This plural law regime is still existing in Nigeria today (section 18(3) of the Evidence Act 2011; the Interpretation Act provides in section 32: (1) Subject to the provisions of this section and except in so far as other provision is made by any Federal law, the common law of England and the doctrines of equity, together with the statutes of general application that were in force in England on the 1st day of January, 1900, shall, in so far as they relate to any matter within the legislative competence of the Federal legislature, be in force in Nigeria; (2) Such Imperial laws shall be in force so far only as the limits of the local jurisdiction and local circumstances shall permit and subject to any Federal law.

With the dominating applicability of the English common law to Nigeria, it became imperative that the colonial government introduced its own English court system. To service this court system, only English trained lawyers and jurists became permitted to practice law in Nigeria.

Period before 1960

The first formal legal link between Britain and Nigeria was the establishment of Lagos as a colony in 1861. Later two different protectorates of Northern and southern Nigeria were created. In 1914 the protectorates and the Colony of Lagos were merged into a nation called Nigeria. In 1863 the Supreme Court of Her Majesty's settlement of Lagos was enacted (Babaloloa [2019]).

In 1876 there was enacted a Supreme Court Ordinance that authorised the Chief Justice under section 74 to approve, admit and enrol to practise as Barristers and Solicitors, persons who have been called to the Bar or admitted as Solicitors in England, Scotland and Ireland; or those who had served articles, that is, those who had worked in the Chambers under Lawyer's supervision; or who had served five years continuously in the Office of practising Barrister or Solicitor residing within Jurisdiction of the Court; and who had passed such examinations of the Principles and Practice of Law before such persons as the Chief Justice (CJ) may from time to time appoint (Babaloloa [2019]). 'Although the Supreme Court Ordinance gave power to the Chief Justice to prescribe some form of examination as a condition precedent to enrolment either in addition to or in substitution for one of the qualifications just mentioned, there was no recorded instance of the exercise of this power by any Chief Justice since the first legislation was first passed in 1876' (Elias [1962]). Following the amalgamation of 1914, the Supreme Court Ordinance of 1876 was replaced with the Supreme Court Ordinance of 1914 but the rules relating to qualification to practice before the court was not strongly altered and no legal training was still in practice provided in Nigeria for those wishing to practice law in Nigeria.

Post 1960

As Nigeria was marching towards independence in 1960, and following many constitutional challenges and reforms, and the clamour to create its own institutions including educational institutions, there was need for local/indigenised content for the legal profession in Nigeria.

In 1959, Nigerian Government set up the Committee on the future of the Nigerian Legal Profession. The Report of that committee became known as the Unsworth Committee Report. The Committee among other things recommended the establishment of a University Law Faculty and the Nigerian

Law School for the professional training of lawyers for legal practice in Nigeria (Jegede [2003]).

Nigeria implemented the Unsworth Committee Report relating to legal education with the establishment of two universities: the University of Nigeria in 1961, and the University of Lagos in 1962 (Ojukwu [2003]). Law Faculties for the training of students for the Bachelor of Law Degree were also part of these two universities. Also in 1962, the Legal Practitioners Act and the Legal Education Act were enacted. The Legal Education Act provided for the establishment of a Council of Legal Education. This led to the establishment of the Nigerian Law School the same year though activities were commenced in 1963 (Ojukwu [2013]).

Dual legal education

Since 1962 there are two parts of training to qualify as a lawyer in Nigeria. The first part that takes place at the university leads to the qualification of a Bachelor of Laws degree (LLB). After this first part, a candidate must then attend the Nigerian Law School and pass the Bar examination.

The Bachelor of Law Degree

The training for the Bachelor of Laws degree is done at the Law Faculties of the Universities. From two law faculties in 1962, there are now 77 Council of Legal Education accredited law faculties of universities offering the LLB course.

From 1962 to 1990, the duration for the LLB programme was four years for a secondary school entry qualification while three years was for a post-secondary school entry qualification. From 1990, the National Universities Commission centralised the establishment and accreditation of universities and university disciplines in Nigeria. From 1991, the duration of the LLB programme became five years for the secondary school qualification and four years for the post-secondary school qualification. The National Universities Commission (NUC) established a uniform curriculum and benchmarks academic statements (BMAS) for all the Law Faculties in Nigeria. From September 2023 the benchmarks academic statements were changed to Core Curriculum minimum academic standards (CCMAS).

The CCMAS for Law

These Core Curriculum and Minimum Academic Standards (CCMAS) are designed for the education and training of undergraduate students wishing to obtain first degree in Law in the Nigerian university system. Presented in this Section are the basic operational elements that serve to define the core curriculum and minimum academic standards required to achieve the cardinal goal of producing graduates in Law with sufficient academic background and professional exposure to face the challenges of a developing economy in the increasingly globalised world economy (National Universities Commission [2022]).

The philosophy of the Law degree programme is

> to contribute significantly to the enrichment and enhancement of legal study and practice. It is designed to provide legal education within a dynamic socio-political environment encompassing national and global trends and challenges. The focus of the Law programme is to create an environment that encourages intellectual rigour, analytical and critical engagement, and profound ethical standards... committed to outcome-based, learner-centred legal education that integrates knowledge, skills, and value competency and ethics to produce law graduates who can compete actively in legal, social, economic, and political developments globally (National Universities Commission [2022]).

The CCMAS for law identifies the following learning outcomes:

1. Analytical skills
2. Research skills
3. Advocacy skills
4. Application skills

The unique features of the LLB programme include the following:

1. Ethical responsibilities: The legal profession's values of justice, fairness, candour, honesty, integrity, professionalism, respect for diversity, and respect for the Rule of Law
2. Problem-solving
3. Pro bono responsibility
4. Entrepreneurships skills to see law practice as a business
5. Alternative dispute resolution

6. Social engineering: The role of the legal profession in society

The Bar Professional Training at the Nigerian Law School

The second part of legal training in Nigeria takes place at the Nigerian Law School that is managed by the Council of Legal Education. The Council of Legal Education has responsibility for the legal education of persons seeking to become members of the legal profession in Nigeria.

The Nigerian Law School was established in Lagos under the Legal Education Act 1962. From 1962 up until December 1997 the Law School remained in Lagos only. In 1997 the Law School was moved to Abuja and in 2001 three additional campuses of the Law School were created. Between 2011 and 2013 two additional campuses were created and in 2022 the seventh campus of the Nigerian Law School was constructed. Today the Campuses of the Nigerian Law School are Abuja (Headquarter), Lagos, Augustine Nnamani Campus Enugu, Kano, Yola, Yenegoa and Nabo Graham Douglas Campus Port Harcourt.

Training at the Nigerian Law School is full time. The training duration is one year. But a person whose LLB degree is from a university outside Nigeria is required to undergo a full time three to six months Bar Part 1 training programme before the person can proceed to the one-year full time Bar Part 2 training programme that entitles one to take the Bar examination.

A candidate that passes the Bar examination shall receive a qualifying certificate issued to him by the Council of Legal Education stating that he is qualified to be called to Bar.

The Nigerian Law School's mission statement (Ojukwu [2013]) include the following:

1. educate and train law graduates in vocational skills as barristers and solicitors;
2. train students to conform to ethics and exhibit the highest sense of integrity and candour in the discharge of their professional calling; and
3. inculcate in its graduates the ideals of rule of law, social justice and community service.

The Nigerian Law School curriculum has the following features and characteristics:

1. It is outcomes-based, learner-centred, and integrative focus on knowledge, skills, and values.
2. It provides good potential and opportunities for experiential learning and clinical legal education.
3. The curriculum provides for 40 weeks of academic work, one week of moot and mock trial before the lessons, 12 weeks of externship programme (placement in the courts and law firms), three weeks of externship portfolio assessment, one week of post lessons moot and mock trial and one week of final examination.
4. An externship programme that is assessed on a pass/fail basis and a failure grade deprives the student a bar certificate.

Conclusion

This article has given a short history of legal education in Nigeria and some insights into the scope of legal education in Nigeria.

ERNEST OJUKWU

References

Aare Afe Babalola (2019). SAN, CON, 'Repositioning Legal Education for National Development (1)', available at https://www.abuad.edu.ng/repositioning-legal-education-for-national-development-1/.

Chief JK. Jegede, SAN, 'A Historical Perspective of the Nigerian Law School', *Nigerian Law School – Four Decades of Service to the Legal Profession*, Chapter 2, Council of Legal Education.

Council of Legal Education. 'A brief Historical profile of the Nigerian Law School'. (2013). *Fifty Years of Legal Education in Nigeria: Challenges and Next Steps,* Chapter 1, p. 8, Council of Legal Education.

Elias, T.O. (1962). 'Legal Education in Nigeria', *Journal of African Law*, 6(2), p. 117.

https://www.nigerianlawschool.edu.ng/index.html.

https://nuc-ccmas.ng/download/ccmas-law/

https://nuc.edu.ng/wp-content/uploads/2015/09/Law%20Draft%20BMAS.pdf

Legal Education Act, sections 1(2), and 5.

National Universities Commission Core Curriculum Minimum Academic Standards (CCMAS) for the Nigerian University System, Law. (2022).

Ojukwu, E. (2003). 'Trends in Legal Education: A Comparative Analysis of Nigeria, USA, UK and South Africa', *Nigerian Law School Four*

Decades of Service to the Legal Profession, Council of Legal education.

Ojukwu, E. (2013). *Legal Education in Nigeria: A Chronicle of Reforms and Transformation under Tahir Mamman,* Council of Legal educa-tion, available at https://www.nigerianlawschool .edu.ng/Notices/AccreditedWithQuotas.pdf.

Preamble. (2022). National Universities Commission Core Curriculum Minimum Academic Standards (CCMAS) for the Nigerian University System, Law.

74. Nigeria (regulation of legal education)

Introduction

As is the case with other concepts, the concept of 'regulation' is often obscurely understood, as it is devoid of a general definition. Regulation 'is often perceived as control or constraint'. However, it 'often imposes no restrictions, but enables, facilitates, or adjusts activities' (Orbach [2016]). In Nigeria, the regulation of legal education is a function of pieces of legislation, which seek to promote quality assurance mechanisms for the assessment, rating, monitoring and evaluation of legal education institutions, with the aim of promoting quality and standards in the training of persons aspiring to be legal professionals. As alluded to in the entry on contemporary legal education in Nigeria (Nigeria (Contemporary Legal Education)), there exists a binate system in the regulation of legal education in Nigeria.

Accordingly, the National Universities Commission (NUC) and the Council of Legal Education (CLE) are vested with powers to regulate legal education in Nigeria. While the NUC is responsible for ensuring minimum academic standards of all Nigerian university programmes, including the LLB programme, by means of accreditation, quality assurance, setting of admission requirements and curriculum development, the CLE regulates the LLB programme in Nigerian universities, using the instrumentality of accreditation, approval of core academic and vocational law subjects, as well as the management of the Nigerian Law School (NLS). The NLS is a centralised law school created for vocational training of law graduates from approved/accredited foreign and Nigerian faculties/colleges of law.

National Universities Commission

The NUC was established in 1962 as an advisory department of the Nigerian federal government on all aspects of university education (Olaleye and Oyewole [2016] at 162). In 1974, it became a statutory body with the responsibility for advising the government on the establishment of universities and programmes offered by them (NUC Act, section 1(1)). The NUC is also vested with 'the power to lay down minimum standards for all universities … and the accreditation of their degrees and other academic awards' (Education (National Minimum Standards and Establishment of Institutions) Act, section 10(1)).

To give effect to the foregoing legal framework, the NUC, in collaboration with the universities, designed and developed the Minimum Academic Standards, Benchmark Minimum Academic Standards and Core Curriculum and Minimum Academic Standards, which were respectively adopted in 1989, 2007 and 2021. The minimum academic standards (MAS) guide Nigerian universities in the design of curricula for their academic programmes, including the LLB programme, by stipulating the minimum requirements (NUC [2018]; NUC [2022]). The MAS contain details of basic courses and elements (including facilities) that a university must have before it can be accredited to award the LLB degree. The NUC also ensures the quality, standards and adequacy of legal education at the postgraduate level (Akpan [2014] at 1293–1294).

In practice, NUC teams of inspectors visit newly established faculties/colleges of law for accreditation to ensure that their facilities meet the MAS requirements before approval for commencement of the LLB programme is given (Akomolafe and Adesua [2019] at 44–45). The NUC also undertakes subsequent interval accreditation visitations to already accredited faculties/colleges of law to ensure that the MAS are sustained and/or enhanced (NUC [2021]). Failure to maintain the standards stipulated in the MAS may lead to the withdrawal of accreditation for the LLB programme, which may eventually result in loss of accreditation (NUC [2021]). A university whose accreditation is withdrawn by the NUC cannot admit new students into the LLB programme until issues raised during the accreditation have been addressed.

Council of Legal Education

The CLE was established in 1962 by the Legal Education Act 1962, based on a recommendation of the Committee on the Future of the Nigerian Legal Profession (Unsworth Committee [1959] para 18). The Legal Education Act was repealed and re-enacted in 1976 and 1992, and is now known as the Legal Education (Consolidation, etc.) Act, Laws of the Federation 2004 (LECA). Section 1 of the LECA confers on the CLE the 'responsibility for the legal education of persons seeking to become members of the legal profession' in Nigeria. The CLE is also vested with the 'power to do such things as it considers expedient for the purpose of performing its functions' (section 2(5)).

Implicit in the provisions of the LECA, is the CLE's power to: (i) develop a system of accrediting law faculties of Nigerian universities to promote quality and standards in academic legal education and (ii) establish and run the NLS.

Accreditation of the LLB Programme

In 2007, in a bid to avoid the setbacks occasioned by the accreditation of the LLB programme by two regulatory bodies and ensure some measures of uniformity in the regulation of academic legal education, the CLE adopted the minimum criteria of academic standards – harmonised NUC and CLE accreditation requirements – for the determination of the status of a university's LLB programme. They include:

- a separate faculty building, with adequate offices and classrooms, moot court rooms, and other recreational facilities;
- adequately qualified and experienced lecturers, including professors;
- the teaching of core law subjects, namely, Nigerian legal system, law of contract, law of tort, constitutional law, law of evidence, criminal law, Nigerian land law, equity and trusts and commercial law;
- an environment conducive for the teaching/learning of law and the grooming of students for the final stage of their training at the NLS;
- strict compliance with admission quota as approved by the CLE for law faculties/colleges in relation to admission of students to the NLS;
- invitation of the CLE for inspection of facilities of a law faculty/college before its establishment (or not later than the second year of its existence);
- the CLE's non-recognition for accreditation of part-time, distant learning and correspondence LLB programme; and
- a minimum score of 70 per cent in the areas of library, staffing, staff development, teaching methods.

A law faculty/college with a cumulative score of: 70 per cent and above attracts a 'full accreditation' status, which lasts for three years; between 55–69 per cent attracts an 'interim or provisional accreditation' status, which lasts for two years; and below 55 per cent attracts a 'deny accreditation' status, for which the exercise will be repeated after one year or as soon as the law faculty/college is ready for a revisit, but it cannot admit fresh students before obtaining a favourable accreditation status (Ojukwu [2013] at 84, 92–93). There are currently 17 federal universities, 21 state universities and 30 private universities approved and accredited by the CLE to offer the LLB programme – the majority of which have provisional accreditation status, a few suspended accreditation status and only one full accreditation status (CLE [2017] at 24). In addition to the imposition of a moratorium on the admission of students into the LLB programme, law graduates from a university with suspended accreditation status may be denied admission into the NLS (Okeh [2023]).

A Nigerian who obtains an LLB degree from a recognised university in a common law country and/or has been called to the Bar in another jurisdiction but desires to practice law in Nigeria, is required to first enrol and participate in the Bar Part 1 programme at the NLS (Ojukwu [2013] at 30, 35).

Management of the Nigerian Law School

The NLS is managed by the CLE to give effect to the latter's powers under the LECA. There are currently seven campuses of the NLS geopolitically located across Nigeria. In addition to qualifying as a graduate of an approved and accredited LLB programme, a person desirous of becoming a lawyer in Nigeria must successfully complete a course of vocational legal education at the NLS as prescribed by the CLE, and 'shall be entitled to have a qualifying certificate issued to him by the [CLE] stating that he is qualified to be called to Bar' (LECA, section 5). Thus, to qualify as a lawyer and be entitled to practice law in Nigeria, a person must successfully complete both the academic and vocational legal education as approved by the CLE (Legal Practitioners Act (LPA), sections 2 and 24).

A law graduate seeking admission into the NLS need not be a Nigerian citizen (LPA section 4(2)(a)). However, a law graduate from a foreign university is required to undertake and pass the Bar Part I programme at the NLS, at which stage he is taught core law courses – Nigerian Legal System, Nigerian Criminal Law, Nigerian Land Law and Nigerian Constitutional Law – before proceeding to the Bar Part II programme. A Nigerian who obtained an LLB degree and is engaged in legal practice for at least five years in a common law country must meet the following requirements to be recommended for induction into the Nigerian Bar:

- enrol and pay the prescribed fees at the NLS;
- participate in the NLS externship programme, which comprises law office and court attachments spanning the same period for Bar II students; and
- attendance at three formal dinners at the NLS (Ojukwu [2013] at 583).

An applicant for admission into the NLS must be adjudged by the CLE to be a 'fit and proper' person worthy of becoming a member of the legal profession in Nigeria (LPA, section 4(1)(c) and (2)(c)). A person who has been convicted of a serious crime, a member of a secret cult or society, a drug addict or peddler, etc, may be considered not a fit and proper person, and therefore denied admission into the NLS irrespective of obtaining the requisite academic legal education qualification from a university (Akinola [2021]). Ultimately, the power to determine who is a 'fit and proper' person lies with the CLE (*Okonjo v Council of Legal Education*). It seems uncertain whether the CLE has been successful in preventing the admission of persons of questionable character into the NLS (and by extension their induction into the legal profession). This is in view of the growing incidences of unethical conducts and unlawful activities by legal practitioners in Nigeria.

At the end of vocational legal training at the NLS (Bar Part II), the CLE recommends students who pass the Bar final examination and satisfy other of its stipulations to the Body of Benchers (BOB) for induction into the Nigerian Bar and enrolment at the Supreme Court of Nigeria as a barrister and solicitor (LPA, sections 10(1)(a), 3(1) & 4(1),(3),(4)). The BOB is a select body of legal practitioners of the highest distinction in Nigeria (LPA, section 3).

Some challenges of the current regulatory system

While the NUC has the authority to approve the establishment of the LLB programme by a university, the CLE is responsible for both academic and vocational legal education for persons seeking to become legal practitioners in Nigeria. There is no legal obligation on the part of the NUC to consult the CLE before approving the establishment of an LLB programme, even though the programme must also satisfy the CLE's academic standards before it is accredited by the CLE.

The implication is that the NUC's accreditation of a university's LLB programme does not automatically translate to accreditation by the CLE (Sunday, Onyekwere and Onochie [2017]). Therefore, the current regulatory framework sometimes creates conflict between the NUC and CLE with respect to the accreditation of the LLB programme. This is essentially a function of the divergence in the objectives for accreditation by both bodies (Herbert and Ole [2023] at 8–13).

Conclusion

There are concerns that the NUC accreditation processes and the reports that emanate from them are questionable and are not a true reflection of the state of the Nigerian university system (Ibijola [2014] at 649). Also, with the growing number of universities approved to offer the LLB programme, it has become impracticable for the CLE, in its present structure, to effectively regulate academic legal education in Nigeria, as the regulation of vocational legal education (for which the CLE is solely responsible) increases with the expansion of the NLS. In this regard, the Nigerian Bar Association has proposed a legislative measure, which seeks, inter alia, to remove the NLS from direct ownership and control of the CLE and to allow for the establishment of private law schools.

Although the NUC and CLE are separate and independent regulatory bodies, their roles in the regulation of legal education in Nigeria are not mutually exclusive. However, the power of the CLE to regulate legal education in Nigeria predates the regulatory authority of the NUC. Regrettably, with the subsequent vesting of regulatory power in the NUC with regard to the design and development of MAS for university programmes, provisions in the

LECA, which appear to vest similar powers in the CLE, have not been repealed. Thus conferring the power of maintaining quality and standards of academic legal education in the CLE and NUC. This suggests that both bodies must improve on their collaborative efforts for the purpose of effective regulation of legal education in Nigeria.

EKOKOI SOLOMON

References

Akinola, O.B. (2021), 'Expanding the frontiers of the concept of fit and proper in the Nigerian law school', *Nile University of Nigeria Law Journal*, 3(1), p. 101.

Akomolafe, C.O. and Adesua, V.O. (2019). 'An evaluative study on the accreditation of academic programmes and quality assurance in public universities in Nigeria', *European Scientific Journal of International Law*, 15(4) p. 40.

Akpan, C.P. (2014). 'Quality assurance in Nigerian universities: The role of the National Universities Commission', in *INTED2014 Proceedings* (8th International Technology, Education and Development Conference, Spain 10–12 March.

Council of Legal Education. (2017). 'List of accredited and approved faculties of law in Nigeria' *Daily Trust*, Lagos, 8 November.

Education (National Minimum Standards and Establishment of Institutions) Act, Cap E63 Laws of the Federation of Nigeria (LFN). (2004).

Herbert, E. and Ole, N. (2023). 'A binate regulatory framework for the accreditation of law faculties in Nigerian universities: A necessity or overkill?', *The Law Teacher*, p. 1.

Ibijola, E.Y. (2014). 'Accreditation role of the National Universities Commission and the quality of the educational inputs into Nigerian

university system', *Universal Journal of Educational Research*, 2(9), p. 648.

Legal Education (Consolidation, etc.) Act, Cap L10 LFN (2004).

Legal Practitioners Act, Cap L11 LFN (2004).

National Universities Commission. (2018). *Monthly Bulletin*, 13(1).

National Universities Commission (2018). 'Benchmark minimum academic standards for undergraduate programmes in Nigerian universities – Law'.

National Universities Commission. (2022). 'Core curriculum and minimum academic standards for the Nigerian university system – Law'.

National Universities Commission. (2021). 'Accreditation', available at https://www.nuc.edu.ng/project/accreditation/.

National Universities Commission. (2021). 'List of illegal universities closed down by NUC', available at https://www.nuc.edu.ng/2224-2/.

National Universities Commission Act, Cap N81 LFN (2004).

Ojukwu, E. (2013). *Legal Education in Nigeria: A Chronicle of Reforms and Transformation under Tahir Mamman*, Council of Legal Education.

Okeh, A. (2023). 'Anxiety as multiple admissions, student backlog frustrate law graduates' *Punch*, available at https://punchng.com/anxiety-as-multiple-admissions-student-backlogs-frustrate-law-graduates/.

Okonjo v Council of Legal Education [1979] Digest of Appeal Cases, 25.

Olaleye, F.O. and Oyewole, B.K. (2016). 'Quality assurance in Nigerian university education: The role of the National Universities Commission as a regulatory body', *International Journal of Academic Research in Progressive Education and Development*, 5(4), p. 160.

Orbach, B. (2016). 'What is regulation?', *Yale Journal on Regulation*, available at https://www.yalejreg.com/bulletin/what-is-regulation/.

Report of the Committee on the Future of the Nigerian Legal Profession. (1959). Lagos, Federal Government Press.

Sunday, E., Onyekwere, J. and Onochie, B.C. (2017). 'NUC, CLE bicker over accreditation of law faculties', *The Guardian*, available at https://guardian.ng/news/nuc-cle-bicker-over-accreditation-of-law-faculties/.

75. Paralegal legal education

Introduction

The American Bar Association defines a 'paralegal' as a member of an adjunct profession, supervised by a licensed lawyer (ABA [2020], Mongue [2017]). This is the conventional understanding and inherent in the 'para' prefix. The complexity of their work, however, may be very high (see e.g. the requirements for a juriste en cabinet d'avocat (France Compétences [2021]).

The division between paralegals and licensed lawyers, including specialist legal professions, is not, however, clear. Depending on local regulation and monopolies over the practice of law, some paralegals are autonomous, albeit practising in a smaller range of fields than that of the principal legal profession(s). Or they may not have full rights of audience. The same could be said of the licensed conveyancer profession in Australia, England and Wales and New Zealand.

Whether adjunct or autonomous, qualification and certification for paralegals often involves multiple routes, online or low-cost study and recognition of work experience. A law degree is often not required, although degrees in Paralegal Studies are available. This may attract a more diverse group of individuals than to the principal legal profession(s). Career progression into the principal profession is, however, sometimes possible.

This entry considers the education of both adjunct and autonomous paralegals before closing with the legal executive profession. Whilst legal executives exist in several common law jurisdictions, in the UK they have successfully made the transition from adjunct to specialist legal profession.

Terminology

Terminology includes auxiliar jurídico; clerc d'avocat; legal adviser; legal assistant; legal clerk; legal executive; legal technician; parajuriste; paralegal; paraprofessional; technicien juridique.

Adjunct paralegals

Perhaps most adjunct paralegals work in legal services organisations or departments and consequently for members of principal legal professions. Where local regulation permits, paralegals may also work in organisations outside the legal services sector. Training may be ad hoc or experiential.

On the other hand, paralegals may be part-qualified for a principal legal profession, or even fully qualified but deregistered. This occurs, for example, where full qualification requires pre-qualification work experience which the paralegal has not secured. Given the resources needed to invest in highly regulated pre-qualification work experience, some employers may demand service as a paralegal before offering it. Where there is no formal pre-qualification work experience requirement, as in India, aspiring lawyers may work as paralegals before completing their bar examination. Further, where there are costs involved in employing a lawyer, such as a practising certificate or minimum salary, employees may deregister in order to work as a paralegal.

Career paralegals may take specific paralegal courses, and their employers or the market may expect this. These may be self-standing degrees or diplomas in Paralegal Studies, but they are normally shorter than those for qualification into the principal legal profession and recruitment can be directly from school. Such qualifications may articulate with other professional qualifications or into law degrees. There are also affinity groups for course providers (e.g. AAFPE [2022]).

Paralegals are often voluntarily regulated. Accreditation may be generic or confined to specific areas of practice such as property or family law work. Sometimes accreditation is by the professional body of a principal profession (e.g. Law Society of Scotland [2023]). Or the professional body may oversee and set standards (e.g. ABA [2022]).

Another option is that a dedicated paralegal organisation accredits. Membership of such a body may confer status, especially if it recognises different levels of seniority. If it requires commitment to a code of conduct and ongoing CPD/CLE, or to a competence statement, it provides quality assurance. It may also offer career development and social support for paralegals and engage in collective bargaining.

Accreditation is usually of a combination of academic study and work experience, and therefore responsive to entrants from a variety of backgrounds. Where experience is accepted, applicants may, as in Scotland, have to demonstrate certain competences, or to certify supervised experience of a certain length. In the USA the National Federation of Paralegal Associations requires a combination of academic study and experience, but accreditation is ultimately by examination.

Autonomous paralegals

One response to unmet legal need has been to license autonomous or semi-autonomous paralegals to assist litigants in person. In several African countries, 'community paralegals', operate in the legal aid sector, including criminal defence (Dereymaeker [2016], Ibe [2021], Wang [2021]). The African Union's 2003 Principles and Guidelines on the Right to a Fair Trial and Legal Assistance in Africa provides specifically for the work, and training, of paralegals. Guideline 14 of the UN United Nations Principles and Guidelines on Access to Legal Aid in Criminal Justice Systems 2012 reinforces the need for 'standardized training curricula and accreditation schemes' for paralegals, albeit often as adjuncts. Recognition for autonomous paralegals was, however, sought in the 2012 Kampala Declaration on Community Paralegals and the 2014 Lilongwe Declaration on Accessing Legal Aid in the Criminal Justice System in Africa exhorted signatories to develop ,standardized training programmes, for them. See further Maru and Gauri [2018] and outside Africa Jingwen [2014], Yeroshenko and Semigina [2017].

Progress, however, has not been without difficulty. Mali has a curriculum developed in conjunction with a Dutch organisation (Avocats sans frontières Canada [2022]). In Nigeria the Legal Aid Act 2011, s 17(3) empowers the Legal Aid Council to grant licences to those who have 'undergone a prescribed course in paralegal services'. Recommendations for 'licensing and regulatory systems for training and paralegal services' were made in 2019 (Legal Aid Council [2020]) and both adjunct and autonomous community paralegals are included. In South Africa there are several paralegal courses, but community paralegals are also trained by their employers or by organisations such as the Community Law & Rural Development Centre (see also Holness [2013], Schönteich [2016]).

Unmet legal need is not confined to criminal law and some community paralegals also practise in civil and non-contentious matters. This has been the focus in the USA where, as a result of the ABA's definition of 'paralegal', different terminology is sometimes used for autonomous paralegals. See Crossett [2017] for an overview. Three states, so far, have introduced autonomous paralegal schemes, as has Ontario in Canada. A pilot project is taking place in Minnesota and Oregon will license autonomous paralegals in housing and family law from 2024.

Washington was the first to do so, in 2012, when it adopted practice rules for 'limited license legal technicians' (LLLTs) with the right to conduct certain tasks in family law litigation (Holland [2013], Nelson [2016]). The scheme has closed to new entrants, however, from July 2023. The Limited License Legal Technical Board oversaw qualification. Study was through accredited courses in legal studies and family law delivered through community colleges and universities, and 3,000 hours of supervised work experience was required. Candidates also had to pass a national paralegal examination and two LLLT examinations, one on family law and one on ethics.

In Utah, paralegal practitioners are licensed in family law, small debt collection and/or landlord and tenant work. They must have a degree in law or paralegal studies from an accredited university, one of several named paralegal accreditations, substantive work experience and pass examinations in the practice area and in ethics.

From 2020 in Arizona legal paraprofessionals work in family, administrative, civil and criminal litigation and, unlike others, do have some rights of audience. There are entry routes recognising degree study and experience and examinations in ethics and in the specific practice area.

The Canadian approach to legal regulation emphasises competences, although it also uses examinations. Autonomous paralegals in Ontario are licensed by the Law Society of Ontario. They must complete an accredited paralegal course, have served at least 120 hours in an 'approved field placement' and passed an open book MCQ examination testing key competences (Law Society of Ontario [2023]). In 2022 the Law Society of Ontario recommended creating autonomous family law paralegals with some rights of audience; setting out the competences they would need to acquire and proposing a course of six to eight months (full time).

Legal executives

This term is confined to a small number of common law countries. Elsewhere, as in South Africa, a 'legal executive' may be a company executive with responsibility for legal matters, but not necessarily a member of a legal profession. Some legal executives are adjuncts but others, at least in England and Wales, are autonomous practitioners.

In Australia the Law Institute of Victoria hosts the Institute of Legal Executives which provides voluntary regulation. Legal executives are adjuncts but may be licensed to carry out certain tasks such as administering oaths. Membership is by case-by-case assessment of a combination of experience and academic legal study.

The Bahamian Legal Profession Act 1992 created a registered adjunct legal executive profession with a protected title, regulated by the Bar Council. The Bar Council may make regulations defining their functions (s 53) and training (s 42).

In Hong Kong there are several courses for legal executives, including those offered through universities. If the course complies with benchmarks set by the Hong Kong Law Society, its graduates may use the title 'legal executive'.

In the Republic of Ireland, the Irish Institute of Legal Executives provides voluntary regulation. They are adjuncts, but, as in Victoria, may have some autonomous licensure, eg for administering oaths. Associate membership can be obtained on completion of a part-time Diploma in Legal Studies and Practice which has an optional progression route into an LLB. Higher levels of membership to Fellow are available on the basis of proven experience.

A similar regulatory context is provided by the New Zealand Institute of Legal Executives. Unlike conveyancers (Lawyers and Conveyancers Act 2006, part 5), the title is not protected, so regulation is voluntary. Membership is acquired by reference to extent and length of experience and education support is by an hours-based CPD system.

Several legal executive qualifications are mentioned on the website of the Institute of Legal Executives in Nigeria. The term is used in Singapore for those working in house, and in particular in the Legal Aid Bureau with some seniority.

In England and Wales, however, the legal executive profession is one of the eight legal professions regulated under the Legal Services Act 2007 with the same official status as that of the more well-known barristers and solicitors. Some of its members may work in what might otherwise be called a 'paralegal' role, but others own law firms, practise autonomously and sit as judges. The profession evolved from the solicitors' 'managing clerks' familiar from Dickens' novels, through voluntary regulation to the Institute of Legal Executives in 1963, granted Chartered status in 2012. From the 1990s its senior members (Fellows) gained increasing practice rights, in particular rights of audience (Francis [2002]). Its ethos is that it provides a route to practice that does not require a law degree (CILEx [no date]). This is multi-layered, so that a school leaver might progress, through a sequence of courses, work experience and assessments, from paralegal to advanced paralegal, to CILEX lawyer. Equally, there are multiple entry routes, so that a law graduate has direct entry to the advanced paralegal stage and an LPC or Bar graduate to CILEx Lawyer stage. Some may choose to remain in these grades. Fellowship and full Chartered status are, however, achieved by completion of three years' qualifying experience and demonstration of competences in a portfolio assessed by the professional body.

The part-time courses are offered by a variety of accredited providers, and may be in person or online, but final assessments are administered by CILEx. Other courses, such as law degrees, can obtain exemption for modules that mirror CILEx qualifications or units. Under a UK government scheme, there are also assessed work-place based apprenticeships both for paralegal and Chartered Legal Executive.

Conclusion

Not all paralegals, then, fulfil the ABA definition, but some do. Not all legal executives are paralegals, but some are. The terms are perhaps best recognised as representing a bundle of roles in legal services, other than that of the principal legal profession(s), and other than purely administrative or financial. Where their education is formalised, it may be more adaptive than that of the principal legal profession(s), offering multiple routes that recognise both classroom and workplace experience in a way that may attract a more diverse workforce. Voluntary regulation may provide comfort and support both to paralegals and to their employers. In due course, as for legal executives in England and Wales, this may evolve into an independent status as a legal profession in its own right.

JANE CHING

References

American Bar Association. (2020). 'Current ABA Definition of Paralegal', *American Bar Association*, available at https://www.americanbar.org/groups/paralegals/profession-information/current_aba_definition_of_legal_assistant_paralegal/.

American Bar Association (2022). 'Standing Committee on Paralegals', *American Bar Association*, available at https://www.americanbar.org/groups/paralegals/.

American Association for Paralegal and Legal Education. (2022). 'Home', *American Association for Paralegal and Legal Education*, available at https://www.aafpe.org/.

Avocats sans frontières Canada. (2022). 'Accès à La Justice Au Mali: Une Réalité à Bâtir', Avocats sans frontières Canada, available at https://ceci.org/uploads/Import/fr-asf-juprec-mali-acces-a-la-justice_2024-03-06-162711_fulk.pdf.

CILEX. (no date). 'About CILEX: Who We Are and What We Do?', CILEx, available at https://www.cilex.org.uk/about_cilex/.

Crossett, L. (2017). 'Regulation of the Paralegal Profession and Programs for Limited Practice by Non-Lawyers', *Journal of the Professional Lawyer*, p. 95.

Dereymaeker, G. (2016). 'Formalising the Role of Paralegals in Africa', CISPRI, *Open Justice Society Initiative*, PASI.

France Compétences. (2021). 'RNCP35602 – Juriste en cabinet d'avocat', France Compétences, available at https://www.francecompetences.fr/.

Francis, A. (2002). 'Legal Executives and the Phantom of Legal Professionalism: The Rise and Rise of the Third Branch of the Legal Profession?', *International Journal of the Legal Profession*, 9, p. 5.

Holland, B. (2013). 'The Washington State Limited License Legal Technician Practice Rule: A National First In Access To Justice', *Mississippi Law Journal*, 82, p. 75.

Holness, D. (2013). 'The Need for Recognition and Regulation of Paralegals: An Analysis of the Roles, Training, Remuneration and Impact of Community-Based Paralegals in South Africa', *Journal for Juridical Science*, 38, p. 78.

Ibe, S. (2021). 'Plugging the Legal Aid Gap in Africa: Paralegals to the Rescue?', *Economic and Social Rights in South Africa*, 22, p. 4.

Jingwen, Z. (2014). 'Data Analysis of Professionalization of Legal Workers in China Data Analysis', *Frontiers of Law in China*, 9, p. 276.

Law Society of Ontario. (2023). 'Entry-Level Paralegal Competencies', *Law Society of Ontario*, available at https://lso.ca/becoming-licensed/paralegal-licensing-process/licensing-examinations/entry-level-paralegal-competencies.

Law Society of Scotland. (2023). 'Accredited Paralegals', *Law Society of Scotland*, available at https://www.lawscot.org.uk/members/membership-and-fees/accredited-paralegals/.

Legal Aid Council. (2020). 'Towards A National Paralegal Movement In Nigeria', *Legal Aid Council*, available at https://legalaidcouncil.gov.ng/2020/07/15/towards-a-national-paralegal-movement-in-nigeria/.

Maru, V. and Gauri, V. (2018). (eds), *Community Paralegals and the Pursuit of Justice*, Cambridge University Press.

Mongue, R.E. (2017). 'From Apprentice to Paralegal: The Rise of the Paralegal Profession in America', *Issues in Legal Scholarship*, 15, p. 41.

Nelson, L.W. (2016). 'LLLT – Limited License Legal Technician: What It Is, What It Isn't, and the Grey Area in between Ethics and Access to Justice in Family Law', *Family Law Quarterly*, 50, p. 447.

Schönteich, M. (2016). 'A Powerful Tool of Justice: Paralegals and the Provision of Affordable and Accessible Legal Services', *South African Crime Quarterly*, p. 21.

Yeroshenko, K. and Semigina, T. (2017). 'Creating a Training Programme for Community-Based Paralegals: Action Research', *Social Work in Education*, 4, p. 33.

76. Poland (contemporary legal education)

Introduction

Every country shapes legal education based on its rich tradition, development, and societal needs. Poland's legal education system is not different. It stands as a testament to the nation's rich legal heritage and its continued traditional commitment to producing well-versed and principled legal practitioners. The primary goal of 'classical legal education' in Poland is to produce well-versed and principled legal practitioners, including future judges, prosecutors, and barristers.

This entry focuses on an exploration of legal education in Poland, delving into its structure, the academic journey from undergraduate to specialisation. It will focus on two fundamental development paths: the classical path, typically leading to the practice of a traditional legal profession, and the academic path, which in Polish legal education implies the necessity of achieving a few academic degrees.

Legal Studies in Poland and a law degree

When beginning to discuss legal education in Poland, it is essential to first consider the entities that are statutorily authorised to provide it. The education system in Poland consists of a variety of educational institutions, with universities playing a significant role. However, it is important to note that private higher education institutions also exist. The regulations in force in Poland (The Law on Higher Education and Science) reserve the term 'university' for an academic institution holding scientific category A+, A, or B+ in at least six scientific or artistic disciplines, spanning at least three fields of science or art. Such a requirement does not apply to higher education institutions (Poland (Regulation of Legal Education)). In Poland, there are primarily public universities, where education is typically tuition-free, private universities (with the first one being SWPS University) as well as private higher education institutions, where education is fee-based. There are a signifi-

cantly larger number of private institutions, and many of them also offer law programmes.

The path of legal education in Poland commences with a five-year programme, divided in 10 semesters. These studies are conducted as integrated master's programmes resulting in the conferral of a master's degree upon successful completion. At the moment due to market demands, many academic institutions also offer undergraduate programmes in the field of law (e.g., business law or new technology law). However, completing these programmes does not confer a Master of Law degree. Therefore, individuals wishing to pursue a legal profession of their choice must further their education through integrated master's programmes. Only a person who has completed master's studies in law is eligible to enter the classical legal profession.

The legal education is available in two forms: full-time and part-time (The Law on Higher Education and Science). Part-time studies are typically conducted on a weekend basis, with classes usually held every two weeks. Part-time students generally have fewer class hours, which requires them to dedicate more time to self-study. Nevertheless, they follow an identical curriculum. Importantly, part-time studies (including those offered by public universities) are always tuition-based. Full-time students have classes during the week. In public universities, this mode of study is tuition-free (students do not pay for study), while at private higher education institutions and private universities, they are tuition-based. The costs vary depending on the institution where the student chooses to study. Importantly, current regulations do not permit the combination of classes for full-time and part-time students. This means that a separate study track and all required classes must be organised independently for each of these forms (The Law on Higher Education and Science).

This leads to the necessity of briefly discussing the curriculum that law students can pursue at various academic institutions. Poland's legal education journey is a compelling narrative, one that has been shaped by the country's complex history, which oscillated between periods of independence, foreign rule, and political transformation. The study of law in Poland is not merely an academic endeavour but a profound exploration of a legal system that bears the imprints of Roman law, Napoleonic codes, and contemporary European legal norms. While Polish legal education is considered traditional and follows a similar pattern in most academic centres, some differences can be observed (Piaskowska and Piesiewicz [2019]). The sources of these differences can be: (1) the chosen educational profile, and (2) individual variances between the academic centres.

Currently, the applicable laws allow for conducting higher education on two profiles: practical and general academic (The Law on Higher Education and Science). The practical profile involves an educational programme with modules designed to equip students with practical skills and social competencies, with the premise that over half of the ECTS credit points in the programme encompass practical classes aimed at developing these skills and competencies, including skills acquired in workshop sessions conducted by professionals with practical experience beyond the academic realm. Conversely, the general academic profile comprises modules linked to the university's research activities, with the assumption that over half of the ECTS credit points in the programme involve classes aimed at enhancing the student's in-depth knowledge (The Law on Higher Education and Science). Importantly, the choice of profile often does not translate into the methods of conducting classes at individual institutions, which tend to be very traditional (Piaskowska and Piesiewicz [2019]). Only one academic centre (the SWPS University) offers legal skills training as part of its curriculum.

Regardless of the chosen profile of studies, there can be differences between various academic centres. The curriculum, consisting of mandatory and elective subjects, along with oral and written exams, is typically predetermined by the university, with slight variations between institutions. These differences typically concern elective subjects and are often related to the specialisation of a particular academic centre based on its geographical location. For example, maritime law may be offered as a lecture subject at the University of Gdańsk (located on the seaside), while geological and mining law may be found at the University of Silesia in Katowice (located in a mining area with active mines).

The classic path of legal education – legal specialisation training

Completing legal studies and obtaining a master's degree does not mean that a graduate can practice one of the classical legal professions. In Poland, the current system mandates that graduates complete specialised training, which includes a preliminary exam covering the entire legal curriculum. Regardless of the choice of a specialised training path, every graduate has also the opportunity for further education, including postgraduate studies, in narrow legal fields such as pharmaceutical law or nutritional law (tuition-based).

The current legal regulations provide exceptions to the requirement of completing a specialised internship, with different criteria for each profession. These exceptions are typically related to the practice of another legal profession for a specified period (for all professions) or having practical experience in a particular profession for a specified number of years (which allows one to sit for the final exam without the need for an internship, for the professions of lawyer and legal advisor), or holding a doctoral degree and practicing for the required period (for the professions of lawyer and legal advisor). Those individuals who hold the academic title of 'doktor habilitowany' (post-doctoral degree) also have the qualifications to practice any legal profession without the requirement of any specialised training. A significant number of legal graduates, right after obtaining a law degree, take the preliminary exams for traineeships, as it is the fundamental and traditional path that enables them to practice their chosen legal profession (Slazak [2007]).

Specialised training is necessary to practice as a barrister or legal advisor, and in both cases, the training is organised by the professional associations and lasts for three years. Trainees are required to participate in training sessions, take exams, and work under the guidance of a mentor to gain practical experience. The training concludes with the bar or the legal advisor exam.

Specialised training is also required to become a judge or prosecutor. The training is organised by the National School of Judiciary and Public Prosecution in Krakow, where all training sessions take place. The judicial traineeship lasts for 36 months and ends with a state exam, after which the graduate can apply for the position of assessor and, after four years, may be appointed as a judge. The prosecutorial traineeship also lasts for 36 months and concludes with a state exam, after which the graduate can be appointed as an assessor. An assessor may hold this position for up to three years, after which they may be appointed as a prosecutor.

In Poland, there are two other significant legal professions that require prior completion of specialised training and a state exam: a notary public and a court enforcement officer (bailiff). The notarial traineeship is organised by the professional association of notaries and lasts for three years and six months, during which the intern participates in training and works under the guidance of a mentor. The traineeship concludes with the notarial exam, after which the graduate awaits appointment and the determination of their office location by the Minister of Justice.

The court enforcement officer traineeship lasts for two years, during which the trainee participates in training and works under the guidance of a mentor. After completing the traineeship and passing the exam, the graduate must work as an assessor for a minimum of two years before being eligible for appointment as a court enforcement officer.

The academic path – from doctoral degree to full professorship

In addition to the traditional legal path leading to one of the legal professions, some graduates of law faculties opt for an academic career path. Therefore, it is impossible not to mention it when discussing legal education in Poland. This path is not easy and typically starts with a four-year doctoral programme during which, apart from attending classes and passing exams, a doctoral candidate works on their doctoral theses under the guidance of an academic supervisor. Regardless of completing the doctoral studies, a doctoral candidate is required to pass three positive doctoral exams: one in their field of specialisation, another in an additional subject such as philosophy, sociology, or economics, and the third in a modern foreign language. They are also required to have previously published at least one academic work (such as a research article or chapter in a book). Subsequently, the doctoral candidate must publicly defend their doctoral theses. Prior to this, the thesis must receive three positive reviews from external (non-affiliated with the university) reviewers

(independent academic employees – typically holding the postdoctoral degree or the title of professor). Following this defence, an authorised body (usually the institute's council) conducts a vote regarding the acceptance of the defence and the conferral of the doctoral degree. Achieving positive results in both votes (eligible voters are council members who are independent academic employees) is equivalent to obtaining a doctoral degree. This is not the only academic degree that a person pursuing an academic path can achieve; it is only the first one. The second is the postdoctoral degree ('doktor habilitowany'), and the third is full professor.

Earning a postdoctoral degree is a more challenging endeavour that necessitates the candidate's engagement with a higher education institution or, at the very least, collaboration with one. To attain the postdoctoral degree, one must demonstrate an impact on the development of the field of law (through their academic achievements, such as numerous scientific contributions in the form of articles, books, or chapters in collective works), engage in international collaboration, and conduct research in more than one scientific centre. Additionally, it is necessary to write a postdoctoral thesis, which is essentially a book containing an original scientific problem's solution. To evaluate the academic achievements and postdoctoral theses, the Council for Scientific Excellence appoints a committee, consisting of seven independent academic employees, including four reviewers. Receiving a minimum of three positive reviews allows for further proceedings, which involve the scheduling of a postdoctoral colloquium. During the colloquium, the candidate presents their theses and answers the committee's questions. The committee's work concludes with a vote on the opinion regarding the conferral of the postdoctoral degree, which is then forwarded to the scientific council of the institute overseeing the postdoctoral procedure. Based on this opinion, the council makes a resolution regarding the conferral of the postdoctoral degree. An individual who holds a postdoctoral degree may be employed as a university professor, and such a title may be conferred upon them. However, it is not an academic title of 'professor,' as a similar path to obtaining it exists in Poland as for the postdoctoral degree. To acquire the title of 'professor,' one must meet the following criteria: hold a postdoctoral degree, possess outstanding scientific achievements at the national or international level, and participate in the work of research teams engaged in projects funded through national or international competitions or complete scientific internships at scientific institutions, including foreign ones, or conduct scientific research or development work at universities or scientific institutions, including foreign ones. The procedure is also overseen by the Council for Scientific Excellence, which designates five reviewers (individuals holding the title of full professor). After receiving positive reviews, the Council for Scientific Excellence applies to the President of the Republic of Poland, via an administrative decision, for the conferment of the title of 'full professor' upon the candidate. The conferment of the title of professor is a prerogative of the President.

Conclusion

Poland's legal education landscape consists of diverse educational institutions, including public and private universities. This diversity in the types of institutions allows students to choose based on their preferences and financial means. It also offers flexible study options (full-time and part-time study), making it accessible to a wider range of students. While legal programmes in Poland generally follow a standard curriculum, variations exist between different centres. These differences can be influenced by the chosen educational profile of the institution or by regional specialisation. Law graduates are required to undergo specialised training to practice classical legal professions. The requirements for specialised training may vary for each profession, including the duration of traineeship. There is also an alternative academic path, which includes pursuing doctoral and postdoctoral degrees to become full professors. This academic path demands rigorous academic achievements, with obtaining a postdoctoral degree being equivalent to gaining the qualifications to practice any legal profession.

OLGA PIASKOWSKA

References

The Law on Higher Education and Science (Poland) 20 July 2018.

Piaskowska, O.M. and Piesiewicz, P.F. (2019). 'Rethinking of law schools in times of systemic change How to bring law school into twenty-first century? Polish perspective', Збірник наукових праць Харківського національного педагогічного університету імені ГС Сковороди Право, 20, pp. 126–153.

Slazak, M. (2007). 'Legal education and training in Poland', European Journal of Legal Education, 4(3), pp. 217–220.

77. Poland (history of legal education)

Introduction

The history of Polish legal education is as old as the history of the Polish academy. The Krakow Academy, founded in 1364, was already educating jurists. Nevertheless, this text aims not to report the history of legal education from that point onward. From a historical perspective, the key to understanding the processes occurring in Poland is to analyse trends and ideas of legal education since the founding of the first modern Polish state (in other words, the Second Polish Republic, which was created in Fall 1918). The starting point for reflection is 1918 when the legal academy of reborn Poland began to be formed by scholars educated in three traditions: Austrian, German and Russian

Interwar legal education

The legal system of interwar Poland was characterised by the fact that in significant areas of legal regulation, until 1939, it was forced to rely on the legislation of foreign occupiers. This, in turn, had a noticeable impact on the legal education system.

Legal studies were conducted at five state universities (Krakow, Poznan, Warsaw, Vilnius, Lviv) and one private Catholic university (Lublin) throughout the Second Polish Republic. Two were established just before or just after Poland regained its independence (Poznań, Lublin). Two originated from the Russian tradition: Warsaw and Vilnius. The Polish department in Warsaw was reactivated to replace the Russian one evacuated during the First War to Rostov-on-Don (and still functioning there today). The Vilnius one was established on the basis of Vilnius academic traditions. However, it is worth noting that, as a result of anti-Polish Tsarist policy, no university had operated in that city since 1842. Consequently, the Stefan Batory University was established in 1919. Institutional continuity was demonstrated by the universities of Lviv and Krakow, which had operated earlier as part of the Austro-Hungarian part of Austria. What's more, in Austrian times, these were mainly Polish-language universities.

Staying in the spirit of the purpose of the individual states in running legal education, it should be considered that, first, the greatest challenge that faced the deans of law faculties throughout the interwar period was the Polishisation of education and the reorientation of the educational system in a way that would suit the needs of the reborn state. Second, the interwar period was not significantly different from the present day when it came to the never-ending dispute over the identity of the legal academy. Similarly to today, it essentially amounted to a struggle over the content of the curriculum. The central focus of the arguments revolved around assessing whether the content lectured was sufficiently applicable for legal practice. In other words, there was an argument over the proportion between legal education's academic and practical elements.

The first document determining how legal education in Poland should be conducted was the Ordinance on the Organization of Studies at State Universities, issued on 16 October 1920, based on Article 114 of the Law on Academic Schools of 13 July 1920 (Dąbrowski [2015] at 36]. In this legal regime, law studies lasted four years and were divided into ten-week trimesters. Within the framework of the top-down programme, a strong accent was placed on propaedeutics and general knowledge. Hence, first-year students attended legal-historical subjects (Roman law, the history of law in Western Europe and the history of Polish law) for a total of 460 lecture hours. The first year's core curriculum was accompanied by 40 hours of legal theory. In subsequent years, they were followed by 180 hours of political economy (2nd year), 40 hours of philosophy of law (3rd year), and 60 hours of statistics (3rd year). Thus, from the 2,000 lecture hours planned for the entire educational cycle, strictly non-dogmatic subjects accounted for 39 per cent of all lecture hours. In addition, 90 hours of ecclesiastical law (2nd year), 60 hours of studies on the state (2nd year), and 60 hours (law of nations – international, also 2nd year) were then provided. That gave 11 per cent of the study programme. Dogmatic subjects (civil, criminal, administrative law) represented half of the content lectured (Dabrowski [2015] at 37–38).

However, this did not mean that the system introduced in 1920 was not criticised. All the more so, considering that the liberal constitution, the so-called March, was adopted a year later. This one was, in turn, overturned by another constitution of 1935. It introduced the domination of the state over the individual and the de facto personal governance of the President, who was neither politically nor legally responsible. In the spirit of this constitution, the efforts to transform legal education began. In 1937, the Minister of Justice explicitly stated that the future of the justice system depended on moving legal education into the right track (ie, corresponding to the 1935 vision of the state) (Dabrowski [2015] at 152). The economic aspect was also important. The bar and judiciary offered 300 annual positions, facing 2,000 law graduates.

Finally, a new regulation appeared on 12 August 1939. Due to the war's outbreak two weeks later, it did not go into force and was not published until 31 December, 1945 (Dabrowski [2015] at 199). It maintained the four-year cycle of education. However, the role of general subjects was reduced in favour of teaching dogmatics earlier and a straight propaedeutic subject (Introduction to Legal Science). Interestingly, the programme designed in this regulation was very close to the curriculum implemented throughout the communist period and most of the 1990s.

The law designed to serve ideology: the period of the Polish People's Republic

The post-war period should be divided into two main periods. The first was from 1944/48 to 1956, when in Poland, the construction of a totalitarian state along the model of the Soviet Union under the strict supervision of Moscow was attempted. The second was from 1956 to 1989, when, with the political thaw, the system evolved toward authoritarianism, and the Communist Party's objective was not to indoctrinate society ideologically but only to operate to prevent the communists from losing power. It should also be noted that a characteristic of the communist system was the dominance of politics over law. In turn, the use of law by the rulers was strictly instrumental (especially in criminal law). The aspiration to maximise political effects, combined with the aversion of the legal community, was the main problem of the new government (Watoła [2015] at 341). Since the beginning of so-called People's Poland, the authorities tried to pursue the reform of legal studies. However, their proposals faced criticism and resistance from academics (Watoła [2015] at 344).

At first, mainstream legal studies were based on the Decree of the Ministry of Education of 31 October 1946 and maintained the pre-war four-year educational cycle. The ordinance modified the catalogue of courses but maintained the trend from the reform first attempted just before the war. Regardless, courses designed to support the new regime or suggest a priority change were added. In the second year, Contemporary Social Doctrines, the view of Social Development appeared. In the third and fourth year, Labor Law and the System and Law of the USSR. The second course could be taught interchangeably with the system and law of Anglo-Saxon countries. Civil, criminology and administrative law specialisations were introduced for the third and fourth years of education.

A significant change was the reform of legal studies, which was introduced in the academic year 1949/1950. At that time, two-degree studies were presented in the 3+1 system. Students were granted to obtain professional licenses after three years. master's studies were supposed to be one year long and intended for the vast minority of graduates [wan346]. The reform's authors attempted to place the four-year degree programme within the new three-year professional degree programme, which involved a reduction in the number of teaching hours [wan347]. However, the problem of overproduction of lawyers was not solved.

However, following the Leninist principle that cadres are crucial, Poland's new rulers aimed to replace the judiciary's staff as soon as possible with people who ideologically suited them. Accordingly, the Teodor Duracz Central Law School [hereafter: CSP] in Warsaw was established on 1 June 1948. It was constituted by an ordinance of the Minister of Justice on 14 May 1948. The CSP was also subordinate to the MS. In common usage, the CSP was referred to as 'Duraczówka'. As was evident from the statute of this School, its ratio was not limited to providing room for theoretical and practical training of candidates for judges and prosecutors. It was also concerned with education in the spirit of 'democratic' ideology and social justice. The education had no fees and was supposed to last two years. The CSP's period of operation ended when the Teodor Duracz Higher School of Law was established in its place. It had a public character. It was a state vocational college. Those who attended the CSP automatically became students of the new school. In 1953, the school was transformed into the Training Centre for Judges and Prosecutors.

The two-degree study system was maintained for three years. In the academic year 1952/53 (Wołodkiewicz [2015] at 243), the studies were again merged into a four-year master's degree. Five five-year degree programmes were introduced in the 1956/57 academic year. In 1965/1966, they were reportedly shortened to four years. The entire period after the 1956 political thaw witnessed a further dispute on balancing practical and academic elements of legal education. In the first half of the 1970s, two reform proposals emerged. The first was drafted by A. Stelmachowski, and the second by J. Baszkiewicz. Stelmachowski proposed concentrating on lawyers' general education during the first two years of training, followed by their two-year specialisation (*ibidem*). Baszkiewicz, on the other hand, sought to make the curriculum more flexible (*ibidem*). The concept of five-year studies was revived from the bottom up in the early 1980s. At that time, the educational cycle was extended at individual universities by resolutions of faculty councils. The last attempt of ideological control over legal education was the Ministry's imposition, in 1982, of a 300-hour block of socio-political subjects in the legal education curriculum (Wołodkiewicz [2015] at 244).

Legal education after the democratic transition: Main challenges

Some point out that the reforms of the Polish political system have hardly touched the academy. As currently emphasised in the literature, law students in Poland must often memorise specific legal regulations taught during particular courses. The problem is not new. It has affected successive generations of students. As Wiktor Osiatyński wrote (whose legal education began in 1962): 'The legal profession and law studies were for those who did not know what to do with themselves. [...] Some of us went to the law faculty to study, and then, when we grew up, to decide what we wanted to do in and with life.' (Osiatyński [2002] at 69).

The dominant model of 'memory-based learning of law' in legal education, which has been in place for years, has been (and is) subject to criticism, even if only because of the low stability of Polish law. This model influences the subsequent passive reproduction of the taught legal regulations. Before the war, the eminent Polish scholar Cz. Znamierowski concluded: 'a legal education based almost exclusively on dogma, commenting on and memorising legal regulations [...] It means that it shapes the mind opposite to the principles on which an academic education should be based, whose task should be precisely to look at things freely, unconstrained by anything, impartial and full of creative imagination.' (Cz. Znamierowski [1938] at 46).

It must be emphasised that the referenced quote has not lost its relevance nowadays. The results of research conducted on law students at the University of Wroclaw by a team of Polish researchers from the CLEST Research published in 2017 show that 73.73 per cent of the surveyed students pointed out that legal studies focus excessively on theory. Almost as many respondents were of the opinion that legal studies involve excessive memorisation learning. This is because students indicated that 'too much is taught by heart' (Czarnota, Paździora, Stambulski (eds.) [2017] at 13). The conclusions of the study emphasised that the Polish system of teaching law appears as a 'tiresome necessity'. It was pointed out that in the Polish system of teaching law, the student is expected to memorise the material. Knowledge is treated as an objective fact. Such a teaching model was equated with inadequate education (*ibidem* at 14).

Although the model of legal education in Poland has been transforming, criticism has been formulated over the years regarding how students are taught. While it was pointed out that the ratio of university studies consists of theoretical learning of the matter taught, it was considered wrong to marginalise the importance of the practical sphere of the subjects taught (Waltoś [1996] at 86; Baszkiewicz [1975] at 35). In previous decades, law students were often not involved in learning about practical issues important to lawyers. Internships taken during university courses did not always provide a chance to approximate what a law student terminating in courts or state administrative bodies should be aware of (Waltoś [1996] at 80). Sometimes, it was ordered that internships be carried out only at the last stage of studies, and such a solution was considered late (*ibidem* at 80).

Considering the current legal framework of Polish legal education, it is essential to emphasise that Poland was among the 29 countries that decided to sign the Bologna Declaration in 1999. Only in 2004, however, did it become a signatory with the status of an EU member state (Wojtczak [2015] at 31). Significant changes were introduced in the 2005 law. The law on higher education adopted at the time was intended to reflect, in particular, the transformational changes that had taken place in Poland (Biernat [2007] at 33). There were sweeping changes in the law at that time. However, it should be added that this legislation is not currently in force and has been profoundly amended twice since that time. Nevertheless, in the case of law studies, we should speak rather about petrification instead of adaptation to modernity. It is particularly visible in the Decree of the Minister of Science and Higher Education of 12 July 2006. It was assumed that law teaching is carried out exclusively in the formula of a single master's (continuing five-year programme) degree (*Ibidem* at 40).

Conclusion

The history of Polish legal education is essentially a dispute between practice and theory, which, although called that, is a dispute over the identity of the legal academy. In other words, no matter what political system or ideology ruled in Poland or whether the country is located inside or outside supranational structures, the content of this disagreement has not changed. This may be because the argument about the nature of legal education is universal and results from its specific nature. On the one hand, it is an academic discipline (such as philosophy). On the other hand, it is a response to the practical needs of the state towards providing concrete specialists (as in the case of medicine).

ALEKSANDRA PARTYK AND FILIP CYUŃCZYK

References

Baszkiewicz, J. (1975). 'O modernizacji studiów prawniczych i administracyjnych', *Państwo i Prawo*, 4, pp. 28, 35.

Biernat, T. (2007). *Polityka prawa a model edukacji prawniczej*, Oficyna Wydawnicza AFM.

Czarnota, A., Paździora, M. and Stambulski, M. (2017). *Tiresome necessity. Reasons for starting the law studies in WPAE UWr and their assessment*, Biblioteka Edukacji Prawniczej i Teorii Społecznej.

Dąbrowski, P. (2015). *Mutationes in Doctrina Iuris. Kwestia praw nad reformą uniwersyteckich studiów prawniczych w Polsce (1918–1939)*, Wydawnictwo GSW.

Osiatyński, W. (2002). 'Czy każdy prawnik musi być uczonym?', in Turska, A. (ed), *Humanizacja zawodów prawniczych a nauczanie akademickie*, Liber.

Siewierski, M. (1946). 'O reformę programu akademickich studiów prawnych i ekonomicznych', *Państwo i Prawo*, 2, p. 64.

Szyszkowska, M. (2002). 'Niezbędność filozofii oraz filozofii prawa w kształceniu prawników', in Turska, A. (ed), *Humanizacja zawodów prawniczych a nauczanie akademickie*, Liber.

Waltoś, S. (1996). 'Od dyplomu uniwersyteckiego do zawodu prawniczego', *Palestra*, 3–4, pp. 79, 80.

Watoła, A. (2015). 'Reforma studiów prawniczych 1949–1950 w Polsce. Zarys problematyki', *Miscelanea Historico-Iuridica*, XIV (2).

Wołodkiewicz, W. (2015). 'Z dziejów nauki i nauczania historii prawa', *Czasopismo Prawno-Historyczne*, LXVII (1).

Wojtczak, K. (2015). 'O reformach studiów prawniczych i nauczaniu prawa w Polsce w latach 1918–2015', *Studia Prawa Publicznego*, 1(9), p. 31.

Znamierowski, C. (2013). *O naprawie studiów prawniczych*, Hoesick, W.F. (1938), quoted in Rodak, L. and Kiełb, M., 'Pamięciowa nauka prawa. W poszukiwaniu straconego czasu', *Prawo i Więź*, p. 72.

78. Poland (regulation of legal education)

The Polish higher education system is subject to statutory regulation. The legal act governing this matter is the Law of 20 July 2018 on Higher Education and Science (consolidated text: Journal of Laws of 2023, item 742, as amended) (hereafter referred to as 'HEaS Law'). Education in the field of law does not have separate legal regulations. This means that the provisions of the aforementioned law and regulations issued by the minister based on this law are applicable to education in this field.

Conducting law studies

Legal studies are classified as so-called uniform master's studies (§ 8 of the Regulation of the Minister of Science and Higher Education of 27 September 2018 on studies, consolidated text: Journal of Laws of 2021, item 661, as amended), which last from nine to 12 semesters, ie, five to six years (Article 64(1)(3) and Article 65(3) of the HEaS Law). Meanwhile, the academic year runs from 1 October to 30 September and is divided into two semesters. The statute of the university may provide for a detailed division of the academic year within semesters (Article 66 of the HEaS Law). Uniform master's studies in law provide specialised knowledge and prepare students for a career in the legal profession, culminating in the award of a Master of Laws degree. Law studies can be conducted with a focus on: (a) practical profile, where more than half of the ECTS (European Credit Transfer and Accumulation System) points are assigned to activities that develop practical skills, or (b) academic profile, where more than half of the ECTS points are assigned to activities related to the university's scientific activities (Article 53(4) of the HEaS Law). Choosing between a practical or academic profile in law studies does not impact the available career paths for students. After completing law studies, graduates can either pursue a scientific career, which is regulated by the HEaS Law, or obtain qualifications to practice as a judge, advocate, legal adviser, notary, prosecutor, tax advisor, or patent attorney. The education and acquisition of qualifications to practice these professions are regulated in separate legal acts governing these professions. The HEaS Law provides for two forms of conducting studies. Law studies can be conducted in either full-time or part-time formats. Full-time study classes take place from Monday to Friday, while part-time study classes usually occur in a student meeting system every two weeks, lasting from Friday afternoon to Sunday. Universities offering education in law are required to assign this field to a specific scientific discipline, in the case of law studies, it would be legal sciences. The establishment of legal studies requires permission from the minister. However, some higher education institutions may be exempt from the need to obtain such permission. Permission is not required to establish law studies if the university has a scientific category of A+, A, or B+ (Article 53 of the HEaS Law). Scientific categories: A+, A, B+, B, or C are awarded by the Minister of Education and Science, taking into account the individual achievements of employees representing the given discipline.

Granting Permission to Establish Law Studies

A university wishing to establish new uniform master's studies in law, whether with a practical or academic profile, must submit an appropriate application. This application should be submitted no later than six months before the planned start of these studies. Before granting permission, the Minister must seek the opinion of the State Accreditation Commission (hereafter referred to as 'SAC'). This opinion concerns whether the university meets all necessary conditions to conduct studies in the proposed field, level, and profile. The Minister issues permission to establish studies if the university meets the requirements specified in the Regulation of the Minister of Science and Higher Education of 27 September 2018 on studies (consolidated text: Journal of Laws of 2021, item 661, as amended) (hereafter referred to as 'MNiSW Regulation'). The application to establish studies must particularly include: an overview of the studies, reasons for initiating them in the chosen field and profile, strategies for enhancing the programme and education quality, details of scientific activities (for academic profile studies), expected competencies of applicants, conditions and organisation of the educational process, including a list of academic staff, class allocation, expected student numbers, infrastructure details, and access to library and electronic resources, a copy of the university senate's resolution on establishing the study programme along with this study programme (§ 9 of the MNiSW Regulation).

Programme of Uniform Master's Studies in Law

There are several requirements set out in the MNiSW Regulation regarding the content of the study programme. First, the programme must specify whether the studies will be conducted in full-time or part-time form, the number of semesters, and the number of ECTS points necessary to obtain a Master of Laws degree. The programme must also define: the professional title to be awarded to graduates (the professional title of Master of Laws); classes or groups of classes, regardless of the form of their conduct, along with the assignment of learning outcomes and programme content ensuring the achievement of these outcomes; the total number of class hours; methods of verification and assessment of learning outcomes achieved by the student during the entire education cycle; the total number of ECTS points that a student must obtain in classes conducted with the direct participation of academic teachers or other persons conducting classes; the scope, rules, and form of professional internships, and the number of ECTS points that a student must obtain as part of these internships (§ 3(1) of the MNiSW Regulation). The law study programme should allow students to choose classes assigned ECTS points, constituting at least 30 per cent of the total number of ECTS points (§ 3(3) of the MNiSW Regulation). If the field of law is associated with more than one discipline, the programme must specify the contribution of each to the number of ECTS points, emphasising the discipline of law as the leading one. The programme must also consider whether these are practical or academic legal studies. The programme for practical legal studies must include classes developing practical skills to a greater extent than 50 per cent of the ECTS points. Meanwhile, academic legal studies must include classes related to the scientific activities conducted at the university in the discipline or disciplines to which the field of

study is assigned, to a greater extent than 50 per cent of the ECTS points. This profile of studies should include student participation in classes preparing for scientific activities or participation in such activities (§ 3(5) of the MNiSW Regulation). The study programme should be subject to systematic evaluation and improvement. However, up to 30 per cent of the overall number of learning outcomes defined in the current study programme on the day of issuing this permission can be changed to improve the programme. When making changes to the study programme, it is necessary to consider feedback from the analysis of the compatibility of learning outcomes with labour market needs and feedback from the results of monitoring, including monitoring conducted by the MNiSW. Changes to the study programme are introduced at the beginning of a new education cycle. In certain cases, it is possible to change the legal studies programme during the education cycle. The first such case is the need to consider the latest scientific achievements or developments related to legal professional activities. The second is the requirement to adjust the study programme to formal requirements, ie, to correct irregularities identified by the SAC or to adapt the study programme to changes in generally applicable regulations (§ 9 of the MNiSW Regulation).

Distance Learning in Law Studies

During the period from the announcement of the state of epidemic threat and later the state of the COVID-19 epidemic, education could be conducted exclusively using distance learning methods and techniques, regardless of whether this was provided for in the study programme. After lifting the state of the COVID-19 epidemic, it is not possible to conduct uniform master's studies in law exclusively using distance learning methods and techniques. The MNiSW Regulation allows this possibility but with certain limitations. The number of ECTS points obtained through distance learning methods and techniques must not exceed 50 per cent of the total number of ECTS points required to complete practical profile studies in law, or 75 per cent in the case of academic profile studies (§ 13 of the MNiSW Regulation). In the field of law, distance learning is permitted if additional criteria are met: academic teachers and others conducting classes must be trained in distance learning, with the university overseeing the implementation's correctness. Both students and instructors need access to IT infrastructure for effective two-way communication. Students must have access to electronic materials and personal consultations with instructors. Continuous monitoring of learning progress is required for outcome verification. Finally, the university must provide training to prepare students for effective participation in distance learning.

Admission to Law Studies

The HEaS Law establishes rules for admitting students to both full-time and part-time studies. These rules apply to both public (state) and private universities. A person who holds a high school diploma, or a certificate or other document recognised as equivalent to a high school diploma under regulations, may be admitted to uniform master's studies in law. In other words, legal studies can only be commenced by individuals who have completed secondary education.

Admission to law studies is possible through three routes: recruitment, validation of learning outcomes, or transfer from another university (domestic or foreign), each with distinct criteria and processes. The university determines recruitment conditions, timing, and methods, as outlined by the university senate's resolution. Admission criteria typically rely on high school exam results, and universities may hold entrance exams to assess candidate suitability, ensuring they don't duplicate secondary education exams (Article 70 of the HEaS Law). Validation of learning outcomes offers access for those with professional experience, with the university verifying previously acquired competencies, potentially reducing study time. This method can account for up to 50 per cent of ECTS points in the study programme (Article 71 of the HEaS Law). Lastly, transferring from another university involves specific regulations ensuring fair procedures and rights for all parties involved.

Academic Teachers

The HEaS Law introduces requirements for academic teachers. Classes in the law department can be conducted by academic teachers employed at the university with the competence and experience necessary for proper class execution, as well as by other persons possessing such competence and experience (Article 73 of the HEaS Law). The law does not specify exact criteria for what constitutes the 'competence and experience necessary for proper class execution.' However, the concept of 'skills' should be understood as defined in Annex I to the Council Recommendation of 22 May 2017 on the European Qualifications Framework for lifelong learning. In this document, 'skills' are defined as the ability to apply knowledge and use know-how to perform tasks and solve problems. The regulation's use of 'experience' should be understood as the 'aggregate of knowledge and skills acquired based on observation and personal experiences' as defined by the PWN Polish Language Dictionary. The statutory regulation allows some freedom in employing persons to conduct classes. There is no direct requirement for employing scientific employees as academic teachers. Classes can be conducted by persons with various qualifications in the field of law, including degrees like doctorate and habilitated doctor, and the title of professor. The professor title, a special distinction awarded by the President of Poland, requires certain statutory requirements. Additionally, classes can be conducted by Masters of Law and practitioners, i.e., persons with professional experience in a specific field of law. It is important to differentiate between academic titles and job positions. The HEaS Law recognises positions such as professor, university professor, adjunct, and assistant (Article 116(1) of the HEaS Law). Specific requirements must be met to be employed in these positions. For example, only a person with a professor title can be employed as a professor, and a person with at least a doctorate and significant teaching or professional achievements can become a university professor. The university's statute may define other positions for academic teachers, such as visiting professor, lecturer, senior lecturer, language teacher, or instructor. Notably, when someone attains the professor title, the university is obligated to employ them as a professor. Other academic advancements are not legally tied to job promotions, and universities have their own rules in this regard.

Evaluation of education quality

The quality of education in studies is subject to evaluation by the State Accreditation

Commission (SAC). SAC conducts evaluations in the form of programme assessment or comprehensive assessment. Programme assessment is a process of cyclic evaluation of the quality of education in a specific field of study. This assessment considers many aspects, including study programmes and education standards, qualifications of teaching and research staff, infrastructure used to implement the study programme, cooperation with the socio-economic environment, internationalisation, and student support in the learning process. A programme assessment can be initiated by the SAC, at the request of the university, or immediately upon the request of the minister. This process ends with issuing a positive or negative assessment. A positive programme assessment is issued for a period of up to six years.

A comprehensive assessment, on the other hand, is a process of evaluating a university's actions to ensure the quality of education, carried out by the SAC. It focuses primarily on assessing the effectiveness of these actions in all fields in which the university provides education. A comprehensive assessment is conducted at the request of a university that has only positive programme assessments or a positive comprehensive assessment. The SAC decides to conduct this assessment, taking into account the results of the university's previous programme assessments. This process ends either with a positive assessment, valid for three to eight years, or with a refusal to issue such an assessment. In the case of a positive comprehensive assessment, the SAC may highlight fields in which the quality of education is particularly high. In such cases, no additional programme assessment is conducted in the study fields related to these areas for the period specified in the assessment unless requested by the minister. If a university receives a refusal for a positive comprehensive assessment, it cannot apply for a re-assessment for five years, unless the SAC specifies a shorter period.

PIOTR PIESIEWICZ

References

Balicki, A., Pyter, M. and Zięba, B. (2021). *Prawo o szkolnictwie wyższym i nauce. Komentarz*, Wydawnictwo, C.H. Beck.

Izdebski, H. and Zieliński, J.M. (2023). *Prawo o szkolnictwie wyższym i nauce. Komentarz*, 3rd edition, Wolters Kluwer Polska.

Jakubowski, A. et al (2023). *Prawo o szkolnictwie wyższym i nauce. Komentarz*, Wydawnictwo, C.H. Beck.

Kierznowski, Ł. (2021). *Stopnie naukowe i stopnie w zakresie sztuki. Komentarz*, Difin.

Woźnicki, J. et al (2019). *Prawo o szkolnictwie wyższym i nauce. Komentarz*, Wolters Kluwer.

79. Police legal education

Police legal education, Higher Education Institutions and 'professionalising' the police

Despite an extensive history of policing in England and Wales, police education is a new concept. Most established professions have long-standing structured relationships with Higher Education Institutions (HEIs) – policing does not. Instead, police legal education has been developed, managed, and delivered 'in house' by police practitioners within police forces. What ensues is a brief overview of the key changes concerning police education in England and Wales and an exploration of police entry routes. The entry examines the challenges in this turbulent field and considers who is best placed to deliver police education.

Policing and legal education

Police officers work in an increasingly complex environment, one which not only includes legal education, such as learning evidence and procedure (i.e. stop and search, house searches), case law and definitional criminal 'points to prove'; but one where the investigator has to be technologically adept (i.e. correct storage and appropriate analysis of mobile phone evidence) as well as highly attuned to the social environment. This means officers are expected to possess more expert knowledge, more analytical capabilities, reflexivity, flexibility and communication skills (Brown [2020]).

'Regional' to 'local' training: IPLDP

Historically, police training in England and Wales comprised of 14 weeks' regionalised residential training before recruits returned to their respective forces for further training and support. Trainers were police officers who needed to attain police-based training qualifications. However, an Inspectorate report criticised the process, arguing it was 'not fit for purpose' and required restructuring (HMIC [2002] at 72). One reason for this is that residential training schools socialised and assimilated new recruits into police culture (Fielding [1988]), embedding the transmis-

sion of often dysfunctional culture and practices. Using concrete examples, officers pass on stories which serve to guide and initiate newer recruits into the prevailing culture (Waddington [1999]). Consequently, officers at the 'sharp end' (on the streets) often tell new recruits to forget what they learned at training school from 'plastics' [the trainers] (Aplin [2019] at 8) leading students to 'unlearn' as they become indoctrinated with the 'old' culture (Hannagan [2005] at 228). More 'localised' training delivery by each force was intended to 'interrupt' these cultural transmissions.

The impetus behind the Initial Police Learning and Development Programme (IPLDP) in 2005 was to modernise training, professionalise the service and 'change' the negative aspects of police culture. However, the global recession (2007–2008), led to priority-based budget cuts for many police forces which led to a freeze on recruitment, civilian redundancies, and the faltering of the IPLDP programme (Ramshaw and Soppitt [2018]).

The professionalisation agenda

Neyroud (2011) recommended a radical change to pre-entry qualifications for policing, suggesting forces recruit individuals with high quality degrees with diverse career experiences. However, it was Flanagan, in an earlier review, who stressed the need to move from police 'training' towards 'education' ([2008] at 53), placing the onus on partnership working with Further and Higher Education Institutions (FE and HEIs) ([2011] at 11). This led to the creation of the College of Policing as a new professional body (2013) to quality assure and provide clear standards for FE and HEIs through a chartered qualification framework and National Curriculum (Neyroud [2011] at 45). The expectation was that from 2020 onwards all officers must hold a degree qualification in policing as a graduate level profession (Bekhradnia and Beech [2018]). The impetus was to elevate policing to the status of a 'profession' (Bryant et al [2014] at 382).

The impact of the global financial market crisis (2007–2008), and the austerity measures that followed, resulted in England and Wales police forces reducing their internal capability and resourcing for officer training and development. In September 2019, the UK

Home Office implemented an uplift policy to reverse the reductions in police numbers caused by austerity measures, by recruiting 20,000 new police officers over a three-year period (Home Office [2020]), supported by almost £750 million in government funding (Home Office [2019]). These events created a 'perfect storm', with forces having neither the capacity to recruit or to train officers in the large numbers needed to meet central government targets, nor the capability to provide this type of HE academic learning, and/or or properly recognised academic qualification.

The four main policing entry routes: DHEP, PCDA, DPP and PCEP

In 2016 the College of Policing created the Policing Education Qualifications Framework (PEQF) as a foundation for developing academic programmes for all forty-three forces in England and Wales (College of Policing [2020]). In response to market demand, from 2019 onwards, a wide range of HEIs began to offer three differing educational routes (Brown [2020]). The first was the two year 'Degree Holder Entry Programme' (DHEP), representing a 'conversion course' for recruits already holding a degree, but not within the discipline of policing (Ramshaw and Soppitt [2018]). The second was the Police Constable Degree Apprenticeship Programme (PCDA), enabling non-graduate recruits to complete a degree program whilst simultaneously undertaking their police training. The third involved students undertaking an undergraduate Degree in Professional Policing (DPP), informally termed a 'pre join degree,' where students might seek recruitment to police forces *after* they completed their degree (Mahruf et al [2020]). All three programmes require providers to adhere to the PEQF framework set by the College of Policing, as continuing delivery requires accreditation and relicensing from the College of Policing.

However, despite the three new entry routes, some forces have remained reluctant to relinquish the 'in house' IPLDP that was formerly in place for new recruits. Although such programmes have been allowed to continue until 31 March 2024 (HE and Policing Forum [2023a]), IPLDP provides only a Level 3 qualification – not a degree. Moreover, the existence of IPLDP sends out a message to all

HEIs that the police are willing and capable of training their own officers, potentially damaging the existing relationships that forces have with higher education.

As a result of consultation between Police and Crime Commissioners and NPCC Chief Constables a new fourth entry route, termed the Police Constable Entry Programme (PCEP), was formally agreed and implemented in April 2024. This does not require the learner to achieve a formal qualification (College of Policing [2023]). Although the NPCC suggests this represents an 'additional' rather than a replacement of established routes, it does not complement the existing framework, indeed, it directly contradicts it (HE Forum in Policing [2023a]). The fourth entry route is arguably divisive, as the other routes require a professional university degree (DHEP/PCDA and DPP) whilst the fourth route allows candidates *without* a degree to become officers, arguably undermining the core principles of the Framework and the 'professionalisation agenda' (HE Forum in Policing [2023a]), inferring that the original aspiration to deliver 'professionalisation' through FE and HEIs has seemingly now been relaxed.

'Whose' knowledge counts in police legal education?

The redistribution of police training from police forces to colleges and universities continues to meet resistance from police forces (Tong and Wood [2011]). There is a distinct air of protectionism from police force trainers around 'who' teaches policing students about the domain that is policing. Currently within higher education, police recruits are being educated by an uneven blend of retired police officers (some of high rank) with little educational training background or higher-level qualifications, 'pracademic' ex officers with higher level qualifications and teaching experience, and pure 'academics' with educational credentials, theoretical knowledge of policing but no direct 'practitioner' experience.

A key requirement when teaching policing students, as stipulated by the College of Policing, is to employ lecturers that possess skills in Law and Criminology (Ramshaw and Soppitt [2018]). Researchers also highlight the scarcity of 'police practitioners' turned 'academics' within the policing field (Mahruf et al [2020]). Observers highlight multiple benefits pracademics can bring, exposing students to 'real world experience(s)', bringing the two worlds of practice and academia together, thereby enabling HEIs to deliver on strategic promises in terms of developing 'work ready' graduates (ibid at 298). Students enjoy the 'war stories' (Van Mannen [1978] at 297) presented by pracademics; but this must be tempered equally by the importance of theoretical underpinnings of criminology along with the legal and procedural elements of 'good policing'.

The greatest tension in terms of police education is the divide between theoretical and practical knowledge, whereby student officers put less credence on theory compared to other apprenticeship programmes, such as teaching or nursing (Werno and Smeby [2018] as cited in Hagen et al [2023]). Research into police culture shows stark scepticism towards book learning (Reiner [2010]). Because pure 'academics' might be teaching new recruits, this can lead some student officers to undermine the academic foundations of policing degrees. Notably, the unruly and disrespectful behaviours policing students showed to lecturers such as 'reading the paper' in the lecture theatre whilst the lecturer tried to control the 'zoo' (Heslop [2011] at 304).

Finally, there is also a disturbing 'them and us' divide between pure academics versus the police practitioner at an internal level within HEI institutions. To police students and police trainers, pure 'academics' may appear theoretical and too remote from the 'coal face' (Punch [2009] at 241) to understand the 'sharp end' of policing (Van Maanen [1978] at 306). Conversely, police practitioners may have the 'street craft' but may not possess the teaching skills necessary to enable effective 'learning.' Recent research from Norway identifies that police educators need to possess *both* practical and theoretical competencies to strengthen the education quality for police officers (Hagen et al [2023]).

At an international level Terpstra and Schaap's study of three countries (Finland, Norway and Germany) recognises the inherently political nature of delivering police education within the HE environment (2021), as is evident within this entry. Indeed the involvement of HE is intended to imbue ethics and *change* the dominant police occupational culture (Brown [2020] at 14; Terpstra

and Schaap [2021]), but as Brown confirms, exposure to Higher Education fails to deliver these ideals ([2020] at 14).

Conclusion

In conclusion, some police practitioners within forces hold the intransigent view that they are in the best position to educate policing students. This may be so on a purely practical level. Unfortunately, the pragmatic demand for 'service' by police forces will always be prioritised above the necessity of educating and professionalising those officers, precipitating stress, burn out and poor retention. In order for Police Education to thrive two elements are necessary. HEIs need to appreciate the unique requirements of the sector and Police Forces must trust HEIs to deliver the aforementioned crucial benefits. If these are relegated Police Education will suffer, as will the service to student officers and the public at large.

RACHAEL APLIN AND HOWARD ATKIN

References

Aplin, R. (2019). *Policing UK Honour-Based Abuse Crime*, Palgrave Macmillan.

Becker, H. (2008). 'Outsiders', in Mclaughlin, E., Muncie, J. and Hughes, G. (eds), *Criminological perspectives*, 2nd edition, London Sage.

Bekhradnia, B. and Beech, D. (2018). *Demand for Higher Education to 2030*, Oxford Higher Education Policy Institute.

Birzer, M. (2002). 'Writing partnership between police practitioners and researchers', *Police Practice and Research*, 3(2), p. 149.

Brown, J. (2020). 'Do Graduate Police Officers Make a Difference to Policing? Results of an Integrative Literature Review', *Policing: A Journal of Policy & Practice*, 14(1), p. 9.

Bryant, R. et al. (2014). 'Police training and education: past, present and future', in Brown, J. (ed), *The Future of Policing*, Routledge.

Charman, S. (2017). *Police socialisation, identity and culture: Becoming blue*, Palgrave Macmillan.

College of Policing. (2020). *Police Education Qualifications Framework (PEQF)*, UK College of Policing, available at https://www.london.gov.uk/programmes-strategies/mayors-office-policing-and-crime/governance-and-decision-making/mopac-decisions-0/policing-education-qualifications-framework#:~:text=The%20Police%20Education%20Qualification

%20Framework,and%20education %20pathways%20from%202020.

Fielding, N. (1988). *Joining forces: Police training and occupational competence*, Routledge.

Flanagan, R. (2008). *The review of policing*. Final report, available at https://assets-hmicfrs .justiceinspectorates.gov.uk/uploads/flanagan -review-of-policing-20080201.pdf.

Hagen, A., Damen, M. and Hermansen, H. (2023). 'Unpacking the Theory-Practice Nexus in Basic Police Education', *Nordic Journal of Studies in Policing*, 10(1), p. 1.

Hannagan, T. (2005). *Management concepts and practices*, 4th edition, Pearson Education Limited.

Her Majesty's Inspectorate of Constabulary (HMIC). (2002). *Training matters*, Home Office.

Heslop, R. (2011). 'Reproducing police culture in a British university: findings from an exploratory case study of police foundation degrees', *Police Practice and Research*, 12(4), p. 298.

Higher Education (HE) Forum in Policing. (2023a). *Letter drafted to Jo Noakes College of Policing around the decision to create a 4th entry route into Policing*, Signed by 62 Higher Education Institutions in England and Wales.

Higher Education (HE). (2023b). *Forum in Policing Online meeting.*

Home Office. (2019). 'National Campaign to recruit 20,000 police officers launches today', available at https://www.gov.uk/government/ news/national-campaign-to-recruit-20000 -police-officers-launches-today.

Home Office. (2020). *Plans for statistical reporting on progress with the recruitment of an additional 20,000 Police Officers in England and Wales*, Statistical Bulletin 04/20.

Mahruf, M. et al. (2020). 'Police Education in the United Kingdom: Challenges and Future Directions', in Nugmanova, M., Mikkola, H., Rozanov, A. and Komleva, V. (eds), *Education, Human Rights and Peace in Sustainable Development*, Intechopen.

Neyroud, P. (2011). *Review of Police Leadership and Training*, London: Home Office, available at https://www.gov.uk/government/publications/ police-leadership-and-training-report-review.

Punch, M. (2009). *Police corruption: Deviance, accountability and reform in policing*, Willan, Devon.

Ramshaw, P. and Soppitt, S. (2018). 'Educating the recruited and recruiting the educated: Can the new Police Education Qualifications Framework in England and Wales succeed where others have faltered', *International Journal of Police Science & Management*, 20(4), p. 243.

Reiner, R. (2010). *The politics of the police*, 4th edition, Oxford University Press.

Terpstra, J. and Schaap, D. (2021). 'The Politics of Higher Police Education: An International Comparative Perspective', *Policing*, 15(4), p. 2407.

Tong, S. and Wood, D. (2011). 'Graduate Police Officers: Releasing the Potential for Pre-Employment University Programmes for Aspiring Officers', *Police Journal*, 84(1), p. 69.

Van Maanen, J. (1978). 'Observations on the making of policemen', in Manning, P. and Van Maanen, J. (eds), *Policing: A view from the street*, Goodyear publishing company inc.

Waddington, P. (1999). 'Police (canteen) sub-culture: An appreciation', *British Journal of Criminology*, 39(2), p. 287.

80. Pre-qualification legal workplace experience

Introduction

The Carnegie Report *Educating Lawyers: Preparation for the Profession of Law* identified the 'apprenticeship of practice' as critical to the formation of legal practitioners (Sullivan et al [2007]). This is often delivered though workplace experience (Wilson [2010] at 15). Its length may be nominal, or up to half the period required to qualify. Regulation of its venue, content and assessment (if any) also varies (Ching [2016]).

In common law countries, however, pre-qualification work experience is not required for attorneys in most of the USA (although it often is for paralegals). Exceptions are the Delaware clerkship of 12 weeks and requirements in some states, such as New York (but vigorously rejected by others), for some pro-bono service, although this is not necessarily perceived as primarily an educational requirement. In New Zealand it was abandoned in the late nineteenth century as an inappropriate obstacle to qualification and has not been reinstated (Spiller [1993] at 226).

Nor is it always required in civil and Muslim law jurisdictions, or where law degrees are longer (for example, Argentina, Bahrain, India, Portugal). In practice, however, many new lawyers have internship or clinic experience, or work as paralegals whilst studying for bar examinations, and employers may expect it in any event (Hewitt et al [2022]). Regulators also sometimes place limits on the licences of newly qualified lawyers until they have acquired some experience or offer targeted support and mentoring in the early years of practice.

Terminology

Terminology includes apprenticeship, articles, clerkship, devilling, induction period, practica forense, pupillage, qualifying employment, referendariat, stage, training contract.

Relationship with classroom study

Historically, common law practitioners qualified through apprenticeship. Courses and examinations were supplemental to learning in a community of practice (Lave and Wenger [1991]). A shift to university study in much of the common law world began in the later twentieth century (Clark [2012]). Practitioners in the UK and Canada, however, retain a strong cultural attachment to work experience (see Law Society of Upper Canada [2017] at 4–5). By contrast, civil law countries emphasise university education (Wilson [2010] at 44), as do India and the USA.

Modern configurations can be divided into:

- Sequential approaches, where classroom activity occurs before work experience (Saunders [1996] at 170).
- Parallel models, where trainees work and study part-time (e.g. British legal executives, English solicitor-apprentices, US law office routes, Brazilian internships) (Sadi [2018] at 175–176).
- Modular approaches, where work experience is embedded into a course (some parts of Australia, France – avocats, the CARICOM Caribbean), or trainees move between blocks of workplace and classroom activity (Republic of Ireland – solicitors).
- Dual approaches, where work experience and a vocational course are alternatives (as in Victoria, Australia; US law office programmes; Ontario, Canada (Jochelson, Gackek and Ireland [2021] at 107; France – notaires).

Length

The length of the period may indicate its intended purpose. A period of hours (USA: New York and elsewhere) or months (Australia) suggests that it is intended to socialise, or serve the community. Periods of a year to three years (China, England, Germany, Hong Kong, Poland, South Africa), suggest that significant learning is envisaged. Nevertheless, periods may be waived or reduced for higher qualifications (Saudi Arabia) or prior experience (Poland). In general, periods are longer where courses are short, law degrees are not required, practice is unsupervised, there is a breadth of experience to be covered and where there is a strongly deregulated market, possibly to assert status and quality by comparison with competitors.

Venue

In modular approaches, the experience can be quality-controlled and, perhaps, assessed more easily than in the employment market. However, sometimes responsibility is in the public sector: German trainees are temporary civil servants, rotated through a variety of posts. In Chile, trainees work in a Corporación de Asistencia Judicial, a pro bono service.

Frequently, however, work experience is obtained through the employment market, though possibly limited to authorised organisations and to particular kinds of 'training contract'. This model is, therefore, dependent on the health of the legal services market and on the recruitment practices of law firms. There may be more candidates seeking work experience than positions, creating a bottleneck. Challenges of fair access are exacerbated if the period is, or can be, unpaid.

Although supervisor training may be required, regulation generally refers only to their length of experience and good standing in the profession rather than to any proven ability to coach or teach. Where there are multiple professions, or where it is possible to serve the period outside the jurisdiction, it is normal for the supervisor to be from the profession and jurisdiction which the trainee wishes to enter. This reinforces the importance of socialisation and induction into the ethics and *habitus* of the specific jurisdiction and profession. The extent to which a supervisor is liable at law, or to disciplinary proceedings, if the trainee is not effectively supervised, is not always clear.

Content

There is a considerable literature on learning in a workplace setting. Nevertheless, there is a tension between fee-earning 'task conscious' activity limiting opportunity for 'learning conscious activity' (Rogers [2003]). Some professions dictate that certain areas of law, or activities, must be experienced – or at least observed – by the trainee (inputs). Others set standards and competences which must be achieved (outputs). Much is, however, tacit and may treat the period as devoted to socialisation and development of a professional identity. There are, however, important things that can only be learned in the workplace (eg working in a hierarchical team, progressing a matter over a period); or contextualising

what has been learned in the classroom (Law [2001] at 467). There is also scope for progression beyond classroom learning, increasing the range of variables used in problem-solving (Blasi [1995]) or specialising.

Assessment

Occasionally, but rarely, the period is summatively assessed, by project (France) or portfolio (England – legal executives) or there is an assessment (as in Turkey and Thailand) at the end of the period. Such assessments are generally administered by the professional body or the state. Certification by supervisors is often limited to the length of service, good character and completion of regulatory requirements such as the required range of experience (by contrast with the level of learning demonstrated).

A self-standing bar exam organised by the licensing authority is not necessarily a summative assessment of what has been learned in the workplace. In China the examination precedes work experience, signalling that the latter is the responsibility of the profession. French avocats, however, take the CAPA examination after their work experience, which may at least allow learning in the workplace to contribute to the examination. In a small number of US states it is possible to become eligible for the state bar examination by studying in a law office or judge's chambers in place of all (or part) of the JD. In New York, for example, a candidate studying in this way must be employed 'as a regular law clerk and student' although they are entitled to receive 'instruction' from their supervisors in law school subjects. In Germany and Poland there are two examinations, one before, and one after work experience, suggesting that the second maybe envisaged as assessing what has been learned in the workplace.

In England, there are currently two routes to qualify as a solicitor for domestic applicants. One is by way of a government sponsored apprenticeship, of up to seven years in duration for school leavers (a shorter period is demanded of graduate apprentices) (Law Society of England and Wales [no date]). These candidates are entitled to 20 per cent of their time in training, and take the same summative examinations as their peers, although their employers pay for both their training and their examinations. Unlike their non-apprentice peers, who can take the professional examinations before, during or after work experience, apprentices can only take the final examination after completion of their work experience and on condition that they have already demonstrated all the competences assessed in the examination. However, given the sequencing of the non-apprentice route, those examinations cannot contain anything that can *only* be learned through work experience. There may, however, be things learned *better*, or more *validly*, or which can be demonstrated over a period in the workplace in a way that is impossible in a self-standing examination.

Conclusion

There is limited empirical research on the learning during mandatory work experience (but see Ching and Henderson [2016], Ali [2017]). That said, a comparative project on the Daniel Webster scheme in USA, New Hampshire, exempting from parts of the bar exam (Gerkmann and Harman [2015]) indicated enhanced competence by those who had taken the workplace route. Emerging evidence in England suggests that apprentices perform better in the solicitors' examination than their peers who have followed the more conventional university-based route. In the USA, however, law office applicants appear to fare worse in the examinations than their peers.

There is potential for workplace exploitation, and possibly as a result, some professions have allocated responsibility for it to the academy or the state. At its best it is an extremely valuable site of authentic learning, contextualisation and socialisation.

JANE CHING

References

Ali, A.S. (2017). 'Summary of Articling Experience Survey Results', Law Society of Upper Canada.

Blasi, G.L. (1995). 'What Lawyers Know: Lawyering Expertise, Cognitive Science, and the Functions of Theory', *Journal of Legal Education*, 45, p. 313.

Ching, J. (2016). 'Pre-Qualification Work Experience in Professional Legal Education: Literature Review', Solicitors Regulation Authority, available at http://irep.ntu.ac.uk/id/eprint/28868/.

Ching, J. and Henderson, P. (2016). 'Pre-Qualification Work Experience in Professional Legal Education: Report', Solicitors Regulation Authority, available at https://irep.ntu.ac.uk/id/eprint/28867/.

Clark, D.S. (2012). 'Legal Education', in Clark, D.S. (ed), *Comparative Law and Society*, Edward Elgar Publishing.

Gerkman, A. and Harman, E. (2015). 'Ahead of the Curve – Turning Law Students into Lawyers', Institute for the Advancement of the American Legal System.

Hewitt, A. et al. (2022). 'Weighing the Cost of Expectations That Students Complete Legal Work Experience', *Legal Education Review*, 32, p. 109.

Jochelson, R., Gacek, J. and Ireland, D. (2021). 'Reconsidering Legal Pedagogy: Assessing Trigger Warnings, Evaluative Instruments, and Articling Integration in Canada's Modern Law School Curricula', *Manitoba Law Journal*, 44, p. 87.

Lave, J. and Wenger, E. (1991). *Situated Learning: Legitimate Peripheral Participation*, Cambridge University Press.

Law, J. (2001). 'Articling in Canada Symposium: A Global Legal Odyssey', *South Texas Law Review*, 43, p. 449.

Law Society of England and Wales. (nd). 'Apprenticeships', *Law Society of England and Wales*.

Law Society of Upper Canada (2017). 'Dialogue on Licensing Discussing the Realities, Challenges and Opportunities of Lawyer Licensing in Ontario Topic 4 Reference Materials: Transitional Training', Law Society of Upper Canada.

Rogers, A. (2003). *What Is the Difference? A New Critique of Adult Learning and Teaching*, 2nd edition, NIACE.

Sadi, R. (2018). 'Legal Education and the Civil Law System', *New York Law School Law Review*, 62, article 7.

Saunders, N. (1996). 'From Cramming to Skills – the Development of Solicitors' Education and Training since Ormrod', *Law Teacher*, 30, p. 168.

Spiller, P. (1993). 'The History of New Zealand Legal Education: A Study in Ambivalence', *Legal Education Review*, 4, p. 223.

Sullivan, W.M. et al. (2007). *Educating Lawyers: Preparation for the Profession of Law*, Jossey-Bass.

Wilson, R. (2010). 'The Role of Practice in Legal Education', American University Washington College of Law, available at http://digitalcommons.wcl.american.edu/fac_works_papers/12.

81. Precarious employment and legal academics

Extent of casualisation in the academy

This entry examines the extent and experience of sessional academics in law. Although reference to 'casual academics' is common, it is increasingly considered inappropriate. Therefore, this entry uses the term 'sessional academics' (RED Report [2008]). Sessional academics are those not appointed on permanent or continuing contracts and includes academics 'employed on an hourly, session-by-session, usually part-time, teaching-only basis' (Cowley [2010] at 29) as well as those on short fixed-term contracts. There are generally two broad types of sessional academics: those pursuing an academic career and industry experts (or practising professionals) [Professional Identities of Legal Academics].

The recent 'massification' and 'corporatisation' of higher education (Coates et al [2009] at 47–49, Richardson et al [2019]) has resulted in high rates of casualisation across the sector (Hitch et al [2018], Burns et al [2015]). Indeed, it is suggested 'precarity has become the norm' (Smither, Harris and Spina [2023]), although accurate data on rates of academic casualisation is not readily available with most statistics understating the number of sessional academics employed in the sector (Bryson [2013] at 3, Klopper and Power [2014], Lama and Joullié [2015], Lopes and Dewan [2014] at 30). Despite this, McComb et al report that 'across the higher education sector in Australia, the UK, and the US, the majority of academic teaching staff are employed on contingent or casual work contracts' ([2021] at 96, Andrews [2016], Ryan et al [2013], May et al [2013]).

The phenomenon of academic casualisation also pervades law schools (Cowley [2010] at 28), where there is a similar paucity of reliable data and statistics (Skead and Rogers [2023]).

Consequences of casualisation in the academy

There are undoubtedly advantages associated with sessional academic employment. These include independence; flexibility; valuable work experience and professional development; and additional income (Richardson et al [2019], Grattan [2018], Lopes and Dewan [2014], Taylor [2017]). However, these advantages are outweighed by the disadvantages, at least for those sessional academics pursuing a career in academia. These disadvantages are both general and discipline-specific.

General Challenges

There is a growing body of scholarship examining the high levels of stress in higher education and the many psychological hazards inherent in academic work (Wray and Kinman [2022]) [Wellbeing/Mental Health of Legal Academics]. These stressors are shared by sessional academics but there are additional stressors arising from the sessional nature of their work. The most significant challenge is the precariousness of sessional work and not knowing whether or how much work is available (Lopes and Dewan [2014], Richardson et al [2019]). This insecurity results in sessional academics commonly not feeling able to refuse work when offered, usually at short notice, and consequently taking on too much work, often at more than one institution (Leatherwood and Read [2020], Richardson et al [2021], Grattan [2018] at 38). This absence of job security also erodes their academic freedom (Ross et al [2021] at 65).

Added to this, sessional academics are commonly appointed at the lowest academic levels and pay scales that do not include paid leave and other benefits (Grattan [2018] at 37). Further, by virtue of being paid hourly for specified activities, much of the invisible work inherent in teaching such as preparation, pastoral care, moderation, and student consultation goes unpaid (Leatherwood and Read [2020], SMH [2023], Ryan et al [2013], Richardson et al [2021], Lopes and Dewan [2014]).

Despite undertaking significant volumes of teaching, it is widely reported that the academic precariat does not have adequate training, supervision, mentoring, guidance or paid professional development opportunities (Sabourin [2021], Andrews et al [2016], Crimmins et al [2017]) and few opportunities for career progression (Lopes and Dewan [2014], Richardson et al [2021]). They have limited access to institutional facilities such as office space, a computer, and printing and little autonomy in what or how they teach (Leatherwood and Read [2020], Brown et al [2006]).

In this 'dehumanised' environment (Mason and Megoran [2021]), it is not surprising that sessional academics report feeling invisible, marginalised and exploited, existing on the outer edges of the academy rather than an integral and valued part of it (McComb et al [2021], Harvey and Fredericks [2016], Lopes and Dewan [2014], Read and Leatherwood [2018], Ryan et al [2013], Richardson et al [2021], Richardson et al [2019]). Inevitably, casualisation causes significant stress and anxiety and impacts negatively on sessional academic wellbeing (Lopes and Dewan [2014]). It is to be expected that this in turn impacts on the quality of their teaching (Leatherwood and Read [2020]).

Law-specific Challenges

In additional to the general stressors shared by all academics (Strevens et al [2023]), there are factors unique to legal education that pose additional discipline-specific challenges for sessional law academics. Heath et al argue that, by its very nature, law teaching 'is the site of significant emotional labour' ([2017] at 431). For example, teaching sensitive content, the inherently adversarial nature of law, navigating the historically gendered and (in many jurisdictions) colonial approach of law, and confronting injustice can result in '[l]aw teaching requir[ing] substantial effort and skill in dealing with emotion' (Heath et al [2017]). Given the precariousness of their employment, the emotional labour in teaching law can be exacerbated for sessional teachers.

Added to this is the vast literature reporting high levels of psychological distress experienced by law students and lawyers, including at the highest levels in the judiciary (Hess [2002], Lewis and Cardwell [2019], Wilson and Strevens [2016], Kelk, Luscombe, Medlow, and Hickie [2009], Field, Duffy, and Huggins [2013], Bergin and Pakenham [2015], Schrever et al [2019]). As Strevens et al note, 'some responsibility for promoting law student wellbeing is falling on law teachers' ([2023] 22) [Wellbeing/Mental Health of Law Students].

Drawing on Morrish's 2019 work on 'the epidemic of poor mental health among higher education staff', Hudson recently commented that '[t]oday there is a crisis in our law schools' (Hudson [2021]) and that (103):

> Some law school staff recognise that they must perform all the essential communal activities that keep a law school functioning: from helping the moot team before a competition to listening to the student in a mental health crisis. The sort of tasks which rarely result in promotion or even thanks.

In this environment, it is not surprising that sessional law academics experience high levels of psychological distress (Skead and Rogers [2023]).

Given the key role sessional academics play in the legal academy and the myriad of challenges they face, law schools need to embed strategies to support their sessional teachers. Doing so will inevitably improve the quality of their academic experience and enhance their teaching practice.

NATALIE SKEAD

References

Andrews, S., Bare, L., Bentley, P., Goedegebuure, L., Pugsley, C. and Rance, B. (2016). *Contingent academic employment in Australian universities*, LH Martin Institute for Tertiary Education Leadership and Management.

Bergin, A.J. and Jimmieson, N.L. (2013). 'Explaining psychological distress in the legal profession: The role of overcommitment', *International Journal of Stress Management*, 20(2), pp. 134–161, available at http://dx.doi.org/10.1037/a0032557.

Brown, T., Goodman, J. and Yasukawa, K. (2006). *Getting the Best of You for Nothing: Casual Voices in the Australian Academy*, South Melbourne: NTEU.

Bryson, C. (2013). 'Supporting sessional teaching staff in the UK – to what extent is there real progress?', *Journal of University Teaching and Learning Practice*, 10(3), p. 1.

Burns, D.J., Smith, Y. and Starcher, K. (2015). 'Adjuncts and mission: Maintaining distinctives in an era of part-time faculty', *Christian Business Academy Review*, 10(Spring), p. 63.

Coates, H., Dobson, I.R., Goedegebuure, L. and Meek, L. (2009). 'Australia's casual approach to its academic teaching workforce', *People and Place*, 17(4), pp. 47, 48.

Cowley, J. (2010). 'Confronting the reality of casualisation in Australia. Recognising difference and embracing sessional staff in law schools', *Queensland University of Technology Law and Justice Journal*, 10(1), pp. 27, 28.

Crimmins, G., Oprescu, F. and Nash, G. (2017). 'Three pathways to support the professional and casual academics', *International Journal for Academic Development*, 22(2), pp. 144–156, available at https://doi.org/10.1080/1360144X.2016.1263962.

Field, R., Duffy, J. and Huggins, A. (2013). 'Supporting transition to law school and student well-being: The role of professional legal identity', *The International Journal of the First Year in Higher Education*, 4(2), p. 15, available at http://dx.doi.org/10.5204/intjfyhe.v4i2.167.

Field, R., Lopes, A. and Dewan, I. (2014). 'Precarious pedagogies? The impact of casual and zero-hour contracts in higher education', *Journal of Feminist Scholarship*, 7(8), p. 28.

Harvey, M. and Fredericks, V. (2016). 'CoPs: Enhancing Quality Learning and Teaching with Sessional Staff', in McDonald, J. and Cater-Steel, A. (eds), *Communities of Practice: facilitating social learning in higher education*, Springer.

Heath, M., Galloway, K., Skead, N., Steel, A. and Israel, M. (2017). 'Learning to feel like a lawyer: law teachers, sessional teaching and emotional labour in legal education', *Griffith Law Review*, 26(3), p. 430.

Hess, G.F. (2002). 'Heads and hearts: The teaching and learning environment in law school', *Journal of Legal Education*, 52, p. 75.

Hitch, D., Mahoney, P. and Macfarlane, S. (2018). 'Professional development for sessional staff in higher education: a review of current evidence', *Higher Education Research and Development*, 37(2), pp. 285–300, available at https://doi.org/10.1080/07294360.2017.1360844.

Hudson, A. (2021). 'Two futures for law schools', *The Law Teacher*, 55(1), p. 101, available at https://doi.org/10.1080/03069400.2020.1862616.

Kelk, N., Luscombe, G., Medlow, S. and Hickie, I. (2009). *Courting the blues: Attitudes towards depression in Australian law students and legal practitioners*, Sydney: Brain & Mind Research Institute of the University of Sydney.

Klopper, C.J. and Power, B.M. (2014). 'The Casual Approach to Teacher Education: What Effect does Casualisation Have for Australian University Teaching?', *Australian Journal of Teacher Education*, 39(4) pp. 101–114, available at https://ro.ecu.edu.au/ajte/vol39/iss4/6/.

Lama, T. and Joullié, J. (2015). 'Casualization of Academics in the Australian Higher Education: Is Teaching Quality at Risk?', *Research in Higher Education Journal*, p. 28.

Leatherwood, C. and Read, B. (2022). 'Short-term, short-changed? Temporal perspective on the implications of academic casualisation for teaching in higher education', *Teaching in Higher Education*, 27(6), p. 756, available at DOI: 10.1080/13562517.2020.1742681.

Lewis, E.G. and Cardwell, J.M. (2019). 'A comparative study of mental health and wellbeing among UK students on professional degree programmes', *Journal of Further and Higher Education*, 43(9), p. 1226.

Mason, O. and Megoran, N. (2021). 'Precarity and dehumanisation in higher education', *Learning and Teaching*, 14(1), p. 35, available at doi: 10.3167/latiss.2021.140103.

May, R., Strachan, G. and Peetz, D. (2013). 'Workforce development and renewal in Australian universities and the management of casual academic staff', *Journal of University Teaching & Learning Practice*, 10(3), available at http://ro.uow.edu.au/jutlp/vol10/iss3/3.

McComb, V., Eatherm N. and Imig, S. (2021). 'Casual academic staff experiences in higher education: insights for academic development', *International Journal for Academic Development*, p. 95, available at https://doi.org/10.1080/1360144X.2020.1827259.

Morrish, L. (2019). 'Pressure Vessels: The Epidemic of Poor Mental Health among Higher Education Staff', Higher Education Policy Institute Occasional Paper, 20, available at https://www.hepi.ac.uk/2019/05/23/pressure-vessels-the-epidemic-of-poor-mental-health-among-higher-education-staff/.

Norton, A. and Cherastidtham, I. (2018). 'Mapping Australian higher education 2018', Grattan Institute (Grattan), available at https://grattan.edu.au/wp-content/uploads/2018/09/907-Mapping-Australian-higher-education-2018.pdf.

Percy, A. et al. (2008). *The RED Report – Recognition, Enhancement, Development – The Contribution of Sessional Teachers to Higher Education* (RED Report), Australian Learning and Teaching Council, available at https://ro.uow.edu.au/cgi/viewcontent.cgi?article=1139&context=asdpapers.

Read, B. and Leatherwood, C. (2018). 'Tomorrow's a Mystery: Constructions of the Future and "un/Becoming" Amongst "Early" and "Late" Career Academics', *International Studies in Sociology of Education*, p. 1, available at doi:10.1080/09620214.2018.1453307.

Richardson, J., Wardale, D. and Lord, L. (2019). 'The "double-edged sword" of a sessional academic career', *Higher Education Research and Development*, 38(3), p. 623.

Richardson, J., Suseno, Y. and Wardale, D. (2021). 'The paradoxical management of casual academics: an Australian case study', *Higher Education Research and Development*, 40(2), p. 370.

Ross, S., Savage, L. and Watson, J. (2021). 'Sessional Contract Faculty, Unionization, and Academic Freedom', *Canadian Journal of Higher Education*, 51(1), p. 57.

Ryan, S., Burgess, J., Connell, J. and Groen, E. (2013). 'Casual academic staff in an Australian university: Marginalised and excluded', *Human Resource Management Journal*, 26(3), p. 235.

Sabourin, B.M. (2021). 'Sessionals' educational development: A review of North American research 2008–2018', *International Journal for Academic Development,* 26(2), pp. 134–149, available at https://doi.org/10.1080/1360144X .2020.1831504.

Schrever, C., Hulbert, C. and Sourdin, T. (2019). 'The impact of judicial work: Australia's first empirical research measuring judicial stress and wellbeing,' *J. of Judicial Administration,* 28, p. 141.

Skead, N. and Rogers, S.L. (2023). 'Sessional Law Teacher Well-Being: An Empirical Australian Study', in Strevens, C. and Jones, E. (eds), Wellbeing and the Legal Academy, Springer Briefs in Education, Springer Nature Switzerland AG.

Smithers, K., Harris, J. and Spina, N. (2023). 'Australian unis could not function without casual staff: it is time to treat them as "real" employees', available at https://theconversation.com/ australian-unis-could-not-function-without -casual-staff-it-is-time-to-treat-them-as-real -employees-203053#:~:text=The%20discussion %20paper%20also%20notes,of%20people %20employed%20on%20contracts.

Strevens, C., Field, R. and James, C. (2023). 'An Analysis of Studies on the Wellbeing of Law Teachers in the UK and Australia Using the Lens of Seven Psychosocial Hazards of Academic Work', in Strevens, C. and Jones, E. (eds), *Wellbeing and the Legal Academy*, Springer Briefs in Education, Springer Nature Switzerland AG, pp. 57–76.

Strevens, C. and Wilson, C. (2016). 'Law student wellbeing in the UK: A call for curriculum intervention', *Journal of Commonwealth Law and Legal Education*, 11, p. 44, available at https:// law-school.open.ac.uk/sites/law-school.open .ac.uk/files/files/Law%20student%20wellbeing %20in%20the%20UK.pdf.

Taylor, M. (2017). *Good work: The Taylor review of modern working practices*, UK, Dept for Business, Energy & Industrial Strategy, UK.

Wray, S. and Kinman, G. (2022). 'The psychosocial hazards of academic work: An analysis of trends', *Studies in Higher Education*, 47(4), p. 771.

82. Pro bono initiatives

Defining student pro bono

Student pro bono (essentially the giving of legal information without charge) benefits persons who could not otherwise afford legal information and assistance, and it confers considerable benefits on law students and law schools (American Bar Association Center for Pro Bono [2010]). It has expanded greatly in the past few decades (see e.g. Dignan et al [2017], and law schools in some jurisdictions are required to offer it (American Bar Association [2023], Standard 303(b)(2)). But what exactly is it? The first definitional task is to distinguish student pro bono from clinical legal education (CLE), as these concepts are sometimes treated as interchangeable (Taylor and Cappa [2016]). Some jurisdictions characterise pro bono as a form of CLE (Ho [2023]), and some law schools offer or require coursework in community legal education (Ho [2023], University of Phayao [2023]), but it is helpful to distinguish the main characteristics of these two kinds of programmes as they offer different benefits and raise different issues. A key difference is that CLE may have a social justice orientation but it is not required, and overall, this model prioritises education. Student pro bono is characterised by service to the community. More specifically, CLE has been defined as activities 'in which each student takes responsibility for legal or law-related work for a client (whether real or simulated) in collaboration with a supervisor' (Bleasdale et al [2020] at 8). Student pro bono is defined here as student activities which serve poor or underserved segments of the community (Grimes [2008]), without charge to the recipient (Dignan et al [2017]) and which do not earn students course credit or payment (American Bar Association Center for Pro Bono [2010]).

In student pro bono, the focus on the public good and the lack of course credit or payment justifies the use of 'pro bono' (American Bar Association Center for Pro Bono [2010]; Booth [2001]), which when done by lawyers is by definition free or low cost. The lack of course credit also helps to distinguish student pro bono from CLE (Booth 2001), because given CLE's more intensive level of supervision, it is normally a for-credit course. The extra-curricular status of student pro bono produces a number of related characteristics, such as less supervision, no assessment, more flexible time frames, and incidental as opposed to formal student reflection (Taylor and Cappa [2016]).

While student pro bono should be distinguished from CLE to appreciate their respective advantages and challenges, the line between them should not be drawn too strictly. Some law schools run legal clinics (Grimes [2008]), and if student participation is paired with CLE teaching methods, then it should be recognised as CLE. It is however possible to run a legal clinic with student participation that comprises student pro bono if the service element is emphasised over education (Whalen-Bridge and Koman [2015]).

Mandatory student pro bono in law schools is something of an exception to the extra-curricular pro bono model. A minimum of 39 US law schools require students to engage in pro bono or public service as a condition of graduation (American Bar Association Standing Committee on Pro Bono and Public Service [2021]), and in Singapore, student pro bono is also a graduation requirement (Whalen-Bridge [2017]). There are different kinds of mandatory programmes, including: a Pro Bono Graduation Requirement, which requires the use of legal skills or the delivery of legal work for particular beneficiaries; a Public Service Graduation Requirement, a more flexible programme that could for example include exposure to poverty law; or a Community Service Graduation Requirement Programme, which accepts law and non-law related service (American Bar Association Center for Pro Bono [2010]). However, a mandatory pro bono programme is usually graded on a pass-fail basis, and this kind of programme is best understood as a graduation requirement, not a fully-fledged, assessed course.

Reasons for student pro bono

Students may take on voluntary pro bono based on a sense of obligation and a concern for justice (Booth [2001]), and some think that doing pro bono will inculcate a public service orientation in law students (Brennan [2005]; Corker [2020]). Law schools may therefore be operating on the assumption that students who do pro bono in law school will do pro bono as lawyers (Adcock [2009]), although this view is not well-supported by empirical research. Deborah Schmedemann found that any amount of law-related volunteering or clinical courses increased pro bono in practice (Schmedemann [2009]), but Deborah Rhode's research did not find a statistically significant correlation between law school policy regarding pro bono and subsequent pro bono work (Rhode [2005]). Per Rhode, the value of pro bono must be 'reflected and enforced throughout the law school experience in both curricular coverage and resource priorities' (Rhode [2005] at 165), a point that conflicts with student pro bono's inexpensive appeal. Robert Granfield also reported that while 'data indicate that lawyers do consider that the pro bono experience in law school contributed to their understanding of marginal groups as well as enhanced their legal skills, [it] also reveals that the impact of that experience on their career was not substantial' (Granfield [2007] at 1380).

It should not be surprising that once lawyers begin professional practice other factors influence their ability to do pro bono (Rhode [2005]), among them the law firm they work for (Cummings [2004]). But there are other compelling reasons for student pro bono. A primary educational reason is that it sends a message that pro bono service is important (Adcock [2009]). If students are not offered opportunities or required to do pro bono, that in itself is an institutional statement that public service is less important (Chaifetz [1993]; Moss [2013]). For some, law school is 'as much a professional socialisation experience as it is 'a scholarly, skills building exercise' (Baille and Bernstein-Baker [1994] at 67), and 'a fundamental part of that socialization is the integration of professional values and ethics', including a lawyer's obligations to the public (Taylor and Cappa [2016] at 123). From this perspective, student pro bono teaches students why pro bono service is an important professional value and demonstrates methods of contribution (American Bar Association Center for Pro Bono [2010]). In addition to helping students connect classroom learning to the real world, students also gain considerable practical benefits, including legal skills, exposure to practice areas, and professional connections (American Bar Association Center for Pro Bono [2010]).

Beyond educational goals, student pro bono programmes allow students to directly contribute to access to justice, by providing or helping others to provide legal information and services to poor or vulnerable persons (American Bar Association Center for Pro Bono [2010]). Students may have greater mobility to reach rural or remote areas with needed legal information and support, e.g. in the Philippines (Ateneo Human Rights Center [2023]). In countries where multiple languages or dialects present challenges, students can provide translation.

Student pro bono programmes can also benefit law schools, by enhancing the law school's stature in the community, strengthening ties to alumni, and supporting the law school's educational mission. Pro bono activities are significantly cheaper for law schools as they do not use the same level of supervision as CLE, so law schools can offer more pro bono opportunities to students.

Varieties of student pro bono

Voluntary pro bono can be categorised as either an informal programme, which refers to student groups or projects in law schools that do not have a school-wide programme, or a formal programme. Formal programmes have two main variations: a referral system with a coordinator that matches students with outside partners, or a programme with administrative support for student groups, in which students often partner with outside organisations (American Bar Association Center for Pro Bono [2010]).

There are relatively few constraints on the type of pro bono activities that can be carried out. Legal profession legislation in some jurisdictions prohibits students or teachers from giving legal advice or going into court. In these jurisdictions, students can comply with restrictions but still use their legal knowledge by engaging in legal literacy projects, also referred to as community legal information. Street Law is a related activity, and while this is defined in the U.S. as a programme in which law students teach law to secondary school students (Arthurs [2015]), it has a wider definition in other jurisdictions. All of these programmes educate the community or parts of the community about law and legal issues.

Because student pro bono frequently does not involve extensive levels of supervision and assessment, it has more flexibility than CLE. It can respond to particular needs and interests of the university, community partners, recipients, students, and the wider community. Pro bono programmes therefore generate a range of different activities, such as research projects, variants of 'McKenzie friend' or unrepresented litigant assistance, judicial shadowing, mediation projects, witness support services, international human rights work, small business set-up and advice (Dignan et al [2017]), and legal support for charitable organisations.

The flexibility of student pro bono potentially offers other benefits. Episodic opportunities can allow students with other commitments to participate, and all students can benefit from activities during university breaks away from the stress of an academic calendar (Taylor and Cappa [2016]). A lower hourly commitment compared to CLE also makes student pro bono doable alongside other activities.

Student pro bono, particularly programmes that rely on student groups, put legal knowledge and skills into action, and so student 'initiative and autonomy' are required to drive the project (Taylor and Cappa [2016]). Students are more likely to be engaged if they run or even initiate the programme themselves, and students can achieve impressive pro bono results (Thickstun [2020]). However, given the level of interaction students have with the community, some level of supervision is usually necessary, e.g. students must be required to advise the group or the supervisor if they cannot attend an event or meet a deadline (Brennan [2005]). Given the extra-curricular character of pro bono, some students may underperform or put an undue burden on fellow participants (Taylor and Cappa [2016]). This would be an issue with any group work, but it appears to be more of an issue in activities like student pro bono due to the absence or low level of assessment. Depending on the programme and other variables, different strategies can be used to address this problem, including a feedback mechanism in which students critique their own and other's performance.

Voluntary student pro bono requires that students be recruited (Booth [2001]) and perhaps vetted. In programmes that work with student groups, pro bono depends more heavily on students for structure and coordination, and this means that student enthusiasm is vital (Booth [2001]). If students hold important positions in pro bono projects, that will support their engagement, but continuity among students must be monitored and coordinated by the law school's advisors or staff.

Conclusion

By all accounts, student pro bono has grown considerably across diverse jurisdictions. It should not be considered CLE's poorer cousin, but rather an important element of legal education in its own right.

HELENA WHALEN-BRIDGE

References

American Bar Association Center for Pro Bono. (2010). 'Everything you wanted to know about law school pro bono but were afraid to ask...', *American Bar Association*, available at https://www.americanbar.org/groups/center-pro-bono/pro-bono-content-directory/.

American Bar Association Standing Committee on Pro Bono and Public Service. (2021). 'A Guide and Explanation to Pro Bono Services', *American Bar Association*, available at https://www.americanbar.org/groups/legal_education/resources/pro_bono/.

American Bar Association Standing Committee on Pro Bono and Public Service. (2013). 'New York's 50-hour Preadmission Pro Bono Rule: Weighing the Potential Pros and Cons', *American Bar Association*, available at https://www.law.upenn.edu/live/files/2420-aba-white-paper-on-ny-pro-bono.

Arthurs, S.G. (2015). 'Street Law: Creating Tomorrow's Citizens Today', *Lewis & Clark Law Review*, 19, p. 925.

Ateneo Human Rights Center. (2023). 'Ateneo Human Rights Center Internship Program goes to Occidental Mindoro to immerse with a Mangyan Community', Ateneo De Manila University, available at https://www.ateneo.edu/news/2023/07/18/ateneo-human-rights-center-internship-program-goes-occidental-mindoro-immerse.

Adcock, C. (2009). 'Shaped by Educational, Professional, and Social Crises: The History of Law Student Pro Bono Service', in Granfield, R. and Mather, L. (eds), *Private Lawyers and the Public Interest*, Oxford University Press.

Baille, J. and Bernstein-Baker, J. (1995). 'In the Spirit of Public Service: Model Rule 6.1, the Profession and Legal Education', *Law and Inequality*, 13, p. 51.

Bleasdale, L. et al. (2020). 'Law Clinics: What, Why and How?', in Thomas, L. and Johnson, N. (eds), *The Clinical Legal Education Handbook*, University of London Press.

Booth, T. (2004). 'Student Pro Bono: Developing a Public Service Ethos in the Contemporary

Australian Law School', *Alternative Law Journal*, 29, p. 280.

Brennan, S. De. (2005). 'Rethinking Pro Bono: Students Lending a Helping Hand', *Legal Education Review*, 15, p. 25.

Chaifetz, J. (1993). 'The Value of Public Service: A Model for Instilling a Pro Bono Ethic in Law School', *Stanford Law Review*, 45, p. 1695.

Corker, J. (2020). 'The Importance of Inculcating the "Pro Bono Ethos" in Law Students, and the Opportunities to do it Better', *Legal Education Review*, 30, p. 1.

Cummings, S. (2004). 'The Politics of Pro Bono', *UCLA Law Review*, 52, p. 1.

Dignan, F., Grimes, R. and Parker, R. (2017). 'Pro Bono and Clinical Work in Law Schools: Summary and Analysis', *Asian Journal of Legal Education*, 4, p. 1.

Granfield, R. (2007). 'Institutionalizing Public Service in Law School: Results on the Impact of Mandatory Pro Bono Programs', *Buffalo Law Review*, 54, p. 1355.

Grimes, R. (2008). 'Why (and How to Do) Pro Bono Work in Law Schools?', *Journal of Commonwealth Law and Legal Education*, 6(1), p. 27.

Ho, Ai Nhan. (2023). 'The Future Possibilities and Perspectives of Clinical Legal Education in Vietnam', *International Journal of the Legal Profession*, 30(2), p. 127.

Koman, R.N. and Whalen-Bridge, H. (2015). 'Clinical Legal Education in Singapore', in Prosun Sarker, S. (ed), *Clinical Legal Education in Asia: Accessing Justice for the Underprivileged*, Palgrave Macmillan.

Latham and Watkins. (2019). 'A Summary of Pro Bono Requirements in 86 Jurisdictions', *Latham and Watkins*, available at https://www.lw.com/admin/upload/SiteAttachments/Survey-Summary-Chart-2019.pdf.

Moss, D.M. (2013). 'The Hidden Curriculum of Legal Education: Toward a Holistic Model for Reform', *Journal of Dispute Resolution*, p. 19.

Rhode, D. (2005). *Pro Bono in Principle and Practice*, Stanford University Press.

Schmedemann, D.A. (2009). 'Priming for Pro Bono: The Impact of Law School on Pro Bono Participation in Practice', in Granfield, R. and Mather, L. (eds), *Private Lawyers and the Public Interest*, Oxford University Press.

Singapore Institute of Legal Education. (2019). 'Pro Bono Programme', *Singapore Institute of Legal Education*, available at https://www.sile.edu.sg/pro-bono-programme.

Smith, L.F. (2020). 'Professional Identity Formation Through Pro Bono Revealed Through Conversation Analysis', *Cleveland State Law Review*, 68, p. 250.

Taylor, M. and Cappa, C. (2016). 'Student Pro Bono and Its Role in Contemporary Australian Law Schools', *Alternative Law Journal*, 41, p. 121.

Thickstun, T. (2020). 'How a Law Student Sparked a Mass Pro Bono Movement', *Student Lawyer*, 49, p. 20.

University of Phayao, Law Clinic School of Law University of Phayao. (2023), available at https://www.facebook.com/LAWCLINIC.UP/ (in Thai).

Whalen-Bridge, H. (2017). 'Student Pro Bono and the NUS Faculty of Law', *Singapore Journal of Legal Studies*, p. 329.

83. Problem-based learning

Origins

'PBL is a pedagogical approach that enables students to learn while engaging actively with meaningful problems' (Yew and Goh [2016]). Originating in medical education in the late 1960s (Servant-Miklos [2018]), it was first introduced in law education at Maastricht University (Moens [2007]). It has been taken up, sometimes partially, in a number of law schools across a range of jurisdictions (Mackinnon [2006]).

PBL's classical six core characteristics have been described as:

- learning is student-centred;
- learning occurs in small student groups;
- a tutor is present as a facilitator or guide;
- the learning process begins with an authentic problem before students have begun study or preparation relevant to that problem;
- the problem is a tool to achieve the knowledge and skills necessary to resolve similar problems in relevant professions; and
- new information is acquired through self-directed learning (Maharg [2015], Houghton [2023]).

In this entry, as well as drawing from the literature on PBL, we have also reflected on the practice at York Law School (YLS). YLS was founded in 2007 and has used PBL for all of its core subjects in its undergraduate LLB since it opened. With Maastricht, it is one of only a handful of law schools to have fully embraced PBL as its pedagogy.

Subject matter of PBL

One of the characteristics of PBL is that problems should be based on 'real-life' problems (Mackinnon [2006]) and which are unclear or ill-defined (Wijnen et al [2017]). Such problems should be interdisciplinary in the sense that they cut across traditional legal categories (Mackinnon [2006], Moust [1998]). This is difficult to achieve in law schools with partial PBL, although that does not prevent the use of PBL single modules – see for example Wong [2003] on using PBL in a criminal law module.

In Maastricht, although there are interdisciplinary modules (Moust [1998]) e.g. a module in 'Unlawful Conduct', where students are confronted with aspects of private and criminal law relating to unlawful conduct, the core modules that are found in all law programmes (criminal law, private law, public law) are still present and taught in isolation.

At YLS the core subjects (reflecting professional requirements) of the law of obligations (contract and tort), property (land and trusts), crime, public (constitutional and administrative) and EU are taught in 6 'Foundations in Law' modules in the first and second years (this is 50 per cent of teaching in each year). Students consider 41 problems across those 6 modules and each problem covers two of the core subjects. Subjects are also mixed randomly so that the students do not know which two subjects they will encounter in each unseen problem.

The following is a first-year problem covering contract and crime (reproduced with permission).

BOX 83.1   EXAMPLE OF PROBLEM-BASED LEARNING TASK

Source: This PBL example comes from a Year 1 YLS PBL problem. It was written by YLS staff for that purpose. It is reproduced by permission of the Head of the Law School.)

Email Dan to Al, 3rd June

Hi Al,

I want my money back. That essay you wrote for me failed! You said in the Student Union café that it would be at least a 2:1. It did not even get 30.

Thanks,

Dan

Email Al to Dan, 6th June

Dan,

Sorry you didn't get the marks, mate. I did what I could but you can't get the money back. What do you think this is, a business? I said over a latte that I would come up with a good essay for £150. It's not like we put anything in writing or signed anything or I promised anything.

Sorry,

Al

Email Dan to Al, 8th June

I know a promise when I hear one. You promised me a good essay and I gave you £150. Deal. The essay obviously isn't good; let's face it, it's crap. So you owe me £150.

Email Al to Dan, 9th June

Yeah, right. What are you going to do? Sue me? Try it. I can't imagine you are going to get a judge to help you out on this one. It was just banter. Besides, I don't think they are supposed to help enforce cheating promises. The moment it comes out that you cheated like this, putting my work in as your own, you will be the one in court being prosecuted.

Email Dan to Al, 10th June

Pay up. You promised and that's the end of it. And don't try and threaten me – I don't think I did anything wrong. I was borrowing your ideas – just like academics do all the time.

Email Al to Dan, 10th June

Jeez, how did they let you in, you muppet? The law is not going to help you get your money and you will be off to jail. It doesn't matter what you think – wrong is wrong!

These are the learning outcomes that the students are working towards in this problem:

1. How does context/circumstance affect whether a binding legal agreement (contract) has arisen?
2. If the subject matter is illegal or improper, does that make a legal agreement unenforceable?
3. What criminal offences might have been committed by someone who breaches university rules about assessments?
4. Should a defendant be held liable for a dishonesty offence despite believing that his or her conduct is not wrong?

The PBL process

The process is core to PBL. Students begin by assigning a member of the group to be the Chairperson ('chair') who will direct the group through the PBL stages. A scribe is also appointed to create a shared group document, capturing the work on all the PBL stages. Ideally, this document is visible to all students on a smartboard (or similar) throughout the process and should be the only document created during the PBL. The students then work through the problem as a group in a set

way in order to achieve their own learning outcomes (Wood [2003]). The Maastricht model has 7 steps (Moust [1998]). At YLS the model has been adapted as follows:

1. Read and clarify the problem – the problem is read out loud by the group and any unclear terms within the problem are clarified. Often someone in the group suggests a definition from their prior knowledge or they can be looked up. 'Legal' terms may be marked for later research.
2. Identify parties and interests – the group identifies all the relevant parties in the scenario and what their respective interests are. This broadens the discussion beyond simply the needs of the 'client' and requires the students to think through law in its full operational context. For example, the interests of the client can be contrasted with those of other possible parties to the dispute or process. The role of the police, the courts, parliamentarians, non-governmental organisations (NGOs) and the wider public may all be relevant practically, legally, socially and normatively.
3. Set out chronology of events – the key facts and sequence of events are then recorded, to focus minds on the link between facts and law and to ensure that no significant development is missed. This is a very important part of the PBL process as it reinforces not only the evidential link, but that the application of the law is determined by what has happened.
4. Summary and name – the group drafts a short summary of the core issues in the problem and gives the problem a memorable name. The purpose is part analysis and part fun. Reducing a problem to its core is an important part of determining the strategy for resolution, while coming up with a clever/funny name (for example a riff on a song title) provides a break from the demands of the process and also aids later recall of the problem.
5. Mind-mapping and synthesis of ideas – the group looks in the broadest sense at what legal issues they might have to address in advancing the interests identified in light of the key facts – this should be done first in a non-compartmentalised way, so it is quick, with all suggestions recorded. The ideas produced by the 'mind-mapping' are then grouped to produce coherent research

themes. Extraneous ideas (e.g. for deferred topics) are excluded at this point.

6. Define learning outcomes from themes – once the themes have been identified, the students should rephrase them as research questions, i.e. the learning outcomes. Typically four to five outcomes may be expected, including occasionally normative questions. See the example above. The learning outcomes may be more or less guided. The open discovery model of PBL allows students a largely free hand in determining their own outcomes whereas the latter expects students to reach predetermined outcomes albeit under their own initiative with some tutor-guidance where necessary (Grimes [2015]). In undergraduate learning it is generally guided – i.e. the tutor identifies learning outcomes in advance (Wood [2003]) to ensure that any regulatory requirements are met in terms of subject coverage.

7. Plan, agree and carry out research – developing independent effective research skills is an essential part of PBL and each student in the group must individually address all the learning outcomes. At YLS, specific help is provided through study guides, linked lectures (one for each core subject) and an 'interim' session (usually with a Graduate Teaching Assistant) where the students can receive help with their research approach. This provides the scaffolding needed to support learners undertaking PBL (Houghton [2023]).

8. Share results – The group members report on their research findings at the next meeting of the group (at YLS this is one week after the initial PBL 'pick up' session). This feedback session is directed by the chair and should be structured so that all firm members make a contribution. Students are expected to give a brief overview of the relevant area of law with reference to appropriate sources and then show understanding by applying their research back to the facts of the problem where appropriate. Areas of misunderstanding should be resolved through group discussion. For normative questions the students should be able to hold a brief debate of the key viewpoints.

9. Consolidation – the students are encouraged to conduct further research after feedback to address any significant gaps in

their research which the group discussion has identified.

Group work

Group work is core to PBL and groups are expected to share their learning. It has been suggested that the optimal group size is six to eight students (Barrows and Tamblyn [1980]). However, given student-staff ratios in law schools, groups are often larger than this (Moust et al [2005], Grimes [2015]). The groups need to be able to create a good dynamic (Wood [2003]), so it is important to consider how long the group continues and how it is supported. At York Law School first year groups are engineered to have a range of characteristics – gender, home/overseas, age, previous knowledge of law (e.g. A level law). In Year 2 the students move into new groups. At YLS, group working is also supported through our compulsory Year 1 and Year 2 legal skills modules which include learning about group roles and dynamics.

Our experience of PBL at YLS is that the roles – chair and scribe (described above) – and the whole process, as Houghton [2023] suggests, 'develops crucial communication and teamwork skills while prompting students to develop an explorative approach to problem-solving.'

Role of the PBL tutors

The PBL tutor's main responsibility is to facilitate the PBL session. This involves many different actions and skills, but essentially it is about creating an environment which encourages engagement by all members of the group. Being a PBL tutor is a very different role to that of the traditional HE lecturer and therefore training for tutors is very important (Wijnen et al [2017]).

At YLS, in the first 'pick up' session (Steps 1–6 above) the tutor should prompt where necessary to ensure that all stages are completed and that the key elements of the problem are identified so that the learning outcomes flow from the process. They also help the group refine those outcomes into appropriate research questions and ensure that all the required legal topics are covered. In the 'feedback session' (Step 8) the tutor should assist the chair to encourage contribution. While the tutor may prompt the students to clarify or expand the discussion so as to cover the essential content (based on the notes provided by the subject leads), the tutor's job is not to teach in the traditional sense of providing information and knowledge. Tutors also encourage reflection on the performance of the group and on individual student research skills.

Assessment

As Wood [2003] notes: 'Student learning is influenced greatly by the assessment methods used. If assessment methods rely solely on factual recall then PBL is unlikely to succeed in the curriculum.' She advises that methods should include assessment of students' activities in their PBL groups.

At YLS a range of assessment methods are used, including reflective portfolios (see Gibbons [2019]) and 'contributions' marks for PBL. Contributions are assessed by tutors on a grading scheme that assesses attitude, co-operative behaviour, contribution and preparation. Our 'traditional' assessments, such as coursework (including short turn around assessments) are aligned to PBL by being centred around a problem with linked questions.

CAROLINE HUNTER, SARAH ARCHER AND CLAIRE ILLINGWORTH

References

Barows, H.S. and Tamblyn, R.M. (1980). *Problem-based learning: An approach to medical education*, Springer Publishing Company.

Gibbons, J. (2019). 'How is reflection "framed" for legal professional identity? Using Bernstein and Leering to understand the potential for reflection in our curriculum as written, experienced and assessed', *The Law Teacher*, 53(4), p. 401.

Grimes, R. (2015). 'Problem-based learning and legal education – a case study in integrated experiential study', *Revista de docencia Universitaria*, 13(1), p. 361.

Houghton, J. (2023). 'Learning modules: problem-based learning, blended learning and flipping the classroom', *The Law Teacher*, 57(3), p. 271.

Mackinnon, J. (2006). 'Problem Based Learning and New Zealand Legal Education', 3, Web JCLI, available at http://webjcli.ncl.ac.uk/2006/issue3/mackinnon3.html.

Maharg, P. (2015). '"Democracy Begins in Conversation": The Phenomenology of Problem-Based Learning and Legal Education', *Nott LJ*, 24, p. 94.

Moens, G.A. (2007). 'The Mysteries of Problem-Based Learning: Combining Enthusiasm and Excellence', *U Tol L Rev*, 38, p. 623.

Moust, J. (1998). 'The Problem Based Education Approach at the Maastricht Law School', *The Law Teacher*, 32(1), p. 5.

Moust, J.H.C., Van Berkel1, H.J.M. and Schmidt, H.G. (2005). 'Signs of erosion: Reflections on three decades of problem-based learning at Maastricht University', *Higher Education*, 50, p. 665.

Servant-Miklos, V.F.C. (2019). 'The Harvard Connection: How the Case Method Spawned Problem-Based Learning at McMaster University', *Health Professions Education*, 5, p. 163.

Wijnen, M., Loyens, S.M., Smeet, G., Kroeze, M.J. and Van der Molen, H.T. (2017). 'Students' and Teachers' Experiences With the Implementation of Problem-Based Learning at a University Law School', *Interdisciplinary Journal of Problem-Based Learning*, 11(2).

Wong, Y.J. (2003). 'Harnessing the Potential of Problem-Based Learning in Legal Education', *The Law Teacher*, 37(2), p. 157.

Wood, D.F. (2003). 'Problem based learning', BMJ, p. 326, available at doi: https://doi.org/10.1136/bmj.326.7384.328.

Yew, E. and Goh, K. (2016). 'Problem-Based Learning: An Overview of its Process and Impact on Learning', *Health Professions Education*, 2, pp. 75–79.

84. Professional identity formation of law students

Introduction

Professional identity formation (PIF) denotes the processes through which students acquire the norms, values and attitudes prevalent in a certain professional occupation (cf Costello [2005] at 28–32). As such, PIF can be regarded as involving processes of socialisation. PIF of law students, then, refers to processes through which law students acquire a *legal* professional identity. Students learn to 'think and act like a lawyer'. These processes continue when students finish law school and start their legal careers. However, this entry is limited to PIF during law school.

Legal education has a strong transformative impact (Scheingold and Sarat [2004] at 57). This does not mean that professional identities are all-encompassing. Rather, people have multiple identities (Costello [2005]; Roccas and Brewer [2002]), and personal identities already exist before one forms a legal professional identity. The manner in which law students internalise a legal professional identity and the specific character of the professional identity may differ in multiple ways due to, among other things, differences in personal characteristics, law schools and national legal cultures. Yet, across these differences, certain patterns and similarities can be discerned which are related to features of the legal profession and legal education. Most of the research on this topic is conducted in a common law setting, usually the United States (US). Therefore, not all of the portrayal provided in this entry is necessarily generalisable to law schools in other jurisdictions.

Professional identity formation in law school curricula

While legal socialisation in law school has been referred to as a largely tacit process or a 'hidden curriculum' that 'lurks behind what is actually said and done' (Crampton [1978] at 247), PIF can also be acknowledged as an explicit learning outcome of legal education. While little explicit attention has traditionally been paid to PIF in law schools, more recently such a movement has been recognised within several curricula of American law schools (Bilionis [2016]; Sullivan [2018]). A focus on PIF often encompasses paying attention to the values or ethics of the legal profession as well as skills or competencies. It also incorporates experiential or clinical learning in educational programmes and promotes reflection and mentoring/coaching (Sullivan et al [2007]). The idea is that incorporating these facets within the educational programmes results in lawyers who are better equipped to enter the legal profession and are aware of – and able to deal with – the responsibilities and fundamental purposes of the profession (Sullivan et al [2007]).

A focus on PIF in law school programmes, as well as in academic research, is predominantly observed in the US. This is not entirely surprising as in the US legal education is in general primarily promoted as professional education, with law schools often being organisationally and physically separate from the rest of the university (Stolker [2014] at 94). In many civil law jurisdictions, such as Germany and France, legal education is primarily regarded as an academic discipline (Stolker [2014]; Wilson [2009]), which can explain why focus on PIF in these countries is less explicit, although it still occurs tacitly.

Legal professional culture and professional identity formation

As one of the traditional professions, the legal profession claims a powerful position in society because of its specialised knowledge concerning a vital social arena. Lawyers are granted certain social and economic privileges that allow them to control their own work. Maintaining self-control and determining the boundaries between insiders and outsiders are regarded as important preoccupations of the profession (Freidson [2001]; Larson [1977]). New lawyers need not only be fit for the job but also fit for legal professional culture. Hence, legal education is aimed at acquiring knowledge and skills as well as the formation of professional identities in terms of norms, values and attitudes (Sullivan et al [2007]).

An essential element of legal PIF is teaching law students to 'think like a lawyer'. This apparently entails a narrow focus on legal-technical and procedural issues, while demarking the emotional, moral, social and political contexts of cases as irrelevant or subjective (Mertz [2007]; Scheingold and

Sarat [2004]). Part of thinking like a lawyer involves the ability to grasp the intricacies of legal language. This is said to be linked to professional boundary work, as legal jargon serves the cultivation of a professional mystique that legitimises the profession's special status (Posner [1998]).

In legal professional culture, a strong commercial paradigm and client-centred focus go hand in hand (Sommerlad [2007]). Accordingly, professional values that tend to receive much emphasis in legal PIF are neutrality and zealous advocacy of client interests. Upholding these values is considered a fundamental part of legal professionals' distinct contribution to the common good. Law students are taught not to confuse professional responsibility and personal convictions (Bliss [2017]; Granfield [1992]; Schleef [2006]).

Forming a credible legal professional identity also includes attitudinal, emotional and physical aspects. Law students learn that they are most likely to be taken seriously if they radiate self-confidence and authority and are eloquent, with a certain degree of emotional toughness (Costello [2005]).

Multiple authors have pointed to the gendered, ethnicised and elitist character of the legal professional habitus (Collier [2021]; Costello [2005]; Gaber [1998]; Granfield [1992]; Guinier, Fine & Baling [1994]; Schleef [2010]; Sommerlad [2007]). The norms, values and attitudes that are fostered within leading professional communities bear the imprint of those who dominated the legal profession for most of the past: white men from elite backgrounds. Therefore, students who are not white or male, are from humble socio-economic backgrounds or are oriented to social justice, are more prone to experience difficulties in their legal PIF.

Factors and actors in legal professional identity formation

Internal (Professors, Pedagogy and Peers)

PIF occurs to a large extent though interaction with others. These others are foremost the law professors and fellow students. Costello (2005), for instance, notes the importance of professors' habitus in acting as role models for students. They 'embody the appropriate demeanour in their styles of dress, manner-

isms, and tastes' and in all this they radiate an aura of authority (Costello [2005] at 44 and 50, see also Chapter 85 (Professional Identities of Legal Academics)).

The role of law professors cannot be separated from their pedagogy. In many law schools, teaching methods are quite teacher-focussed. A distinct aspect of legal pedagogy is the case dialogue method, also referred to as the Socratic method, which is especially central in common law jurisdictions (see Chapter 99 (Socratic Method)). The case dialogue method teaches students about the case-based nature of legal reasoning. Yet, this method has been criticised for upholding some of the problematic features of the legal profession by stripping cases from their moral dimensions and creating an overly competitive and stressful environment that favours white male students (for an overview see, Mertz [2007] at 26–30).

Law school programmes, including outside of the US, generally consist of lectures in large-sized classrooms. These are currently regularly complemented with smaller tutorials or somewhat larger seminars (Stolker [2014] at 162). Kortleven, Holvast and Besic [2024], therefore, also point to the important role that tutors can play in forming a legal professional identity, as tutors tend to be more approachable and stand closer to students.

Fellow students are also indicated as important actors in PIF. They play a key role in reproducing traditional norms and existing images of the legal profession (Costello [2005]; Bliss [2017]; Granfield [1992]). Granfield ([1992] at 79) shows, for example, how students affirmed legal education's narrow focus on legal-technical issues by labelling classmates as naïve for making moral arguments on the basis of equity or social justice.

External (Internships, Legal Clinics and Clerkships)

In many law school programmes, gaining professional experience is regarded as an important element. It is intended to supplement the more 'scientific' and cognitive case dialogue method and serves as a way for students to acquire professional skills. Gaining professional experience can either be a formal part of the curriculum, for which students receive credits, or it can take the form of extracurricular activities.

The effect of professional experience on law students' PIF depends greatly on the type of experience. Bliss [2017], for instance, demonstrated how large law firm internships, in which many American elite law school students engage, can steer students toward a private interest orientation. Conversely, involvement in legal clinics or in internships at public interest organisations can result in 'public interest persistence' (Albiston, Cummings and Abel [2021]). Judicial clerkships can be expected to result in yet another PIF.

If there is a close relationship between law school faculty and legal practitioners (via e.g career events, guest lectures and academic collaboration) this can further strengthen the influential role that practicing lawyers already play in the PIF of law students. Also in this regard, differences can be denoted between jurisdictions. Gaining professional experience is generally a less essential part of law school training in various civil law countries, and clinical experience is especially strong in numerous low- and middle-income countries.

The transformative impact of legal professional identity formation

PIF can evidently have various transformative impacts. We briefly elaborate on two impacts that are well documented in the empirical literature.

Public Interest Drift

First, the way in which law students are introduced to the profession during law school appears to result in many students losing their initial interest in working in the public-interest sector; they end up applying for jobs at large, commercial law firms (Bliss [2018]; Granfield [1992]; Sherr and Webb [1989]; Rhode [2000]). This 'public interest drift' is associated with a combination of factors, such as legal education's propensity to render moral and social issues irrelevant, its focus on neutrality and zealous advocacy of client interests, and the hiring pressure of large law firms at law schools.

However, some studies question the extent to which such a drift occurs. These studies suggest that students' self-professed public interest orientations at the start of legal education might be less sound than strategic (for an overview, see Bliss [2017]). This can mean that students change vocabularies of motive rather than lose their ideals (Schleef [2006]).

Friction Between Personal and Professional Identities

Second, various studies have found that legal PIF can have repercussions for law students' performances and wellbeing. Students whose personal identities and values fit well with the professional habitus and dominant values tend to flourish in law school and beyond (Costello [2005]). Students whose identities deviate (for instance, by being female or being from an ethnic minority, working-class background or public interest orientation) are more likely to struggle due to friction between their personal identities and developing a legal professional identity (Bliss [2017]; Clydesdale [2004]; Guinier, Fine and Baling [1994]; Granfield [1992]; Sommerlad [2007]).

Such friction can be coped with in different ways, but often at significant personal or professional cost (Costello [2005]; Granfield [1992]). One such coping strategy is role distancing. Drawing on Goffmann's role theory, Bliss [2017] and Sommerlad [2017] analysed how law students and young professionals tried to manage friction between identities by playing the role of legal professional. They behaved and dressed the part yet did not feel like lawyers. This strategy can have several drawbacks, such as internal conflicts and diminished job satisfaction, as well as lack of commitment toward clients, the profession and society (Bliss [2017]; Costello [2005]).

Public interest drift and friction between personal and professional identities could be expected to occur with less frequency once law school environments become more diverse and inclusive (Kortleven, Holvast and Besic [2024]). Yet, this assumption warrants further empirical substantiation.

NINA HOLVAST AND WILLEM-JAN KORTLEVEN

References

Albiston, C., Cummings, S.L. and Abel, R.L. (2021). 'Making public interest lawyers in time of crisis: an evidence-based approach', *Georgetown Journal of Legal Ethics*, 34(2), p. 223.

Bilionis, L.D. (2016), 'Professional formation and the political economy of the American law school', *Tennessee Law Review*, 83(3), Article 12.

Bliss, J. (2017). 'Divided selves: Professional role distancing among law students and new lawyers in a period of market crisis', *Law & Social Inquiry*, 42(3), p. 855.

Bliss, J. (2018). 'From idealists to hired guns: an empirical analysis of public interest drift in law school', *U.C. Davis Law Review*, 51(5), p. 1973.

Clydesdale, T.T. (2004). 'A forked river runs through law school: Toward understanding race, gender, age, and related gaps in law school performance and bar passage', *Law & Social Inquiry*, 29(4), p. 711.

Collier, R. (2021). 'Rethinking masculinities in the legal academy: Men, gender and legal careers (Or, whatever happened to the 'nutty professor'?)' in Schultz, U., Shaw, G., Thornton, M. and Auchmuty, R. (eds), *Gender and careers in the legal academy*, Hart Publishing, p. 513.

Costello, C.Y. (2005). *Professional identity crisis: Race, class, gender, and success at professional schools*, Vanderbilt University Press.

Cramton, R.C. (1978). 'The ordinary religion of the law school classroom', *Journal of Legal Education*, 29(3), p. 247.

Freidson, E. (2001). *Professionalism, the third logic: On the practice of knowledge*, University of Chicago Press.

Gaber, P. (1998). 'Just trying to be human in this place: The legal education of twenty women', *Yale Journal of Law & Feminism*, 10, p. 165.

Granfield, R. (1992). *Making elite lawyers: Visions of law at Harvard and beyond*, Routledge.

Guinier, L., Fine, M. and Balin, J. (1994). 'Becoming gentlemen: Women's experiences at one Ivy League law school', *University of Pennsylvania Law Review*, 143(1), p. 1.

Kortleven, W.J., Holvast, N.L. & Bešić, A (2024) 'From adaptive to reflective law school socialisation: a theoretical and empirical contribution from the Netherlands', Legal Ethics – pre-publication online DOI: 10.1080/1460728x.2024.239991. ---- with Legal Ethics italicsed.

Larson, M.S. (1977). *The rise of professionalism: A sociological analysis*, University of California Press.

Mertz, E. (2007). *The language of law school: Learning to 'think like a lawyer'*, Oxford University Press.

Posner, R.A. (1998). 'Professionalisms', *Arizona Law Review*, 40, p. 1.

Rhode, D.L. (2000). 'Legal education: Professional interests and public values', *Indiana Law Review*, 34, p. 23.

Roccas, S. and Brewer, M.B. (2002). 'Social identity complexity', *Personality and Social Psychology Review*, 6(2), p. 88.

Scheingold, S.A. and Sarat, A. (2004). *Something to believe in: Politics, professionalism and cause lawyering*, Stanford University Press.

Schleef, D. (2010). 'Identity transformation, hegemonic masculinity and research on professionalization', *Sociology Compass*, 4(2), p. 122.

Schleef, D. (2006). *Managing elites: Professional socialization in law and business schools*, Rowman & Littlefield.

Sherr, A. and Webb, J. (1989). 'Law students, the external market, and socialization: Do we make them turn to the city', *Journal of Law and Society*, 16, p. 225.

Sommerlad, H. (2007). 'Researching and theorizing the processes of professional identity formation', *Journal of Law and Society*, 34(2), p. 190.

Stolker, C.J.J.M. (2014). *Rethinking the law school. Education, research, outreach and governance*, Cambridge University Press.

Sullivan, W.M., Colby, A., Wegner, J.W., Bond, L. and Shulman, L.S. (2007). *Educating lawyers: Preparation for the profession of law*, John Wiley & Sons.

Sullivan, W.M. (2018). 'After ten years: The Carnegie Report and contemporary legal education', *University of St. Thomas Law Journal*, 14, p. 331.

Wilson, R.J. (2009). 'Western Europe: Last holdout in the worldwide acceptance of clinical legal education', *German Law Journal*, 10(6–7), p. 823.

85. Professional identities of legal academics

Introduction

This entry reflects on the professional identities and 'private lives' of legal academics (Cownie [2004]) within the context of changes in universities that have reshaped understandings of what it means to 'feel academic' (Taylor and Lahad [2018]). There has been change and continuity with regard to the professional identity of legal academics and examination of the topic raises important questions about what, ultimately, university law schools are considered to be for.

The contingencies of gender, race and ethnicity, age, sexuality, stage of career, health, disability, socio-economic background and relative wealth, for example, mediate how structural changes in the field of higher education internationally are experienced 'on the ground' by individuals in specific academic settings. There are different permutations of the legal academy across jurisdictions as well as of the prestige accorded to it within civil law and common law traditions (Schultz et al [2022]). University law schools vary greatly across countries in terms of institutional context, location in markets for legal education, academic reputation/ranking and function within discrete legal, political, local and wider communities. Professional identity is relational and discussion of legal academics cannot be separated from changes in the working lives of others who inhabit the law school such as professional services staff, librarians, security workers, undergraduate and postgraduate students.

It is nonetheless possible to identify in the extant literature central themes with regard to shifts associated with the marketisation of universities (Brown and Carasso [2013]) that have served to remodel or refashion the professional identities of legal academics in ways aligned to the new world in which global universities are now seen to operate.

The shifting terrain of legal education: academic identity in the marketised university

Research into university law schools and legal academics has become a more established and respected feature of law scholarship than in the not-so-distant past (see, for example, Bradney [2003]; Cownie [2004]; Jones and Cownie [2020]; Thornton [2012]). Changes in the professional identities of legal academics reflect the shifting political and theoretical terrain of legal scholarship itself; the growing impact, for example, on teaching and research in many law schools of socio-legal studies and methods, of feminist legal theory, critical legal studies, sexualities/gender scholarship and critical race theory. The law curriculum has evolved in ways that embrace philosophical and moral approaches and engagement with cultural and political questions. Academic identities in law, for some, align with an institutional and disciplinary embrace of a model of 'liberal legal education' (Bradney [2003]; Cownie [2004]) that engages with the political, economic and cultural context in which legal research is undertaken and law is taught.

University law schools have become more reflective of their own history, culture and social practices and legal studies has sought to subject the changing culture of knowledge production in law to critical scrutiny. This has included an exploration of how academic professional identities have been reshaped within the marketised university (Thornton [2012]). Work across jurisdictions has interrogated multifarious dimensions of changes in the political economy in which universities operate that have impacted upon contemporary academic life (see, for a flavour Barcan [2016]; Hall [2018]; Pesta et al [2017]; in law Thornton [2012]; Collier [2021, 2020]). Distinctive academic subjectivities and 'structures of feeling' (Burrows [2012]) in universities have emerged as a result of processes aligned to the marketisation of higher education including, of particular significance in England and Wales, changes to the structure of funding (on the 'neo-liberal university' see Thornton [2012]). A reconfiguring of the institutional function and goals of universities via the introduction of entrepreneurial competition has reinforced a model of the 'student as consumer' and institutional view that law is an essentially applied subject and relatively in-demand commodity within the new educational marketplace that has arisen.

With regard to the experience of legal academics, scholarship has explored the consequences of a proliferation of metric assemblages (Burrows [2012]) and the impact of new models of metric driven performance management that have resulted in a commodification of the outputs of academic labour (Davies and Bansel [2010]; Pack [2018]; Taberner [2018]). Concerns have been expressed across countries about a reshaping, if not eradication, of the academic cultures and values (including knowledge for its own sake) that marked university law schools at earlier historical moments (Chubb [2017]); Collier [2020]). The growth of national and global ranking industries has crystallised the idea that academic identities are shaped within an overarching culture of competition between institutions and individuals (whether competition for higher league table rankings, for students or esteem (Robertson [2010])). The seeming hegemony of a market model of education has redrawn the relational boundaries between academic staff and students (Chory and Offstein [2016]), bringing an acute ambivalence to the role of academics as 'educators and performers' (Wong and Chiu [2017]). Marketisation has fostered the idea of legal education as a *private* good with the focus of much academic labour increasingly pitched at securing student 'satisfaction' measured against a range of indices including employability and future earnings potential (Thornton [2012]).

There is a need to be more precise, however, about what these broader changes and macro-perspectives on the academy have meant for the professional identities of legal academics. Three themes are of especial note.

(Over) Work, Life and Professional Commitment

First, studies have unpacked the changing relationship between 'work' and 'life' in legal academia and the subjective impact of an incremental ratcheting up of workplace pressures; of the need to meet demands attached to new models of performance management and processes of audit around teaching and research; of 'becoming' entrepreneurial subjects, 'technopreneurs' who will seek grant money and self-promote on the world stage (Thornton [2022]) within the culture of competition fostered by the logic of the market and 'university as business'. Legal academics experience a multiplicity of demands associated with navigating a workplace in which hyper-performance and long working hours have been normalised and in which ideas of professional commitment and academic

vocation align with the institutional goals of the neoliberal university.

The 'Hidden Injuries' of Academic Life

Second, studies have addressed how changes in professional identity interweave with growing concerns about poor wellbeing and mental health in the legal community generally and university law schools (Jones et al [2020]; Strevens and Field [2019]). Research has explored links between the organised practices, structures and cultures of universities and the emotional and affective consequences of marketisation. Professional identities have been reshaped within a context in which distinctive psychosocial hazards attach to increasing job demands, diminishing autonomy, low levels of self-determination and poor manager and peer support (Peake and Mullings [2016]; Morrish [2019]; Wray and Kinman [2021]). The professional identity of many academics appears to be marked by often significant levels of anxiety (Berg et al [2016] and emotional distress (Smith and Ulus [2019]). Studies describe experiences of being constantly monitored and assessed, of imposter syndrome, fear of rejection, psychosocial insecurity and associated anxieties around risk management. Notwithstanding institutional commitments to improving legal academic and law student wellbeing significant 'hidden injuries' have attached to the rise of the neoliberal university (Gill [2009]).

Intersectionality: Whose Professional Identity Are We Talking About?

Finally, work has explored the intersectional dimensions of academic identity within the context of the multiple factors such as gender, race, ethnicity, socio-economic background, disability and sexual orientation; how assumptions about the interconnections between gender, care practices and commitment, for example, shape the paths of academic careers and perceptions of what 'success' means. As the once elite role of professor is feminised and displaced, an 'uber-elite' of 'top-down, authoritarian and masculinist' senior managers has emerged (Thornton [2022] at 467) whilst the corporatisation of universities has had a distinctly gendered and masculinist character (Collier [2022]). As in the legal profession particular difficulties can be experienced by members of the legal academic community who are younger, female, from an ethnic minority or disabled. Notwithstanding changes in the social profile of legal academics and law students the trajectories of legal academic careers continue to be shaped by the contingencies of gender, race, social background and differential access to social, cultural and economic capital, including, increasingly, intergenerational shifts around wealth transfer (Davies [2018]; Schultz et al [2022]).

The professional identities of those on insecure, part-time contacts, of 'pracademics' in university law schools – those who entered academia from legal practice and who continue to be predominantly women (Anonymous, 2019) – or postgraduate students engaged in teaching are by no means the same as other groups. The professional identities of young/er academics can be distinct to those of previous generations (Archer [2008]). Against the backdrop of structural divides between academic and professional services staff, and between academics whose role may be teaching only; teaching and research or occasionally research only (where a 'teaching-only' position may be perceived as less prestigious), it is early career academics and casualised staff who can face particular problems relating to the need to 'prove oneself' in a hyper-performance culture.

Resistance, change and continuity: the contradictions of professional identity

These processes should not be seen as a fixed or finished process. For all the pressures described above it could be argued many legal academics experience, to varying degrees, relatively high levels of self-determination and workplace autonomy. Recent histories of women in law schools (Schultz et al [2022]), of sexualities in the law school (Ashford [2021]) and interrogations of masculinities in the legal academy (Collier [2022]) highlight the complexities of professional identities in law. Increasingly encompassing voices from the global south work addressing experiences of disability, sex, race and age discrimination, transphobia and homophobia in law schools reflects a legal academy that has become, in some jurisdictions, more reflective of issues of equality, diversity and inclusion. Academics have sought to resist the processes of marketisation by rethinking academic

labour conceptually (Hall [2018]), challenging the boundaries of 'proper' knowledge and exploring different, healthier, ways of working (Mountz et al [2015]).

Conclusion

The longer-term impacts of the COVID-19 pandemic on the legal academy are unknown. What is clear, however, is that professional identities are being redrawn by the new platforms of knowledge production and education wrought by COVID-19, new ways of working, new forms of collegiality, of belonging and a transformation in the relationship between 'work' and 'home'. Academic identities are being recast in a multiplicity of ways as new forms and models of teaching and learning come into existence; by the growth of online and blended platforms, 24/7 digital communication, online storage, streaming services and use of social media that is transforming models of knowledge production and the management of academic performance. Each of these developments has the potential to reshape professional identities in as yet unknown ways.

RICHARD COLLIER

References

Anonymous. (2019). 'The glass box: a law teacher's experience of structural discrimination', *The Law Teacher*, 53(1), p. 119.
Archer, L. (2008). 'The New Neoliberal Subjects? Young/er academics' constructions of professional identity', *Journal of Education Policy*, 23(3), p. 265.
Ashford, C. (2021). 'Gender, Sexuality and the Law School', *Amicus Curiae*, 2(3), p. 450.
Barcan, R. (2016). *Academic Life and Labour in the New University: Hope and Other Choices*, Routledge.
Berg, L., Huijbens, E. and Gutzon Larsen, H. (2016). 'Producing Anxiety in the Neoliberal University', *The Canadian Geographer*, 2, p. 168.
Bradney, A. (2003). *Conversations, Choices and Chances: The Liberal Law School in the Twenty-First Century*, Hart Publishing.
Brown, R. and Carasso, H. (2013). *Everything for Sale? The Marketization of UK Higher Education*, Routledge.
Burrows, R. (2012). 'Living with the h-index: metric assemblages in the contemporary academy', *The Sociological Review*, 60(2), p. 355.
Chory, R. and Offstein, E. (2016). '"Your Professor Will Know You as a Person": Evaluating and

Rethinking the Relational Boundaries between Faculty and Students', *Journal of Management Education*, 41(1), p. 9.

Chubb, J. (2017). 'Academics fear the value of knowledge for its own sake is diminishing', The Conversation, available at http://theconversation.com/academics-fear-the-value-of-knowledge-for-its-own-sake-is-diminishing-75341.

Collier, R. (2022). 'Rethinking Masculinities and the Legal Academy: Or, Whatever Happened to the "Nutty Professor?"', in Schultz, U., Shaw, G., Thornton, M. and Auchmuty, R. (eds), *Gender and Careers in the Legal Academy*, Hart Publishing.

Collier, R. (2021). 'Blackstone's Tower Revisited: Legal Academic Wellbeing, Marketization and the Post-pandemic Law School', *Amicus Curiae*, 2(3), p. 474.

Collier, R. (2020). '"Left Pessimists" in Rose Coloured Glasses? Reflections on the Political Economy of Socio-Legal Studies and (Legal) Academic Wellbeing', *Journal of Law and Society*, 47(52), p. 244.

Cownie, F. (2004). *Legal Academics: Culture and Identities*, Hart Publishing.

Davies, B. and Bansel, P. (2010). 'Governmentality and Academic Work: Shaping the hearts and minds of academic workers', *Journal of Curriculum Theorizing*, 26(3), p. 5.

Davies, M. (2018). 'Educational background and access to legal academia', *Legal Studies*, 38, p. 120.

Gill, R. (2009). 'Breaking the Silence: The Hidden Injuries of the Neoliberal University', in Flood, R. and Gill, R. (eds), *Secrecy and Silence in the Research Process: Feminist Reflections*, Routledge.

Hall, R. (2018). *The Alienated Academic: The Struggle for Autonomy Inside the University*, Palgrave.

Jones, E. and Cownie, F. (2020). (eds), *Key Directions in Legal Education National and International Perspectives*, Routledge.

Jones, E., Graffin, N., Samra, R. and Lucassen, M. (2020). *Mental Health and Wellbeing in the Legal Profession*, Bristol University Press.

Morrish, L. (2019). *Pressure Vessels: The Epidemic of Poor Mental Health Among Higher Education Staff*, HEPI.

Mountz, A. (2015). 'For Slow Scholarship: A Feminist Politics of Resistance through Collective Action in the Neoliberal University',

ACME: An International E-Journal for Critical Geographies, 4(4), p. 1235.

Pack, J. (2018). *How the Neoliberalization of Academia Leads to Thoughtlessness: Arendt and the Modern University*, Lexington.

Peake, L. and Mullings, B. (2016). 'Critical Reflections on Mental and Emotional Distress in the Academy', *ACME: An International Journal for Critical Geographies*, 15(2), p. 253.

Pesta, T., Barrie, S. and McLean, J. (2017). 'Academic Life in the Measured University: Pleasures, Paradoxes and Politics', *Higher Education Research and Development*, 36(3), p. 453.

Robertson, S. (2010). 'Corporatisation, Competitiveness, Commercialisation: New Logics in the Globalising of UK Higher Education', *Globalisation, Societies and Education*, 8(2), p. 191.

Schultz, U., Shaw, G., Thornton, M. and Auchmuty, R. (2022). (eds), *Gender and Careers in the Legal Academy*, Hart Publishing.

Smith, C. and Ulus, E. (2019). 'Who cares for academics? We need to talk about emotional well-being including what we avoid and intellectualise through macro-discourses', available at https://doi.org/10.1177/1350508419867201.

Strevens, C. and Field, R. (2020). (eds), *Educating for Well-Being in Law: Positive Professional Identities and Practice*, Routledge.

Taberner, A. (2018). 'The Marketisation of the English Higher Education Sector and Its Impact on Academic Staff and the Nature of Their Work', *International Journal of Organizational Analysis*, 26(1), p. 129.

Taylor, Y. and Lahad, K. (2013). (eds), *Feeling academic in the neoliberal university: feminist flights, fights and failures*, Palgrave Macmillan.

Thornton, M. (2022). 'The First and Last(?) Feminist Law Professors in Australia', in Schultz, U., Shaw, G., Thornton, M. and Auchmuty, R. (eds), *Gender and Careers in the Legal Academy*, Hart Publishing.

Thornton, M. (2012). *Privatising the Public University: The Case of Law*, Routledge.

Wong, B. and Chiu, Y.L. (2017). 'Let Me Entertain You: The Ambivalent Role of University Lecturers or Educators and Performers', *Educational Review*, 71(2), p. 218.

Wray, S. and Kinman, G. (2021). 'The challenges of COVID-19 for the well-being of academic staff', *Occupational Medicine*, available at https://doi.org/10.1093/occmed/kqab007.

SLSA. (2024). *Precarious Employment Survey Report*, available at https://slsa.ac.uk/images/slsadownloads/SLSA_Board_2023/SLSA_Precarious_Employment_Survey_Report_FINAL_24.04.23.pdf.

86. Professional legal education

The purpose of university legal education

University legal education originally developed in different jurisdictions at different historical points. In some it was conceived as a way of preparing individuals for legal practice, improving on earlier ad hoc methods whereby apprentice lawyers were inducted. In others it was conceived primarily as an academic discipline, and then often used as a step in the preparation for practice. In most jurisdictions, law is a university discipline in its own right, with aspirant lawyers undertaking an undergraduate law degree before turning to training focussed on preparation for practice. Major exceptions include the USA where law is undertaken at postgraduate (JD) level, but generally covering similar content to undergraduate degrees studied elsewhere.

Whether the law degree should be perceived purely as a liberal academic discipline or as a preparation for practice is hotly contested, and different stakeholders take different perspectives. While many university legal academics strongly resist the idea that their task is to prepare practitioners, it seems that most law students, when starting their degree, have professional qualification as at least a possible, if not a probable goal. Many legal professionals perceive the main function of the law degree as preparation for practice, and professional regulators, where they are influential, adopt a similar approach. Higher education regulators may well expect the law degree to serve both functions.

As a result, there is pressure on the law degree to achieve a degree of conformity while also developing the individual to have the freedom of perspective to be critical.

> There is no such thing as a *neutral* educational process. Education either functions as an instrument that is used to facilitate the integration of the younger generation into the logic of the present system and bring about conformity to it, *or* it becomes 'the practice of freedom,' the means by which men and women deal critically and creatively with reality and discover how to participate in the transformation of their world. (Shaull, in Freire, [1996] 16)

Some regard these as mutually inconsistent, while others propose ways in which recognition of both functions can be mutually enhancing. This entry to the encyclopedia will provide information about the expectations of professional legal education in some selected jurisdictions with this question in mind.

The legal profession(s)

To consider what professional legal education is preparing students for, we should enquire into what the profession is. Inevitably, it is many things that are organised differently in different jurisdictions.

Lawyers

In most jurisdictions there is one formal category of 'lawyer', and qualification entitles the new lawyer to choose any area or type of practice. In practice, most lawyers specialise in terms of an area of practice (for example, conveyancing real property; criminal prosecution or defence; commercial transactions; family matters) and of a type of activity (focussing, for example on advising in an office, settling disputes or conducting trial advocacy). In some jurisdictions the profession is formally divided into solicitors and barristers, with different qualification requirements for each. In France, for example, *avocats* are independent lawyers while notaires act as agents of the State for many legal functions. Where these distinctions exist it still remains normal for students to pursue a law degree, even if subsequent training diverges.

Judges

In most civil law jurisdictions there is a career pathway through legal education directly into the judiciary. This generally involves special competitive examinations after the law degree and specific training courses. By contrast, in most common law countries, judges are appointed from experienced practitioners, either by an independent selection panel or (in the USA) by election or political appointment. In either case, all judges will have experienced the academic legal education of their jurisdiction.

Legal Executives

Lawyers' work is usually supported by others who may have their own professional bodies

(Chartered Institute of Legal Executives (CILEx) in the UK). Graduate status is not compulsory but is increasing, and qualification may be organised around on-the-job training or apprenticeships.

What professional legal education involves

To consider this question we need to identify what might reasonably be expected of lawyers. Whether practitioners or judges, they hold key roles in ensuring an effective system of justice. In order to perform these roles effectively they need:

- an understanding of general principles of law;
- a detailed knowledge of the law in the areas in which they practise;
- a critical analytical ability to apply that knowledge and understanding to practical problems;
- the independence necessary to represent client interests against possibly powerful opponents;
- the ethical commitment to respect confidentiality while maintaining their duty of candour amongst other duties;
- the ability to communicate effectively to a variety of others in advising and persuading; and
- the administrative ability to manage complex and changing circumstances.

It is argued that a law degree alone is unlikely to provide all these to the level that a client, court or society is entitled to expect. However, a law degree is capable of being an excellent foundation for all these essential characteristics.

A useful analysis of the key characteristics of legal education is provided by the US Carnegie Foundation publication *Educating Lawyers* (Sullivan et al [2007]). This identifies professional legal education as offering three apprenticeships.

- A cognitive (or intellectual) apprenticeship. This addresses the knowledge and understanding which lawyers must acquire, including the ability to interpret and apply Code and statutory provisions and to make use of court decisions insofar as they establish the law (as in Common Law jurisdictions) and to research the

law when their existing knowledge is inadequate.
- A practical apprenticeship. This develops the skills required to practise law effectively, including the ability to draft legal documents, write letters on behalf of clients and provide written advice; and to communicate effectively in order to discover what is necessary to prepare advice on legal problems, give oral advice to clients, test evidence through examination of witnesses, persuade judges and juries, and conduct effective negotiation on a client's behalf.
- An apprenticeship of professional identity and purpose. This is an ethical and social apprenticeship whereby the aspirant lawyer learns the professional values and the requirements of the Codes of Conduct that will bind them in practice, how to respond ethically to conflicts that arise between elements of the Codes, and a commitment to the Rule of Law.

Each jurisdiction has its own requirements before an individual may practise law. Information as to the requirements is generally available through the government or professions' websites in each jurisdiction. A useful source for EU jurisdictions is the factsheet *Lawyers' Training Systems* published by the European Union (E-justice Europa [2023]). It is common for this process to incorporate three conceptually different stages:

- An academic legal education at university level;
- Professional education and training to prepare for the transfer to practice;
- A period of supervised work experience.

A university academic legal education

This is not always required, for example, in Germany, and, recently, for the solicitors' profession in England and Wales (E&W). Here, standards are ensured through centrally set examinations, and degree-level study of some sort is expected. Where a law degree is required, its character will differ between jurisdictions depending on the conventions of that state. Thus, for the Bar in England and Wales it generally constitutes a three-year LLB, while in Scotland it is a four-year LLB and in many Australian states it is a longer degree combined with other subjects in order to provide a broader academic education. In USA students undertake a three-year undergraduate degree and the law degree is a three-year postgraduate JD. In most civil law jurisdictions a three-year undergraduate degree is expected.

The content may vary considerably, as might the approach to teaching and learning. Most jurisdictions however recognise 'core' subjects, likely to include study of the legal system, criminal law, the law of obligations (contract and tort), constitutional and administrative law and the law of real property. Company law will also often be offered. In Common Law jurisdictions the study of Equity is usually also expected. In EU jurisdictions study of European Union law is required.

An example of a 'core' is the Australian 'Priestley Eleven' (Law Admissions Consultative Committee [2008]). These are:

- Administrative Law
- Civil Procedure
- Company Law
- Contracts
- Criminal Law and Procedure
- Equity (including Trusts)
- Ethics and Professional Responsibility
- Evidence
- Federal and State Constitutional Law
- Property
- Torts

In addition, most degrees offer optional subjects and there may be a wide range. This will usually permit students to focus on particular areas of interest such as commercial law, the law affecting ordinary citizens, international or human rights law; to approach the law from different perspectives such as jurisprudence or critical theory; or to introduce other disciplines such as criminology.

The approach to teaching and learning may differ according to the prevalent pedagogic culture or the resources available. In most civil law jurisdictions, students have a right to a place at university, and pay little or no fees, leading to large initial enrolments, with teaching dominated by large lectures. Elsewhere, student fees may fund a higher proportion of small group work. Active learning, including problem-based learning has been introduced to augment the more didactic lecture approach. The widespread introduc-

tion of clinical learning methods has provided opportunities for both skill development and experience on which to build critical perspectives. Further, the introduction of educational technology services, speeded up as a result of the pandemic, has prompted development of more varied approaches to blended learning.

Assessment approaches are also varied, with a move towards assessment criteria that address transferable skills and the ability to apply knowledge as well as simple knowledge acquisition.

Professional education and training to prepare for the transfer to practice

This is generally designed to develop the transferable skills and apply the knowledge of key elements of the law that students have acquired during their undergraduate studies, to practice situations. Not all jurisdictions require this stage, and its content varies. Where it is required, the content is generally controlled by an overarching body, sometimes by the legal profession itself, by a professional regulator or some other body appointed by the state, or by the judiciary. Content may also vary depending on the nature of the profession for which the student is preparing themselves.

For example, in a jurisdiction like England and Wales, where there is a divided profession, solicitors and barristers have different requirements. A recent (2021) development by the Solicitors' Regulation Authority replaces a compulsory year of professional education with control only through centrally set assessments called SQE 1 and SQE 2. SQE 1 addresses 'Functioning Legal Knowledge' and covers what used to be expected of the undergraduate law degree plus business law and practice, dispute resolution, solicitors' accounts and the practice element of other subjects.

SQE 2 addresses 'Practical Legal Skills' and assesses six skills:

- Client interview and attendance note/legal analysis
- Advocacy
- Case and matter analysis
- Legal research
- Legal writing
- Legal drafting

It does so across five practice areas:

- Criminal Litigation (including advising clients at the police station)
- Dispute Resolution
- Property Practice
- Wills and Intestacy, Probate Administration and Practice
- Business Organisations (SRA [2023])

By contrast, the Bar Standards Board sets a syllabus covering skills and knowledge areas particularly relevant to barristers' practice:

- Advocacy
- Civil Litigation
- Criminal Litigation, Evidence and Sentencing
- Professional Ethics
- Conference Skills
- Opinion Writing
- Legal Research
- Drafting (BSB [2021])

A further contrast may be seen in some Australian states, where all students become solicitors first and may choose to become barristers once they have some experience. Students will have completed a degree that covers the 'Priestley Eleven' and may then be prepared for practice through a discrete Practical Training Course or through supervised workplace training, which may take place in a university law clinic.

In the USA, given that the JD is a postgraduate degree, there is no discrete period of professional training. Instead, most students will undertake clinical programmes which may include internships: placements within law firms or with judges. Each State has its own Bar Examination, and in addition there are central exams offered by the National Conference of Bar Examiners, which provides, for example, a Uniform Bar Examination incorporating essay, multiple choice and practical tasks, and a multiple-choice question Multi-State Professional Responsibility Examination (NCBE [2023]). Many students augment their JD with specific courses designed to prepare them for these tasks.

In Germany, where no law degree is required, students must pass the 1st State Exam before being permitted to commence the two-year Referendariat. This includes training on legal and non-legal professional skills and a number of theoretical courses. It concludes with the 2nd State Exam.

In other EU jurisdictions beyond a requirement for a law degree, there is a further examination, organised either by the State or the professional association. Possession of a higher degree such as a Doctor of Laws may provide exemption from these exams (as, for example, in Bulgaria).

Supervised work experience

Most jurisdictions require a period of work experience or induction. This may be tightly controlled, such as the solicitors' two-year Qualifying Work Experience or the Bar's one-year pupillage in England and Wales. It may involve combining work with study as in the CILEx process or in apprenticeships. Control is often by the Bar Association (as in Lithuania, where induction concludes with an exam organised by the Ministry of Justice). Where no induction is required (as in Bulgaria) a period of practice (for example as a judge or prosecutor) may be required. Supervision is generally undertaken by the employing organisation, to standards set by the professional association or the state.

Work experience provides employers with an opportunity to influence trainees to adopt the values of the firm. In many jurisdictions, global commercial firms dominate the market for traineeships and there may be a tension between commercial pressures and professional values. This requires constant vigilance by professional regulators, the judiciary and states to minimise the development of unethical cultures.

Conclusion

It is clear from the degree of control that is applied formally by professional bodies, by regulators and governments, and informally by, for example, the pulling power of the big commercial law firms, that much of professional legal education is designed to induce conformity to the present system. Indeed, in a world where inducements for unethical behaviour abound, there is much of value in this. But if Shaull's 'practice of freedom' receives no encouragement whatsoever, the scope for improvement and development is damaged. A creative combination of planning and praxis from university educators, practitioners and their regulators and influencers may be the best way forward, but this needs nurturing.

NIGEL DUNCAN

References

Bar Standards Board. (2021). *Curriculum and Assessment Strategy*, available at https://www.barstandardsboard.org.uk/training-qualification/curriculum-and-assessment-strategy.html.

E-Justice Europa. (2023). *Lawyers' Training Systems*, available at https://e-justice.europa.eu/407/EN/lawyers__training_systems.

Law Admissions Consultative Committee. (2008) *Uniform Admission Rules*, available at https://www.legalservicescouncil.org.au/uniform-framework/uniform-rules/admission-rules.html.

National Council of Bar Examiners. (2023) *NCBE Exams*, available at https://www.ncbex.org/exams.

Shaull, R. (1996). Foreword, in Freire, P. *Pedagogy of the Oppressed*, Penguin.

Solicitors' Regulation Authority. (2023), *What is the SQE*, available at https://sqe.sra.org.uk/about-sqe/what-is-the-sqe/.

Sullivan, W.M., Colby, A., Welch Wegner, J., Bond, L. and Shulman, L. (2007). *Educating Lawyers*, Jossey-Bass.

87. Professional support staff in law schools

'Professional Services' is a term which can encompass a multitude of roles, not all of which will necessarily be housed directly within a Law School. Roles can include Programme Support and Module Support; External Engagement (such as with alumni, sponsors, and/or potential employers in the legal sector and beyond); Assessment or Exam Boards (providing administrative support to the School, and/or support to students requiring information about re-sits, progression etc, as well as ensuring any requirements of regulators such as the Bar Standards Board are adhered to); Timetabling (which, during the COVID-19 pandemic, extended to ensuring the 'in-person' contact requirements of international regulators of law degrees were met); Student Support (potentially including providing support with mitigating circumstances, extensions, referrals to central University support services, and/or mental health support); Employability, Careers, or Placements (providing support to students seeking future employment within the legal professions and elsewhere, including arranging events such as law fairs, conducting mock interviews/assessment days, checking CVs and other components of applications, and/or arranging on-site events/external placements); Human Resources; Student Records (maintaining accurate records of e.g. attendance, academic attainment, registration, enrolment and module choices); Media/ Communications officers (maintaining social media channels on behalf of the School, producing newsletters and/or magazines, distributing School-wide programme-related information etc); Student Experience officers (working on e.g. welcome week activities and extra-curricular activities); Digital Learning roles (such as providing initial IT support, or supporting academics with learning management systems); Research Support and Research Project officers; Study Abroad officers (developing links with Universities overseas for placement purposes and/or supporting students during a study abroad year); Clinical Legal Education Support officers (which could include directing Clinics, developing and supporting pro bono opportunities within the community, and/or supporting the assessment of pro bono work); Operational Directors responsible for managing multiple teams across a service; and Health and Safety officers.

It would be unlikely that a Law School would contain every such role, or be able to draw upon such roles from elsewhere within the institution: the roles will be defined and divided up differently at each University. For example, at some institutions the Communications Officer might not solely deal with social media and internal messaging, but rather also with alumni communications.

Depending upon the size, type and approach of each University, there might be more or less consistency in roles across different Schools/ disciplines. Universities which are more centralised might not see much diversity between how specific roles are implemented in different areas e.g. Communications Officers might have the same job description regardless of the specific team in which they work. In contrast, a University which is historically larger and/or less centralised, in which different disciplines/Schools have had greater autonomy to respond to their specific needs, might see roles varying to a great degree. Wolf and Jenkins (2020) suggest pre-1992 Universities have traditionally been less centralised than post-1992 Universities, but that there is a shift occurring towards greater centralisation.

It is also the case that Universities, including Law Schools, will employ varying numbers of Professional Services staff proportionate to other staff members. Certain Professional Services staff, such as those providing administrative support to academic staff, have been more likely to be subject to restructuring and redundancies (Wolf and Jenkins [2020]). Others claim that Universities are experiencing 'administrative bloat,' in the form of too many roles which they argue are not central to the core teaching and research purposes of institutions (Jack [2022]), particularly as many Universities have moved towards a 'full-service ethos' (incorporating, for example, additional support with mental health challenges). A widespread complaint is certainly that academics have experienced an 'administrative creep' within their roles over the last 5–10 years (Wolf and Jenkins [2020]): to take one example, some Law Schools will require academics to mark assessments and to input their marks on the relevant learning management system (such as BlackBoard, or Moodle), with Professional Services colleagues then inputting those marks into student records, calculating the average mark for the module, etc. Other Law Schools will require the latter roles to be performed by the academics themselves. It has also been suggested that this 'administrative creep' can be attributed to increased regulation, including the creation of the Office for Students (Greatrix [2023]).

It is clear that Professional Services roles will vary greatly both within and between Law Schools and the institutions of which they are part, potentially complicating expectation management on the part of students and colleagues of Professional Services staff. Levels of understanding of Professional Services roles and remits have the potential to be negatively impacted by the overt or covert hierarchical structure of many Universities, in which the academic can be seen as superior to colleagues performing more 'administrative' roles – an exclusionary culture which can be exacerbated by the use of language such as 'backroom staff' (Greatrix [2018]). Although Professional Services colleagues are often a valued first point of contact for student queries about mitigating circumstances, extensions, and timetabling matters for example (Bleasdale and Humphreys [2018]), the power dynamics vis-à-vis academics can leave Professional Services staff feeling 'invisible' within Higher Education institutions (Akerman [2020]).

Such power dynamics are evident when considering institutional promotion structures. Whereas academic promotion structures are more likely (although not universally) to allow for promotion to the next grade at the point when the relevant criteria are met, for Professional Services staff there is often less opportunity to be promoted within their current role. For example, a role relating to pro bono will have been designated as being at 'X' grade, and in order to be promoted the individual will need to change to a different role (Marsden [2021]; Holmes [2020]). This can involve moving between service areas within a University, or even to another institution, which is highly problematic for the individual potentially having to leave a role which they enjoy, and when combined with precarity in legal academia (Blackham [2020]).

Most importantly, it also risks the loss of discipline-specific expertise such as programme knowledge (which is particularly critical where there are regulatory requirements, as with LLB programmes); and knowledge of the student cohorts. In their study across six Undergraduate disciplines, including Law, Bleasdale and Humphreys (2018) identified differences between student cohorts, with Law students being more likely to compare themselves negatively to other students, and being more likely to be anxious about their workload. Although students across the disciplines also shared some characteristics – with disciplines attracting larger numbers of international students being more likely to see timetabling requests linked to a desire to be home before dark, as just one example – it was concluded that discipline-specific understanding of student cohorts was important for advisory and other work with students.

In conclusion, there is no possibility of offering a definition of 'Professional Services' which neatly encapsulates the positions held within all Law Schools, and the structures within which such positions sit. The haphazard development of institutions and their processes, alongside the varying approaches taken to external factors such as regulatory requirements from the Office for Students; the increase in internationalisation; and the increased focus upon wider student support not directly related to the development of academic skills, means that 'Professional Services' roles will vary to a great extent between Universities. Nevertheless, there are some common factors, including the fact that localised knowledge can be supportive of the student experience, and that colleagues in such roles can feel overlooked or 'invisible' within their institutions – including when it comes to their future career paths. It is incumbent upon academic colleagues to ensure they understand the roles played by their Professional Services colleagues in their own institutions (Melling [2019]), and that they recognise their value through, for example, advocating for clearer progression routes and not feeding into institutional hierarchies through exclusionary language.

LYDIA BLEASDALE

References

Akerman, K. (2020). 'Invisible Imposter: Identity in Institutions', *Perspectives: Policy and Practice in Higher Education*, 24(4), p. 126.

Blackham, A. (2020). 'Unpacking precarious academic work in legal education', *The Law Teacher*, 54(3), p. 426

Bleasdale, L. and Humphreys, S. (2018). 'Undergraduate Resilience Research Project', University of Leeds.

Greatrix, P. (2018). 'Academics and administrators: No more "us and them"', *WonkHE*.

Greatrix, P. (2023). 'The unbearable heaviness of regulation', *WonkHE*.

Holmes, A. (2020). 'What are the barriers and opportunities for continuing professional development for professional services staff in UK HE?', *Perspectives, Policy and Practice in Higher Education*, 24(3), p. 79.

Jack, A. (2022). 'Are Universities suffering from management bloat?', *Financial Times*.

Marsden, S. (2021). 'Meeting the needs of professional services staff', *WonkHE*.

Melling, L. (2019). 'What's in a name? Job title and working identity in professional services staff in higher education', *Perspectives, Policy and Practice in Higher Education*, 23(2–3), p. 48.

Wolf, A. and Jenkins, A. (2020), 'Why have Universities Transformed their Staffing Practices? An Investigation of Changing Resource Allocation and Priorities in Higher Education', available at https://www.kcl.ac.uk/policy-institute/assets/why-have-universities-transformed-their-staffing-practices.pdf.

88. Public legal education (community)

The case for improving the general public's awareness of the law as it affects daily life has been made for some time (see for example PLEAS Task Force [2007]). The logic is not hard to establish – more informed citizens may be better placed to identify, address, uphold and possibly avoid or resolve legal problems and issues. A basic level of legal literacy can be said to be as essential as the ability to read, write, handle money or maintain a healthy lifestyle.

Whilst many make this a priority in their work there is still very patchy provision worldwide. In some places government agencies have taken the lead (for example in Canada see www.plecanada.org) and in other instances non-governmental organisations (NGOs) promote and deliver PLE initiatives (for example see the work of Bridges without Borders South East Asia (BABSECLE) available at: www.babseacle.org; and the work of Lawforlfe, www.advicenow.org.uk/lawforlife). Increasingly law schools have become involved in PLE provision (and other pro bono and clinical legal education initiatives, see entry 46 – Clinical legal education (general) and entry 42 – Pro bono initiatives) and are well placed to do so given their resource-base (LawWorks [2020]). Whilst there may be uneven provision of PLE globally and nationally the fact remains that PLE initiatives can now be found in many jurisdictions across the civil, common, Shari'a and customary law worlds (see Bloch [2010] at Ch 15). The common denominator is the provision of information to the public of their legal rights and responsibilities.

PLE takes a variety of forms and formats. This can be in hard copy form such as posters, leaflets and toolkits. Increasingly, however, this is being done through e-technology with the information on relevant rights and responsibility being found on dedicated websites, through social media and in other online formats. The use of television, radio and newspapers is also a common form of PLE delivery.

Face-to-face PLE work is also regularly found, with one particular model being used in many jurisdictions. Originating at Georgetown University, Washington DC, USA, the *Street Law* model of PLE has proven to be both a popular and effective means of educating the public on legal matters – so much so that this form of public education is now to be found in over 40 countries (Bloch [2010] at Ch 15). *Street Law* works on the basis of taking PLE into the community at their invitation and working in an interactive way with community groups on issues of law that directly affect them. Some *Street Law* programmes use qualified lawyers and trained teachers to deliver the sessions but many such initiatives are conducted through law schools where the law students (under the supervision of qualified lawyers) research, prepare and deliver the sessions themselves. The concept and process is described elsewhere. Street Law Inc, also in Washington DC, has pioneered much of this work and its website provides relevant resources and guidance (see www.streetlaw.org).

Whilst, by definition, PLE focuses on matters relating to law and the legal system its coverage can include anything that stands to be of public use (see, for example, the practical lessons in a range of legal subjects (US-specific), in Arbetman et al [2021]). As has been demonstrated, PLE tends to centre on those subjects that are of immediate concern often to relatively disadvantaged and/or marginalised communities (again see Bloch [2010] at Ch 15 and Grimes [2021]). What might be broadly termed 'social welfare' or 'poverty' law is often the substantive focus. Housing, consumer, employment, family, discrimination, disability, migration, health and social security benefit issues frequently form the core of PLE work. That said, capacity-building efforts have seen PLE address such important issues as economic development, job creation and environmental protection. The substance of PLE endeavours can and often does lead to wider campaigning work and, what has been referred to as cause lawyering (for this development in an international context see Sarat et al [2001]) and attempts to reform and improve legal provisions. Research has shown that the effectiveness of PLE largely and understandably depends on the relevance of what is being covered in the PLE sessions to the communities and individuals concerned (Giddings et al [2001]). Understandably perhaps, if people have immediate issues around what is being discussed there is likely to be a greater appreciation of the issues at hand with possibly an application of the new awareness taking place in consequence.

In a nutshell therefore PLE can cover any legal topic that is of interest to the targeted audience.

The beneficiaries of PLE are many and varied. If, as seen above, PLE can, in principle, cover any relevant topic then similarly it can be directed at any audience having need of information on a given matter. School pupils are often involved in PLE work as part of their overall curriculum through subjects such as civic education and citizenship studies. The original and many subsequent *Street Law* classes are delivered in schools. Whilst this may be an obvious and helpful focus for PLE – educating young people on the law – PLE has also many other actual and potential beneficiaries. Many *Street Law* programmes have for example worked in prisons especially with those prisoners about to be released. Work was done in the transition years in then apartheid South Africa (McQuoid-Mason [2019]).

Perhaps the best way to explain this is to take specific issues of current social concern. For example, domestic abuse is regrettably a common problem in many countries. PLE work can be carried out with communities who suffer from this serious problem or with groups established to support abuse victims. As seen above this can take the form of resources setting out the relevant legal provisions and/or educational classes that explain the law and procedures involved. Similarly, housing disrepair issues or high unemployment rates might call for an increased awareness of rights and responsibilities under the law and groups of tenants or the unemployed might be targeted to see if they would like to know more about their entitlements. Such PLE activity can be directly with the individuals concerned and/or in partnership with NGOs who support those most affected. PLE work therefore can, in principle cover anything and anyone from school children to the elderly, from the unemployed to those wanting to set up their own business and from those directly experiencing legal problems to NGOs trying to help them. Many of the most effective PLE initiatives have focused on a 'training of trainers' model so as to build the capacity of the NGO by increasing the legal awareness of the staff in turn supporting the work they can do with their service users. The biennial conferences held by the Global Alliance for Justice Education (see www.gaje .org) regularly feature a training of trainers component aimed at capacity-building. As in many other aspects of life providing what is being done is practically relevant, culturally appropriate and suitably engaging, then the possibilities are considerable.

PLE provision varies considerably across jurisdictions in both form and content and in terms of who is responsible for its provision. If legal literacy is as important as suggested here and elsewhere then it follows that it should be a concern at governmental level to ensure that the public at large have at least a basic understanding of their and others' legal rights and responsibilities. In some countries this has resulted in the relatively recent inclusion of 'civics' in the school curriculum (for example the introduction of citizenship into the National Curriculum for schools in England in 2002, see www.teachingcitizenship.org .uk). Whilst the rationale for this may be compelling few school-teachers in fact had or have legal training and in any event the overall curriculum is often crowded with little room for a detailed examination of matters legal. In addition, many, especially those with limited formal education experience, may not have been able to benefit from such classes or if they did it is not foremost in their thoughts. They may also now face problems that were never addressed by such early educational experiences. It is interesting to note that the importance of and responsibility for PLE has been accepted by statutory agencies such as the Legal Services Board in England and Wales. How this materialises on the ground however does not always match up with legislative intent. The bottom line is often a resource one and public expenditure is, more often than not, under pressure and scrutiny, as currently (2023) being witnessed worldwide. There are however some powerful examples of government-led PLE initiatives where responsibility for promotion and delivery is accepted and acted upon (again see www.plecanada.org).

In many countries, however, the practicalities of PLE fall to the non-governmental sector and in particular not-for-profit organisations such as charities and community groups. It is here that law schools in universities and colleges have come to the fore. Largely following the *Street Law* model university law schools have been actively involved in PLE for at least 50 years and that involvement is growing worldwide (again see Bloch [2010] at Ch 15). The reasons for this are both interesting and compelling. In essence and to quote a somewhat hackneyed phrase, 'everyone is a winner' – providing the quality of provision is to the appropriate standard and this can be ensured with relevant professional supervision. The use of *Street Law*, where students are required to identify, research, prepare, deliver and evaluate PLE provision gives them a unique opportunity to apply theory to practice using what is termed 'experiential' educational methods (see entries Clinical Legal Education (Overview) and Reflection and Legal Education). Enhancing students' knowledge, skills and values can bolster CVs and improve subsequent job prospects. For the public concerned there is the obvious benefit of improving levels of legal literacy. For the institutional provider social and corporate responsibility aspirations can be served as well as aiding learning and possibly influencing recruitment, retention and the eventual employability of graduates. Employers (within and beyond the legal profession) stand to take on graduates with the ability to 'hit the ground running' and government sees its own citizenship agenda supported.

Public legal education is therefore an important dimension of education generally and one that if society is serious about inclusion, equality and even democracy, we should be concerned about. Whilst government has responsibility for overseeing provision the reality is that institutions such as NGOs and law schools are well placed and able to deliver much of what is needed on the ground.

RICHARD GRIMES

References

Arbetman, L. and O'Brien, E. (2021). *Street Law: A course in practical law*, 10th edition, McGraw Hill.

Bloch, F. (2010). (ed), *The Global Clinical Movement: Educating Lawyers for Social Justice*, Oxford University Press.

Giddings, J. and Robertson, M. (2001). 'Informed litigants with nowhere to go: Self-help legal aid services in Australia', *Alternative Law Journal*, 26(4), p. 184.

Grimes, R. (2021). *Public legal education: the role of law schools in building a more legally literate society*, Routledge.

LawWorks. (2020). *Law School Pro Bono and Clinic Report 2020*, LexisNexis.

McQuoid-Mason, D. (2019). *Street Law and Public Legal Education*, Juta Press.

Public Legal Education and Support (PLEAS) Task Force. (2007). Developing capable citizens: the role of public legal education, available at https://www.advicenow.org.uk/sites/default/files/uploads/2013/05/pleas-task-force-report-14.pdf.

Sarat, A. and Scheingold, S. (2001). *Cause Lawyering and the State in a Global Era*, Oxford University Press.

89. Public legal education (prisons)

Public legal education targets citizens who have not been professionally trained as lawyers, offering them a basic knowledge of how the legal system works, including an understanding of their rights and duties. Its relevance for those serving sentences in prison is obvious, given the huge importance that the law has in their lives. This entry is about public legal education in prisons (LEiP). It covers legal education delivered in any kind of correctional institution but does not cover inmates studying professional law degrees via on-line or distance education.

This entry is based on the findings of specific projects about LEiP that have been conducted in different countries. Although the realities of life in prison and the legal and administrative organisation of the penal system differ significantly in different jurisdictions, there is nonetheless a substantial common ground in educational projects across the world in recognising possibilities for action, identifying the problems usually encountered by those who venture in them, and summarising the most promising outcomes.

There is a noticeable lack of quantitative evidence about legal education in prisons. This is a problem of prison education in general, basic research on which is 'still in its infancy internationally' (Rangel Torrijo and De Maeyer [2019] at 676). Most of the literature on LEiP deals with the description and qualitative analysis of particular educational projects, often written by the professors who were conducting the projects. Valuable as these sources are, there is need for a more systematic, objective and scientifically reliable body of literature, especially since policy makers and resource allocators rely on this kind of literature.

Legal education in prison: methodologies

The need for legal knowledge in prisons is justified, among other reasons, by the interest it sparks in the incarcerated population. When given access to higher education, law and criminology are popular choices among prisoners. How is that demand met? The different formats and methods that have been tried can be broadly organised around two main groups, here identified as the 'shared-classroom' and the 'clinical legal education' models.

The shared-classroom model reproduces conventional face-to-face teaching: inmates and students sit in the same room – always within the facilities of the correctional institution – and learn alongside one another ('inmates' here refers to those studying law as 'in-prison' students, while 'students' refers to regular university students based outside the prison). Typically, each group makes up for half of the total student body, and the course runs for a term. Several such initiatives have developed throughout the years. The oldest and most widespread is The Inside-Out Prison Exchange Program. Pioneered during the 1990s by a professor from Temple University, it currently involves a network of over 150 higher education institutions and over 200 correctional facilities worldwide (although mostly in the US) (https://www.insideoutcenter.org/network.html). Many other initiatives that reproduce the same philosophy have spread around the world. The content of the teaching can be legal or non-legal. In fact, at its inception Inside-Out was not specifically devised for legal education, although the model was later used to offer specific legal content.

The clinical legal education model brings the well-known methodology of law clinics to prisons. The aim is twofold: to provide students with experiential learning that gives them immediately applicable real life professional skills in a context that is especially relevant for future lawyers, and to offer direct assistance to prisoners in gaining access to their rights for purposes that can be as diverse as planning their appeal or getting advice on how to set up a business once released. This model may also include additional educational activities, such as classes, seminars and talks. An interesting development of the clinical model is that it allows those detainees who are the initial recipients of assistance to act themselves as informal legal experts and peer-advisors for fellow prisoners, achieving a sort of ripple effect that expands its benefits.

Main problems

Funding and Institutional Arrangements
Almost inevitably, any action in LEiP will face a significant scarcity of funds that may

thwart the educational project altogether or affect its proper functioning. In most countries prisons are publicly run by the state, and investing in them rarely pays off politically, since a part of public opinion is always 'fanaticised' against improving the living conditions of inmates or advancing their rights (De Maeyer [2019] at 819). As for private prisons, data indicates that they do even worse in terms of investing in education.

A further problem of LEiP lies in its specialised nature. Although the need for education in prison is recognised in the official documents of international organisations such as the United Nations, there is more awareness of the need for basic mandatory education. With a prison population that disproportionately suffers from deficits in literacy and numeracy, it is easy to dismiss higher and specialised education as a luxury product.

Nevertheless, alternative opportunities for funding emerge as new experiences in LEiP are able to attract media attention and the interest of public and private stakeholders, advocacy groups and even individual donors. The most common institutional arrangement for successful LEiP is cooperation between a prison and a university, with the latter providing educational know-how, students, teaching staff and possibly financing. Moreover, this institutional duo facilitates further partnerships, such as with charities and non-for-profit organisations, thus enhancing the possibilities of financing.

The Correctional Institution as a Problem

Prisons do not provide the best environment for education to flourish, as they operate under policies of incapacitation, coercion and punishment. Educating in prison brings to the forefront the intrinsic paradox between rehabilitation and retribution that faces any modern penal system, pointing towards aims 'which at best seem competing or at worst even diametrically opposed' (Bright and McNicholl [2021] at 96).

In that context, any educator designing a pedagogical action in jail must confront the fact that the specific idiosyncrasy of the institution will affect the whole process. Limitations to face-to-face encounters may frustrate the educational project from its inception or limit its scope of action, as can restrictions on the inmates' access to the digital world. Even in the most permissive correctional envi-

ronments, emphasis on control and security can disrupt education. The potential use as weapons of basic classroom material such as pencils or spiral notebooks explains restrictions that outside students may perceive as ridiculous, if not humiliating. Institutional constraints are not only physical and immediate. The implementation of educational programmes in prison can also be frustrated by over-zealous administrative actions.

However, the institutional hardship may have positive effects on university students by placing them in an uncomfortable new setting out of the relative comfort of the campus. Even if with the privileged status of external visitors, students have to go through some correctional routines – meeting with prison officers, clearing security checks, and so on – that add an invaluable experiential element to their learning. In the words of the founder of Inside-Out: '[h]aving class inside a prison is compelling – an experience that's hard to shake. ... I do not want my students to shake these encounters easily; in fact, I want the students to be shaken *by* them' (Pompa [2005] at 173).

Knowledge of Law and Attitudes Towards Law

The life of prisoners is totally determined by law and law enforcement. This may explain both the interest in, and the need for, legal education in jail. But it has also important consequences once a LEiP action is in place. Because of their life story, inmates tend to have previous knowledge of law – and strong opinions about it – and may be willing to let the students know how the law really works in action. This is one of the potential benefits of LEiP, with inmates contributing with 'a practical understanding of the application of the law, real-world examples and the reality of life ... inside prisons ... often in stark contrast to the theory of statutory provisions' (Bright and McNicholl [2021] at 110). However, over-reliance on the inmates pre-acquired legal knowledge may be counterproductive. Too much insistence on the legal story of convicts can strengthen barriers between both groups if 'sessions stray into conversation areas that objectify the in-prison students with their personal experiences' (Gray, Ward and Fogarty [2019] at 13). Furthermore, inmates' legal knowledge is frequently confused, inaccurate and overcharged with negative emotions and prejudice against law and lawyers. This can generate frustration for law students and professors, as previous legal experience turns into an obstacle to legal education. Preventing these problems demands from educators careful previous planning as much as flexibility during delivery.

A summary of positive outcomes

Although there is a noticeable gap in the objective and quantitative measurement of results in this area there is also a remarkable amount of common ground in the qualitative results reported by those who have studied different actions of LEiP, participants included. The literature shows that these educational projects mutually benefit both groups of participants – inmates and students – having a legitimising effect rather than the (ethically objectionable) temptation of using inmates for the major benefit of the students.

Research evidence also points to the fact that education in prison results in lower recidivism and better reintegration into the labour market. This is an effective argument to persuade authorities and funders of the value of LEiP actions, but the end goal should aim at the more elusive and more ambitious dimension of holistic human development. Solely concentrating on the acquisition of knowledge and professional skills without changing attitudes may result in producing 'qualified criminals' (De Maeyer [2019] at 825).

The literature also reveals that positive results on the part of prisoners are in the form of self-confidence and self-esteem are very important. There is a whole reimagining of their identity as active learners, rather than passive recipients of coercive policies and occasional benefits. This is enhanced when LEiP leads to the creation of communities of learning, be it with the outside students or with fellow inmates. In the shared-classroom model in particular, inmates frequently emphasise how their participation in a free and equal dialogue with outsiders allows them to leave behind their role as convicts – at least for some hours.

For students, a clear benefit is a better understanding of the functioning of law in action and of the many problems involved in its implementation, but here again the real outcomes go beyond the merely technical. Many students refer to their participation in

LEiP as a decisive experience in defining their own role and professional responsibility as lawyers. And this is not only relevant for those who aim at careers as defense attorneys, but especially for those who are never again going to walk into a prison but whose roles as judges, legislators, state attorneys or public officials may have a crucial effect on the life of the incarcerated population.

This sharpened consciousness of professional responsibility is related to the fact that prejudices against prisoners are at the very least questioned. LEiP offers university students the opportunity to see legal life through the eyes of others – precisely those who suffer the harshest consequences of the legal system, which from a learning perspective amounts to a truly 'decentering pedagogy' (Butin [2007] at 181). There are innumerable first-hand accounts of students describing their evolution during the term as a journey from prejudice to empathy.

But questioning of prejudices works both ways. There is qualitative evidence suggesting that studying law and working with law students actually helps convicts to get a more complex and nuanced view of the legal system and to gain a better sense of their own individual responsibility. For those serving a sentence, accessing and understanding legal knowledge may put them 'in the position to appreciate the reason for judgments of the Court', which besides its significance for their particular situation contributes 'to build confidence in the legal system' (Oludayo [2018] at 118).

Finally, despite all its problems and difficulties, LEiP contributes to the attainment of social justice. This is self-explanatory for those actions that, following the clinical model, effectively provide prisoners with free legal advice. But these educational actions are justice-oriented in a wider sense. It is by questioning mutual prejudices and building communities of thought and learning that they contribute to create more conscious and ethically oriented legal professionals and more active and responsible citizens. And it is precisely because of the constitutional values embedded in modern legal systems that education in law provides an excellent opportunity to move prison education beyond the aims of lowering recidivism and enhancing employability – valuable as they are – into a broader and deeper conception of personal and civic development.

CÉSAR ARJONA

References

Abenoza, S. and Arjona, C. (2017). 'Socrates behind bars: a report on an experimental course on justice and philosophy', *The Law Teacher*, 51, p. 3.

Armstrong, R. and Ludlow, A. (2016). 'Educational Partnerships Between Universities and Prisons: How Learning Together can be Individually, Socially and Institutionally Transformative', *Prison Service Journal*, 225, p. 9.

Blengino, C. (2018). 'Interdisciplinarity and Clinical Legal Education: How synergies can improve access to rights in prison', *International Journal of Clinical Legal Education*, 25, p. 210.

Bright, K.L. and McNicholl, M. (2021). 'The Open University Law School's Public Legal Education in Prisons: Contributing to Rehabilitative Prison Culture', *International Journal of Public Legal Education*, 5, p. 94.

Butin, D.W. (2007). 'Justice-Learning: Service-Learning as Justice-Oriented Education', *Equity & Excellence in Education*, 40, p. 177.

Codd, H. (2020). '"The Best of times and the Worst of Times": Reflections on Developing a Prison-Based Business Law and Tax Clinic in the Midst of a Global Pandemic', *International Journal of Public Legal Education*, 4, p. 39.

De Maeyer, M. (2019). 'L'éducation en prison à la périphérie de l'éducation pour tous', *International Review of Education*, 65, p. 811.

Gray, N., Ward, J. and Fogarty, J. (2019). 'Transformative Learning Through University and Prison Partnerships: Reflections from "Learning Together" Pedagogical Practice', *Journal of Prison Education & Reentry*, 6, p. 7.

Oludayo, J.B. (2018). 'Access to Prison Law Libraries as a Precursor to Effective Administration of Justice in Nigeria: Lessons from the United States of America', *International Journal of Legal Information*, 42, p. 110.

Pompa, L. (2005). 'Service-learning as crucible: Reflections on immersion, context, power, and transformation', in Butin, D.W. (ed), *Service-learning in higher education: Critical issues and directions*, Palgrave.

Rangel Torrijo, H. and De Maeyer M. (2019). 'Education in prison: A basic right and an essential tool', *International Review of Education*, 65, p. 671.

Shay, G. (2012). 'Inside-Out as Law School Pedagogy', *Journal of Legal Education*, 62, p. 207.

90. Reflection and legal education

Introduction

The most ambitious forms of legal education aim to produce individuals and legal professionals who have well-developed and robust capacities for reflective learning and inquiry, critical reflection, self-reflection, collective reflection, and a commitment to integrative forms of reflective practice (Leering [2017a/b, 2023]). Effective learning about law, justice systems, and how to be a legal professional is enabled and facilitated by law professors who are learner-centred and model reflective practice through their teaching, research, and scholarship – their professional practice.

In educational theory, reflection is a key enabler of learning at every stage of the professional learning journey. Building students' reflective capacity supports self-directedness and self-management, deeper learning outcomes, higher order thinking, and prepares them for lifelong learning. It strengthens the ability to learn from experience. Furthermore, nurturing students' critically reflective capacity is fundamental to ensuring they can effectively reflect on case law, legal instruments and institutions, the rule of law, and theories of justice and professional practice. Reflective inquiry is essential for understanding how the *law is lived*, how best to prevent legal problems and resolve disputes, and nurture the creative thinking needed to ameliorate gaps in access to justice. Yet, in legal education in many countries, a 'pedagogy of reflection' (Russell [2014]) has been undertheorised and undervalued, and lacks whole-of-law school approaches, although this is slowly changing. Similarly, reflective practice as a professional competency has been poorly conceptualised and implemented.

A strong reflective capacity integrates substantive and technical legal knowledge with practice- and evidence-based knowledge to generate more holistic and actionable professional knowledge and expertise. It helps refine the skills of legal reasoning, research, and advocacy, while developing ethical awareness, refined levels of judgement, wise action, and a positive professional identity.

Reflective practice

Since it first entered the learning lexicon, the meaning of the term reflective practice (Schön [1983]) has been significantly expanded by scholars in every discipline. Noting that professionals must be able to apply their theoretical and technical knowledge to the 'confusing messes' and 'swampy lowlands' of practice, Schön [1983] described what was required as professional artistry. Intuitive 'knowing-in-action' must be developed through integrating theory and practice, and by reflecting in and on action. To overcome professional schools' narrow focus on technical rationality, Schön called for a new epistemology of practice to deal with the complexity and uncertainty characteristic of professional roles and responsibilities. In a professional learning context, reflection is disciplined, rigorous and systematic. Reflective practice helps build professional knowledge and professionalism to ensure effective action across all forms of professional practice. In law, these forms include teaching, researching, or engaging in traditional legal practice, negotiating, dispute resolution, or legislative drafting, judicial decision making, or the myriad of other professional paths open to those who possess a law degree.

For three decades, Australian law teachers have been articulate about the benefits of reflective practice for educators (Le Brun and Johnstone [1994]). Kift [1997] extended this analysis to students, identifying reflection as a metacognitive skill, and reflective practice as instrumental in developing intellectual and vocational lawyering skills. Strengthening the capacity for reflective learning became an important focus (McNamara and Field [2007]). Reflective practice is essential for developing emotional intelligence (James [2005]), promoting student wellbeing and positive professional identity (Field, Duffy and Higgins [2014]), and mitigating the impact of vicarious trauma (Burton and Paton [2021]). A best practice guide for introducing it was created to help students acquire the Threshold Learning Outcomes for Law (McNamara, Cockburn and Campbell [2013]). Clinical educators, and those teaching dispute resolution and legal ethics also incorporate reflective practice capacity building (Copeland [2017]; Spencer [2012]). Critical reflection and critically reflective practice have also been promoted (James and Burton [2017]).

Law professors' commitment to their reflective practice is exemplified by their scholarship of teaching and learning, including 17 empirical studies since 2002 exploring the effectiveness of methods for introducing reflective practice (Leering [2023]).

Although there is less scholarship in Canada, understanding of the professional learning concept has been advanced by clinical educators (Voyvodic [2001]; Buhler, Marsden and Smyth [2016]), those providing experiential learning opportunities, and teaching legal ethics, substantive law, and dispute resolution (LeBaron [2002]). The evolving Canadian narrative has included Buchanan [1993] advocating for critical theories to be applied to poverty law practice, Macfarlane and Manwaring [1998] advancing problem-based learning in contract law, and Macfarlane [1998] explaining how it constructs legal knowledge. The emphasis on critical reflection and reflexivity continues to grow (Nussbaum [2021]). Developing the systematic capacity for reflection, noted Rochette and Pue [2001], supports a more holistic approach to professional education. To develop this capacity, Leering [2023] identified ten benefits, seven opportunities to advance reflective practice during law school, and 15 categories of methods or reflective practices to enable it, introduced iteratively. Methods include introductory sessions or guides; role modelling; reflective writing; reflective questioning; structured reflective learning cycles; self-assessment, self-awareness, planning, and debriefing exercises; reflective assignments; portfolios; aesthetic and contemplative practices; and feedback, supervision, and assessment practices. Lowenberger [2019] provided guidance for supporting rigorous assessment. To improve teaching practices, Rochette [2020] has encouraged law professors to develop reflective professionalism.

In England and Wales, Beck [1985] was an early proponent of the formative importance of critical reflection. Early adopters of reflective practice understood its merits for enhancing skills training (Webb [1995]), experiential learning and clinical legal education (Grimes [1996]; Ledvinka [2006]). Calling for more reflective and holistic legal education, Macfarlane [1992] and Webb [1996] engaged deeply with Schön's theories and the notion of reflective practicums. The UK Centre for Legal Education produced a helpful guide to reflective practice (Hinett [2002]) and sponsored conferences and research projects. Empirical studies include Brooman and Darwent [2012] researching how reflection supports transition into the first year. Gibbons [2019] reported on how York Law School's guided-discovery problem-based learning curriculum integrated reflective practice across the curriculum. In 2019, a special issue of *The Law Teacher* featured the first ever international collection of writings about reflective practice.

In the US, where notably Schön [1995] spoke with clinical educators about reflective practicums in the 1990s, the scholarship reveals important applications. Neumann [2000] extensively reviewed Schön's theory and its practical implications for law, cataloguing 14 insights, and how it strengthened professional learning. Neumann also connected Schön's concept of *reflection-in-action* to students' learning the art of critique. Ogilvy [1986] explained how it supports higher order learning outcomes and could be advanced by student learning journals. Its seminal role in professionalising teaching practice was explored by Hess [2002]. Reflection's role in supporting the three apprenticeships for law – cognitive, practical, and particularly the ethical-social – was recognised in the influential Carnegie Report (Sullivan et al. [2007]). Self-directed and reflective learning was promoted by a persuasive report on best practices in legal education (Stuckey et al. [2007]). Anzalone [2010], in an international cross-disciplinary compendium about reflective practice, described how reports like Carnegie's and Stuckey's helped pave the way for its acceptance in law. Cogently setting out the benefits, Anzalone described introducing it as one of the most exciting developments in legal education pedagogy. Hamilton [2022] outlined its role in forming professional identity. The American Bar Association's law school accreditation requirements for experiential learning have further increased awareness of its merits. The field of dispute resolution has adopted it, evidenced by Lang's [2019] guide to reflective practice in conflict resolution, as has externship education (Scherr and Barry [2016]). Incorporating insights from educational, cognitive, and moral development theory, clinical educator Casey [2014] constructed a framework to support reflection. Capulong, King-Ries and Mills [2021] provided an example of how to encourage critically reflective practice by incorporating critical race theory in a course. Balsam, Brooks and Reuter [2017] offered useful assessment advice.

Barriers and challenges have been identified for introducing a reflective practice pedagogy. However, like all pedagogical challenges, these can be surmounted. Leering [2019] outlined ten perils and pitfalls to avoid including not being clear about why reflection is being required, choosing a reflective method that is not fit for purpose, assuming students know how to reflect, ignoring scepticism about the value of reflection, underestimating the value of modelling reflective practice, avoiding reflective practice overload, naivety about the challenges students face being reflective in law school (particularly in the self-reflection domain), promoting superficial or formulaic reflection, being inattentive to issues raised by assessment, and not evaluating whether the method is effective and achieves the desired result.

Despite these challenges, reflective practice in law is now broadly conceptualised to maximise its implementation and impact. It has both instrumental and transformative aims. Leering [2017] identified five domains for thinking about reflective practice in law, leading to praxis, embedding reflection in all professional action. The intention behind the first, reflection on practice, is to improve the capacity to learn, develop skills and competence, and to build professional knowledge. Reflecting in this domain helps mature professional judgement and seeds lifelong learning. Critical reflection, in its many forms, is a fundamental skill. It includes developing critical perspectives on law and the rule of law, legal institutions, human rights, and philosophies of practice. Self-reflection creates the space to foster self-awareness, professionalism, cultural competence, ethical action, trauma-informed approaches, and responsiveness to societal need. Increasingly, its value is being acknowledged, including for supporting mental health and well-being. Integrative reflection helps question assumptions, interrogate espoused theory versus theory-in-use, and enable personal authenticity and professional integrity. It consolidates and deepens the insights from other domains to transform practices, increase professionalism and support praxis. And finally, nurturing the capacity for collective reflection ensures that despite law's reputation for adversarialism, prospective legal professionals can engage in reflective and generative dialogue appropriately and productively.

Conclusion

In summary, the benefits of engaging in *instrumental* and *transformative* reflective practice – the systematic and disciplined use of reflection to improve learning and practice and create professional knowledge – are well-documented in other professions, and increasingly in law. There are many imperatives for becoming more vigilant and strategic about enhancing students' capacity to be more reflective and raising awareness of the benefits of reflective practice during law school. Students are better positioned to develop professional competence and sustain their commitment to professional learning, ethics, and values. Future legal professionals will be better supported in their quest to become more client-centred and responsive to societal needs, and with a stronger *access to justice consciousness* and commitment to the rule of law. Thus, reflective practice as a professional learning concept is essential to studying and practicing law – in its many manifestations (as educators, researchers, scholars, barristers, solicitors, lawyers, judicial decision makers, policy makers, etc.). Leadership on how to develop this capacity has emerged in many countries from clinical educators, professors supporting experiential, active, and problem-based learning, and those offering dispute resolution, legal ethics, and substantive law courses. Many seminar-type courses explicitly encourage critical reflection on law, legal theory, and legal institutions. Fifteen types of pedagogical methods have been identified to encourage it.

MICHELE LEERING

References

Anzalone, F.M. (2010). 'Education for law: Reflective education for the law', in Lyons, N. (ed), *Handbook of Reflective Inquiry: Mapping a Way of Knowing for Professional Reflective Inquiry*, Springer.

Balsam, J.S., Brooks, S.L., and Reuter, M. (2017). 'Assessing Law Students as Reflective

Practitioners', *New York Law School Law Review*, 62(1), p. 49.

Beck, A. (1985). 'Legal Education and Reflection', *The Law Teacher*, 19(3), p. 193.

Brooman, S. and Darwent, S. (2012). 'A Positive View of First-year Undergraduate Reflective Diaries: Focusing on What Students Can Do', *Reflective Practice*, 13(4), p. 517.

Buchanan, R.M. (1983). 'Context, continuity, and difference in poverty law scholarship', *University of Miami Law Review*, 48(5), p. 1000.

Buhler, S. and Marsden, S. (2017). 'Lawyer Competencies for Access to Justice: Two Empirical Studies', *Windsor Yearbook of Access to Justice*, 34(2), p. 186.

Buhler, S., Marsden, S. and Smyth, G. (2016). *Clinical Law: Practice, Theory and Social Justice Advocacy*, Emond Montgomery.

Burton, K. and Paton, A. (2021). 'Vicarious Trauma: Strategies for Legal Practice and Law Schools', *Alternative Law Journal*, 46(2), p. 94.

Capulong, E.R.C., King-Ries, A. and Mills, M. (2021). 'Antiracism, Reflection, and Professional Identity', *Hastings Race and Poverty Law Journal*, 18(1), p. 3.

Casey, T. (2014). 'Reflective Practice in Legal Education: The Stages of Reflection', *Clinical Law Review*, 20(2), p. 317.

Copeland, A. (2017). 'Reflective Practice: The Essence of Clinical Legal Education', in Evans, A., Cody, A., Copeland, A., Giddings, J., Joy, P., Noone, M.A. and Rice, S. (eds), *Australian Clinical Legal Education: Designing and Operating a Best Practice Clinical Program in an Australian Law School*, ANU Press.

Field, R., Duffy, J. and Huggins, C. (2014). *Lawyering and Positive Professional Identity*, LexisNexis.

Gibbons, J. (2019). 'How is Reflection "Framed" for Legal Professional Identity? Using Bernstein and Leering to Understand the Potential for Reflection in our Curriculum as Written, Experienced, and Assessed', *The Law Teacher*, 53(4), p. 401.

Grimes, R. (1996). 'The Theory and Practice of Clinical Legal Education', in Webb, J. and Maughan, C. (eds), *Teaching Lawyers' Skills*, Butterworths.

Hamilton, N. (2022). 'The Foundational Skill of Reflection in the Formation of Professional Identity', *St. Mary's Journal on Legal Malpractice & Ethics*, 12(2), p. 254.

Hess, G.F. (2002). 'Learning to Think Like a Teacher: Reflective Journals for Legal Educators', *Gonzaga Law Review*, 38(1), p. 129.

Hinett, K. (2002). *Developing Reflective Practice in Legal Education*, UK Centre for Legal Education.

James, C. (2005), 'Seeing Things as We Are: Emotional Intelligence and Clinical Legal Education', *International Journal of Clinical Legal Education*, 8, p. 123.

James, N. and Burton, K. (2017). 'Measuring the Critical Thinking Skills of Law Students Using a Whole-of-Curriculum Approach', *Legal Education Review*, 27(1), p. 1.

Kift, S. (1997). 'Lawyering Skills: Finding Their Place in Legal Education', *Legal Education Review*, 8(1), p. 43.

Lang, M.D. (2019). *The Guide to Reflective Practice in Conflict Resolution*, Rowman & Littlefield Publishing Group.

LeBaron, M. (2002). *Bridging troubled waters: Conflict resolution from the heart*, John Wiley & Sons.

Le Brun, M. and Johnstone, R. (1994). *The Quiet Revolution: Improving Student Learning in Law*, The Law Book Company.

Ledvinka, G. (2006). 'Reflection and Assessment in Clinical Legal Education: Do You See What I See?', *International Journal of Clinical Legal Education*, 9, p. 29.

Leering, M.M. (2017a). 'Integrated Reflective Practice: A Critical Imperative for Enhancing Legal Education and Professionalism', *Canadian Bar Review*, 95(2), p. 47.

Leering, M.M. (2017b). 'Enhancing the Legal Profession's Capacity for Innovation: The Promise of Reflective Practice & Action Research for Increasing Access to Justice', *Windsor Yearbook of Access to Justice*, 34(1), p. 189.

Leering, M.M. (2019). 'Perils, Pitfalls, and Possibilities: Introducing Reflective Practice Effectively in Legal Education', *The Law Teacher*, 54(4), p. 431.

Leering, M.M. (2023). *Integrative Reflective Practice in Canada and Australia: Enhancing Legal Education, Pedagogy, and Professionalism* (Doctoral dissertation, Queen's University), available at https://qspace.library.queensu.ca/items/c50f6ac8-05f2-4198-8282-f326bc24b993.

Lowenberger, B. (2019). 'Advancing Rigorous Reflective Practice in Legal Education Through Assessment: A Guide for Educators', *The Law Teacher*, 53(4), p. 446.

Macfarlane, J. (1992). 'Look Before You Leap: Knowledge and Learning in Legal Skills Education', *Journal of Law and Society*, 19(3), p. 293.

Macfarlane, J. (1998). 'Assessing the Reflective Practitioner: Pedagogic Principles and Certification Needs', *International Journal of the Legal Profession*, 5(1), p. 63.

Macfarlane, J. and Manwaring, J. (1998). 'Using Problem-based Learning to Teach First Year

Contracts', *Journal of Professional Legal Education*, 6(2), p. 271.

McNamara, J., & Field, R. (2007). 'Designing for reflective practice in legal education', *The Journal of Learning Design*, 2, 66–77.

McNamara, J., Cockburn, T., & Campbell, C. (2013). *Good practice guide (bachelor of laws): Reflective practice* (Australian Learning and Teaching Council), available at http://www.lawteachnetwork.org/resources/gpg-reflection.pdf.

Neumann, R.K. Jr. (2000). 'Donald Schön, the Reflective Practitioner, and the Comparative Failures of Legal Education', *Clinical Law Review*, 6(2), p. 401.

Nussbaum, S. (2021). 'Critique-inspired Pedagogies in Canadian Criminal Law Casebooks: Challenging "Doctrine First, Critique Second" Approaches to First-year Law Teaching', *Dalhousie Law Journal*, 44(1), p. 209.

Ogilvy, J.P. (1996). 'The Use of Journals in Legal Education: A Tool for Reflection', *Clinical Law Review*, 3(1), p. 55.

Rochette, A. (2010). *Teaching and Learning in Canadian Legal Education: An Empirical Exploration* (Doctoral dissertation, McGill University), available at https://escholarship.mcgill.ca/concern/theses/12579x59g.

Rochette, A. and Pue, W.W. (2001). '"Back to Basics?" University Legal Education and 21st Century Professionalism', *Windsor Yearbook of Access to Justice*, 20, p. 167.

Russell, T. (2014). 'One teacher educator's career-long development of a pedagogy of reflection', in Crain, C. J. and Orland-Barak, L. (eds), *Advances in Research on Teaching: International Teacher Education: Promising Pedagogies*, Emerald Group.

Scherr, A. and Barry, M.M. (2016). 'Reflection and Writing Journals', in Wortham, L. Scherr, A., Maurer, N. and Brooks, S.L. (eds), *Learning from Practice: A Text for Experiential Legal Education*, 3rd edition, West Academic Publishing.

Schön, D. (1983). *The Reflective Practitioner: How Professionals Think in Action*, Basic Books.

Schön, D.A. (1995). 'Educating the Reflective Practitioner', *Clinical Law Review*, 2(1), p. 231.

Spencer, R. (2012). 'Holding Up the Mirror: A Theoretical and Practical Analysis of the Role of Reflection in Clinical Legal Education', *International Journal of Clinical Legal Education*, 18, p. 179.

Stuckey, R. et al. (2007). *Best Practices for Legal Education: A Vision and a Roadmap*, Clinical Legal Education Association.

Sullivan, W.M., Colby, A., Wegner, J.W., Bond, L. and Shulman, L.S. (2007). *Educating Lawyers: Preparation for the Profession of Law*, The Carnegie Foundation for the Advancement of Teaching, Jossey-Bass.

Voyvodic, R. (2001). 'Considerable Promise and Troublesome Aspects: Theory and Methodology of Clinical Legal Education', *Windsor Yearbook of Access to Justice*, 20, p. 111.

Webb, J. (1995). 'Where the Action Is: Developing Artistry in Legal Education', *International Journal of the Legal Profession*, 2(2/3), p. 187.

Webb, J. (1996). 'Why theory matters', in Webb, J. and Maughan, C. (eds), *Teaching Lawyers' Skills*, Butterworths.

91. Research into legal education (empirical)

Introduction

This entry is concerned with empirical, as compared with theoretical or other analyses of legal education. Research topics are varied, ranging from legal education in universities and colleges, to law professional courses and legal professional and judicial training, along with research into basic issues such as student numbers, assessment outcomes, pedagogy and levels of student satisfaction. Illustrative projects in this entry are drawn from many jurisdictions, though the structures and traditions of legal education vary considerably.

Empirical research provides information about how the legal education system is working in reality, how it is responding to challenges and change and the key 'actors'. It has also been influenced by the application of empirical research methods to law itself (Cownie [2010], Ogloff et al. [2000]). Empirical research requires researchers to become actively involved in their topic by applying either quantitative methods, usually surveys of various types, or qualitative methods. The latter include face-to-face, telephone and on-line interviews, observation/ monitoring, active participation and focus groups (Kritzer [2021]; Pannebakker et al [2022]). Quantitative-based research is well established, with records of student numbers, their assessment and professional qualification dating back to medieval universities and records belonging to long-standing legal professional bodies such as the Inns of Court and Bars and other regulatory bodies.

Empirical research methods inevitably have implications for funding, skills development, cooperation and ethical issues. However, their strength is that, properly undertaken, the reality of legal education emerges and findings can counter assumptions about, for example, why people study law, what they find most useful, their learning experiences and the problems/issues they face (Kritzer [2021]). Well-designed and executed empirical projects can identify the strengths but also weaknesses of curricular, pedagogic, assessment and other practices and the broader culture of legal education. We have such research from many jurisdictions, providing interesting contrasts. Arguably, despite a global research agenda emerging, there remain wide variations regarding legal education itself, both in terms of direct issues such as its content and pedagogy but also several structural aspects, such as its regulation, funding and management. All aspects have been increasingly affected by heightened competition and the application of management theories.

Empirical research inevitably requires not only funding and skills development, along with on-going management but also researcher interaction with others, typically those from the legal education system itself and its 'recipients'. Importantly, it requires their support and participation. This is especially the case with qualitative research, such as observation and participation projects and case studies where the researchers are closely involved with their research subjects and must gain their trust, much as required by effective team building. Empirical methodologies are sometimes controversial. Probing 'realities' may raise ethical issues and findings can sometimes make uncomfortable reading, especially in a context where education institutions are subject to a competitive environment, 'league tables', social media and official scrutiny. Empirical research into legal education became more widely established from the1960s, though interestingly in the UK, it was into further education institutions, such as technical colleges and colleges of commerce rather than universities (Wilson [1966]).

Today, research into university legal education dominates. Research has been growing, with new topics emerging, though many gaps remain. For example, law plays a key role on many professional and other courses (and in schools), yet empirical data is limited, even regarding legal professional training programmes. Projects on post-graduate and, say, doctoral programmes remain relatively rare. So, inevitably, this overview of empirical research into legal education is inhibited by its concentration, to date, on university law programmes and, to a lesser extent, legal professional issues. Research findings are available in a growing number of journals, for example, The Journal of Legal Education, Asian Journal of Legal Education, European Journal of Legal Education, International Journal of the Legal Profession, Law and Society and The Law Teacher, along with many journals associated with specific Law Schools, such as the Griffith Law Journal, the

Maastricht Law Journal and the Sydney Law Review.

What has been researched and how?

Many topics have been researched using quantitative empirical methods, though interviews and focus groups are also widely used. Observation/participation projects remain rare despite their being especially useful for, say, student experiences and professional legal training. Many of these projects have gathered basic data, such as the nature of providers, the legal courses offered, curriculum content, student numbers and characteristics, assessment data and to an extent, post qualification careers. Although there are major differences between jurisdictions, important projects have mapped legal education in a more systematic way. There are a few overviews of legal education, for example, from the USA (Ogloff et al [2000]). Interestingly, from the UK, Wilson's survey referred to above, was published in the first edition of The Law Teacher in 1967. Out of 353 colleges that then taught law, some 275 completed a questionnaire. It not only provided basic data but triggered interest in legal education more widely and the establishment or re-focusing of law academic associations which had interests in legal education. The first survey was followed by a series of similar surveys in the UK, covering higher as well as further education (Wilson [2006]). All had very good response rates, for example, Harris and Beinhart [2004] had a 71 per cent response rate such that empirical research became better established, and knowledge of the nature of legal education deepened. It is important to note that these surveys were undertaken by law academics, who were able to decide on the surveys' aims, content and significance. They often had different priorities than the more recent 'official' surveys that tend to focus on performance and satisfaction issues.

A second topic that has generated interesting research has been the characteristics, experiences and aspirations of law teachers themselves. Some early projects were into pre-university law teachers. One explored the question of how law teachers self-identified. Are they 'academics' or (legal) 'professionals'? (Leighton, Mortimer and Whatley [1995]). This question highlights many of the continuing complexities and tensions of legal education. An interesting study from the USA

explored the role of academic publications, in terms of both individual expectations and law school reputation (Cofone and Male [2021]). An emerging topic for research on law teachers has been the role of so-called 'shadow'/private law teachers or 'crammers', who are an important and often long-established feature of legal education. They are well established, for example, in Germany, Norway, Denmark and the Netherlands, are widely used in Asia and are one indicator of high levels of competition to enter the legal profession/achieve top awards. Surveys confirm the high numbers of students who resort to 'shadows' largely because of perceived inadequate or insufficient formal teaching (Nielson [2023]). The research findings raise interesting questions. These include a possible mismatch between teaching and assessment, confused learning objectives and student lack of confidence regarding the relevance of often costly formal legal education. But also the possible effects of increased business competition by private and international providers and their effective marketing.

Specific teaching methods feature to an extent, for example, how to engage students in an on-line learning environment, and problem-based and blended learning, along with research into types of assessment. Some of this research was 'COVID-driven', with some clear findings emerging. For example, one 'COVID' project found that students wanted more clarity regarding expectations of them, effective engagement with staff, and more advice. Although a critical topic, the response to the questionnaire was only c. 24 per cent, indicating difficulties in achieving good response rates (St Val [2021]).

In terms of specific 'schools' of legal education such as socio-legal studies, clinical legal education has probably been the most researched (Alexander [2023]. Data are drawn from many or even most jurisdictions and despite the 'case' for developing clinics having wide support research does reveal many tensions and unresolved issues. A relatively new yet well-established research topic has been the relationship between the learning environment and student well-being or lack of it (Skipper and Fay [2023]; Ferris [2022]). In addition to personal characteristics that might heighten risk, such as ethnicity, gender, sexual orientation and class, especially perhaps on legal professional programmes, aspects of pedagogy emerge as relevant. For example, the socratic/case method approach arguably heightens risk because it assumes extrovert personalities (Spencer [2022]). There are also surveys of students on professional training programmes which highlight stress factors, here not only based on traditional 'disadvantages' but educational background and aspects of class (Mason, Vaughan and Weil [2023]). This has particular impact where a career in law is seen not only as high status but hugely competitive. Interestingly, law students do not feature as strongly in empirical research beyond official surveys as might be expected, especially in terms of why they study law, what their expectations of it are and what they want to use their education for. There are, though, some notable exceptions (Bone [2009]) and a longitudinal study of law students in New Zealand (Taylor et al [2023]).

What has not been extensively researched?

Some topics relatively neglected have already been referred to, such as law in schools, on interdisciplinary programmes, and importantly, critiques of the regulation and management of legal education itself. Competition is seen in many jurisdictions as the route to improved quality. However, we have little data on whether that is correct or not. The proliferation of league tables, arguably some of variable quality and commercially influenced, has led to huge discrepancies in the ranking of even well-known university law schools. The marketing of legal education is a topic crying out for more detailed empirical analysis, along with analysis of the processes of decision-making and development. Interestingly, wider empirical research into the law curriculum, assessment and pedagogy is not extensive, though is sometimes the topic for official enquiries (e.g. LETR [2013]). In some jurisdictions enquiries into professional legal education, such as apprenticeships of various forms and training contracts, judicial training etc are a priority but very limited in others. The relative neglect of legal education outside universities, especially perhaps in business schools and the like, on joint degrees, and at sub degree level is interesting. It may be a reflection of the question raised by some as to whether law, seen by some as simply a rules-based discipline is truly

an 'academic' subject (Beecher and Trowler [2001]). In some ways law is still perceived as professional-driven, like medicine and engineering (heightened by the fact that we have relatively little data on what law graduates do aside from entering the legal profession or teaching). But perhaps more importantly, given the arguable dominance of the legal profession over legal education, relatively little research is published on the future of the profession though there has been some trailblazing research on technological advances (Susskind [2023]). Today, debates around AI are raging and are critical for the profession and for legal education itself. How will both need to change and what has been done to date? (Armour and Sako [2021]). Another area of neglect is that of the training and development of so many who provide legal advice and support, although not as lawyers. This includes a wide range of charities, trade unions, specialist advice centres and via various on-line activities.

Some reflections

Empirical research into legal education appears, though thriving, to be generally relatively self-contained. Only rarely is research and publication inter-disciplinary or a part of the generality of educational research into higher, professional or, say further education. For example, links between legal education researchers and the UK's Society for Research into Higher Education (SRHE) and publications in the European Educational Research Journal from a legal education perspective appear limited. Yet such organisations and publications often have research agendas with considerable relevance for legal education.

Empirical research can be costly and often requires the development of some distinctive research skills. There seems some evidence of a growing reluctance of students, teachers and employers to participate in empirical projects. This is in no way confined to legal education, with currently low responses to, for example, labour market and environmental surveys. It is vital, therefore that funders and researchers explain clearly why we need data, why the data needs to be well informed and robust and, critically, what we have gained from it, especially its practical implications.

PATRICIA LEIGHTON

References

Alexander, J. (2023). 'Modelling employability through clinical legal education, building confidence and professional identity', *The Law Teacher*, 57(2), p. 135.

Armour, J. and Sako, M. (2021). *AI assisted law technology; Its impact on law firms*, Oxford University Press.

Bell, F. (2026). 'Empirical research in Law', *Griffith Law Review*, 25(2), p. 141.

Bone, A. (2009). 'The twenty first century law student', *The Law Teacher*, 43(3), p. 222.

Brutus St. Val, A. (2021). 'How to engage students in an online learning environment', *Journal of Legal Education*, 70(2–3), p. 297.

Cofone, I. and Male, P.-J. (2022). 'How to choose a law review: An empirical study', *Journal of Legal Education*, 71(2), p. 311.

Cownie, F. (2012). 'Legal education and the Academy', *The Oxford Handbook of Empirical Legal Research*, ch 36.

Ferris, G. (2022). 'Law students well-being and vulnerability', *The Law Teacher*, 56(1), p. 5.

Hamilton, N. and Morrison, V. (2012). 'Legal education and the ethical challenge: empirical research on how most effectively to foster each student's professional formation', *University of St Thomas Law Journal*, 9(2), p. 327.

Harris, P. and Beinhart, S. (2004). 'A Survey of Law Schools in the United Kingdom', *The Law Teacher*, 39(3), p. 299.

Kritzer, H. (2021). *Advanced Introduction to Empirical Legal Research*, Edward Elgar Publishing.

Legal Education Training Review (LETR). (2013). 'Setting Standards: the future of legal services education and training regulation in England and Wales', IPS, BSB and SRA.

Leighton, P., Mortimer, T. and Whatley, N. (1995). *Today's Law Teachers: Lawyers or Academics?*, Anglia Polytechnic University.

Mason, M., Vaughan, S. and Weil, B. (2023). 'The possible forms of professional credibility and the performance of queer sexualities among barristers in England and Wales', *Journal of Law and Society*, 50(1), p. 77.

Nielson, R.G. (2023). 'Law teaching for sale: legal shadow education in Denmark from an historical and current perspective', *European Journal of Legal Education*, 4, p. 71.

Ogloff, J., Lyson, D., Douglas, K. and Rose, G. (2000). 'More than learning to think like a lawyer', *Creighton Law Review*, p. 76.

Pannebacker, E., Pluut, H., Voskamp, S. and de Zanger, W.S. (2022). 'Empirical legal studies in the law school curriculum in the Netherlands: what is the state of the art and where do we go from here?', *The Law Teacher*, 56(3), p. 384.

Skipper, Y. and Fay, M. (2023). 'The relationship between a sense of belonging, mental well being and stress in students of law and psychology in an English University', *European Journal of Legal Education*, p. 5.

Spencer, R. (2022). 'Hell is other people-Re-thinking the Socratic method for quiet law students', *The Law Teacher*, 56(1), p. 90.

Susskind, R. (2023). *Tomorrow's Lawyers*, 3rd edition, Oxford University Press.

Taylor, L., Baird, N., Cheer, U., Sotandi, V. and Broght, E. (2023). 'The making of Aoteroa l New Zealand lawyers; a longitudinal study of law students and law graduates', *The Law Teacher*, 57(1), p. 309.

Wilson, J. (1967). 'Law teaching at colleges of further education', *The Law Teacher*, 1(2), p. 3.

Wilson, J. (2006). 'A third survey of legal education in the United Kingdom', *Legal Studies*, 13(2), p. 143.

Zeiler, K. (2016). 'The future of empirical legal scholarship: Where do we go from here?', *Journal of Legal Education*, 66(1), p. 78.

92. Research into legal education (non-empirical)

Introduction

Academic freedom is usually seen as a right (Russell [1993]). As a right, on occasion it receives legal protection (Barendt [2010]). Yet academic freedom can also usefully be conceived as an obligation; an obligation on academics to say only that which they believe to be true and, in some sense, consequential (Bradney [2016]). If this is so then reading and reacting to research into legal education is synonymous with being a legal academic no matter what specific area of legal expertise the academic claims to have (Cownie and Bradney [2017]). Only by responding to such research can a legal academic fully articulate their justifications for their choices as to how and what they teach or the agenda that they set for their research.

All legal academics, as with all other academics, need a principled position to justify what they choose to do as academics. As members of what Perkin has suggested is the key profession they must take responsibility for their choice of action (Perkin [1969]). Professionalism has been described as being 'a set of institutions which permit members of an occupation to make a living while controlling their own work' (Friedson [2001] at 17). If this is so then what governments, vice-chancellors, the practising professions or others want legal academics to do may be of interest to them but cannot in itself be determinant of their behaviour. This is particularly so in the present day when much that has previously been thought about law and legal institutions has increasingly come to be questioned.

Traditional doctrinal conceptions of law and legal institutions are still seen as plausible by some legal academics (see Doctrinal Legal Education) but for others the challenges of, amongst other things, critical legal studies, feminist legal education, empirical legal education, indigenous legal education, law and economics and socio-legal education (see Socio-Legal Approaches to Legal Education) which sometimes interlock and at other times compete with each other, suggest other ways of thinking and thus other ways of learning and teaching. In addition to this, legal academics continue to need to consider the long running tensions between providing a liberal education in law and training students for either the legal professions or other forms of employment. How does each legal academic respond to Owen Fiss' final contribution to the 'Of Law and the River' exchange?

'Law professors are not paid to train lawyers, but to study the law and to teach their students what they happen to discover. The law school is…is an integral part of the university and must be pure in its academic obligations' (Martin [1985] at 26).

Attending to both empirical and non-empirical research into legal education is a necessary prerequisite to giving reasoned as opposed to merely personal, anecdotal responses to these pressing urgent issues. Thinking about such research is thus the very essence of being an academic.

Empirical and non-empirical research into legal education

Determining the factual landscape which forms the background to legal education is a fundamental element to inquiry. No reflection on legal education can be entirely abstract. The distinction between empirical and non-empirical research into legal education is in this sense of limited utility. Yet reading and evaluating empirical research into legal education is itself not straightforward. Questions of methodology are a vital consideration in assessing the value of individual pieces of research; such matters are complex and challenging. But beyond and behind empirical questions there are the theoretical issues which trouble and divide legal academics. Non-empirical research can usefully be seen as research which focusses on these debates.

Issues for non-empirical research into legal education

The most basic question for legal education is what such education should be about. Historically this has often been seen as being about how far, if at all, the education should relate to particular types of employment. Should the education be about professional legal education or should it be a liberal education? Is a professional legal education the same thing as vocational education? Can either providing either professional education or vocational education be justified in a university setting? Is university legal education by its very definition purely academic legal education? Even if conducted in a university can the education be about other forms of employment such as paralegal education, social workers' legal education or police legal education? More than this is legal education limited to undergraduate or postgraduate education? What place is there for, for example, children's legal education (see Children, Schools and Legal Education) and once again does the university have any role in such education?

The issues outlined above historically have all usually taken as their starting point the idea that the concept of law that forms the basis for legal understanding is state law. Whether that law is seen through doctrinal or socio-legal eyes it is still that which functions as the official state legal system within a jurisdiction that is the focus of discussion. However, this view has increasingly been met with arguments about the importance of legal pluralism (Griffiths [1986]). Legal pluralism puts forward the notion that alongside state law there might be a series of other legal systems that find their basis within non-state norms and which might be complementary or contradictory to state legal systems.

One historical source for arguments about legal pluralism is the longstanding study of legal anthropology with its interest in laws to be found in traditional societies which have become parts of colonial empires (see, for example, Malinowski [2013]). Such studies are empirical in their nature but their analyses can have powerful theoretical consequences. Malinowski's idea of law as reciprocity is a long way from traditional doctrinal legal conceptions. Legal anthropology can in turn lead to an interest in the study of indigenous legal education and to decolonising the legal curriculum. But legal pluralism goes beyond this. Religious systems, for example, can have their own law or their own particular concepts of notions of dispute settlement and dispute avoidance (see, for example, Greenhouse [1986]). Even in largely secular societies significant religious minorities can see legal legitimacy as having a very different source to state authority. Religions, however, are not the only site for legal pluralism. Individual universities, for example, each have their own legal system. For legal pluralists everywhere is 'a world of multiple, overlapping normative communities' (Berman [2009] at 226).

Conclusion

Many commentators in different jurisdictions have noted the way in which legal academic work has become more professionalised over the years (see, for example, Cownie and Bardney [2020], Schlegel [1985]). This can be seen in an increasing requirement for doctorates for legal academics before appointment as well as a stress on the need for publications. In this the legal academy is doing little more than mirror what has already happened in other parts of the university. The number of legal education journals, academics who have as part of their own research agenda research into legal education and quantity of research into legal education can also be seen as part of this process of professionalisation. This phenomenon seems to be only tangentially related to the increasing external audit of universities which is also widespread. Instead, research into legal education is at the same time both an acceptance of the need for the legal academy to reflect on itself as part of an examined life and the result of increasing doubts about matters that were once seen as unquestionable verities.

ANTHONY BRADNEY

References

Barendt, E. (2010). *Academic Freedom and the Law: A Comparative Study*, Hart Publishing.

Berman, P.S. (2009). 'The New Legal Pluralism', *Annual Review of Law and Social Sciences*, 5, p. 225.

Bradney, A. (2016). 'The Necessary Loneliness of Teaching (and of Being a Legal Academic)', in van Klink, B. and de Vries, U. (eds), *Academic Learning in Law: Theoretical Positions, Teaching Experiments and Learning Experiences*, Edward Elgar Publishing.

Cownie, F. and Bradney, A. (2020). 'The Changing Position of Legal Academics in the United Kingdom: Professionalization or Proletarianisation?', *Journal of Law and Society*, 47, pp. S227–S243.

Cownie, F. and Bradney, A. (2017). 'An Examined Life: Research into University Legal Education and the Journal of Law and Society', *Journal of Law and Society*, 44, p. S129.

Friedson, E. (2001). *Professionalism: The Third Logic*, Polity Press.

Greenhouse, C. (1986). *Praying for Justice: Faith, Order, and Community in an American Town*, Cornell University Press.

Griffiths, J. (1986). 'What is Legal Pluralism', *Journal of Legal Pluralism and Unofficial Law*, 24, p. 1.

Malinowski, B. (2013). *Crime and Custom in Savage Society*, Routledge.

Martin, P. (ed). (1985). '"Of Law and the River,"

and of Nihilism and Academic Freedom', *Journal of Legal Education*, p. 1.

Perkin, H. (1969). *Key Profession: The History of the Association of University Teachers*, Routledge.

Russell, C. (1993). *The Ideal of Academic Freedom*, Routledge.

Schlegel, J.H. (1985). 'Between the Harvard Founders and the American Legal Realists: The Professionalization of the American Law Professor', *Journal of Legal Education*, 35, p. 311.

93. Scholarship and legal education

Introduction

This entry sets out the core tenets of the evolution of scholarship in legal education, as separate from learning and researching the substantive law (Storr and McGrath [2023]). It explores the impact of the scholarship of legal education, addressing the duality of curricula and pedagogical development. It also reflects on global influences, challenges, and changes (Jamin and van Caenegem [2016]). In doing so this work engages with the green shoots of global legal education, and examines how the traditional boundaries of legal education, can evolve to meet the needs of twenty-first century lawyers (Williams [2021]).

The notion of 'scholarship' is subject to varying interpretations within legal education and has frequently been conflated with 'research' (Cownie [2020]). For the purposes of this entry, scholarship into legal education will be defined as pedagogic investigations into the uses and applications of pedagogy (the art and practice of teaching) within law schools and other settings where the law is taught and learnt. This includes, for example, evaluation of a specific teaching initiative on a particular module or programme. As Cownie explains, such scholarship is a 'valuable endeavour' which can 'stimulate others to engage in similarly effective teaching or assessing and be of great potential value to students'. This is despite it not adding to 'the sense of human knowledge' in the way research into substantive legal topics does, because it is instead focused upon 'applying existing knowledge to a particular teaching "problem"' (Cownie [2020]).

Legal education globally

To understand the evolution of scholarship in legal education it is important to contextualise its development. The term 'legal education' can be interpreted differently across jurisdictions and has developed in differing ways. In England and Wales, legal education has a broad identity, which includes courses taught at post 16 Education, with academic and vocational content (Leighton [2021]). It also includes the re-emergence of the apprenticeship, with students working and undergoing graduate level study, as well as vocational qualifications often studied whilst at work [Pre-Qualification Legal Workplace Experience].

As for other jurisdictions, especially common law, the position is often dependent on state or professions centred approaches to legal education. In India for example, legal education commences in post year 12 and then like in the UK, will progress on to study both the traditional common law degree and then progress to professional qualification Law School (Ramaswamy HHS [2020], Srinivasan and Yadav [2022]).

In China (Wang, Liu and Li [2017], Xianyuan [2015]), the nature of legal education is one which has undergone significant changes to reflect the development and vision of those in power (Wu, Lo and Liu [2020]). This has meant that although the curriculum is still state controlled, the position is now that the country needs competent lawyers, rather than state officials. Yet it is also apparent that knowledge and understanding of the role of lawyers within the socio legal and political environment is also a vital part of their education. This contrasts with Hong Kong, where currently the mechanism of legal education is very much driven by output and the production of lawyers and reflects the common law traditions. The development of Legal Education in Saudi Arabia, amongst others has been influenced heavily by a mix of colonial heritages, from the US (United States), France, and Egypt. These support change in cultural expectations of a legal education, to encourage a more global approach, moving away from a banking pedagogy a metaphor, where students receive, file and store information (Freire [1970]) one which embraces interaction and practice focused learning (Alanza [2020]).

Although legal education is often associated with building lawyers, there are wider expectations to evolve curriculum and pedagogy to support the development of student skills and competences as global citizens. These include the articulation of sustainable development goals (Karim [2023]), digital skills and technology (Thanaraj [2018]). Whilst understanding these influences, there is also vital work to decolonise the curriculum and pedagogy (Morrison and Guth [2021]).

To understand how diversity of content is delivered, it is time to consider the evolution and influence of scholarship into different pedagogical approaches. The next section explores the evolution of pedagogy, and the infusion of innovative ideas which students will need (Salameh [2023]).

The development of scholarship

In the earliest commentaries about legal pedagogy, Blackstone indicated that where the student learns solely the practical application of law, then this will undoubtedly limit their understanding of first principles, which would limit their capacity to critically evaluate the law. There were real concerns evidenced in the nineteenth century journal, the Jurist stating, 'We would have used the expression system of legal education, but that there is nothing whatever in existence deserving the name of system' (The Jurist [1840]). What existed in terms of professional education was free market driven, there being no desire to include practice skills at university. In some respects, it is remarkably similar to the current position, where students wishing to progress to the profession will focus on the practical application of the law rather than theory and principle (Saunders [1996]).

The development in the USA of law schools with a graduate professional focus, meant that the traditional teaching of law as a philosophical study – i.e., as Jurisprudence – was challenged (O'Brien [2022]). The debate and the power struggle in terms of connection to practice as opposed to the development of theory – the very identity of the study of law – was now engaged (Leighton [2021]).

In England and Wales, it was not until the 1971 Ormrod reforms, that the English law degree became tied to needs of the profession. The impact was a reductionist programme of study, which relied on traditional pedagogy lecture-based delivery, some interaction through workshops and of course formal written assessments. The professional qualification courses provided even less scope for interaction, simply a banking pedagogy was applied. Law post-1971 borrowed its pedagogy from professional scholarly activity – the doctrinal approach, being seen as the most robust way of studying the law. Variety in pedagogy was limited, assessment even more so essays. And for the more adventurous lecturers found that problem questions were of benefit in certain areas (Ferris [2009]). Novel approaches to scholarship within legal education began to explore and examine the wider more practical connections between content and practice and sought to adopt the US model of clinical legal education where students work with clients and obtain contextualised learning experiences, an opportunity to learn and develop much needed practice-based skills before being let loose in practice (Mkwebu [2017]).

In the USA, the development of law's signature pedagogy – based on Socratic doctrinal mechanisms (see Socratic Method) championed by Langdell, created a structured and cost-effective teaching process (Shulman [2005]). Here the professor held the information and the students accepted the knowledge (Hyland and Kilcommins [2009]). This emphasises the lecturer's control over materials, activities sources and outcomes – in practice challenge was rare. Whilst the Socratic methods may be valuable in some cases, it is right to say that its application has diminished over time, especially in undergraduate legal education (Cramton [1986]).

Newer approaches provided students with an opportunity to extemporise with the law, rather than accept the rigid principles and practices as propounded by the doctrinal approach. It is right to say that both mechanisms are well used in USA law schools today, but as tools rather than a restrictive approach to learning and exploring the law.

Posner suggests that pedagogical transformation had more to do with law being integrated in university life, and the attack of other disciplines, than student pressures. He alludes to the development of interdisciplinary influences which provide scope to understand not just the law, but social consequences and its constructs. In terms of the wider claims as to the reduction in importance of doctrinal approach, in the USA, it is suggested that this has been influenced by the limited numbers of law professors active in the profession, or indeed judiciary, and the reduced requests for professorial perspectives of the law when seeking expert guidance. The infusion of socio-legal approaches into teaching and learning has also impacted on the development of pedagogy, as reflected by the embeddedness of clinical legal education (CLE) as a pedagogy of choice in both the USA and globally (Rhode [2001], Wilson [2017]).

New directions in scholarship

There are several global influences upon legal education which are likely to influence trends in scholarship.

The United Nation's Sustainable Development Goals (United Nations [2015]) may provide positive influences on curriculum transformation (Karim [2023]), although there is limited evidence of law schools' willingness to use the Goals as pedagogical tools for curricula design.

Digital pedagogical development has been more rapidly absorbed into law, with universities embracing Virtual Learning Environments, hybrid and asynchronous courses, and MOOCs (Massive Open Online Courses) (Blissenden [2015]). These challenge legal educators to develop and embrace new ways of learning – in and outside the classroom – as well as innovative assessment methods which capture learning moments (Woolley, et al [2021]).

The final and perhaps most encompassing evolution is pedagogical decolonisation. In revising curricula and pedagogical processes to reflect the inherent biases of traditional law teaching, legal educators are focused on unpacking pedagogical history that fails to recognise or even challenge colonial and post-colonial practices. In doing so they face challenging and uncomfortable conversations, to address the implications of pedagogy which reinforce stereotypes and biased behaviours (Barkaskas and Buhler [2017], Adebisi [2020]).

Conclusion

In this entry, the ebb and flow of scholarship within legal education has been explored, reflecting national, international, and global developments, the role and practice of legal education, as well as current influences on curricula and pedagogy.

CAROLINE GIBBY

References

Adebisi, F. (2020). 'Decolonising the law school: presences, absences, silences… and hope', *The Law Teacher*, 54, p. 471.

Alanzi, A.A. (2020). 'The Models of Legal Education: Implication for Saudi Arabia', *Journal of Education and e-Learning Research*, 7, p. 235.

Barkaskas, P. and Buhler, S. (2017). 'Beyond reconciliation: Decolonizing clinical legal education', *Journal of Law and Social Policy*, 26, p. 1.

Blissenden, M. (2015). 'Teaching Undergraduate Law Students in the 21st Century-Pedagogy in a Technological Era', *Athens JL*, 1, p. 213.

Bloch, F.S. (2011). (ed), *The Global Clinical Movement: Educating Lawyers for Social Justice Xxiii*, Oxford University Press.

Cramton, R.C. (1986). 'Demystifying legal scholarship', *Geo LJ*, 75, p. 1.

Cownie, F. (2020). 'The Reception of Legal Education Research in the (Legal) Academy', in Golder, B., Nehme, M., Steel, A. and Vines, P. (eds), *Imperatives for Legal Education Research: Then, Now and Tomorrow*, Routledge.

Dixit, A.K. et al. (2023). *Education 4.0 and IOT: Leveraging LSRW skills & research in the legal arena*, AIP Publishing.

Dongbei Nongye Daxue Xuebao. (2016). *Journal of Northeast Agricultural University*, 14(2), p. 68.

Ferris, G. (2009). 'The legal educational continuum that is visible through a glass Dewey', *The Law Teacher*, 43, p. 102.

Freire, P. (1972). *Pedagogy of the Oppressed*, Penguin Education.

Fotouh, J.A. (2017). 'The development of legal education in the Kingdom of Saudi Arabia', *Fiat Justisia: Jurnal Ilmu Hukum*, 11, p. 289.

Ge Xianyuan (Falü zhiye zige kaoshi Beijing xia benke faxue jiaoyu gaige yanjiu, *Analysis of the reform of undergraduate law education against the background of the legal profession examination*.

Hyland, Á. and Kilcommins, S. (2009). 'Signature pedagogies and legal education in universities: epistemological and pedagogical concerns with Langdellian case method', *Teaching in Higher Education*, 14, p. 29.

Japanese Bar Association (2023). Available at https://www.nichibenren.or.jp/en/about/judicial_system/attorney_system.html.

Jamin, C. and van Caenegem, W. (2016). 'The Internationalisation of Legal Education: General Report for the Vienna Congress of the International Academy of Comparative Law, 20–26 July 2014', in Jamin, C. and van Caenegem, W. (eds), *The Internationalisation of Legal Education*, Springer International Publishing.

Leighton, P. (2021). 'Legal education in England and Wales: what next?', *The Law Teacher*, 55, p. 405.

Mkwebu, T. (2017). 'Unpacking Clinical Scholarship: Why Clinics Start and How They Last', *Asian Journal of Legal Education*, 4, p. 33.

Morrison, D. and Guth, J. (2021). 'Rethinking the neoliberal university: embracing vulnerability in English law schools?', *The Law Teacher*, 55, p. 42.

O'Brien, C. (2022). 'Bringing EU Law Back down to Earth', *International Journal of Law in Context*, 18, p. 450.

Posner, R.A. (1992). 'Legal scholarship today', *Stan L Rev*, 45, p. 1647.

Ramaswamy, H.H.S. (2020). 'The Prospect of Legal Education: An India Overview', *Journal of Legal Studies 'Vasile Goldiş'*, 25, p. 31.

Rhode, D.L. (2001). 'Legal scholarship', *Harv L Rev*, 115, p. 1327.

Saunders, N. (1996). 'From cramming to skills – the development of solicitors' education and training since Ormrod', *The Law Teacher*, 30, p. 168.

Shulman, L.S. (2005). 'Signature Pedagogies in the Professions', *Daedalus*, 134, p. 52.

Srinivasan, B. and Yadav, S. (2022). 'Default Rules Theory: Implications on Teaching Contract Law in India', *Asian Journal of Legal Education*, 9, p. 200.

Storr, C. and McGrath, C. (2023). 'In search of the evidence: digital learning in legal education, a scoping review', *The Law Teacher*, 57, p. 119.

United Nations. (2015). 'Transforming our world: The 2030 Agenda for sustainable development', available at https://sustainabledevelopment.un.org/post2015/transformingourworld.

Thanaraj, A. (2018). 'Making the case for a digital lawyering framework in legal education', *International Review of Law*, 2017, p. 17.

Wang Z, Liu, S. and Li X. (2017). 'Internationalizing Chinese legal education in the early twenty-first century', *Journal of Legal Education*, 66, p. 237.

Williams, J.J. (2015). 'Internationalizing Legal Education: A Cooperative Tool In A Globalized World', *Indonesian Journal of International Law*, 12.

Wilson, R.J. (2017). *The global evolution of clinical legal education: More than a method*, Cambridge University Press.

Woolley, E., Yammouni, D. and Rayner, G. (2023). 'Taking the Law Into their Own Hands: Innovative Digital Video Assessment in a Law Degree', in *Integrating Digital Literacy in the Disciplines*, Routledge.

Wu, R.W.-S., Lo, C.W.-H. and Liu, N. (2020). 'Legal Professionalism and the Ethical Challenge for Legal Education: Insights from a Comparative Study of Future Lawyers in Greater China', *The China Quarterly*, 244, p. 1118.

94. Service teaching in legal education

What is service teaching?

Service teaching in legal education is the delivery of legal modules on non-law degrees, both undergraduate and postgraduate, by academics from the law school. Sometimes, a non-law department may engage an academic lawyer to deliver the necessary legal content required by the curriculum, in which case the teaching would not be described as service teaching. There are a large variety of degree courses which contain legal modules. These include business, accountancy, social work, health sciences, built environment and civil engineering degrees. Often, including these modules is a requirement of accreditation by a professional body. Law may also be a required component of specific subjects' external quality assurance benchmarks. In the UK, for example, the Quality Assurance Agency for Higher Education benchmark statements significantly influence degree programmes' curriculum.

The content of such service modules will vary according to the nature of the degree but will usually include the legal system and how legal disputes are resolved, as well as substantive law topics as appropriate. For example, business students are likely to study contract, agency, and tort law. In addition, elements of employment law, company law and intellectual property are also likely to feature in business degrees. Service modules may also include elements of how to avoid legal disputes and how best to engage the services of lawyers should a dispute arise (Allison [1991] at 242). There is a wide array of literature on service teaching in various disciplines written by scholars from various countries.

Staff and student perceptions of service modules

Perceptions of Staff

Teaching law to non-lawyers has sometimes been characterised as a secondary activity from the point of view of law school staff (Bradney [1998] at 81). Research has shown that legal academics prefer teaching law students than any other form of student (Leighton, Mortimer and Whatley [1995]).

Perceptions of Students

The fact that law is often a component of a degree prescribed by an accrediting body lends considerable credibility to including law modules within the curriculum. Research has also shown that students can see the importance of law to everyday life, their chosen subject, and future careers (Endeshaw [2002]). However, unlike a second subject in a joint honours degree, the student does not usually choose a law module within a single honours degree. The law module is only included because it is deemed a necessary part of that subject and may be essential to students' professional lives after graduation.

Whilst students from other disciplines understand the relevance of law, they often find the study of law difficult and boring, and in some studies, students have reported it less enjoyable than their other modules (Endeshaw [2002]). They find the amount of reading overwhelming, which can result in poor quality assessment scores that result in disappointment for students and lecturers alike (Allen [2007]). Legal language is a challenge for law students. Still, it is even more of a barrier to understanding for students from other disciplines whose exposure to legal language is limited to one or two modules. It is not merely the individual items of vocabulary that create problems but also how legal meanings of words and phrases may differ from those seen in common usage. How lawyers construct sentences may also present challenges to students from other disciplines (Tanner [2010]).

Challenges in delivering service modules

The Problem with the Doctrinal Approach

The traditional doctrinal approach (see Doctrinal Legal Education) to teaching law to law students, focusing on the study of legal judgments, may be inappropriate for students from other disciplines (Endeshaw [2002] at 31), particularly as those students may only have one or two modules of law in which to assimilate this approach. Law students will get used to reading judgments in a wide variety of substantive law modules, whereas this will not be the case for students who only study one or two law modules. Students from other disciplines also have to juggle the contrasting conventions of their primary discipline with the very different approach required for law. This may include engaging with a different writing style and referencing scheme. This issue may be exacerbated by the approaches taken in textbooks, which, even if designed with non-law students in mind, may still take a largely 'black letter law' approach (Lampe [2006]).

Although a doctrinal law approach may not be appropriate for students from other disciplines, it may be challenging for the academics teaching these modules to move away from this approach. Academics teaching service modules may teach law students the same area of law as they teach to students in the other discipline. Still, there is a danger that what is delivered within the service module is a diluted version of what is being delivered to law students. For example, an academic teaching company law to law students may use the module learning outcomes and even the module assessment as a starting point for the company law module they deliver to business students. Lampe, writing about the business school context in the United States, has suggested that law courses within business schools can be described as 'law school lite' (Lampe [2006] at 3). This approach may be the worst of all worlds, where the students are subjected to a considerable volume of content, which is simplified to such an extent that it results in inaccuracy (Batty [2013]). Whilst a broader and less in-depth approach in service teaching is acknowledged as necessary, an approach which merely attempts to squeeze the same content that is delivered to law students into fewer credits and a shorter time is likely to result in overloaded students and poor outcomes. Furthermore, a content-heavy module may result in memorisation and 'surface' learning as students try to determine what is required for the assessment.

The Disparity Between Law and Other Disciplines

One of the criticisms of service teaching highlighted in some literature is that law academics teaching students from other disciplines do not sufficiently understand the primary discipline (Hannigan and Afterman [1971]). This problem is reflected in literature dating back many decades (see, for example, Hannigan and Afterman [1971]) across several jurisdictions (see, for example, Batty [2013] in Australia, Lampe [2006] in the US, Butler and Madhloom [2016] in England, and Skwarok [1995] in Hong Kong) and in various disciplines (see, for example, Allison [1991] and Endeshaw [2002] in the context of business and Bennett [2009] and Morris [2010] in the context of real estate education). The issue is exacerbated by the fact that those teaching the law modules are not usually involved in curriculum and course level decisions and may, therefore, not have access to the overall decision-making process or understand where the module fits into the more significant learning outcomes of the degree programme.

Assessing Service Modules

Working in the business world or the real estate sector for example, necessitates understanding pertinent aspects of the law. However, the university curriculum must assess more than knowledge or understanding of the law, as these are insufficient learning outcomes for undergraduate or postgraduate study. In a law module taught to law students, it is common to assess the application of the law to a problem in which a client is given advice or to assess critical analysis of the law in the form of an essay question. Academics designing law modules for non-law students will be very familiar with these modes of assessment. While more innovative approaches are also taken, the skill of application and analysis remains important. However, where the student has no ambitions towards a career in law, assessing their ability to advise a client as if they were a lawyer is inappropriate. Numerous multiple-choice questions may test legal knowledge, but more is needed to meet the requirements of undergraduate or postgraduate study. Multiple choice questions, unless very carefully drafted, can result in learning the rules without the ability to apply those rules. Therefore, academics from the law school have to consider how the learning outcomes and assessment of their service module will align with the course learning outcomes in a discipline with which they are relatively unfamiliar. As Byles and Soetendorp [2002] suggest, this may be liberating as it allows the academic to move away from traditional types of assessment. However, it will also be time-consuming as it will require a whole new approach to assessment.

Pedagogy and solutions

Environmentalist Approach

Recommendations have been made regarding how the delivery of individual service modules can be improved to meet the needs of students from non-law disciplines (see, for example, Byles and Soetendorp [2002]; Endeshaw [2002]; Batty [2013]). Byles and Soetendorp [2002] suggest that the best approach to teaching law to students from other disciplines is the contextual environmental approach in which the students' subject area forms the context within which law is delivered (Byles and Soetendorp [2002]). This approach aims to increase the student's motivation to engage with the law, as the relevance of the law is highlighted when it is put into the context of the student's chosen discipline. To successfully design a module taking this approach, it is, according to Byles and Soetendorp, necessary for the academic to question their values and develop a rapport with the programme leaders from the non-law discipline and work with the profile of the students. An environmentalist approach will reduce the volume of the law taught and change the focus towards understanding the rules and procedures to avoid costly disputes (Batty [2013]).

Problem-Based Learning

Another popular approach to improving the delivery of service teaching is to adopt Problem-Based Learning (PBL) as the pedagogy. Some law schools have used PBL as the primary mode of delivery for the law curriculum, and some elements have been included in some modules by others both in the UK and elsewhere. PBL is also popular in disciplines other than law and, as such, may be an approach used within the student's primary discipline. PBL starts with a problem the learner wishes to solve, and then the students work towards resolving the problem (Barrows and Tamblyn [1980]). It has been suggested that PBL enhances learning, knowledge retention, and knowledge recall. Students are also more active in the process of knowledge construction, which aids understanding (Batty [2013]). Furthermore, it has been suggested that PBL can create a more authentic learning experience where students can appreciate the untidy nature of legal problems in their chosen discipline rather than focusing on discrete rules devoid of context.

Ongoing Challenges

Although the recommendations found within the literature are interesting and have undoubtedly been adopted to various degrees by academics in the preparation of their service modules, challenges remain. The time allocated to designing the service module may be the same as for a module within their own department, even though there may be different and novel considerations to take into account. For example, Byles and Soetendorp [2002] suggest that in designing a module for non-law students, it is important to understand the nature of the student's discipline and to work with colleagues within the discipline better to understand the students' needs (p. 147). Working more closely with colleagues from a different discipline to better embed the service module into the broader curriculum is desirable but may be difficult within the time constraints experienced. The service module will be one of several modules designed and delivered by the academic. If, as research suggests, it is viewed less favourably by the academic than the modules delivered to law students, it seems unlikely that the academic will wish to spend significantly more time perfecting the module. Particularly if the academic is not confident that changing the module will improve student satisfaction or results.

Conclusion

Law will always form a part of studies in other disciplines, and academics from the law school will likely continue to deliver most of this content. Service teaching has generated considerable research and commentary from a range of jurisdictions and has been considered in the context of various disciplines. There is considerable consensus about the problems, but the solutions are more contested.

EMILY WALSH

References

Allen, V. (2007). 'A Critical Reflection on the Methodology of Teaching Law to Non-Law Students', Web Journal of Current Legal Issues,

4, available at http://webjcli.ncl.ac.uk/2007/issue4/allen4.html.

Allison, J.R. (1991). 'The Role of Law in the Business School Curriculum', *J. Legal Stud Educ*, 9, p. 239.

Barrows, H. and Tamblyn, R. (1980). *Problem Based Learning: An Approach to Medical Education*, Springer Publishing Company, p. 1.

Batty, R. (2013). 'Well There's Your Problem – The Case for using PBL to Teach Law to Business Students', *The Law Teacher*, 47(2), p. 243.

Bennett, L. (2009). 'Why, What, how? Case Study on Law, Risk, and Decision Making as Necessary Themes in Built Environment Teaching', *Journal of Legal Affairs and Dispute Resolution in Engineering and Construction*, 1(2), p. 105.

Bradney, A. (1998). 'Law as a Parasitic Discipline', *JLS*, 25, p. 71.

Butler, N. and Madhloom, O. (2016). 'Teaching Company Law to Business Students: an Effective Framework', *The Law Teacher*, 50(2), p. 160.

Byles, L. and Soetendorp, R. (2002). 'Law Teaching for Other Programmes', in Burridge, R., Hinett, K., Paliwala, A. and Varnava, T. (eds), *Effective Learning and Teaching in Law*, Kogan Page.

Endeshaw, A. (2002). 'Teaching Law to Business Students: An Inquiry into Curriculum and Methodology', *The Law Teacher*, 36(1), p. 24.

Hannigan, A.St.J and Afterman, A.B. (1971). 'The Teaching of Business Law Subjects in Non-Law Faculties', *The Law Teacher*, 5, p. 166.

Lampe, M. (2006). 'A New Paradigm for the Teaching of Business Law and Legal Environment Classes', *The Journal of Legal Studies Education*, 23(1), p. 1.

Leighton, P., Mortimer, T. and Whately, N. (1995). *Today's Law Teacher: Lawyers or Academics?*, Routledge-Cavendish.

Morris, R.J. (2010). 'The Teaching of Law to Non-Lawyers an Exploration of Some Curriculum Design Challenges', *International Journal of law in the Built Environment*, 2(3), p. 232.

Skwarok, L.M. (1995). 'Business Law for Non-Lawyers: Setting the Stage for Teaching, Learning and Assessment at Hong Kong Polytechnic University', *The Law Teacher*, 29, p. 189.

Tanner, E. (2010). 'Legal Language and the Non-Law Research Student', *Journal of the Australasian Law Teachers Association*, 3, p. 77.

95. Sexuality and legal education

Introduction

This entry outlines how sexuality is a subject of, and constitutes, legal education, with a particular focus on non-normative sexualities marginalised in law. This entry begins by exploring critical theories and definitions of sexuality. The next section considers how sexuality, particularly homosexuality, has been an object of legal interest and regulation. The following section explores how sexuality has become a subject of legal education across different modules/units. The final section discusses how sexuality shapes legal education by combining personal, political, and pedagogic interests.

Defining sexuality

There is no fixed or universal definition of sexuality. Some people claim that sexuality is an immutable characteristic of human identity. They believe that whether someone is gay or heterosexual is associated with their biological characteristics. Common psychological explanations or definitions of sexuality are anchored by ideas of genitals (the sexed body) and their uses (the sexual activity) (Freud [1949]). However, sexuality is a complex phenomenon that traverses social, bodily, and environmental factors. As a concept or idea, sexuality is culturally, geographically, and historically variable. It is defined differently and debated across disciplines like medicine, psychology, sociology, theology, and law.

While sexuality is an elusive concept to define, it is typically contextualised in terms of erotic attraction, sexual behaviours, personal identifications, social organisation, and/ or interpersonal relationships. The concept of sexuality is one which operates as a historically specific set of knowledges (Foucault [1978]). In places like England and United States (sometimes caricatured as 'the West') during the nineteenth century, sexuality became a site of 'historical rupture' as sex became organised through an array of disciplinary fields like psychology, law, religion, and education. These disciplines surveilled non-heterosexual desires, and individuals that did not conform to matrimonial ideals or reproductive relations, in order to police and punish them.

Sexuality, then, is implicated in structures of power and history. While biological capacities impact upon sexual desires and practices, they are limited in explaining our sexual identity in terms of its complexities (Rubin [1984]). Bodies or body parts are not without socialisation as they are implicated by social institutions. In other words, language and its relationship to bodies produce what we think about as sexuality.

Gender affects the operation of sexual system, and sexuality manifests itself in gendered ways. Gender and sexuality are linked but they are also distinctive social practices and are discussed as such in this entry.

Sexuality as an object of law

Sexuality features explicitly and implicitly in all areas of law. Given that sexuality encapsulates the social organisation of human life in terms of identities, attractions, relationships, and bodies, legal regulation is inextricable from sexuality. The interaction of law and sexual minorities can be observed through criminal law that prohibits homosexuality, employment law that addresses anti-gay discrimination, family law that recognises non-nuclear family structures, and constitutional law that determines the permissibility of same-sex marriage. Historically and currently, there are laws that criminalise consensual and kinky sex, prohibit sex work, regulate the use and distribution of sex toys, and limit the availability of sexual material in public spaces.

Broadly speaking, law regulates sexual behaviour by creating and enforcing moral stigmas. Non-procreative sex has – and in many places still is – condemned as a threat to the social order that warrants legal attention and regulation. While marriage, reproduction and love are secured as the basis for 'legitimate' coupling, those acts or bodies that fail to subscribe to this norm are rendered deviant or social contaminants. In other words, law encourages certain behaviours or practices by affirming them through legal rights, such as marriage and marital procreation. Law also discourages certain behaviours or practices by stigmatising them, such as pre-marital sex, procreation outside of marriage, sex work, and homosexuality.

Sexual regulation also sustains extra-legal forms of governance and control. Intimates as well as strangers, in private and public, for example, play a crucial role in ensuring sexual conformity. For example, gay boys who are effeminate and lesbian girls who are masculine have experienced abuse or rejection from parents or siblings because they refuse gendered assumptions of heterosexuality. Another example includes trans people who are perceived to transgress social expectations about their body and encounter violence and harassment from others in public places such as workplaces, schools, and streets (Stanley [2021]).

Homosexuality as an object of legal prohibition can be traced to figures such as Henry VIII. Henry VIII criminalised homosexual 'buggery' (anal penetration between men) in approximately 1533 in England and Wales. This was amended by the Criminal Law Amendment Act 1885 that removed the death penalty for gay sex but introduced the offence of 'gross indecency' which included other acts of sexual intimacy between men (Moran [1996]). The writer Oscar Wilde was one of the most famous individuals prosecuted under this law in 1895. Anti-buggery or gross indecency laws were also introduced to several countries in Asia, Pacific, and Africa through colonialism (many of which are still in force today). These laws are subject to ongoing legal scrutiny and debate through litigation, judicial review, political advocacy, legislative intervention, and social activism.

Sexual regulation, however, is subject to cultural and legal change. Social acceptance of gay, lesbian, bisexual, and transgender (LGBT) people has resulted in laws that not only decriminalise gay sex but also permit same-sex couples to marry and have children. There are laws that allow some trans and non-binary people to register their gender without medical or surgical interventions. Sexuality as an object of law, much like sexuality itself, is dynamic and fluid (Kapur [2005]).

Sexuality as a subject of legal education

Sexuality organises legal curriculums. Subjects of law that deal with human behaviour and relationships foreground sexuality in either explicit or implicit terms. The teaching of presumptions of advancement in equity,

assumptions about care and affection in civil liability claims, ideals of relationships in marital contracts, beliefs about deviancy in criminal law, and norms of sovereignty in international human rights disputes are sexualised (as well as raced, gendered, etc). All forms of legal study are in some way constituted by ideas about, and experiences of, sexuality.

While sexuality has always been present in legal education, the emergence of sexuality as a discrete subject in legal education can be traced to the rise of the Critical Legal Studies movement that gained momentum across law schools in the United States during the 1980s. This movement aimed to understand and critique the ways in which law functioned as a system of power that marginalised certain groups of people on the basis of their race, class, gender, sexuality, etc (Crenshaw [1989]). In more 'traditional' law schools, discussions of gendered and sexual subjectivity, individual emotion, and identity were met with institutional suspicion because they would function to politicise the curriculum and threaten the 'objectivity' and 'neutrality' that were central to traditional legal method. While this belief was not universally held then or now, notions of objectivity, rationality, and dispassion frame dominant views not only about the exercise of law but also how law should be studied as a discipline (Bandes [2021]). In the social sciences more broadly, sexuality scholarship is considered 'dirty work' because it relates to abject topics (gay sex, bodily fluids, etc) and scholars who engage in it are sometimes stigmatised by their association with sexual perversities (Irvine [2014]).

Over the last 40 years, numerous monographs, curriculums, edited collections, and conferences have sought to highlight the existence (and production) of LGBT people within law while problematising the relationship between such people and the legal systems (Herman and Stychin [2000]; Moran [1996], [2009]; Raj and Dunne [2020]; Stychin [1995]). In the UK and comparable countries, several law schools now offer specific units, including postgraduate degrees, specialising in gender and sexuality. English legal scholarship focused on sexuality has canvassed topics relating to the policing of homosexuality, cruising, religious exemptions, asylum, HIV criminalisation, legal gender recognition, prisons, relationships, and parenting.

These scholarly engagements vary in theoretical orientation and methodological choices. Some scholarship and curricula focus on doctrinal analyses of law with prescriptions for reform. This kind of scholarship and teaching examines why same-sex couples should be able to parent without legal discrimination or why trans people should be free to self-declare their gender without medical or bureaucratic hurdles through reference to progressive legal norms and human rights doctrines (Raj and Dunne [2020]). Other forms of legal research and teaching on sexuality, however, take a more radical or critical posture to the legal system. This kind of work seeks to deconstruct how law is structurally biased against 'queer' minorities (those who challenge prevailing social norms about sex and gender) and queries how categories of sex and gender are relevant to law (Herman and Stychin [2000]).

These differences in scholarly and pedagogical approach are not static or mutually exclusive. They reflect varying attachments to feminist theories that seek to understand and challenge how gender is socially conceptualised, structured, and hierarchised (MacKinnon [1989]), and queer theories that seek to expose how social norms organise and marginalise bodies, relationships, and identities (Zanghellini [2014]). Unsurprisingly then, women (studied through the lens of 'gender') and LGBT people (studied through the prism of 'sexuality') are core subjects of concern in feminist and queer legal research and teaching.

Sexuality and desire in pedagogy

Contemporary legal education literature on sexuality also foregrounds the 'queer' desires that animate the inclusion of LGBT rights in law school. Queer desires here refer to both sexual desires that are non-heterosexual as well as pedagogical desires that disrupt the organisation of legal education as an 'objective' discipline. In *Sappho Goes to Law School*, Ruthann Robson reflects on how desire structures lesbianism in law and the pedagogical style of lesbian legal scholarship. The novelty of her intervention is she refuses to sideline the anxieties that emerge when discussing sex in a classroom and the 'messiness' of her anxieties as a lesbian scholar in a heteronormative law school. As such, her account helps to make explicit how lesbian

sexual desires complicate the study of conventional legal topics (like indecency laws), particularly when students feel comfortable enough to disclose their personal sexual experiences when contributing to discussions of jurisprudence (Robson [1998] at 215–224).

Chris Ashford (2021) has observed how the inclusion of gender and sexuality in the legal curriculum is not simply about the inclusion of additional topics. Gender and sexuality units reshape the architecture of a 'traditional' law school because feminist and queer legal scholars engage students in broader questions about activism, policy, and law reform rather than simply insisting on a doctrinal study. Legal academics who teach about sexuality also subvert the 'professionalism' of law school etiquette. Gender, Sexuality and Law units encourage students to recognise and share relevant anecdotes, desires, and experiences that disrupt assumptions of the status quo (Ashford [2021] at 454–457). In a survey about international human rights law teaching relating to sexual orientation and gender identity, Paula Gerber and Claerwyn O'Hara (2019) argue that critical legal teaching has come to embrace the lives of those the law seeks to speak about by paying close attention to language, identities, interdisciplinarity, different spaces of law, diverse issues and actors, and social contextualisation.

'Queering legal education' has emerged as a practice in response to these critical engagements with sexuality in law. As such, 'queering' legal pedagogical conventions involves challenging the idea there is a dispassionate teacher and disengaged student in a classroom or subjects of legal curricula are 'neutral' about sex. A queer pedagogy encourages law teachers to reimagine what they think of as 'successful' classrooms and scholarship (Robson [2018] at 277). This pedagogy involves co-creation with students, foregrounding how LGBT students engage with law in ways that make space for their passions while refusing to censor their emotional responses (Ricciardo et al. [2022]). Legal education literature on this topic is still emerging and provides normative and critical context for locating desires in the teaching of LGBT rights in legal curricula.

Conclusion

Sexuality is central to law and legal education. It functions as an object, subject, and mode of legal pedagogy. This entry has explained how sexuality is an elusive concept that generates enormous debate across a range of disciplines. It has shown how sexuality is the site of intense legal regulation – an object of law's focus – particularly in relation to sexual minorities. This entry has also demonstrated how legal education has taken up sexuality as a specific subject of study, through a critical study of both law and sexuality. The entry concluded by showing how sexuality enables law teachers to re-imagine how they teach law by threading together the personal, political, and pedagogic.

SENTHORUN RAJ

References

Ashford, C. (2021). 'Gender, Sexuality and the Law School: (Re)Thinking *Blackstone's Tower* with Queer and Feminist Theory', *Amicus Curiae*, 2, p. 450.
Bandes, S. (2021). 'Feeling and Thinking Like a Lawyer: Cognition, Emotion, and the Practice and Progress of Law', *Fordham Law Review*, 89, p. 2427.
Crenshaw, K.W. (1991). 'Mapping the Margins: Intersectionality, Identity Politics, and Violence against Women of Colour', *Connecticut Law Review*, 43, p. 1253.
Foucault, M. (1978). *The History of Sexuality: The Will to Knowledge*, Pantheon Books.
Freud, S. (1949). *Three Essays on the Theory of Sexuality*, Imago Publishing.
Gerber, P. and O'Hara, C. (2019). 'Teaching Law Students about Sexual Orientation, Gender Identity and Intersex Status within Human Rights Law: Seven Principles for Curriculum Design and Pedagogy', *Journal of Legal Education*, 68, p. 416.
Herman, D. and Stychin, C. (2000). (eds), *Sexuality in the Legal Arena*, Bloomsbury Academic.
Irvine, J.M. (2014). 'Is Sexuality Research "Dirty Work"? Institutionalised Stigma in the Production of Sexual Knowledge', *Sexualities*, 17, p. 632.
Kapur, R. (2005). *Erotic Justice: Law and the New Politics of Postcolonialism*, Glass House Press.
MacKinnon, C. (1989). *Toward a Feminist Theory of the State*, Harvard University Press.
Moran, L. (1996). *The Homosexuality of Law*, Routledge.
Moran, L. (2009). 'What Kind of Field is "Law, Gender and Sexuality"? Achievements, Concerns and Possible Futures', *Feminist Legal Studies*, 17, p. 309.
Ricciardo, A., Rogers, S.L., Puttick, S.D., Skead, N., Tarrant, S. and Thomas, M. (2022). 'Understanding, Promoting and Supporting LGBTQI+ Diversity in Legal Education', *The Law Teacher*, 56, p. 307.
Robson, R. (1998). *Sappho Goes to Law School: Fragments in Lesbian Legal Theory*, Columbia University Press.
Robson, R. (2018). 'Educating the Next Generation of LGBTQ Social Justice Attorneys', in Ashford, C. and McKeown, P. (eds), *Social Justice and Legal Education*, Cambridge Scholars Press.
Rubin, G. (1984). 'Thinking Sex: Notes for a Radical Theory of the Politics of Sexuality', in Vance, C. (ed), *Pleasure and Danger: Exploring Female Sexuality*, Routledge & Keegan Paul.
Stanley, E.A. (2021). *Atmospheres of Violence: Structuring Antagonism and the Queer/Trans Ungovernable*, Duke University Press.
Senthorun, R. and Dunne, P. (2020). (eds), *The Queer Outside in Law: Recognising LGBTIQ People in the United Kingdom*, Palgrave Macmillan.
Zanghellini, A. (2009). 'Queer, Antinormativity, Counter-Normativity and Abjection', *Griffith Law Review*, 18, p. 1.

96. Social justice, citizenship and legal education

Introduction

The concepts of social justice and citizenship are both used to inform legal education pedagogies. Bell defines social justice as both a process and a goal (Bell [1997]). The former involves 'full and equal participation of all groups in a society that is mutually shaped to meet their needs' (Bell [1997] at 3), while the process of social justice 'should be democratic and participatory, inclusive and affirming of human agency and human capacities for working collaboratively to create change' (Bell [1997] at 4). Nevertheless, social justice and citizenship remain contested normative terms. This entry seeks to draw on the work of John Rawls, Martha Nussbaum and Nancy Fraser (among others), in order to explore the normative contours of social justice and citizenship, particularly within the context of legal education. It will ultimately conclude that these two concepts can be taught using a holistic approach informed by various pedagogies such as critical theories, emotions, and cosmopolitan education. It will also contend that an optimal methodology for teaching these pedagogies is Clinical Legal Education.

Social justice

The earliest attempt to map the normative contours of social justice can be traced back to Aristotle, who distinguished between 'corrective justice' and 'distributive justice' (Aristotle [2009] at Book V paras 3:1131a–4:1132b). The former deals with whether one party has suffered transactional injustices as a result of another's actions e.g. in contract law or tort law. Distributive justice, for Aristotle, is related to the idea of desert rather than what individuals need. A paradigm desert claim is where a person deserves something by virtue of possessing a particular feature. For example, a student deserves a high grade by virtue of the fact that they are known to their lecturer to have produced work of exceptionally high standard. Aristotle's view of distributive justice can be contrasted with the contemporary view that individuals have a claim to satisfy basic needs irrespective of their actions or character (Jackson [2005] at 361).

While the concept of social justice can be found in the work of various philosophers, such as John Stuart Mill ([1861]) and Henry Sidgwick ([1874]), those commentators did not distinguish it from distributive justice (Miller [1999] at 3). In any case, the term 'social justice' did not emerge until the nineteenth century (Miller [1999] at 4), with the first book entitled *Social Justice: A Critical Essay* published in 1900 (Willoughby), where the author seeks to identity the general principles of right which underpin the ethics of social systems.

Social justice eventually entered mainstream political and public debates in the twentieth century, when advanced liberal democracies adopted some form of welfare state (Brodie [2007] at 95). With regards to the 'social' dimension, the emergence of industrial capitalism led to the contemporary understanding of this concept as being associated with 'society and the collective' (Brodie [2007] at 95). Therefore, according to Brodie ([2007] at 97), social justice consists of two key elements. First, it can be viewed as a virtue that applies to a 'society' and not merely to individual behaviour. Second, social justice has a substantive political element that is concerned with alleviating poverty and inequality. Adam Smith ([2008]) propounds the idea that the indigent are the equals of the wealthy, and that those who suffer deprivation are subject to significant harms caused by their poverty (Fleischacker [2004] at 62–68). Distributive justice, therefore, can be described as being concerned with bringing about a fair or just distribution of benefits and burdens in society, and was associated with the development of the welfare state (Fook and Goodwin [2019] at 4).

One of the most influential theories of social justice is that of John Rawls. Although Rawls sets out his theory of justice as fairness in his book, *A Theory of Justice* ([1972]), its foundations were published in an earlier work (Rawls [1963]). Rawls defines social justice as 'the way in which major social institutions distribute fundamental rights and duties and determine the division of advantages from social cooperation' (Rawls [1971] at 7). In other words, his theory of justice is concerned with just or fair political institutions. It is a theory of distributive justice, but only in a limited sense; in that it seeks to maximise equal liberty of individuals without disadvantaging the least well-off in a community.

Along with Rawls's theory of justice, a second theory of social justice is applied in order to influence social justice education and its moral commitments (Grant and Gibson [2013] at 93). This second theory is informed by the normative concept of 'recognition'. Iris Marian Young ([1990]), for example, is of the view that social justice theories ought to be underpinned by the goal of recognition. In contrast to Rawls's theory of justice, Young argues that structural inequalities can be redressed by the recognition of social groups. Consequently, the 'politics of recognition' involve aspiring for a 'difference-friendly world' where 'assimilation to majority or dominant cultural norms is no longer the price of respect' (Fraser [2001] at 21). Justice, therefore, entails the redistribution of material resources as well as promoting pluralism (Grant and Gibson [2013] at 93).

Citizenship and legal education

While there is no universally accepted definition of citizenship (Ivic [2016] at 65], the concept derives from the Greek polis and the Roman res republica (Pocock [1998] at 35). Thus, its origins can be traced to the Greeks and Romans, where citizens (unlike slaves), enjoyed certain rights but also had obligations towards the state and other citizens (Pring [2016] at 9). In other words, a citizen is a member of a community that enjoys certain rights but also has certain duties. In a plural society, citizenship entails (Figueroa [2000] at 57):

> [A] commitment to the society in its diversity; openness to, and indeed solidarity with and respect for, the different other, in particular the 'ethnically' different; acceptance of the basic equal worth of all people, of the rights and responsibilities of all; and a rejection of any form of exploitation, inequitable treatment or racism.

The above highlights that citizenship can include elements of social justice, namely a commitment to respecting diversity, beyond merely the reluctant acceptance of diversity. Thus, citizenship education ought to provide students with the conceptual tools to identify and work towards addressing discrimination.

In relation to legal education and citizenship, the law school mission, according to Brownsword, ought to be framed in terms of producing 'really good citizens' (Brownsword [1992] at 48). He echoes Bradney ([1996] at 153), who argues that the aims of the law school are less concerned with producing skilful lawyers and more concerned with producing graduates who are capable human beings. Brownsword conceives the notion of law schools for citizens, or the 'liberal project' (Brownsword [1999] at 26), as having four distinct features (Brownsword [1999] at 27). First, the mission of the law school is framed in terms of understanding the concept (or practice of) law. Second, understanding law entails an inquiring multi-disciplinary approach that contributes to one's appreciation of law. The third feature involves producing graduates who are equipped to engage in rational debates regarding socio-economic and political matters and able to form their own independent conclusions on such matters. Finally, legal academics ought to act as exemplars of the inquiring approach. Brownsword's vision of liberal legal education is one which seeks to equip students with the ability to intelligently engage in the 'politico-legal life of the community' (Brownsword [1999] at 29). However, Brownsword does not provide a definition of the term 'community'.

A community can include either one's nation state or cosmopolitan community. In 'Patriotism and Cosmopolitanism', Martha Nussbaum ([1994] at 7) draws on the work of Stoic philosophers to address the concerns of proponents of nationalism and patriotism (Rorty [1994]). Writing in relation to US education, Nussbaum advocates an approach to education which allows students to not only continue, should they wish, to regard themselves as partly defined by their family, religious, ethnic, or even their country, but also to 'learn to recognize humanity wherever she encounters it, undeterred by traits that are strange to her, and be eager to understand humanity in its "strange" guises' (Nussbaum [1994] at 9). Legal education, therefore, ought to teach students to view the entire world of human beings as a single community (Nussbaum [1994] at 4). Nussbaum presents four arguments in favour of making 'word citizenship' education's main focus. First, students are, through a cosmopolitan education, able to learn about themselves and question their norms through the lens of the other.

Second, this type of education promotes dialogue with others, which can act as a first step towards international cooperation, the aim of which is to address global challenges such as addressing climate change and the refugee crisis. Third, cosmopolitan education promotes the idea that persons owe moral obligations to the rest of the world. This justification is underpinned by Kant's Categorical Imperative (Kant [1993] at paras 4:420–421), which can be used in education to highlight to students that certain matters cannot be universalised, such as the high living standards enjoyed in developed countries. Nussbaum does not presuppose universalism, but rather she makes an argument in its favour. Thus, educating students to believe that all human beings are created equal and possess certain inalienable rights requires educating students to think about what this conception requires them to do for the rest of the world. Finally, persons make consistent arguments based on distinctions they are prepared to defend. Consequently, students ought to be taught that respect should be 'accorded to humanity as such' and not merely to their fellow citizens.

Incorporating social justice and citizenship into legal education

Social justice education and world citizenship can be taught through Clinical Legal Education (CLE), which is a form of experiential learning. Indeed, CLE is recognised as an optimal methodology or vehicle to teach social justice and citizenship (Bloch [2010]; Wilson [2016]; Ashford and McKeown [2018]). CLE, including live-client clinics can foster a sense of social responsibility towards one's clients, for example those from a low socio-economic background (Wizner [2002] at 1934–1935) [Public Legal Education (Community)].

Additionally, CLE can provide students with the opportunity to engage in collaborative work, ethical deliberation, and reflective lawyering (Madhloom and Antonopoulos [2022] at 24). Madhloom and Antonopoulos ([2022] at 32) contend that the key tenets of CLE, such as social justice, are aligned with those of the Universal Declaration of Human Rights (UDHR). In addition to highlighting positive obligations towards others, the UDHR, as a non-binding instrument, provides a 'single source of values that is

codified and recognized at an international level' (Madhloom and Antonopoulos [2022] at 25). While at first glance, the UDHR does not appear to promote pluralism, in its Preamble, it recognises 'that inherent dignity and of the equal and inalienable rights of all members of the human family is the foundation of freedom, justice and peace in the world' (Universal Declaration of Human Rights [1948] at Preamble). The UDHR is, therefore, aligned with Nussbaum's idea of cosmopolitan education, whereby a person is a member of a moral community. In addition to adopting the UDHR into legal education, it is also recommended that social justice education integrates a holistic approach through the use of other pedagogies such as critical pedagogy (Freire [2017]), critical feminist pedagogy (hooks [2000]; English and Irving [2015]), critical race theory, and emotions (Jones [2019]; Madhloom [2022]).

OMAR MADHLOOM

References

Aristotle. (2009). *Nicomachean Ethics*, David Ross tr, Oxford University Press.

Ashford, C. and McKeown, P. (2018). (eds), *Social Justice and Legal Education*, Cambridge Scholars Publishing.

Bell, L.A. (1997). 'Theoretical foundations for social justice education', in Adams, M., Bell, L.A. and Griffin, P. (eds), *Teaching for diversity and social justice: A sourcebook*, Routledge.

Bloch, F.S. (2010). (ed), *The Global Clinical Movement Educating Lawyers for Social Justice*, Oxford University Press.

Bradney, A. (1996). 'The quality of teaching quality assessment in English law schools', *The Law Teacher*, 30(2), p. 150.

Brodie, J.M. (2007). 'Reforming social justice in neoliberal times', *Studies in Social Justice*, 1(2), p. 93.

Brownsword, R. (1992). 'Teaching Contract: A Liberal Agenda', in Birks, P. (ed), *Examining the Law Syllabus: The Core*, Oxford University Press.

Brownsword R. (1999). 'Law Schools for Lawyers, Citizens, and People', in Cownie, F. (ed), *The Law School – Global Issues, Local Questions*, Routledge.

Crenshaw, K. (1989). 'Demarginalizing the intersection of race and sex: a Black feminist critique of antidiscrimination doctrine, feminist theory and antiracist politics', *University of Chicago Legal Forum*, 1(8), p. 31.

English, L.M. and Irving, C.J. (2015). 'Critical Feminist Pedagogy', in English, L.M. and

Irving, C.J. (eds), *Feminism in Community*, Springer.

Figueroa, P. (2000). 'Citizenship education for a plural society', in Osler, A. (ed), *Citizenship and democracy in schools: Diversity, identity, and equality*, Trentham Books Ltd.

Fleischacker, S. (2004). *A Short History of Distributive Justice*, Cambridge University Press.

Fook, J. and Goodwin, S. (2019). 'Introducing social justice', in Mealey, A.M., Jarvis, P., Doherty, J. and Fook, J. (eds), *Everyday Social Justice and Citizenship*, Routledge.

Fraser, N. (2001). 'Recognition without ethics?', *Theory, Culture & Society*, 18(2–3), p. 21.

Freire, P. (2017). *Pedagogy of the Oppressed*, Penguin.

Grant, C.A. and Gibson, M.L. (2013). '"The path of social justice": A Human Rights History of Social Justice Education', *Equity & Excellence in Education*, 46(1), p. 81.

hooks, b. (2000). *Feminist Theory: From Margin To Center*, Pluto Press.

Ivic, S. (2016). *European Identity and Citizenship: Between Modernity and Postmodernity*, Palgrave Macmillan.

Jackson, B. (2005). 'The Conceptual History of Social Justice', *Political Studies Review*, 3(3), p. 356.

Jones, E. (2019). *Emotions in the Law School: Transforming Legal Education Through the Passions*, Routledge.

Kant, I. (1993). *Grounding for the Metaphysics of Morals: On a Supposed Right to Lie because of Philanthropic Concerns*, first published 1785, James W. Ellington tr, 3rd edition, Hackett Publishing Company.

Madhloom, O. (2022). 'A Kantian Moral Cosmopolitan Model for Teaching Professional Legal Ethics', *German Law Journal*), p. 1139.

Madhloom, O. and Antonopoulos, I. (2022). 'Clinical Legal Education and Human Rights

Values: A Universal Pro Forma for Law Clinics', *Asian Journal of Legal Education*, 9(1), p. 23.

Mill, J.S. (2014). *Utilitarianism*, first published 1861, Cambridge University Press.

Miller, D. (1999). *Principles of Social Justice*, Harvard University Press.

Nussbaum, M.C. (1994). 'Patriotism and Cosmopolitanism', in Cohen, J. (ed), *For Love of Country: Debating the Limits of Patriotism*, Beacon Press.

Pocock, J.G.A. (1995). 'The Ideal of Citizenship Since the Classical Times', in Beiner, R. (ed), *Theorizing Citizenship*, SUNY Press.

Pring, R. (2016). 'Preparing for citizenship: Bring back John Dewey', *Citizenship, Social and Economics Education*, 15(1), p. 6.

Rawls, J. (1963). 'Constitutional liberty and the concept of justice', in Fredrich, C.J. and Chapman, J.W. (eds), *Nomos, VI Justice*, Atherton Press.

Rawls, J. (1972). *A Theory of Justice*, Oxford University Press.

Rorty, R. (1994). 'The Unpatriotic Academy', New York Times, available at http://www.nytimes.com/1994/02/13/opinion/the-unpatriotic-academy.html.

Shafir, G. (1998). (ed), *The Citizenship Debates. A Reader*, University of Minnesota Press.

Sidgwick, H. (2011). *The Methods of Ethics*, first published 1874, Cambridge University Press.

Smith, A. (2008). *An Inquiry into the Nature and Causes of the Wealth of Nations*, first published 1776, Oxford University Press.

Universal Declaration of Human Rights, available at https://www.ohchr.org/en/human-rights/universal-declaration/translations/english.

Willoughby, W.W. (1900). *Social Justice: A Critical Essay*, Macmillan and Co.

Wilson, R.J. (2018). (ed), *The Global Evolution of Clinical Legal Education: More than a Method*, Cambridge University Press.

Wizner, S. (2002). 'The Law School Clinic: Legal Education in the Interests of Justice', *Fordham L Rev*, 70, p. 1929.

Young, L.M. (1990). *Justice and the Politics of Difference*, Princeton University Press.

97. Social workers' legal education

Introduction

The legal education of social workers is often overlooked, not only in terms of legal pedagogy but also in the context of the broader education of social workers. The first specialist and discursive textbook was not published until 1990 when Hugh Brayne and Gerry Martin recognised the need for a clear and practical guide to the law for trainee social workers (Brayne and Martin [1990]). This book has been regularly updated since it was first published (see, for example Carr and Goosey [2021]).

The book was originally written in anticipation of the implementation of the Children Act 1989 and in the immediate aftermath of the Cleveland child abuse scandal when more than 120 children were taken into care by local authority social workers because of concerns about sexual abuse. The subsequent inquiry, chaired by Judge Elizabeth Butler-Sloss found (inter alia) that insufficient attention had been paid to legal proprieties and individual rights (*Report of the Inquiry into Child Abuse in Cleveland*). This entry considers the legal status of the social worker, the scope of the legal knowledge required by those practicing social work and the challenges of educating 'legally literate' and effective social workers.

What is a social worker?

In England, the title 'social worker' is prescribed by the Social Workers Regulations 2018. To practise as a social worker, one must be registered with Social Work England. Similar provisions apply in the other three UK countries. Thus, law and regulation broadly define what social workers are and do. The Local Authority and Social Services Act 1970 established the role of social services in local government and provides a list of relevant prior Acts and by amendment, Acts after 1970 which have created a social services function in local government. These functions are in general carried out by social workers. The law thus frames social work in specific governmental contexts and defines its roles and tasks. Social workers must understand this if they are to recognise their position in society

and their relationship with those people who they seek to help.

The State has increasingly assumed a role in governing family life and social relations so that in the twenty-first century there is a complex array of legal provisions. This contrasts with the late nineteenth century and early twentieth century when the role of the State was minimal. In 1920 Clement Atlee (who became the post-World War Two Labour Prime Minister) published *The Social Worker* in which he noted, that 'much of the doctrines of the classical economists hampered the efforts of social reformers by practically forbidding all action by the state outside the narrowest lines' (Atlee [1920] at 13). Nonetheless, he went on to note

> We claim the right to as full an opportunity of expressing our personalities as has anybody else, and that implies the duty of securing as good an opportunity for others as we have for ourselves. Society is built upon a series of rights and duties express or implied; they may vary at different stages of human development and between different classes, but at our present stage of development in which all do at least lip service to democracy, our ideal is the fullest opportunity for the development of every human soul. (Atlee[1920] at 16)

So even in 1920, significant social work values were being articulated alongside the rights and duties that all citizens should enjoy. The essential desire and mission for social work is to improve human experience and this is often the motivation for people to join the profession. However, in the modern context, the law increasingly defines how that help should be offered. The law describes the social workers' powers and duties as well as a series of obligations. Most social workers in the UK are employed by statutory bodies predominantly made up of local authorities. It is these authorities, with social services functions, that require social workers to carry out key tasks associated with those authorities' responsibilities. Local authorities themselves are tightly controlled by central government such that they should not carry out any functions unless primary legislation has been enacted which gives those authorities permission to do so. Thus, local authorities have very little discretion to spend public money on anything other than that which is prescribed in law.

Social workers are essentially local government officers and are thus obliged to adhere to what the law and regulations tell them. But local authorities are also bureaucratic and frequently experience financial shortages. Local authority social services functions are inspected and sometimes publicly criticised. And many social work tasks require complex collaboration with other professions. This complex context sometimes leads social workers into dangerous territory where they can act outside of the law. Furthermore, social workers' powerful motivation to help highly vulnerable children and adults, where they are trying to do the 'right thing' can sometimes lead to unlawful actions. Thus, a sound legal understanding is fundamental in social work.

Law for social workers

Sound legal understanding is challenging because the scope of the law that social workers need to know is extensive. It comprises different types of law, from the overarching legal requirements contained for instance in Human Rights obligations or data protection laws, to the detailed statutory provisions which prescribe how social workers must carry out their everyday statutory functions, such as Working Together to Safeguard Children or the Care Act 2014 Guidance. Alongside the areas of law where a social worker should acquire expertise – children's law, adult social care, mental health law etc, a general knowledge of law relating to domestic abuse, debt, housing and homelessness and immigration is expected as vulnerable service users are likely to face a range of problems and legal challenges. Social workers need at least to be able to point people in the right direction for help in solving the complex problems they face.

Social workers' legal knowledge must include understanding when and how the law will hold a social worker accountable for their actions or inactions, as an agent of the state and/or personally, and closely linked to accountability, the laws around whistle blowing. Social workers need to know how to use the outcomes of judicial reviews, public inquiries and local serious case reviews to improve their professional practice, turning what can seem like scapegoating of the front-line social worker into valuable lessons. The law that social workers use can align closely to the professional values they are taught, for instance anti-discriminatory practice and the Equality Act 2010, or it can feel counter-intuitive, for instance preventing intervention or information sharing when social work instincts to protect the service user may suggest failure to act, or share could be detrimental.

Knowing the law is not sufficient; social workers need to know how the law works, the difference between common law and statute, between public law and private law, and statutory guidance and best practice, and how this differs from practice guidance provided by their employers. They need to understand court procedures and evidence, and how to present evidence in court. They must learn how to reason in a lawful way and record those reasons so that there is an effective audit trail of decisions made in a case. In principle being able to locate the law and how it is updated is important but limited local authority resources means that in reality they are unlikely to have access to the necessary legal databases.

The law that social workers use is not only complex, but frequently controversial. There have been longstanding controversies around, for instance, the relationship between lawful decision making about adult social care services and the availability of resources, which have become increasingly acute over the last decade as local authorities have faced dramatic funding cuts. The question that social service authorities must address, and individual social workers are required to implement, is whether needs drive resource allocation, or the other way round. How the human rights of those who lack mental capacity and can therefore not consent to deprivations of liberty should be protected has proved equally difficult to resolve with a second set of statutory mechanisms currently awaiting enactment. The rapidly developing law concerning gender self-identification and gender critical beliefs is another minefield for social workers working with vulnerable service users. The considerable public debate and the proposals to reform the legal status of those seeking to re-categorise their birth gender can conceal the need to balance individual rights to freedom of expression and the broader public good. Our argument is that a grasp of the law and legal reasoning and an understanding of the principles of coherent and transparent decision-making provides invaluable tools for managing these controversies.

HELEN CARR AND DAVID GOOSEY

Social work and legal pedagogy

Legal education in this context is challenging, bearing in mind that the law is only a small fraction of the social work syllabus. Teaching black letter (doctrinal) legal rules is important. Social workers need to understand the legal limits of their role, when to get advice from local authority lawyers, and what that advice means. They should also have the confidence to challenge department guidance and advice if they think the law is not being correctly applied. This is likely to be difficult if, as is often the case, the law teacher is not legally qualified. When law is not taught by a lawyer it can be all too easy for a fear of law, its difference and authority, to be communicated. At the same time social workers must have a critical appreciation of law, understanding the tensions between the law and the ethical values that inform social work, and recognition that the legalistic model of social work is not the only or even dominant framework for ethical social work practice (Braye and Preston-Shoot [2020]. These tensions are not easy to resolve, but legal rigour is essential for proper decision making and proper decision making should be the priority of the legal education of social workers. The role of law and its significance in social work decision making is perhaps best exemplified by the President of the Family Division, Sir James Munby's critical observations in *Re A (A Child)* [2015] EWFC 11. This was a case where the father of a child who had been placed in foster care and was being considered for adoption, was seeking to take responsibility for the child's care. The father's application was opposed by the local authority which alleged that the child was likely to suffer significant harm in the care of the father by way of neglect. It was supported by the Children's Guardian who had met the father only once, for about 45 minutes. What Munby made clear is that local authority decision making must be legally literate. This involves the following:

- Findings of fact must be based on evidence (including inferences that can properly be drawn from the evidence) and not on suspicion or speculation.
- If a local authority is challenged on some factual point, it must adduce proper evidence to establish what it seeks to prove.
- Allegations that a parent 'appears' to have done something or that various people have 'stated' or 'reported' or that there is 'an allegation that... something has happened' are wrong and should never be used. The relevant allegation is not that someone 'appears' to have done something, it is that he 'did' it.
- A local authority needs to demonstrate why facts A + B + C justify the conclusion that the child has suffered, or is at risk of suffering, significant harm of types X, Y or Z.

There is a lot of sympathy for the difficult role that social workers play in an increasingly unequal society where vulnerable people face complex social challenges. That sympathy is forfeit if social workers exceed their powers or make decisions that are not rooted in proper evidence. Effective legal education of social workers is essential to avoid this outcome.

HELEN CARR AND DAVID GOOSEY

References

Atlee, C. (1920). *The Social Worker*, Bell and Sons Ltd.

Braye, S. and Preston-Shoot, M. (2016). *Practising Social Work Law*, 4th edition, British Association of Social Workers.

Brayne, H. and Martin, G. (1990). *Law for Social Workers*, Blackstone Press.

Carr, H. and Goosey, D. (2021). *Law for Social Workers*, 16th edition, Oxford University Press.

Department for Education. (2023). *Working Together to Safeguard Children*, Statutory Guidance.

Department for Health and Social Care. (2023). *Care and Support Statutory Guidance*.

Department for Social Services. (1988). *Report of the Inquiry into Child Abuse in Cleveland 1987* (Cm 412).

Local Authority and Social Services Act 1970.

Re A (A Child) [2015] EWFC 11.

The Equality Act 2010.

The Social Workers Regulations 2018, S.I. 2018/893.

98. Socio-legal approaches to legal education

Definition of socio-legal studies

Socio-legal studies does not have a precise or unified definition. Commentators disagree on whether it is an approach to legal study and legal research or whether it is a discipline in its own right. We can be sure what the 'legal' encompasses; it is the 'socio' part that causes more discussion. At its narrowest it is seen as an approach that draws upon sociology, social policy and social admin-istration to explore legal concepts (Harris [1983]) whilst not offering its own critique (Campbell and Wiles [1976]) or an alternative explanatory classification (Cotterell [1984]). Wider interpretations see the 'socio' as an interface 'with a context in which law exists, be that a sociological, historical economic, geographical or other context' (Wheeler and Thomas [2000]). To this list of disciplinary contexts in which we can situate the legal, a whole raft of others such as anthropology, natural and life sciences, gender studies and other humanities subjects could be added. At its widest socio-legal studies would embrace law and humanities, law and economics, law in context and feminist legal education. The label 'Law and Society' is more commonly used in the US and Australia but in the context of legal education they are both describing a broadly similar paradigm.

It might no longer be obvious what turns on the definitional debate, but what it explains is the story of the establishment within the Academy of a new interdisciplinary way (Scott [1995]) of thinking about what to teach (and research) in law – a discipline that had previously been anchored to the acquisition of knowledge and skills thought to be rele-vant to a professional career in law and often taught by practitioners (Cownie and Bradney [2017]). Then in terms of what was taught, it was primarily doctrinal principles through, in the UK, the case and problem method (Capper [2019]), distinguishable from problem-based learning, and in the US the rather more elab-orate and staged Socratic method (Weaver [1991]). In terms of research what was under-taken was an analysis of these principles in case notes, short articles and student text-books (Wilson [1987]). Establishing intellec-tual rigour and standards through a considered genealogy were all important for socio-legal studies in challenging these prevailing ortho-doxies. The success of socio-legal studies in terms of its penetration of the Academy is documented by Cownie in her work on the professional identities of legal academics where she extrapolates from her data that around half of legal academics identify as socio-legal and more still work in that way without self-identifying (Cownie [2004]).

Early engagement with doctrinal legal education

We can view socio-legal studies 'negatively' (but not pejoratively) in terms of something other than a doctrinal structured contribution (Sommerlad [2015]). This helps to construct its distinctive contribution to legal education in higher education. From a historical per-spective the first impact socio-legal studies had on legal education was through the inclusion in the curriculum of research done under the Socio-Legal subset label of Law in Context. This involves essentially empirical work carried out on law and legal institu-tions with a view to providing an account that distinguishes between law as experienced (context or law in action) and law as a formal structure (the law in the books). Indeed there is a book series entitled *Law in Context*, now published by Cambridge University Press, that from its very first volume published in 1970 (Atiyah's *Accidents, Compensation and the Law*) offered a vehicle from which students could access law in context material. This was often presented as a supplement to the accounts of doctrinal law they were served as primary reading (Lacey [2020]).

However intellectually stimulating and educationally broadening the early Law in Context accounts, often termed 'gap' studies (Gould and Barclay [2012]) were, their essen-tially empirical base prevented them from being considered as mainstream texts. They offered an account of the gap or space between the doctrinal law in the leading textbooks and the law as it was experienced by users, advo-cates and professional groups. Knowledge of doctrinal principles was a necessary prior step in engaging with 'gap' accounts. These accounts explained, often in micro terms, why the gap existed (Feeley [2001]); to wit discretionary behavior by a class of gatekeepers, unmanageable workloads for policy officers or poor record keeping by court officials. Doctrinal texts, at a time when legal education was heavily influenced by the demands of the legal profession, were seen as providing the necessary explanations for 'how legal concepts fit[ted] together [and] the extent to which general principles [could] be extracted from legal reasoning' (McCrudden [2006]). This internally focused perspective, drawing almost exclusively on sources such as decided cases and legislation, was seen as the natural order of legal education (Guth and Ashford [2014]); it was solutions focused rather than critically inspired and the ideal site of self-replication for practicing lawyers.

Second wave socio-legal studies in the curriculum

Sitting alongside Cownie's pioneering work about the professional identities of legal academics (Cownie [2004]) are accounts of how the relationship between the legal academy and the legal profession has changed in terms of the prescription of teaching content, how research is funded and valued within the academy and how legal academics are more likely to hold academic qualifications post their first degree than professional ones (Collier [2004], Cowan and Wheeler [2020]). These developments have led to a UG legal education curriculum in which 'the big socio-legal questions' are much more likely to be asked (O'Brien [2012]) and used to critically analyse doctrinal legal categories. These questions move socio-legal inquiry from illustrative empirically informed 'gap' studies towards an interrogation of fundamental, large scope questions about the nature of law from broader theoretical and externally derived perspectives. So for example small scale studies about access to justice in particular areas of the immigration system might now be core reading in a course or module on the same where the focus is on contextually informed and interdisciplinary based discussions of migration, borders, delegated decision making and ideas of bureaucracy.

In general terms the things that might be focused on are substantive topics like citizenship, the relationship between institutions, the state and individuals and ideas of property. Themes such as power, accountability and governance might be captured alongside perspectives such as feminism, gender and colonialism. Both topics and perspectives would be informed by ideas and methods taken from the disciplines suggested above. This disciplinary list is non-exhaustive as more interfaces between law and other disciplines are constantly being suggested and mined. In a classroom in which a socio-legal approach was being taken to legal education, students would be encouraged to think about who is and who is not being regulated by law and how that regulation occurs and about how and when laws are enforced and in relation to whom. They would place legal concepts in a broad societal landscape that included socio-economic context but also ideas of historical and geographical context. Some subjects within the curriculum perhaps lend themselves more readily to a socio-legal approach than others. Halliday argues persuasively in a UK example which has global resonance that Public Law or Constitutional Law has to be delivered through a socio-legal lens if it is to make sense of the relationship between the constitution, the state and the citizen (Halliday [2012]). A socio-legal approach to Secured Transactions might be more difficult to conceptualise in this way. However textbooks and other materials (casebooks and online resources) that take a socio-legal approach are now much more common than they were and in addition to research based socio-legal journals they are several Legal Education journals, for example *The Law Teacher*, that offer discussions of course and module content and assessment strategies (see also Hunter [2012]).

Further directions

Two interconnected issues are worthy of further consideration if socio-legal studies is to continue to expand its reach within the Law School curriculum. Engagement with disciplines other than law is the foundation for socio-legal studies but students in a law school classroom are usually studying law as a standalone discipline. A key question is how much they need to understand about the substantive debates and methods of inquiry within the other disciplines that the content they are presented with draws upon to be able to engage critically with it. Whilst presenting legal topics and categories informed by other disciplines enriches those topics and categories, there needs to be thought given to not presenting the content of other disciplines as facile and/or fixed. Allied to this is the question of understanding the research methods employed in empirically based socio-legal studies research and research of legal issues founded in other disciplines. Opinions vary on the degree to which knowledge of methods is necessary (Bradney [2010] cf Hunter [2012]). However, some knowledge must be required for law students to engage effectively and yet there is little evidence that this is taught within Law Schools either in substantive or standalone modules.

Socio-legal studies has undeniably broadened the conceptions of law that students engage with. It makes clear the idea that law is both a social practice and a social construct and that the nature of intellectual endeavor within the study of law is about inquiry rather than the search for authority. However, what remains undeveloped is the 'socio' part of socio-legal studies (Lacey [1996]). There is an absence of both a clear ethical or political underpinning to socio-legal studies and a conceptual framework (Silbey [2013]). The turn to more theoretically informed socio-legal studies, second wave socio-legal studies as they are labelled here, has improved this position somewhat but much remains to be done. Students risk obtaining a fragmented view of the world which does not give them any clear standpoints from which to survey the field in which law is situated. We might contrast this with the deconstructive project of Critical Legal Studies.

SALLY WHEELER

References

Bradney, A. (2010). 'The Place of Empirical Legal Research in the Law School Curriculum', in Cane, P. and Kritzer, H. (eds), *The Oxford Handbook of Empirical Legal Research*, Oxford University Press.

Campbell, C. and Wiles, P. (1976). 'The Study of Law in Society in Britain', *Law and Society Review*, 10, p. 547.

Capper, D. (2019). 'Contract Law Teaching: teaching from the case law', in Swain, W. and Campbell, D. (eds), *Reimagining Contract Law Pedagogy*, Routledge.

Collier, R. (2004). 'We're all socio-Legal Now? Legal Education, Scholarship and the Global Knowledge Economy: Reflection on the UK Experience', *Sydney Law Review*, 26, p. 503.

Cotterrell, R. (1984). *The Sociology of Law*, Butterworths.

Cownie, F. (2004). *Legal Academics: Culture and Identities*, Hart Publishing.

Cownie, F. and Bradney, A. (2017). 'Socio-Legal Studies', in Watkins, D. (ed), *Research Methods in Law*, Routledge.

Cowan, D. and Wheeler, S. (2020). 'The Sociology of Housing Law', in Priban, J. (ed), *Research Handbook on the Sociology of Law*, Edward Elgar Publishing.

Feeley, M. (2001). 'Three Voices of Socio-Legal Studies', *Israel Law Review*, 35, p. 175.

Gould J. and Barclay, S. (2012). 'Mind the Gap: The Place of Gap Studies in Sociolegal Scholarship', *Annual Review of Law and Social Science*, 8, p. 323.

Guth, J. and Ashford, C. (2014). 'The Legal Education and Training Review: Regulating Socio-Legal and Liberal Legal Education?', *The Law Teacher*, 48, p. 5.

Halliday, S. (2012). 'Public Law', in Hunter, C. (ed), *Integrating Socio-Legal Studies into the Law Curriculum*, Palgrave Macmillan.

Harris, D. (1983), 'The Development of Socio-Legal Studies in the United Kingdom', *Legal Studies*, 3, p. 315.

Hunter, C. (2012). *Integrating Socio-Legal Studies into the Law Curriculum*, Palgrave Macmillan.

Lacey, N. (1996). 'Normative Reconstruction in Socio-Legal Theory', *Social and Legal Studies*, 5, p. 131.

Lacey, N. (2020). 'William Twining and the *Law in Context* Series: a personal reflection', *International Journal of Law in Context*, 16, p. 464.

McCrudden, C. (2006). 'Legal Research and the Social Sciences', *LQR*, p. 632.

O'Brien, C. (2012). 'European Union Law', in Hunter, C. (ed), *Integrating Socio-Legal Studies into the Law Curriculum*, Palgrave Macmillan.

Scott, P. (1995). *The Meanings of Mass Higher Education*, Open Uni Press.

Silbey, S. (2013). 'What Makes A Social Science of Law: Doubling the Social in Socio-Legal Studies', in Feenan, D. (ed), *Exploring the 'socio' of socio-legal studies*, Palgrave Macmillan.

Weaver, R. (1991). 'Langdell's Legacy: Living with the Case Method', *Villanova Law Review*, 36, p. 517.

Wheeler, S. and Thomas, P. (2000). 'Socio-Legal Studies', in Hayton, D. (ed), *Law's Futures*, Hart Publishing, p. 267.

Wilson, G. (1987). 'English Legal Scholarship', *MLR*, 50, p. 818.

99. Socratic method

Introduction

The Socratic Method is perhaps the feature of American legal education that has most captured the imagination, attracted passionate comments, and garnered cultural meanings in and outside of legal academia from its inception in the 1870s to today. It has also been the focus of countless academic essays for a century and a half; popular culture movies like *The Paper Chase* (1973) and *Legally Blonde* (2002) have also illustrated this pedagogical approach in law classrooms, perhaps in a caricatural way.

The following entry first provides an overview of the introduction of the Socratic Method at Harvard Law School in the 1870s and its later spread across the United States. It highlights the pedagogical goals of its founder, Christopher Langdell. It then summarises the main criticisms against the Socratic Method as well as the key achievements that are attributed to it. Finally, the entry offers a snapshot of the contemporary vigour of the Socratic Method in and outside of the United States.

Defining the Socratic Method

The Socratic Method is the combination of two distinct but intertwined elements: the Case Method and the Socratic Dialogue method of teaching. The Case Method refers to the inductive study of law from original sources (judgments) rather than from academic treatises. The Socratic Dialogue method of teaching refers to building the content of the class not from the instructor's recitation of material but from the accumulation of students' answers elicited by the instructor's questioning. While 'Socratic Method' may sometimes refer only to the second component, it is best understood as the combination of both.

The Socratic law teacher faces the students and interacts with them one by one by way of question and answer for most of the class time. The teacher asks questions regarding the facts of the cases, the reasons put forth by the judges to justify their decision, the underlying policy principles and varying hypothetical scenarios to apply and test the limits of the rules thus idehtified. This method was designed to teach students to identify under-lying legal principles, and not simply discrete rules, as well as to 'think like a lawyer.' The judicial opinions are studied as primary sources, and the method prioritises the depth of understanding of organising principles rather than the breadth of information coverage that might be otherwise better achieved by uninterrupted lecturing. The instructor does not deliver their own description of the course's subject for students to listen to. Rather, students should learn legal knowledge and legal analysis skills by induction, from the observation of the dialogue between the teacher and another student about the cases they should have all read in preparation for class. The indirect praise or blame of students' answers, whether the teacher develops further the idea and continues the train of thought or criticises, ignores or solicits other answers are all cues for the students as to how they should think about the cases.

In many law schools, this pedagogy is facilitated by the lay out of the classroom arrangement as a semi-circle where students can see the instructor, who remains the focal point of attention, but also most other students. The students may be assigned seats for the entirety of the term, and the teacher would thus be provided with a seating chart allowing them to easily call by name any of the several dozens of students in the room.

Inception at Harvard in 1870 and development

The Socratic Method was the brainchild of CC Langdell, appointed Dean of Harvard Law School in 1870 by Harvard's new president CW Eliot. The Socratic Method was one of many innovations pioneered at Harvard Law School at the time, alongside high standards for admission, sequenced coursework, written examinations and full-time teaching and full-time study.

At the time, the dominant method of instructions in university and proprietary law schools alike was lecturing to the students. Most often, the teacher would read out existing treatises and provide additional commentary along the way. Students would then be tested by way of recitations or quizzes asking for general definitions or restatements of rules.

Langdell aimed to establish the study of law as a scientific enterprise, in the hopes of legitimatising the discipline. With the

Socratic Method, he first intended to deploy a rational mode of inquiry onto appellate court decisions, seen as the lawyer's primary material, so as to identity and analyze principles of the common law rather than a myriad of rules (Stevens [1983] at 52–53). It was later presented as a mode of active learning leading students to think like lawyers. The Socratic Method created a new genre of legal literature, the casebook; it also led to a new form of examination by way of problem solving on hypotheticals (Kimball [2009] at 160–164).

Initially opposed by most students, teachers, and practitioners alike, Langdell's Socratic Method soon garnered increasing recognition. Langdell's obstinacy, president Eliot's support, and Langdell's student and successor JB Ames's own proselytism helped the Socratic Method establish itself as the leading innovation in legal pedagogy. This was also in large part due to Harvard's intellectual and cultural prestige as well as the financial efficacy of his approach to teach large groups of students. Through the 1890s, the Socratic Method was spreading to most elite law schools in the United States and criticisms from the bar abated (Stevens [1983] at 57–64). By the early twentieth century, it was seen as the standard across the United States and beyond, notably in Canada (Pue [2016] at 197).

Main criticisms and achievements

Early critiques of the Socratic Method feared that it encouraged students to read overruled cases and argue any point of view, thus shaping litigators rather than counsel knowing when to advice a client not to go to court. Others recognised the intellectual merit of the method, but objected to its generalisation as they thought it too demanding and unsuited to the average student (Stevens [1983] at 57–58).

A few decades later, the Legal Realists criticised the Socratic Method for its exclusive reliance on the printed opinions of appellate judges to learn the law. For the Realists, published judicial opinions are only a fractional explanation of the judge's decision in any given case. Relying exclusively on this material of study to learn how to predict what courts would decide in a new situation or how to induce them to make a ruling most favourable to one's clients would be akin to 'future horticulturists confining their studies to cut flowers' (Frank [1932] at 912).

While Frank's grand clinical model proposal for legal education would only gain traction decades later, and in rather marginal fashion in the law school curriculum, the Realists' critique nonetheless bore fruits in the diversification of materials used for law teaching. Instead of the pure casebooks from the early days of Socratic Method, it is now more frequent to find 'Cases & Materials' books where excerpts of statutes, academic papers from law or other disciplines and the editors' commentaries on some aspect or ambiguity of the materials presented will accompany cases. Despite this evolution, the Carnegie Foundation Report on legal education formulated the same critique as Frank three quarters of a century later: the focus on appellate opinions obscures the reality of the professional roles that lawyers play for their clients as well as the ethical implications and limit law students' exposure to the reality of situations leading to judicial decisions (Sullivan et al [2007] at 55–57).

Another vein of criticisms against the Socratic Method targeted the Socratic Dialogue aspect of this pedagogy. Kennedy in the early 1980s, followed by many since, described the experience of a law student in this environment as frightening and humiliating (Kennedy [1982] at 593; Sullivan et al [2007] at 57). The students are expected to learn the requisite skills by osmosis, picking the implicit cues from the dialogue between the teacher and other students. The teacher may call on any student at any point and the student does their best to read the teacher's mind in search of the answer expected of them; any failure to do so exposes the student's struggle to the large audience of his peers. Kennedy further denounced how this approach reinforces and normalises social hierarchy, instilling deference in a way that prepares students to reproduce it in workplace relationships between junior associates and senior partners as well as between lawyers and judges. Finally, Kennedy blamed the Socratic Method, alongside 100 per cent examination and curve grading, for fostering a stressful and competitive rather than collaborative relationship between students and for silencing students whose personal background or characteristics (e.g. gender, socio-economic or cultural background) does not predispose to answering questions on the spot in front of others.

Other scholars have highlighted the achievements of the Socratic Method. Through anthropological observation and linguistic analysis, Mertz described how the Socratic Method teaches students to read legal texts in a way that filters out certain facts, emotions and ideas. She showed how it frames legal thinking in terms of relationships with previous authorities (mostly judicial precedents and statutes) so as to teach students 'to reason and speak using the categories and analogies that are salient withing this legally delimited view of the conflict at issue in a particular case' (Mertz [2007] at 59). Similar observations led the authors of the 2007 Carnegie Foundation Report on legal education (who were not lawyers) to conclude that American law schools' heavy reliance on the Socratic Method achieves in a short period of time an effective socialisation process into 'thinking like a lawyer' (Sullivan et al [2007] at 185–188). While also offering recommendations to address the shortcomings of this approach, the report framed this conclusion as a laudable achievement.

The Socratic Method today in and outside of the United States

The Socratic Method is a distinctive feature of American law schools. It remains widely in use in American law schools, primarily in first-year core courses, but is almost nonexistent abroad.

In a 1994–95 survey of US law professors (Friedland [1996] at 27), 97 per cent of the participants teaching in first year courses reported using the Socratic Method, compared to 31 per cent for lecturing. On average in first year classes, participants reported using the Socratic Method during 59 per cent of the class time, compared to 25 per cent for lecturing. The numbers for Socratic Method and lecturing were much closer for upper-level courses. This study confirmed that the Socratic Method dominates law teaching in US law schools, especially in first year courses. A decade later, the Carnegie Foundation Report on legal education came to the same conclusion (Sullivan *et al* [2007]). Despite all the changes to the landscape and political economy of higher education since 1870, even though a more numerous and more diverse student population attends law schools nowadays, and in spite of recurring critiques, the Socratic Method has thus remained firmly established as a salient and distinctive feature of American legal education.

The general prestige of American legal education and the personal experience of foreign graduates of elite American elite law schools returning back home to teach spurred several attempts to implement some version of the Socratic Method abroad. Nearly always, these attempts met enough resistance or differing local conditions that led to adaptations no longer resembling the original (see e.g. the chapters on England, Australia and Israel in Sandomierski and Bartie [2021]). A recent example is the 2004 reform of legal education in Japan. The restructuring was heavily inspired by the American model and led to much greater emphasis on the study of cases, but the enthusiasm for the Socratic dialogue aspect of the Method was short-lived and has since mostly disappeared from Japanese law school classrooms (Matsuura [2021] at 227). Matsuura points to the Japanese legal culture of advocacy through written documents rather than oral exchanges, and preference for uniformity over innovation to explain this failure (Matsuura [2021] at 238–239). Even in Canada, a neighbouring country much closer in culture and legal structure to the United States, the Socratic Method is barely used. Rochette found that only nearly half of Canadian law teachers rarely or never used the Socratic Method, and another 15 per cent only used it occasionally, whereas the teaching methods used most often are lecture, class discussion and question-answer (Rochette, [2010] at 138–146). The only jurisdiction outside of the United States and its territories where the Socratic Method is well-established seems to be the Philippines, where the modern regime of legal education was developed while the country was an American colony (Salcedo [2021]). Elsewhere in the world, the Socratic Method is absent or very marginal and the main pedagogy in law schools is the lecture with diverse levels of interactions with students (Stolker [2014] at 164).

Conclusion

Revered or vilified, the Socratic Method remains the signature pedagogy of American legal education. Introduced by Langdell at Harvard in 1870, it soon spread and maintains a strong pre-eminence today in core law courses in US law schools, despite several waves of harsh critiques over the past century and half. However, it achieved only limited success and outside of the US it never replaced locally dominant pedagogies. A mode of teaching principles and shaping lawyerly minds as well as socialising process, the Socratic Method remains a focal point when discussing contemporary issues in legal education, such as the possibility of distance education through interactive technology.

ADRIEN HABERMACHER

References

Frank, J. (1932–1933). 'Why Not a Clinical Lawyer School', *U Pa L Rev*, 81, p. 907.

Friedland, S.I. (1996). 'How We Teach: A Survey of Teaching Techniques in American Law Schools', *Seattle U L Rev*, 20, p. 1.

Kennedy, D. (1982). 'Legal Education and the Reproduction of Hierarchy', *J Legal Educ*, 32(4), p. 591.

Kimball, B.A. (2009). *The Inception of Modern Professional Education C. C. Langdell, 1826–1906*, UNC Press.

Legally Blonde. (2002). Robert Luketic (dir), MGM Home Entertainment.

Matsuura, Y. (2021). 'The American Case method and New Japanese Legal Education', in Sandomierski, D. and Bartie, S. (eds), *American Legal Education Abroad Critical Histories*, NYU Press.

Mertz, E. (2007). *The Language of Law School*, Oxford University Press.

Lapiana, W.P. (1994). *Logic and Experience: The Origin of Modern American Legal Education*, Oxford University Press.

Pue, W.W. (2016). *Lawyers' empire: Legal professions and cultural authority, 1780–1950*, UBC Press, ch 6.

Reed, A.Z. (1921). *Training for the Public Profession of the Law: Historical Development and Principal Contemporary Problems of Legal Education in the United States with Some Account of the Conditions in England and Canada*, Arno Press.

Rochette, A. (2010). 'Teaching and Learning in Canadian Legal Education: An Empirical Exploration', DCL, McGill University.

Sanchez Salcedo, E. (2021). 'Socratic-Method, Philippine-style', in Sandomierski, D. and Bartie, S. (eds), *American Legal Education Abroad: Critical Histories*, NYU Press.

Sandomierski, D. and Bartie, S. (2021). (eds), *American Legal Education Abroad: Critical Histories*, NYU Press.

Stevens, R. (1983). *Law School: Legal Education in America from the 1850s to the 1980s*, UNC Press.

Stolker, C.J.J.M. (2014). *Rethinking the Law School. Education, Research, Outreach and Governance*, Cambridge University Press.

Sullivan, W.M. et al. (2007). *Educating Lawyers: Preparation for the Profession of Law*, The Carnegie Foundation for the Advancement of Teaching, John Wiley & Sons.

The Paper Chase. (1973). James Bridges (dir), 20th Century Fox.

100. South Africa (contemporary legal education)

Legal education in South Africa consists of two phases: (1) the academic degree offered at university law faculties (the Baccalaureus Legum (LLB)), which is the pre-requisite for entry to the legal profession; and (2) the vocational phase, delivered by the Schools for Legal Practice for attorneys (solicitors), and the General Council for the Bar for advocates (barristers).

The law degree is a four-year undergraduate Bachelor of Laws (LLB) degree. The subsequent vocational phase is undertaken by graduates wishing to enter legal professional practice. A period of articles of clerkship for candidate attorneys, or a year of pupillage for advocates, must be completed before the practice admission exams may be taken.

The LLB degree is offered at 17 law faculties at state universities in the country: the University of Cape Town, the University of Fort Hare, the University of Free State, the University of Johannesburg, the University of KwaZulu-Natal, the University of Limpopo, the Nelson Mandela Metropolitan University, the University of the North, the University of Pretoria, Rhodes University, the University of Stellenbosch, the University of Venda, Walter Sisulu University, the University of the Western Cape, the University of the Witwatersrand, the University of Zululand, and the University of South Africa, which offers only distance education. Two recently opened universities do not yet offer a law degree. The LLB is now also offered at a small number of private tertiary institutions. In 2021, 15,999 students entered LLB study, while a total of 68,459 students were registered over the four-year qualification (Law Society of South Africa Data [2022]).

At most law schools the language of instruction is now English: however, at Stellenbosch University and at the University of the North (Potchefstroom), law courses are still offered in both English and Afrikaans. In previous years, Afrikaans was the language of teaching and assessment at Stellenbosch University, University of the Free State, Pretoria University and the University of the North (Potchefstroom). For many African students whose first language is neither English nor Afrikaans, the language of instruction at universities presents a challenge. Many students must study in a second or third language, an impediment which is compounded by a weak secondary school system that does not adequately equip students to adapt to the academic demands of tertiary education (Greenbaum [2009]).

Up until 1995, all law students were required to pass a course in English, Afrikaans and Latin during their degree studies. The Admission of Advocates Amendment Act 55 of 1994 and the Admission of Legal Practitioners Amendment Act 33 of 1995 abolished Latin and any other language requirements. The previous statutory language provisions had served as barriers to Black candidates. Although there is a constitutional imperative to recognise the 11 official languages of South Africa, English and Afrikaans remain as the two 'official languages'. In 2017, English was declared to be the language of record in South African courts by former Chief Justice Mogoeng.

During the apartheid (racial 'separateness') era (1948 to 1994) when races were strictly segregated, universities were established for particular race groups, with less funding being given to historically Black universities (HBUs) (South Africa (History of Legal Education)). Universities during apartheid were designated separately for whites, Africans, Indians and Coloureds (mixed race persons). In South Africa, African, Indian, and Coloured persons are still classified as being 'Black', for the purposes of educational data collection. As a result of these historical racial distinctions, inequalities relating to under-resourcing, poor facilities, low research output and limited qualifications of lecturing staff were evident between these HBUs and the historically white universities (HWUs). Typically, the HBUs are situated in outlying rural areas, which diminishes their popularity and the interactions between their staff and students and the mainstream legal profession. Although almost 30 years have passed since the transition to democracy, the deficit in resources of the HBUs has not been rectified by additional state funding (Greenbaum [2016]).

The four-year undergraduate LLB degree is now the only law qualification in South Africa, but it is often completed as a second degree by graduates who have completed a primary degree in another faculty, such as

Arts or Commerce. The undergraduate degree was introduced in 1998, after the transition to democracy in South Africa. The purpose of an attenuated degree was to provide greater and more affordable access to the legal profession by students who had been disadvantaged during the dark years of apartheid. Further, it was intended as a vehicle that would expedite transformation, to enhance the representativity of the national law student body and the legal profession. Prior to 1998, a three-year postgraduate LLB and other degrees, such as the four-year undergraduate Baccalaureus Procurationis (B Proc) and a three-year B Iuris were offered. These degrees were often considered to be inferior qualifications which prepared graduates for careers as attorneys only (B Proc) or magistrates and court officials (B Iuris). The requirement of a postgraduate LLB to practice as an advocate, or to be appointed as a judge ensured the domination of white (mostly males) in those two areas of the legal profession.

In 1998 the four-year LLB degree was introduced at law faculties, on the understanding that each faculty would have the discretion to include and sequence the subjects within the degree according to their individual curriculum design plan, to align with their mission and vision. Law Deans agreed on the core courses to be taught in the LLB, including the following subjects:

Constitutional Law (including fundamental rights), Corporate Law, Criminal Law, Law of Contract, Law of Delict (Torts), Law of Persons, Family Law, Law of Succession, Property Law, Criminal Procedure, Civil Procedure, Evidence, Interpretation of Statutes, Administrative Law, Law of Insolvency, Law of Negotiable Instruments, Mercantile Law (including Sale, Lease, Insurance, Suretyship and Consumer Protection), Labour Law, Conflict of Laws, African Customary Law, Public International Law, Jurisprudence, Roman Law, Legal History, Legal Skills (including language, communication, writing and legal reasoning skills) (Greenbaum [2009]).

Frequently, some of the subjects were combined, and taught within one module, in order to fit all the different topics into the curriculum.

A decade after the introduction of the undergraduate LLB, complaints from the judiciary, members of the legal profession and the media about the poor quality of law graduates began to surface (Sedutla [2013]). In response to these criticisms a meeting, 'Crisis in legal education', was held in May 2013, convened by the South Africa Law Deans' Association (SALDA).

Consensus on a way forward for legal education was reached among stakeholders: SALDA; the General Council of the Bar (GCB); the Law Society of South Africa (LSSA); Department of Justice (DOJ); Department of Higher Education and Training (DHET) and the Society of Law Teachers of Southern Africa (SLTSA). A national review of the LLB degree offered by each law faculty would be conducted by the quality assurance body for higher education, the Council on Higher Education (CHE) (Whitear and Freedman [2015]). An LLB qualification standard was drafted by a panel of legal education experts in the period 2013–2015. This standard prescribed the graduate attributes to be developed in law students, categorising them into knowledge, skills and applied competences. Law faculties were assessed for accreditation, based on a self-evaluation report (SER) drafted by each university, but it was agreed that the standard should serve primarily as an 'instrument for programme development' (The State of the Provision of the Bachelor of Laws (LLB) Qualification in South Africa [2018]). The process began with a desktop evaluation of each SER, followed by a peer-driven site-visit to each law faculty.

In the Preamble to the LLB Standard, a central focus is on embedding 'transformative constitutionalism' pervasively in law curricula. The notion was described by Karl Klare in 1998 as:

> a long-term project of constitutional enactment, interpretation, and enforcement committed... to transforming a country's political and social institutions and power relationships in a democratic, participatory, and egalitarian direction. (Klare [1998] 150)

The LLB review report noted that a completely different way of teaching and studying law must be adopted, alerting students to the fact that the Constitution is the supreme law and that all other sources of law are subservient to it (The State of the Provision of the Bachelor of Laws (LLB) Qualification in South Africa, Council on Higher Education, CHE [2018]).

LESLEY GREENBAUM

The Chief Justice, Pius Langa (at that time) stated:

> A truly transformative South Africa requires a new approach that places the Constitutional dream at the very heart of legal education. It requires that we regard law as part of the social fabric and teach law students to see it as such. They should see law for what it is, as an instrument that was used to oppress in the past, but that has that immense power and capacity to transform our society (Langa [2006] 356).

A framework for 'transformative legal education' (TLE) was outlined by Professor Geo Quinot in 2012 (Quinot [2012]). It is founded upon a three-pronged approach: (1) to introduce a fundamental shift from formalistic legal reasoning to substantive reasoning under a transformative constitution; (2) to encourage a shift towards a constructivist student-centred teaching model; (3) for the recognition of a paradigm shift in knowledge from linear to non-linear, relational or complex. These tenets should now shape and inform legal education.

In the 2018 CHE report of the National LLB review it was recommended that the degree be extended by a year to accommodate the inclusion of more discipline-based non-law modules. Further, a recommendation was made that all faculties endeavour to include a course on Clinical Law and Information Technology in their curricula.

A SALDA task team was appointed in 2015 to interrogate the infusion of ethics into the curriculum. In their report of November 2016, a proposal for a model of curriculum was presented for the academic phase of legal education. Ethics and integrity were included as applied competencies in the LLB standard, but no recommendation was made in the report of the National LLB Review.

Between 2015 and 2017 student protests spread across South African university campuses, initially driven by the #Rhodesmustfall campaign and thereafter by the #Feesmustfall campaign. As part of the latter protests, a call came for the decolonisation of university curricula, including those offered in law faculties (Andrews [2016]). Serious reflection on what is meant by decolonisation of higher education has not produced consensus on the meaning of the term.

SALDA appointed a Task team and convened a conference in 2017, but no consensus was reached on the meaning of Africanisation and decolonisation in legal education. Academics (Campbell [2019]) have suggested that it is also a political process over and above being a curriculum issue.

Tshivase proposes the following principles regarding decolonisation of legal education in South Africa: (1) decolonisation requires an interrogation of the history of the legal system and legal education; (2) not all principles, doctrines and practices that have come through colonisation need to be discarded; (3) a revisiting of some undesirable aspects of the law and legal education, taking into account the African and South African context, may be required; (4) there is a call for substantive and deliberate inclusivity in conception and teaching of the law as a constitutional imperative (Tshivhase [2019] 81–2).

The current status of legal education in South Africa is that since the COVID-19 pandemic, when law teaching moved into online pedagogical formats, most faculties are grappling with the challenges of decolonising curricula, adopting methods of blended learning and online engagement with students, as well as addressing unacceptably high staff to student ratios. Each law school prescribes the content of their curricula and assessments and regulates the admission criteria. In general, applications for the LLB degree far exceed the number of places available at universities, but still too many law graduates are being produced by law faculties. Students experience difficulties in securing articles of clerkship in law firms and in obtaining employment in the legal profession and associated careers.

The future of legal education in South Africa presents challenges as well as opportunities for improvement. Most law schools have in place programmes to increase access to students of colour as a redress measure for previous disadvantage, taking into account the poor secondary schooling that many black students experience. Some law schools offer extended curriculum programmes which provide academic support and provide for students to take an additional year to complete the LLB.

With the implementation of the LLB standard and since the LLB review, it seems that there is reduced diversity among the offerings of law schools. Elective courses toward the end of the degree allow for the study of specialist law courses, but students wishing to pursue a specific career path in law often undertake a Master of Laws (LLM) to focus on a particular subject, such as tax law, shipping law, international law or environmental law.

The LLB degree remains a rigorous qualification, which many students do not complete within four years. Demographics in law schools have changed dramatically in the past decade, but challenges remain in establishing acceptable equity profiles in accordance with national population data (CHE [2021]).

LESLEY GREENBAUM

References

Admission of Advocates Amendment Act 55 of 1994.
Admission of Legal Practitioners Amendment Act 33 of 1995.
Andrews, P. (2017). 'Race, Inclusiveness and Transformation of Legal Education in South Africa', available at SSRN: https://ssrn.com/abstract=3110039 or http://dx.doi.org/10.2139/ssrn.3110039.
Andrews, P. (2016). 'Race, Inclusiveness and Transformation of Legal Education in South Africa', available at SSRN: https://ssrn.com/abstract=3110039 or http://dx.doi.org/10.2139/ssrn.3110039.
Campbell, J. (2020). 'Decolonising Clinical Legal Education', in Tshivhase, A.E., Mpedi, L.G. and Reddi, M. (eds), Decolonisation and Africanisation of Legal Education in South Africa, Juta.
CHE Standards for Bachelor of Laws_ LLB final version_20150921.pdf, available at https://www.che.ac.za/sites/default/files/Standards%20for%20Bachelor%20of%20Laws_%20LLB%20final%20version_20150921.pdf.
CHE The state of Provision of the LLB Qualification (CHE), available at https://www.che.ac.za/sites/default/files/publications/CHE_LLB%20National%20Report_2018_DD_REV2-05.pdf.
CHE Vital Stats for Public and Private Higher Education 2021, available at https://www.che.ac.za/sites/default/files/publications/PUB_VitalStats%202021_Public%20and%20Private%20Higher%20Education%20Data_2023%5B66%5D.pdf.
Greenbaum, L. (2009). 'A History of the Racial Disparities in Legal Education in South Africa', J Marshall LJ, 3, p. 1.
Greenbaum, L. (2009). 'The undergraduate law curriculum: Fitness for purpose', Unpublished PhD thesis, University of Kwa-Zulu Natal.
Greenbaum, L. (2015–2016). 'Legal Education in South Africa: Harmonizing the Aspirations of Transformative Constitutionalism with Our Educational Legacy', N.Y.L. Sch. L. Rev., 60, p. 463.
Klare, K.E. (1998). 'Legal Culture and Transformative Constitutionalism', South African Journal on Human Rights, 14(1), p. 146.
Langa, P. (2006). 'Transformative Constitutionalism', Stellenbosch L. Rev., 17, pp. 351, 356.
Mpedi, G. and Reddi, M. (2019). (eds), Decolonisation and Africanisation of legal Education in South Africa, Juta.
Quinot, G. (2012). 'Transformative Legal Education', South African Law Journal, 129, p. 411
Sedutla, M. (2013). 'LLB summit: legal education in crisis?', De Rebus, 113.
Tshivhase, A.E. (2019). 'Decolonisation and Africanisation of Legal Education in South Africa: Background and Introduction', in Tshivhase, A.E., Mpedi, L.G. and Reddi, M. (eds), Decolonisation and Africanisation of Legal Education in South Africa, Juta.
Whitear, N. and Freedman, W. (2015). 'A historical review of the development of the post-apartheid South African LLB degree – with particular reference to legal ethics', Fundamina, 21(2), p. 234.

101. South Africa (history of legal education)

An historical outline of legal education in South Africa from 1652 when the Dutch colonisers arrived at the Cape of Good Hope, through the period of British colonial rule (1795–1910), the Union of South Africa, including apartheid, then the transition to democracy in 1994 and up to the present time will be undertaken.

The first Dutch settlers arrived at the Cape in 1652, establishing a refreshment station for Dutch trading ships sailing to and from the East. Representatives of the Dutch East India Company (VOC) settled around the area that is currently Cape Town. The indigenous occupants, the Khoi and San peoples, were dispossessed of much of their grazing land, which was taken over by settlers for farming activities. Indigenous law was not recognised by the colonisers, other than as an inferior and subsidiary set of customary rules applicable to the inhabitants that were already living at the Cape (Iya [2001]).

Roman-Dutch law, as practiced in the province of Holland in the Netherlands, was applied to Dutch residents at the Cape through the Raad van Justitie, a body made up of the Commander and additional lay persons (Kruuse [2021]). The legal profession was divided into two categories, following the distinction made in Roman-Dutch law. Advocates (advocaten) typically argued cases in court, while attorneys (procureurs) carried out largely day-to day commercial and land transactions. Notaries formed a third class of legal practitioner. In 1688, the first advocate was appointed at the Cape (Gauntlett [2010]). Due originally to a shortage of legal practitioners, both advocates and attorneys were permitted to argue cases in court. No professional qualification or legal education was required for attorneys, but advocates were required to hold a doctorate in law from Holland. In 1791, as a result of a complaint that practitioners were ignorant and indifferent, a Code of Conduct for attorneys was drafted (Church [1998]). No provision was made for educating lawyers at the Cape.

In 1795, the British took over the Cape as a British colony, but no changes to the regulation of the legal profession were made. During a brief period of Batavian rule from 1803 to 1806, advocates were expressly required to be law graduates of Holland, while attorneys were required to undergo an examination conducted by the Cape courts' commissioners (Church [1998] at 110).

During the second British occupation of the Cape, Roman-Dutch law in Holland was superseded by the Code Napoleon in 1809, which meant that there was no longer a 'parent' source of law to refer to (Cowen [1959]). The development of Roman-Dutch law would from this time onwards take place in South Africa. The British government introduced two Royal Charters of Justice (1827 and 1832), establishing a Supreme court and lower courts modelled along English lines. These changes affected the administration of justice and introduced many aspects of English procedural law, while retaining Roman-Dutch law as the common law at the Cape (Cowen [1959]).

In 1828, advocates had to 'have been admitted as barristers in England or Ireland or Advocates in the Court of Session of Scotland, or to the degree of Doctor of Laws at the Universities of Oxford, Cambridge or Dublin...' (Church [1998] at 109). Consequently, many aspiring South African advocates went to study at the Inns of Court in London, before returning to practice at the Cape (Sachs [1973]). In 1829 a rule of court was introduced, which required attorneys to serve five years of articles. No system of legal education was established and local advocates and attorneys were left to provide the necessary training for aspirant lawyers.

Formal legal education at the Cape commenced in 1858, when the British governor, Sir George Grey, established a Board of Examiners in Literature and Science in Act 4 of 1858 (Church [1998] at 111). The purpose was to regulate admission to practice of persons holding the 'Certificate of the Higher Class in Law and Jurisprudence' (Church [1998]; Cowen [1988] at 6; Visser [1992]). In order to be admitted to practice at the side bar, attorneys were required to have a matriculation and a second-class Certificate in Law and Jurisprudence awarded by the Board, as well as having served two years of articles. Notaries were required to serve four years of articles and then pass an examination. Although the Board of Examiners suffered from the usual criticisms levelled at external examining bodies, it did establish a formal qualification for practising law at the Cape.

Students were tutored in law at the South African College, which had been established in 1828. Thereafter they were examined by the Board of Examiners. Johannes Henricus Brand LLD, a barrister, was appointed in 1859 as the first professor of law at the South African College. His first class of eight students attended two lectures a week. This marked the beginning of formal legal teaching in South Africa with the purposes of improving the quality of practitioners locally and supporting the development of Roman-Dutch law at the Cape (Cowen [1959]).

The Board of Public Examiners was replaced in 1873 by the University of the Cape of Good Hope, which was the forerunner of the University of South Africa. The university was authorised to award a Certificate in Proficiency in Law and Jurisprudence, as well as a Bachelor of Laws degree (LLB). It was the first time that a law degree could be conferred in South Africa. The university awarded the degree, but tuition continued to be provided by the South African College, which became the University of Cape Town in 1916. Tuition was also provided at the Victoria College in Stellenbosch, which became the University of Stellenbosch in 1916. LLB students were required to pass a course in Roman law, Colonial and Dutch law, English law, international law, the law of evidence and to study the maxims of conflicts of laws (Church [1998]).

By the early 1900s the number of practising lawyers at the Cape who had South African degrees began to exceed those who held overseas qualifications. However, in the ensuing 17 years, five different proposals for the reform of legal education were made. Reports were drafted by the Laurence Commission, the Thompson Commission, the Lewis Committee, the report of the under-secretary for education GR Hofmeyr, and the Howes memorandum drafted by the committee of the law board (Cowen [1959]).

The proposals highlighted the following critical areas in legal education that required attention:

1. The appropriate physical accommodation for the teaching of law;
2. the provision of an adequate South African law school library;
3. whether law should be taught as a professional discipline or as part of a general education in the humanities;
4. the content of an appropriate professional law syllabus;
5. the size of an adequate teaching staff and the maintenance of manageable staff/student ratios;
6. whether the qualification should be a four-year LLB, or a postgraduate degree, following an undergraduate degree in another faculty, such as in the faculty of arts or commerce;
7. the linguistic requirements for practising law in South Africa, and specifically the role of Latin;
8. the extent to which the judiciary, the bar and the side-bar should be involved in policy-making of the law faculty (Cowen [1988]).

In 1910 the four colonial territories in South Africa: Cape, Natal, and the two independent Boer (Afrikaans farmer) states: the Transvaal and the Orange Free State, joined to form the Union of South Africa, comprising four provinces. A central Supreme court was established in Bloemfontein (Kruuse [2021]).

Two law faculties were established by Acts 13 and 14 of 1916. The University of Cape Town, incorporating the South African College, and the University of Stellenbosch were created by statute. Each faculty appointed full-time professors of law. The opening of these law schools in 1918 heralded the formalisation of university legal education.

In the judgment in *Ex parte Van der Willigen* [1920] CPD 302 Sir John Kotze noted:

> The future of the legal profession is a matter of great public concern to the country, and what that future is to be, will greatly depend upon the systematic and scientific teaching of law in our law schools.

Other institutions that were incorporated as constituent colleges with the University of the Cape of Good Hope, later the University of South Africa, were: Grey College of Bloemfontein (later the University of the Free State), Huguenot College of Wellington, Natal University College of Pietermaritzburg, Rhodes University College of Grahamstown, the Transvaal University College of Pretoria, the South African School of Mines and Technology of Johannesburg which subsequently become the University of the Witwatersrand and the Potchefstroom

University College. Most of these colleges had become independent universities by the 1930s (Church [1998]). The University of South Africa (UNISA) subsequently became one of the largest distance learning universities in the world. Notably, Nelson Mandela was able to complete his LLB degree through UNISA while he was incarcerated on Robben Island.

Legislation governing the admission of advocates was introduced in 1921 (Act 3 of 1921). This Act required an applicant to be 'fit and proper', to be at least 21 years old, have the necessary qualifications, and be a South African citizen or a permanent resident (Kruuse [2021]). In 1934 in terms of the Attorneys, Notaries and Conveyancers Admission Act 23 of 1934, in order to be admitted to the profession as an attorney, one had to be 'fit and proper', be at least 21 years old, have completed an LLB degree, and have completed a two-year articles period (Kruuse [2021]).

During apartheid (1948 to 1994), attendance at universities was restricted to students belonging to designated racial categories in South Africa. Students of colour: African, Indian and Coloured (or mixed race) were only permitted to attend historically 'White' universities (HWUs) with the express permission of the Minister of Education. HWUs were better resourced and situated in urban areas. These institutions are still today referred to as HWUs, because of the lingering effects of a racially differentiated tertiary education system. African students were required to attend the University of Zululand and Fort Hare University. Coloured students attended the University of the Western Cape and Indian students attended the University of Durban-Westville. Post-apartheid, these institutions are still referred to as 'historically Black universities' (HBUs). These restrictions on attendance at any university were lifted in the 1990s as South African moved toward democracy.

Today, 21 universities are in existence, but the HBUs still remain under-resourced and are located in areas outside of major urban areas (Greenbaum [2009]).

Up until 1998 students completed a three-year undergraduate degree in Arts or Commerce, before obtaining a postgraduate LLB degree. At some universities a three-year undergraduate B Iuris which qualified graduates as magistrates was offered, while other universities offered a four-year undergraduate B Proc Degree, which qualified graduates for practice as attorneys only. In 1998, the LLB was made a four-year undergraduate degree, qualifying graduates for all branches of the legal profession. This change was implemented as a strategy to transform the composition of the legal profession and to increase access and affordability of the degree for black students who had been disadvantaged during the apartheid era. Much criticism from the legal profession, judges and the media has been levelled at the quality of the attenuated curriculum and its graduates (Greenbaum [2016]). As a result, some law faculties encourage their students to complete an undergraduate arts or commerce degree before studying for an LLB.

In 2015, a national review of the LLB offered at 17 law faculties was undertaken (Whitear and Freedman [2015]). The purpose was to address complaints about deficiencies in the degree. An LLB standard was generated by a team of legal experts and the degree at each university was measured against that standard. The outcome of the review was that only one university was not re-accredited, but this situation has since been remedied (South Africa (Contemporary Legal Education).

During the COVID pandemic (2020–2022) most law faculties moved their teaching online to accommodate students working remotely. Increasingly, legal education in South Africa has integrated new technology into teaching activities as students are prepared for changed post-university legal practice.

Following on the student protests (2015 to 2017) initiated by the #Rhodesmustfall and #Feesmust fall movements at universities in South Africa, increasing pressure has been applied in law faculties to decolonise the LLB curriculum. Academics are engaged in infusing African Customary law throughout the curriculum and in addressing the need to Africanise and decolonise traditional law subjects.

The history of legal education in South Africa reflects a development that has been shaped by colonisation, apartheid and more recently, a democratic constitutional dispensation. Emerging from a deeply fractured past, legal education must now meet the challenges of producing graduates and professionals qualified to serve the needs of a diverse society.

Lesley Greenbaum

References

Admission of Advocates Act 3 of 1921.
Attorneys, Notaries and Conveyancers Admission Act 23 of 1934.
Church, J. (1998). 'Legal Education in South Africa – An Historical Overview', *Fundamina*, 4, p. 108.
Cowen, D.V. (1988). 'Taught Law Is Tough Law: The Evolution of a South African Law School', *THRHR*, 51, p. 4.
Cowen, D.V. (1959). 'The History of the Faculty of Law in the University of Cape Town, 1859–1959', *Acta Juridica*, p. 1.
Creating a Board of Public Examiners in Literature and Science Act 4 of 1858.
Gauntlett, J. (2010). 'The rule of law and an independent legal profession: A South African perspective', *Advocate*, p. 55.
Greenbaum, L. (2009). 'A History of the Racial Disparities in Legal Education in South Africa', John Marshall Law Journal, 3, p. 1.
Iya, P.F. (2001). 'The Legal System and Legal Education in Southern Africa: Past Influences and Current Challenges', *Journal of Legal Education*, 51(3), p. 355.
Kruuse, H.J. (2021). 'Legal ethics and the lawyer-client relationship in South Africa: A proposal for reform using local values', Unpublished PhD thesis, Rhodes University.
Sachs, A. (1973). *Justice in South Africa*, University of California Press.
University of Stellenbosch Act 13 of 1916.
University of Cape town Act 14 of 1916.
Ex parte Van der Willigen [1920] CPD 302.
Visser, D.P. (1992). 'As durable as the mountain: The story of the Cape Town Law School since 1859', *Consultus*, p. 32.
Whitear, N. and Freedman, W. (2015). 'A historical review of the development of the post-apartheid South African LLB degree – with particular reference to legal ethics', *Fundamina*, 21, p. 234.

102. South Africa (regulation of legal education)

Introduction

This brief overview of legal education regulation in South Africa has two sections. In the first section, it identifies that the minimum qualification required to practice law in South Africa is the Baccalaureus Legum (LLB). Given that such qualification must be awarded by a university, this section describes the regulatory framework impacting the LLB qualification and sets out the requirements for recognition of the qualification against the statutes and the policy framework underpinning higher education in South Africa. Unlike the accountancy profession in South Africa for example, and the legal profession in certain other jurisdictions, South African LLB programmes are not accredited by the legal profession's regulatory body, the Legal Practice Council (set up in terms of the Legal Practice Act 28 of 2014), nor their professional associations (the Law Society of South Africa and the General Council of the Bar, amongst others).

The second section, characterised as 'practical vocational training' in the legislation, describes the competency-based assessment that LLB graduates must complete during their articles or pupillage before a court will admit them as an attorney (solicitor), advocate (barrister) or trust advocate. It is at this stage that the regulatory authority involves itself in legal education – but only while the LLB graduate is undergoing articles or pupillage and only as a way of gaining admission to the side bar or bar.

The minimum qualification required by the Legal Practice Act: The LLB

In order to practice law, section 24 of the Legal Practice Act sets out the specific requirements that must be met before a person can be admitted to practice law. These requirements include being 'duly qualified' which in turn is described in section 26 of the Act as 'the minimum qualification and practical vocational training' required in order to meet the requirement in section 24. Section 26 describes that 'minimum qualification' as the LLB degree. The section goes on to acknowledge that the LLB degree can be obtained at any university registered in the Republic, after pursuing for that degree in two ways: either as '(i) a course of study of not less than four years; or (ii) a course of study of not less than five years if the LLB degree is preceded by a bachelor's degree other than the LLB degree ....'. While these courses of study are the only current pathway to practice, the Act is prospective in force, and so any persons who obtained a legal qualification under the previous legislation will still be able to practice law (section 114 of the Legal Practice Act). Historically, an undergraduate Baccalaureus Procurationis (B Proc) and a three-year Bacculaureus Iuris were offered as a pathway to practice, albeit with the caveat that only those persons with an LLB could be admitted as an advocate or be appointed as a judge.

Section 26 also sets out that a person may meet the Act's requirement of a minimum qualification where they have 'satisfied all the requirements for a law degree obtained in a foreign country, which is equivalent to the LLB degree' and is recognised by the South African education regulatory framework. However, this path to practice is limited by section 24(2)(b) of the Act which sets out that only South African citizens or permanent residents in the Republic can be admitted to practice. This means that foreign nationals may not practice law in South Africa unless permanent residency is acquired. This particular provision was subject to a constitutional challenge in *Rafoneke and Others v Minister of Justice and Correctional Services and Others (Makombe Intervening)* [2022] ZACC 29. However, South Africa's Constitutional Court found that the discrimination against foreigners was not unfair. The current position thus remains that – despite obtaining a South African LLB degree, or a foreign degree recognised as its equivalent – only those persons who are citizens or permanent residents may be admitted to practice law in South Africa.

The Higher Education Act 101 of 1997 is the enabling legislation for all higher education in South Africa, including legal education at universities. In general, the Act deals with the establishment of the Council on Higher Education (the CHE); management of public and private universities; and governance and financing of higher education. The CHE is particularly important as it advises the Minister of Education and Training on all higher education issues and is responsible for quality assurance and promotion through the Higher Education Quality Committee.

The LLB degree, along with all other university degrees in South Africa, must comply with the requirements of the National Qualifications Framework Act 67 of 2008 (NQFA). Any university that wishes to offer the LLB must register such degree under the South African Qualifications Authority (SAQA) (see https://www.saqa.org.za/) which is empowered by the NQFA. This process entails accreditation within the policy processes of the Higher Education Qualifications Sub-Framework (HEQSF) determined in terms of section 27(k)(iv) of the NQFA.

In 2017, the meaning of 'university' in section 26 of the Legal Practice Act was the subject of litigation. One of the then legal profession regulators (the KwaZulu-Natal Law Society) refused to register articles of clerkship of aspirant attorneys with an LLB degree from a private higher education institution (the Independent Institute of Education (Pty) Ltd – the 'IIE'). The Law Society contended that a private higher education institution – even if accredited by SAQA to teach an LLB as the IIE was – was excluded by the reference to 'university' in section 26 of the Legal Practice Act. It contended that the Act only contemplated public universities or those private universities that were registered in terms of the Higher Education Act. However, it was common cause that it was impossible for the IIE to register as a private university since the Minister of Education had not yet finalised regulations setting out criteria that had to be met, as required by the Act. The matter reached South Africa's apex court in *Independent Institute of Education (Pty) Limited v Kwazulu-Natal Law Society and Others* [2019] ZACC 47 where the Constitutional Court simply found that the word 'university' in section 26 should be given its ordinary grammatical meaning, and not that ascribed in the Higher Education Act, thus allowing the regulator to recognise the LLB qualification.

In applying for accreditation of an LLB degree, a university must consider the South African Qualifications Authority level descriptors which are set out in the SAQA *Level Descriptors for the South African National Qualifications Framework* (2012) and seek to adhere to these descriptors. These Level Descriptors can be described generally as 'a statement of learning achievement at a particular level of the NQF that provides a broad indication of the types of learning outcomes and assessment criteria that are appropriate to a qualification at that level' (SAQA 'Level Descriptors' 2012). While many degrees are programme-based, the LLB qualification is listed as 'generic': Bachelor of Laws. This effectively means that the essential minimum required outcomes and their assessment criteria have been identified in an abstract way and are not linked to a preconceived curriculum (content) – as is the case in other jurisdictions vis-à-vis their LLB degrees (for eg, in England and Wales, an LLB law degree covers seven compulsory core modules). These level descriptors are complemented by critical cross-field outcomes (CCFOs) which are generic in nature. They can be described as the broad, overarching outcomes towards which all SAQA programmes work – not only the LLB programme (Dednam [2012]). They are intended to provide the basis for lifelong learning, personal growth, honest business acumen, critical, creative thinking and aesthetic appreciation. However, as seen below, these CCFOs appear to have been overtaken by the Council on Higher Education's work on the LLB programme from 2014 onwards.

Thus, while the design of an LLB curriculum at a university in South Africa is expected to reflect the progressive nature of the SAQA level descriptors and CCFOs, it has really been the two relatively recent documents produced by the Council on Higher Education (CHE) that has influenced the sequencing and content of the curriculum. It is probable that section 16(1)(d) of the South African Constitution informs this structure since it guarantees 'academic freedom and freedom of scientific research'. Nevertheless, universities have to follow the principle of these two CHE documents. The first document is the *Higher education qualifications sub-framework: Qualification standard for Bachelor of Laws (LLB)* (2015) and the second document is *The state of the provision of the Bachelor of Laws (LLB) qualification in South Africa* (2018). The former document was produced in 2015, in consultation with the stakeholders in legal education and the profession. The second document was produced as a report of the national review of LLB programmes in South Africa in November 2018.

The focus of a standards statement – such as the one drafted for the LLB – is the relationship between the purpose of the qualification, the attributes of a graduate that manifest the purpose, and the contexts and conditions for assessment of those attributes (LLB Standards Framework [2015]). These ideas are captured in the two main sections of the LLB standards framework. The first section sets out the CHE's perspective on the context and process for the development of the LLB standards. It is then further sub-divided into two parts: one setting out the broader process of developing standards and another setting out the process for the LLB specifically. Section 2 sets out the actual standards for the LLB degree. It is, in turn, divided into three parts, namely a preamble, the standards and guidelines. The preamble requires that all LLB degrees in South Africa have to address the values of transformative constitutionalism, responsiveness to social justice, responsiveness to globalisation and responsiveness to ever-evolving information technology. In general, the standards framework sets out the LLB degree's stated purpose as offering 'a broad education that develops well-rounded graduates'. To achieve this goal, the sub-goals include knowledge of the values and principles of the Constitution of the Republic of South Africa, 1996; a critical understanding of the basis of the discipline of law; the ability to apply this knowledge; and the ability to be accountable and responsible. The standards for the evaluation of the LLB are then set out as follows: (1) graduates of the LLB must show *knowledge of the law* and this includes both the 'black-letter law' and 'some knowledge of a discipline other than law'. The latter reference is further qualified as requiring 'sufficient breadth and depth to provide understanding of a coherent range of fundamental concepts in the discipline and competence to perform basic tasks involving relevant knowledge and skills'. (2) LLB graduates should also *exhibit certain skills.* These include both critical thinking skills and research skills. And research skills, in turn, specifically include appropriate referencing skills. (3) LLB graduates should also include *applied competences* and these include ethics and integrity; communication skills and literacy; numeracy; information technology; problem solving; self-management and col-laboration; transfer of acquired knowledge; and 'agency, accountability and service to the community' which further includes 'social justice imperatives'.

As set out in the entry on South Africa (Contemporary Legal Education), the content of the LLB and even the CHE standards framework has been subject to contestation primarily on the need for decolonised teaching (Madlalate [2022]) and being fit for purpose (CHE [2018]).

Practical vocational training

Section 27 of the Legal Practice Act requires the Legal Practice Council (the regulatory authority of the legal profession) to draft rules determining the minimum conditions and procedures for the registration and administration of practical vocational training.

These Rules (originally published under General Notice 401 in Government Gazette 41781 of 20 July 2018 but amended from time to time) set out that any person wishing to qualify to be admitted and enrolled as an attorney– apart from the education requirement set out in the Legal Practice Act (viz inter alia have an LLB as set out below) will be required to have passed a competency-based assessment. This assessment covers – at a minimum – the practice and procedure in the Magistrates' and High Courts of South Africa; the practice and procedure relating to the winding up and distribution of the estates of deceased persons; the practice, functions and duties of an attorney, including the ethical duties of an attorney; and a knowledge of accounting necessary for the keeping of accounting records referred to the Legal Practice Act.

Similarly, those persons with an LLB wishing to practice as an advocate are required to pass a competency-based assessment which also covers the practice and procedure in the Magistrates' and Highs Courts and the practice, functions and duties of an advocate, including the ethical duties of an advocate. Where the person intends to practice as an advocate conducting a trust account practice, that person must also pass an assessment on the accounting necessary for the keeping of accounting records referred to in the Legal Practice Act.

HELEN KRUUSE

References

Council on Higher Education. (2015). *Higher Education Qualifications Sub-Framework Qualification Standard for Bachelor of Laws (LLB)*.

Council on Higher Education. (2018). *The state of the provision of the Bachelor of Laws (LLB) qualification in South Africa*, available at https://www.che.ac.za/publications/reports/state-provision-bachelor-laws-llb-qualification-south-africa.

Carmichael, T. and Stacey, A. (2006). 'Perceptions of SAQA's critical cross-field outcomes as key management meta-competencies', *South African Journal of Business Management*, 37, p. 1.

Dednam, M.J. (2012). 'Knowledge, skills and values: Balancing legal education at a trans-forming law faculty in South Africa', *South African Journal of Higher Education*, 26, p. 926.

Higher Education Act 101 of 1997.

Independent Institute of Education (Pty) Limited v Kwazulu-Natal Law Society and Others [2019] ZACC 47.

Legal Practice Act 28 of 2014.

Madlalate, R. (2022). 'Legal Education in South Africa: Racialized Globalizations, Crises, and Contestations', in Garth, B. and Shaffer, G. (eds), *The Globalization of Legal Education: A Critical Perspective*, Oxford University Press.

Rafoneke and Others v Minister of Justice and Correctional Services and Others (Makombe Intervening) [2022] ZACC 29.

South African Qualifications Framework, 'Level Descriptors for the South African National Qualifications Framework', available at https://www.saqa.org.za/level-descriptors-for-the-south-african-national-qualifications-framework/.

103. Sustainability and legal education

Introduction

Achieving a sustainable future is one of the grand challenges of our times. The current climate emergency and recurrent human rights violations in global supply chains are just two topical issues that demonstrate why sustainability is of such significance in the twenty-first century. However, whilst sustainability is an important concept, there is no specific UK Act of Parliament for sustainability, nor a clearly defined Law of Sustainability. Including sustainability in the legal curriculum is therefore not a straightforward matter.

However, law has several important interactions with sustainability. Promoting 'sustainability' or 'sustainable development' is not only the goal of some (new) laws; rather, these concepts are expressly included in the letter of laws. For example, Article 3(3) of the Treaty on European Union stipulates the European Union's aim that it 'shall work for the sustainable development of Europe'. Also, the 17 UN Sustainable Development Goals – which were adopted by the United Nations in 2015 'as a universal call to action to end poverty, protect the planet and improve the lives and prospects of everyone, everywhere' – highlight the global importance of sustainable development at the highest political level.

This entry analyses both the present and the possible future role of sustainability in legal education. It first establishes the definition of sustainability, before analysing how the concept overlaps with different areas of law. The next part discusses to what extent sustainability is already (knowingly or unknowingly) part of the legal curriculum. Based on this, it is argued that there is scope to develop a new area of law called 'Sustainability Law'. More generally, including sustainability aspects in the legal curriculum would contribute to the work of UNESCO to promote Education for Sustainable Development.

What is sustainable development?

The terms 'sustainability' and 'sustainable development' are frequently used in political and public discussions, but do not necessarily carry the same meaning for everyone. To reflect practical reality and to avoid confusion, this chapter uses both terms interchangeably (Rühmkorf [2018]).

Until the last decade, the term 'sustainability' was mainly shaped at the international level, particularly by the UN Environmental Conferences, starting with the first UN Conference on the Human Environment in Stockholm in the year 1972 (Michelsen and Adomßent [2014]). The UN World Commission on Environment and Development, set up in 1983 and led by the Norwegian Minster President Gro Harlem Brundtland, developed the following definition in its final report in 1987: 'Sustainable development meets the needs of the present without compromising the ability of future generations to meet their own needs' (Brundtland [1987]).

This definition understands sustainable development as a process. Based on this definition, the common understanding of 'sustainable development' focusses on the three dimensions of environmental, social and economic sustainability (Purvis, Mao and Robinson [2019]). These three dimensions are linked with each other (Sieben [2003]). Some argue that sustainability means more than simply adding the three dimensions to each other (Ekardt [2009]). Otherwise, the global and intergenerational aspect could easily be overlooked (Halfmaier [2016]).

More recently, it was argued that 'definitions of sustainable development must be revised to include the security of people and the planet' (Griggs et al 2013]). Consequently, Griggs et al. propose amending the definition from the Brundtland Commission to 'development that meets the needs of the present while safeguarding Earth's life-support system, on which the welfare of current and future generations depends'. According to this amendment the three-pillar model of sustainable development would need to be understood as an interlocked concept. This entry adopts the proposal from Griggs et al. because it recognises that sustainability can only be pursued within an overarching framework that puts the safety of the planet first. This approach is also in line with the concept of planetary boundaries which constitute the boundaries within which humanity can safely act (Rockström et al [2009]).

A new field of law? Towards 'sustainability law'

There is no established 'Law of Sustainability' in the same way there is Criminal Law, Property Law or Company Law. This means that no clearly defined field of law exists (yet) in this area. However, it does not follow from this that there is nothing that could be taught, learnt and researched in law under the umbrella of 'Sustainability Law'. Indeed, it will be argued below that there is scope to develop a new area of law.

Given the important role of sustainability at both the international and national level, one can expect a growing number of laws aimed at promoting sustainability. The UN Sustainable Development Goals, the reference to sustainable development in the EU Treaty and in EU Directives (e.g. the Corporate Sustainability Reporting Directive) as well as national laws (e.g. section 87 of the German Joint Stock Corporations Act) are all part of a developing trend towards using law as an instrument to promote greater sustainability.

In light of this, the question is whether it can be argued that there is already a 'Law of Sustainability' or, at least, whether there is scope to develop such an area of law. Due to space constraints, this issue can only be touched on here. New areas of law have been developed over time as law had to keep up with societal developments and new technical innovations. Environmental Law, IT Law and Medical Law are all examples of areas of law that did not exist a century ago, but which are now widely taught and researched areas of law (Hope [1991]).

There is literature on the question of how to determine whether a new field of law has been developed. Hamilton [1990] applies two necessary criteria for determining whether a scholarly field exists. These two criteria are: (i) academic scholarship, and (ii) law school courses. Related to the area of food law & policy, Linnekin and Broad Leib [2014] build on Hamilton's work and apply ten criteria to assess the state of the field. In addition to the two criteria from Hamilton, they also assess issues such as 'academic conferences' and 'academic centres'.

The two criteria from Hamilton [1990] will be applied here, but a limitation of this analysis is that a full-scale assessment of all the different criteria is not possible within the space limits of this chapter. Regarding the first cri-

terion – academic scholarship – a brief search for the term 'Sustainability Law' produced 743 hits on Google Scholar since 2019. The search term 'The law of sustainable development' yielded 282 results. On Westlaw UK, similar searches were conducted for articles that contain these two terms. Here, 'sustainability law' produced 14 results and 'law of sustainable development' seven hits. Whilst the numbers on Westlaw are significantly smaller, this search engine is more focussed on UK law journals than Google Scholar. Yet, the fact these two search terms are already expressly used in legal articles supports the argument that there is, indeed, an evolving field of law.

A first small-scale general Google search related to the second criterion from Hamiliton – law school courses in the area – also produced, inter alia, the following relevant results: A short online course called 'Law and Sustainability: Tackling Global Environmental Challenges' by the University of Oxford; a module called 'Law and Policy for Sustainability' at the University of Exeter; an LLM called 'Law – Environment, Sustainability and Business (LLM)' at the University of Essex. The latter finding also supports the third criterion from Linnekin and Broad Leib 'degree programmes'.

As noted, these are just snapshots rather than full-scale assessments of the criteria. However, these initial findings are important indications that the criteria from Hamilton are likely to be met and that, at least, some of the further criteria from Linnekin & Broad Leib would also be met. Given the increasing societal and political importance attached to the different pillars of sustainability and recent legislative developments, one can expect more journal articles, modules and also degree programmes in this area.

Defining the actual contours of this evolving new field of law will be an issue for future research and this question will be shaped by practices in modules, related degree programmes and indeed by future textbooks. As a starting discussion, this chapter will contribute some initial suggestions for topics that could be part of a module 'Sustainability Law', focussing on commercial/private law. Starting from the three-pillar understanding of sustainable development, this module would include the social, environmental and economic aspects of sustainability. Hence, it would principally cover a broad range of legal areas and issues which is illustrated by the following examples:

i.   Social pillar: This does not only include human rights generally (as protected by the state), but also encompasses the role of business with regards to human rights. For example, it includes transparency laws that require companies to publish their record on social aspects (e.g. the duty to publish an annual modern slavery and human trafficking statement pursuant to section 54 of the UK Modern Slavery Act 2015) and it also includes human rights due diligence laws (e.g. The 2021 Act on Corporate Due Diligence Obligations in Supply Chains in Germany).
ii. Economic pillar: This particularly overlaps with laws that require businesses to take a more long-term approach to business as opposed to pursuing short-term strategies such as section 172 of the UK Companies Act 2006.
iii. Environmental pillar: This is broader than what was traditionally understood as 'Environmental Law'; it also covers regulation that is aimed at addressing climate change.

There are several Directives in the European Union aimed at promoting more sustainability which were either recently passed or proposed. These include the right to repair in contract law, new rules on greenwashing and on sustainable finance. Both these new regulations and the examples above show that there is scope to comprehensively and systematically study the range of interactions of legal regulation with the concept of sustainability. Such a thorough study of the manifold relationships of law with sustainability can only be achieved through a separate new legal field called 'Sustainability Law'.

Education for sustainable development in the legal curriculum

In addition to creating a new field of law, the concept of sustainability can also be addressed in other individual modules. Such an integration would complement the creation of a new field of law. The pedagogical reason for this parallel approach is that promoting sustainability is such a significant issue in the twenty-first century that it should not purely

be looked at on its own, but additionally should also feed into all relevant modules across the legal curriculum. This approach would mean that existing modules would both: (i) address new regulation in their area that are aimed at promoting sustainability, eg the 'right to repair' in contract law, and (ii) scrutinise whether existing debates in their area already address topics that overlap with the three dimensions of sustainability.

The latter point (ii) is not to be underestimated. Longstanding debates can be linked with sustainability but use different terminology. A concrete example are discussions in company law and corporate governance about the role of stakeholders (as opposed to shareholder value) and long-termism. These discussions overlap with the economic pillar of sustainability. Whereas those debates should, of course, continue to use the terminology that they are accustomed to (the common terminology here could include: stakeholder value; pluralism; long-termism), module leaders could also alert students, overlaps with sustainability. Such a practice would help students appreciate the manifold dimensions of sustainability. More importantly, this would also be appropriate in light of the UN and EU's focus on the concept of sustainable development. In fact, the United Nations Educational, Scientific and Cultural Organization (UNESCO) focusses on promoting Education for Sustainable Development (ESD). The UN has tasked UNESCO to be leading on ESD globally. The current global framework is called 'ESD for 2030'.

UNESCO defines ESD as giving

> learners of all ages the knowledge, skills, values and agency to address interconnected global challenges including climate change, loss of biodiversity, unsustainable use of resources, and inequality. It empowers learners of all ages to make informed decisions and take individual and collective action to change society and care for the planet. ESD is a lifelong learning process and an integral part of quality education... (UNESCO, 2020)

Some universities have already expressly taken up this idea by working towards integrating the concept of sustainable development into the teaching of all university subjects (e.g. University of Sheffield [2023]). The aim is to make the concept relevant to all students as part of their journey to graduation. Law schools can make a significant contribution to this development both through pointing out overlaps of existing debates with sustainability and through creating new modules called 'Sustainability Law' which are aimed at systematically and comprehensively studying the increasing overlap between the concept of sustainability and legal regulation.

ANDREAS RÜHMKORF

References

Brundtland, G.H. (1987). 'Our Common Future: Report of the World Commission on Environment and Development', UN-Dokument A/42/427.
Ekart, F. (2009). 'Nachhaltigkeit und Recht – Eine kurze Anmerkung zu Smeddinck, Tomerius/ Magsig und anderen juristischen Ansätzen', Umweltpolitik & Umweltrecht, p. 233.
Griggs, D. et al. (2013). 'Sustainable development goals for people and planet', Nature, 496, p. 305.
Halfmaier, A. (2016). 'Nachhaltiges Privatrecht', Archiv für civilistische Praxis, 216, p. 717.
Hamilton, N. (1990). 'The Study of Agricultural Law in the United States: Education, Organization, and Practice', Arkansas Law Review, 43, p. 503.
Hope, R.A. (1991). 'Review: The Birth of Medical Law', Oxford Journal of Legal Studies, 11, p. 247.
Linnekin, B. and Broad Leib, E. (2014). 'Food Law & Policy: The Fertile Field's Origins and First Decade', p. 557.
Michelsen, G. and Adomßent, M. (2014). 'Nachhaltige Entwicklung: Hintergründe und Zusammenhänge', in Heinrichs, H. and Michelsen, G. (eds), Nachhaltigkeitswissenschaften, Springer.
Purvis, B., Mao, Y. and Robinson, D. (2019). 'Three pillars of sustainability: in search of conceptual origins', Sustainability Science, 14, pp. 681–695.
Rockström, JJ. et al. (2009). 'A safe operating space for humanity', Nature, 461, p. 472.
Rühmkorf, A. (2018). (ed), Nachhaltige Entwicklung im deutschen Recht: Möglichkeiten und Grenzen der Förderung, Nomos.
Sieben, P. (2003). 'Was bedeutet Nachhaltigkeit als Rechtsbegriff', Neue Zeitschrift für Verwaltungsrecht, p. 1173.
UNESCO, 'What you need to know about education for sustainable development', available at https://www.unesco.org/en/education-sustainable-development/need-know#how-does-unesco-work-on-this-theme-.
University of Sheffield, 'Education for Sustainable Development', available at https://www.sheffield.ac.uk/sustainability/education-sustainable-development.

104. Transnational legal education

Introduction

The transnational character of the legal academic community – hinted at in the range of nationalities of contributors to publications such as this one, as well as of participants at numerous international legal academic meetings in any given year – both reflects and projects the transnational character of legal education. As it happens, professors tend to be privileged workers in the global economy – among those for whom the promise of the free movement of people, goods, services, money, and ideas dependably delivers. That is, for those scholars who also happen to carry the right passport, who do not get denied travel visas or turned away at airports on their way to these international academic conferences.

Transnational legal education is not experienced by everyone in the same way. That is in part because of the various ways to theorise, practice, fund, design and teach transnational legal education. This entry aims to offer an introduction to this variety of approaches, while identifying and explaining certain cross-cutting themes. Two broad orientations to this subject stand out. On the one hand, 'transnational legal education' has emerged as something of a term of art, referring to programmes of study in 'transnational law.' On the other hand, 'transnational legal education' speaks to the cross-border character of the legal educational undertaking itself.

Education in transnational law

American jurist Philip Jessup coined the term, 'transnational law' in the 1950s to encompass private and public international law, as well as 'all law which regulates actions or events that transcend national frontiers' (Jessup [1956]). More recently, Carrie Menkel-Meadow has defined transnational law as 'the study of legal phenomena, including lawmaking processes, rules, and legal institutions, that affect or have the power to affect behaviors beyond a single state border' (Menkel-Meadow [2011]). More recently still, Peer Zumbansen refers to the 'flows of humans, data, viruses, goods, services, capital and other risks' in whose legal regulation a range of 'actors, norms and processes' are implicated (Zumbansen [2021]).

Conventionally, though, it is cross-border commercial transactions that enjoy pride of place in transnational law. Central is the flow of capital – the exchange of goods and services – in a global, neo-liberal normative context. On this account, the question of how to equip future providers of legal services with the requisite competencies for helping service ever-expanding capitalist needs takes primacy. As Darian-Smith notes, the emergence of this focus 'has accompanied the decentralization of state power and correlative privatization and deregulation of legal norms over the past forty years' (Darian-Smith [2021]). As she, and the other authors cited above argue, transnational law need not be conceived so reductively, however.

Understood more pluralistically, transnational law is concerned with the exercise of power in a global context, and more specifically, the norms, actors and processes involved in the exercises of, resistances to, and the disciplining of that power. Transnational legal education refers to the sites and modes in which knowledge is disseminated and acquired – and therefore created and questioned – about such phenomena. It is not just corporate profit-making that stands to benefit from legal professionals (or indeed people in any line of work) having a solid grounding in transnational law. The most pressing and complex challenges of our day – whose political and economic, as well as cultural, social and environmental effects have begun to reverberate already – demand every effort to instill a comprehensive and critical education in transnational law. That is, an education suitable to a legal world where the exercise of authority and the effects of injustice cut through and overcome, while weighing on the legal institutions, processes and norms of individual nation states as well as international systems.

Transnational education in law

From international student exchange programmes, academic conferences, and visiting professorships to institutionalised programmes of study built around one or more legal system, transnational legal education denotes the process of teaching and learning law defying unique jurisdictional containment. This entails programmes established in Irish law faculties in the 1990s to equip students with German and French legal and linguistic knowledge in light of opportunities in the burgeoning area then known as European Community Law. It also includes United Kingdom and Australian law faculties in the 2010s investing in new courses (and degrees) catering to the Federation of Law Societies of Canada curricular requirements to attract Canadian law students who pay international fees.

Transnational legal education predates the emergence of the discipline of transnational law, but nevertheless reflects the very tensions in economic forces, political values, and intellectual commitments constituting this field of research, study, and practice. The physical movement, social connections, cultural experiences and institutional opportunities transnational education in law offers stokes the fires of comparative analysis and critical self-reflection. Such border crossing has both formal and informal, purposive and unintended consequences for law teaching and learning. It is deeply tied to the virtues of the comparative method in legal research.

An historical perspective on transnational legal education shows a variety of factors shaping the manner in which the law and legal education proper to one jurisdiction come to have an impact on the people and institutions in another. Military, diplomatic, and imperial power, for example, do not just shape how borders come to be drawn; these factors also affect who or what traverses these borders, as well as when, why, and how they make their crossing. The Treaty of Paris in 1898 saw the United States take possession of Spain's archipelago colony in east Asia, marking the beginning of a period of major American influence on political, legal, and educational institutions in the Philippines (Sanchez Salcedo [2021]). In 1891, the French Minister of Foreign Affairs funded the establishment of the French law school in Cairo and in 1919, a homologous institution in Beirut, to serve as tools of French cultural diplomacy (Fillon [2011]). The efforts of Western countries to exercise influence on the legal and legal educational institutions in post-colonial African is evident in the work of the British Committee on Legal Education for Students from Africa, as well as that of the US agencies, the Ford Foundation and the Rockefeller foundation (Harrington and Manji [2003]). Recent critical histories challenge any assumption as

to the totalising nature of such influences, however (Bartie and Sandomierski [2021]).

The exportation (importation, appropriation or adaptation) of one nation's legal educational model to another shows broader ideological and political forces shaping transnational dimensions to legal education. Meanwhile, the establishment of specific academic programmes to entice domestic or international students seeking legal careers at home or abroad shows how markets for legal services and quests for increased institutional revenue sources shape educational structures, philosophies and practices. Imperialism and colonialism have deeply shaped the transnational character of legal education, both in forging transnational law and equipping legal educational activities with transnational dimensions. The global context of transnational law informs the institutional realities of transnational legal education.

Conversely, the global orientation of transnational law programmes also reflects market considerations in curricular design and delivery. The share of public investment, in the form of government dollars, for university education continues to decrease in many countries throughout the world. Law faculties find themselves in competition (within and across national borders) to attract tuition money, philanthropic donations, top students, and professorial talent. Supplying multinational corporations, law firms, and consultancy companies with workers to staff their coveted, highly paid positions means equipping students with the knowledge and skills those businesses are seeking. Importantly, as scholarship in the Third World Approaches to International Law tradition has laid bare for years, legal and educational institutions in the global south flow into and trickle down from conditions of startling inequality. As Muna Ndulo has observed, '[u]nless measures are taken to enable poor countries to participate in the process of internationalising legal education, globalisation is bound to marginalise poor countries' (Ndulo [2014]).

Defining and legitimating the legal in transnational legal education

Ideas such as universalism, liberalism, and nationalism have been – and continue to be – implicated in institution-building as well as legal theorising. In recent decades, anti-imperial, anti-colonial and anti-globalisation discourses have endeavoured to recognise and valorise otherwise suppressed legal orders, including those of First Nations in Canada (Cameron, Sari Graben and Val Napoleon [2020]). This has exposed just how 'transnational' the law (and legal education) can be, even within the jurisdictional borders of a given nation-state. Integrating multiple legal traditions, orders and systems into curricular design and pedagogical models may be as much a response to local values and intellectual necessities, as any market pressures – as witnessed in the development of the trans-systemic programme at the McGill University Faculty of Law (Morissette [2002]).

The identification and the legitimisation of law are two touchstones for transnational legal education, in both broad senses of the term. What law is and under what conditions it should serve as the authoritative guide to human interaction are questions that take on a global scale when pursued with a suitably broad context in mind. While the sky may be the limit on possible answers, the impact of those responses will invariably be felt under somebody's roof.

Inquiring into transnational legal education means turning to the international, and indeed globalising, context in which law is made, practiced, lived, learned, and taught. A more capacious, perhaps colloquial, interpretation of the expression transnational legal education permits a wide range of activities, institutional forms and pedagogical approaches to come into view – beyond the kinds of courses and pedagogies pitched to be useful to an enterprising global, legal professional elite. Ironically, perhaps, law faculties (and indeed, any university-based legal educational institution worth its salt) teaching transnational law (or teaching law transnationally) cannot escape exposing students to the contradictions, hypocrisies, and injustices prevalent within what might be called the transnational legal order. At the same time, such pedagogical engagement can help develop the conceptual tools and intellectual commitments necessary to imagine and build more just legal orderings. For that's what true education (as opposed to mere training) implies in relation to any legal order.

Conclusion

This look at transnational legal education acknowledges that there is no such thing as a view from nowhere. Although this entry aims to provide an overview of transnational legal education, it is rooted, nevertheless, in the author's own limited perspective. The specific handful of examples of transnational legal education cited present a partial, illustrative account, as opposed to a compendious, let alone comprehensive, treatment of the subject. The sheer range of potential vantage points is vast and the key to a solid grasp is never accepting a kind of generic, point-of-view-less formulation of what transnational legal education is, let alone what it could or, indeed, what it should be.

Transnational law – with its contested hierarchies and uneven experience by, say, migrants crossing the Mediterranean Sea at night and corporate board members ratifying international mergers over zoom by day – demands attention be paid to formal legal institutions as well as informal social impacts, implicit legal norms in addition to explicit political commitments. Transnational legal education requires the formation of human communities of teaching and learning that transcend not only geographical borders, but the cleavages that enable one segment of human beings to navigate such boundaries with an ease unknown to the bulk of the world's population. The major, complex questions arising from the widescale challenges confronting humanity commend a look at transnational law; discovering what institutions, norms and processes – and most importantly, transformative practices – will respond meaningfully to these questions is the work also of transnational legal education.

THOMAS MCMORROW

References

Bartie, S. and Sandomierski, D. (2021). (eds), *American Legal Education Abroad: Critical Histories*, NYU Press.

Cameron, A., Graben, S. and Napoleon, V. (2020). (eds), *Creating Indigenous Property: Power, Rights, and Relationships*, UTP.

Darian-Smith, E. (2021). 'Transnational Legal Education', in Zumbansen, P. (ed), *The Oxford Handbook of Transnational Law*, Oxford University Press.

Fillon, C. (2011). 'L'enseignement du droit, instrument et enjeu de la diplomatie culturelle française: L'exemple de l'Égypte au début du xxe siècle',

Mil neuf cent. Revue d'histoire intellectuelle, 1(29), p. 123.

Harrington, J. and Manji, A. (2003), 'Mind with mind and spirit with spirit: Lord Denning and African legal education', *Law & Society Review*, 30(3), p. 376.

Jessup, P.C. (1956). *Transnational Law*, Yale University Press.

Menkel-Meadow, C. (2011). 'Why and How to Study "Transnational" Law', *UC Irvine Law Review*, 1(1), p. 97.

Minas, S. (2021). 'Transnational Legal Education in China', in Zumbansen, P. (ed), *The Oxford Handbook of Transnational Law*, Oxford University Press.

Morissette, Y.-M. (2002). 'McGill's Integrated Civil and Common Law Program', *Journal of Legal Education*, 52, p. 14.

Ndulo, M. (2014). 'Legal Education in an Era of Globalisation and the Challenge of Development', *Journal of Comparative Law in Africa*, 1(1), p. 1.

Salcedo, S. (2021). 'Socratic Method, Philippine-style: To Unhave or Uphold?', in Bartie, S. and Sandomierski, D. (eds), *American Legal Education Abroad: Critical Histories*, NYU Press.

Zumbansen, P. (2021). 'Introduction', in Zumbansen, P. (ed), *The Oxford Handbook of Transnational Law*, Oxford University Press.

THOMAS MCMORROW

105. Trauma-informed legal education

Law schools have begun to integrate trauma theory into legal education following research showing that many lawyers have poor mental health (International Bar Association [2021]), and that one of the causes relates to lawyer's exposure to traumatic situations and distressed clients in their work (Levin et al [2011], Maguire and Byrne [2017]). Psychological trauma is a mental wound, or a 'psychic injury' from a distressing event or experience where the person feels seriously threatened, such as a near-death experience. Most adults have had at least one experience of trauma in their lives, and while symptoms are diverse, often subclinical and most people recover, in some cases the effects are serious and ongoing.

Many organisations have adopted the six guiding principles for a trauma-informed approach: safety, trust, connections, collaboration, empowerment, and culture, including gender and historical issues (Center for Disease Control and Prevention [2018]). These principles offer a framework for introducing trauma theory and emphasising aspects that are most relevant to the subject or area of practice. No one can be fully trauma-informed because trauma theory is constantly developing and there are many perspectives and opinions. Trauma theory is one of the rare domains about which a little knowledge is beneficial, making it accessible for all human service professions, including legal practice.

In the legal profession, trauma theory is particularly relevant to legal education because some habits and attitudes of lawyers contributing to poor mental health begin in law school, and an early understanding of trauma theory can be helpful (Thomson and Richardson [2023]). Among the problems emerging in law students are a cognitive bias with stigma against emotions and mental health concerns, tendencies to overwork, a fixed rather than growth mindset, motivations and values that are more extrinsic rather than intrinsic, and most worrying, a growing depressive mood with increased reliance on alcohol and drugs (Young [2021], Weiss [2022]) [Wellbeing/Mental Health of Law Students]. Trauma theory includes developmental strategies for coping with stress and can help students manage current and future challenges.

Before graduation, law students need to know that trauma is common in legal practice and they will need self-awareness and the skills to work with distressed people. Law is conventionally taught as a transactional process while many lawyers discover their work is largely relational and requires interpersonal skills. Areas of practice where clients are most likely to be traumatised include criminal law, family law, immigration law involving refugee/asylum clients, as well as social security law involving homelessness and poverty, personal injury law, and other areas involving highly distressed people. Legal clients in any area, including business, financial and corporate law, may have experienced distressing events that impact their emotions and thinking, affecting their decisions and behaviour. Trauma-informed lawyers are likely to be more effective in communicating with traumatised clients and witnesses, building trust and establishing a lawyer-client relationship less likely to re-traumatise or aggravate symptoms (Maki et al [2023]).

Trauma symptoms are potentially diverse, subject to the situation and personal issues. In serious cases a diagnosis of PTSD may be appropriate and a range of treatments, including counselling and medication is indicated (Graziano et al [2023], El Jowf et al [2023]). Common trauma symptoms involve three categories:

- Psychological (depressive mood, dissociation, reduced concentration, communication difficulties, and memory disturbance including blocked, chronological order and priorities);
- Behavioural (avoidance of topics or places, alcohol and substance abuse, sleep disturbance, reduced work efficacy, suicidal attempt); or
- Physical (rapid pulse, gut disturbances, hormonal changes, shallow breathing, increased sweating, metabolic disturbances, and inflammation).

Law students should know that trauma can be contagious and that lawyers working with distressed clients can develop secondary symptoms affecting their wellbeing and productivity. Lawyers may become distressed after working with survivors of violent assaults, or with perpetrators of violence and abuse. Lawyers may ruminate over their clients' suffering, or they may feel saddened or distressed about their prospects or following a bad outcome after spending significant time and effort on a case. Lawyers' exposure to trauma in their work can lead to related conditions including secondary trauma stress, burnout, compassion fatigue and vicarious trauma (James [2020]).

Learning trauma theory can begin by encouraging first year law students to start strategic self-care habits to maintain their wellbeing and develop the resilience that will help them during law school and later in legal practice. Self-care habits can lead to improved self-awareness to work effectively with traumatised people and stressful situations. The most beneficial habits include having a reflective practice, not over-working, maintaining a good diet, physical fitness, sleep hygiene, and recognising the need for professional help when required (Scott et al [2023], Albrecht [2023]). Common problems for law students include finding the time to follow through with a fitness regime and having rest breaks, and minimising the use of alcohol and drugs which can develop into a dependency and avoidance of important concerns. Early discussions of trauma theory with students can help to reduce the stigma against emotions and mental health issues that is common in law schools, and which prevents some students and graduates from getting help, disclosing symptoms or discussing their feelings or concerns about cases or other distressing events.

Some students have traumatic experiences in their backgrounds and may be vulnerable to retraumatising from case content and discussions in class. As these students learn trauma theory, including reasons for their vulnerability, they will be less likely to be 'ambushed' by their emotional responses and more inclined to get help if needed. Similarly in legal practice, some legal clients are vulnerable to traumatic events due to past experience or pre-existing conditions, especially adverse childhood experiences (ACE), depressive mood or another psychological condition. New lawyers should avoid judging clients or comparing their abilities to manage stressful events because they cannot know the person's history.

Trauma may develop from acute stress, following a single experience such as an assault or witnessing a car accident or a natural disaster. Chronic trauma may follow repeated experiences of abuse or exposures to violence, leading to ongoing symptoms that impact a person's overall well-being, including their ability to communicate and function. Complex trauma can develop from situations of ongoing stress as with survivors of domestic violence, child abuse, and refugee/asylum seekers escaping persecution. Some people develop a range of symptoms, which can aggravate or develop comorbid with pre-existing conditions.

Competency in legal practice requires lawyers to have at least a basic understanding of trauma theory so they can recognise the effects of trauma on clients and witnesses, to be able to work effectively and compassionately with distressed and traumatised people, and to avoid secondary harm in themselves. Graduating law students need to know that trauma symptoms are highly contextual, depending on the circumstances of the event, including the intensity, significance and nature of violence, the level of risk, and the person's background, preparedness, knowledge and well-being.

Trauma informed legal education integrates trauma theory and legal theory to enable students to learn the law in real-world contexts, since many clients have backstories with potentially traumatic circumstances relevant in some way to their legal situation. Students should know that in legal practice 'the facts' of a case may not be provided clearly and with useful detail as if read from a text, and it can be difficult to get the necessary information from a distressed client, or a client with a disability or someone who is recovering from trauma. Traumatised clients may need time to process a question during an interview, or to reflect and recover repressed details which they find distressing or painful to describe but are legally relevant. Surfacing those details may re-traumatise the client unless the lawyer has first established trust and created an environment where the client feels safe.

Some law schools offer clinical legal education [Clinical Legal Education (Overview)], which enables students to work under supervision directly with clients, including distressed or trauma-affected clients in some cases (Halder and Katz [2023], Kenny and Copeland [2021], Rose and Maylea [2023], Smyth et al [2021]). Clinical legal supervision encourages students to develop *reflective practices* to cope with emotionally challenging and difficult situations, and to develop the personal skills in self-management that will help them in legal practice (Leering [2023]). *Mindfulness*, for example, is a particularly useful life-skill for law students and lawyers (Rogers [2023]) [Contemplative Practices in Legal Education].

Law teachers need to be competent in interpersonal communications, and to engage with students beyond legally substantive or procedural issues. In classrooms and doctrinal courses, students can learn that laws and legal processes are inevitably human and political, and that justice and fairness cannot be guaranteed. Some students may be surprised to learn that legal systems are fallible and can contribute to traumatic experiences. For example, in criminal law, not-guilty clients may be found guilty and guilty clients acquitted, and in immigration law, asylum-seeking clients may be held in long-term detention for apparent political expedience. In everyday legal practice, clients coping with stress or trauma may have difficulty listening, concentrating, or understanding questions or advice. Shortness of time can cause additional stress to some clients, causing some to 'give up' their case, not wanting to persist or give evidence, regardless of the consequences. Witnesses and survivors of assaults may have confused memories, including 'gaps' in their recall of significant events. Lawyers who have a basic knowledge of trauma theory are more likely to understand a client's hesitancy, to engage with them effectively and find a way to build trust and hope in the legal process.

Law students need to be cautioned that some legal workplaces do not provide trauma-informed supervision and some are poorly managed, which can lead to workplace stress which in turn increases the risk of lawyers developing secondary trauma from distressed clients or traumatic cases. Some workplaces are internally competitive, with lawyers having high workloads and quantitative performance measures such as billing targets; some lawyers are exposed to bullying, discrimination, or sexual harassment which can be highly stressful and impact their work efficacy and wellbeing. Knowledge of trauma theory and its attendant developing self-awareness can help lawyers have the confidence to identify inappropriate behaviour in the workplace and to decide on appropriate responses and getting support.

Fortunately, a growing number of legal workplaces have adopted trauma theory into their management systems which helps to improve the milieu with a supportive and positive atmosphere. In particular, some legal managers are careful not to overwork lawyers and they encourage a collegial atmosphere rather than competitive, which can lead to high stress in some lawyers and poor decision-making. Many workplaces have trauma-informed supervisors who help lawyers develop strategies in difficult cases, to recognise and accept what they cannot change, and to learn from their experiences.

A growing number of legal workplaces have trauma-informed Employee Assistance Programme services and some supervisors encourage new lawyers to get regular counselling with an outside psychologist, not necessarily for therapy, but to support the lawyer as a knowledgeable and trusted friend. Individually, lawyers can use trauma theory to help resolve and integrate distressing thoughts and feelings, remembering to engage their character strengths, to accept the limitations of their role and the legal system, and to recover and maintain their confidence, competence and wellbeing despite the challenges of their work. Rather than learning 'on the job' after graduation, it is safer for everyone and more effective for law students to integrate trauma theory into their understanding of legal practice as they develop their professional identity in law school.

COLIN JAMES

References

Albrecht, E.A. (2023). 'The Importance of Self-Care for New and Young Lawyers', American Bar Association – GP Mentor.

Al Jowf, G.I., Ahmed, Z.T., Reijnders, R.A., de Nijs, L. and Eijssen, L.M.T. (2023). 'To Predict, Prevent, and Manage Post-Traumatic Stress Disorder (PTSD): A Review of Pathophysiology, Treatment, and Biomarkers', *International Journal of Molecular Sciences*, 24(6), p. 5238.

Atkinson, M. and Castles, M. (2023). 'Supporting Reflective Practice and Writing in Clinical Legal Education in a Digital Technological Era', in Atkinson, M. and Livings, B. (eds),

Contemporary Challenges in Clinical Legal Education, Routledge, p. 24.

Center for Disease Control and Prevention (CDC). (2018). 'Infographic: 6 Guiding Principles To A Trauma-Informed Approach'.

GERS. (2020). 'Trauma Informed Legal Practice Toolkit', Golden Eagle Rising Society – The Law Foundation of British Columbia.

Graziano, R.C., Brown, W.J., Strasshofer, D.R., Yetter, M.A., Berfield, J.B., Haven, S.E. and Bruce, S.E. (2023). 'Posttraumatic stress symptoms, posttraumatic growth, and personality factors: A network analysis', *Journal of Affective Disorders*.

Haldar, D. and Katz, S. (2023). 'Preventing Vicarious Trauma and Encouraging Self-Care in Clinical Legal Teaching', in Atkinson, M. and Livings, B. (eds), *Contemporary Challenges in Clinical Legal Education*, Routledge.

International Bar Association. (2021). *Mental Wellbeing in The Legal Profession: A Global Study*, International Bar Association.

James, C. (2020). 'Towards trauma-informed legal practice: A review', *Psychiatry, Psychology and Law*, 27(2), p. 275.

Kenny, M.A. and Copeland, A. (2021). 'Teaching clinic within a practice of injustice', *Teaching Migration and Asylum Law: Theory and Practice*.

Leering, M. (2023). 'Integrative Reflective Practice in Canada and Australia: Enhancing Legal Education, Pedagogy, and Professionalism', Queen's University.

Levin, A.P., Albert, L., Besser, A., Smith, D., Zelenski, A., Rosenkranz, S. and Neria, Y. (2011). 'Secondary Trauma Stress in Attorneys and their Administrative Support Staff Working with Trauma-Exposed Clients', *The Journal of Nervous and Mental Disease*, 199(12), p. 946.

Maguire, G. and Byrne, M.K. (2017). 'The Law Is Not as Blind as It Seems: Relative Rates of Vicarious Trauma among Lawyers and Mental Health Professionals', *Psychiatry, Psychology and Law*, 24(2), p. 233.

Maki, H., Florestal, M., McCallum, M. and Wright, J.K. (2023). (eds), *Trauma-Informed Law: A primer for lawyer resilience and healing*, American Bar Association.

Rogers, S.L. (2023). *The Mindful Law Student: A Mindfulness in Law Practice Guide*, Edward Elgar Publishing.

Rose, M. and Maylea, C. (2023). 'The case for implementing legal clinical supervision within legal practice, and recommendations for best practice', *Griffith Law Review*, p. 1.

Scott, H., Killian, K., Roebuck, B.S., McGlinchey, D., Ferns, A., Sakauye, P., Ahmad, A., McCoy, A. and Prashad, N.A. (2023). 'Self-care and vicarious resilience in victim advocates: A national study', *Traumatology*, 29(3), p. 368.

Smyth, G., Johnston, D. and Rogin, J. (2021). 'Trauma-Informed Lawyering in the Student Legal Clinic Setting: Increasing Competence in Trauma Informed Practice', *International Journal of Clinical Legal Education*, 28(1).

Thomson, C. and Richardson, K. (2023). 'Wellbeing and vicarious trauma: personal reflections on support for students, practitioners and clinicians in family law', in Jones, E. and Strevens, C. (eds), *Wellbeing and Transitions in Law: Legal Education and the Legal Profession*, Springer, pp. 225–251.

Weiss, D.C. (2022). '11% of law students had suicidal thoughts in the past year, survey finds; what can law schools do?', *ABA Journal*.

Young, K.M. (2021). 'Understanding the Social and Cognitive Processes in Law School that Create Unhealthy Lawyers', *Fordham Law Review*, 2575, p. 89.

106. USA (contemporary legal education)

In 2022, 196 accredited US law schools educated 116,723 students in a three-year graduate education programme leading to the conferral of a Juris Doctor ('JD') degree (American Bar Association ('ABA') [2023a]). Most US law schools are, or are affiliated with, private non-profit educational institutions but about 44 per cent (86 total) are public institutions (ABA [2024a]). A tiny fraction are for-profit entities.

Student body diversity presents a mixed picture. In 2016, the gender balance among law school students switched from majority male to majority female; by 2023, 56 per cent of US law students were female (Pisarcik [2024]). Some racial minorities are underrepresented as compared to their percentages in the national population. For example, 12.4 per cent of the national population and 8.4 per cent of law school graduates are African American, and 18.4 per cent of the national population and 13.2 per cent of graduates are Latinx. Meanwhile, individuals of Asian descent comprise 5.6 per cent of the national population and 6.4 per cent of law graduates (Nelson et al. [2023] at 81). Social stratification is pronounced, as shown by the strong correlation between parents' social class and the rankings of the schools that students attend (Nelson et al. [2023] at 85).

Unlike in many countries, US legal education takes place among students who already have their four-year bachelor's degree (ABA [2024b]). A lucrative sub-industry involves the advanced training of lawyers who already have their law degrees, in programmes that award LLM or SJD degrees (Silver and Ballakrishnen [2018] at 42). Many LLM students hold law degrees from non-US law schools. LLM programme revenue has traditionally bolstered US law school budgets, especially in the higher ranked schools LLM students tend to attend (Silver and Ballakrishnen [2018] at 42 n.13).

In JD programmes, first year students typically study torts, contracts, property, constitutional law, civil procedure, criminal law, and legal writing (Law School Admissions Council ('LSAC') [2024]). Professional responsibility, upper-level legal writing, and skills credits are also mandatory to complete these programmes [ABA, Standards 303(a)(1) and 303(a)(2) [2024b]). In recent decades, law schools have added more international perspectives [Ribstein [2011] at 1656), along with electives in rapidly developing areas of law including environment, intellectual property, cyberspace, technology, health care, and more (Georgetown [2024]). Students also continue to select courses with an eye toward the traditional subjects tested on state bar exams, such as corporate law and secured transactions (Kuris [2023]).

After graduating, students seeking licenses to practice law must take the bar exam of the state in which they wish to practice (ABA [2018]). Unlike many other countries with Anglo-derived legal systems – such as Canada – US law graduates must find their first jobs on their own (Girard [2021] at 70); there is no formal apprenticeship phase. Some students obtain judicial clerkships, which confer prestige on the graduates selected (Simon [1986] at 129–30).

US legal education is highly stratified. The law schools that are regarded as the most elite tend to send their graduates into the law jobs regarded as most elite – this includes large law firms, commonly called 'big law,' and the most prestigious non-profit and public sector positions (Nelson at al. [2023] at 69, 89, 119). Since 1990, the publication of ordinal law school rankings by a for-profit magazine called the *US News & World Report* has exacerbated a rankings 'war.' As a result, law schools often allocate resources to improving their performance in accordance with the indices the magazine weighs most heavily (Solimine [2006] at 300). These indices include law faculty reputation, employment rates nine months after graduation, bar passage rates, admitted applicants' undergraduate grade point averages ('GPAs'), and students' scores on the standardised Law School Admission Test ('LSAT') (LSAC 2024b). Law schools' heavy reliance on LSAT scores continues to elicit controversy. Some argue that these scores objectively compare students coming from different educational backgrounds, but others argue that the scores are insufficiently predictive of future success in law practice, among other problems (Caron and Gely [2006] at 8).

Mounting criticism of the *US News* rankings led top-ranked Yale Law School to announce in 2023 that it would cease providing proprietary data to *US News* for use in their ranking evaluations (Hartocollis [2022]). Yale Law's dean criticised *US News'* reliance on students' full-time employment rates at graduation and nine months after graduation as devaluing new graduate employment in the public service and public interest sectors, where finding the jobs *US News* classifies as full-time and long-term tends to take more time (Farrell [2022]). Forty law schools followed Yale in ceasing to cooperate with *US News* in 2023 (Hartocollis [2023]). The magazine continues to publish rankings, relying on publicly available information for law schools that do not provide proprietary information (Hartocollis [2022]). The magazine has been changing its algorithm from year to year, such as by placing more weight on bar passage rates and average student loan debt burdens, and decreasing the weight given to faculty reputation. As a result, rankings outside the top tier have been swinging widely, though the top tier has remained fairly stable (Hartocollis [2023]).

Another important development stems from the US Supreme Court's 2023 decision restricting US educational institutions' use of race as an 'affirmative action' factor in admissions decisions (*Students for Fair Admissions v. Harvard* [2023]). Observers predict this recent decision may accelerate a pre-existing trend of placing less weight on, or no longer requiring, LSAT scores for admissions.

US law schools have been undergoing economic upheaval. Law schools traditionally served as reliable revenue generators for the universities with which they were affiliated (Wu [2013]), but this began to change after the Great Recession of 2008–09. The recession exacerbated shrinkage in the job market for US law graduates (US Bureau of Labor Statistics [2019]), already begun by globalisation, the deskilling of legal work, technological innovation, and other pressures that have restructured the legal profession throughout the world (Susskind [2010] at 19–22; Polden [2016] at 951–52). News that law graduates were finding it harder to obtain jobs has led fewer students to apply to law schools (Fuller et al. [2021]; Polden [2016] at 951). With decreases in the size of the applicant pool, many law schools have encountered financial problems. Some, seeking to maintain high undergraduate GPA and LSAT scores, have opted to shrink their overall class size, further reducing tuition revenues (Jones [2013]). Simultaneously, law schools have to compete more aggressively for students. To do so, law schools, especially those outside the top tier, have begun offering higher tuition discounts than they had previously (Burk et. al [2018] at 586). Most ceased offering need-based financial aid, concentrating their resources on so-called 'merit' awards to compete for talent (Reynolds [2021] at 96).

This move to 'merit'-based tuition discounting has had further ramifications. Because high LSAT scores correlate strongly with socio-economic advantage (Nelson et al. [2023] at 85–86), this strategy exacerbated problems of access to, and affordability of, legal education for students from less privileged backgrounds (Reynolds [2021] at 97). So-called 'merit' tuition discounting has perversely resulted in students with the most modest family resources graduating with the highest educational debt (Ward [2017]). Observers predict that disruption will eventually cause a shake-up resulting in fewer surviving law schools (Henderson and Morriss [2006] at 165–66; Burk et al [2018] at 587), but this has not yet occurred outside the lowest rankings tier.

Even with the economic shakeup in US legal education, law schools retain a relatively resource-rich advantage as compared to legal education in many other countries (Carle [2021] at 360). This is especially true of law schools higher in the rankings, which remain comfortably funded through high tuitions, endowments, and private contributions. As a result, they can operate high-profile academic centres, enrichment programmes, and pay high faculty salaries (Carle [2021] at 361). Ample research funds further support faculty and reduce teaching loads. Virtually all US law schools manage to fund at least a few and sometimes more than a dozen student-edited law journals, in which faculty throughout the US and beyond can publish their work (Carle [2021] at 361). The number of such US publications totaled more than 650 in 2024 (Max Planck Law [2024]).

Nonetheless, budget demands lead many schools to continue to offer an initial tuition sticker price that only socio-economically advantaged students can pay without heavy borrowing through student loans. The rationale for high tuition has been the expectation that graduates will increase their earning power by a margin far greater than the cost of their student loans (Tretina and Hahn [2022]). But as prospects for highly-paid employment decline, the economic rationality of paying high tuition for a law degree declines too (Tretina and Hahn [2022]).

Social inequality manifests itself not only in law school rankings and student career prospects, but also in the demographics of the legal professoriate. Unlike in many countries, the core instructors in US law schools are full-time career professors who tend to have graduated from top-tier schools, augmented with non-tenure track and adjunct faculty (Syverud [2002] at 14–15). Tenure is typical for the more privileged full-time, career law professors, though it is currently under threat across US academia (Worthen [2021]).

Gender stratification is likewise evident, with men tending to dominate doctrinal teaching and tenure-line positions and women concentrated in legal writing and other typically non-tenured jobs (Tiscione [2019] at 117–19). This is especially true in institutions at the top of the prestige hierarchy (Tiscione [2019] at 98–99). Faculty members have filed, and sometimes prevailed, in lawsuits alleging sex and race discrimination in compensation and other terms of employment (Hodder and Li [2022]). A major challenge to US legal education going forward is eliminating all forms of inequity reflected by and perpetuated through its institutions (Rhode [2013]; Nelson et al. [2023]).

SUSAN CARLE

References

Students for Fair Admissions v. Harvard, 143 S. Ct. 2141 (2023).

American Bar Association ('ABA'), List of ABA-Approved Law Schools [2024a] available at https://www.americanbar.org/groups/legal_education/resources/aba_approved_law_schools/public_law_schools/.

ABA, 2023–2024 Standards and Rules of Procedure for Approval of Law Schools [2024b], available at https://www.americanbar.org/groups/legal_education/resources/standards/.

ABA, Profile of the Legal Profession [2023] https://www.abalegalprofile.com/legaled.html#:~:text=In%202022%2C%20for%20the%20first,%25%2C%20from%20the%20previous%20year.

Burk, B.A., Organ, J.M. and Rasiel, E.B. (2018). 'Competitive Coping Strategies in the American Legal Academy: An Empirical Study', *Nev. L.J.*, 19, p. 583.

Carle, S.D. (2021). 'Rethinking Assumptions about the Global Influence of US Legal Education', in

Bartie, S. and Sandomierski, D. (eds), *American Legal Education Abroad: Critical Histories*, p. 353, New York University Press.

Caron, P. and Gely, R. (2006). 'Symposium: Dead Poets and Academic Progenitors: The Next Generation of Law School Rankings', *Indiana L.J.*, 81, p. 1.

Farrell, H. (2022). 'Yale Law School Pulled Out of the U.S. News Rankings. Here's Why', *The Washington Post*, 18 November, available at https://www.washingtonpost.com/politics/2022/11/18/collegesrankingsyale/.

Fuller, A., Mitchell, J. and Randazzo, S. (2021). 'Law School Loses Luster as Debts Mount and Salaries Stagnate', Wall Street Journal, 3 August, available at https://www.wsj.com/articles/law-school-student-debt-low-salaries-university-miami-11627991855.

Georgetown, 'Course Offerings', available at https://www.law.georgetown.edu/tech-institute/academics/course-offerings/.

Girard, P. (2021). 'American Influences, Canadian Realities', in Bartie, S. and Sandomierski, D. (eds), *American Legal Education Abroad: Critical Histories*, p. 67, New York University Press.

Hartocollis, A. (2022). 'Yale and Harvard Law Schools Withdraw from the U.S. News Rankings', *New York Times*, 16 November, available at https://www.nytimes.com/2022/11/16/us/yale-law-school-us-news-rankings.html.

Hartocollis, A. (2023). 'Elite Law Schools Boycotted the U.S. News Ranking. Now, They May Be Paying the Price', *New York Times*, 21 April, available at https://www.nytimes.com/2023/04/21/us/21nat-us-news-rankings-law-medical-school.html.

Henderson, W.D. and Morriss, A.P. (2006). 'Student Quality as Measured by LSAT Scores: Migration Patterns in the U.S. News Rankings Era', *Indiana L. J.*, 81, p. 163.

Hodder, R. and Li, I. (2022). 'U-M Law Professor Sues UMich, Claims Racial- and Gender-based Discrimination', *Michigan Daily*, 29 August, available at https://www.michigandaily.com/news/news-briefs/u-m-law-professor-sues-umich-claims-racial-and-gender-based-discrimination/.

Jones, A. (2013). 'Top Law School Cuts Admissions', *The Wall Street Journal*, 11 March, available at https://www.wsj.com/articles/SB10001424127887324281004578354490114584144.

Kuris, G. (2023). 'Law School Applicants and the Bar Exam', *U.S. News*, 18 September, available at https://www.usnews.com/education/blogs/law-admissions-lowdown/articles/what-law-school-applicants-should-know-about-the-bar-exam.

Law School Admission Council ('LSAC'). (2024a). 'What You Can Expect from Your Law School Experience', available at https://www.lsac.org/

discover-law/what-you-can-expect-your-law
-school-experience.

LSAC, 'The LSAT'. (2024b), available at https://
www.lsac.org/lsat.

Max Planck Law. (2024). 'The American Law
Review Market: Background and Publication
Strategies', available at https://law.mpg.de/event/
the-american-law-review-market-background
-and-publication-strategies/.

Nelson, R.L. et al. (2023). *The Making of Lawyers'
Careers: Inequality and Opportunity in the
American Legal Profession*, University of
Chicago Press.

Pisarcik, I. (2024). 'Women Outnumber Men in
US Law School Classrooms, but Statistics Don't
Tell the Full Story', *Jurist*, 17 January, available at https://www.jurist.org/commentary/2024/
01/women-outnumber-men-in-us-law-school
-classrooms-but-statistics-dont-tell-the-full
-story/.

Polden, D.J. (2016). 'Leading Institutional Change:
Law Schools and Legal Education in a Time of
Crisis', *Tenn. L. Rev.*, 83, p. 949.

Reynolds, L. (2021). 'A Vehicle to Inequity: Law
School Merit Scholarships', *Conn. Pub. Int. L.J.*,
21, p. 96.

Rhode, D.L. (2013). 'Legal Education: Rethinking
the Problem, Reimagining the Reforms',
Pepperdine L. Rev., 40, p. 437.

Ribstein, L.E. (2011). 'Practicing Theory: Legal
Education for the Twenty-First Century', *Iowa L.
Rev.*, 96, p. 1649.

Silver, C. and Ballakrishnen, S.S. (2018). 'Sticky
Floors, Springboards, Stairways and Slow
Escalations: Mobility Pathways and Preferences
of International Students in U.S. Law Schools',
*University of California at Irvine J. International,
Transnational, and Comparative Law*, 3, p. 39.

Simon, W.J. (1986). 'Judicial Clerkships and Elite
Professional Culture', *J. Legal Educ.*, 36, p. 129.

Solimine, M.E. (2006). 'Status Seeking and the
Allure and Limits of Law School Rankings', *Ind.
L. J.*, 81, p. 299.

Susskind, R. (2010). *The End of Lawyers?
Rethinking the Nature of Legal Services*, revised
edition Oxford University Press.

Syverud, K.D. (2002). 'The Caste System and Best
Practices in Legal Education', *J. Ass'n of Legal
Writing Directors*, 1, p. 12.

Tiscione, K.K. (2019). 'Gender Inequality
Throughout the Legal Academy: A Quick Look
at the (Surprisingly Limited) Data', available at
https://scholarship.law.georgetown.edu/facpub/
2396.

Tretina, K. and Hahn, A. (2022). 'Is Law School
Worth It? 5 Factors to Consider', *Forbes Advisor*,
available at https://www.forbes.com/advisor/
education/law/is-law-school-worth-it/.

United States Bureau of Labor Statistics. (2019).
'Producer Prices in the Legal Services Industry
after the Great Recession', available at https://
www.bls.gov/opub/mlr/2019/article/producer
-prices-in-the-legal-services-industry-after-the
-great-recession.htm.

Ward, S.F. (2017). 'Affluent Students Get Law
School Merit Scholarships While Others Foot
the Bill, Study Finds', ABA Journal, available at https://www.abajournal.com/news/
article/affluent_students_get_law_school_merit
_scholarships_while_others_foot_the_b.

Worthen, M. (2021). 'The Fight Over Tenure is Not
Really About Tenure', *NYT*, available at https://
www.nytimes.com/2021/09/20/opinion/tenure
-college-university.html.

Wu, F.H. (2013). 'Where Law Schools Get Their
Money: Where Does All the Law School
Money Come From?', Above the Law, available at https://abovethelaw.com/2013/10/where
-law-schools-get-their-money/#:~:text=First
%2C%20law%20schools%20are%20what,they
%20receive%20to%20financial%20aid.

107. USA (history of legal education)

Legal education in the United States currently consists of a three-year graduate degree programme, the use of some form of the Socratic method in doctrinal classes, written examinations, the use of case books of appellate decisions, and the requirement of a Bar examination administered by a state in order to be admitted to the practice of law in that state. This model developed slowly over the course of the past two and a half centuries. Moreover, the fact that women now outnumber men in law schools, that women and racial minorities are law professors, and that many law schools strive for some form of racial diversity would have shocked early lawyers. Such developments occurred relatively recently and were a result of second wave feminism and the long Civil Rights Movement for racial equality. Other issues influencing the history of legal education include the desire of elite lawyers and academics to professionalise the law school and for it to function as a gate-keeper to the legal profession.

Early legal education: apprenticeship and proprietary law schools

As a young country the US lacked developed centres of legal learning such as the UK's Inns of Court, Oxford and Cambridge Universities or Continental Europe's medieval universities. Following the UK the US imported the Common Law, but lawyers had scant access to legal materials, making treatises such as that by William Blackstone a cornerstone of legal knowledge. The US's nascent legal profession was also primarily unregulated and entirely within the purview of individual states and not the federal government.

From the founding of the US and throughout the first half of the nineteenth century, lawyers primarily trained through apprenticeships where they worked as clerks in lawyers' offices and often paid a fee to do so. Although many of the US's leading judges, lawyers, and politicians received training though apprenticeships, the quality of training varied greatly. Since the apprenticeship system was based on the determination of a lawyer deciding to take on an apprentice, few women or racial minorities were provided with such an opportunity. But there were cracks in the system, and some were able to apprentice with family members or particularly open-minded lawyers. Macon Bolling Allan, a Black man who had apprenticed with an abolitionist attorney in Maine was admitted to the Maine Bar in 1844, eventually becoming a judge in North Carolina in the 1870s.

As discussed by Daniel R. Coquilette and Bruce Kimbell, in *On the Battlefield of Merit: Harvard Law School, The First Century*, a number of stand-alone proprietary law schools grew out of the apprenticeship system. Litchfield Law School, opened in 1784, was the first law school in the country. It arose from the popularity of students apprenticing with attorney Tappings Reeve whose office was located in Litchfield, Connecticut, a thriving commercial town. As the number of young men seeking to be apprentices to Reeves outgrew the space and time for individualised attention, Reeve established Litchfield, which attracted pupils from across the still small country. The teaching method at Litchfield was through morning lectures with students taking notes during the lecture and then carefully rewriting them. Other proprietary law schools were established, and often perished, in a number of states. None of these law schools accepted women who were considered ill-suited and too delicate in mind and body to be lawyers.

Legal education after the Civil War

The impact of the Civil War (1861–1865) on education as a whole was enormous. In its aftermath, education at all levels became more generally available and a host of Black colleges as well as women's colleges opened. Black colleges sought to educate formerly enslaved people who, in slave states, were often prohibited by law from becoming literate. Likewise, Black people and other racial minorities were routinely excluded from law schools in practice or by law. In the North such exclusions were informal, part of the admissions process. In the South, in the decades following the Civil War, such segregation was enacted into law. However, in 1869, before Jim Crow segregation descended over the South, Congress chartered Howard University, along with its law school, to specifically provide an institution that would accept Black students. Howard's first class of law students included former slaves. John Mercer Langston, the first dean of Howard Law School, had himself been denied admission to two law schools because of his race. The longstanding goal of Howard was to produce graduates who would help fight for racial equality and social justice. The importance of Howard cannot be overstated in terms of graduating Black lawyers, both men and women, who formed the backbone of a Black Bar. The first Black woman attorney to graduate from Howard was Charlotte E. Ray who received her law degree in 1872. Although underfunded, Howard graduated lawyers such as Thurgood Marshall and later Pauli Murray who would seek to dismantle segregation and discrimination during the long Civil Rights Movement. Other schools devoted to educating Black attorneys included Central Tennessee College from which Lutie Lytle graduated in 1897. Lytle, the daughter of former enslaved people, became one of the first women teaching law in the US.

Elite legal education was also being transformed. Bruce Kimbal in *The Inception of Modern Professional Education: C.C. Langdell, 1826–1906* examines how Charles Eliot, the President of Harvard, appointed Christopher Langdell as the first dean of Harvard Law School in 1870. Although there is some question as to whether Langdell was an innovator or populariser, he instituted a new method of teaching law whereby students would learn through reading appellate cases instead of treatises and Langdell's *Cases on Contracts* was the first such casebook. As explained by Kimbal, Langdell expected students to extract the principle or rule from such cases and apply it to other cases. For Langdell and his successors, law was a logical, scientific system. In the classroom, Langdell employed the Socratic method in which he would ask a question or provide a hypothetical scenario and guide students through a series of questions to test potential answers. This would come to be known as 'thinking like a lawyer' and would be one of the hallmarks of US legal education. Through the Socratic method students became active participants rather than passive recipients of legal knowledge. Langdell and his successors also transformed the law school faculty from consisting of lawyers who were primarily legal practitioners to one in which faculty were hired based on their academic success

in an elite law school. The elite reproduced the elite.

The continuing quest for equality in the twentieth century

Through the turn of the twentieth century and beyond, numerous law schools opened to educate immigrant and working-class students. Such schools often had night classes for working students. Elites feared these law schools and the lawyers that they graduated, claiming that they produced unethical and ill trained lawyers – the proverbial ambulance chasers. Yet these schools allowed large numbers of immigrant, working class, women and minority students to receive a legal education. Their graduates began diversifying the Bar at a time when elite schools often remained closed or unreceptive to women, Jews, Blacks, and a host of other minorities.

Phyllis Eckhaus in a 1991 ground-breaking law review article, 'Restless Women: The Pioneering Alumnae of New York University School of Law', explores how beginning in 1890, New York University Law School opened its doors to women, affirmatively welcoming them and graduating a cadre of women lawyers, who would become active social reformers and prominent in the long campaigns for women's suffrage, worker rights, and the peace movement. A few women also created their own law schools. In 1896, two women lawyers in Washington D.C. founded the Women's Law Class with approximately ten women students as many Washington law schools remained closed to women. Three years later, they incorporated the Washington College of Law which was a coeducational institution run by women and which employed female as well as male professors, administrators, and trustees. Some of their women graduates had successful careers in government and even the judiciary. Whereas the school ran on the principle of the importance of equality between men and women, such equality did not extend to race. No Black person attended the school until 1950. Even with the education of a small cadre of racial minorities and women attending law school, the reality is that their numbers remained small until the late twentieth century.

Still, elites continued their drive to create higher standards for legal education that included requiring an undergraduate degree to attend law school and creating increased barriers to enter the legal profession. As discussed by G. Edward White, in *American Legal History: A Very Short History*, the primary mission of the American Bar Association (ABA), founded in 1878, was to tighten state requirements regarding Bar admission while also ensuring that law schools acted as gatekeepers to the profession. Eventually the ABA would accredit law schools and sought to have states require graduation from an ABA accredited law school in order to take state Bar examinations. In 1915, the ABA spun off the American Association of Law Schools which focused upon creating greater uniformity in the content of legal education. These mandarin projects would take decades to complete.

Meanwhile, in the South, many law schools only admitted white law students. In 1950, Heman Marion Sweatt sued the all-white University of Texas Law School for violation of the Equal Protection Clause of the Fourteenth Amendment of the Unites States' Constitution. The Texas constitution specifically reserved the University of Texas for white students. Sweatt, in Sweatt v Painter, won the case in the United States Supreme Court and entered the University of Texas Law School in 1950. After being subjected to racial harassment, including cross burnings, he withdrew in 1951. For decades thereafter the Law School had no Blacks. Similar stories occurred throughout the South with some law schools refusing to admit Black people even after plaintiffs won numerous court cases challenging segregation. Throughout the 1970s, law school enrolment numbers for Black people and other minorities such as Chicanas, Indigenous people, and Asians were minute.

In contrast, the number of white women attending law school steadily increased with the rise of second wave feminism. However, as explored by Lani Guinier and her co-authors in *Becoming Gentlemen: Women, Law School, and Institutional Change*, for decades women still faced significant hostility both within law school and in the profession. Faculties and law school administrators remained significantly white and male. As late as 1998, women (primarily white) constituted only 20 per cent of fulltime law school faculty with the majority of such women in nontenured legal writing jobs. Throughout the 1990s and into the 2000s, dozens of studies were conducted showing women law students' discontent with their legal education and a profound sense of alienation. Derrick Bell, who was a Black Harvard Law School professor, describes in his autobiography, *Confronting Authority*, one of the most dramatic episodes in which he staged a year-long sit-in in his office, and eventually left Harvard, when Harvard Law School refused to hire a Black female professor under the rationale that no such woman was qualified. Likewise, the activism of women and minorities within the legal academy slowly changed the law school curriculum itself, pressuring schools to include classes in such topics as women and the law, race and the law, and race and feminist critical legal theory. Related to this was the creation of new law journals and student organisations devoted to civil rights, women, and gender and the law.

Efforts to bring racial minorities into law school to create true equality have had mixed success and reflect the larger social, economic, and political discrimination that still prevails. In 2023, the US Supreme Court, in *Fair Admissions v Harvard*, ruled that affirmative action, which is the ability of universities to use race conscious admissions to create diversity, is unconstitutional. Precisely what effect this will have on the ability to truly diversify law schools and the Bar remains to be seen but many are not hopeful.

FELICE BATLAN

References

Sweat v Painter, 339 U.S. 629 (1950).

Students for Fair Admissions v President and Fellows of Harvard, 600 U.S. 181 (2003).

Bell, D. (1994). *Confronting Authority: Confessions of an Ardent Protestor*, Beacon Press.

Coquilette, D.R. and Kimbell, B. (2015). *On the Battlefield of Merit: Harvard Law School, The First Century*, Harvard University Press.

Eckhaus, P. (1991). 'Restless Women: The Pioneering Alumnae of New York University School of Law', *NYU L. Rev*, 66, p. 1996.

Guinier, L., Fine, M. and Balin, J. (1997). *Becoming Gentlemen, Women, Law School, and Institutional Change*, Beacon Press.

Kimball, B.A. (2009). *The Inception of Modern Professional Education: C.C. Langdell, 1826–1906*, University of North Carolina Press.

White, G.E. (2013). *American Legal History: A Very Short History*, Oxford University Press.

108. USA (regulation of legal education)

Introduction

Regulation of legal education in the United States reflects the federal system generally characteristic of the US legal system, with federally authorised and state regulators operating simultaneously. These national and state regulations address different aspects of legal education and in this way form an intersecting web governing law schools and their activities and graduates. Further, states are not uniform in their approach to regulating legal education – certain states issue complex and detailed provisions and others do not, and in addition their regulations may address different topics. The result is a multifaceted approach to regulating legal education that can seem overly complicated and, at the same time, leaves certain important aspects relatively unregulated.

Federal regulatory authority is housed in the United States Department of Education, which has designated the Council of the American Bar Association's Section of Legal Education and Admissions to the Bar (the 'Council') as the official accreditation body for law schools. The Council is referred to here as a regulator by virtue of its accrediting function pursuant to Department of Education authority. Through the mechanism of accreditation, the Council accredits on the basis of one particular degree that law schools offer – the three-year JD degree that serves as a necessary condition in most US states to qualification for the right to practice law (ABA Standards [2023–2024]). Schools that satisfy this accreditation standard are referred to as ABA-approved law schools. Law schools that cannot satisfy the accreditation requirements must look to more general accrediting bodies for regulatory oversight; these may be regional rather than national.

Operating simultaneously to accreditation is regulatory oversight exerted by the states. Unlike the Council, state regulation does not generally take the form of accreditation; in fact, the states typically refrain from *direct* regulation of law schools at all. Rather, they exert regulatory influence over legal education through their control of the process to become licensed as a lawyer. The states determine the conditions necessary for licensure, which

almost always begins with legal education in the US, although certain states permit private study or training apart from a law school, for example (NCBE ABA Comprehensive Guide [2024]). State bar admission rules generally build on the accreditation regime of the Council – they accept graduation from an accredited JD programme as satisfying one of the basic conditions for Bar eligibility. In addition, certain states impose additional substantive requirements for eligibility to become a lawyer, from pro bono requirements (New York Rules §520.16) and additional training and course-work provided outside of law school (Delaware Supreme Court Rules), both of which apply to all graduates seeking admission in the state, to rules governing only a particular cohort of law graduates such as those who have not earned a US JD in an ABA-approved law school (New York Rules §520.6). Finally, Bar examiners also shape legal education, albeit not by directly imposing regulations. But topics tested on the Bar exam and the rapid coalescence around a uniform Bar exam has lent the National Conference of Bar Examiners important influence in this regard around which topics are taught in law school.

Regulators

The Council, the primary regulator of US legal education, is comprised of twenty individuals from four main professional backgrounds: legal education (administrators and faculty), higher education (university administrators and faculty, typically with no expertise or education in law, and members of higher education professional associations), practicing lawyers, and state supreme court judges and justices. The inclusion of members of the state supreme court judiciary is particularly relevant to the issue of regulation because it is the state supreme courts that generally have regulatory authority over licensing and admission – which in turn works as a direct or indirect influence over legal education. Council members are nominated by the nominating committee of the Section of Legal Education and Admissions to the Bar and elected by ABA members.

At the state level, while each state may adopt its own approach, it is common that the highest court in the state has authority over lawyer admission and licensing, either alone or in combination with the state legislature (Comprehensive Guide, Chart 1). In New York, for example, the state's highest court, the Court of Appeals, issues rules governing eligibility for admission that impact legal education in several respects (New York Rules). That court may designate particular organisations to help administer its rules and the admission and licensing process. In Illinois, for example, the Supreme Court has designated the Illinois Board of Admissions to the Bar in this role (Illinois Supreme Court Rules).

Content of regulation

The accreditation regime established by the Council focuses on just one aspect of contemporary US legal education: the three-year JD degree. To gain accreditation, a law school must comply with rules addressing a wide variety of matters including faculty governance (shared between the faculty and the dean); financial resources; general curricular requirements that specify course requirements regarding topic, nature of the course (doctrinal, experiential etc) and credit hours; overall credit hours required for the degree; faculty (focusing on full-time faculty); library and the facilities – including equipment and technology, and space for classes, collaborative learning and faculty offices, among others (ABA Standards). These mandatory rules shape the curriculum for law schools across the country and serve to tie together law students' experiences through common core experiences.

The consequence of a law school's JD programme being accredited is twofold: first, a JD from an ABA-approved law school satisfies the education requirement for bar eligibility in every US jurisdiction (Comprehensive Guide, Chart 3); second, students enrolled in degree programmes accredited by the Council have access to federally financed loans. (Barton [2019])

But the Council's accreditation regime leaves important aspects of legal education essentially unregulated because it does not address the degrees other than the JD. Law schools very commonly award such additional degrees, including Masters degrees for law graduates whose first degree in law was earned outside the United States (LLM, MCL, etc), doctoral degrees in law (SJD or JSD), and Masters degrees in law awarded to students who have not studied law in a bachelors

programme (MSL, for example). While every law school does not award each of these additional non-JD degrees, they are exceedingly common: according to the Section of Legal Education's statistics, in 2023 nearly 73 per cent of all ABA-approved law schools had students enrolled in one or more non-JD degree programmes, accounting for more than 16 per cent of law students overall (ABA JD/Non-JD Enrolment Data). The Council does not affirmatively accredit or otherwise regulate these non-JD degree programmes, but it requires its acquiescence in them. The standard for acquiescence is that the non-JD degree programme 'not interfere with the ability of the law school to operate in compliance with the Standards and to carry out its program of legal education' – meaning that offering the non-JD degree programme not interfere with the law school's JD degree programme (ABA Standards, Standard 313(c)). Apart from acquiescence, these non-JD programmes might be accredited by organisations that accredit other non-law degrees granted by universities and colleges, such as the Higher Learning Commission; the same organisations might accredit law school JD programmes that cannot satisfy the ABA Council's standards.

States also may fill in the gap left by the accreditation-acquiescence regime through Bar eligibility rules. This is most common with regard to the LLM degree that is commonly pursued by individuals who have earned their first degree in law outside of the US. The LLM, a one-year degree programme at most law schools, is sufficient, combined with legal education outside of the US, for Bar eligibility in certain states if its graduates have satisfied particular course and credit hour requirements, among other things. Course requirements might include certain substantive areas – such as professional responsibility and courses on the American legal system such as constitutional law or civil procedure – and certain skills-focused courses such as legal writing and analysis. Further, tested substantive fields might be targeted in the rules for these graduates, too (New York Rules §520.6(b)(3)(vi)). In this way, state regulation adds to that of the Council by addressing the legal education of a distinct cohort. Reflecting forces affecting higher education generally, international students – the majority of whom have enrolled in Masters degree programmes – have comprised an important part of the US law student population for the last few decades and have contributed to the financial health of the law schools (Silver and Ballakrishnen [2018]).

Even combining national and state regulation, however, leaves areas of legal education relatively unregulated. This includes degrees described by the American Bar Association as 'academic Masters degrees for nonlawyers', meaning the graduates have no intention of using the degree to qualify as a lawyer (ABA, Post-J.D. & Non-J.D.). These degree programmes require acquiescence but are not subject to affirmative regulation through the accreditation process, and also are not addressed through state regulation related to Bar admission.

Conclusion

US regulation of legal education is not static. It is subject to forces shaping regulation of higher education generally, such as oversight of costs of higher education by the federal government and regulation of admission considerations that recently have been overturned by the United States Supreme Court. New initiatives in regulating lawyers also may influence the regulation of legal education, such as concerns about the availability of legal services for populations currently underserved by lawyers. Further, experiences during the pandemic with remote learning offer the basis for reconsidering rules mandating in-person learning. Finally, the Council has recently taken a more accepting approach to changes and experiments that law schools make to their programmes, which suggests important consequences may follow in the future.

CAROLE SILVER

References

American Bar Association Section of Legal Education and Admissions to the Bar, JD/Non-JD Enrollment Data (2023), available at https://www.americanbar.org/content/dam/aba/administrative/legal_education_and_admissions_to_the_bar/statistics/2023/2023-jd-non-jd-enrollment-final.xlsx.

American Bar Association Section of Legal Education and Admissions to the Bar, Post-J.D. & Non-J.D, available at https://www.americanbar.org/groups/legal_education/resources/llm-degrees_post_j_d_non_j_d/.

American Bar Association Section of Legal Education and Admissions to the Bar, Standards and Rules of Procedure for Approval of Law Schools. (2023–2024), available at https://www.americanbar.org/products/inv/book/433733786/.

Barton, B.H. (2019). *Fixing Law Schools*, NYU Press.

Delaware Supreme Court Rules, Part V, Subpart A, Rule 52, available at https://courts.delaware.gov/forms/download.aspx?id=182608.

Illinois Supreme Court Rules, Rule 702, available at https://ilcourtsaudio.blob.core.windows.net/antilles-resources/resources/7ae8a196-2a43-4484-9666-43098da60282/S_Ct_Rules_full.pdf.

National Conference of Bar Examiners and American Bar Association Section of Legal Education and Admissions to the Bar, Comprehensive Guide to Bar Admission Requirements. (2024), available at https://reports.ncbex.org/comp-guide/.

New York Rules of the Court of Appeals for the Admission of Attorneys and Counselors at Law, available at https://nycourts.gov/ctapps/520rules10.htm#B16.

Silver, C. and Ballakrishnen, S.S. (2018). 'Sticky Floors, Springboards, Stairways & Slow Escalators: Mobility Pathways and Preferences of International Students in U.S. Law Schools', *U.C. Irvine Journal of International, Transnational and Comparative Law*, 3, p. 39.

Students for Fair Admissions, Inc. v. President & Fellows of Harvard College and *Students for Fair Admissions, Inc. v. University of North Carolina* [2023] 600 U.S. 181.

109. Values and ethics in legal education

This entry opens by distinguishing broadly between values and ethics and their relationship with law. It then describes the various ways in which values and ethical discourse arise in legal education, distinguishing the general study of ethics and values in the curriculum from studying the specifics of lawyers' professional ethics.

Values, ethics, and law

Values can be understood as guiding beliefs, both moral and non-moral that motivate people to act in particular ways (Campbell [1935]). They are distinct from subjective preferences in that they operate as a higher ('second') order basis for evaluating wants and needs. Values tend to be seen as necessarily reflective of actual social practices and social relationships (e.g. Raz [2003]; Selznick [1992]) and to that extent offer some non-arbitrary though nonetheless plural and competing bases for action. We can also talk of institutional values in the sense that institutions like 'the law', or the courts, law schools and legal profession reflect certain terminal and instrumental values through their form and practices. This also means that, in the role of lawyer, or law student, or teacher, an individual may experience conflict between their personal and institutional (role) values, and one important question that might arise is how far, by opting-in to the role of law teacher, lawyer, judge, etc, one commits to adopting its values over one's own in cases of value conflict (see, e.g., Wendel [2014]).

Ethics can be seen as part of the solution to such value conflict. Ethics may be distinguished from values insofar as ethical norms give people a reason to select one of a set of competing values. To that extent a system of professional ethics is perhaps closer to a system of law than it is to the terrain of values per se, though ethical codes are often expressed more abstractly and at a higher level of generality than legal rules.

Values in legal education

Classical legal doctrinalism has been criticised for encouraging students to take a narrow, technocentric, view of the law. Outside of legal theory, it is said, moral questions about legal doctrine are overlooked or even discouraged, and critique is limited to questions about the logic and coherence of legal rules. This approach seems to leave students under-equipped to deal with moral complexity in legal settings. Research further suggests it may cause some reduction in students' public service values and motivations, and a loss of connection with feelings, personal values, and sense of self, with potentially negative consequences for student wellbeing (see, e.g., Sheldon and Krieger [2004]).

The narrow position has been increasingly challenged by scholarship in both public and private law theory, which seeks to uncover the work done by fundamental (social and moral) values in shaping specific legal fields and doctrines. While there is inevitable debate about the specific values implicit in and advanced by law, concepts such as human dignity, personal autonomy, equality, security, distributive and corrective justice are widely discussed in the literature. The question that follows for legal education is: what institutionally-speaking is the function or responsibility of legal educators when it comes to teaching (about) these legal values (Burridge and Webb [2007])?

The historically dominant approach in higher education, advanced by classical liberal education theory, is to advise moral neutrality on value debates, rather than see the university's role to inculcate specific values. In its strongest version, as advanced by nineteenth-century educationalists such as John Henry (Cardinal) Newman, university was seen as a process of educating the mind rather than building moral character, though as Bradney [2003] notes, there is a certain, important, slippage in Newman's thought whereby educating the mind should somehow result in a set of appropriate dispositions.

Critics of the classical position point to its tendency to be blind to its own moral location and valuations. Liberalism, it is said, cannot be morally neutral about its own values, and this is necessarily reflected in the values and practices of liberal legal education. This critique grounds two (related) alternatives to the narrow, classical, position. First, a number of scholars within the broadly liberal tradition acknowledge that the liberal mission is purposive; that it functions to develop in students what is variously described as a 'democratic intellect', 'democratic imagination' or sense of self as (global) citizen (see, e.g., Ward [2009]; Nussbaum [2003]). Secondly, scholars from both within the liberal tradition and beyond (particularly those operating through the lens of critical legal studies or 'outsider' jurisprudence) argue that legal education must also focus on alternative values, that are not valued in established legal discourse, as a way of demonstrating both how law currently responds (or not) to the complexities of value pluralism, and as a way of actively demonstrating how different value priorities could re-shape the law and individual legal outcomes.

Taken together these various approaches seem to emphasise four things: (i) the process aspects of values education, as enabling a way of thinking about and engaging with the world; (ii) relatedly, that the imaginative capabilities required make values education an education in sentiment, as well as reason; (iii) that an academic legal education is deeply contextual, and not just about learning the law and 'legal' values (strictly construed), and (iv) that it may be legitimate to *advance* certain value positions that relate to the conceptions of law being studied. This last point takes seriously the idea of the university as a public space for the exploration of oppositional ideas and values. Some writers caveat this by suggesting that even an education *in* values must stop short of imposing a single notion of the good on all others, otherwise it breaches the principle of 'permissive neutrality' and undermines the core liberal value of toleration (Burridge and Webb [2007]).

A problem with much 'values talk' in legal education is that it is implicit and often presented under the guise of 'public policy' (Cownie [2004]; Rochette [2011]). The pedagogical response to this has been to argue that a more explicit legal values education needs to be advanced via a range of strategies that pervade the student learning experience. At the core is dialogue – what Bradney [2003] describes as a conversation between student and teacher about legal values, and how to choose between values. This requires a concomitant commitment to training in normative reasoning across (more of) the curriculum. Experiential legal education is also valued for its ability to support students in developing empathy, and an appreciation of the lived reality of legal problems. Values education requires cross-cultural awareness and sensitivity to issues of cultural safety. Exposure to a wide range of literature and media, not just standard legal texts is encouraged, as a further way of strengthening 'narrative imagination' (Nussbaum [2003]) and building that (multi-) cultural competence.

Ethics in legal education

In talking about ethics in legal education it is helpful to distinguish between metaethics and applied and professional ethics. The term 'legal ethics' is sometimes used in ways that crosses the metaethical-professional divide. This entry follows prevailing practice in using it to focus on teaching the ethical obligations and professional responsibilities of the practising legal profession. It should also be noted that law programmes may also contain specialist subjects that address the relationship between law and other areas of applied ethics, such as health law, media law, and law and technology (including the ethics of artificial intelligence).

Legal ethics is a relatively young sub-discipline and addition to the law school curriculum, having emerged in its modern form only since the 1970s (Webb and Hard [2023]). As a matter of regulation, legal ethics is required in most of the major common law jurisdictions, as a part of either professional or academic legal education, and sometimes both. It is thus a mandatory component on degree courses in Australia, Canada (since 2015, though a graduation requirement of most law schools before that), New Zealand, and the USA. It is not currently mandated at degree level across the UK jurisdictions, though it does form part of professional legal training requirements. Globally, however, there remains significant variation, with many jurisdictions lacking a systematic approach to teaching legal ethics as an academic or professional subject.

The purposes of legal ethics teaching, correspondingly, tend to be conceived of in various ways. Many courses offer a relatively narrow 'survey' approach which focusses on understanding and applying the detailed 'law on lawyering'. This doctrinal emphasis is sometimes supported by some consideration of philosophical legal ethics or jurisprudence as a way of presenting a deeper basis for justification and critique, e.g., in terms of examining the idea of a role morality, or understanding the interplay between professional, legal and societal values and value priorities. Increasingly, however, enabling students simply to know the rules and their ethical foundation has been seen as insufficient, and course design is recognising that students need to engage more deeply with professional context and/or the processes of professional judgement and decision-making (e.g. Green [1997]; Rhode [2009]). These newer approaches draw on a variety of interdisciplinary bodies of knowledge, including empirical research into the legal profession and its organisational practices, moral development theory, and behaviourial ethics (see, e.g., O'Grady [2014]) as well as on experiential learning methods.

This diversity of objectives also tends to flow through into the selection of one or other of four curriculum models:

- The dedicated course, where the subject is taught through a single subject or unit, which may be either mandatory or elective; this remains probably the most common approach.
- The integrated or combined model, where legal ethics and professionalism is integrated into another subject or concentration, such as legal research and writing, legal system, civil and/or criminal litigation, or a course more generally on the legal profession.
- The 'pervasive' method, whereby there is no single specialist course, but ethical issues are integrated across the curriculum offering (Rhode [1992]). This is often seen as the 'gold standard' approach, especially if combined with a clinical offering (Rhode [2009]), though it does create significant challenges as regards coordination and assuring proper curriculum coverage.
- The clinical legal studies method, whereby all students have some exposure to working with clients in a live or simulated clinical setting. Some formal teaching of legal ethics may be incorporated into clinic preparation, or provided pervasively, or required as a pre- or co-requisite to the clinic.

Notwithstanding these developments, the subject is widely regarded as a difficult one to teach and to locate in the curriculum. Concern has been expressed that it suffers from confusion regarding its mission, that conventional legal pedagogies are ill-suited to it, and that,

in an academic context, it remains difficult to contextualise. Even in more professionalised course settings, teachers may lack the time and skills to effectively discuss conflicts of personal and professional values, or to help students develop strategies for having effective value-based conversations or dealing with poor ethical work climates and the wellbeing issues those can raise (McMorrow [2022]).

These difficulties are likely exacerbated outside the established common law jurisdictions that dominate the academic literature, because the transferability of concepts and teaching approaches that they have adopted cannot simply be assumed. Civil law systems, for example, do not have a unitary legal profession, and while the core ethical values attached to the advocate's role tend to be similar, systems of regulation and the values attached to different legal functions can vary significantly (Goldstein Bolocan [2002]). There is also growing debate in Africa and Asia as to how received professional ethics might be adapted to take better account of distinctively African or Asian value priorities (e.g., Senghore [2018]). Nonetheless, as with values-based learning more generally, there is strong cross-national interest in the use of experiential learning and reflective practice techniques as an emerging form of best practice.

JULIAN WEBB

References

Bradney, A. (2003). *Conversations, Choices and Chances: The Liberal Law School in the Twenty-First Century*, Hart Publishing.

Burridge, R. and Webb, J. (2007). 'The Values of Common Law Legal Education: Rethinking Rules, Responsibilities, Relationships and Roles in the Law School', *Legal Ethics*, 10, p. 72.

Campbell, C.A. (1935). 'Moral and Non-Moral Values: A Study in the First Principles of Axiology', *Mind*, XLIV, p. 273.

Cownie, F. (2004). *Legal Academics: Culture and Identities*, Hart Publishing.

Goldstein Bolocan, M. (2002). (ed), *Professional Legal Ethics: A Comparative Perspective*. CEELI Concept Paper, American Bar Association.

Green, B.A. (1997). 'Less is More: Teaching Legal Ethics in Context', *William & Mary Law Review*, 39, p. 357.

McMorrow, J.A. (2022). 'Teaching Legal Ethics in a Client-Centred Profession', in Jacobs, R.M. (ed), *Educating in Ethics Across the Professions:*

A Compendium of Research, Theory, Practice, and an Agenda for the Future, IAP.

Nussbaum, M.C. (2003). 'Cultivating Humanity in Legal Education', *University of Chicago Law Review*, 70, p. 265.

O'Grady, C.G. (2014). 'Behavioral Legal Ethics, Decision Making, and the New Attorney's Unique Professional Perspective', *Nevada Law Journal*, 15, p. 671.

Raz, J. (2003). *The Practice of Value*, Oxford University Press.

Rhode, D.L. (1992). 'Ethics by the Pervasive Method', *Journal of Legal Education*, 42, p. 31.

Rhode, D.L. (2009). 'Legal Ethics in Legal Education', *Clinical Law Review*, 16, p. 43.

Rochette, A. (2011). 'Values in Canadian Legal Education', *European Journal of Current Legal Issues*, 2, available at https://www.bailii.org/uk/other/journals/WebJCLI/2011/issue2/rochette2.html.

Sanghose, A.A. (2018). *Democracy, Human Rights, and Governance in The Gambia: Essays on Social Adjustment*, CENMEDRA.

Selznick, P. (1992). *The Moral Commonwealth: Social Theory and the Promise of Community*, University of California Press.

Sheldon, K.M. and Krieger, L.S. (2004). 'Does Legal Education Have Undermining Effects on Law Students? Evaluating Changes in Motivation, Values, and Well-Being', *Behavioral Science and Law*, 22, p. 261.

Ward, I. (2009). 'Legal Education and the Democratic Imagination', *Law and Humanities*, 3, p. 87.

Webb, J. and Hard, N. (2023). 'Introduction: Surfing the Waves of Legal Ethics Scholarship', in Webb, J. (ed), *Leading Works in Legal Ethics*, Routledge.

Wendel, W.B. (2014). *Ethics and Law: An Introduction*, Cambridge University Press.

110. Wellbeing/mental health of law students

The World Health Organization defines mental health as '[a] state of mental well-being that enables people to cope with the stresses of life, to realise their abilities, to learn well and to work well, and to contribute to their communities' (World Health Organization [2022] at 8). Across time, jurisdictions and measures, empirical studies have assessed law students' self-reported likely mental health and wellbeing at levels that are lower than those reported by the general population and/ or the subset of the general population that best reflects the law student sample from which data was collected. This is not to suggest that all or even most law students have a mental health condition, but that law students as a group may be at greater risk of suffering from a mental health condition. The term 'mental health condition' is used in this entry to include recognised mental health disorders and psychosocial disabilities, and 'mental states associated with significant distress, impairment in functioning or risk of self-harm' (World Health Organization [2022] at 8).

Empirical studies of law students' mental health and wellbeing

Law students' mental health and wellbeing has been studied in the United States of America (USA) since the 1960s (Sheldon and Kreiger [2004], [2007]). This body of knowledge is now supplemented by empirical studies from Australia (Kelk et al [2009]), Germany (Rabkow et al [2020]), New Zealand (Sotardi et al [2022]), and the United Kingdom (UK) (Jones, Samra and Lucassen [2019]).

There are many variations in methodology of the empirical studies of law students' mental health and wellbeing. Some have focused on single law school populations. Others have drawn a student sample from several law schools. The nature of the law schools from which student samples have been drawn vary in ranking, reputation, and predominant teaching method. For example, in older studies from the USA, the Socratic dialogue was the predominant teaching method experienced by law student sample groups. Some studies have focused on law students in their first-year or final year of study. Others have reported on a sample group drawn from the general population of law students at a university or universities. Some studies are longitudinal, others focus on a point in time. In either case there is variation in the time in the academic year at which data is collected. Older studies have relied on law students completing paper surveys, with more recent studies collecting data from law students via online surveys.

Due to variations in the professional study of law across jurisdictions, empirical studies from the USA have collected data from law students who have completed undergraduate study prior to enrolling in the professional study of law. In other jurisdictions, such as Germany, New Zealand and the UK, prior undergraduate study is not required for enrolment in the professional study of law, meaning that data has been collected from law students who are likely to be comparatively younger than their USA counterparts. In Australia, the professional study of law may be undertaken at undergraduate or postgraduate (JD) level, and data has been collected from law students studying at one or both levels.

In many studies, particularly older studies, law student sample groups were undertaking their law studies face-to-face and on campus, but some recent studies have collected data from law students engaged in distance study.

The measures used to assess law students' self-reported mental health and wellbeing across jurisdictions also vary. Measures employed include the Kessler–10 or Kessler–6 scales which screen for non-specific psychological distress (including anxiety, depression or rage) in large populations; the DASS–21 Depression, Anxiety and Stress Scale which, as its name suggests, is designed to measure likely levels of depression, anxiety and stress; the BEES (Brief Emotional Experience Scale), used to measure positive or negative influences on individuals and their predominant emotional state; the PHQ-9 Patient Depression Questionnaire; the GHQ-12 (General Health Questionnaire) which screens for general mental health disorders; the Warwick-Edinburgh Mental Well-being Scale; and the BDI (Beck Depression Inventory). All these instruments indicate a likelihood, rather than a diagnosis, of a mental health condition.

Notwithstanding the variations described above, law students are consistently reported as having a higher likelihood of occurrence of the mental health condition under investigation than does the general population and/or the subset of the general population from which the law student sample is drawn (Kelk [2009]). There is also consistency in findings from empirical studies from the USA and Australia that law students' self-reported higher risk of experiencing a mental health condition occurs a short period after they have begun their studies, and that this risk does not decrease across their time at law school (Sheldon and Krieger [2004]).

Empirical studies of university students' mental health and wellbeing

There is less universality in the results from the fewer empirical studies that have compared the self-reported mental health and/or wellbeing of law students with that of students from other disciplines. As is the case with the empirical studies of law students, there is variation in the methodology and focus of the cross-disciplinary studies. Some have compared law students with students engaged in other professional courses of study, such as medicine, engineering, or veterinary science. Some have focused on students studying at a single university, others on students studying across several universities. Most studies report that law students have a greater likelihood of a mental health condition than do students studying other disciplines (Lewis and Cardwell [2019]). However, it is important to consider these results in the light of consistent findings across time, jurisdictions and measures that university students have a greater likelihood of suffering a mental health condition than the general population and/or the subset of the general population that best reflects the student sample group (Auerbach [2016]). Possible explanations for this are that: (1) period of university study is associated with social and academic transitions not necessarily experienced by the non-university student population, and (2) university students appear more likely to report university related factors, rather than non-university related factors, as adversely affecting their mental health and wellbeing.

Female and minority students' mental health and wellbeing

Female students, including female law students, are generally reported to have a higher risk of a mental health condition than male students (Kelk [2009]), but three additional factors are relevant to these findings. The first is that many recent general and law student focussed empirical studies report greater numbers of female participants than male participants. The second is a generally recognised trend for females to be more willing to admit to a mental health condition. Finally, there is evidence that male and female students may have different experiences of university and law school with female students being more likely to report negative experiences. There is also some evidence that students from lower socio-economic backgrounds and minority students are also more likely to self-report a score on a screening instrument that indicates a likelihood of increased risk of a mental health condition.

Consequences of suffering a mental health condition

Suffering from a mental health condition may affect detrimentally a student's ability to make the most of their abilities, and to work and study well. A small number of empirical studies have reported law students' self-reported alcohol consumption or use of prescription and non-prescription drugs, but it is not clear whether the law students who report frequently engaging in these behaviours also self-report a greater likelihood of suffering from a mental health condition. Studies conducted in the early 2000s report that some law students indicate they would be reluctant to seek help if they experienced a mental health condition because of the adverse impact they perceive this might have on their study or employment prospects (Kelk [2009]).

Explanations for law students' reported mental health and wellbeing

Non-empirical studies have offered several explanations for law students' self-reported likely rates of mental health conditions including the use of the Socratic dialogue teaching method; assessment practices such as heavily weighted final examinations or (conversely) too many assessments, the use of grading curves, and a lack of feedback; competition between students to attain high grades to gain an advantage when seeking employment; learning to think rationally and analytically, or in other words, 'like a lawyer'; and the adversarial nature of law. Some of these factors may feature across jurisdictions, but others are not necessarily a characteristic of legal education outside the USA, such as for example, the Socratic dialogue teaching method. Further, given that university students are at greater risk of a mental health condition than the general population, it is less certain, if at all, that there is something about the professional study of law across time and jurisdictions that creates a greater likelihood of risk of law students experiencing a mental health condition.

In the empirical studies focusing on law students, self-determination theory (SDT) is the theoretical model most frequently used to explain students' self-reported levels of likelihood of suffering a mental health condition. SDT is a theory of human motivation which holds that positive or intrinsic (internal) motivation and goals are linked to optimal wellbeing which, in turn, is generated by regular experiences of autonomy, competence, and relatedness. As Sheldon and Kreiger ([2007] at 885) explain:

> ... people need to feel they are good at what they do or at least can become good at it (competence); that they are doing what they choose and want to be doing, that is, what they enjoy or at least believe in (autonomy); and that they are relating meaningfully to others in the process, that is, connecting with the selves of other people (relatedness).

In instances where findings relating to law students' likelihood of suffering from a mental health condition are analysed through a SDT lens, aspects of the law school curriculum and/or learning environment in which the student sample was engaged have been suggested as likely to lower one, more, or all of students' experiences of competence, autonomy, and relatedness and so reduce their intrinsic motivation and goals and, in turn, their reported wellbeing (Sheldon and Kreiger [2004]). For example, a learning environment where a strict grading curve is used so that the number of students who are able to achieve high grades is limited may adversely affect students' feelings of competence. A curriculum with few options or that does not foster student engagement in a choice of active or deep learning activities may reduce students' feelings of autonomy. A learning and social environment that allows students limited opportunities to build constructive and positive relationships with teachers and peers may negatively affect relatedness.

How should law schools respond?

The variation in curriculum and learning environments for the professional study of law across jurisdictions suggests there is unlikely to be a 'one-size' approach for law schools to adopt to improve and/or protect law students' mental health and wellbeing. Nevertheless, and consistent with newly developed international guidelines, law schools can educate their students about practices and strategies to achieve mental health and wellbeing (IBA International Guidelines for Mental Wellbeing in Legal Education [2023]). Law Schools can also collect data from their students and, in the light of this information, review and adapt their curriculums and/or learning and social environments to better promote students' mental health and wellbeing (ABA International Guidelines for Mental Wellbeing in Legal Education [2023]).

LYNNE TAYLOR

References

ABA International Guidelines for Mental Wellbeing in Legal Education. (2023).

Auerbach, R. et al. (2016). 'Mental disorders among college students in the World Health Organization World Mental Health Surveys', *Psychological Medicine*, 46, p. 2955.

Jones, E., Samra, R. and Lucassen, M. (2019). 'The world at their fingertips? The mental wellbeing of online distance-based law students', *The Law Teacher*, 53(1), p. 49.

Kelk, N., Luscombe, G., Medlow, S. and Hickie, I. (2009). *Courting the Blues: Attitudes to Depression in Australian Law Students and Lawyers*, Brain & Mind Research Institute, University of Sydney.

Lewis, E.G. and Cardwell, J.M. (2019). 'A comparative study of mental health and wellbeing among UK students on professional degree programmes', *Journal of Further and Higher Education*, 43(9), p. 1226.

Rabkow, N. et al. (2020). 'Facing the truth – A report on the mental health situation of

German law students', *International Journal of Law and Psychiatry*, 71, p. 101599.

Sheldon, K.M. and Krieger, L.S. (2004). 'Does Legal Education Have Undermining Effects on Law Students? Evaluating Changes in Motivation, Values, and Well-Being', *Behavioral Sciences & the Law*, 22(2), p. 261.

Sheldon, K.M. and Krieger, L.S. (2007). 'Understanding the Negative Effects of Legal Education on Law Students: A Longitudinal Test of Self-Determination Theory', *Personality and Social Psychology Bulletin*, 33(6), p. 883.

Sotardi, V., Taylor, L., Brogt, E., Cheer, U. and Baird, N. (2022). 'Influences of Students' Intentions for a Legal Career, Satisfaction with Law School, and Psychological Distress', *The Law Teacher*, 56(1), p. 67.

World Health Organization. (2022). *World mental health report: transforming mental health for all*, World Health Organization.

111. Wellbeing/mental health of legal academics

This entry focuses specifically on the wellbeing and mental health of legal academics. However, in terms of definitions of wellbeing and mental health it is aligned to the separate entry on the wellbeing/mental health of law students. The scholarship on this topic is less developed than the literature relating to law students. It rests in part on the scholarship on the wellbeing and mental health of academics in general and reflects a variety of approaches to measurement. As explained below, the concept will be summarised by using the word flourishing. The entry will explain the importance of the wellbeing of legal academics, what we mean by the term legal academics, and what the research tells us about flourishing when working in the legal academy.

Definitions

The constitution of the World Health Organization (WHO) states that health includes mental health and is more than the absence of disease. Much current scholarship has adopted the WHO definition of wellbeing (WHO [2022] Mental Health section) which is: 'Mental health is a state of well-being in which an individual realises his or her own abilities, can cope with the normal stresses of life, can work productively and is able to make a contribution to his or her community'. This entry adopts this definition because it prioritises the positive, and we summarise it using the word 'flourishing' (Seligman [2011]).

The imprecise science of wellbeing has been stated and bemoaned by leading psychologist and scholar Huppert [2014]. In 2014 there was a danger of wellbeing being linked with economic performance. According to Fleuret et al [2011] 'In Europe, use of the term was found in domains of economy, social welfare or social cohesion, and only penetrated wider policy discussions including health in the 1990s'. There was, and to a lesser extent still is, a need for clear definitions, not least to enable clear measurement of factors that have an impact on legal academic wellbeing.

It should also be noted when referring to legal academics that they are not all on the same employment contract. There are significant differences between the context of staff on permanent contracts and those on fixed term or casual contracts who are known as 'the precariat' (Skead and Rogers [2023]). The teaching and learning and teaching scholarship career paths provides a more uncertain prospect to the teaching and research version with substantial differences to esteem and workload and much clearer, well-defined and well-recognised routes to promotion applying to the latter. Any strategy aimed at addressing the wellbeing of legal academics must take account of these inequalities.

Why the wellbeing and mental health of legal academics is important

Wellbeing has been correlated with many positive indicators. According to Huppert and So ([2013] at 838): 'In cross-sectional, longitudinal and experimental studies, high levels of well-being have been shown to be associated with a range of positive outcomes, including effective learning, productivity and creativity, good relationships, pro-social behaviour, and good health and life expectancy.' Thus, we can regard achieving higher wellbeing for legal academics not only as an end in itself but as a means to realise linked goals such as improving learning, and teaching and research outcomes. Ensuring that law teachers flourish in law schools can also be considered a critical starting place for sustaining the wellbeing of law students, many of whom will go on to practice law. Therefore, starting within law school, there is potential to enhance the mental health of the profession into the future (Wilson and Strevens [2018]; James et al [2019] and [2020]).

The link between the flourishing of staff and students was recognised in the 2020 Universities UK publication *Stepchange: Mentally Healthy Universities*. This document calls for greater training for all academic staff to ensure the appropriate recognition of mental ill health in students and for the development and implementation of strategies that align staff and student mental health.

It is often academic staff who students turn to for initial and ongoing support for their wellbeing, as these are the staff with whom they have most contact and feel they can trust. Universities should ensure that there is access available to mental health support services for academics themselves, acknowledging the impact that supporting students can have on academics' own mental health (Spear et al [2020]).

Irrespective of this link, it is important that law schools evaluate policies and activities to ensure balanced support for both law student and legal academic wellbeing.

Development of the field

Early in the twenty-first century, legal scholars interested in gender and emotional labour highlighted the gap in scholarship relating to legal academics. Writers such as Collier [2002] and Cownie [2004] started to comment on the position of legal academics within the changing context of higher education in the UK. The existing scholarship at that time was generated by writers such as Thornton [1996] in Australia, and Fineman [1998] and Farley [1996] in the USA. For a full review of this literature see Collier [2002].

Some of the earlier work on the wellbeing/mental health of legal academics can be categorised under the umbrella term of 'affect' with a full section of chapters concerning legal educators appearing in *Affect and Legal Education* (Maharg and Maughan [2011]). However, the editors shied away from using the definition of 'affect' from Martin and Briggs [1986] that encompasses concepts of motivation, values, mental health and personal growth, preferring to limit the idea of 'affect' to the study of emotion. The lack of scholarship on the emotional life of legal academics, the editors argued, was due to the need to understand concepts outside one's discipline; a lack of recognition that the wellbeing of staff had an important impact on students; a lack of funding for research in the area; and the prioritisation of rational approaches to legal scholarship leading to under-theorisation. This deficit has been corrected as the importance of considering the emotional life of legal academics has been cogently and comprehensively argued in 'Emotions on the Law School' by Jones [2020].

One of the earliest publications on law teacher perceptions of wellbeing, based upon a survey conducted in 2015 and funded by the Legal Education Research Network (Wilson and Strevens [2018]), reported on what legal academics themselves thought about the word wellbeing and contrasted it with the concept of stress. At this time research had emerged from the USA and Australia that highlighted the impact that studying law might have on increasing the psychological distress of students (Kelk [2010]; Sheldon and Krieger [2007]; Field et al [2015]). Sheldon and Krieger's work moved the direction of scholarship towards concepts of positive psychology in order to enable the use of measurement scales to analyse empirical data, and this approach was adopted by Wilson and Strevens in relation to UK legal academics. The term 'psychological wellbeing' was adopted by Wilson and Strevens and was defined as including general psychological wellbeing, living according to one's values, and spanning concepts such as hope, depression, anxiety and stress. Each of these concepts had a validated measurement scale. One of the authors, Wilson, a psychologist with substantial experience of quantitative research methods, ensured that the interdisciplinary collaboration enabled a snapshot assessment of the participants (albeit with the limitation of a small sample size for the research) with the large majority of legal academic participants in the study falling within the normal range for stress, anxiety and depression. The dearth of similar interdisciplinary work has restricted the range of subsequent quantitative scholarship.

Strevens and Wilson also adopted the framework of Self-Determination Theory ('SDT') in order to analyse responses to open-ended questions thereby helping to import into the UK a theory that was well used in the USA (Sheldon and Krieger [2004], [2015]) and in Australia (Field et al [2015]). The use of this theory enables the analysis of social contexts that might promote or obstruct wellbeing using the framework of three basic psychological needs: autonomy, competence and relatedness and moves the locus of responsibility for poor wellbeing away from the individual.

Since this study, the term legal academic wellbeing has increased in frequency of use with chapters in *The Legal Academic's Handbook* (Ashford and Guth [2016]), *Wellness for Law: Making Wellness Core Business* (Sifris and Marychurch [2019]), *Mental Health and Higher Education in Australia* (Francis and Carter [2022]) and a recent volume dedicated to the subject of

Wellbeing in the Legal Academy (Strevens and Jones [2023]) and in numerous peer reviewed journal articles.

Contemporary issues in legal academic wellbeing and mental health

The wellbeing of academics in higher education generally has come under greater scrutiny in recent times. Studies conducted in various countries around the world have established 'evidence that academic staff in particular experience significant levels of stress from various aspects of their work' (Wray and Kinman [2020] at 771).

Among recent publications related to academic wellbeing are the reports by the UK's Higher Education Policy Institute (Morrish [2019] and [2020]) which found escalating rates of poor mental health in university staff. There were significant increases in several indicators including referrals for occupational health, excessive workloads often dominated by 'audit and metrics' rather than teaching and student support, reduced employment security and heightened 'performance management' linked to short-term outcomes that many teachers found unattainable.

In the UK and Australia, universities have been subjected to reduced government support, requiring them to seek increased funding from private sources including sponsorships and direct student fees. The effects of this seemingly simple change have been deep and broad, including increased austerity in university programmes, reduced funding for staff activities and support, and a focus on efficiencies intended to improve productivity by cutting costs and increasing measurable outputs. Part of the neoliberal strategy includes shifts in language so that students are now customers, consistent with the shift towards a market model of selling education as the product of universities.

A collaboration between members of the UK Advancing Wellness in Law Network and the Australian Wellness Network for Law, commencing in 2017 and continuing throughout the pandemic period, has explored how legal educators experience working life in law school in both countries, with a view to developing a better understanding of the structural and cultural workplace stressors arising in the legal academic workplace (James et al [2019], [2020]; Strevens et al [2023]).

In both countries the results have confirmed one of the main findings in the original 2015 UK study, that law teachers are more focused on their students' wellbeing than on their own. A majority of the study participants in 2015 reported being satisfied in their role at work. However, significant minorities showed symptoms and signs of being at risk of mental illness. The qualitative data provided rich information to help understand some of the causes of law teacher stress. In particular, the SDT analysis produced two main themes. First, poor management styles in law schools, related to structural changes, cause confusion about strategic reputation and priorities for research and teaching. Second, structural changes reflecting a lack of transparency and a lack of respect, lead to reduced autonomy, increased workload and administrative burdens.

Increased workload, particularly teaching-related activity, was consistently seen as a growing and key stressor. As the workload demands grow, the time for staff collaboration, mutual support and collegiality shrinks with adverse consequences for wellbeing, and later studies by the research team found this was particularly so at the time of working from home during the pandemic.

Autonomy support is of particular importance where there is a hierarchical relationship as experienced in employment by legal academics (Krieger and Sheldon [2014]). Autonomy support is experienced where the employer provides meaningful choice and where this is not possible explains the reason as to why it is not possible and, most importantly, acknowledges the perspective of the employee. Furthermore, recent scholarship (Strevens and Jones [2023]) has highlighted four themes that impact upon academic staff flourishing: workload, communication, competence and community (James et al [2019]). However, most effective of all (Dollard and Bakker [2010]) may be a law school management style that balances the psychological health of staff with the objectives of the institution.

This entry has highlighted some key areas of knowledge and many opportunities for future research. Legal academics have an important role to play in society in educating the legal professionals of the future who will uphold the rule of law. Achieving the goal of the wellbeing of legal academics is furthered when each individual, as well as the institutions of legal education, have an understanding of how to flourish.

CAROLINE STREVENS AND RACHAEL FIELD

References

Collier, R. (2002). 'The changing university and the (legal) academic career – rethinking the relationship between women, men and the "private life" of the law school', *Legal Studies*, p. 1.

Cownie, F. (2004). *Legal academics: Culture and identities*, Hart Publishing.

Dollard, M. and Bakker, A. (2010). 'Psychosocial safety climate as a precursor to conducive work environments, psychological health problems, and employee engagement', *Journal of occupational and organizational psychology*.

Duncan, N., Field, R. and Strevens, C. (2022). 'Ethical Imperatives for Legal Educators to Promote Law Student Wellbeing', *Legal Ethics*.

Farley, C. (1996). 'Confronting expectations: Women in the legal academy', *Yale JL & Feminism*, p. 8.

Field, R., Duffy, J. and Huggins, A. (2015). 'Teaching independent learning skills in the first year: A positive psychology strategy for promoting law student well-being', *Journal of Learning Design*.

Fineman, M. (1998). 'The New "Tokenism"', *Vermont Law Review*, 23(2), p. 289.

Fleuret, S. and Atkinson, S. (2007). 'Wellbeing, health and geography: a critical review and research agenda', *New Zealand Geographer*, 63, p. 106.

Huppert, F. (2014). 'The State of wellbeing science: Concepts, measures, interventions, and policies', in Huppert, F. and Cooper, C. (2014). *Interventions and Policies to Enhance Wellbeing: A complete reference guide*, John Wiley & Sons Inc.

Huppert, F. and So, T. (2023). 'Flourishing across Europe: application of a new conceptual framework for defining Well-being', *Social Indicators Research*, 110(3), p. 837.

James, C. et al. (2019). 'Student wellbeing through teacher wellbeing: A study with law teachers in the UK and Australia', *Student Success*, 10(3), p. 76.

James, C., Strevens, C. and Field, R. (2020). 'Law teachers speak out: What do law schools need to change', in Legg, M., Vines, P. and Chan, J. (eds), *The Impact of Technology and Innovation on the Wellbeing of the Legal Profession*, Intersentia.

Jones, E. (2019). *Emotions in the law school: Transforming legal education through the passions*, Routledge.

Kelk, N., Medlow, S. and Hickie, I. (2010). 'Distress and depression among Australian law students: Incidence, attitudes and the role of universities', *Sydney L. Rev.*

Krieger, L. and Sheldon, K. (2014). 'What makes lawyers happy: A data-driven prescription to redefine professional success', *Geo. Wash. L. Rev.*

Maughan, C. and Maharg, P. (2016). (eds) *Affect and legal education: Emotion in learning and teaching the law*, Routledge.

Morrish, L. (2019). 'Pressure vessels: The epidemic of poor mental health among Higher Education staff', *HEPI*, available at https://www.hepi.ac.uk/2019/05/23/pressure-vessels-the-epidemic-of-poor-mental-health-among-higher-education-staff/.

Perret, B. (2002). 'Social indicators, current situation and perspectives', The CERC papers, 1.

Seligman, M. (2011). *Flourish: A visionary new understanding of happiness and well-being*, Simon and Schuster.

Sell, A. (2023). 'Contextual factors associated with the morale of academic and support staff in universities', *Perspectives: Policy and Practice in Higher Education*, 27(2), pp. 41–50.

Sheldon, K. and Krieger, L. (2004). 'Does legal education have undermining effects on law students? Evaluating changes in motivation, values, and well-being', *Behavioural Sciences & the Law.*

Sheldon, K. and Krieger, L. (2007). 'Understanding the negative effects of legal education on law students: A longitudinal test of self-determination theory', *Personality and Social Psychology Bulletin*, 33, pp. 883–897.

Skead, N. and Rogers, S. (2023). 'Sessional law teacher well-being: An empirical Australian study', in Strevens, C. and Jones, E. (eds), *Wellbeing and the Legal Academy*, Springer International Publishing.

Sointu, E. (2005). 'The rise of an ideal: Tracing changing discourses of wellbeing', *The sociological review*, 53(2), pp. 255–274.

Strevens, C. and Wilson, C. (2015). 'LERN Final report Perceptions of wellbeing in Law Teachers', Institute of Advanced Legal Education, available at https://web.archive.org/web/20220302221330/https://ials.sas.ac.uk/sites/default/files/files/About%20us/Leadership%20%26%20Collaboration/LERN/LERN_Final_Report(CS)_Perceptions_of_wellbeing_in_Law_Teachers.pdf.

Thornton, M. (1996). *Dissonance and distrust: Women in the legal profession*, Oxford University Press.

Wilson, C. and Strevens, C. (2018). 'Perceptions of psychological well-being in UK law academics', *The Law Teacher*, 52(3), pp. 335–349.

World Health Organization. (2004). 'Promoting mental health: Concepts, emerging evidence, practice: Summary report', World Health

Organization, available at https://www.who.int/ publications/i/item/9241562943 .

World Health Organization. (2022). 'Mental health', WHO, available at https://www.who .int/news-room/fact-sheets/detail/mental-health -strengthening-our-response.

Index